Europe TravelBook

The Guide to Premier Destinations

Seventeenth Edition

Written by Des Hannigan, Sally Roy, Nia Williams.
Seventeenth edition verified by Mark Baker, Big World Productions Ltd,
Anne Braathen, Sue Dobson, Mary-Ann Gallagher, Mike Gerrard, Sally Roy,
Dorothy Stannard, Ann Stonehouse.

Project Editor: Sheila Hawkins.

Published by AAA Publishing, 1000 AAA Drive, Heathrow, Florida 32746.
The *AAA Europe TravelBook* was created and produced for AAA Publishing by
AA Media Limited, Fanum House, Basing View, Basingstoke, Hampshire,
RG21 4EA, UK.

Text © AAA Publishing 2016, 17th edition.
AAA Editor: Janet Reddick.

Maps © AA Media Limited 2016.
Contains Ordnance Survey data © Crown copyright and database right 2016.

Maps created using data from openstreetmap.org © OpenStreetMap contributors.

ISBN: 978-1-59508-572-6

Main cover photo and spine: Gondola in Venice, Italy
© iStockphoto.com/samards.
Back cover: Extract from Europe map © AA Media Ltd 2016.

Cataloging-in-Publication Data is on file with the Library of Congress.

Color separations by Digital Department AA Publishing.
Printed and bound in China by 1010 Printing Group Ltd.

A05321

The soaring towers of the Cathedral of St. James dominate the Santiago skyline, Spain

Foreword

Every traveler has a favorite destination in Europe. Its capitals have enraptured visitors for centuries: Paris, with its exceptional museums, superb food and broad 18th- and 19th-century boulevards; London, where tradition and royal pageantry coexist with a robust arts scene; Prague, with its medieval grandeur; Rome, cradle of one of the world's great civilizations; and Vienna, with its heritage of world-renowned music.

The smaller cities hold their own enchantments. Odense, in Denmark, welcomes visitors to famed storyteller Hans Christian Andersen's birthplace, now a charming museum. In England, the old center of York, webbed with ancient cobbled streets lined by leaning half-timbered shops and pubs, envelops guests in atmosphere. And Santiago de Compostela, in Spain, continues its centuries-old tradition of receiving Christian pilgrims journeying from the far corners of Europe to its monumental cathedral built around the reputed grave of St. James; today they are still drawn by the myth and beauty of this holy place.

To make your travels in Europe memorable and enjoyable, we've selected places that have special appeal, particularly for a first- or second-time visitor. This book will enable you, whether a seasoned or novice traveler, to get the most out of your trip. Its wealth of practical information includes tips about what to bring and about getting around, maps to help you find your way, detailed descriptions of things to see, and suggestions of where to stay and eat. Our insider advice is sure to increase your enjoyment of the fascinating cultures that make up Europe.

4

Contents

Key to symbols

✚	map page number and coordinates
✉	address or location
☎	telephone number
🕐	opening times
Ⓠ	nearest subway/overground train station
🚍	nearest bus/trolley bus/tram/funicular route
⛴	ferry
🍴	restaurant
💰	admission charge (per adult, unless otherwise stated)
ℹ	information

For conversion charts, see the inside back cover

CONTENTS

Before You Go

Passports and Visas

The most important document you'll need to arrange before you travel is a passport. Passport application forms can be obtained at any AAA office. They also are available from many federal, state and probate courts, post offices, some public libraries and county and municipal offices authorized to accept passport applications.

Passport information and downloadable application forms are available on the website for Passport Information at www.travel.state.gov. Travel warnings, consular information sheets, public announcements, publications information and information about individual countries also can be accessed.

If you need a passport urgently (in fewer than three weeks) contact a passport agency located in major cities (see the *Yellow Pages* for the one nearest you). You also can request an application form from the National Passport Information Center (NPIC) at 1-877-487-2778. Automated information is available daily 24 hours; operators are available Mon.–Fri. 8 a.m.–10 p.m. (Eastern Time), excluding federal holidays.

Passport and consular/emergency services for Canadian citizens traveling abroad can be accessed at the Government of Canada internet site at www.travel.gc.ca.

Each person traveling must have a valid passport; apply early, since processing can take several months. Expedited service is available for an extra charge. Before departure, make sure your passport is valid for at least six months prior to the expiration date; some European countries require this.

You'll need your passport whenever you board an international flight, train or ferry. In some countries, you will be required to leave your passport with the hotel when you check in; this is to satisfy regulations requiring the hotel to register all foreign visitors with local police authorities. In addition, you may be required to show your passport whenever you cash a traveler's check.

Passports also need to be shown whenever national borders are crossed, although in practice border controls have been relaxed between many European Union (E.U.) member countries. In Geneva, the city transportation system crosses national borders and the airport also straddles the border, so you'll need a passport simply to get around.

Make two photocopies of the identification page; leave one copy with a friend in case of emergency and carry one with you in case your passport is lost or stolen while traveling. If this occurs, inform local police immediately and contact the nearest U.S. Embassy or consulate. The U.S. Department of State has a 24-hour travelers' hotline; phone 1-888-407-4747 or 1-202-501-4444.

In addition to a passport, some countries require a visa. Travel visas are not necessary when visiting any of the countries covered in this book, but if you'll be traveling to other nations, check their entry requirements; AAA offices have visa information.

AAA and CAA members will want to visit www.AAA.com before setting out on

---

U.S. CITIZENS

The information in this guide has been compiled for U.S. citizens who are traveling as tourists.

AAA recommends travelers consult online U.S. State Department travel advisories when planning travel abroad. Find this information at http://travel.state.gov/content/passports/english/alertswarnings.html.

Travelers who are not U.S. citizens, or who are traveling on business, should check with their embassies and tourist offices for information on the countries they wish to visit.

Entry requirements can be subject to change on short notice, and travelers are therefore advised to check the current situation before they travel.

Show your Card!

their international travels. Check for merchants who will accept your AAA or CAA membership card in order to obtain member savings at thousands of locations throughout the world. Members visiting their club's www.AAA.com website should look under the "Discounts" link for the "AAA Discounts & Rewards[SM]."

Travel and Health Insurance

Before leaving, make sure you are covered by insurance that will reimburse travel expenses if you need to cancel or cut short your trip due to unforeseen circumstances. You'll also need coverage for property loss or theft, emergency medical and dental treatment, and emergency evacuation if necessary. Before purchasing additional insurance, check to see whether your current homeowner's or medical coverage already covers you for travel abroad.

If you make a claim, your insurance company will need proof of the incident or expenditure. Keep copies of any police report and related documents, or doctor's or hospital bills or statements, to submit with your insurance claim.

Weather and When To Go

The European continent occupies a far more northerly location than its overall moderate climate would suggest. Different factors affect the weather at any given destination. The warming influence of the Gulf Stream affects all countries with an Atlantic coastline, from Spain and Portugal north through the British Isles into Scandinavia. The North and Baltic seas also affect temperatures and rainfall on the coastal areas they border.

Another definer is altitude, and Europe's great mountain ranges affect local temperatures and rainfall as well. The Pyrenees divide the Iberian Peninsula and France, while the Alps form an immense natural barrier across Austria, Switzerland and northern Italy south into France, where they descend to the Mediterranean Sea at Monaco. This entire region is popular with winter skiers, while summer visitors can expect clouds, mist and cool temperatures. The Apennines cut down the boot of Italy, also creating somewhat changeable conditions.

Destinations bord[...] Mediterranean are id[...] vacations, with mostly [...] warm temperatures and [...] flip side can be the heat [...] southern Spain and Gree[...] yourself from overexposure [...] and carry drinking water for [...] outdoor excursions. Winters i[...] Mediterranean region are cool [...] but temperatures are not usually [...] and snow is rare in coastal areas.

Summer also is the main vacation season in central Europe, which has warm, mainly dry summers and cold winters with snow at higher elevations. The weather in spring is generally more unpredictable than in the fall.

The British Isles can have weeks of dry conditions in summer, although it's best to come prepared for rain; a collapsible umbrella should be an essential traveling companion. British winters are rainy, although temperatures can be extremely cold and snow is not uncommon. However, snow is most common in northern England and Scotland.

Scandinavia has varying weather and overall lower temperatures. Daytime highs in the summer months rarely exceed 75 degrees Fahrenheit, and the coastal locations of Copenhagen, Oslo, Stockholm and Helsinki increase the probability of unsettled conditions. Winters are uniformly severe, with significant snowfall the rule.

European school vacations are a factor in planning when to travel. Schools in most countries are in session from September until early July, making May and June good months to visit.

What To Pack

Electrical appliances will require an adapter that changes the arrangement of the plug prongs, as well as an electrical voltage converter that will allow a normal 110-volt American appliance to take 220- to 240-volt European current. Two-in-one adapter/converters are available at some hardware stores and also at many AAA Travel Stores.

Bring a first-aid kit with adhesive bandages, sunblock, insect repellent and

ver-the-counter remedies for
ailments. Include written
iptions for prescription medicines
e you need more or need to show
rescription to customs officials.
ues will come in handy, as local
rooms in some areas may be
equipped or below U.S. standards.
ropean hotel rooms provide towels
t often no washcloth.

Check with your airline carrier prior
o your flight to determine specific
carry-on restrictions.

While You Are There

Emergencies
See the Essential Information section,
pages 493–569, for information about
a specific country.

Health
Take sensible precautions during hot
weather. Wear a hat, sunglasses and
sunblock, especially if you are on or near
the water. Drink plenty of fluids, and
remember that alcoholic beverages and
the caffeine in coffee, tea and some sodas
has a dehydrating effect.

The tap water in northern Europe is
generally safe to drink, although its high
mineral content can cause minor upsets if
you're not used to it. Bottled water, still
or carbonated, is inexpensive and widely
available. In an area where the tap water
is unsafe, avoid ice cubes and salads with
ingredients that are likely to have been
washed in water.

Pharmacists are a good first source for
dealing with minor health problems; a
pharmacist will be able to direct you to a
doctor if necessary. For advice pertaining
to specific topics, see the "Health"
subheading under individual countries
in Essential Information.

Language
Traveling is always more enjoyable if you
can converse a bit in the local language.
"Yes," "no," "please" and "thank you,"
accompanied by a pleasant smile and

polite manner, will go far toward oiling
social wheels. Refer to the "Useful Words
and Phrases" subheading under
individual countries in Essential
Information for a helpful list.

English is most likely to be spoken in
Scandinavia, The Netherlands, Belgium,
Luxembourg, Germany, Austria and
Switzerland. In Britain and Ireland you
may encounter strong regional accents, as
well as unfamiliar words and expressions.

To some Europeans – particularly the
French and the British – good manners
are a social necessity. "Please" and "thank
you" should be part of every request in
Britain; in France, anyone you don't know
personally (including the staff in stores
and restaurants) should be addressed
as *monsieur* (sir), *madame* (madam) or
mademoiselle (miss).

If you're really stuck with
communications, remember that hotel
receptionists very often speak English,
and are invariably helpful and friendly;
you can ask them to phone for taxis and
arrange for cleaning and similar personal
services on your behalf.

Media
Room televisions in the larger hotels have
satellite or cable connections and
broadcast BBC channels, the British Sky
network or CNN. On the radio you may
be able to pick up Voice of America,
Radio Canada or BBC broadcasts.

In larger cities, American newspapers
(usually previous-day editions) and
magazines are widely available; the most
common publications are *USA Today*, the
International Herald Tribune and *Time*
magazine. They can be purchased at
airports and central train stations, as well
as at newsstands, tobacconists and
"stationers," shops that also sell books
and stationery.

Money and Valuables
The euro (€) is the common currency of
19 European Union countries (Austria,
Belgium, Cyprus, Estonia, Finland,
France, Germany, Greece, Ireland, Italy,
Latvia, Lithuania, Luxembourg, Malta,
The Netherlands, Portugal, Slovakia,
Slovenia and Spain). For additional

information see the "Money" subheading in the Essential Information sections for the countries featured in this guide.

Currency exchange facilities are widely available in Europe. There are exchange offices at airport and central train and bus stations, in the central business districts in cities, and at seaports and other internal border crossing points. Most hotel reception desks also will exchange currency. A fee is usually charged for each exchange transaction. Although the fee is likely to be a little higher at hotels, it may be worth paying extra for the convenience and safety while traveling. For lower commissions, it is advisable to exchange currency at a travel office or bank before you leave on your trip.

When traveling in highly developed countries or frequently visited tourist destinations, you will find ATMs abound. Prepaid travel cards are recommended for use in these areas because they allow the withdrawal of useable amounts of local currency from ATMs without allowing access to checking or savings accounts. Your exchange and ATM fee is usually lower since it is set by your prepaid card provider, however, you may be charged an additional ATM fee by the ATM provider. Many merchants prefer Chip and Pin cards in Europe, instead of magnetic stripe cards typically used in the U.S., however most merchants will accept the magnetic stripe with a little insistence by the cardholder.

It may be useful to travel with a second prepaid card in case your first card is lost or stolen. Keep a record of the card numbers and international phone numbers in order to report any lost or stolen cards, and always carry your second card in a separate place.

Credit cards are another method of payment when traveling abroad. American Express, MasterCard and Visa are the most widely accepted (Discover/ Diners Club are accepted less often). Be sure to notify your credit card company before departure to let them know where and when you will be traveling. Often, credit card companies will block your card if the transaction is not a "usual and customary" transaction on your card.

You can get cash advances with your credit card from ATMs, but you will most likely incur cash advance charges in addition to your ATM and exchange fees.

Leave valuable jewelry at home; ostentatious displays mark you as a prospective target for theft. Make sure your luggage is lockable and labeled both outside and inside. Never leave your bags unattended. Train and bus stations normally provide lockers or check desks where you can leave a heavy bag while sightseeing. If you're traveling by car, keep your doors locked in slow-moving traffic or when driving through busy urban areas, and put everything in the trunk while the car is parked.

If you do have any belongings stolen, report the incident to the police immediately and obtain a police report or written statement to provide to your insurance company as evidence to support your claim.

Personal Safety

Most of the rules for personal safety constitute common sense. Keep valuables (passport, money, checks, credit cards) hidden when you're on the move; a money belt or neck purse worn inside clothing is the safest option. Put money in different places so that if one bag is lost you have another source of funds. Fanny packs and pockets are not safe places to carry valuables. Any bag you'll be carrying with you during the day should have a secure fastener, with a sturdy strap that goes over your neck and crosses your body – not simply over the shoulder. This helps ensure that bulkier items (cameras, phones, tablets, etc.) will be safe from pickpockets and petty thieves in crowded urban areas or on buses or trains.

The big tourist attractions are prime territory for pickpockets, as are buses, trains, subways, markets and airports. Be on guard for people who "accidentally" bump into you, or watch while you use an ATM. In large cities, be on the lookout for gangs of youngsters who create a commotion and then steal bags from tourists while their attention is distracted.

Street beggars can be quite persistent; walk quickly away without responding or making eye contact. Contact a police officer if anyone becomes particularly aggressive or threatening.

In general, avoid walking alone after dark. In southern European city centers during the summer, however, you'll almost certainly find locals out walking and shopping late into the evening.

Phone Service

You can make international calls from most European telephones; for specific information see "Telephones" under individual countries in the Essential Information section (see pages 493–569). To place a call to another country, first dial the international code, then the country code, then the area code (minus any initial zero) and the local number. Sometimes you'll need to wait for another dial tone after dialing the international code. In some countries the telecommunications infrastructure is fragile, and it may take a few attempts to get through.

The least expensive way to make an international call is to use a prepaid calling card. Dialing the appropriate access number (numbers differ according to country) will connect you with an English-speaking operator who can place a collect call or a call credited to your card. To obtain a card and a list of country access numbers, contact your telephone service provider. Credit cards (American Express, Diners Card, MasterCard and VISA) are accepted in many public phones. If you use a pay phone, you may need to insert coins in the local currency (a minimum fee applies) to get an outside line to make the call.

The convenience of making a phone call from your hotel room will be offset by the hefty surcharges tacked onto the bill. It's always less expensive to use the pay phone in the lobby or even cheaper to use the phone on the street; ask the hotel staff for assistance if you can't figure out how the phone works.

Some cell phones may be adaptable for use in Europe, but the operating frequencies are different; check with your service provider. You can rent cell phones for use during your trip. Check with your AAA office for information. Most U.S. "smart" phones will not work if not configured to European networks, so you may have to use WiFi hotspots to access web-based services. WiFi is widely available in many cafés, bars and hotels as well as at airports and in many other public places.

If you're staying in one country for a few days, it may be worthwhile to obtain a local prepaid telephone card, which can be used with phones that accept them. They can normally be purchased at small stores called "tobacconists" that also sell cigarettes, candy, snacks, magazines and sometimes postage stamps.

Travelers with Disabilities

Facilities for visitors with disabilities in northern and central European countries are generally very good, but old castles, palaces, cathedrals and historic houses may not be adapted for special access. Facilities in the Mediterranean countries, the Czech Republic and Hungary are improving, but if you need help it is advisable to check in advance with local tourist offices. The old central cores of European cities are often difficult to change or adapt to make them suitable for those with special needs. Expect steps and stairways in city centers (some stairways have no handrails), in addition to cobbled and uneven street and sidewalk surfaces.

Almost all of the old buildings that you come across in Europe – including those that house hotels, restaurants and museums – are likely to contain stairways, narrow halls and doorways, and other access irregularities. Make certain that accessibility standards meet your requirements when reserving your accommodations.

In many instances hotels will be able to provide a room with adequate access if they know your needs in advance. Telephone ahead to museums, attractions and restaurants as well to ascertain the nature of their facilities and accessibility.

There are usually motorized carts at airports that will whisk you to and from arrival and departure gates – these can be quite far apart within an airport.

Getting Around

City Transportation

A good first stop when you arrive at your destination is either a central public transportation information center or the tourist information office (see the Essential Information boxes in the introduction to each featured city). Spend time here and obtain information on how to get around the city, including transportation maps and detailed city maps. You also may be able to purchase tickets for public transportation, including those valid for multiple rides or for one or more days; they will save you money and the inconvenience of having to buy a new ticket for every trip. The information office may be able to provide public transportation schedules also.

AAA has partnered with Gray Line to provide members with sightseeing tours in more than 700 destinations worldwide. Discounts are offered on tours lasting one day or less. Tours are available in Amsterdam, Dublin, Florence, Lisbon, Munich, Paris, Rome, Venice and Zurich, among other E.U. locations. In addition, there are a variety of public transportation options in Europe:

■ Subways (metros) are underground trains that travel beneath city centers, emerging to ground level in suburban areas, or to cross rivers.
■ Private bus companies operate along designated routes in city centers; double-decked buses are common for carrying larger numbers of passengers.
■ Long-distance buses are commonly known as "coaches" in Britain and Ireland.
■ Trams are vehicles that travel on rails set into the street surface. They are often powered by overhead electric cables that run along the route; be especially careful of trams since they have the right of way.
■ Trolley buses run on tires, but are powered by overhead electric cables running above the route, like trams. They have right of way and run quietly.
■ Funiculars are passenger cars that ascend and descend hills or cliffs on a track set into the ground, where there are steep inclines.

■ Cable cars are suspended from tension cables attached to the top of the cars. They are common at ski resorts, and in some cities.
■ Rack railways are a feature in Switzerland, where trains that climb steep mountains connect with a cog system between the rails and give extra power to get up the steep slopes.

In many continental European countries you buy a travel ticket at a ticket office, booth or ticket machine and validate it by pushing it into a special machine, either at the stop or on the vehicle, which will give the ticket a date and time stamp for the appropriate trip or time period. If you buy a tourist ticket valid for a number of days, you will usually need to validate it only once before you first use it.

Between Cities

Trains Most countries in Europe have a national train system, with trains operating across national borders. Service is generally efficient, although local routes with frequent stops can be slow. If your entire trip is going to be by train it may be worth obtaining a Eurail pass from your AAA travel agent in the United States before you go. It is important to note that they are not on sale in Europe and must be purchased before you travel. Passes are valid for periods from a few days to three months. In addition, many national rail systems have their own passes for travel within a country; these also are available from travel agents in the United States and Canada, and in Europe too. Some trains require reservations.

Tickets for most trains are available either in advance or just before travel. For special trains (some express trains – for instance, in Spain; overnight sleeper trains; the Orient Express; or the Eurostar trains between Britain, France and Belgium that travel through the tunnel beneath the English Channel) you may need to buy tickets a few days in advance to be sure of getting a seat. This is especially the case during busy vacation times.

Information about main city train stations is in the Essential Information panel for each city.

Airlines Most countries have a national airline, as well as independent operators that operate internationally, based on hub cities within the country. Additionally, smaller airlines serve smaller destinations, usually functioning within the country. Schedules, fares and availability are subject to frequent change.

If you have a specific itinerary in mind, your travel agent is the best place to start for flight information.

For the best choice of flights and prices, reserve your tickets well in advance. Big airports in major cities – Paris, London and Rome, for example – will have the largest choice of flights, but also are the busiest. For this reason it can be a good idea to begin your trip at a smaller, less busy destination.

Ferries Services transport individual passengers as well as cars, and in some cases trains (the cars of the train actually travel on the boat). Ferry companies offering longer-distance trips of two or three days have comfortable ships, and they promote these services as "minicruises" as a change to city sightseeing.

Ferries operate regularly in the Scandinavian archipelago and along the Norwegian fjords; among the Scottish islands; between Britain and Ireland, Scandinavia, Germany, The Netherlands, Belgium, France and Spain; and throughout the islands and coastal ports of Mediterranean countries and islands.

Generally speaking, transfers from ports to city centers are less straightforward than from airports and train stations. If you intend to carry a lot of luggage, it may be advisable to ask tourist information offices about this when planning your trip.

European Customs and Immigration

Each country has its own customs import regulations; see the Essential Information section beginning on page 493. For the purposes of customs and duty-free allowances, the countries of the European Union are considered as one customs area, and there are no limits on goods for personal use when traveling between any of the member countries. However,

customs restrictions do apply when traveling between E.U. countries and non-E.U. countries.

The E.U. member countries include all the countries in this book, with the exception of Norway and Switzerland.

At the immigration barrier in E.U. countries, travelers are separated into two lanes – one for E.U. citizens and one for non-E.U. citizens. Border controls between E.U. countries are gradually being relaxed. You will probably pass through an immigration desk when arriving in a new country by plane, train or ferry, but road-barrier checkpoints within the E.U. have largely disappeared in recent years. There are still border controls in place between the E.U. and the rest of Europe, however.

Driving in Europe

European Automobile Clubs

For the benefit of members traveling abroad, AAA maintains reciprocal agreements with motoring clubs in Europe. Presentation of your valid AAA membership card at participating motoring clubs allows you to receive services they provide to their own members. Operating philosophies and facilities differ from country to country, however, so services may not be the same as back home. AAA members will need to visit their local club to obtain information

AAA TRAVEL AGENCIES
AAA Travel Agencies offer various member services to help simplify the logistics of international travel planning, especially for the first-time visitor. They can make airline reservations, book accommodations, set up escorted tours and independent travel packages, offer passport and visa assistance, arrange for car rentals and an official International Driving Permit, and provide fee-free VISA traveler's checks.

AAA members also are eligible for discounts on selected hotels and motels and receive exclusive savings on cruising vacations.

about services that can be expected from a specific European motoring club.

Refer to the Essential Information pages for each country for motoring club contact details, as well as documentation requirements and driving regulations.

Car Rental

If you intend to drive across national borders tell the rental company. This will affect all insurance documentation required. Some rental agencies may require advance notice to supply a car for travel to continental Europe. Most car rental companies in Europe limit car rental to persons over 25, a very few companies will rent to persons over 21.

To rent a car you will need a valid U.S. driver's license and preferably an International Driving Permit, necessary insurance and your passport. Some rental companies may require you to produce an additional credit card or further proof of identity for renting luxury cars.

European cars are generally small with manual transmissions; you will need to specify in advance if you want an automatic. Most rental companies offer vehicles equipped with air conditioning. Rates vary, but a AAA travel agent should be able to give you an accurate estimate of cost. Reciprocal arrangements with European motoring clubs may not apply if you are driving a rental car (see the Driving section under Essential Information for each country). Be sure to inquire about local taxes; in France, for example, taxes increase rental rates by up to one-third. Find out exactly what insurance coverage is included, and check whether you need a collision damage waiver (CDW) – you might already be covered through your personal car insurance policy or credit card company. A CDW may not cover certain types of damage; for example, in Greece damage to the underside of a car caused by a rough road may not be covered.

AAA Travel Agencies can make rental car reservations, provide prepayment arrangements, or reserve a car for you for specified dates and destinations. Rates are generally lower if reservations are made in the United States prior to your departure. They also are guaranteed in U.S. dollars if you prepay; it is recommended that you reserve well in advance. If you plan to travel through several countries, make certain that the rental company has been informed, and that you have the necessary documents.

Hertz Europe offers discounts in many European countries (including all those listed in this guide). Benefits include low competitive rates; free unlimited mileage; a 24-hour toll-free telephone information line; 24-hour emergency roadside assistance; enhanced computerized driving directions; and English-speaking personnel at every location. Hertz operates a fleet of more than 80,000 vehicles in more than 2,000 convenient locations in more than 40 European countries. There are free drop-offs between many major cities within the country of rental. For reservations contact a AAA Travel Agency at www.AAA.com or Hertz at 1-800-654-3001 in the United States or 1-800-263-0600 in Canada.

Green Card

If you drive a car in Europe you will need a Green Card (sometimes called an International Insurance Certificate) to prove that you have liability insurance. Most car rental agencies will provide this with the vehicle; most companies include it in the rental price.

A Green Card also is advised for motorists taking their own vehicle overseas; for additional information contact your automobile insurer.

International Driving Permit (IDP)

An International Driving Permit is a document containing your photograph and confirming that you hold a valid driver's license in your own country. It has a standard translation in several languages and is a useful document to carry if you plan to drive in Europe, even if it is not specifically required by the country. The permit is available from AAA Travel Agencies.

Driving Regulations

Driving in busy European cities can be challenging. If you are renting a car, get as much information about the country's driving conditions from the rental company as possible, including a chart of common road signs and an area road map. If you visit a city by car, park outside the city center, preferably close to a public transportation link, and travel to the center by public transportation.

Check parking signs where you leave your car: Ensure that there are no restrictions, that you pay for and display a parking sticker if necessary, and check closing times if you use a multistory parking garage or a gated street parking area. Parking regulations are strictly enforced in city centers throughout Europe and penalties, including the immobilization or the removal of your vehicle, can be the consequence of leaving your car in an unauthorized place. Some European cities offer free evening and weekend parking, but it is advisable to check before leaving your vehicle.

If you enter central London by car during the week you will incur a daily congestion charge of £11.50. Vehicles entering the charging zone (visit www.tfl.gov.uk to see the Congestion Charging zone map) must be registered; an area license permits drivers to enter and leave the zone an unlimited number of times within a particular day. The charging zone is clearly defined by signs and road markings at entrance and exit points. The daily charge must be paid by midnight on the day of travel if not already prepaid; between midnight on the day of travel and midnight on the next charging day, the fee goes up to £14. Payment can be made at pay stations, selected gas stations, retailers displaying the PayPoint logo and online. The charge is in effect Mon.–Fri. 7–6 (excluding public holidays and Dec. 25–Jan. 1). For more information telephone 0343 222 2222 (Mon.–Fri. 8 a.m.–10 p.m., Sat. 9 a.m.–3 p.m.) or go online to Transport For London at www.tfl.gov.uk.

Specific driving regulations for each country are provided in the Essential Information section (see pages 493–569). In some European countries, police can levy on-the-spot fines for serious offenses – including speeding and drunk-driving.

Returning to the United States

Confirming Return Travel

If you are flying, contact the airport the day before your departure to check flight details. Some carriers require you to reconfirm flights after an extended stopover of more than a few days; check the information that was supplied with your ticket.

Allow plenty of time for check-in and clearing security. You may be able to check in online up to 24 hours in advance – check with your airline.

Tax-free Shopping

Some major stores offer "tax-free shopping" to tourists. Although specific procedures differ slightly between countries, this enables you to make purchases and have them either sent to the airport of your departing flight, or directly to your home address. Such shopping saves the (often substantial) sales tax, but these items are still subject to any applicable U.S. import duty, plus postage and handling charges.

U.S. Customs

During your flight or voyage returning to the United States, you will be required to complete a customs declaration form. Returning to the United States you are allowed $800 worth of personal goods and gifts (including items purchased in duty-free shops); keep sales slips and have them ready for inspection. The duty-free exemption can include 100 cigars and 200 cigarettes, as well as one liter of wine, beer or liquor if you are 21 or over. (Check the current situation with products originating from Cuba at www.cbp.gov.) Any purchases in excess of the $800 exemption will be subject to duty.

There is no restriction on the importing or exporting of currency.

For more information contact the U.S. Customs and Border Protection Info Center at 1-877-CBP-5511 or 202-325-8000 (Mon.–Fri. 9 a.m.–12 p.m., 1–4 p.m.) or visit www.cbp.gov where "Know Before You Go" has details.

Premier Destinations

Austria

Opposite: Detail of cherubs on the Mozart memorial at the Hofburg (Imperial Palace) in Vienna

Austria

Small yet beautiful, Austria has unrivaled Alpine scenery, some of Europe's finest baroque architecture, and a long musical and cultural tradition. Straddling the center of Europe, the country has exerted a critical influence on the history of the European region through the centuries, becoming a major player in world politics.

Today, despite loss of territory and power after two world wars, Austria retains its status as the crossroads of modern Europe. The grandeur of the mountains draws visitors from all over the world, while the combination of efficiency and charm makes Austria one of Europe's most beguiling tourist destinations.

The Land

Austria is one of the most mountainous countries in Europe, with more than 70 percent of the land occupied by the Alps and Alpine valleys. This section of the eastern Alps is characterized by massive mountain chains with sheer rock faces and jagged ridges broken by deep valleys. The Tyrol region, bordering the Swiss and Italian Alps in western Austria, is renowned for its stunning scenery and is an extremely popular skiing and hiking area. Below the tree line the mountains are heavily forested, giving way to lush Alpine meadows, grazed in summer by gentle-faced cattle and carpeted with vivid wildflowers.

Picturesque villages sit amid the pastures and along the valley bottoms, each with distinctive churches, clusters of traditional shuttered houses and wooden farm buildings. The Danube (Donau) river dominates northeastern Austria, and most of the country's people inhabit the rolling terrain around the river. The flat fields of the Vienna basin are intensely cultivated, producing grain, fruit and vines.

The Habsburg Legacy

Throughout six centuries of Habsburg rule, Austria dominated the politics of much of Europe. The Habsburg Empire spread from Spain to Hungary, with sons and daughters of the ruling families

More Top Destinations in Austria

- Baden E2
- Bad Ischl C2
- Eisenstadt E2
- Eisriesenwelt C2
- Graz D1
- Grossglockner Hochalpenstrasse C1
- Hallstatt C2
- Kitzbühel B2
- Maria Saal D1
- Melk D2
- Mondsee C2
- Ötztal B1
- Riegersburg D1
- St. Anton A2
- Salzkammergut C2
- Stein D3
- Wachau D3
- Zillertal B2

marrying into other European ruling houses, thus furthering its influence. Vienna, with its grandiose architecture, splendidly illustrates Austrian prestige, and the entire country is rich in buildings from the days of the empire.

The Viennese Court sent administrators and army officials into the provinces; they brought along Viennese customs, attitudes and manners, as did the nobility who spent time both in the capital and on their country estates. The high-handed approach of these outsiders throughout the provinces has left a legacy of mistrust of the Viennese still discernible today. But, because of the terrain, the different areas of Austria were, and remain, immensely varied, each valley having its own dialect, dress, habits and way of life.

Crossroads of Europe

At the end of World War II, Austria was divided into four zones of occupation, with the Allied powers occupying most of the western half. With economic aid provided by the Marshall Plan after the war, this area was able to industrialize more efficiently than the Soviet-occupied zone, and the east–west divide continued even after the Second Republic was founded in 1945 and the country became independent 10 years later, in 1955.

Present-day Austria shares boundaries with eight European countries: Germany, Italy, the Czech Republic, Hungary, Slovakia, Slovenia, Switzerland and Liechtenstein. Its 8.5 million inhabitants are spread across nine distinctive provinces, each one with attractions for the visitor.

A view over the rooftops of Salzburg

manifests itself in an easy friendliness to everyone, and it's one of the first things visitors notice. Every region sees itself as the best, and people proudly wear regional dress and enjoy traditional music and festivals. So, if you encounter people wearing *Lederhosen* (leather pants) and *Dirndls* (bodiced dresses), it's for their benefit, not yours.

There's an elegance and ease to much Austrian life; cafés buzz with the chatter of people, a *Bierkeller* (tavern) is likely to be packed with young and old, and streets are full of strolling crowds. Manners are conservative, even old-fashioned; this is a country where children open doors for adults, and outside of the cities nearly every stranger is greeted with an amicable *"Grüss Gott."*

Environmental Issues

It's not only the magnificent tree-clad mountain slopes and verdant valleys that make Austria green; this is one of the most environmentally aware countries in Europe. Austria banned all nuclear power use in the 1970s, and since then its green policy has made giant strides.

Heavy investment in public transportation has considerably lessened the use of cars. This is a huge benefit to visitors, making travel in Austria, with its seamless connections between different forms of public transportation, very easy. Despite the Alpine terrain, Austrians cycle a lot, and every town has bike routes and parks.

Recycling is a way of life in Austria; there are many different types of garbage cans, each clearly labeled for the appropriate trash.

More than half the working population is employed in the service sector: education, tourism, administration and health. Traditional agriculture continues thanks to large subsidies, and employs less than 10 percent of the workforce.

The vast majority of Austrians speak German or a German dialect. Austria was only slightly affected by the Protestant Reformation and is still a Catholic country. Its fine baroque churches still have congregations for Sunday Mass.

Proud Traditions

Despite sharing a common language, Austrians are very different from their German neighbors – more lighthearted, and generally more relaxed in their approach to life. They see themselves, correctly, as hospitable and cordial, thus defining the term *Gemütlichkeit*. This

Sauerkraut and Strudel

Austrians take food seriously, and waiters are genuinely interested to know whether you've enjoyed a meal and are alarmingly downcast if you can't cope with the vast portions served. Mealtimes are closer to American schedules than elsewhere, with lunch around noon and dinner any time after 6 p.m.

Each region has its own specialties, but the emphasis everywhere is on heavy soups, plenty of meat, *Knödel* (a kind of dumpling) and noodles, and cream, cream, cream. The latter appears in sauces, soups, coffee and whipped mounds decorating just about every dessert. *Sauerkraut* (pickled cabbage) frequently accompanies main courses, along with piles of potatoes. Salads are drenched in creamy dressings.

Austrians indulge their passion for coffee and cakes between meals, and you should certainly sample *Apfelstrudel* (apple strudel), the delicious fruit dessert that is the hallmark of the country's pastry-making, and *Sachertorte,* a wickedly rich chocolate cake oozing apricot jam.

There are many different types of beer, and some excellent wines. Austria has been cultivating vines for thousands of years, particularly in Styria, Lower Austria and The Burgenland. *Veltliner,* made from the Grüner Veltliner grape, is the country's best-known white wine. You should also try *Schnapps,* a strong fruit- or herb-based liqueur, drunk as a digestive aid.

Coffee is the national drink, with cafés sometimes serving as many as 20 or more different variations; hot chocolate is good, too. And on the healthy side, there are outstanding fruit and vegetable juices.

Summer and Winter

Austria offers visitors as much in the winter as in the summer. For Europeans, the Austrian Alps have been a favorite skiing destination for many years, with impeccably organized facilities, trails ranging from gentle slopes to world-class diamond runs, and wonderful après-ski dining and nightlife.

Summer sees the Alpine pastures at their best, and the whole country is crisscrossed with hiking trails through glorious mountain scenery. It's in summer, too, that the cities come alive, with strolling crowds, colorful flowers

and a plethora of music and folk festivals. Spring starts late, so it's best to plan a visit in May or later.

In early spring and again in fall, you may experience the dreaded *Föhn* wind in western Austria; this is a fierce, warm, dry wind from the south that is notorious for making people generally tired and grumpy, so be prepared.

A quiet spot in Vienna's Schloss Schönbrunn

Timeline

15 BC to AD 50	Romans establish frontier provinces along the Danube and found the legionary fortress of Carnuntum.
500–700	After the final withdrawal of the Romans, Alamanni and Bavarian tribes settle lower Alpine regions.
966	Marcha orientalis (Ostmark), established as a bulwark against attacks from the east, is first referred to as Ostarrîchi.
1278	Founding of Habsburg Dynasty, beginning 640 years of power.
1493–1519	Foundations of the Habsburg world empire laid by marriage contracts of Maximilian I.
1683	Second Ottoman siege of Vienna is beaten back.
1699	Conquest of Hungary; Habsburgs gain hereditary right to the Hungarian throne in the male line.
1805–1806	Napoleon defeats the Austrians at Battle of Austerlitz; end of Holy Roman Empire.
1814–15	Congress of Vienna restructures the political map of Europe.
1905	Berta von Suttner is the first woman to receive the Nobel Peace Prize.
1914	Assassination of heir to Austrian throne at Sarajevo leads to outbreak of World War I; Austria fights on losing side.
1919	Dissolution of Austro-Hungarian monarchy; loss of territories.
1938	Hitler incorporates Austria into the German Reich.
1939–45	World War II; Austrians fight in German army; following defeat, Austria is divided into four zones of occupation.
1955	Full sovereignty and neutrality of Second Republic; Austria is admitted to the United Nations.
1986	Kurt Waldheim is elected president.
1995	Austria joins European Union.
1999	Austria enters European Monetary Union.
2010–11	Celebrations for the life of composer Gustav Mahler (1860–1911).
2012	The 150th anniversary of the birth of artist Gustav Klimt. Skydiver Felix Baumgartner sets multiple world records in his jump to earth from a balloon at an altitude of more than 128,000 feet.
2015	Refugees and migrants fleeing Syria's war zone arrive from Hungary and cross Austria's border into Germany.

The Last of the Knights

Maximilian I ruled from 1493 until 1519; these years saw the establishment of his family, the Habsburgs, as hereditary emperors of the Holy Roman Empire and rulers of Austria and far beyond, a dynasty that continued until 1918. Maximilian, through two strategic marriages, gained control over Burgundy (a region in eastern France) and the Low Countries. He married his son into the Spanish royal family, giving the Habsburgs rights over Spain, Naples and Spanish America and thus laying the foundations for the vast empire that was to come. Maximilian reformed the governmental administration, patronized the arts, loved hunting and jousting, and was known as "the last of the knights" who led Austria from the Middle Ages to the bright light of the Renaissance and the empire.

This street café on Kohlmarkt Square in Vienna offers welcome shade in summer

Survival Guide

- Always return greetings; hospitality is Austria's most important national characteristic. A polite reply to their welcoming "*Grüss Gott*," meaning "God's greeting." would be "*Guten Tag*," meaning "good day."

- For the opera, men should wear a jacket and tie; women, a dress, suit or fashionable pants.

- When going into churches, remember that it's disrespectful to show bare shoulders or upper arms.

- Take an umbrella; it can rain heavily, anywhere, at any time of year.

- For a day in the mountains, remember that the temperature drops as you gain altitude. Take water and food, and wear warm clothes and suitable footwear.

- Austrians are very litter-conscious and streets are immaculately clean; do your part to leave them that way.

- It's considered polite to stand in line when waiting for a bus or at an attraction, and to defer to the older members of society.

- Bedding in Austria generally consists of a large, puffy feather quilt in a cotton cover. This will be folded on your bed, waiting to be opened up.

- Austrians eat and drink with gusto, and spirits as well as the noise level will rise during the evening. Drunkenness, however, is always considered uncouth.

- All cafés, bars and restaurants have coat hooks and umbrella stands, and it's considered more respectful to leave coats and umbrellas there rather than on your chair.

- It's acceptable to spend up to an hour lingering over one or two drinks in a café.

- Public restrooms are free, numerous and spotless; you'll find them in most public buildings, and you can also use bathrooms in cafés and restaurants.

- Always cross the street at official crossings and wait for the green man signal. It's illegal, though seldom prosecuted, to cross anywhere else.

Vienna

For much of the 20th century, Vienna (Wien) had an air of fading grandeur, a city whose days of imperial glory had passed. But in the 1980s Vienna began to redefine itself, and continues to do so. In the last two decades the population has increased for the first time since 1919; a vibrant youth culture has emerged; and the imperial architecture of the 18th and 19th centuries has been joined by exciting modern designs, such as the huge museum quarter built on the site of the emperor's former stables. Now, in the 21st century, Vienna seems to be shaking off its torpor and styling itself, once again, as a vibrant, dynamic European cultural center.

Finding Your Way

Between 1857 and 1865 Emperor Franz Josef I had the bastions surrounding Vienna's Old Town (Innere Stadt) demolished, and laid out a vast boulevard known as the Ring. Within the Old Town and the Ring are Vienna's most important sights, including St. Stephen's Cathedral (Stephansdom, see page 32) and the Imperial Palace (Hofburg, see pages 29–30).

It's possible to take in the main sights on foot, but the "Hop on, Hop off" buses are a flexible alternative, allowing you to hop on or off anywhere along their route. There also are trams and subway (U-Bahn), rapid transit and rail (S-Bahn) trains running through and around the

area. A more expensive option is a horse-drawn carriage (*Fiaker*) at Stephansplatz, Heldenplatz or Albertinaplatz. Be sure to agree the price and route before your journey starts.

An outer ring road, the Gürtel (belt), links the city with major freeways. East of Vienna, the Danube (Donau) river and the Danube canal cut through some 23 Austrian districts, and on the

---

The Third Man

One of Vienna's favorite parks is the Prater, situated on the former imperial hunting grounds. It was opened to the public in 1766, and its attractions now include racing tracks, a fairground and a Ferris wheel built in 1897. This is where Joseph Cotten and Orson Welles had their confrontation high over the city in the 1949 film *Der dritte Mann (The Third Man)*.

southern outskirts are the Vienna Woods (Wienerwald). Maps showing walking routes through the woods are available from the efficient and helpful information center at the corner of Albertinaplatz and Maysedergasse.

Architecture

Wandering Vienna's streets is a treat for lovers of architecture. Styles range from the Gothic pointed arches of St. Stephen's Cathedral and the neo-Gothic arcades of the New City Hall (Neues Rathaus) to the baroque of the 17th and 18th centuries.

Imperial 19th-century majesty is typified in buildings lining the Ring and also in the art nouveau edifices, known here as the "Secession" style because its practitioners seceded from the staid

Association of Fine Artists in 1897. They later set up their own exhibitions in the Secession Building on Friedrichstrasse.

There also are modern styles, such as the 1990 Haas-Haus by Hans Hollein; and a postmodern housing block by Friedensreich Hundertwasser. The city has skyscrapers, like the Millennium Tower (663 feet) on the waterfront and Danube City (DC) Tower 1 (826 feet) on the north bank of the river.

Viennese Music

Vienna is proud of its long history as a center of classical music, and celebrates with a busy schedule of concerts, balls and café concerts. The grandest of the annual balls is the February's Opera Ball at the State Opera (Staatsoper).

Some classical music venues are worth seeing just for their decoration: the State Opera (on Opernring); the Konzerthaus (on Lothringerstrasse); the Musikverein (at Karlsplatz); and the Royal Chapel (Burgkapelle) where the Vienna Boys' Choir sings at Sunday Mass.

Viennese Shopping

Expect high prices. Clothes are especially expensive – the best options are chain stores such as Humanic, H&M and Pimkie on Mariahilfer Strasse, the "shopping mile" that also features most major department stores.

Porcelain and glassware have been produced in Vienna for more than 200 years. Outlets on Kärntner Strasse (near central Stephansplatz), include J. & L. Lobmeyr (No. 26). Wieden is noted for its hip stores and galleries. The section of Gumpendorfer Strasse closest to the MuseumsQuartier is known for its trendy style. The Old Town is great for window-shopping. Except for some museum shops, stores are closed on Sunday.

Essential Information

Tourist Information
Tourist-Info Wien (Tourist-Info Vienna)
Albertinaplatz, corner of Maysedergasse (daily 9–7) ☎ 01 24 555 (information and hotel bookings); www.wien.info

Urban Transportation
Vienna has a network of U-Bahn (subway) lines, tram (Strassenbahn) lines and buses. U-Bahn lines 1, 2 and 4 meet at central Oper/Karlsplatz. Subways are marked with a U on the city map. Rapid transit railroad, the S-Bahn, travels into the city center from the suburbs. Buses 1A, 2A and 3A stop near major Old Town sights. Pick up transportation maps at the Opern Passage/Karlsplatz U-Bahn

information counter (☎ 01 79 09 100; www.wienerlinien.at). Order taxis at: ☎ 01 31 30-0, 01 40 10-0 or check www.wien.info.

Airport Information
Vienna International Airport (☎ 01 7007 22233; www.viennaairport.com) is a 20-minute bus ride from the City Air Terminal, in the city center. Shuttle buses run between the two sites (☎ 01 7007 32300), plus from the airport to Südbahnhof and Westbahnhof railroad stations. There also are S-Bahn trains (line 7) and the faster nonstop city airport train CAT (☎ 01 25250; www.cityairporttrain.com) half-hourly from the airport to the city center.

Climate – average highs and lows for the month

Jan.	Feb.	Mar.	Apr.	May	Jun.	Jul.	Aug.	Sep.	Oct.	Nov.	Dec.
2°C	3°C	9°C	14°C	19°C	22°C	25°C	24°C	20°C	14°C	7°C	4°C
36°F	37°F	48°F	57°F	66°F	72°F	77°F	75°F	68°F	57°F	45°F	39°F
-3°C	-2°C	2°C	5°C	9°C	13°C	15°C	15°C	12°C	6°C	2°C	-1°C
27°F	28°F	36°F	41°F	48°F	55°F	59°F	59°F	54°F	43°F	36°F	30°F

Vienna Sights

Albertina

Housed within the beautiful Hofburg
(Imperial Palace), the Albertina is
named for its founder, Duke Albert von
Sachsen-Teschen (1738–1822), who
lived in the palace at the end of the 18th
century. The Albertina's collection of
more than a million drawings, prints
and engravings dates from the 14th
century and includes exquisite pieces by
Raphael, Michelangelo, Goya and
Cézanne, plus studies of children by
Rubens. Also here is the world's most
important collection of work by German
artist Albrecht Dürer, which includes his
beautiful masterpieces *Young Hare* and
Praying Hands. An ultramodern study
and research center uses a state-of-the-
art storage system to protect all of the
invaluable works of art. There also is an
interesting architecture collection.

➕ C2 ✉ Albertinaplatz 1 ☎ 01 534 83-0;
www.albertina.at ⏰ Daily 10–6 (also Wed. 6–9 p.m.)
🚇 U-Bahn: Stephansplatz or Karlsplatz 🚌 2A
🍴 Restaurant 💶 $$$ 🚹 Guided tours; audio guide
in English

Hofburg

Blue and gold domes top the magnificent
Hofburg (Imperial Palace), which took
more than six centuries to build. The
original fortress, built in 1275, made
way for the Schweizerhof (Swiss
Courtyard), whose Schweizertor (Swiss
Gate) was built in the 16th century.
Other sections were added during the
17th and 18th centuries, including the
gorgeously decorated Hofbibliothek
(Library) and the world-famous
Hofreitschule (Riding School), where
white Lipizzaner horses perform for
visitors (see page 32).

The Kaiserappartements (Imperial
Apartments) were built in the 19th
century, and new sections were added
on as late as 1913 to create today's
enormous complex of 18 wings, 2,600
rooms and 19 courtyards. Many of the
Habsburg opulent trappings are on
display, including the imperial crowns
in the Kaiserliche Schatzkammer
(Imperial Treasury). Located between
the Kaiserappartements and the Silver
Collection, the Sisi Museum is dedicated
to the life of Empress Sisi (1837–98).

Kaiserappartements ➕ C2 ✉ Michaelerplatz
(entrance: beneath Michaelerkuppel cupola)
☎ 01 533 7570; www.hofburg-wien.at ⏰ Daily 9–6,
Jul.–Aug.; 9–5:30, Sep.–Jun. 🚇 U-Bahn: Herrengasse,
Stephansplatz or Volkstheater 🚌 2A, 3A
🍴 Augustinerkeller restaurant, see page 463; café on
site 💶 $$$ 🚹 Guided tours

The Large Salon of Empress Elisabeth, a reception room in the Kaiserappartements of the Hofburg

A statue in the grounds of Schloss Schönbrunn

Kaiserliche Schatzkammer ✉ Schweizerhof
☎ 01 525 240; www.kaiserliche-schatzkammer.at
🕐 Wed.–Mon. 9–5:30 🚇 U-Bahn: Herrengasse,
Stephansplatz or Volkstheater 🚌 1, 2, 2A, 57A
🍴 Augustinerkeller restaurant, see page 463 🍷 $$$
ℹ Guided tours; audio guide in English

Kirche am Steinhof

Huge copper angels guard the portico of
the eccentric, domed Kirche am Steinhof
(Steinhof Church), built between 1904
and 1907 for people suffering from
mental illness. Its white interior is full of
light, with colored glass, and windows
by Secessionist artist Kolo Moser to
brighten the vault and side altars.
Running water was provided in the
stoop (entranceway) to lessen the risk of
infection and a ceiling under the cupola
gives the lovely effect of a starry sky.
✚ Off map at A2 ✉ Baumgartner Höhe 1, Penzing
☎ 01 91060 11007 🕐 Interior Sat. 4–5 p.m., Sun.
noon–4; guided tour (in German only) Sat. 3 p.m.,
Sun. 4 p.m. 🚌 47A, 48A 🍷 $$

Schloss Belvedere

The spectacularly baroque Schloss
Belvedere (Belvedere Palace) was built
for Austrian general and prince, Eugene
of Savoy, who led his army to many
victories over the French. Begun in
1714, building was in two phases: the
Unteres Belvedere (Lower Belvedere),
where Eugene's military triumphs are
celebrated in a ceiling fresco; and the
Oberes Belvedere (Upper Belvedere),
which housed his collection of paintings
and later became the Imperial Picture
Gallery. Archduke Franz Ferdinand,
whose assassination sparked the events
leading to World War I, lived here for
20 years until his death. The permanent
collection in the Upper Belvedere
displays Austrian art from the Middle
Ages to the present. Among the
highlights are Secessionist masterpieces
of the late 19th and early 20th centuries,
including *The Kiss* by Gustav Klimt and
superb French Impressionist paintings
by Manet, Renoir and Van Gogh. The
Lower Belvedere and Orangery are used
for special exhibitions.
✚ D1 ✉ Rennweg 6 (Unteres Belvedere);
Prinz-Eugen-Strasse 27 (Oberes Belvedere) ☎ 01
79557-134; www.belvedere.at 🕐 Palace and gardens:
daily 10–6 (gardens closed in bad weather)
🚇 Karlsplatz, Stadtpark 🚋 Tram 71 (Unteres
Belvedere); 🚌 69A; tram D, O, 18 (Oberes Belvedere)
🍴 Café 🍷 $$$ ℹ Tours by appointment; audio
guide in English

Schloss Schönbrunn

Empress Maria Theresa's (1717–80)
dreams of creating a Habsburg Versailles
at Schloss Schönbrunn resulted in this
magnificent baroque palace with more
than 1,400 rooms. Nikolaus Pacassi
designed this imperial summer residence
between 1743 and 1749; the imposing
facade looks out onto ornamental
gardens, fountains and a park stretching
into the distance. Here you will find the
world's oldest zoo and the palm house.
The main attractions are the state rooms
and private apartments, inhabited by
Maria Theresa and her 16 children, and
later by Emperor Franz Joseph and his
consort, the Empress Elisabeth ("Sisi").
The opulent surroundings form a vivid

City of Composers

Many 17th- and 18th-century Habsburg rulers were music lovers and musicians: Leopold I was a composer; Charles VI was a violinist; and Maria Theresa played the double bass. Royal patronage drew some of the world's greatest composers to Vienna, including Beethoven and Brahms. In 1772, at age six, Mozart gave a concert for the Empress Maria Theresa in Schönbrunn's Hall of Mirrors.

The waltz is inextricably linked to Vienna thanks to Johann Strauss, the "Waltz King," and every New Year's Day the Vienna Philharmonic Orchestra plays his waltzes to television viewers around the world. A statue of Strauss stands in City Park (Stadtpark).

In 1498 Emperor Maximilian I engaged 12 young male choristers to sing with the court orchestra. Over the centuries some of Austria's greatest composers served their apprenticeships with the Court Choir Boys, including Franz Schubert and Joseph Haydn. Beethoven and Mozart composed works especially for the choir. Today known as the Vienna Boys' Choir, their naval-style dress dates back to the 1920s.

The elaborate and gilded Musikverein was built in the 19th century as a concert venue for the city's Society of the Friends of Music. (It's here that the Vienna Philharmonic performs its New Year concert.) In 1913 the hall was the scene of a brawl between conservatives and radicals of musical taste, at a concert conducted by Arnold Schönberg.

Schönberg was responsible for changing the face of modern musical composition by abandoning the standard eight-tone scale familiar to the Western ear and devising a complex 12-tone system. Together with his former pupils Alban Berg and Anton von Webern, he formed the Second Viennese School of Music. Their contemporary, Gustav Mahler (1860–1911), studied at the Conservatory and became artistic director at the Vienna State Opera House (Staatsoper).

The unassuming entrance of the Beethoven-Haus in a courtyard on Probusgasse in Vienna backdrop for the displays of Indian and Persian miniatures, Gobelin tapestries, 18th-century porcelain, furniture and landscape paintings and frescoes.

A1 ✉ Schönbrunner Schlossstrasse 47 ☎ 01 81113 239 (palace); 01 52524-4702 (coach collection); 01 877 9294-0 (zoo); 01 8775 087-0 (palm house); www.schoenbrunn.at; www.zoovienna.at ⚙ Palace: daily 8:30–5:30, Apr.–Jun. and Sep.–Oct.; 8:30–6:30, Jul.–Aug.; 8:30–5, rest of year. Coach collection: daily 9–6, Apr.–Oct.; 10–4, rest of year. Zoo: daily 9–6:30, Apr.–Sep.; 9–5:30, Mar. and Oct.; 9–4:30, Nov.–Jan.; 9–5, Feb. 🚇 U-Bahn: Schönbrunn 🚌 10A; tram 10, 58 🍴 Tyrolean Restaurant in grounds of zoo; cafés 💷 $$$ (palace, zoo and palm house); $$ (coach collection) ℹ Audio-guided tours. Concerts ☎ 01 812 50 040

Spanische Hofreitschule

In a glittering white arena of the Imperial Palace the fine white Lipizzaner horses of the Spanische Hofreitschule (Spanish Riding School) strut to the gavotte, quadrille and waltz and show off the leaping, rearing and trotting of the high school of dressage. Originally the horses were brought from Spain and bred at a 16th-century stud farm at Lipica, Slovenia (hence the name).

The nave of Stephansdom, looking to the high altar

Full performances, complete with music and uniformed riders, are booked well in advance, but same-day tickets for morning training sessions or a final rehearsal can be purchased at the visitor center, Michaelerplatz 1, daily 9–4.

C2 ✉ Michaelerplatz 1 ☎ 01 533 9031; www.srs.at ⚙ Performance: selected Fri. at 7 p.m., some Sat. and Sun. at 11 a.m., Feb.–Jun. and Sep.–Dec. Training: Tue.–Sun. 10–noon, early Feb.–late Jun., Sep.–Oct. and Dec. Final rehearsal: selected Fri. at 10 a.m. 🚇 U-Bahn: Herrengasse, Stephansplatz or Karlsplatz/Oper 🚌 2A, 3A 💷 $$$ ℹ Check well in advance as performance times vary

Stephansdom

Stephansdom (St. Stephen's Cathedral) is an unmistakable landmark, with its black-, yellow- and green-tiled roof and the 449-foot-tall Gothic South Tower, known to locals as "Steffl," or "Little Steve." Relics of earlier churches are incorporated into the building, including the Giant's Door and the Tower of Heathens, supposedly the site of a pagan shrine. Inside, St. Stephen the Martyr is represented on a baroque 17th-century altar painting by Tobias Pock. The catacombs house an ossuary containing the remains of many victims of the plague.

D2 ✉ Stephansplatz 3 ☎ 01 515 52-3054; www.stephanskirche.at ⚙ For tourists: Mon.–Sat. 6 a.m.–10 p.m., Sun. and public holidays 7 a.m.–10 p.m. 🚇 U-Bahn: Stephansplatz 🚌 1A, 2A, 3A ℹ Guided tours in English

Uhrenmuseum

In 1917 Vienna's city councillors set up a museum devoted to timepieces across the ages in the Obizzi Palace, once home to Count Ernst Rüdiger von Starhemberg, who defended Vienna against the 1683 Turkish siege; it is in a side street by the Am Hof Church. The Uhrenmuseum (Clock Museum) displays over 3,000 fascinating items.

C2 ✉ Schulhof 2 ☎ 01 533 22 65; www.wienmuseum.at 🚌 1A, 2A, 3A ⚙ Tue.–Sun. 10–6 🚇 U-Bahn: Herrengasse or Stephansplatz 💷 $$ (free first Sun. of the month)

Viennese Flavors

Coffeehouses and pastry shops (*Konditoreien*) are two pretty good reasons for visiting Vienna. At the turn of the 20th century, artists, musicians and writers gathered in cafés to swap ideas, work, read or just sit, and some of their old haunts are still going strong. Stop by Bräunerhof (Stallburggasse 2, ☎ 01 512 38 93); Central (Herrengasse 14, ☎ 01 533 37 63-24); or the grand old Imperial (Kärntner Ring 16, ☎ 01 501 10 389), in the former city mansion of the Duke of Württemberg. Customers are generally left alone to linger in the grandiose surroundings, sipping one of the many different types of coffee drinks on offer.

On average, Austrians consume almost 15 pounds of coffee a year, and the menu usually offers many different varieties. *Mocca* is strong black coffee; a *kleiner* or *grosser Brauner* has a little milk, a *Melange* has more; a *Fiaker* is mocca with rum or brandy; and an *Einspänner* is a mocca with whipped cream. The *Café-Konditorei*, or pastry-shop-cum-café, is a showcase for Vienna's pastry makers. The most famous is Demel at Kohlmarkt 14, a must for visitors who love these light, fluffy edibles.

Wine made from the most recent grape harvest is known here as *Heuriger*, and this also is the name for the Viennese taverns that serve it. These *Heurigen* stand in their own vineyards in the Vienna Woods, and serve food – usually roast meat, cheese and salad – to complement and soak up the wine. A small music band is more than likely to be playing rousing folk music, and in summer there are often long tables and benches set outside. A bunch of fir twigs is traditionally hung outside the tavern door to show that it's open.

Viennese cooking is plain, simple and filling. It's collectively known as *Beisl* – a Yiddish word introduced by traditionally Jewish tavern owners. Dishes might include boiled beef (*Tafelspitz*), steak with crispy onions (*Zwiebelrostbraten*), chopped calves' heart and lungs in sauce (*Beuschel*) and – perhaps the best-known export – *Wiener Schnitzel*, a fried veal cutlet coated with egg and breadcrumbs. For dessert the popular choice is *Strudel*, fruit-filled baked dough with raisins and cinnamon (a perfect choice with a Viennese coffee).

The Demel coffeehouse has a view toward the St. Michael's Gate entrance to the Hofburg

Innsbruck

Strategically and beautifully situated on the Inn river, at the heart of the Alps, Innsbruck stands on a great European crossroads. The 19th-century construction of the east–west railroad through the Arlberg valley, in combination with the city's historic control of the north–south trade route through the Brenner Pass, placed it firmly on the trans-European map. Today, travelers from across Europe pass this way, and Innsbruck, with its excellent tourist and winter sports facilities, is well worth more than a brief stop en route.

Innsbruck Through Time

Innsbruck has had a checkered past. By the 12th century a fortified town was growing up beside the bridge over the Inn river, close to the site of an old Roman garrison.

By the 1360s, when the Habsburgs had acquired the Tyrol region, the settlement had outgrown its original fortifying walls.

Under Maximilian I, Holy Roman Emperor from 1493 to 1519, Innsbruck was the administrative and cultural center of the Habsburg empire.

The next 200 years encompassed a golden age that continued through the reign of Empress Maria Theresa from 1740 to 1780. When Napoleon conquered Tyrol in 1806, Innsbruck became part of Bavaria, but was handed back to Austria in 1814.

After World War I Italy got the southern part of Tyrol (Bozen) and the Brenner Pass became the new frontier. The city suffered a great deal of damage during World War II, but since then it has prospered, and today it is a university city as well as a popular tourist destination.

Exploring Innsbruck

The center of Innsbruck is small, and it's likely your hotel will be within easy walking distance of the historic Old Town (Altstadt), a pedestrianized maze of picturesque streets.

Attractions outside the city are served both by regular local buses and special tourist shuttles that take you right to where the action is.

It's worth buying the Innsbruck Card, which gives you free entry to many museums and other attractions, plus free use of public transportation and four mountain cable-car systems, the latter otherwise very expensive. It's valid for 24, 48 or 72 hours and available at the tourist office (www.innsbruck.info).

A Rich Culture

Due to its long history, Innsbruck is richly endowed with some marvelous buildings, churches and museums.

The Old Town is a tiny area packed with handsome houses and narrow arcaded streets.

Outside this fascinating, ancient core you'll find splendid Renaissance, baroque and rococo architecture. Many

A street in the Old Town (Altstadt) area of Innsbruck, where tables have been set out on the sidewalk for sunny summer dining

of these fine buildings house Innsbruck's museums, some devoted to history and the arts, others offering insights into such subjects as Tyrolean railroads, bells and hunting. The cathedral and churches are packed with interesting artistic treasures.

Landmarks along the 17th- and 18th-century street, Maria-Theresien-Strasse, include a column topped by a statue of the Virgin (the Annasäule, built 1706), and a resplendent arch, the Triumphpforte, built in 1765.

Nowadays, six bridges span the Inn river – originally called the Innbrücke – from which the city gets its name, leading to the riverfront houses of the Mariahilf neighborhood. This area is also home to a botanic garden.

You can stroll beside the river, with mountains towering in the background, to the Hofgarten – a colorful and attractive garden which was first laid out in 1410 but later refined by Archduke Ferdinand II in the 16th century.

Located southeast of the city center, in a wonderful position overlooking the Inn valley, is Ferdinand's great palace, Schloss Ambras.

Mountain Scenery

Dramatic mountains encircle the city of Innsbruck, their lower slopes scattered with picturesque villages. The surrounding countryside offers year-round opportunities for fresh air and exercise amid some of Europe's loveliest upland scenery. The best way to experience this landscape is on foot, and the tourist office arranges good daily guided hikes outside the city in the summer; boots and a backpack can be rented. You can swim, ride, play golf, go rafting or summer skiing, or just enjoy the Alps from the comfort of a sightseeing airplane flight. Winter brings the skiing season, when sports fans flock to Innsbruck from all over the world and the city's architecture looks particularly beautiful under a fresh blanket of snow.

Tyrolean Tastes

Visitors can sample a wide range of Austrian and Tyrolean specialties at

Innsbruck's restaurants, taverns and cafés (see pages 463–464). The food is good and portions are generous, and you'll find the warm welcome that is so common all over the country.

In the summertime, follow your dinner with a cable-car ride up the Seegrube mountain where you can enjoy a drink while watching the sparkling lights of the city far below, or you can take a lantern-lit hike to a party held inside a hillside hut.

Year-round you can take in a Tyrolean folklore evening, which includes traditional dances, yodeling and a performance on brass instruments; during the summer, *Schuhplattler* dancers and brass bands perform in the center of town.

Innsbruck's casino offers a more sophisticated evening, and there's always a choice of classical music, and often opera.

Woodcarvings and *Christkindlmarkt*

Some of Innsbruck's most appealing stores are tucked away in the narrow, winding streets of the Old Town, where you'll find ethnic Austrian souvenirs, clothes, knitwear, antiques and interior design pieces. Woodcarvings make ideal presents, as do dried-flower garlands and baskets – especially charming decorations for Christmas and Easter – and intricately made national costumes.

Maria-Theresien-Strasse has a range of department, home furnishing and linen stores. Excellent bookstores offer English-language illustrated books about Austria, as well as beautiful calendars that make good gifts.

The atmospheric Christmas market (*Christkindlmarkt*) sets up in the Old Town, its stalls brimming with gifts, traditional decorations, cookies and a range of tempting sweetmeats.

Essential Information

Tourist Information
Touristinformation Innsbruck (Innsbruck Tourist Board)
Burggraben 3 ☎ 0512 59850;
www.innsbruck.info
Accommodations reservation (same address)
☎ 0512 562000

Urban Transportation
Many of Innsbruck's main sights are grouped together within walking distance in and around the Old Town (Altstadt); use the excellent tram and bus service (operated by IVB ☎ 0512 5307-500); to venture farther afield. You can buy a day-use ticket, book of tickets or weekly transportation card from the tourist information office, some tobacconists and other outlets. Validate your ticket when boarding the bus or tram. Press the illuminated button near the door to open the doors when you want to get off. There are taxi stands throughout the city center, or you can call a taxi (☎ 0512 292915, 0512 5311).

Airport Information
Innsbruck Airport (☎ 0512 22525-0; www.innsbruck-airport.com), with domestic and some European flights, is just 2 miles west of the city center. Bus F runs throughout the day to the central railroad station and the city center, or you can pick up a taxi outside the terminal.

Climate – average highs and lows for the month

Jan.	Feb.	Mar.	Apr.	May	Jun.	Jul.	Aug.	Sep.	Oct.	Nov.	Dec.
1°C	4°C	10°C	15°C	20°C	23°C	25°C	24°C	20°C	14°C	8°C	2°C
34°F	39°F	50°F	59°F	68°F	73°F	77°F	75°F	68°F	57°F	46°F	36°F
-7°C	-4°C	0°C	4°C	8°C	11°C	13°C	12°C	9°C	4°C	0°C	-4°C
19°F	25°F	32°F	39°F	46°F	52°F	55°F	54°F	48°F	39°F	32°F	25°F

Innsbruck Sights

The Golden Roof, Innsbruck's most famous sight

Goldenes Dachl

Innsbruck's Goldenes Dachl (Golden
Roof) shimmers above a viewing balcony
added onto the front of the previous
ducal palace to commemorate Emperor
Maximilian I's marriage to Bianca Maria
Sforza of Milan in 1493. Beautifully
decorated with reliefs of the Emperor, it
is roofed with 2,657 gilt copper tiles –
hence its name. The building now hosts
a small museum of the life and times of
Maximilian I, a heroic figure who was
dubbed "the last knight."

➕ A2 ✉ Herzog-Friedrich-Strasse 15 ☎ 0512 5360
1441; www.goldenes-dachl.at 🕐 Daily 10–5,
May–Sep.; Tue.–Sun. 10–5, Oct.–Apr.
🚋 A, C, J, O, TS, W; tram 1, 3 🎟 $$

Hofkirche

The Gothic Hofkirche (Court Church)
was built by Ferdinand I in 1553 to
house the mausoleum of his grandfather,
Emperor Maximilian I. Considered the
most important monument in the Tyrol
region, the magnificent tomb is
decorated with marble reliefs and
flanked by 28 larger-than-life-size
bronze statues. See also the Sliberne
Kapell (Silver Chapel) and 1560 Ebert
organ still used for concerts.

➕ B2 ✉ Universitätsstrasse 12 ☎ 0512 5948 9514;
www.tiroler-landesmuseen.at 🕐 Mon.–Sat. 9–5,
Sun. 12:30–5 🚋 A, C, J, O, TS, W 🎟 $$

Hungerburgbahn and Nordkettenbahn

These connecting mountain
transportation systems take you from
Innsbruck city center up the Nordkette
to 6,250-foot Seegrube; from here you
can go to an even higher altitude, to
the 7,400-foot Hafelekar.

The original Hungerburgbahn
transportation system was a steep
funicular, built in 1906 to link lower
and upper Innsbruck. Designed by
architect Zaha Hadid, the
Hungerburgbahn/Nordkettenbahn lines
opened at the end of 2007. The cable
cars run up Hungerburg mountain over
precipitous slopes to the Seegrube
station, with ever-widening views over
Innsbruck, the valley and the high
Alpine peaks.

➕ Off map at B3 ✉ Hungerburgbahn: Rennweg 41;
Nordkettenbahn: Höhenstrasse 145
☎ Hungerburgbahn and Nordkettenbahn: 0512
293344; www.nordkette.com 🕐 Sektion I Hungerburg
(Alpenzoo–Hungerburg): Mon.–Fri. 7 a.m.–7:15 p.m.;
Sat.–Sun. 8–7:15 (some seasonal variations). Sektion II
Seegrube (Hungerburg–Seegrube): daily 8:30–5:30
(also Fri. 6 p.m.–11:30 p.m.). Sektion III Hafelekar
(Seegrube–Hafelekar): daily 9–5 🚋 D, E, TS
🍴 Cafés and restaurants at top and bottom of cable
car 🎟 Hungerburgbahn: $$; Nordkettenbahn: $$$

Schloss Ambras

Schloss Ambras (Ambras Castle) lies
outside Innsbruck, a beautiful 16th-
century conversion of a medieval castle
standing in a landscaped garden above

the Inn valley. It was the home of Archduke Ferdinand II from 1563 to 1595; an avid collector and patron of the arts, he built the superb Spanish Hall, with its colorful frescoes and beautiful ceiling, and amassed a collection of curiosities. They are displayed in the Chamber of Art and Curiosities, an early museum that offers great insight into the Renaissance mind.

The castle also contains an armory and a large portrait gallery dedicated to the imperial Habsburg family; many visitors also find interest in Ferdinand's wife's bathroom, a perfect and rare example of a 16th-century bathroom, complete with sunken copper bath.

🔢 Off map at C1 ✉ Schlossstrasse 20 ☎ 01525 24-4802; www.schlossambras-innsbruck.at
🕐 Daily 10–5 🚌 C, TS; tram 3 🍴 Castle restaurant and café 🎫 $$; children under 19 free

Stadtturm

For a bird's-eye view of Innsbruck, climb (148 steps, there's no elevator) the 167-foot-high Stadtturm (Town Tower), built between 1442 and 1450 as a watchtower. The bulbous cupola was added in the 16th century.

🔢 B2 ✉ Herzog-Friedrich-Strasse 21 ☎ 0512 58-7113 🕐 Daily 10–8, Jun.–Sep.; 10–5, rest of year
🚌 A, C, J, O, TS, W 🎫 $$

Swarovski Kristallwelten

One of the Innsbruck area's most visited attractions, Swarovski Kristallwelten (Swarovski Crystal Worlds) in Wattens, 9 miles east of Innsbruck, has to be experienced to be believed. This multimedia theme park centers around the magic of crystal and features moving walls, sculptures and sparkling crystals in underground caverns. You enter this experience through the Giant, a leafy face on the side of a hill.

🔢 Off map at C1 ✉ Kristallweltenstrasse 1, Wattens
☎ 05224 51080; http://kristallwelten.swarovski.com
🕐 Daily 9–6:30 (last admission 5:30 p.m.)
🚌 Kristallwelten shuttle bus every two hours from the city railroad station 🍴 Restaurant and café 🎫 $$$

Tiroler Volkskunstmuseum

The Tiroler Volkskunstmuseum next to the Hofkirche (see page 37) offers to visitors a great introduction to the traditional way of life in Tyrol. There are displays on aspects of rural life, as well as displays of complete Gothic and Renaissance house interiors. Don't miss the charming nativity scenes depicted in busy Alpine villages.

🔢 B2 ✉ Universitätsstrasse 12 ☎ 0512 59489-510; www.tiroler-landesmuseen.at 🕐 Daily 9–5
🚌 A, C, J, O, TS, W 🎫 $$

Ambras Castle stands in delightful landscaped grounds above the Inn valley

Winter Sports in Innsbruck

Innsbruck and its surrounding villages offer superb skiing amid beautiful Alpine landscapes. Winter sports enthusiasts will find something for every taste, and some excellent all-inclusive deals can be arranged through the Innsbruck tourist office.

Skiing and Snowboarding

You can ski at spots throughout the Innsbruck area as well as at surrounding resorts such as Kitzbühel and St. Anton am Arlberg, giving access to some 435 miles of well-maintained downhill runs served by 210 lifts. Every skill level is accommodated, from gentle runs of hard-packed snow for families and beginners to extreme slopes and off-run skiing for experts. Special areas are designated for snowboarding and carving, and for the truly tough and experienced backcountry skier there are superb high-altitude itineraries.

Cross-country skiing is very popular in Europe, and 12 different cross-country areas are accessible around Innsbruck, offering 186 miles of tracks. Ski and snowboard schools operate daily, and ski guides can be hired on a daily basis. Several areas have snowmaking equipment to supplement early winter snow. Access to the slopes is by a combination of bus, funicular, cable car, chairlift and surface lift. Free buses take skiers from the city center to their chosen ski area and collect them at the end of the day; these buses also run to Kitzbühel and St. Anton am Arlberg. Innsbruck's season runs from mid-December to mid-April.

Winter Fun

There are plenty of other activities on offer here besides hitting the slopes. With its Olympic facilities, Innsbruck offers skating and curling, or you can take a piloted bobsled ride down the Olympic run. Dog- and horse-drawn sleigh rides give you a chance to appreciate the natural beauty of the mountains, and tobogganing and winter walking provide a gentler pace. Events take place throughout the season, culminating on New Year's Day with torchlit celebrations in the Old Town and on the mountains.

ℹ️ Information on ski packages is available from the tourist information office (✉️ Touristinformation Innsbruck, Burggraben 3, A-6021 Innsbruck, Austria ☎️ 0512 59850; www.innsbruck.info)

Snowboarding is increasingly popular in Austria, and several schools run courses for novices

Salzburg

The beautiful little city of Salzburg, stretching along the Salzach river and tucked beneath the Mönchsberg hill, is a delightful combination of medieval, Renaissance and baroque architecture, the birthplace of Wolfgang Amadeus Mozart, its most famous son, and the gateway to some of Austria's most splendid landscapes. Add to this friendly people, a relaxed way of life and one of

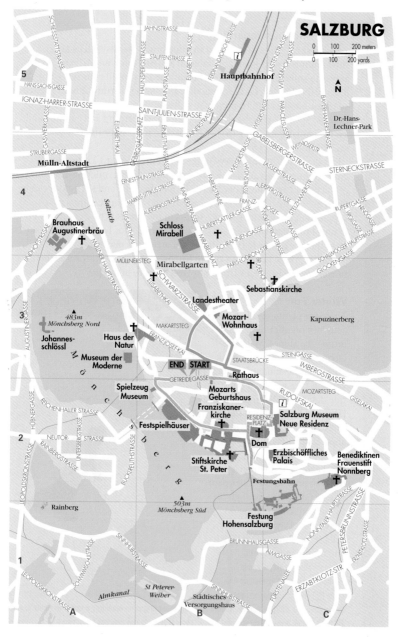

SALZBURG

| 0 | 100 | 200 meters |
| 0 | 100 | 200 yards |

SCHIESSSTATTSTRASSE

JAHNSTRASSE

STAUFFENSTRASSE

HAUNSPERGSTRASSE

PLAINSTRASSE

ELISABETHSTRASSE

FERDINAND-PORSCHE-STRASSE

LASTENSTRASSE

WEISERSTRASSE

BAYERHAMERSTRASSE

5

HANS-SACHS-GASSE

IGNAZ-HARRER-STRASSE

GASWERKGASSE

PARACELSUSSTR.

Hauptbahnhof

N

Dr.-Hans-Lechner-Park

SAINT-JULIEN-STRASSE

RAINERSTRASSE

GABELSBERGERSTRASSE

WETTINGGASSE

STERNECKSTRASSE

STRUBERGASSE

Mülln-Altstadt

ELISABETHKAI

ERNEST-THUN-STRASSE

MARKUS-SITTIKUS-STRASSE

AUERSPERGSTRASSE

HABERSTRASSE

WÖLFGANGWEBERSTR

LASSERSTRASSE

STELZHAMERSTR

RUPERTGASSE

4

Salzach

ELISABETHKAI

AUERSPERGSTRASSE

RAINERSTRASSE

HUBERT-SATTLER-GASSE

FRANZ JOSEF GASSE

PARIS-LODRON-STR.

SCHANNENGASSE

SCHALLMOOSER HAUPTSTRASSE

GLOCKENGASSE

Brauhaus Augustinerbräu

Schloss Mirabell

MÜLLNER HAUPTSTRASSE

MÜLLNERSTEG

Mirabellgarten

MIRABELLPLATZ

SCHWARZSTRASSE

ELISABETHKAI

Sebastianskirche

AUGUSTINERGASSE

LINDHOFSTRASSE

483m
Mönchsberg Nord

Landestheater

MAKARTSTEG

Mozart-Wohnhaus

Kapuzinerberg

3

Johannes-schlössl

Haus der Natur

FRANZ-JOSEF-KAI

Museum der Moderne

END **START**

STAATSBRÜCKE

STEINGASSE

IMBERGSTRASSE

HÜBNERGASSE

REICHENHALLER STRASSE

Mönchsberg

GETREIDEGASSE

Rathaus

RUDOLFSKAI

MOZARTSTEG

GISELAKAI

Spielzeug Museum

Mozarts Geburtshaus

Franziskaner-kirche

RESIDENZ-PLATZ

Salzburg Museum Neue Residenz

NEUTOR-STRASSE

UNTERSBERGSTRASSE

BLASIUSGASSE

BLOCKREUTH-STRASSE

Festspielhäuser

Dom

Erzbischöffliches Palais

Benediktinen Frauenstift Nonnberg

LEOPOLDSKRONSTRASSE

RAINBERGSTRASSE

Stiftskirche St. Peter

Festungsbahn

NONNTALER HAUPTSTRASSE

PETERSBRUNNSTRASSE

ERZABTKLOTZSTRASSE

2

Rainberg

503m
Mönchsberg Süd

Festung Hohensalzburg

BRUNNHAUSGASSE

ERZABTKLOTZ-STR.

SCHWARZGRABENWEG

SINNHUBSTRASSE

1

LEOPOLDSKRONSTRASSE

Almkanal

St Peterer-Weiher

SINNHUBSTRASSE

Städtisches Versorgungshaus

ALMGASSE

FÜRSTENALLEE

A   **B**   **C**

the world's greatest music festivals, and it's easy to see why Salzburg is popular year-round with tourists.

For fans of the movie *The Sound of Music*, there's the added bonus that the city was home to the Von Trapp family; you can find several of the movie's locations scattered around the city and various tour companies operate trips with English guides that take you to some of the sites associated with the popular film.

Mozart's Footsteps
For Mozart lovers, a visit to Salzburg is little short of a pilgrimage. You can see the composer's birthplace, the house the family rented when he was growing up, and the Residenz (see page 46) where he was literally kicked out by a steward for "getting above himself."

For classical music lovers, festivals are the other main draw (see pages 42 and 45); the city is packed during festival season and it's hard to find accommodations, so make reservations well in advance. Salzburg's charming cityscape, however, can be enjoyed any time of year. Late spring and autumn are good times to visit, but whenever you come it will probably rain: Salzburg has a reputation for being the country's wettest city.

Getting Your Bearings
Salzburg is an easy city to negotiate. The historic center on both banks of the Salzach river is pedestrianized. Although you can walk from end to end in roughly half an hour, you'll doubtless want to spend more time enjoying the medieval streets and spacious baroque squares. Most of what you'll probably want to see is on the left bank, with a few sights across the river.

Tourist offices sell the Salzburg Card, valid for 24, 48 or 72 hours, which offers free single admission to all museums and attractions and discounts on various services, and provides free access to public transportation.

Various companies will take you on city tours or farther afield to see the landscape of the Salzkammergut, one of the loveliest parts of Austria, with its shimmering lakes. There are fascinating walking tours around Salzburg, concentrating on different aspects of the city. If you just want to sit back and relax, you can take a trip in a horse-drawn carriage (*Fiaker*); pick one up on Residenzplatz.

Cosmopolitan Cuisine
You'll eat extremely well in Salzburg, which has dozens of restaurants, inns, taverns and cafés where you can enjoy anything from local and regional specialties to Japanese sushi. Traditional cooking is hearty and filling: plates of meat with dumplings, soups and spicy *Gulasch* (meat stew). The local specialty is *Salzburger Nockerl* (an egg dessert), and a variety of drinks and open wines (available by the glass) also are offered.

Make a point of lingering an hour or so in one of Salzburg's traditional cafés, which specialize in coffee and cream cakes served in elegant surroundings. Many cafés and restaurants have summertime beer gardens, some in beautiful settings.

Austrian Cafés
There's no better way to get the feel of the country than by spending an hour or so in a café, a quintessential Austrian experience. Café decor ranges from chandelier-hung baroque splendor to wood-paneled coziness, but the basic elements are always similar: excellent service, a vast range of coffees, and a wide choice of feather-light cream cakes and pastries, all indulged in by well-dressed locals chatting or reading the newspapers. Reading materials are provided by the establishment and hung on wooden poles. Cafés often serve beer and wine, and some offer savory snacks. Many have summertime terraces, the perfect place to write your postcards and rest your feet.

Salzburg Souvenirs

Salzburg is filled with tempting stores, many of them lining Getreidegasse (see page 44) and its surrounding streets, although there's a good cluster on the left bank of the river. Traditional women's clothes are appealing buys, but keep in mind that what looks lovely here might not look so good back home. Also look for wooden carvings, delicate porcelain and crystal, and bright china and linens, all with an Austrian theme, as well as big European designer names. Don't forget Austria's well-organized tax-free shopping service.

Music and Marionettes

Although classical music is the heart of the entertainment scene, it's not the only attraction. Folk, blues and jazz concerts take place year-round across the city or you can enjoy a traditional dinner in the largest preserved fortress in central Europe, the Festung Hohensalzburg (Hohensalzburg Fortress, see page 43), followed by a Mozart serenade played by musicians in period dress. The main festival season runs from late July through August, but something happens most months. Tyrolean entertainments include a jazz festival in the fall and fairs in September and the weeks before Christmas.

To keep the whole family happy, adults can visit the city's casino, while children will enjoy watching one of the famous puppet performances at the Marionette Theater.

Essential Information

Tourist Information

Tourismus Salzburg

Mozartplatz 5 ☎ 0662 889 87-330; daily 9–7, May–Sep.; Mon.–Sat. 9–6, rest of year Hauptbahnhof (Railroad Station): Südtiroler Platz 1 ☎ 0662 889 87-340; daily 9–6, Jan.–Apr. and Oct.–Dec.; 9–7, May and Sep.; 8:30–7, Jun.; 8:30–8, Jul.–Aug.; www.salzburg.info

Urban Transportation

Salzburg's small central core is easy to walk around but there are good bus and trolley bus services covering the city. Buy your ticket before boarding, at the main bus stops or from any tobacconist, and remember to validate it as soon as you board the bus. Validation machines are marked *Entwerter*. There is no need to validate them again if you change buses. To open the doors from either outside or inside the bus you must press the illuminated button beside the door. For service information contact StadtBus ☎ 0662 4480 1500; www.salzburg-ag.at. There are taxi stands outside the historic center, or you can call Taxi "2284" (☎ 0662 22 84) or Salzburger Funktaxi (☎ 0662 81 11). If you are driving to Salzburg, do not bring your car into the city center as parking is a problem. There are supervised parking lots outside the city from which you can take a shuttle bus to the center.

Airport Information

Salzburg's W. A. Mozart Airport (☎ 0662 85 80-0; www.salzburg-airport.com), with domestic and some European flights, is 4 miles west of the city center. Bus No. 2 runs every 10–20 minutes throughout the day to the railroad station and there is a taxi stand outside the terminal.

Climate – average highs and lows for the month

	Jan.	Feb.	Mar.	Apr.	May	Jun.	Jul.	Aug.	Sep.	Oct.	Nov.	Dec.
	2°C	4°C	10°C	14°C	19°C	22°C	24°C	24°C	20°C	14°C	7°C	2°C
	36°F	39°F	50°F	57°F	66°F	72°F	75°F	75°F	68°F	57°F	45°F	36°F
	-5°C	-4°C	-2°C	2°C	8°C	12°C	13°C	13°C	9°C	4°C	-2°C	-3°C
	23°F	25°F	28°F	36°F	46°F	54°F	55°F	55°F	48°F	39°F	28°F	27°F

Salzburg Sights

Dom

The ornate facade of the Dom (Cathedral), the first truly Italian-style church to be built north of the Alps, dominates Domplatz, its four marble statues indicating the magnificent interior splendors. There's been a cathedral here since the eighth century; today's structure is the third on the site. It was built between 1614 and 1628, damaged during World War II, and restored by 1959.

The huge interior, accommodating 10,000 people, is a riot of stucco, marble and gilding, whereas the simple 14th-century font provides a serene aesthetic contrast. In the crypt see the medieval foundations and remains of the original Roman church. The museum has superb treasures such as an eighth-century cross.

➕ B2 ✉ Domplatz ☎ Dom: 0662 8047-7950; www.salzburger-dom.at 🕐 Cathedral: Mon.–Sat. 8–5 and Sun. 1–5, Jan.–Feb. and Nov.; Mon.–Sat. 8–6 and Sun. 1–6, Mar.–Apr., Oct. and Dec.; Mon.–Sat. 8–7 and Sun. 1–7, May–Sep. 🚊 3, 5, 6, 7, 8, 20, 25, 28 💶 Cathedral free; Museum $$$ 🛈 Guided tours on request; audio guides available

Festspielhäuser

Even if you're not musically inclined, the Festspielhäuser (Festival Theaters) are well worth visiting. They stand on the site of the old court stables, the winter riding school that was converted to form the Kleines Festspielhaus (Little Theater). The Grosses Festspielhaus (Large Theater) was built in 1960 and runs right into Mönchsberg hill; vast amounts of rock were removed during its construction. To see the theaters, unless you attend a performance, take a guided tour; this will allow you to experience the acoustics of the 2,000-seat Large Theater, among the best in the world.

➕ B2 ✉ Hofstallgasse 1 ☎ 0662 80450; www.salzburgerfestspiele.at 🕐 Guided tours daily at 2 p.m. 🚊 1, 4, 7, 8, 10, 22 💶 $$ 🛈 Entry is only with a guided tour; tour time is subject to change if rehearsals are in progress. Check before you visit

Festung Hohensalzburg

The massive Festung Hohensalzburg (Hohensalzburg Fortress) dominates Salzburg from atop Mönchsberg hill. This fortress was built and extended between 1077 and 1681. Walk up or take the funicular to admire the views from the fortress before joining one of the guided tours. WIthin the building you'll see winding passages and ornate state rooms, including the Golden Room with its gilded tracery, and the Golden Hall, with a superb gold-and-blue coffered ceiling. The Rainer Museum displays weapons and coats of arms.

➕ C1 ✉ Mönchsberg 34 ☎ 0662 842 430-11; www.salzburg-burgen.at 🕐 Grounds: daily 9–7, May–Sep.; 9:30–5, Jan.–Apr. and Oct.–Dec. Interior (by guided tour only): closes 30 minutes earlier. Rainer Museum: daily same hours as interior 🚠 Festungsbahn funicular: daily 9–8, May–Jun. and

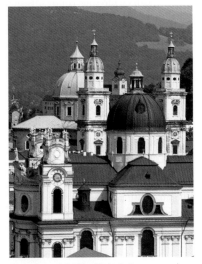

The rooftops of the Dom (Cathedral)

Sep.; 9 a.m.–10 p.m., Jul.–Aug.; 9–5, Oct.–Apr. 🍴 Café and restaurant (see page 465) located in fortress 🎫 Combination ticket $$$

Franziskanerkirche

A short distance from the cathedral stands the Franziskanerkirche (Franciscan Church), a peaceful and lofty building dedicated to the Virgin, which served as Salzburg's parish church until 1635. The nave, with its Romanesque details, is the oldest part, its dimness set off by the airy Gothic choir, built in the 15th century. Be sure to go behind the altar to admire the ring of baroque chapels that encircle it.

🚩 B2 ✉ Franziskanergasse 5 ☎ 0662 843 629; www.franziskanerkirche-salzburg.at 🕐 Daily 6:30 a.m.–7:30 p.m. 🚌 1, 4, 5, 22

Getreidegasse

The medieval street known as Getreidegasse runs through the center of old Salzburg and is lined with stores, each with a distinctive wrought-iron sign hanging above.

Most of the houses date from the 15th through the 18th centuries and were built by prosperous burghers for their businesses and to house their families. Passages run through the buildings to connect with picturesque courtyards and squares; these are called *Durchhäuser*, meaning "through the houses."

Crowds throng the street and its continuation, Judengasse, and there's no better place to come to soak up Salzburg's unique atmosphere.

🚩 B3 ✉ Getreidegasse 🚌 1, 4, 5, 22

Haus der Natur

A few hours in Salzburg's Haus der Natur (Natural History Museum) provides a splendid antidote to an excess of fine architecture and Mozart.

Popular with families, the museum's more than 90 rooms house a wide range of scientific and nature displays, including a reptile zoo, European animal exhibits and an excellent aquarium; among the many fish here is a black-

tipped reef shark. Children of all ages will enjoy the Space Research Hall, with its dioramas, models and mock-up of a future space city.

🚩 A3 ✉ Museumsplatz 5 ☎ 0662 842 653; www.hausdernatur.at 🕐 Daily 9–5 🚌 1, 4, 7, 8, 10, 22 🍴 Café in museum 🎫 $$

Mirabellgarten

The beautiful Mirabellgarten (Mirabell Garden) spreads around the Schloss Mirabell (Mirabell Palace), built in 1606 by Archbishop Wolf Dietrich von Raitenau as a palace for his mistress, Salome Alt. The terraces and grounds around the house are a splendid example of baroque garden design, where trees and flowers contrast with statues and fountains to create a truly civilized landscape. Concerts of Mozart's music are held in the Marble Hall.

🚩 B3 ✉ Mirabellplatz ☎ 0662 8072-0 🕐 Daily 6:30 a.m.–dusk 🚌 1, 2, 3, 5, 6, 20, 25, 28

Mozarts Geburtshaus

Wolfgang Amadeus Mozart was born in a modest middle-class apartment in the heart of Salzburg on January 27, 1756. These rooms are among Salzburg's most visited sights, a place of pilgrimage for music lovers from all over the world.

Climb the stairs to enter the Mozarts Geburtshaus (Mozart's Birthplace), today a simple museum containing family portraits and mementos of the composer, including his first violin. The next-door apartment has been filled with period furniture to give an idea of the appearance of 18th-century living quarters, where each room opens from its adjoining room and communal wooden balconies overlook a courtyard.

One floor down, you can study stage sets and costumes from festival productions of Mozart's works while listening to his sublime music.

🚩 B2 ✉ Getreidegasse 9 ☎ 0662 844 313; www.mozarteum.at/museen 🕐 Daily 8:30–7, Jul.–Aug.; 9–5:30, rest of year. Last admission 30 minutes before closing 🚌 1, 4, 5, 22 🍴 Café on ground floor of museum 🎫 $$

Mozart and the Salzburg Festival

The facade of the Mozarts Geburtshaus in Salzburg where the composer was born in 1756

Although Mozart spent much of his adult life in Vienna, his name is inextricably linked with his birthplace, Salzburg. Considered by many to be the world's greatest composer, Mozart left a spiritual legacy to his native city that is exemplified by one of the world's greatest music festivals, the Salzburg Festival, an annual program of musical events.

Mozart

Wolfgang Amadeus Mozart was born in Salzburg in 1756, the son of a respected court musician, himself a fine violinist whose treatise on violin technique is still respected. The boy soon showed signs of genius, playing a variety of instruments by sight and ear and starting to compose at an early age. Mozart's father touted his talented son all around the European courts, keeping a stern eye on his behavior, spending and morals, and thus storing up trouble for the pair's future relationship.

Eventually the small-town atmosphere of Salzburg, with its reliance on the bishops for employment, proved too stifling, and Mozart moved to Vienna, where he married Constanze Weber. He composed prodigiously and was capable of writing scores as if by divine dictation, while chatting to his friends. Unfortunately, Mozart's genius did not extend to managing his finances; weighed down by money worries and stress, he died in 1791 and was buried in a pauper's grave.

The Salzburg Festival

The Salzburg Festival is held annually from late July through August. Founded in 1920 by poet Hugo von Hoffmannsthal and theater director Max Reinhardt, famous names associated with the festival have included composer Richard Strauss and conductors Arturo Toscanini, Bruno Walter and Herbert von Karajan, who became its artistic director in 1956. The music festival attracts audiences and renowned performers from all over the world. Its main venues are the Festspielhäuser (Festival Theaters) complex (see page 43), but performances are held in buildings around the city. The program always includes Mozart operas and orchestral works, but many other composers are featured, as well as plays – in particular *Everyman*, which is traditionally performed outside in the Domplatz.

If you want to attend the festival it is essential to book far ahead; reservations start in December, when you should also reserve your accommodations.

Salzburg Ticket Service ✉ Salzburg Information, Mozartplatz 5, A-5020 Salzburg, Austria
☎ 0662 840310; www.salzburgticket.com or www.salzburgerfestspiele.at

Mozart-Wohnhaus

In 1773 the Mozart family left their modest apartment on Getreidegasse and moved across the river to Makartplatz to occupy a far more spacious and elegant place, now the Mozart-Wohnhaus (Mozart's Residence). The building was badly damaged in World War II and was finally renovated and reopened in 1996 for the 240th anniversary of Mozart's birth. The result is a superb, state-of-the-art museum with evocative displays of Mozart memorabilia.

A true picture of the composer emerges – a man who loved games and jokes, who had an earthy sense of humor but who also had a difficult relationship with his father. Here are scribbled letters, musical manuscripts, books and instruments, all brought to life through an English-language commentary. Two rooms are devoted to audiovisual programs about Mozart's early life and his travels through Europe.

➕ B3 ✉ Makartplatz 8 ☎ 0662 874 227-40; www.mozarteum.at/museen 🕓 Daily 8:30–7, Jul.–Aug.; 9–5:30, rest of year. Last admission 30 minutes before closing 🚌 1, 2, 3, 5, 6, 20, 25, 28 🎫 $$ ℹ Audio guide

Residenzplatz

Residenzplatz is the triumphant architectural landmark of the inner city, splendidly adorned with an ebullient baroque fountain (the largest in central Europe) complete with water-spouting horses and dolphins and topped by a conch-blowing triton.

Opposite rises the Residenz (Archbishop's Palace), built between 1595 and 1619, and set around three courtyards. See the impressive baroque interiors on an audio-guided tour that leads through rooms of ornate decoration with stucco, gilding, marble and astonishing painted ceilings, to sense of the scale of grandeur enjoyed by Salzburg's prince bishops. The palace also contains a gallery of European art. Concerts are held in the state rooms.

➕ B2 ✉ Residenzplatz 1 ☎ Palace: 0662 8042-2690; www.residenzgalerie.at. Art Gallery: 0662 840 4510 🕓 Palace and Art Gallery: daily 10–5, Jul.–Aug.; Wed.–Mon. 10–5, rest of year 🚌 3, 5, 6, 7, 8, 20, 25, 28 🎫 Palace $$; Art Gallery $$; reduced combination ticket $$$ ℹ Guided tours of Palace; audio guide

Salzburg Museum Neue Residenz/Spielzeug Museum

Salzburg's primary museum has collections housed in two buildings. The Neue Residenz specializes in antiquities, art and musical instruments. The Spielzeug Museum (Toy Museum) has a charming collection of toys, dolls and musical instruments.

You can trace Salzburg's history from Roman times and admire some lovely 17th-century paneled rooms. Among the highlights is a beautiful Celtic ewer (pouring vessel). The toys and dolls, some 250 years old, include train sets and puppet theaters.

➕ C2, B2 ✉ Neue Residenz, Mozartplatz 1. Toy Museum: Bürgerspitalgasse 2 ☎ Neue Residenz: 0662 620 808-700. Toy Museum: 0662 620 808-300; www.salzburgmuseum.at 🕓 Tue.–Sun. 9–5. 🚌 Neue Residenz: 3, 5, 6, 7, 8, 20, 25, 28; Toy Museum: 1, 4, 5, 22 🎫 $$ (each museum) ℹ Combination ticket available for both buildings

Stiftskirche St. Peter

The lovely Stiftskirche St. Peter (St. Peter's Church) was built between 1131 and 1147 but altered to its present rococo appearance in the 18th century. A simple Romanesque west door leads into a sumptuous interior, with 16 marble altars in its side chapels and decorated with green and pink molding and golden cherubs.

Make time to see the monument to Mozart's beloved sister Nannerl before leaving to explore the charming old Friedhof (cemetery), with its flower-bedecked graves.

➕ B2 ✉ St. Peter-Bezirk 1 ☎ 0662 8445 760; www.stift-stpeter.at 🕓 Church: daily 8 a.m.–noon and 2:30–6; no admission during services. Catacombs: daily 10–6, May–Sep.; 10–5, Oct.–Apr.; may be closed 3 weeks each Nov. 🚌 1, 4, 5, 22 🍴 St. Peter Stiftskeller, see page 465 🎫 Catacombs $

A Day in Salzburg

Although several companies offer a variety of tours in and around Salzburg, the city is small enough to find your way around easily, so it makes sense to plan your own day's sightseeing.

A view across Salzburg from Festung Hohensalzburg

A Mozart Morning

After a hearty breakfast, spend the morning concentrating on Wolfgang Amadeus Mozart, Salzburg's most famous son. His father, employed as a musician in the city, lived in a house on Getreidegasse, where Mozart was born in 1756 (see page 44). After visiting the house and its museum you may be ready for a cup of coffee and a break; head for the atmospheric Café Tomaselli on Alter Markt. It was here that Mozart's widow came with her second husband to write the composer's biography in 1820.

Next, cross the Staatsbrücke and walk along the river to Mozart's House (Mozart-Wohnhaus, see page 46) on Makartplatz, a far grander house where Mozart lived between 1773 and 1780 in a spacious apartment. Nearby you'll find the Mozarteum, the music university that holds the Mozart archives. The hut on the grounds is the Little Magic Flute House (Zauberflötenhäuschen) which once stood in Vienna. Here, Mozart composed the opera in less than five months.

An Afternoon in the Altstadt

Back across the river, have lunch in one of the cafés or restaurants and then spend the afternoon exploring the Old Town (Altstadt). Most sights are clustered around the trio of lovely squares known as the Residenzplatz, Domplatz and Mozartplatz. Behind the cathedral (Dom, see page 43), take the funicular up to the massive fortress of Hohensalzburg (see page 43).

After this, visit the fine Salzburg Museum Neue Residenz (see page 46). En route, stop at the Pferdeschwemme (literally "horse-swim"), a frescoed fountain-cum-pool where horses were once led down sloping ramps in order to be washed. Leave time to enjoy the stores along Getreidegasse (see page 44) and in the alleys leading off it, where you'll find every imaginable Austrian souvenir.

A Salzburg Evening

No Salzburg visit would be complete without some music; many visitors enjoy special Mozart evenings, with dinner followed by a performance of the composer's works played by costumed musicians. Then wander back through the atmospheric streets to your hotel with music ringing in your ears. For details of the walk route, see the city map on page 40.

Belgium

Opposite: The striking facade of one of the beautiful guildhalls surrounding the Grand' Place, Brussels

Belgium

Belgium is a young country in terms of "old" Europe. Its name derives from a prehistoric tribe, the Belgae, but there is no racial or cultural link with such a distant past. The country has been in the melting pot of European history for centuries and only achieved true national identity in 1830 after the Belgian Revolution. Yet nowhere else on the continent will you be so close to such a powerful sense of European history.

Influential Neighbors

The Belgium of today is a nation born out of a divided Europe, surviving in spite of differences in politics, territory and language that remain within its own borders. Too often it is seen as the administrative focus of the European Union, a country preoccupied with international politics and commerce. Geographically, it is tiny (about the size of Maryland) relative to the size of Europe's larger nations. The Netherlands lies to the north; Germany to the east; France to the south; and Luxembourg, an independent Grand Duchy linked historically to Belgium, to the southeast.

The northwestern coastline of Belgium faces Britain across the narrow English Channel. The influences and interests of all of these European countries have had an impact on Belgium and, in the case of France and the Netherlands, have radically shaped the country's north–south linguistic and cultural divide.

Landscape of History

Apart from the canals in the north, Belgium has no outstanding landscape features that define it in the way that Norway is defined by its fjords, Greece by its islands or Switzerland by its Alps. Yet Belgium has a powerful identity expressed through historic cities and a peerless artistic legacy. You will be seduced by medieval Bruges and old Brussels; feel a sense of history in Ghent,

Antwerp and regional cities such as Leuven and Mechelen; and be enchanted by the castles in the Ardennes region. The dazzling works of art of early Flemish Masters and medieval painters will fascinate you: Prepare yourself for Jan van Eyck, Hans Memling and Peter Paul Rubens, as well as the Bruegels, Anthony van Dyck and Jacob Jordaens.

Belgium is about the landscape of history rather than of scenery. Yet outside the cities and towns lies a quietly charming countryside of fruitful

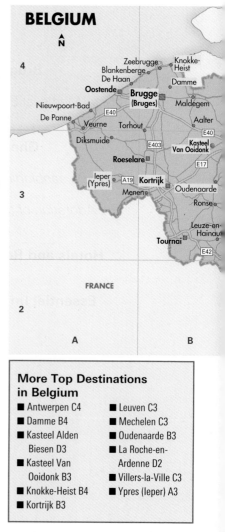

BELGIUM

More Top Destinations in Belgium

- Antwerpen C4
- Damme B4
- Kasteel Alden Biesen D3
- Kasteel Van Ooidonk B3
- Knokke-Heist B4
- Kortrijk B3
- Leuven C3
- Mechelen C3
- Oudenaarde B3
- La Roche-en-Ardenne D2
- Villers-la-Ville C3
- Ypres (Ieper) A3

farms, serene waterways and flower-filled meadows. On the immediate outskirts of Brussels to the south is the Forêt de Soignes, a superb beech forest that is an oasis of peace. In the Haspengouw region to the west of Brussels are several historic castles, such as the stately Gaasbeek with its formal gardens and the 13th-century, moated Alden Biesen. A more somber yet compelling aspect of Belgium is enshrined in the poem *In Flanders Fields* by Canadian poet John McCrae (1872–1918), who was a medical officer in World War I. Throughout Europe's turbulent history this northwestern corner of the continent has seen conflict, none so bitter as World War I. Towns such as Mons and Ypres still resonate with memories, and you will find many war memorials and graves in the now-healed landscape.

Beaches, Woodlands and Parks
Along Belgium's relatively short 42-mile coastline there are attractive sand dunes,

The Atomium is in Heysel, northern Brussels

beaches and resorts, lively towns such as Oostende, quaint resorts like De Haan and stylish hangouts like Knokke Le Zoute, all connected by a tram line. There may be no dramatic mountains, but the hilly country of the Ardennes in southern Belgium offers a varied landscape of woods, rivers and soft moorland where you can walk or bicycle around Dinant and Rochefort.

Brussels has plenty of green spaces, such as the popular Bois de la Cambre, and the vast beech woodland of the Forêt de Soignes. For more gardens and floral displays, check out the Royal Greenhouses at Laeken or the National Botanic Garden in Meise, about 7 miles north of Brussels.

Belgium has a variety of theme parks to appeal to children and adults alike. At Wavre, near Brussels, is Walibi Belgium (www.walibi.com), a huge theme park with thrilling roller-coaster rides such as "Buzzsaw" and "Cobra," as well as a fabulous water park, Aqualibi, adjacent; at Boudewijn Seapark

(www.boudewijnpark.be), just outside Bruges, is one of Europe's largest indoor dolphinariums.

Exploring Belgium

Public transportation in Belgium is universally efficient, but the railroad network is by far the best way to travel. It is well integrated with systems in neighboring countries, and trains are frequent. Inter-city trains are fast and comfortable; local trains tend to be slower, and you may feel that some of the older equipment seems a little spartan and drab. However, the high standards that distinguish rail travel throughout northern Europe prevail.

City transportation systems also are well run. Trams are a northern European institution, and the larger cities in Belgium have good tram and bus services. Brussels and Antwerp have well-organized subway systems that visitors will find useful.

Renting a car will give you independence, but driving in Belgium can be a challenge due mainly to the small size of the country and, in part, to its congested urban nature. The road system is excellent, but because distances between built-up areas can be short, you are frequently faced with busy intersections. Traffic in Brussels and in many of the larger cities is hectic, and navigation can be complicated for visitors because road signs are in French and Flemish. Out on the road, along the east–west dividing line between French-speaking and Flemish-speaking Belgium, destination names on road signs change suddenly and confusingly between French and Flemish.

Diverse Foods

Food in Belgium is often characterized as being French in quality and German in quantity. The reality is more subtle. Wallonian cuisine shares the French penchant for wine-based sauces, but traditional Belgian cuisine focuses particularly on beef and pork, and

The Last Post ceremony takes place at 8 p.m. daily at the Menin Gate war memorial in Ypres

specializes in seafood on the coast, and game in the Ardennes.

In most good hotels you will find the generous buffet breakfasts that are an international staple, consisting of a variety of cereals, cheeses and hams, along with fish and smoked meats. For lunch and dinner, be adventurous. Try *maatjes*, marinated raw herring swallowed whole, but not quite the raw experience it seems. Or settle for *mosselen/moules*, Belgian mussels in a variety of tangy sauces. For a truly filling meal, try *waterzooi*, the traditional Flemish stew of fresh vegetables with rabbit, chicken or fish, originating in Ghent, or *anguilles au vert/paling in 't groen*, freshwater eels in a green herb sauce, or *carbonnades*, beef stewed in beer. And do not miss Ardennes *pâté*, the region's excellent *jambon d'Ardennes* (smoked ham) or some of the many delicious local cheeses, little known outside Belgium.

In spring look for an asparagus dish with a butter-based sauce, as well as chopped boiled egg and chopped ham. This goes nicely with one of Belgium's many excellent beers, which tend to be rich, mellow and smooth. In the Flemish and the Liège regions of Belgium the specialty is *jenever* (*genièvre*), a grain spirit like gin, flavored with juniper berries and other herbs and spices.

For those with a sweet tooth, Belgium's famous *chocolatiers* will be irresistible. The specialties are individually made pralines with liqueur or cream fillings, and truffles with the utterly indulgent ingredients of butter, cream and sugar. The shopfront displays are an art form in themselves and are guaranteed to tempt you inside. *Gaufres wafels*, tasty waffles, are a Belgian treat that you can buy from street vendors.

Traditional Courtesy

Throughout Belgium, visitors will find the local people unfailingly helpful. This is a conservative country with a strongly Roman Catholic religious tradition, factors that make people courteous yet reserved. The language divide (see page 54) lends a certain rivalry to relations between Flemings and Walloons, yet such cultural diversity seems to make most Belgians amenable to, and interested in, visitors. The people may seem busy and preoccupied, but they will respond politely if you ask for advice or information about their country, which is, after all, a distillation of the most significant aspects of old and new Europe.

Timeline

57 BC	Romans in northern Europe conquer Iron Age Belgae tribe territory.
AD 751	Carolingian Dynasty is formed; during reign of Charlemagne, Holy Roman Emperor, the Low Countries prosper.
993	King Baudouin I dies, and his brother, Albert II, becomes king.
1419	Central government established at Bruges; the city becomes a center of the cloth trade and a focus of early Flemish painters.
1519	Charles V of Spain is crowned Holy Roman Emperor; the Netherlands comes under Spanish control.
1581	The Netherlands divides into United Provinces of the Netherlands and Spanish Netherlands (Belgium).
1713	War of Spanish Succession ends; Austria controls Belgium.
1815	Congress of Vienna; Belgium and the United Provinces of the Netherlands form the Kingdom of the Netherlands, ruled from the Hague by the Dutch William of Orange.
1839	Belgian independence recognized by the (Dutch) Netherlands.
1914–18	World War I: most of Belgium is occupied by Germany.
1940–44	World War II: Belgium again occupied by Germany.
1957	European Economic Community (now the European Union) establishes its headquarters in Brussels.
1967	NATO sets up headquarters in Brussels.
2006–present	Belgian politics is characterized by deep rifts based on Flemish/French language and cultural differences.
June 2010	A general election results in no overall majority for any one party. Negotiations begin to form a coalition government comprising the French- and Flemish-speaking parties.
October 2011	Agreement is reached on constitutional changes to allow a coalition government to take power.
December 2011	New Belgian government sworn in with Elio de Rupo as Prime Minister.
June/July 2013	King Alfred II abdicates. The crown passes to his son, Prince Phillippe. King Phillippe is sworn in as ruling monarch of Belgium.
October 2014	A new Federal government takes office headed by Reformist Movement party leader Charles Michel.

Language Divide

There is a dramatic linguistic divide between north and south Belgium, a legacy of the country's formation from a southern French-influenced area and a northern Flemish-influenced area. In northern Belgium the dominant language is Flemish, a Germanic language similar to Dutch. In southern Belgium, in the area known as Wallonia, the prevailing language is a French dialect. Brussels lies within the Flemish half of Belgium and is officially bilingual, but within the city French is the dominant language. Be careful in associating Flemish too closely with Dutch. Brugeans (residents of Bruges) will tell you that theirs is a far subtler language. And Antwerpenaars (residents of Antwerp) will tell you that they speak better Flemish than Brugeans; if you visit more remote rural districts you will find even more regional differences.

Survival Guide

- Flemish and French are both spoken in Brussels, where even street signs are in both languages. You can try out your French in Brussels and Wallonia and your Flemish in Ghent, Bruges and in the north, but to use either language in the wrong area may elicit a frosty reaction. However, many Belgians speak English, and this is often the wisest option, particularly in the city of Brussels, where it is now lingua franca.

- You will usually find that the Flemish and French proper names have similarities; for example, Bruges is Bruges (French) and Brugge (Flemish), Louvain is Louvain (French) and Leuven (Flemish). But there are problematic differences. For example, Ghent is Gand (French) but Gent (Flemish), and Mechelen is Malines (French) but Mechelen (Flemish). If in doubt, especially when checking train or bus destinations, confirm the destination with an English-speaking official.

- There are a few public restrooms in Belgian cities, but they are often not very clean. Railroad and bus stations, restaurants and the bigger cafés tend to have public bathrooms with attendants, where you are expected to pay about 20 to 50 cents per person.

- In restaurants, the *menu* usually signifies the dish of the day. If you want to choose from a selection of dishes, ask for the *kaart* (Flemish) or *la carte* (French).

- In the rue des Bouchers area of Brussels you may find that prominently displayed menus at reasonable prices become suddenly replaced as soon as you are seated. You may be repeatedly offered house specialties at inflated prices. If this is not what you want, move on to another restaurant.

King's House Café in Grand' Place, Brussels

- For a quick snack there are numerous fast-food outlets, stalls and, in large shopping malls, café counter service. Apart from the universal hamburgers and french fries, there is usually a big selection of *broodjes*, rolls crammed with mouthwatering fillings. Belgians' favorite snack, whether it be day or night, is a packet of *frites/frietjes* (fries) from their local *frietkot* or fries to-go outlet. *Gaufres wafels*, tasty, vanilla-flavored waffles, are another favored treat, bought fresh from street stalls and spread with chocolate sauce and/or fresh cream.

- Beer brewing is a Belgian specialty, and there are hundreds of different Belgian brews to choose from. Have a beer at lunchtime or try a *bière/bier* with your meal at a restaurant. It is perfectly in keeping with the local cuisine, which incorporates beer in many dishes. Some of the best Belgian beers can be as distinctive as wine and some have a high alcohol content.

Brussels

Brussels (Brussel or Bruxelles) takes most people by surprise. The city's name is so closely associated with the modern trappings of the European Union (E.U.) that for many it is synonymous with modern high-rise buildings and the world of suited bureaucrats.

The real Brussels has a far more colorful and resonant life. It is an exciting, modern city, yet rich in beautiful medieval and art nouveau buildings, outstanding museums and galleries, and a cultural life vibrantly international in character.

Life in the City

You may feel intimidated at first by the hectic pace of the busy streets, but Brussels is genuine "old Europe" at heart – open, friendly and welcoming. Life between the busy boulevards is engagingly relaxed. There is a wonderful variety about Brussels, a sense of its being several urban "villages" within a whole. The heart of the city lies within a barrier of encircling main roads known

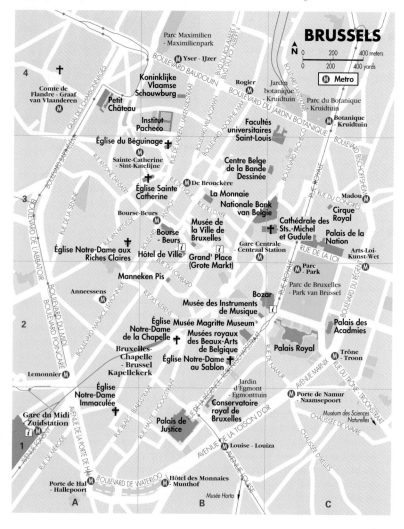

as the *Petit Ring/Kleine Ring*. You should be able to reach the inner city's finest features easily, and you should have no difficulty finding your way around; another option is to join one of the many guided tours.

For areas outside the *Petit Ring/Kleine Ring*, use the city's subway system, one of the easiest ways of getting around greater Brussels.

Medieval Townscape

Historic Brussels is celebrated by the breathtaking Grand' Place (Grote Markt, see page 61), the best-preserved medieval townscape in Europe. North of here you will find the rue des Bouchers area, where narrow cobbled streets are lined with competing restaurants more reminiscent of Mediterranean cities. Nearby are the elegant, glass-roofed shopping malls of the 19th-century Galeries St.-Hubert.

A short distance west of Grand' Place, along rue au Beurre, is the massive neoclassical Bourse, the city's stock exchange, its front facing busy boulevard Anspach. Nearby is rue Neuve, a lively shopping street.

Head west from boulevard Anspach and discover Brussels' very old heartland of place St.-Géry, with its covered market, and place Ste.-Cathérine and place du Béguinage, old cobbled squares with slightly worn but still splendid baroque churches. Between St.-Géry and Ste.-Cathérine lies rue Antoine Dansaert, a street which is home to many Belgian fashion stores.

Sightseeing and Shopping

Outside the Grand' Place area there are other atmospheric and stylish areas.

Le Sablon, near the southern edge of the *Petit Ring/Kleine Ring*, is convenient to the Royal Fine Arts Museums of Belgium (Musées royaux des Beaux-Arts de Belgique, see page 60). The leafy place de Grand Sablon is the center of Brussels' antiques trade, and it has some fine restaurants and antiques shops. Just south of Le Sablon is the busy and fashionable shopping street of avenue Louise, at the heart of the upscale area of Ixelles/Elsene. This is where many of the trendy shops and restaurants are located.

Brussels has much to see and you'll need to use your time efficiently to visit as many of the attractions as possible.

Branch out beyond the *Petit Ring/ Kleine Ring* to places like Heysel, four miles north of Grand' Place. Here stands the striking Atomium, by architect André Waterkeyn, a vast model of a metal crystal, its steel spheres gleaming in the sun. At its foot the popular Mini-Europe (www.minieurope.be) presents scaled-down versions of Europe's most famous buildings.

Visit the Parc du Cinquantenaire, Leopold II's 1880 celebration of the Golden Jubilee of the Belgian State. The park has a central avenue, named after John F. Kennedy, that leads to a triumphal arch linking monumental halls. Several major museums are located here.

Petit Julien
South of Grand' Place on rue du Chène (reached via rue Charles-Buls and Stoofstraat) stands the famous *Manneken-Pis* (right), a bronze fountain statuette of a naked little boy happily urinating. *Petit Julien*, as he is properly called, dates from 1619 and has long been an irreverent and endearing symbol of "carefree" Brussels.

Belgium

Cuisine and Culture

Make sure you sample classic Brussels cuisine at gourmet restaurants such as Comme Chez Soi (see page 465); or try a less pricey local *geuze* or *kriek* beer in any of the café bars in and around Grand' Place and St.-Géry. Try mussels, of course, but also enjoy *anguilles au vert/paling in 't groen*, freshwater eels in sauce, or *waterzooi*, fish or chicken stew with vegetables and creamy sauce, and spoil yourself with Belgian chocolate.

Enjoy great music in the superb national opera house, Théâtre de la Monnaie (www.lamonnaie.be), or in one of the rock and jazz venues. There also are colorful street theaters, festivals and puppet theater events for kids.

Essential Information

Tourist Information
Brussels Tourist Information Office
Hôtel de Ville, Grand' Place (Grote Markt)
Brussels Info Place, rue Royale 2
☎ 02 5513 8940; www.visitbrussels.be
Flanders Region & Brussels Tourist Office
Marché des Herbes/Grasmarkt 61 ☎ 02 504 0300; www.toerismevlaanderen.be
Arrivals Hall TGV/Thalys/Eurostar, Gare du Midi/Zuidstation

Urban Transportation
Brussels has three main railroad stations: the Gare du Nord/Noordstation (Brussels North), Gare Centrale/Centraal Station (Brussels Central) and Gare du Midi/Zuidstation (Brussels South). Eurostar service from London's St. Pancras International station (1 hour 51 minutes) arrives at Brussels Midi station, as does the TGV/Thalys train (1 hour 25 minutes) from Paris. For international rail information call (toll call) ☎ 070 79 79 79 (Mon.–Fri. 8–8, Sat.–Sun. and public holidays 9–4:30); www.b-europe.com. For domestic services ☎ 02 528 2828 (daily 7 a.m.–9:30 p.m.); www.belgianrail.be. There are metro (subway) stops at all three stations. Metro stations are marked on the map as "M"

and are identified at entrances by a white letter "M" on a blue background. Brussels has a metro, buses and an underground tram system (same ticket for all), and taxis. The metro lines have stations near major attractions. For general information about city transportation call (toll call) ☎ 070 23 2000 (Mon.–Fri. 7–7, Sat. 8–4); www.stib.be. Licensed, metered taxis can be hailed in the street or from a taxi stand at rue du Marche aux Herbes (Grasmarkt) for Grand' Place and at Gare Centrale; rates double when traveling outside the city. Call Taxis Bleus ☎ 02 268 0000; www.taxisbleus.be.

Airport Information
Brussels International Airport is located at Zaventem, 8 miles northeast of the city. There is an Airport City Express train that runs to/from all of Brussels' main stations at 15-minute intervals (journey time 17–30 minutes, depending on time of day), daily 5:24 a.m.–12:24 a.m. from the airport and 4:39 a.m.–11:06 p.m. from the city. For flight information call ☎ 0900 70000 (Mon.–Fri. 7 a.m.–10 p.m.; Sat.–Sun. 7 a.m.–8 p.m. toll call); ☎ 32 2 753 7753 outside Belgium; www.brusselsairport.be.

Climate – average highs and lows for the month

Jan.	Feb.	Mar.	Apr.	May	Jun.	Jul.	Aug.	Sep.	Oct.	Nov.	Dec.
4°C	6°C	10°C	13°C	18°C	22°C	22°C	22°C	20°C	15°C	9°C	5°C
39°F	43°F	50°F	55°F	64°F	72°F	72°F	72°F	68°F	59°F	48°F	41°F
-1°C	0°C	2°C	5°C	8°C	11°C	12°C	12°C	10°C	7°C	3°C	0°C
30°F	32°F	36°F	41°F	46°F	52°F	54°F	54°F	50°F	45°F	37°F	32°F

Brussels Sights

🚋 Tram 93 🍴 Museum restaurant 🎟 $$$ (includes reading room); Library only $ ℹ️ Library: visitors over age 16 only. "Tintin" themed walks available

Key to symbols
➕ map coordinates refer to the Brussels map on page 56 🎟 admission charge:
$$$ more than €7.50, $$ €4–€7.50, $ less than €4
See page 5 for complete key to symbols

Musée Horta

This is the house that Belgium's famed art nouveau architect, Victor Horta, built for himself. The art nouveau style, popular in Europe and especially in Brussels between 1893 and 1918, typically used industrial materials like steel and iron in the visible parts of houses. Art nouveau originated in England with the Arts and Crafts movement, and it became known as Jugendstil in Germany and Modernismo in Spain. The movement was inspired by nature, and was a reaction against growing industrialism.

From outside, Horta's house and studio look much like the neighboring terraced houses, but the interior is light and sensuous. The beautiful stained-glass ceiling floods the superb wrought-iron stairwell with light, and gives the house a wonderfully airy feel. At the top floor is a glass-roofed conservatory with a winter garden.

➕ Off map at B1 ✉️ rue Américaine 23–25 ☎ 02 543 0490; www.hortamuseum.be 🕐 Tue.–Sun. 2–5.30. Last admission 15 minutes before closing 🚇 54; tram 81, 91, 92, 97 🎟 $$$

Cathédrale des Sts.-Michel et Gudule

Work began on the construction of the Cathédrale des Sts.-Michel et Gudule (Cathedral of St. Michael and St. Gudula) in the 13th century. Architecturally, the building shows the various forms of Brabantine Gothic that evolved over the 300 years it took to complete the work.

Inside, baroque style is lavishly celebrated by giant figures of the Apostles, while Renaissance influence shines from the fine stained glass of the 16th-century west window.

The Romanesque remains of an 11th-century church can be seen down in the crypt.

➕ C3 ✉️ place Ste.-Gudule ☎ 02 217 8345; www.cathedralisbruxellensis.be 🕐 Cathedral: Mon.–Fri. 7:30–6, Sat. 7:30–3:30, Sun. 2–6. Treasure Museum: Mon.–Fri. 10–12:30 and 2–5, Sat. 10–3, Sun. 2–5. Crypt: by appointment only 🚇 Gare Centrale 🎟 Cathedral free; Museum $; Crypt $$

Musée des Instruments de Musique

The excellent Musée des Instruments de Musique (Museum of Musical Instruments) is housed in a former department store, one of Brussels' most striking art nouveau buildings. The Old England store was built in 1899 by architect Paul Saintenoy in glass and steel. The well-adapted space holds one of the largest and most varied collections of musical instruments in the world. The galleries feature more than 1,000 of the 9,000 items in the museum's collection, dating from antiquity to modern day. Visitors are given infrared headphones that allow them to hear the sound of the musical instruments on display.

Centre Belge de la Bande Dessinée

The unusual Centre Belge de la Bande Dessinée (Belgian Comic Strip Center) encompasses a dazzling celebration of the strip cartoon, the *bande dessinée*. The strip cartoon is closely associated with Belgium, not least in the shape of Hergé's (Georges Rémi's) character Tin Tin, created in 1929. The museum building is a delight, designed as a department store in 1906 by architect Victor Horta (see Musée Horta, right).

➕ B3 ✉️ rue des Sables 20 ☎ 02 219 1980; http://www.comicscenter.net/en/home 🕐 Tue.–Sun. 10–6 (library: Tue.–Thu. noon–5, Fri. noon–6, Sat. 10–6) 🚇 Gare Centrale, De Brouckère, Botanique or Rogier

On the top floor is a pleasant tearoom-restaurant with a delightful terrace offering extensive views over Brussels.
🚩 B2 ✉ rue Montagne de la Cour 2 ☎ 02 545 0130; www.mim.be ⏰ Tue.–Fri. 9:30–5, Sat.–Sun. 10–5. Last admission 45 minutes before closing 🚇 Gare Centrale, Porte de Namur 🚌 27, 38, 71, 95; tram 92, 94 🍴 Rooftop restaurant 💶 $$$; free first Wed. of the month after 1 p.m.

Musée Magritte Museum

Belgian artist René Magritte was a central figure in the Surrealist movement of the early 20th century, working with groups of artists in Brussels and in Paris until his death in 1967. The Magritte Museum, one of the Royal Museums of Fine Arts of Belgium, is home to the world's largest collection of the artist's work, with important and pivotal pieces including *The Secret Player* (1927), a canvas that propelled Magritte into Surrealism proper.

The museum is housed in the renovated former Hôtel Altenloh, with its neoclassical facade disguising a state-of-the-art gallery interior.
🚩 B2 ✉ place Royale 1 ☎ 02 508 3211; www.musee-magritte-museum.be ⏰ Tue.–Fri. 10–5, Sat.–Sun. 11–5 🚇 Gare Centrale 🚌 27, 29, 38, 71, 95; tram 92, 94 🍴 Restaurant and café 💶 $$$; free first Wed. of the month after 1 p.m. Combined ticket available for all Royal Museums of Fine Arts ℹ Audio guide ($$)

Musées royaux des Beaux-Arts de Belgique

Three of the six Musées royaux des Beaux-Arts de Belgique (Royal Fine Arts Museums of Belgium) are housed within this former court of Charles Lorraine.

The Musée Oldmasters Museum concentrates on pieces from the 15th to 18th centuries, with Flemish Primitives, and Renaissance and baroque masterpieces. The collection by Pieter Bruegel the Elder is considered superb.

The Musée Fin-de-Siècle Museum displays works from the late 10th to early 20th centuries, during which time Belgium was at the very center of the exciting and important art nouveau and art deco movements.

The collections of the Musée Modern Museum span the 19th century to the present day (renovation works ongoing).
🚩 B2 ✉ rue de la Régence 3 ☎ 02 508 3211; www.fine-arts-museum.be ⏰ Tue.–Fri. 10–5, Sat.–Sun. 11–5 🚇 Gare Centrale 🚌 27, 29, 38, 63, 65, 66, 71, 95; tram 92, 93, 95 🍴 Museum café and brasserie/restaurant 💶 Individual museums $$$; combined tickets available; free first Wed. of the month after 1 p.m. ℹ English audio guide ($$) is available

Musée de la Ville de Bruxelles

The Musée de la Ville de Bruxelles (City of Brussels Museum) is a local celebration of Brussels. It merits a visit for its porcelain, pottery and tapestry collections as well as its paintings, including Brueghel the Elder's splendid piece *The Marriage Procession*.

The museum is on Grand' Place in the handsome building known as La Maison du Roi (The King's House). On the top floor there is a display of some of the more than 800 costumes comprising the "wardrobe" of the *Manneken-Pis* (see box page 57), which have been donated by heads of state and others since 1698.
🚩 B3 ✉ rue du Poivre 1 (entrance from Grand' Place) ☎ 02 279 4350; www.museedelavilledebruxelles.be ⏰ Tue.–Wed. and Fri.–Sun. 10–5, Thu. 10–8 🚇 Bourse, Gare Centrale 💶 $$; free first Sun. of the month ℹ Very little information in English

Muséum des Sciences Naturelles

Europe's largest dinosaur exhibition is the centerpiece of the Natural History Museum. Actual skeletons include nine of the dozens of iguanodons discovered in Bernissart in the Belgian countryside in 1878. The state-of-the-art galleries here shed light on our natural world and the forces that have shaped the earth's history. Others explore the biodiversity that shapes our contemporary world.
🚩 Off map at C1 ✉ rue Vautier 29 ☎ 02 627 4211; www.sciencesnaturelles.be ⏰ Tue.–Fri. 9:30–5, Sat.–Sun. 10–6. Last admission 30 minutes before closing 🚌 34, 38, 80, 95 🍴 Café 💶 $$$; free first Wed. of the month from 1 p.m.

Grand' Place

The late medieval Grand' Place, or Grote Markt in Flemish, is one of the most glorious sights of urban Europe. These are buildings that seem wrought from nature, yet their symmetry and elegance is ravishing. Any debate about the competing merits of traditional or Modernist architecture melts away in the face of such adventurous style.

What you see in Grand' Place today are some of the finest examples of Flemish Renaissance and Gothic architecture, most of which are 17th-century replacements of older wooden-framed guild houses. The originals were destroyed in 1695 during a devastating bombardment of Brussels by the troops of a spiteful Louis XIV. The citizens rebuilt the heart of their city in a bold act of defiance.

The late Gothic-style Town Hall (Hôtel de Ville), dating from the 15th century, is the focus of Grand' Place. Its soaring tower dominates the Brussels skyline; its facade is crammed with statues of dukes, duchesses, monks, saints and sinners.

The guild houses, which make up the remaining sides of the square, are named and represented by a collection of gilded statues, bas-reliefs, motifs and classical orders. They are a riot of exquisite forms and interesting symbols. Look for No. 7, Le Renard (The Fox), the Haberdasher's guild house; and No. 6, Le Cornet (the Horn), the guild house of the Boatmen, whose gable suggests the stern of a 17th-century sailing ship.

Opposite the Town Hall is La Maison du Roi (The King's House), known also as the Broodhuis (Bread House) and home to the City of Brussels Museum (Musée de la Ville de Bruxelles, see page 60).

On the east side of Grand' Place is the restored facade of the house of the Dukes of Brabant, six individual houses united by the cool elegance of a single Renaissance facade.

Finally, in the southeast corner to the left of the Town Hall, is No. 10, L'Arbre d'Or (The Golden Tree). This is the headquarters of the Brewers' Guild, the Knights of the Mash Staff, and also houses a Brewery Museum. Next door is Le Cygne (The Swan), complete with a graceful swan motif that rounds off the magnificent Grand' Place with a flourish.

⊕ B3 ✉ Grand' Place ☎ (Town Hall) 02 548 0447; www.brucity.be 🛈 Guided tours of Town Hall in English Wed. at 2, Sun. at 11, 3 and 4. Register at least 15 minutes before tour begins. Carpet of the Flowers mid-Aug. biennialy on even numbered years; medieval festival, the Ommegang in early Jul.; Planting of the May Tree procession in Aug.

Every two years a fabulous "carpet" of begonias is laid out in Grand' Place

Bruges

In Bruges (Brugge), the survival of exquisite medieval buildings provides a vivid architectural record of 16th-century Europe. Yet that survival is the result of a commercial decline that lasted for nearly 400 years. By the early 16th century, the Zwin river, which linked Bruges and its elegant canals to the North Sea, could not be navigated because of silting; the successful cloth trade had declined, and local and foreign traders moved their businesses to the flourishing port of Antwerp. There was

no wealth with which to modernize the venerable townscape. We can thank the rough handling of history for a city that delights with the completeness of its medieval street plan and its ornate buildings, now a UNESCO World Heritage Site.

Finding Your Way

If you arrive at Bruges railroad station you will find a small tourist information office on Stationsplein, outside the station to the right. It is only a short bus ride from Stationsplein to Bruges' grand central square, the Markt (see pages

BRUGES

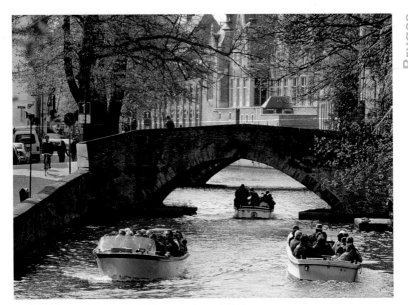

Sightseeing boats glide along a canal to pass under Groene Lei bridge

66–67), a good place to start sightseeing. A short walk along Breydelstraat, the street that begins at the southeast corner of the Markt, is the Burg (see pages 68–69), the historic heart of Bruges.

You can enjoy Bruges through guided tours, on foot, by bicycle, by bus or by canal boat (daily Mar.–Nov.). Trips on the famous horse-drawn carriages and trams of Bruges are enjoyable but more expensive. The city is easy to explore on your own, however.

A City of Canals

A few steps south of the Burg, along the narrow alley known as Blinde Ezelstraat (Blind Donkey Street), will bring you to the colonnaded Vismarkt (fish market), a lively scene Tuesday to Saturday mornings. From here proceed right to Huidenvettersplein, and then along Rozenhoedkaai (Rosary Quay) to the Dijver, a pretty, tree-lined walkway running alongside the canal. There is a splendid complex of museum buildings here, including the Groeningemuseum (see page 66), with a wonderful collection of paintings by the Flemish

Primitives, the Gruuthusemuseum (see page 66), which displays decorative arts, and the Church of Our Lady (Onze-Lieve-Vrouwekerk; see page 67). All are centered around Bonifaciusburg (St. Boniface Bridge), itself a reminder of medieval Bruges.

Across the road from the church is the Sint-Janshospitaal, the medieval St. John's Hospital, decorated by artist Hans Memling (see page 67). Also nearby is the old Begijnhof (Beguinage; see page 65), and from there you can explore the city's ancient walls and gates. The many canals lend Bruges the nickname "the Venice of the north."

Lace
Bruges has long been famous for its lace. Since the 16th century, lace-makers here specialized in bobbin lace, a method that used weaving and plaiting with thread-loaded bobbins, with the threads pinned to the pattern. In Italy, they made needlepoint lace, a method of embroidering with buttonhole and other stitches.

Cosmopolitan Tastes

Amid this historical splendor, modern Bruges has its own delights. The city's social life is centered on the Market Square and 't Zand, both lined with sidewalk cafés and bars.

There is a Wednesday market on the first square and a larger Saturday Market on the latter. Between 't Zand and the Markt lie Bruges' busiest streets, Noordzandstraat and Zuidzandstraat, the latter leading into the shopping area of Steenstraat, with connecting squares and narrow streets harboring cafés and several bistros.

Eating out in Bruges is a diner's delight. You will find every type of international restaurant, but make sure you try Belgian specialties such as *kalfsblanket*, veal ragout, or *lapin à la gueuze*, which is rabbit cooked in *gueuze* beer. A warming winter specialty is *hutsepot*, a delicious hotpot made with vegetables (usually potatoes, carrots and onions) and lamb.

Lace, Chocolate and Music

If you like lace, make sure you do not miss the Gruuthuse lace shop on the Dijver for intricate, authentic work, or the many lace shops on Wollestraat, which is the street running south from the Markt.

For antiques and craft stores, Mariastraat running south from Simon Stevinplein on Steenstraat is the place to browse; and for mouthwatering chocolates, which make a good souvenir, try the locals' favorite store, Spegelaere at Ezelstraat 92 (see page 466), where all the chocolates and marzipan are made on the premises.

At night, Bruges spectacularly lights up; the buildings in the Markt and elsewhere are illuminated and there is plenty to keep you entertained. Find out what's happening at Cultuurcentrum (www.ccbrugge.be) in St. Jakobsstraat, or catch one of the summer concerts performed each year on the open-air stage on the Burg.

Essential Information

Tourist Information

Toerisme Brugge (Bruges Tourism)
Concertgebouw (Concert Hall), 't-Zand 34
☎ 050 44 4646; www.brugge.be
🕙 Mon.–Sat. 10–5, Sun. 10–2
Stationsplein, Bruges railroad station (opening times and contact details same as above)
Markt (Historium), Markt 1 🕙 Daily 10–5

Urban Transportation

Bruges railroad station lies a mile southwest of the Markt. There also is an efficient bus service that caters to the city and its environs (☎ Information 070 220 200, toll call;

Mon.–Fri. 7–6, Sat. 10–6). Taxis: Rony's (☎ 050 344 344; www.ronystaxis.com). There are stands at the Markt and at Stationsplein.

Airport Information

Bruges does not have an airport; the nearest one is Brussels International Airport at Zaventem (see page 58). For flight information ☎ 0900 70000; 32 2 753 7753 (outside Belgium, Mon.–Fri. 7 a.m.–10 p.m., Sat.–Sun. 7 a.m.–8 p.m., toll call); www.brusselsairport. be. Train connections for Bruges are made at Brussels' Nord/Noord (North), Centrale/Centraal (Central) and Midi/Zuid (South) stations.

Climate – average highs and lows for the month

Jan.	Feb.	Mar.	Apr.	May	Jun.	Jul.	Aug.	Sep.	Oct.	Nov.	Dec.
5°C	6°C	8°C	11°C	15°C	18°C	19°C	20°C	18°C	15°C	10°C	6°C
41°F	43°F	46°F	52°F	59°F	64°F	66°F	68°F	64°F	59°F	50°F	43°F
1°C	2°C	3°C	5°C	9°C	11°C	12°C	12°C	11°C	8°C	4°C	2°C
34°F	36°F	37°F	41°F	48°F	52°F	54°F	54°F	52°F	46°F	39°F	36°F

Bruges Sights

Key to symbols

map coordinates refer to the Bruges map on page 62 admission charge:
$$$ more than €7.50, $$ €4–€7.50, $ less than €4
See page 5 for complete key to symbols

Basiliek van het Heilig Bloed

The Basiliek van het Heilig Bloed (Basilica of the Holy Blood, see pages 68–69) has been a place of pilgrimage for centuries. The basilica consists of two chapels; the lower St. Basil's Chapel, which displays a Romanesque style, and the upper 15th-century Gothic-style chapel with the famous Relic of the Holy Blood. In the Middle Ages, this vial, containing drops of Holy Blood, brought to Bruges in 1150, was considered one of the holiest relics in Europe.

Veneration takes place daily (except Wednesday, November to March) whereby a priest presents the vial to the awaiting congregation so that they may show their respects. The vial is on display throughout the year.

B2 Burg 10 050 336 792; www.holyblood. com Basilica and museum: daily 9:30–noon and 2–5, Apr.–Oct.; Mon.–Tue. and Thu.–Sun. 2–5, rest of year All buses to station and market Chapels free; museum $ Contact tourist office for information regarding Ascension Day Procession

Begijnhof

The Begijnhof (Beguinage) complex, a wonderful testimony to a more sedate, spiritual age, has retained its tranquil atmosphere. It was founded in 1245 to accommodate pious single women, many of them lace makers, who lived reclusive lives. These inhabitants, known as Beguines, abandoned the complex in the 1920s, but Benedictine nuns later settled in the Beguinage and still live here today. The 17th-century little whitewashed cottages surround a peaceful square.

You can visit the Begijnhuisje (Beguine's House), a museum house that has old-style furnishings and a delightful little cloister. The Begijnhof Church of St. Elizabeth has a simple grace.

B1 Wyngaardstraat 050 44 87 23 (museum reservation number) or 050 33 00 11 (monastery) Beguinage: daily sunrise–6:30 p.m. Beguine's House: Mon.–Sat. 10–5, Sun. 2:30–5. Church: daily 7–12:15 and 3–6 1 Beguinage and church free; Beguine's House $

Belfort

Bruges' famous medieval Belfort (Belfry) dominates the Markt. You can reach the top of the 272-foot tower by climbing the 366 steps. You may marvel at the vast number of bricks and the tons of mortar holding everything together, including the 27 tons that the 47-bell

After climbing the Belfort (Belfry) you can look down on the café-restaurants on the Markt

Allegorical Figure of the Christian Church by Master of the Legend of St. Ursula, in the Groeningemuseum

with *Canon Joris van der Paele*, the works of Pieter Pourbus and Hans Memling, and the nightmarish *The Last Judgment* by Hieronymus Bosch.

➕ B2 ✉ Dijver 12 ☎ 50 448 711; www.museabrugge.be ⏰ Tue.–Sun. 9:30–5 🚌 11 💷 $$$ (includes audio guide)

Gruuthusemuseum

The 15th-century city palace of the Gruuthuse family houses a collection of fine Flemish decorative arts, including a stunning display of 16th- and 17th-century tapestries. It features an interesting oratory overlooking the altar of the church next door. There also is a collection of paintings by the Bruges-born British artist Frank Brangwyn. As well as grand objects, the vast kitchen is a revelation, with a large range of crockery, cutlery and pottery.

➕ B2 ✉ Dijver 17 ☎ 50 448 711; www.museabrugge.be ⏰ Closed for renovation work until mid-2017

Huisbrouwerij de Halve Maan

Step into the Huisbrouwerij de Halve Maan (The Half Moon Brewery), where the local Strong Henry beer has been brewed since 1546 and a new brew, Brugse Zot, has been flowing since 2005. The present building dates from 1856. The air of the brewery is so aromatic that it might make your head spin, although a visit to the roof will clear it. To complete your visit there is a guided tour of the museum and a complimentary drink of beer at the bar.

➕ B1 ✉ Walplein 26 ☎ 050 444 222; www.halvemaan.be ⏰ Guided tours: Mon.–Fri. and Sun. 11–4, Sat. 11–5 (tours begin on the hour) 🚌 1 💷 $$$

carillon weighs. Below the belfry is the chamber containing the clock mechanism and copper carillon drum. The bells ring each quarter hour. You have time to watch the ingenious system whir and click into life, like a great mechanical beast, before the short climb to the belfry to enjoy the surprisingly muted peals and the view.

➕ B2 ✉ Markt ☎ 50 448 711; www.museabrugge.be ⏰ Daily 9:30–5. Last admission 45 minutes before closing 🚌 All buses to station and market 💷 $$$ ℹ️ Only 70 people are allowed into the tower at a time. Check with the tourist office for carillon recitals

Groeningemuseum

The Groeningemuseum is housed in a former Augustinian monastery on the Dijver and contains Bruges' superb civic collection of 15th- to 20th-century Flemish, Dutch and Belgian paintings. There are exceptional works here, including Jan van Eyck's *The Madonna*

Markt

The Markt (Market Square) is a superbly atmospheric square, the heart of Bruges. The Gothic buildings of the Provinciaal Hof, seat of the government of West Flanders, and the adjoining Central Post Office dominate the east side of the impressive square.

The Belfort (Belfry, see pages 65–66) stands on the south side. The crow-stepped gables of a row of guild houses stand behind a statue of Jan Breydel and Pieter de Coninck, heroes of the 1302 uprising against French overlordship.

The west side of the Markt has a collection of handsome buildings, including the 15th-century Maison Bouchoute and the Craenenburg House (now the Café Craenenburg) flanking the entrance to Sint Amandstraat. At Markt 1, Historium is a walk-through attraction re-creating some of the medieval highlights of the city.

🔀 B2 ✉ Markt 🚍 Most buses 🎠 Horse-drawn carriage trips ($$$) and mini-bus tours ($$$) start from the Markt

Onze-Lieve-Vrouwekerk

The brooding Onze-Lieve-Vrouwekerk (Church of Our Lady) plays host to several important objects. The superb Gothic stonework protects the gilded Renaissance mausoleum of Charles the Bold, the powerful ruler of the region as Duke of Burgundy. The pulpit designed by Bruges artist Jan Antoon Geramijn is a marvelous rococo extravaganza but the major artistic draw is Michelangelo's masterpiece sculpture *Madonna and Child*. Originally intended for a church in Siena, Italy it was bought by two wealthy Bruges merchants. The church is undergoing renovation but will remain open. Michelangelo's sculpture is still on view, however, some areas are closed to the public.

🔀 B2 ✉ Mariastraat 🕿 50 448 711; www.museabrugge.be 🕓 Church and museum: Mon.–Sat. 9:30–5, Sun. 1:30–5. Last admission 30 minutes before closing 🚍 1 🎟 Church free; Museum $ (during renovation work). Combined ticket for all Bruggemuseum sites available

Sint-Janshospitaal

St. John's Hospital, founded in the 12th century, was one of Europe's oldest surviving medieval hospitals, but it has been renovated into a spectacular background for Hans Memling's work.

A German painter, Memling settled in Bruges in 1465 and soon was in great demand. The chapel, which contains magnificent 15th-century Memling decorative panels and the St. Ursula Shrine, is the highlight of the complex, but the fascinating old hospital pharmacy also is worth a visit. Look for masterpieces such as the *Madonna with Child* and the *Lamentation of Christ*.

🔀 B2 ✉ Mariastraat 38 🕿 50 448 711; www.museabrugge.be 🕓 Tue.–Sun. 9:30–5 (pharmacy closed 11:45–2) 🚍 1 🎟 $$$ (includes audio guide)

Sint-Salvatorskathedraal

Bruges' churches reflect a sober Flemish style, but Sint-Salvatorskathedraal (St. Saviour's Cathedral) has many features to counteract its Gothic vastness. The high altar and the 15th-century choir stalls add a richly decorative note; the rood loft, beneath the organ case, contains a superb baroque sculpture of God the Father in white marble by Arthur Quellin the Younger. Visit the Cathedral Museum; among its treasures is the vivid realism of Dirk Bouts' 15th-century triptych *The Martyrdom of St. Hippolytus*.

🔀 B2 ✉ Steenstraat 🕿 050 336 841; www.sintsalvator.be 🕓 Cathedral: Mon.–Fri. 10–1 and 2–5:30; Sat. 10–1 and 2–3:30; Sun. 11:30–noon and 2–5. Museum: Sun.–Fri. 2–5 🚍 1–5, 13, 89 and all buses that go to the market 🎟 Cathedral free; museum $ 🎵 Major concerts held in cathedral

Stadhuis

The Stadhuis (Town Hall) stands in the medieval Burg (see pages 68–69) and dates from the 14th century. It has undergone renovation work over the years and has a superb carved Gothic facade. Inside this important building is the splendid former council chamber, the Gotische Zaal (Gothic Hall), where local policies were once decided.

🔀 B2 ✉ Burg 12 🕿 50 448 711; www.museabrugge.be 🕓 Daily 9:30–5 🚍 All buses to the Markt 🎟 Gothic Hall $; museum $$. Combined ticket for all Bruggemuseum sites available

A Medieval Experience: The Burg

The Burg is medieval Bruges at its most tangible. Once it was a jealously guarded enclave, walled and with locked gates. Today it is the city's finest public square, an intimate space flanked by a series of exquisite historic buildings offering a unique perspective on the secular and religious importance of the city during its heyday. The northern side of this outstanding architectural complex contained the 10th-century Romanesque Church of St. Donatian, demolished in 1799 during the French occupation of the region. The only remaining element of the complex is the handsome facade of the Provost's House of St. Donatian.

On the east side of the Burg is the Paleis van de Brugse Vrije (Palace of the Liberty of Bruges; www.museabrugge.be; open daily 9:30 a.m.–12:30 p.m. and 1:30 p.m.–5 p.m.), once the seat of the Bishop of Bruges and now the administrative headquarters of West Flanders, the westernmost province of the Flemish region of Belgium. This was once the ruling seat of the Bruges Vrije, a territorial precinct of Flanders. One wing harbors a magnificent Renaissance chimneypiece created in honor of Charles V, Count of Flanders and Holy Roman Emperor. The lower section is in black marble with an alabaster frieze depicting the biblical story of Suzanna and the Elders. The main section is in exquisitely carved wood and depicts the Emperor and members of the Habsburg family, the male contingent endowed with embellished Habsburgian codpieces.

To the right of the palace across narrow Blinde Ezelstraat (Blind Donkey Street) is the Stadhuis (Town Hall of Bruges, see page 67). This exquisite building dates from the 14th century but has been rebuilt and renovated over the centuries. The turreted, Gothic sandstone facade is a lyrical evocation of the mason's craft. Inside is the council chamber, the Gotische Zaal (Gothic Hall), with 19th-century romantic wall paintings that illustrate important events in the history of Bruges, and a handsome chimneypiece. Its glorious vaulted ceiling is all gilded wooden arches with slender ribs and hanging keystones. Fortunate couples are married here.

To the right of the Town Hall in the southwest corner of the Burg is the most medieval building of all, Basiliek van het Heilig Bloed (the Basilica of the Holy Blood; see page 65). In the building is a sacred vial believed to contain drops of Christ's blood, brought to Bruges in 1150 from the Holy Land by Diederik van den Elzas, count of Flanders. The Holy Blood is still venerated daily (except Wednesday, November to March). Each Ascension Day in May or June, the relic is the focus of one of the most important events in West Flanders, the Heilig-Bloedprocessie (Holy Blood Procession), a colorful and theatrical costume pageant depicting religious events, where the relic is taken around the center of town.

There is something strangely compelling about the Basilica of the Holy Blood. It has a medieval authenticity that is irresistible, even to the ungodly. The building contains an upper and lower chapel. You enter the lower chapel through a modest doorway and it is as if you are stepping straight into the Middle Ages. The basilica dates from the 12th century and was built to house the relics of St. Basil. It has been partly restored, but is still one of the finest surviving examples of Romanesque architecture in Flanders. Wall carvings are simple, almost primitive. The air is dense and exterior sounds are muffled and resonant.

Gothic Mood

You reemerge into the daylight, pass through an enchanting Gothic doorway in the ornate facade of the main chapel and then mount a wide staircase beneath shallow vaults. The upper chapel is a breathtaking contrast to the somber Romanesque below the stairs. It is lavishly decorated in a late Gothic style that overlays original Romanesque themes. A rococo white marble altar, barrel roof, luminous stained glass, carved wood, and gold and silver artifacts all create a mood that is reminiscent of the heavy decoration of Orthodox churches.

There is a delightful spherical oak pulpit with disk canopy but with no visible access. The secret is a small door to the side of the Holy Blood altar, which opens onto hidden stairs. The Holy Blood is contained within a crystal sheath with a gold crown stopper and is supported by gilded copper and silver angels. Adjoining the upper church is a small museum with the gold and silver reliquary for the Holy Blood.

Above left to right: The Holy Blood Procession takes place in the town center on Ascension Day each year; outdoor café tables in Eiermarkt in the heart of the old city

Ghent

At first glance Ghent (Gent or Gand), the fourth-largest city in Belgium, may seem slightly rough around the edges, a city lacking the sparkle of Luxembourg or the carefully preserved splendor of Bruges.

Ghent has been an industrial and commercial center throughout its long history, and the fabric of the city has suffered because of this. But apart from the urban realities, this is Belgium's "City of Flowers," containing some of the finest historical and cultural artifacts in Europe, along with architecture that encompasses soaring towers and exquisitely decorative domestic buildings.

Its citizens, the friendly Gentenaars, are shrewd, down to earth and personable. Many speak some English and are always ready to oblige the visitor with guidance and advice.

A tram on Korenmarkt makes its way through Ghent's busy historic center

First Impressions

Ghent's main railroad station, Sint-Pietersstation (St. Peter's Station), is just over a mile south of the city center. The station can be a sobering experience for the first-time visitor. It is a busy place and has reasonable facilities, including a digital information port offering tourist information. For comprehensive visitor information head to the heart of the city and the helpful tourist information center in Sint-Veerlpein, close to Het Gravensteen and just off Kraanlei.

Buses, trolley buses and trams leave regularly for Korenmarkt from a covered terminal on the east side of Sint-Pietersstation. Ghent's trams run along extremely narrow streets – a mildly alarming experience at first – but they do so with great efficiency. Almost 75 acres of downtown Ghent is traffic free; the area encompasses some of the city's most important historical attractions.

The great central squares are the best places to get a handle on Ghent. Here are the powerful Gothic churches of Sint-Baafskathedraal (see page 74) and Sint-Niklaaskerk. Civic buildings between them include the Belfort (Belfry), the Lakenhalle (Cloth Hall) and the Stadhuis (Town Hall), with their distinctive mix of architectural styles. Take the glass elevator to the top of the Belfort (www.belfortgent.be) for superb views of this city of towers and steeples.

Old Ghent

For a taste of old Ghent, go west from Sint-Niklaaskerk, past the neo-Gothic, neo-Renaissance flamboyance of the 1910 former post office, to the bridge of Sint-Michielsbrug that spans the Leie river. Look back from the bridge for a breathtaking view of the skyline. North of the bridge is Tussen Bruggen, once a busy harbor and still lined by the gabled buildings of Graslei, a popular place for taking photographs, and Korenlei.

North of Graslei is Groentenmarkt, a tree-shaded square flanked by the sturdy 15th-century Groot Vleeshuis (Great Butchers' Hall), though meat is no longer sold there. Today the Groentenmarkt is the scene of a bio-produce market on Friday mornings, and an open-air art forum between 10 a.m. and 6 p.m. on Sundays, April through September.

A few steps farther is Sint-Veerleplein, with a monumental baroque archway to the old fish market and handsome gabled houses. However grand, these houses are all overshadowed by the brooding mass of Het Gravensteen, the 12th-century Castle of the Counts (see page 73).

Across the street, to the east of Het Gravensteen, is the narrow, waterfront street of Kraanlei, an attractive row of late medieval buildings lining a stretch of the Leie river. This is one of Ghent's finest streetscapes. From Kraanlei's far end, the Zuivelbrug (Zuivel Bridge) crosses the canal into the square of Vrijdagmarkt, where there is a popular and large market on Fridays.

Shopping in Ghent

Ghent's main commercial and shopping area lies to the south of Korenmarkt and Botermarkt. The busy Veldstraat has stores of all types, but if you walk through the network of little streets just east of here, including Mageleinstraat, Sint-Niklaasstraat, Kortedagsteeg and Koestraat, you'll find numerous specialty shops. These include chic fashion boutiques, delicatessens, *chocolateries*, antiques and crafts shops. At the heart of the area is the Kouter flower market, held daily, but at its colorful best on Sundays, a vivid indication of Ghent's fame as the "City of Flowers."

Night Lights

Eating out in Ghent is an essential experience. Try such local specialties as *Gentse hazenpeper* (jugged hare) or *Gentse waterzooi van riviervis* (freshwater fish stew). There are many intimate restaurants in the Patershol area to the north of Kraanlei.

Enjoy Ghent by night, when the buildings are lit up and the streets hum with life. Spend an evening at the trendy and busy Handelsbeurs at Kouter 29 (www.handelsbeurs.be); at Opera Gent (www.operaballet.be) on Schouwburgstraat; or at the classical music venue Stedelijke Concertzaal De Bijloke (www.debijloke.be) on Josef Kluyskensstraat.

Essential Information

Tourist Information
Toerisme Stad Gent (Ghent Tourism)
Oude Vismijn Sint-Veerleplein 5
☎ 09 266 5660; www.visitgent.be

Urban Transportation
Ghent railroad station (Sint-Pietersstation) is one mile south of the city center. For international rail information ☎ 070 79 79 79 (toll call, Mon.–Fri. 8–8, Sat.–Sun. and public holidays 9–4:30); www.b-europe.com, domestic services ☎ 02 528 2828 (daily 7 a.m.–9:30 p.m.); www.belgianrail.be. Ghent's main bus and tram stations adjoin the railroad station. Tram, trolley bus and bus service times are available from the tourist office or bus information offices, or call Delijn ☎ 070 220 200 (toll call, Mon.–Fri. 7–6, Sat. 10–6); www.delijn.be. There are taxis at the Korenmarkt and outside Sint-Pietersstation or call ☎ 09 333 3333; www.taxigent.be.

Airport Information
The nearest airport is Brussels International Airport at Zaventem (see page 58). For flight information, call ☎ 0900 70000; 32 2 753 7753 (outside Belgium, Mon.–Fri. 7 a.m.–10 p.m., Sat.–Sun. 7 a.m.–8 p.m., toll call). Train connections to Ghent can be made at Brussels' Nord/Noord (North), Centrale/Centraal (Central) and Midi/Zuid (South) stations. The trip from the airport to Ghent takes 30 minutes.

Climate – average highs and lows for the month

Jan.	Feb.	Mar.	Apr.	May	Jun.	Jul.	Aug.	Sep.	Oct.	Nov.	Dec.
5°C	6°C	9°C	11°C	17°C	21°C	22°C	22°C	20°C	15°C	9°C	5°C
41°F	43°F	48°F	52°F	63°F	70°F	72°F	72°F	68°F	59°F	48°F	41°F
0°C	1°C	2°C	5°C	8°C	11°C	12°C	12°C	11°C	7°C	4°C	2°C
32°F	34°F	36°F	41°F	46°F	52°F	54°F	54°F	52°F	45°F	39°F	36°F

Ghent Sights

Key to symbols
✚ map coordinates refer to the Ghent map
on page 70 💷 admission charge:
$$$ more than €7.50, $$ €4–€7.50, $ less than €4
See page 5 for complete key to symbols

Het Huis van Alijn museum occupies several houses

Design Museum Gent

The Design Museum Gent is a Ghent experience not to be missed. Housed in the handsome old Hotel de Coninck, and with a stunning contemporary extension, the museum exhibits international and Belgian decorative and applied art, crafts and design from the Renaissance to 20th-century art deco, art nouveau and contemporary work, including a Pininfarina-designed Coca-Cola® Freestyle® machine.

The older part of the museum displays superb period interiors and has lucid explanations of baroque, rococo and classical styles.

✚ A3 ✉ Jan Breydelstraat 5 ☎ 09 267 9999; www.designmuseumgent.be 🕔 Tue.–Sun. 10–6 🚊 3, 17, 18, 38, 39; tram 1, 4, 24 💷 $$$

Graslei en Korenlei

Graslei and Korenlei are the wharves flanking the medieval harbor Tussen Bruggen ("between the bridges") that lies to the north of the bridge of Sint-Michielsbrug. Their names relate to their role in the grain trade; their buildings were the trade and guild houses of the medieval period, carefully restored for the World Exhibition of 1913. The facades of these magnificent buildings offer an impression of Ghent in the days when the wharves were alive with the bustle of medieval trade.

✚ A3 ✉ Graslei en Korenlei 🚊 3, 17, 18, 38,39; tram 1, 4, 24

Het Gravensteen

Magnificent Gravensteen (Castle of the Counts) has all the authentic menace of 12th-century feudalism. A visit to this well-restored building is irresistible,

made even better by the "movieguide" visual tour companion (included in the ticket price). The main castle is a series of intriguing rooms linked by staircases.

In the upper rooms you will find historical exhibitions, including the Wapenmuseum (Weapons Museum) with historical weapons, and the Gerechtsmuseum (Museum of Instruments of Torture), which displays tools of torture and execution.

✚ A4 ✉ Sint-Veerleplein ☎ 09 243 9730; www.gravensteengent.be 🕔 Daily 10–6, Apr.–Oct.; 9–5, rest of year. Last admission 45 minutes before closing 🚊 Tram 1, 4, 24 💷 $$$ (includes museums)

Het Huis van Alijn

The intriguing Het Huis van Alijn (Alijn House) owes much of its charm to its location among the old buildings of the 14th-century Kinderen Alijns Hospitaal (Hospital of the Alijns Children), on the canalside street of Kraanlei. Children will be thrilled with the museum's marionette theater company, 't Spelleke van de Folklore, and other delights. The collections are spread throughout some quaint little houses surrounding a central square. The domestic and commercial life of Ghent through the ages is exhaustively represented in excellent set-piece tableaux and displays.

✚ B4 ✉ Kraanlei 65 ☎ 09 269 2350; www.huisvanalijn.be 🕔 Tue.–Sat. 11–5:30, Sun. 10–5:30 🚊 3, 17, 18, 39; tram 1, 4, 24 🍽 Museum tavern 💷 $$ 🎭 Puppet shows Sat. at 2:30 (also Wed. in school holidays) ($$); tickets at www.uitbureau.be

Architectural gems along the Leie river in Ghent

Kraanlei

Kraanlei is one of Ghent's finest canalside streets. Its name derives from a wooden crane that unloaded cargoes. The baroque facades of Kraanlei's buildings, with touches of Gothic, are survivors of an exuberant age of prosperity and Flemish culture. The houses have stepped gables and pediments. Look for Ghent's version of Brussels' *Manneken-Pis* (see page 57), perched above a restaurant door at the beginning of the street. Halfway along is the Het Huis van Alijn (Alijn House, see page 73). Three of the finest facades are at the far end of Kraanlei and include the exquisite 17th-century house known as "The Flying Deer."

Lively Patershol, a few steps north of Kraanlei, is a warren of cobbled streets with art galleries and trendy restaurants.

➕ B4 ✉ Kraanlei 🚌 3, 17, 18, 39; tram 1, 4, 24 🍴 Restaurants nearby

Museum voor Schone Kunsten

The Museum voor Schone Kunsten (Museum of Fine Arts) is one of Belgium's oldest art galleries. It offers an overview of local Flemish art from the Middle Ages to the first half of the 20th century. Exhibits also offer an insight into the tastes of the local bourgeoisie who were strongly connected with France but interested in the rest of Europe. The collection includes works by Flemish and other European masters from the 14th to mid-20th centuries.

Of special note are the works by Hieronymus Bosch. Other superb pieces include Pieter Brueghel the Younger's *Wedding Feast* and Frans Hals' evocative *Portrait of a Woman*.

➕ Off map at B1 ✉ Fernand Scribedreef 1, Citadelpark ☎ 09 240 0700; www.mskgent.be 🕐 Tue.–Sun. 10–6 🚌 34, 35, 36, 55, 57, 58, 70, 71, 72, 73, 74 🍴 Museum café 🖐 $$$

Sint-Baafskathedraal

The tall four-stage tower of Sint-Baafskathedraal (St. Bavo's Cathedral) dominates the east end of Botermarkt. Externally, the cathedral is a mix of Gothic styles beneath a patina of city grime. Inside is one of the great art treasures of the world, the multipaneled *Het Lam Gods (The Mystic Lamb),* known as the Ghent Altar (see page 75). Other treasures include the rococo pulpit in Carrara marble and Danish oak, with its carved staircases like twisted tree roots. The 12th-century Romanesque crypt of the cathedral is full of religious artifacts and works of art.

➕ B2–C2 ✉ Sint-Baafsplein ☎ 09 269 2045; www.sintbaafskathedraal.be 🕐 Cathedral and crypt: Mon.–Sat. 8:30–6, Sun. 1–6, Apr.–Oct.; Mon.–Sat. 8:30–5, Sun. 1–5, rest of year. *The Mystic Lamb*: Mon.–Sat. 9:30–5, Sun. 1–5, Apr.–Oct.; Mon.–Sat. 10:30–4, Sun. 1–4, rest of year 🚌 Tram 1, 4, 22, 24 🖐 Cathedral and altar free; *The Mystic Lamb* $$ (includes audio guide) ♿ A panel may be missing due to renovation work

Stedelijk Museum voor Actuele Kunst (S.M.A.K.)

Opposite the Museum of Fine Arts (see left) is the Stedelijk Museum voor Actuele Kunst (Municipal Museum of Contemporary Art), or S.M.A.K., Belgium's finest post-1945 art collection. It includes works by Andy Warhol, Francis Bacon, Joseph Beuys, David Hockney, Christo and Belgian artist Marcel Broodthaers, and often has outstanding temporary exhibitions.

➕ Off map at B1 ✉ Citadelpark ☎ 09 240 7601; www.smak.be 🕐 Tue.–Sun. 10–6 🚌 34, 35, 36, 55, 57, 58, 70, 71, 72, 73, 74 🍴 Museum café 🖐 $$$

De aanbidding van Het Lam Gods – The Adoration of the Mystic Lamb

The famous Ghent Altar, *Het Lam Gods (The Mystic Lamb)*, lives up to your highest expectations. A visit to Sint-Baafskathedraal (St. Bavo's Cathedral) and a view of the altar should not be missed. This luminous work unveiled in 1432 has an impact that can change lives and attitudes.

The Ghent Altar is a polyptych, a painting made up of many panels. It is allegedly the work of two 15th-century Flemish painters, brothers Hubert and Jan van Eyck. There are doubts over whether or not Hubert van Eyck even existed, although Jan van Eyck was unquestionably the most famous painter of his generation.

Two rows of paintings, one above the other, make up the altar. The centerpiece in the upper row is of Christ the King, who is flanked by the Virgin Mary, St. John the Baptist, singing angels, a musician and nude portraits of Adam and a pregnant Eve within the wing panels. The focus of the lower row is the Adoration of the Lamb of God. The flanking panels depict processions of the faithful, judges, knights, hermits and pilgrims. The painted wing panels fold over to enclose the central panels. All of this is presented in breathtaking color against detailed Flanders landscapes.

The altar has survived the meddling of history. Iconoclasts sought to destroy it. In the 1780s the panels showing the nude Adam and Eve were removed from view during a visit by Emperor Joseph II. In the late 1800s two panels showing the couple clothed in bear skins were displayed to take into account more prudish sensibilities of the times. Two panels were stolen in 1934. The panel depicting John the Baptist was found in Brussels Central railroad station. The panel of the Righteous Judges has never been traced and was replaced by a copy painted by a Belgian artist, Jef van de Veken. During World War II, German soldiers stole this particular work but it was later liberated by American troops.

A five-year restoration program of the Ghent Altar is under way and is scheduled to continue until 2017. One panel will be removed at a time for restoration.

Lord in Majesty between the Virgin Mary and St. John the Baptist by Hubert and Jan van Eyck

Britain

Opposite: Hampton Court Palace, in the London Borough of Richmond upon Thames, Greater London

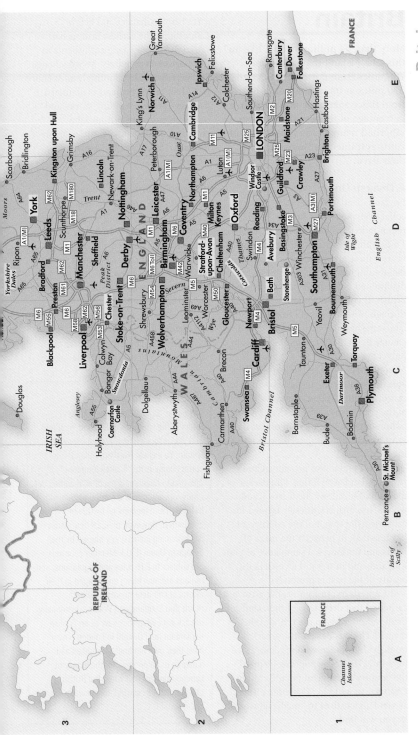

Britain

More than 64 million people live on this small island that spans only 700 miles from north to south and 350 miles at its widest point. But from this remarkable nation, a large percentage of the world's population inherited many of the linguistic and cultural influences that shaped their lives.

A Diverse Unity

England, Scotland and Wales – collectively known as Britain – each retain individual cultural characteristics. To complicate matters further for the visitor, there are distinct regions within regions, all reflecting the resilient and determined individuality that is typically British. If you spend any time traveling through Britain, you will find that the landscape and the customs of the people change dramatically, sometimes within only a few miles.

People have been arriving at all points around Britain's corrugated coastline for centuries, but London is now the focus of the country as a whole. Here history, politics and culture meet in one of the most invigorating and exciting cities in the world.

Beyond London lies provincial and rural England. You'll find a landscape of moors and meadows, hedgerows and woods, its earth relentlessly farmed for centuries. But much of the countryside has retained, in between the maze of roads and highways, a semblance of Old England, and in treasured corners the beauty of the past is preserved.

At Canterbury, in Kent, is the great cathedral that drew tens of thousands of medieval pilgrims to the relics of the revered Thomas Becket, the great English churchman who was murdered here in 1170. These pilgrims inspired the country's first great poet, Geoffrey Chaucer, to write his *Canterbury Tales*, as vivid a picture of the medieval world as you will find.

Yet before Chaucer and before Canterbury, the earliest Britons had raised their own pagan equivalents to the Christian cathedrals. At Stonehenge, and perhaps more hauntingly at Avebury in Wiltshire, in the heart of southern England, are the standing stones and burial chambers of Britons who commanded England centuries before Romans, Danes, Anglo-Saxons and Normans ever did.

Village Greens and Seaside

Throughout scores of picturesque villages in southern and western England, you will find the essence of the country; where people still play cricket on village greens, dance around maypoles on May Day and sell jars of local honey at village festivals – weather permitting, of course.

Yet England also boasts great cities and historic towns that bustle with energy. The great seaport of Bristol is one. The Georgian city of Bath, where

---

Britain Explained

The name "Britain" (or "Great Britain") refers to the countries of England, Scotland and Wales located on the main island of Britain. To include Northern Ireland, the correct name is the "United Kingdom." The United Kingdom is the official unified entity, governed by the central parliament in London and (nominally) by Queen Elizabeth II. However, political boundaries are becoming increasingly blurred by the European Union (E.U.). Member countries are subject to E.U. rules and regulations, and regions are now being encouraged in their efforts at self-determination, with the result that Scotland and Wales – historically uneasy with what they saw as an English parliament (and Queen) in London – now have their own national assemblies and a degree of autonomy. But the legacy of London remains, and when the British talk about "this country" they usually mean Britain.

Stonehenge stone circle, on Salisbury Plain in Wiltshire, was built around 5,000 years ago

warm Cotswold stone and the classical elegance of 18th-century fashion conspired to create one of the world's most astounding cityscapes, seems consumed with golden light in the summer sun.

Miles of coastline fringe the English Channel. On the southern coast are the cliffs of Beachy Head, and famous resorts like Brighton and Bournemouth, as well as long stretches of undulating green and peaceful coast that run westward past Dorset's limestone cliffs and the rich red cliffs of Devon to the golden beaches of Cornwall.

From Oxford to the Lakes

North and west of London, in the counties of Oxfordshire and Warwickshire, are such cities as Oxford, university town par excellence, matched only by its rival Cambridge in the fen country of eastern England. Here, too, you will find the Cotswolds, with its honey-colored limestone villages and the historic town of Stratford-upon-Avon, birthplace of William Shakespeare.

Progress through the cultural heart of England is not an idyllic rural journey

by any means. Yet the cities of Manchester, Leeds, Birmingham and Liverpool are vibrant and exciting places, while historic cities such as Chester, on the Welsh border, and York in the east have managed to preserve their medieval townscapes.

Beyond this great sprawl an unspoiled England survives. Derbyshire's Peak District, the Yorkshire Dales, the exquisite Lake District of Cumbria and

More Top Destinations in Britain (see map pages 78–79)

- Avebury D2
- Bath D1
- Caernarfon Castle C3
- Cambridge E2
- Canterbury E1
- Chester C3
- The Cotswolds D2
- Dartmoor C1
- Deeside C5
- Glen Coe C5
- Isle of Skye B6
- Lake District C4
- St. Andrews C5
- St. Michael's Mount B1
- Snowdonia C3
- Stonehenge D1
- Stratford-upon-Avon D2
- The Trossachs C5
- Windsor Castle D2
- Yorkshire Dales D3

Urquhart Castle perches on the banks of the famous Loch Ness, near Inverness, in Scotland

the lonely heights of Northumberland appear like magic in the landscape.

Wild Wales

Wales is renowned as a land of poetry and song, and as a part of Britain that seems older than time. In these green borderlands, the ruined castles of Norman Britain survive, relics of a time when England failed to entirely subdue the Welsh communities. Strongholds of the Anglo-Norman conquerors, such as Caernarfon Castle, are reminders of a later age of determined feudalism. But in the beautiful countryside of central Wales, on the rugged west coast and in the great mountains of Snowdonia, the spirit of the ancient Welsh lives on, the powerful identity of modern Wales a token of that endurance.

North to the Highlands

North of Northumberland and Cumbria, the Southern Uplands guard Scotland's borderland, once infamous for its violent robber clans. It was this raw border country that gave courage to heroic Scottish patriots like Robert Bruce and William Wallace as they pitted themselves against England's might. And across these hills in 1745 marched Charles Edward Stuart – Bonnie Prince Charlie, the last of a moribund royal line – supported by the cream of the Highland clans in a doomed final gesture of defiance by Scotland against English domination.

North of the Southern Uplands are the Central Lowlands of Scotland, with the capital city of Edinburgh to the east and Glasgow, the great powerhouse of old industrial Scotland, to the west. Edinburgh is the historic distillation of all things Scottish, the political and cultural focus of the nation from a time when poet Robert Burns and novelist Sir Walter Scott graced fashionable 18th-century salons, to the vigorous and progressive Edinburgh International Festival of today.

Across the Forth river (Firth of Forth) from Edinburgh lies the region of Fife, often referred to as the "Kingdom of Fife," home to the university town and golfing mecca of St. Andrews. To the north and west are the Scottish Highlands, Britain's most dramatic landscape, and some of the last great wilderness areas of Europe.

At the edge of the Highlands are the Trossachs, Scotland's equivalent to England's Lake District, steeped in the history of real-life characters like Rob Roy Macgregor, inspiration for the classic novels of Sir Walter Scott. Farther north are the mountains of Aberdeenshire. Here, on Royal Deeside, sits Balmoral Castle, traditional summer retreat of the Queen and her family.

Scotland's most spectacular mountain country lies to the far west and north, at the Pass of Glen Coe, and then for more than 100 miles northward along the west coast to Kintail and Wester Ross. Out to sea lie the Isle of Skye and the misty Hebrides, romantic islands at Britain's far western edge.

Seeing the Country

Britain's essence lies in its diversity and in the hidden corners between the most popular places. Traveling independently by train or bus is one way to explore off the beaten track, but you will need to plan carefully. Britain's long-distance bus network is generally good, but away from major cities and main roads service can vary greatly. Organized bus tours, on the other hand, will whisk you efficiently to all the major tourist sights. Traveling by car is another option; Britain is so diverse that you can drive for a few hours on a main highway and then veer off onto quieter byways.

London is a year-round destination, but outside the main summer season and major vacation periods, Britain's hidden corners are quiet. May and June are good months to visit – the freshness of early June is invigorating in England's upland areas, northern Wales and the Scottish Highlands. Winter is quite another story, but even in December and January Britain's larger cities are vibrant; London, Manchester, Liverpool, Cardiff, Edinburgh and Glasgow all pulse with British fashion and style.

Great classical music can be savored year-round in London, Manchester and Edinburgh. Attend world-class theater in Cardiff and Glasgow. Outstanding choirs fill England's cathedrals with truly heavenly music, and the open-air performances by Welsh and Cornish choirs are enchanting. Enjoy folk music or a live rock band at a neighborhood pub, or discover a colorful local festival or time-honored custom in a Devonshire hamlet or Yorkshire town.

The Taste of Britain

The same variety applies to shopping. The British were dismissed by Napoleon as a "nation of shopkeepers," but the intended slight is actually a compliment. The British engaged in trade the world over, and today that spirit of enterprise, curiosity, good business sense and eclectic style is maintained. Fashion salons rival those in France and Italy. Britain has some of the finest antiques shops, art galleries and auction houses in Europe. Traditional and modern styles are blended to produce some colorful and out-of-the-ordinary clothing and craft items, and it is often in the provinces that the best examples are found.

Not so long ago, British food was seen as uninspired and overcooked. Today, British modern cuisine is exciting yet still essentially British, the ingredients fresh and flavorful. British beer has rediscovered great traditions, too; every English county has a lively range of local ales to back up the standard brews. English wine is also worth sampling.

In Scotland, sample the best from the country's huge range of superb single malt whiskies.

Timeline

8000 BC	Mesolithic hunter-gatherers journey into southern Britain.
4000 BC	Neolithic people settle in southern Britain in the Stone Age.
circa 500 BC	Iron Age culture develops in Britain.
55–54 BC	Julius Caesar makes expeditions to Britain.
AD 43	Roman conquest of Britain begins including a settlement of London.
circa 400	Roman army and administration withdraws from Britain.
1066	Battle of Hastings; Norman Conquest of Britain.
1314	Battle of Bannockburn, in which England suffers disastrous defeat at the hands of Scotland's Robert Bruce.
1534	Henry VIII appoints himself head of the Church in England; beginning of English Reformation.
1649	King Charles I executed; Commonwealth established until the restoration of the monarchy in 1660.
1707	Scotland and England unite by Act of Union.
1776	American colonies declare independence from Britain.
1815	Battle of Waterloo; Napoleon defeated by combined European force led by Duke of Wellington.
1914–18	Britain plays major part in World War I.
1939–44	World War II begins; Winston Churchill becomes Prime Minister of Britain; D-Day, Allied forces invade Normandy.
1945	War ends; Churchill loses in national elections.
1973	Britain joins European Economic Community, now known as the European Union.
1994	The Channel Tunnel opens.
2008	Global banking crisis leads to recession in Britain.
2012	Britain hosts the Olympic Games and celebrates the Queen's Diamond Jubilee.
July 2013	The Duchess of Cambridge gives birth to a son, named George Alexander Louis Windsor, who is third in line to the British throne.
September 2014	Scottish people vote "no" to independence in the historic Independence Referendum held on September 18, 2014.
May 2015	The Duchess of Cambridge gives birth to a daughter, named Charlotte Elizabeth Diana Windsor, who is fourth in line to the British throne.
September 2015	Queen Elizabeth II becomes the longest reigning British monarch.

Protected by Sea

Britain's island location has protected it from invasion over the centuries. The country has experienced two definitive "invasions;" by the Romans in the first century AD and by the Normans in 1066. The Danes, or Vikings, steadily occupied eastern England during the ninth century but were later repulsed. The Anglo-Saxons did not invade in the sense of armed occupation, but rather by a slow and steady immigration and integration after Roman withdrawal left chaos and uncertainty within the country. In later centuries Britain developed a powerful military and naval force, and although almost constantly at war with various European powers during the medieval period was itself never invaded. In more recent times both Napoleon and Hitler tried and failed to conquer. The English Channel and the surrounding seas have been Britain's greatest strategic blessing.

Watch the Changing the Guard ceremony outside Buckingham Palace in London

Survival Guide

- If visiting London, try to see one of the city's pageants, such as Trooping the Colour on Queen Elizabeth II's "official" birthday in June, or the Lord Mayor's Show in November. For something far more informal, join the fun at the fantastic Notting Hill Carnival during the last weekend (Saturday to Monday) of August.
- In York and Bath, be careful where pedestrian zones end and traffic begins. As in all cities, watch out for pickpockets on crowded streets.
- Try Britain's various regional foods. The national dish – fish and chips – can be found almost anywhere. In London, seek out genuine East End whelks (chewy marine molluscs). In Cornwall, look for Cornish pasties (savory pastry), a true hand-held meal. In Wales, sample Caerphilly cheese; in Yorkshire, try roast beef and Yorkshire pudding; and don't miss steak-and-kidney pie in any English country pub. In Scotland, tackle haggis, tatties (potatoes) and neeps (turnips), or kippers (smoked herring) – all accompanied by a thick and creamy regional beer or a good strong cup of tea with milk.
- Be prepared for dramatic changes in the weather. They say that Britain has no climate, it just has weather. The truth is that the country is caught between the extremes of northern and southern Europe, while its island nature allows vast amounts of condensed Atlantic seawater to be deposited as wind-blown rain at regular intervals. Expect rain, and if it comes, enjoy it and carry on with your plans.
- Make sure you always know what county of England you are in, and try not to confuse counties, especially not Yorkshire and Lancashire. Never refer to Welsh or Scottish people as English.
- In southwest England especially, enjoy a cream tea. This grand traditional indulgence consists of a pot of tea and fresh, fluffy scones (cakes) spread with jam and delicious, thick clotted cream. The cream is either slathered on top of the jam or jam is dolloped on top of the cream.
- The strength of the summer sun can deceive, often because there are passing clouds. Guard against sunburn even if there is a breeze.

London

London is one of the world's great experiences, a city that is always exhilarating, sometimes bewildering, sometimes exhausting, but never disappointing. This political, financial and commercial center is a year-round tourist city. The excitement is palpable.

There is a feeling that something is always happening, that you are in one of a handful of truly great cities.

London needs to be taken very much on its own terms; if you do so, you will enjoy it. It is an expensive and sometimes stressful place; admission prices to major attractions are steep and the crowds of fellow visitors can be huge.

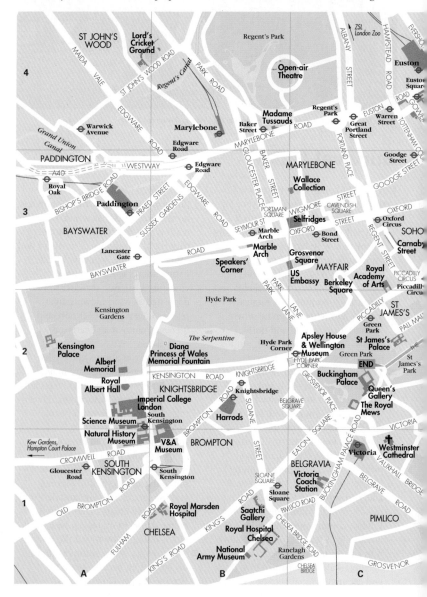

There are excellent guided tours, and bus tours are an easy way to sample all London (and beyond) has to offer. Exploring independently can be hugely rewarding, however, provided you plan well. Many attractions are some distance apart, and if you set out blindly determined to see everything you may end up frustrated and exhausted. Orient yourself by establishing two or three familiar focal points from which you can connect to other parts of the city.

Trafalgar Square to Big Ben

Trafalgar Square should be one of these focal points. It is the symbolic center of London; the towering pillar of Admiral Lord Nelson's column rises 169 feet into

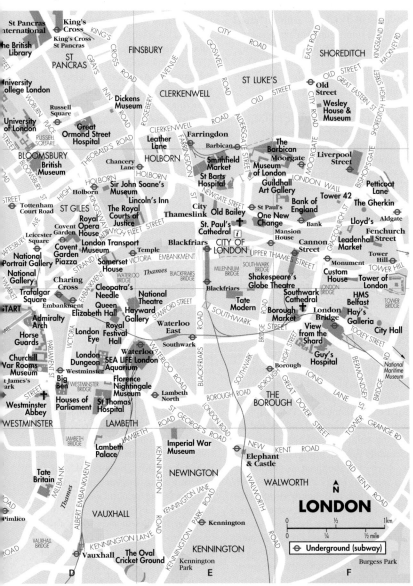

the London sky. At the base of the column are fountains and monumental guardian lions. All around the central square a constant throng of people is besieged by fluttering pigeons. Trafalgar Square is overlooked from the north by the National Gallery. At the southwest corner of the square is Admiralty Arch, through which you reach The Mall and progress toward Buckingham Palace.

Whitehall, London's "political" street, runs due south from Trafalgar Square. You'll see such landmarks as Big Ben, the clock tower of the Palace of Westminster, as you walk past the Old Admiralty Building and the Horse Guards, where helmeted troopers in scarlet or blue sit immobile on their sleek, black, patient horses. Soon you pass the gates of Downing Street, where Britain's Prime Minister and Chancellor of the Exchequer have their homes. In the middle of Whitehall is The Cenotaph, a stark and simple memorial to the dead of two world wars. Beyond The Cenotaph, Whitehall merges with Parliament Street and then meets Bridge Street. To the left is Westminster Bridge and the River Thames; straight ahead are the Houses of Parliament and to the right is Westminster Abbey.

Piccadilly Circus to Covent Garden

Another focus of central London is busy Piccadilly Circus, with the elegantly poised statue of *Eros* at its center. You can reach Piccadilly from Trafalgar Square by walking along Pall Mall from in front of the National Gallery and then turning right up Haymarket. From Piccadilly you can plunge into London's world of great shopping. To the north lies Soho, the long-established heart of late-night London, slightly risqué but full of character. Here are some of the capital's best theaters, restaurants and cafés, offbeat and specialty stores, and a resident population that maintains a tradition of eccentricity, style and eclectic fashion. Soho spills eastward

through the small Chinatown area around Gerrard Street to reach Leicester Square, lined with movie theaters and restaurants. To the east, along Cranbourne and Garrick streets, is Covent Garden, a lively area with stores, cafés, restaurants and street entertainers.

Beyond the Center

Once familiar with central London, you can start to venture beyond the focal points. This is where the city's excellent subway network, the Underground or "Tube," comes in handy. Use of the subway does mean you lose some grip of how London lies above ground; sometimes it is more rewarding if you walk to your destination, and London buses also supply excellent service.

Head northeast from Trafalgar Square, by subway or on foot, along the Strand, Fleet Street and Ludgate Hill, to St. Paul's Cathedral. Then proceed east to the Tower of London and Tower Bridge. Or go west from Trafalgar Square, beyond Buckingham Palace, to the great green space of Hyde Park and exclusive Knightsbridge, where you will find Harrods department store and three great museums: the Victoria and Albert Museum, the Science Museum and the Natural History Museum.

Venture northwest for a stroll around Regent's Park, or continue on to ZSL London Zoo, still drawing crowds as it has done since it opened in 1847.

Crossrail

When it opened in 1863, London's Metropolitan railway was the world's first underground line, and the start of a complex transportation network beneath London's surface. The latest addition is currently being constructed: Crossrail, a brand-new underground west–east rail link. When completed (due 2018), it will offer an efficient and speedy way to travel across the city. It's a vast project, with new stations being built and some upscaling of older stations, so some disruption to travel is likely at times.

Essential Information

Tourist Information

Visit London www.visitlondon.com
Visit England
City Information Centre (CIC), St. Paul's
Churchyard, London EC4M 8BX
☎ 020 7332 1456; www.visitbritain.com

Urban Transportation

The London Underground or "Tube" (subway)
trains operate Mon.–Sat. 5 a.m.–12:30 a.m.,
Sun. 7 a.m.–12:30 a.m. (some Tube lines
operate 24 hours Fri.–Sat.); Docklands Light
Railway (DLR), connecting the Docklands
(southeast London) with the Underground,
runs Mon.–Sat. 5:30 a.m.–12:30 a.m., Sun.
7 a.m.–11:30 p.m. Services are every few
minutes. The 11 Tube lines plus the DLR are
named, color-coded and shown on maps
divided into nine zones (Zone 1 is the central
zone) posted in all subway stations. Buy
tickets from attended booths in some station
entrance halls or from machines – contactless
payment cards also are an option. For more
than two trips, it is cheaper to buy a
Travelcard or an Oyster card (an electronic
smartcard) – both also are valid on suburban
rail services and buses. The subway symbol is
a red circle crossed by a horizontal line.
London's red buses cover central London and
its suburbs and run from 5 a.m.–12:30 a.m.;
many major routes operate 24 hours. London
buses are cash free so you must have a valid
ticket or Oyster card before you board a bus.
For information on London's public
transportation call Transport for London (TFL)
☎ 0343 222 1234 (24 hours daily); www.tfl.
gov.uk. London's black cabs (various colors)
are metered and can be flagged in the street
or at designated taxi ranks.

Airport Information

London is served by two major airports;
Heathrow (www.heathrowairport.com),
15 miles west of the city, and Gatwick
(www.gatwickairport.com), 30 miles south.
Rail services below operate Mon.–Sat. 5 a.m.–
midnight, Sun. 6:25 a.m.–midnight; at night
services will be less frequent. From Heathrow,
the Heathrow Express (☎ 0345 600 1515;
www.heathrowexpress.com) nonstop
train goes to Paddington Station every
15 minutes; journey time is 15 minutes.
The Heathrow Connect (☎ 0345 604 1515;
www.heathrowconnect.com) makes the same
journey every 30 minutes; journey time around
25 minutes. The subway's Piccadilly line to
central London departs every 5–10 minutes,
Mon.–Sat. 5 a.m.–11:45 p.m., Sun. 5:45 a.m.
–11:25 p.m.; journey time is around an hour.
National Express buses (www.national
express.com) go to Victoria Coach Station,
up to two buses an hour, travel time from
40 minutes. Between 10:30 p.m. and 6 a.m.
take the N9 night bus to Trafalgar Square.
Taxis (expensive) are available 24 hours; travel
time to central London is about an hour. From
Gatwick, the Gatwick Express (☎ 0345 850
1530; www.gatwickexpress.com) and
Southern trains (☎ 03451 272920; www.
southernrailway.com) go to Victoria Station
every 15–20 minutes; travel time 30–40
minutes. Thameslink trains (☎ 0345 026
4700; www.thameslinkrailway.com) go
to four central London stations up to every
15 minutes; travel time is 30 minutes. National
Express buses go to Victoria Coach Station
every hour and through the night; travel time
is around 90 minutes.

Climate – average highs and lows for the month

Jan.	Feb.	Mar.	Apr.	May	Jun.	Jul.	Aug.	Sep.	Oct.	Nov.	Dec.
6°C	6°C	10°C	13°C	16°C	20°C	21°C	21°C	18°C	14°C	10°C	7°C
43°F	43°F	50°F	55°F	61°F	68°F	70°F	70°F	64°F	57°F	50°F	45°F
2°C	2°C	3°C	5°C	8°C	11°C	13°C	13°C	11°C	7°C	5°C	3°C
36°F	36°F	37°F	41°F	46°F	52°F	55°F	55°F	52°F	45°F	41°F	37°F

Britain

London Sights

British Museum

The British Museum, founded in 1753, is a treasure house of global artifacts, many of them the riches of Britain's imperial past.

There are 8 million exhibits here, including the Elgin Marbles, the fifth-century BC relief sculptures taken from the Parthenon in 1801 by Thomas Bruce, the Earl of Elgin, and still the subject of Greek demands for their return.

Other highlights are the Rosetta Stone, the key to the understanding of Egyptian hieroglyphics; the 2,000-year-old Lindow Man, whose preserved body was found in an English peat bog; the Mildenhall Treasure, a collection of Roman silver; and Anglo-Saxon artifacts from a ship burial discovered at Sutton Hoo on England's eastern coast during the outbreak of World War II. Don't miss the Egyptian Galleries, the finest collection outside Egypt itself.

The Queen Elizabeth II Great Court, enclosed by a massive glass roof, is the largest covered public square in Europe. It houses galleries, an education center, cafés, information desks and the fine Reading Room, resplendent in blue and gold. This is where Karl Marx wrote parts of *Das Kapital*.

➕ D3 ✉ Great Russell Street, WC1B 3DG ☎ 020 7323 8299; www.britishmuseum.org 🕐 Galleries: daily 10–5:30 (also selected galleries Fri. 5:30–8:30 p.m.). Great Court: Sat.–Thu. 9–6, Fri. 9–8:30 Ⓜ Holborn, Russell Square, Tottenham Court Road or Goodge Street 🚌 38, 59, 188 🍴 Restaurant and cafés 🎟 Free (also free tours); charge for special exhibitions ($$$)

Houses of Parliament

The Houses of Parliament, also known as the Palace of Westminster, are mainly to be admired from the outside. The present building replaced an older palace dating from the 11th century. Most of this earlier building burned down in 1834. The structure's linear form is doubly enhanced by the vertical thrust of Victoria Tower and the clock tower known as Big Ben.

Inside access is limited because it is the workplace of British government. You can attend debates in the House of Lords and House of Commons on a first-come-first-served basis; join the line for the "Strangers' Galleries" (public galleries) outside Cromwell Green Entrance. On Saturdays and during the Easter, summer and Christmas recesses, tours

The Houses of Parliament seen across the River Thames from the South Bank

of the Houses of Parliament are available to overseas visitors. Advance reservations are recommended.

⊞ D2 ✉ Parliament Square, SW1A 0AA ☎ 020 7219 4114; www.parliament.uk 🕐 Public galleries Mon.– Thu. and some Fri. (times vary; phone for details), Oct. 13–late Jul. Closed 3 weeks at Christmas, 1 week in mid-Feb., 2 weeks at Easter and 1 week in late May; guided tours Sat. and during Easter, summer and Christmas recesses only 🚌 11, 24, 148, 159, 453 🚢 Westminster Millennium Pier 🍴 Café in Westminster Hall Ⓜ Westminster 💷 Free; tours $$$

Imperial War Museum

Two vast guns stand in front of the handsome Ionic portico of the Imperial War Museum, where the story of modern conflict is documented in a fascinating and varied collection, which includes more than 50 historic aircraft, tanks and other field weapons. The cruel lessons of conflict are not shirked, especially in the permanent exhibition on the Holocaust. Opened in 2014, the First World War Galleries are particularly evocative.

The museum was formerly the Bethlehem Royal Hospital, the notorious asylum for the insane that was known as "Bedlam."

⊞ E1 ✉ Lambeth Road, SE1 6HZ ☎ 0207 416 5000; www.iwm.org.uk 🕐 Daily 10–6 Ⓜ Elephant and Castle, Lambeth North, Southwark or Waterloo 🚌 59, 148, 159, 188, 433 🍴 Café 💷 Free; charge for special exhibitions 🚩 First World War Galleries (free) may be timed admission during busy periods

Kew Gardens

A World Heritage Site, the Royal Botanic Gardens at Kew date from 1759 and represent one of the finest collections of plants in the world, all contained within a 300-acre site. The vast Temperate House contains plants from every continent, and the architectural wonders are just as fascinating. Highlights include the Palm House, a billowing pavilion in glass and wrought iron that is a classic expression of creative 19th-century design, and the Princess of Wales Conservatory, which opened in

1987. Scattered throughout the gardens are such interesting buildings as a 10-story, 18th-century pagoda (closed to the public) and Kew Palace, used as a country retreat by George III. Also here is Queen Charlotte's Cottage, given by George III to his wife Charlotte and a superb example of "cottage ornée" style.

⊞ Off map at A1 ✉ Kew Road, Kew TW9 3AB ☎ 020 8332 5655 (24-hour recorded information); www.kew.org 🕐 Daily 10–6:30, Apr.–Aug. (to 7:30 p.m. weekends and public holidays); 10–6, Sep.–Oct.; 10–5:30, Feb.–Mar.; 10–4:15, Nov.–Jan. Ⓜ Kew Gardens 🚌 65, 237, 267, 391 🚢 Kew Pier (Apr.–Oct.) 🍴 Restaurant and cafés 💷 $$ (Kew Palace additional $$) 🚩 Kew Explorer land train tour ($$), guided and self-guiding walking tours

London Eye

Built as part of the city's millennial celebrations, the London Eye is a superb feat of construction. A huge Ferris wheel-like structure, it rotates slowly (once every 30 minutes), giving visitors a bird's-eye view across London and up to 25 miles toward the horizon from within 32 glassed capsules. At 443 feet high, it is Europe's tallest cantilevered observation wheel.

⊞ D2 ✉ Jubilee Gardens, South Bank ☎ 0871 781 3000 (bookings). Calls cost 13p per minute plus your phone company's access charge; www.londoneye.com 🕐 Daily 10–8:30, but extended hours during Jul. and Aug. Closed for 10 days in mid-Jan. Ⓜ Waterloo 🚌 RV1, 59, 139, 188 🚢 London Eye Pier 🍴 Cafés 💷 $$$ (includes 4D cinema experience)

Madame Tussauds

Visit Madame Tussauds wax model museum and "rub shoulders" with the rich and famous. Just about everyone is here: royalty, presidents, politicians, celebrities, stars, heroes and villains. The collections change all the time – recent additions include Prince Harry, British actor Benedict Cumberbatch, and figures from the *Star Wars* movies. The Chamber of Horrors, including SCREAM, has hideous charm, although not for under-12s; the murderous are still menacing, even in effigy, and live actors make it all the scarier. Other attractions include Spirit of London, a quick trip through 400 years of London's history as glimpsed from a miniature city taxicab.

➕ B4 ✉ Marylebone Road, NW1 5LR ☎ 0871 894 3000. Calls cost 13p per minute plus your phone company's access charge; www.madametussauds.com 🕐 Mon.–Fri. 9:30–5:30, Sat.–Sun. 9–6 (daily 8:30–7 during school vacations) 🚇 Baker Street 🚌 74, 139, 205, 274, 453 🍴 Café 💲 $$$ ℹ️ Reserve ahead by credit card (or online for a discount) to avoid long lines

Museum of London

This rewarding museum tells the story of London's history from prehistoric times to the present through set-piece galleries focusing on important periods.

The Roman section is superb; its reconstructed rooms, one with a fabulous mosaic floor, and its sculptures are not to be missed. Another highlight is the Lord Mayor's State Coach dating from the 1750s, a glittering golden extravaganza that is still used during the Lord Mayor's Show each November and for the coronation of a new sovereign.

The museum's second site, in Docklands, highlights London's growth as one of the world's great ports. Displays include the walk-through 19th-century "Sailortown" and a moving exhibition about slavery.

➕ E3 ✉ 150 London Wall, EC2Y 5HN; West India Quay, Canary Wharf, E14 4AL ☎ 020 7001 9844; www.museumoflondon.org.uk 🕐 Daily 10–6; last admission at 5:40 p.m. 🚇 Barbican, St. Paul's; Canary Wharf for Docklands site 🚌 8, 11, 23, 25, 43 🍴 Café 💷 Free; charge for some exhibitions

National Gallery

London's National Gallery contains one of the finest collections of Western European art in the world. You may find most of the world here on a busy day, but "the National" seems able to absorb the crowds. The collection is displayed chronologically from 1250 to 1900. You will need a floor plan to navigate or join a free guided tour (daily, 11:30 a.m. and 2:30 p.m.). Portable audio guides

are available ($), with random-access commentaries about more than 1,200 paintings. They also can be used to follow a range of thematic tours.

Among the highlights are: Leonardo da Vinci's *Virgin of the Rocks*; Sandro Botticelli's *Venus and Mars*; Titian's vivid and agile *Bacchus and Ariadne*; Jan van Eyck's *The Arnolfini Portrait*; Diego Velázquez's sensual *The Rokeby Venus*; Rembrandt's haunting *Self Portrait at the Age of 34*; Paul Cézanne's *Bathers*; and Vincent van Gogh's *Sunflowers*.

Head to Room 34, the Sackler Room, where you are surrounded by British paintings from the late 18th century to the early 19th century – the works of English masters such as Thomas Gainsborough, Sir Joshua Reynolds, George Stubbs and J. M. W. Turner.

➕ D3 ✉ Trafalgar Square, WC2N 5DN ☎ 020 7747 2885; www.nationalgallery.org.uk 🕐 Daily 10–6 (Fri. to 9 p.m.) 🚇 Charing Cross, Embankment or Leicester Square 🚌 9, 11, 15, 23, 24, 139, 159, 453 🍴 Restaurant and cafés 💷 Free; charge for some temporary exhibitions ℹ️ Free concerts take place in the gallery on Friday evenings

National Maritime Museum

A visit to the world's largest maritime museum offers insight into Britain's past maritime expertise. The Nelson, Navy Nation display celebrates the great admiral, with his bullet-pierced coat from the Battle of Trafalgar adding drama. In the glass-roofed Neptune Court is the gilded state barge created for Frederick, Prince of Wales in 1732. Themed galleries tell of early explorers, the age of ocean liners, lighthouses and Britain's historic maritime trade with Asia, Africa and the Americas. The restored *Cutty Sark* tea clipper ($$) lies close by, on King William Walk.

➕ Off map at F2 ✉ Park Row, Greenwich SE10 9NF ☎ 020 8858 4422; www.rmg.co.uk 🕐 Daily 10–5, (to 6 p.m. during school vacations). Last admission 30 minutes before closing 🚇 Docklands Light Railway: Cutty Sark 🚌 53, 54, 177, 180, 188, 199, 202, 286, 380, 386 ⛴ Greenwich Pier 🍴 Restaurant and café 💷 Free; charge for special exhibitions

Covent Garden Through Time

London is an ever-changing city and, over the years, has evolved from surprising origins. A classic example of London's fascinating development is Covent Garden, today a lively and fashionable focus of entertainment, dining and shopping. The area gets its name from being the medieval-era "Garden of the Convent," when vegetables were grown here for the kitchens at Westminster Abbey.

During the 17th century it was laid out as the first and finest square in London, complete with the Church of St. Paul and arcaded houses. The architect was Inigo Jones, who planned it in Italianate style, with the square known as The Piazza. Then the owner of Covent Garden, the Earl of Bedford, decided to hold a market in the square. Commerce overcame culture; buildings were erected – first the older fruit and vegetable market and then the floral market. The Opera House building was added later.

In 1974 the market moved to new premises in south London and the square's market halls were renovated and filled with new stores, cafés and restaurants that have transformed the old "Garden of the Convent" into a major leisure area.

From Covent Garden subway station, turn right and walk southeast, past the Crabtree & Evelyn store (renowned for bath oils and soaps) on your right, into the heart of Covent Garden. This is an excellent place to browse and wander at your leisure. There are fashion boutiques for all tastes. These line the cobbled piazza, tastefully blending in with the Italianate architecture and elegant columns. On the eastern side of The Piazza, the bustling Real Food Market takes place each Thursday. Under the glass-and-iron roof of the renovated market building set in the middle of the square, you'll find stalls selling crafts, jewelry, different types of clothing and accessories. On the western side of the market, in front of St. Paul's Church, also known as the Actors' Church because of its long association with the acting profession, street performers often entertain the crowds with comedy or magic tricks. You're likely to see clowns, fire-eaters, musicians and acrobats. It all adds to the exciting bustle of this area.

If you walk back toward the Covent Garden subway and head two blocks north, you will find yourself in the maze of small streets that intersect with Neal Street. Neal's Yard Dairy sells some of the best cheese in the country – it's all British or Irish made.

Covent Garden market extends across two levels, with stalls selling an eclectic mix of goods

The Millennium Bridge near St. Paul's Cathedral

Natural History Museum

The Natural History Museum shouldn't be missed and is a great favorite with children. The exhibitions display some fascinating specimens from the museum's incredible collection of more than 80 million items (not all on display), from the tiniest of preserved insects to a reconstruction of a huge blue whale. The museum is divided into four zones (Blue, Green, Red and Orange). The Blue and Green zones cover life on Earth, the highlight of which is a huge, animatronic Tyrannosaurus rex, complete with smelly breath. The Cadogan Gallery showcases a selection of 22 remarkable items spanning 4.5 billion years. The Red Zone deals with the world beneath our feet and is every bit as fascinating; the Orange Zone contains a wildlife garden. At the state-of-the-art Darwin Centre visitors can share the experience of exploring the complex natural world.

🔲 A1 ✉ Cromwell Road, SW7 5BD (Blue, Green and Orange zones entrance), Exhibition Road (Red Zone entrance) ☎ 020 7942 5000; www.nhm.ac.uk ⏰ Daily 10–5:50. Last admission at 5:30 p.m. 🚇 South Kensington 🚌 14, 74 🍴 Restaurant and cafés 💲 Free; charge for special exhibitions

St. Paul's Cathedral

St. Paul's Cathedral is one of architect Sir Christopher Wren's greatest achievements, and is easily reached from the Tate Modern on the South Bank by a walk over the Millennium Bridge. The twin towers and baroque elements of its facade and the crowning glory of its dome are still breathtaking. The bright interior is full of stately monuments, memorials and statues. You can descend to the crypt, where you will find the tomb of Sir Christopher Wren among others, or ascend heavenward up 528 steps, first to the famous Whispering Gallery, on to the Stone Gallery and then to the Golden Gallery for superb views over London. The movie theater in the crypt offers virtual tours if you don't want to climb that high.

🔲 E3 ✉ St. Paul's Churchyard, EC4M 8AD ☎ 020 7246 8357; www.stpauls.co.uk ⏰ Mon.–Sat. 8:30–4:30; closed during some services 🚇 St. Paul's 🚌 4, 11, 15, 23, 25, 26, 100, 242 🍴 Restaurant and café 💲 $$$ 🎫 Guided tours at 10, 11, 1 and 2, and multimedia guides (included in admission fee)

Science Museum

Every aspect of science and technology is covered in this vast collection, and you will find everything from atoms to the *Apollo 10* command module. The museum's official guidebook will help you find your way around the seven floors, including the Information Age gallery and a new gallery devoted to math (opens 2016). On display are George Stephenson's early locomotive, the *Rocket*, and Charles Babbage's enormous prototype computer. The huge Flight gallery contains ranks of aircraft, and in the Energy Hall great steam engines from the Industrial Revolution hiss and revolve. Many of the exhibits have a hands-on element. Check for any special events on the day you visit. The Wellcome Wing is a groundbreaking complex of up-to-the-minute interactive scientific exhibits.

🔲 A2 ✉ Exhibition Road, SW7 2DD ☎ 020 7942 4000; www.sciencemuseum.org.uk ⏰ Daily 10–6 (to 7 p.m. during school vacations) 🚇 South Kensington 🚌 14, 74 🍴 Restaurant and cafés 🎫 Free; IMAX 3D cinema $$; flight simulators $; charge for some exhibitions

Tate Britain

Tate Britain exhibits the world's greatest collection of British art, from 1500 to the present, in a mixture of chronological and thematic displays. Works by major artists as diverse as Barbara Hepworth, William Hogarth and David Hockney are on display.

The Turner Collection in the Clore Gallery includes oil paintings, sketches and watercolors by J. M. W. Turner. ✚ D1 ✉ Millbank, SW1P 4RG ☎ 020 7887 8888; www.tate.org.uk/visit/tate-britain 🕐 Daily 10–6 (last admission at 5:15), selected Fri. 6–10 p.m. also 🚇 Pimlico 🚌 2, 36, 87, 88, 185, 436, C10 ⛴ Tate Boat to Millbank Pier (from Tate Modern and London Eye) 🍴 Restaurant and café 🎫 Free; charge for special exhibitions 🛈 Guided tours (free), talks and films

Tate Modern

Housed in the former Bankside Power Station, on the south bank of the River Thames, Britain's national museum of modern and contemporary art features an international collection from 1900 to the present, and draws around 5 million visitors each year. It includes works by major figures such as Salvador Dalí, Pablo Picasso, Henri Matisse, Edvard Munch, Piet Mondrian, Jackson Pollock, Andy Warhol and Roy Lichtenstein, as well as such contemporary artists as Damien Hirst. In a break with tradition, the collection is presented in themed groups rather than chronologically or by school. Adventurous and often controversial conceptual works and installations also are a feature.

You can approach Tate Modern from north of the Thames across the pedestrian-only Millennium Bridge. In 2016, a new six-story building to the south will extend the gallery further. ✚ E2 ✉ Bankside, SE1 9TG ☎ 020 7887 8888; www.tate.org.uk/visit/tate-modern 🕐 Sun.–Thu. 10–6, Fri.–Sat. 10–10. Last admission 45 minutes before closing 🚇 Southwark, Blackfriars or St. Paul's 🚌 RV1 ⛴ Tate Boat to Bankside Pier (from Tate Britain) 🍴 Restaurant and café 🎫 Free; charge for special exhibitions $$$ 🛈 Guided tours (free), multimedia guides ($), events and talks

Tower of London

There are crowds of visitors at London's foremost historical sight most of the year, and you may find yourself being hurried through some of the sections. Many of the nation's most daring personalities ended up here, as prisoners or as reluctant "guests," or, like Henry VIII's wives Anne Boleyn and Catherine Howard, on a final trip to the executioner's block. Tours conducted by the Yeoman Warders, or "Beefeaters," give an excellent introduction, after which you can wander at your own pace to see the Medieval Palace, White

The Tower of London, once a place of incarceration, was built in the 11th century

ORS' GATE

Tower, Bloody Tower, Traitors' Gate, the Jewel House (for the Crown Jewels), the Tower Ravens and the execution site at Tower Green.

⊞ F3 ⬚ Tower Hill, EC3N 4AB ☎ 020 3166 6000; www.hrp.org.uk/TowerOfLondon ⏰ Tue.–Sat. 9–5:30, Sun. and Mon. 10–5:30, Mar.–Oct.; Tue.–Sat. 9–4:30, Sun. and Mon. 10–4:30, rest of year. Last admission 30 minutes before closing 🚇 Tower Hill 🚌 RV1, 15, 188 ⛴ Tower Pier 🍴 Restaurants and cafés 💷 $$$ (discount for online purchase) 🚹 Guided tours, every half hour, included in price of ticket; audio guide ($)

V&A Museum

The V&A is recognized as being the world's greatest repository of applied and decorative art, containing ravishing collections of jewelry, silverware, ironwork, glass, ceramics, textiles, costume and dress, furniture, sculpture, paintings, books, photographs and prints from all over the world.

The British Galleries (Level 2), a chronological survey of British art and design from 1500 to 1900, are an attraction in themselves. The Medieval and Renaissance galleries alone are worth a whole day, and the Asia, Ceramics, Glass, Sculpture, Metalwork and Jewellery galleries, along with the superb art collection, are all worth seeing. The Fashion Collection is the biggest in the world, spanning from the 1750s to the present.

⊞ B1 ⬚ Cromwell Road, SW7 2RL ☎ 020 7942 2000; www.vam.ac.uk ⏰ Daily 10–5:45; selected galleries also Fri. 5:45–10 p.m. Last admission 10 minutes before closing 🚇 South Kensington 🚌 14, 74 🍴 Cafés (one in garden, summer only) 💷 Free; charge for some exhibitions and events

View From The Shard

The coolest view over the city doesn't come cheap, but the experience of seeing London from 802 feet up, on the 72nd floor of Western Europe's highest building, is surely worth every penny.

Designed by Renzo Piano, the spectacular glass tower block dominates the skyline south of the Thames. There are three viewing platforms on different levels, and the top one is open-air. Security is strict, with airport-style scanners, so leave large bags behind. Entry is by timed ticket, but stay as long as you like.

⊞ F2 ⬚ 96 Tooley Street, SE1 2TH ☎ 0344 499 7222; www.theviewfromtheshard.com ⏰ Daily 10–10, Apr.–Oct.; Sun.–Wed. 10–7, Thu.–Sat. 10–10, rest of year. Last entry 90 minutes before closing 🚇 London Bridge 🚌 RV1, 43 🍴 Restaurants 💷 $$$ (buy e-tickets ahead online for discount and priority entry info); free entry for children up to age 3 🚹 Children under 16 must be accompanied by an adult

Westminster Abbey

Westminster Abbey has been the ceremonial site of almost every British coronation, from William the Conqueror in 1066 to Queen Elizabeth II in 1953. Monarchs that are buried here include Henry VII, Elizabeth I and Mary, Queen of Scots. The abbey is full of monuments and memorials to famous people from Britain's history. The Quire and Sanctuary are the ceremonial heart of the abbey, where Queen Eizabeth II was crowned and where Prince William married Katherine Middleton in 2011. The present abbey dates, in part, from the 13th century and is a powerful expression of English Gothic style.

Henry VII's chapel has a style of airy elegance that represents Gothic at its finest. Tiered sculptures line the walls, and there is exquisite fan vaulting in the roof. The Tomb of the Unknown Warrior is dedicated to the many thousands of British servicemen killed in World War I. In the south transept is Poets' Corner, resting place of great writers including Geoffrey Chaucer, Alfred Tennyson and others.

⊞ D2 ⬚ Broad Sanctuary, SW1P 3PA ☎ 020 7222 5152; www.westminster-abbey.org ⏰ Mon.–Fri. 9:30–4:30 (Wed. until 7 p.m.), Sat. 9:30–2:30. Last admission 1 hour before closing. Cloisters: daily 9:30–6. Abbey Museum: Mon.–Sat. 10:30–4. College Garden: Tue.–Thu. 10–6, Apr.–Sep.; 10–4, rest of year 🚇 Westminster or St. James's Park 🚌 11, 24, 148, 159, 453 🍴 Café 💷 Abbey $$$. Cloisters and College Garden free 🚹 Abbey tours ($); audio guide (free)

A Royal Stroll

Royal London begins at Admiralty Arch, at the southwest corner of Trafalgar Square. The arch dates from 1911 and was erected as part of a general celebration of Queen Victoria's life and reign. Beyond the arch is The Mall, a broad open avenue that runs southwest, directly toward Buckingham Palace. It was first laid out by Charles II in the 1660s as part of St. James's Park. It is open to traffic, but as soon as you pass beneath Admiralty Arch the city's character becomes less frantic.

Keep to the sidewalk on the left of the avenue and you'll soon pass a statue of the seafarer Captain James Cook. St. James's Park spreads out to the left – a great sweep of open lawns, trees and gardens with a lake at its heart. The right (north) side of The Mall is lined with stately buildings. First is Carlton House Terrace, broken halfway by the Duke of York's Steps that lead up to the Duke of York's Column. At St. James's Palace, sentries guard the Tudor Tower. Next to the palace is Clarence House, the official London residence of the Prince of Wales and the Duchess of Cornwall. Five of the rooms are open to the public for guided tours Mon.–Fri. 10–4:30, Sat.–Sun. 10–5:30 in August (tickets must be reserved in advance; ☎ 020 7766 7303; www.royalcollection.org.uk; $$).

On your way to the large open area in front of Buckingham Palace is Lancaster House (a building now used by the government). In front of the palace is the spectacular bronze and marble Victoria Monument, erected in 1911 and constructed with more than 2,300 tons of marble. The exuberant gilded bronze winged Victory crowns the monument.

Beyond the monument and behind railings and gates stands Buckingham Palace. The Royal Standard (the Queen's flag) flies when the Queen is in residence. Changing the Guard takes place daily at 11:30 a.m. from May through July and on alternate days the rest of the year (weather permitting). The ceremony takes around 30 minutes to complete (free).

Nineteen of Buckingham Palace's state rooms are open from early August through September (daily 9:30–5:30 or 6:30) when the royal family is not in residence. Buy a ticket on the day of your visit or in advance online at www.royalcollection.org.uk, or by calling ☎ 020 7766 7300 ($$$).

The Royal Mews are worth a visit for their state carriages and splendid horses. For the walking route, see the city map on pages 86–87.

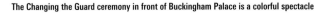

The Changing the Guard ceremony in front of Buckingham Palace is a colorful spectacle

Edinburgh

Edinburgh is Scotland in microcosm. In this lively capital city, buildings do not overpower the spectacular landscape of hills and crags that march across the southeastern horizon. Yet Edinburgh's buildings – from the old houses of the Royal Mile to the elegant Georgian terraces and crescents of the New Town – are outstanding complements to the city's natural setting. Few other capitals seem to reflect the history and culture of their country so potently.

Edinburgh's famous castle sits high on a craggy promontory, Castle Rock, made inaccessible on three sides by steep cliffs and with a long descending ridge on its fourth side. The city's layout is linear, a pattern set by Castle Rock and Castle Ridge, down which the magnificent Royal Mile descends to the Palace of Holyroodhouse.

North of the Royal Mile lies a shallow valley once covered by swampy Nor' Loch, and now occupied by the lovely Princes Street Gardens, with Waverley Station, the city's main railroad station, at their eastern end. Above the gardens and to the north is Edinburgh's main thoroughfare, Princes Street, its south

EDINBURGH

Greyfriars Bobby

This Skye terrier's devotion to his dead master is enshrined in Edinburgh folklore. The famous Greyfriars Bobby was a trained police dog who worked with his master, Constable John Gray, guarding livestock at Edinburgh's city market, the Grassmarket, during the 1850s. When Gray died at age 45 he was buried in Greyfriars churchyard, and his devoted terrier took up what began a 14-year vigil by his grave. Bobby was cared for and beloved by everyone in the neighborhood. A statue of Greyfriars Bobby stands at the intersection of Candlemaker Row and the George IV Bridge, near the church gate and opposite a pub named after the faithful dog.

side uncluttered by buildings and thus serving as a splendid place from which to view the castle and Old Edinburgh.

First Impressions

Many visitors arrive by train at Waverley Station. Perfectly located between the old town and modern Edinburgh, Waverley Station first opened in 1846, but then was rebuilt at the end of the 19th century. Some detail of the original structure can still be seen on the domed ceiling, which is adorned with cherubs amid the fine ironwork trusses.

From the station you emerge onto Waverley Bridge and get an immediate first impression of the city's visual drama. The castle and the dark soaring back walls of the buildings that enclose the Royal Mile rise to the south.

From the northern exit of the station, a stairway takes you to Princes Street. Here, the Scott Monument, a towering Gothic steeple, dominates one view while the bulk of The Balmoral Hotel, itself castle-like, dominates the other.

Royal Botanic Garden Edinburgh

Royal Yacht Britannia

York Place

LONDON ROAD

Royal Terrace Gardens

ROYAL TERRACE

Omni Edinburgh

Regent Gardens

Bus Station

St Mary's RC Cathedral

National Archives of Scotland

City Observatory

Calton Hill

American Consulate

Scottish National Portrait Gallery

St Andrew Square

National Monument

General Register House

Dugald Monument

Nelson Monument

The Scott Monument

Assembly Rooms

Royal Scottish Academy

East Princes Street Gardens

Princes Mall

Edinburgh Waverley Station

The People's Story

White Horse Close

Palace of Holyroodhouse

NEW TOWN

Princes Street

Scottish National Gallery

Edinburgh Dungeon

John Knox House

Royal Mile

Scottish Parliament

Queen's Gallery

END

Arthur's Seat

Auditorium

Museum on the Mound

Museum of Edinburgh

Scottish Poetry Library

Tartan Weaving Mill

Camera Obscura

Loch Ness Discovery Ctr

Museum of Childhood

Museum of Edinburgh

Dynamic Earth

The Scotch Whisky Experience

National Library of Scotland

St. Giles' Cathedral

University of Edinburgh

Edinburgh Castle

START

OLD TOWN

Sheriff Court

University of Edinburgh Old College

Holyrood Park

Regimental Museums

Greyfriars Tollbooth & Highland Kirk

National Museum of Scotland

Festival Theatre

Salisbury Crags

Edinburgh College of Art

University of Edinburgh

George Square Gardens

C   D   E

Up to the right looms Calton Hill, topped by neoclassical monuments.

From Waverley Bridge you can take an instant Edinburgh open-top bus tour that will introduce you to the city. Details about city transportation are available from Lothian Buses City Centre Travelshops at Hanover Street and Waverley Bridge. You also can find out about other guided tours from the Edinburgh and Scotland Information Centre on Princes Street, close to Waverley Station. They include walking tours that take you through the Old Town's historic lanes and courtyards and the entertaining Cadies and Witchery Tours (ghost tours and murder and mystery tours).

Two Edinburghs

Exploring the city on your own is straightforward. Old Edinburgh is the southern part, encompassed by the castle and the Royal Mile; beyond them are the areas of Southside, the Grassmarket and Canongate. To the south of the Royal Mile you will find the National Museum of Scotland (see page 102) and the Edinburgh Festival Theatre, a venue presenting fine drama, ballet and opera. Edinburgh Castle (see page 101) and the Royal Mile (see pages 104–105) are Old Edinburgh's main attractions.

You can easily spend an entire day here, and amid the souvenir shops and tourist spots there is a potent sense of history embodied by the splendid clutter of tall old sandstone buildings.

Also take time for a walk in Holyrood Park (see pages 101–102), a lovely green world of spectacular craggy hills, lochs and glens that is a genuine slice of Highland Scotland.

North of Waverley Bridge is Edinburgh's New Town, where Old Edinburgh expanded during the 18th century as part of a typically Georgian exercise in town planning. Above Princes Street is George Street, center of Scotland's financial district, with Charlotte Square and St. Andrew Square at either end. The elegance and unity of Georgian architecture – an exhilarating contrast to the equally splendid Royal Mile – can be appreciated at such locations as Queen Street Gardens, the Royal Circus (a circular residential street), Great King Street and Drummond Place – all north of George Street – as well as around Moray Place, west of Queen Street Gardens.

Life in Edinburgh

George Street and Princes Street, and the short connecting streets between them, are Edinburgh's main shopping streets. On Princes Street you will find an Edinburgh institution, Jenners, a labyrinthine department store that sells luxury items and has a wonderful food hall. This street also has branches of Marks & Spencer as well as big-name brands like Gap. St. Andrew Square is the home of Harvey Nichols, the first Scottish outlet for the famous London store. For refreshment, visit Rose Street, which has more pubs than any other street in Scotland.

Edinburgh is crowded during the summer, but the cultural feast of the Edinburgh International Festival, in the second half of August and early September, is well worth taking in. There also are good alternatives outside the festival season – modern Scottish drama at the Traverse Theatre, or musical performances at Usher Hall.

Stylish Edinburgh restaurants offer distinctive Scottish dishes such as wild salmon, Aberdeen Angus beef or game, such as grouse and venison.

Local residents are friendly and Scottish reticence is replaced here by a style that reflects sophistication without pretension, and by pride in the city's internationalism. And with a historic return to the Royal Mile by the Scottish Parliament, Edinburgh has renewed stature and optimism.

Essential Information

Tourist Information

Edinburgh and Scotland Information Centre
3 Princes Street, EH2 2QP ☎ 0131 473 3868;
www.visitscotland.com

Edinburgh International Airport
International arrivals area

Urban Transportation

Waverley Station is on Princes Street (see National Rail at www.nationalrail.co.uk). For bus information contact Lothian Buses City Centre Travelshops at Hanover Street or Waverley Bridge (☎ 0131 554 4494). The city's tram system opened in 2014; for details see www.edinburghtrams.com. Taxis can be hailed on the street, at Waverley Station or Waverley Bridge stands, or call Central Taxis (☎ 0131 229 2468) or City Cabs (☎ 0131 228 1211).

Airport Information

Edinburgh Airport (www.edinburghairport.com) is 8 miles west of the city center. Airlink 100 buses go to Waverley Station every 10 minutes (20 minutes early morning), daily 4:30 a.m.–12:22 a.m.; travel time 30 minutes. Night Bus N22, departing every 30 minutes, operates daily 12:47 a.m.–4:17 a.m. The new tram link to the city center takes around 35 minutes.

Climate – average highs and lows for the month

Jan.	Feb.	Mar.	Apr.	May	Jun.	Jul.	Aug.	Sep.	Oct.	Nov.	Dec.
5°C	6°C	7°C	10°C	13°C	16°C	18°C	17°C	15°C	12°C	9°C	6°C
41°F	43°F	45°F	50°F	55°F	61°F	64°F	63°F	59°F	54°F	48°F	43°F
1°C	1°C	2°C	4°C	6°C	9°C	11°C	11°C	9°C	6°C	4°C	2°C
34°F	34°F	36°F	39°F	43°F	48°F	52°F	52°F	48°F	43°F	39°F	36°F

Edinburgh Sights

Edinburgh Castle

You can tackle Scotland's most visited attraction in several ways. There are official guided tours (included in admission), which are entertaining and informative. A self-guiding audio tour ($) is a good option, and helps focus the mind amid inevitable crowds.

You will need to brace yourself for the One O'Clock Gun, a 25-pounder that blasts off a single blank charge from the Half Moon Battery at 1 p.m. from Monday through Saturday.

Highlights are the tiny, 12th-century St. Margaret's Chapel (dedicated to Margaret, mother of David I); the Stone of Destiny; the Prisons of War exhibition in the Vaults; the mighty medieval siege gun, Mons Meg, which stands in grim splendor like some huge black beast; and the 16th-century Great Hall with its glorious hammerbeam roof and masses of weaponry. Take time also to see the interesting Honours of Scotland exhibition and Scotland's Crown Jewels.

➕ C2 ✉ Castlehill, EH1 2NG ☎ 0131 225 9846; www.edinburghcastle.gov.uk ⏰ Daily 9:30–6, Apr.–Sep.; 9:30–5, rest of year. Last admission 1 hour before closing 🚌 23, 27, 41, 42, 67 🍴 Cafés 💵 $$$

ℹ The Royal Edinburgh Military Tattoo show takes place on the Castle esplanade every August. For more information see www.edintattoo.co.uk

The Georgian House

The Georgian House is the showplace of New Town's Charlotte Square and one of the most prestigious addresses in Scotland. Designed in 1791 by Robert Adam, this masterpiece of urban architecture was once home to the chief of the Lamont clan. Three floors are open, all full of 18th-century furnishings and beautiful paintings. The basement houses the wine cellar and kitchen.

➕ B2 ✉ 7 Charlotte Square, EH2 4DR ☎ 0131 225 2160; www.nts.org.uk ⏰ Daily 10–6, Jul.–Aug.; 10–5, Apr.–Jun. and Sep.–Oct.; 11–4 Mar. and Nov.; Thu.–Sun. 11–4, early to mid-Dec. Last admission 30 minutes before closing 🚌 36, 47 💵 $

Holyrood Park

Few cities are blessed with such a marvelous open space as Holyrood Park, or Queen's Park as it is also known. The park is dominated by the Salisbury Crags

Edinburgh Castle overlooks the city from atop the volcanic crag known as Castle Rock

The Royal Yacht Britannia remains a striking looking vessel

and by Arthur's Seat, a high, rounded hill. You can enter the park from the bottom of the Royal Mile (see pages 104–105), just beyond the Palace of Holyroodhouse (see below). The high ground is encircled by a public road, the Queen's Drive, but the area is better enjoyed on foot. A slanting path slices up the slopes below Salisbury Crags, where the views are outstanding. Arthur's Seat can be climbed, but it is challenging. However, you can still enjoy the splendid sights if you keep to the low ground of the park.

🔳 E1 ✉ Queen's Drive, EH8 8HG ☎ 0131 652 8150; www.historic-scotland.gov.uk 🚌 35, 36 🎧 Free 🛈 Maps and information from information center (open daily 9:30–3) by New Scottish Parliament

National Museum of Scotland

The National Museum of Scotland incorporates what used to be known as the Royal Museum in a bold space completed in 2011. The older part of the museum has retained its impressive Victorian ironwork Grand Gallery. Ten new galleries (open 2016) are dedicated to technology and design.

Along with the dramatic modern buildings, in golden stone, the museum tells the story of Scotland from its geological beginnings to the 21st century, and the relationship between Scotland and the wider world. Historical highlights include the Lewis Chess Pieces and artifacts relating to Bonnie Prince Charlie and Robert Burns. The core of the complex contains several levels, each displaying a particular era of Scotland's history. Pick up a copy of the floor plan from the information desk in the entrance hall. You also can check the plasma screens for information.

🔳 D1 ✉ Chambers Street, EH1 1JF ☎ 0300 123 6789; www.nms.ac.uk 🕐 Daily 10–5 🚌 9, 23, 27, 35, 41, 42, 45, 67 🍴 Restaurant and cafés 🎧 Free; charge for some exhibitions 🛈 Free guided tours daily

Palace of Holyroodhouse

Her Majesty Queen Elizabeth II's official residence in Scotland, Holyroodhouse was part of the Abbey of Holyrood, but much of the present palace was built during the reign of King Charles II. The severe neoclassicism of the courtyard block reflects the distinctly English fashion of the time; nevertheless it exudes Scottish history. The State Apartments are luxurious and grand, with artifacts and paintings elegantly displayed beneath superb stucco ceilings. Deep in the historic apartments is the bedchamber of Mary, Queen of Scots, and the adjoining closet where, in 1566, her secretary and confidante, David Rizzio, was stabbed to death by associates of the Queen's delinquent husband, Lord Darnley. The Queen's Gallery, in an adjacent building, has exhibitions of art from the Royal Collections. Behind the palace is Holyrood Park (see pages 101–102).

🔳 E2 ✉ Canongate, EH8 8DX ☎ 0131 556 5100; www.royalcollection.org.uk 🕐 Daily 9:30–6, Apr.–Oct.; 9:30–4:30, rest of year. Last admission 90 minutes before closing 🚌 6, 35 🍴 Café 🎧 $$$ (includes audio tour) 🛈 Closed for state functions. See the website for details

Edinburgh

Royal Botanic Garden Edinburgh

The Royal Botanic Garden Edinburgh is just a mile north of the New Town. Rhododendrons are the highlight here, at their colorful best from late April to early June. Other attractions are the glasshouses, where orchids and other exotics flourish in defiance of Scotland's less than tropical climate; the Chinese Hillside; a decidedly Scottish heath garden; and the café's outdoor terrace with great views of the city.

✚ Off map at C3 ✉ Inverleith Row, EH3 5LR ☎ 0131 248 2909; www.rbge.org.uk 🕐 Daily 10–6, Mar.–Sep.; 10–5, Feb. and Oct.; 10–4, rest of year. Glasshouses: 10–5:30, Mar.–Sep.; 10–4:30, Feb. and Oct.; 10–3:30, rest of year. Last admission 30 minutes before closing 🚌 8, 9, 23, 27 🍴 Restaurant and cafés 💲 Free; glasshouses $ 🚹 Guided tours Apr.–Oct. at 11 a.m. and 2 p.m. ($)

Royal Yacht Britannia

See how the British royal family once traveled the world in this venerable queen of the seas, now permanently anchored in the harbor at Leith. The visitor center at Ocean Terminal will fill you in on the history of royal craft before you enter the historic ship itself, which was built in Scotland on the Clyde, and launched in 1953. It served as the ultimate floating royal residence for state occasions and holidays, before being decommissioned in 1994. Visit the State Apartments where celebrated guests were entertained, and the bedrooms where the Queen and her family resided. The other side of life onboard may be seen in the laundry and in the gleaming engine room.

✚ Off map at D3 ✉ Ocean Terminal, Leith ☎ 0131 555 5566; www.royalyachtbritannia.co.uk 🕐 Daily 9:30–4:30, Apr.–Sep.; 9:30–4, Oct.; 10–3:30, Nov.–Mar. 🚌 10, 11, 16, 22 🍴 Café 💲 $$ (includes self-guiding audio tour)

St. Giles' Cathedral

St. Giles' Cathedral (or the High Kirk of Edinburgh) is the mother church of Scottish Presbyterianism and a powerful feature of the Royal Mile (see pages 104–105). The Kirk is a mix of medieval Gothic and Georgian Gothic, the latter grafted on in the early 19th century; the interior reflects an enthusiastic Victorian restoration. There are some superb external features, including the 19th-century west door and the late medieval tower and spire. Inside, the cathedral has many fine features and memorials. The Thistle Chapel was built in 1911 as a private chapel for the Knights of the Most Ancient and Most Noble Order of the Thistle. Richly carved stonework enlivens the interior of the chapel. Look near the entrance door for the tiny bagpipe-playing angel.

✚ D2 ✉ Royal Mile, EH1 1RE ☎ 0131 225 9442; www.stgilescathedral.org.uk 🕐 Mon.–Fri. 9–7, Sat. 9–5, Sun. 1–5, May–Sep.; Mon.–Sat. 9–5, Sun. 1–5, rest of year 🚌 23, 27, 35, 41, 42, 67 🍴 Café 💲 $ (donations) 🚹 Rooftop tours ($)

Scottish National Gallery

The Scottish National Gallery is a large, 19th-century neoclassical building with a good selection of works from the early Renaissance to the end of the 19th century, including Botticelli's *The Virgin Adoring the Sleeping Christ Child* and John Singer Sargent's *Lady Agnew of Lochnaw*. Most of the major names in 17th-century European art are represented; there are some fine landscapes by Claude Lorrain, and Nicholas Poussin's *Seven Sacraments* are on display. There is a powerful work by Frederick Edwin Church, *Niagara Falls, from the American Side*. Scottish painting is well represented by Gavin Hamilton and Allan Ramsay. Sir Henry Raeburn's *The Reverend Dr. Robert Walker Skating on Duddingston Loch* and Alexander Carse's *The Penny Wedding* are lively and very typical Scottish narrative works.

✚ C2 ✉ The Mound, EH2 2EL ☎ 0131 624 6200 or 0131 624 6336 (24-hour recorded information); www.nationalgalleries.org 🕐 Daily 10–5 (also Thu. to 7 p.m.), Sep.–Jul.; daily 10–6 in Aug. 🚌 All city center buses 🍴 Restaurant and café 💲 Free; charge for some exhibitions 🚹 The Gallery Bus Link to the Scottish National Gallery of Modern Art ($)

Stroll Down the Royal Mile

Edinburgh's Royal Mile is the epitome of Old Edinburgh. Made up of four linked streets – Castlehill, Lawnmarket, High Street and Canongate – it descends the sloping back of a long, steep-sided ridge from Edinburgh Castle (see page 101) at the west end to the Palace of Holyroodhouse (see page 102) at the east end. On either side of the Royal Mile are tall buildings, riddled with courtyards and passageways known as "closes" and separated by narrow streets known as "wynds," all of it a delight to explore. All the way down the Royal Mile historic buildings punctuate the streetscape, and there are numerous stores, cafés, restaurants and pubs.

You can begin a relaxed descent of the Royal Mile from the entrance to the Castle Esplanade, starting with Castlehill. Attractions beckon from both sides. On the left is the Tartan Weaving Mill and Exhibition, with its masses of tartan cloth and working mill (free). On the right is the Scotch Whisky Experience, which offers a fun barrel-ride tour and tasting ($$). Next on the left and well worth a visit is the fascinating Camera Obscura and World of Illusions, where moving images of the surrounding area are projected onto a white viewing table ($$). The street is narrow here, but opens up just past the powerful Highland Tolbooth, a handsome Gothic building with the tallest spire in Edinburgh. It is now The Hub, home of the Edinburgh International Festival and a focus of the city's cultural life. At this point, the Royal Mile becomes the much wider Lawnmarket, once the city's linen market.

Keep to the left side of the street, where steps rise from street level to the sidewalk. There are several stores here selling woolen and tartan goods. Soon you come to Gladstone's Land, a 17th-century merchant's house now restored by the National Trust for Scotland ($). The house's Painted Chamber is stunning. Just a bit farther is the entrance to Lady Stair's Close. A narrow alleyway leads to an open square and to Lady Stair's House, now The Writers' Museum (free), a quiet little corner housing memorabilia associated with Scotland's finest writers, including Robert Burns, Robert Louis Stevenson and Sir Walter Scott. The spiral stairs have an uneven step halfway up, a common trick in medieval houses aimed at tripping an intruder in the dark.

The Lawnmarket reaches an intersection with Bank Street and the street called George IV Bridge, where the Royal Mile becomes High Street. Here you will find a remarkable concentration of historic buildings. On the east corner with Bank Street is the High Court, with a bronze statue of Scottish philosopher David Hume in front of it. Next to the High Court is Edinburgh City Chambers, with an arcaded entrance screen. Opposite is St. Giles' Cathedral (see page 103). Behind the cathedral is Parliament Square and the old Parliament House, seat of the Scottish Parliament until the union with England in 1707. Directly opposite St. Giles' is The Real Mary King's Close, a historically accurate interpretation of life in Edinburgh from the 16th to the 19th centuries ($$).

High Street then descends gently to a junction with North and South Bridge streets. Stay on the north side of High Street, past the entrances to various alleys, and look for Chalmer's Close. Go through the entrance and down the steps to the preserved apse of the 15th-century Trinity College Church, home to the Brass Rubbing Centre (free).

On the other side of High Street, opposite Chalmer's Close, is the entertaining Museum of Childhood (free). Farther down High Street, just before an intersection is the John Knox House, a celebration of the 16th-century religious reformer who brought the Protestant Reformation to Scotland with more than a whiff of fire and brimstone. It is now part of the Scottish Storytelling Centre ($). Beyond Jeffrey Street the Royal Mile becomes Canongate and narrows once more.

Halfway down Canongate is the old Tolbooth, with its wonderful clock and conical-roofed towers. Canongate Tolbooth was once a courtroom and jail and is now The People's Story Museum, an exhibition of Edinburgh life (free). Just opposite is The Museum of Edinburgh, a beautifully restored late 16th-century building containing an excellent collection of artifacts of Edinburgh life (free).

Diagonally opposite the Museum of Edinburgh is the 17th-century Canongate Kirk and Kirkyard. The church has close royal connections; the royal family worship here when they are in residence at nearby Holyroodhouse, and the royal coat of arms can be seen decorating one of the church benches, or pews. Just past the church the Royal Mile passes The Scottish Parliament building to the right (free tours; see www.scottish parliament.uk for details), and continues as Abbey Street to end at the gates of the Palace of Holyroodhouse (see page 102). For the walking route, see the city map on pages 98–99.

Above left to right: Many visitors buy a tartan garment. Those with Scottish ancestors can choose a clan tartan; St. Giles' Cathedral and a view down the Royal Mile

Looking down onto the soaring spires of All Souls College from the Church of St. Mary the Virgin

Oxford

Oxford, 56 miles northwest of London, is a typical English market town at heart. It is located within a hollow amid low hills at the gentle confluence of the River Thames and River Cherwell.

What makes Oxford exceptional is its university, the oldest in the English-speaking world, an institution that consists of not one single campus but 38 independent colleges that are scattered throughout the city. They represent elegant seats of learning, but they also are blessed with beautiful, historic buildings.

The history of Oxford is said to have begun with the founding of a priory by the Saxon St. Frideswide, near where the River Thames and River Cherwell meet. Christ Church Cathedral supplanted the priory, and in time wealth from the medieval wool trade led to the founding of other religious houses, where learning was revered. Scholars were drawn to Oxford, and from these beginnings the university evolved.

Unless you're a student, Oxford is more of a journey through history and great architecture than through academia. For the visitor, the experience may seem faintly voyeuristic. You visit the colleges, picking your way through elegant quadrangles, chapels, arched passageways, gardens and libraries, and at times you may feel you are intruding on a select world of academic privilege and of cultural paradigms. Yet the physical integration of Oxford's colleges with the realities of Oxford as a city dispel any sense of intrusion. This is a living, working city that retains its own identity and commercial life.

Take a ride on an open-top bus to see the principal sights, leaving the bus where and when you like, or take a

The Original Alice

The children's books *Alice in Wonderland* and *Alice Through The Looking Glass* were inspired by Oxford life. Charles Lutwidge Dodgson, a writer, mathematician and ordained deacon at Christ Church, wrote the books during the latter part of the 19th century. Dodgson was the oldest of 11 children born to his clergyman father and he loved to entertain his siblings with stories and poems. He formed an intense friendship with Alice Liddell, the daughter of the Dean of Christ Church, and enjoyed entertaining her and her two sisters with his stories of Wonderland. Dodgson later published his stories under the pseudonym Lewis Carroll. Alice's Shop is where the real-life Alice bought her candy. It also sells Alice memorabilia (✚ A1 ✉ 83 St. Aldates, OX1 1RA ☎ 01865 723793; www.aliceinwonderlandshop.co.uk ◷ Daily 9:30–6:30, Jul.–Aug.; Sun.–Fri. 10:30–5, Sat. 9:30–6, rest of year).

guided walking tour of historic Oxford or of the colleges. Stroll by the Thames or take a river cruise.

Oxford's Colleges

You can walk around central Oxford in less than an hour, but it is the density and complexity of colleges and great buildings that is so absorbing. The heart of the university lies between High Street and Broad Street and is enclosed by the colleges of Brasenose, All Souls, Hertford and Exeter. The University Church of St. Mary the Virgin (see page 110) is on High Street. Behind St. Mary's is Radcliffe Square, which has the elegant 18th-century Renaissance rotunda of the Radcliffe Camera (chamber) at its heart. On the east side of the square is All Souls College. On the west side is Brasenose College, named after a traditional brass "mask" door

knocker and a treasured college possession; a replica can be seen on the great oak doors.

From Radcliffe Square you can walk into the Schools Quadrangle of the Bodleian Library, with its superb Jacobean entrance tower and decorative inner walls. Through the arch on the north side of the quadrangle is the Sheldonian Theatre, where the *Encaenia* (the ceremony to confer honorary degrees each June) and the degree ceremony for Oxford graduates are held.

The Radcliffe Square area is the heart of the university, but try to visit some of the colleges when their grounds are open to the public (get the free leaflet *Visiting the University of Oxford* from the Tourist Information Centre or check www.ox.ac.uk). Include Christ Church (see page 109), the largest and most famous of the colleges, and do not miss nearby Merton College, reputedly the oldest of them all and certainly one of the finest, with its delightful gardens, ancient quadrangle, medieval library and chapel. Adjoining Merton Street, cobbled and quiet, is one of the finest parts of the city. Merton counts among its alumni 14th-century religious reformer John Wycliffe, poet T. S. Eliot and actor-singer Kris Kristofferson. Then head east toward Magdalen (pronounced "Maudlin") and its superb tower, Cloister Quad, gardens and riverside walks. Magdalen alumni include playwright Oscar Wilde.

The Market Town

Oxford itself is famous for automobile manufacturing, and is the home of the Morris Oxford and the T-series MG sports car. They were produced at Oxford's Cowley factories, built up by William Richard Morris, later Viscount Nuffield, a self-made man who founded Oxford's Nuffield College among his numerous charitable acts. Visit the Museum of Oxford (see page 109) and discover the history of the city, and take in the Pitt Rivers Museum and the Oxford University Museum of Natural History (see page 110). Climb to the top of Carfax Tower for great views.

The streets radiating from Carfax constitute Oxford's main shopping area. Cornmarket has a range of well-known stores. Off Cornmarket's east side is Golden Cross, where Shakespeare's plays are said to have been performed. Just beyond is the celebrated covered market, with more than 50 shops and outlets under one roof.

Oxford's university population and townspeople exhibit a fascinating contrast of lifestyles. In medieval times this duality led to occasional bloody battles, but although today's students are noted for their boisterous post-exam antics, Oxford is an eminently civilized place where the traditions of "town and gown" rest easily side by side.

Essential Information

Tourist Information

Tourist Information Centre
15–16 Broad Street, OX1 3AS ☎ 01865 252200; www.visitoxfordandoxfordshire.com

Urban Transportation

Oxford railroad station, Park End Street (☎ 03457 000125) offers regular train connections to and from London Paddington. Central Oxford is a 10-minute walk from the station. Local bus services in and around the city are frequent. Two companies provide all local services: The Oxford Bus Company (☎ 01865 785400; www.oxfordbus.co.uk) and Stagecoach Oxford (☎ 01865 772250; www.stagecoachbus.com). Taxi stands are located at the railroad station, Carfax and the Gloucester Green bus station. Alternatively, try 001 Taxis (☎ 01865 240000).

Airport Information

The Airline buses (☎ 01865 785400) depart every 20 or 30 minutes for London Heathrow Airport (every two hours at night), and every hour for London Gatwick Airport (every two hours at night). Birmingham Airport has daily rail (www.nationalrail.co.uk) connections to and from Oxford.

Climate – average highs and lows for the month

Jan.	Feb.	Mar.	Apr.	May	Jun.	Jul.	Aug.	Sep.	Oct.	Nov.	Dec.
7°C	7°C	10°C	13°C	16°C	16°C	21°C	18°C	18°C	14°C	10°C	8°C
45°F	45°F	50°F	55°F	61°F	61°F	70°F	64°F	64°F	57°F	50°F	46°F
3°C	3°C	4°C	5°C	8°C	10°C	13°C	13°C	11°C	8°C	6°C	4°C
37°F	37°F	39°F	41°F	46°F	50°F	55°F	55°F	52°F	46°F	43°F	39°F

Oxford Sights

```
Key to symbols
🔠 map coordinates refer to the Oxford map
on page 107 💲 admission charge:
$$$ more than £15, $$ £10–£15, $ less than £10
See page 5 for complete key to symbols
```

Ashmolean Museum of Art and Archaeology

The Ashmolean is a fascinating museum of grand oddities and elegant art, housed in a neoclassical building dating from the 1840s. It is the oldest museum in Britain, founded in 1683, and its extensive collection includes much medieval material; Greek, Roman and Egyptian artifacts; and Asian porcelain.

Five floors of gallery space include the 2009 modern development that more than doubled the original space, around a central atrium and staircase. The state-of-the-art galleries of Ancient Egypt and Nubia, in which visitors are taken on a journey through 5,000 years of history, are just one highlight.

🔠 A2 ✉ Beaumont Street, OX1 2PH ☎ 01865 278 000; www.ashmolean.org ◉ Tue.–Sun. and public holidays 10–5 🚌 All city center buses 🍴 Restaurant and café 💲 Free; charge for some exhibitions

Christ Church College and Christ Church Cathedral

Oxford's largest college, Christ Church, is the most visited of all the university's colleges. It is recognizable to many as a location for the *Harry Potter* movies. Entry to Christ Church College is via the Meadow building, off St. Aldates.

Tom Quad is Christ Church's glorious central quadrangle; Mercury Pond, with Mercury Fountain at its center, adds an elegant accent. The figure of Mercury often sprouts neckties and other "outfits" donated by students. The entrance to Tom Quad and to Christ Church is the mighty gate tower, Tom Tower, that holds a massive seven-ton bell, Great Tom. Visit Christ Church's vaulted Great Hall, the Picture Gallery

of Old Master works of art, and Canterbury and Peckwater quadrangles.

The present cathedral dates from the 12th century. Among its fine features are exquisite stained-glass windows.

🔠 A1–B1 ✉ College and cathedral: St. Aldates, OX1 1DP. Picture Gallery: Canterbury Quad ☎ College and cathedral: 01865 276492; www.chch.ox.ac.uk. Picture Gallery: 01865 276172; www.chch.ox.ac.uk/gallery ◉ College and cathedral: Phone ahead or check website as opening times are amended weekly. Picture Gallery: Mon.–Sat. 10:30–5, Sun. 2–5, Jul.–Sep.; Mon., Wed.–Sat. 10:30–5, Sun. 2–5, Jun.; Mon., Wed.–Sat. 10:30–1 and 2–4:30, Sun. 2–4:30, Oct.–May 🚌 All city center buses 💲 College and cathedral $; Picture Gallery $$ 🅸 May close at short notice. Free gallery tours Mon. 2:30 p.m.

Museum of Oxford

The Museum of Oxford has well-arranged and interactive displays and gives an excellent account of Oxford's history. Everyone who played a part in the making of Oxford is here, from prehistory through the Roman, Saxon and Norman periods to the present day. The realities of town life from both sides of the tracks are depicted through 19th-century house interiors from middle- and working-class districts. There is a program of changing exhibitions covering subjects from Roman times to space travel.

🔠 A1 ✉ Town Hall, St. Aldates, OX1 1BX ☎ 01865 252334; www.oxford.gov.uk/museumofoxford ◉ Mon.–Sat. 10–5 🚌 All city center buses 💲 Free

Oxford Castle Unlocked

Eleventh-century Oxford Castle, a place of incarceration for many souls from 1071 to 1996 was once as notorious as Colditz. Visitors can experience something of the austere confines of prison life over the centuries as people and events from the site's turbulent past are brought to life by costumed guides in character. Those who climb the 101 steps of the Saxon St. George's Tower (children aged under 5 not permitted) are rewarded with panoramic views of Oxford and beyond. The 19th-century wing of the prison has been converted to a fine hotel.

🕂 Off map at A2 ✉ 44–46 Oxford Castle, OX1 1AY
☎ 01865 260666; www.oxfordcastleunlocked.co.uk
🕐 Daily 10–5 (last tour 4:20) 🚌 3, 5, 13, X3 🍴 Café
🍷 $$ ⓘ Opening times subject to change

Oxford University Museum of Natural History

This museum is housed in an Italianate-Gothic-style 19th-century building. The interior is a single open space, surrounded by an ambulatory and forested with slender iron columns that support a wrought-iron vault and glass roof. Exhibits range from dinosaur skeletons to minerals and fossils.

You can access the Pitt Rivers Museum from the rear of the building.

🕂 B3 ✉ Parks Road, OX1 3PW ☎ 01865 272950;
www.oum.ox.ac.uk 🕐 Daily 10–5 🚌 2, 7A, 27
🍴 Café 🍷 Free

Pitt Rivers Museum

Founded in 1884, this fascinating museum is a marvelous example of 19th-century museum culture. It has a full program of changing exhibits and events, and houses more than half a million objects from many cultures around the world, including jewelry, pots, masks, boats, armor and weaponry, textiles, toys, and medical and musical instruments. The museum includes also the often wildly eccentric collection of Lieutenant General Augustus Henry Lane Fox Pitt Rivers, who served throughout the British Empire and gathered many artifacts along the way.

🕂 B3 ✉ South Parks Road, OX1 3PP (enter through the Oxford University Museum of Natural History)
☎ 01865 270927; www.prm.ox.ac.uk 🕐 Mon.
noon–4:30, Tue.–Sun. 10–4:30 🚌 2 🍷 Free

University Church of St. Mary the Virgin

St. Mary the Virgin is both the parish church of Oxford and the university's church. It forms the southern side of Radcliffe Square. The early 14th-century tower rises above Oxford's dreaming

The splendid interior at the Pitt Rivers Museum

spires, domes and cupolas. The south porch, facing High Street, is a 17th-century addition that trumpeted Italian influence with its twisted columns and heavily decorated segmented arch.

For fantastic views over the city, climb up the tower's 127 steps as far as the base of the spire – there is a resting place halfway up, and it can be busy.

🕂 B2 ✉ High Street, OX1 4BJ ☎ 01865 279111;
www.university-church.ox.ac.uk 🕐 Daily 9–6,
Jul.–Aug.; 9–5, rest of year. Tower: Mon.–Sat. from
9:30 a.m., Sun. from 11:45 a.m. 🚌 All city center
buses 🍴 Café 🍷 Church free; tower $$

University of Oxford Botanic Garden

The University of Oxford Botanic Garden was founded as a "physic garden" in 1621 and is Britain's oldest botanic garden. This delightful enclave has a collection of around 5,000 plant species. The River Cherwell and Magdalen College's tower enhance the setting. There also are splendid greenhouses with 100-year-old cacti.

🕂 C1 ✉ Rose Lane, OX1 4AZ ☎ 01865 286690;
www.botanic-garden.ox.ac.uk 🕐 Daily 9–6, May–
Aug.; 9–5, Mar.–Apr. and Sep.–Oct.; 9–4, rest of year.
Last admission 45 minutes before closing 🚌 All city
center buses 🍷 $ ⓘ Free audio trails with "smart"
map available 10–3 (refundable deposit required)

Shakespeare's Stratford-upon-Avon

Stratford-upon-Avon was the birthplace of William Shakespeare and today the town is something of a shrine to the poet-playwright, its numerous Tudor and Jacobean half-timbered houses enhancing the Shakespearean theme. Shakespeare's Birthplace on Henley Street has been restored with late 16th-century furnishings and is full of memorabilia. Another fine old building in the town is the Elizabethan Harvard House, which, although having no connection to Shakespeare, is interesting as the birthplace of John Harvard, who founded Harvard University in Massachusetts.

After an intriguing life, Shakespeare died in 1616 at the age of 52 in a house called New Place in Stratford. The original house no longer exists as it was demolished by the owner in 1759 because he found visitors a nuisance. The foundations remain and are adjoined by the Elizabethan-style Knott Garden and Nash's House, the superbly restored 17th-century home of Thomas Nash, husband of Shakespeare's granddaughter, Elizabeth Hall (admission with Birthplace Museum $$$).

Another famous Stratford building is the 13th-century Holy Trinity Church, where Shakespeare was baptized in 1564, located on the banks of the River Avon. Here you will see the remarkable alabaster bust of Shakespeare, modeled on a wax impression of the playwright's face at his death. Nearby is Shakespeare's tomb and those of his wife, Anne Hathaway, and their daughter, Suzanna. On the banks of the River Avon to the north of the church is the Royal Shakespeare Theatre, where the Royal Shakespeare Company performs the Bard's plays. Attending a performance here or at the more intimate Swan Theatre nearby is a highlight of any visit.

Arrange day trips to Stratford at the Oxford Tourist Information Centre.

Oxford Tourist Information Centre ✉ 15–16 Broad Street, Oxford OX1 3AS ☎ 01865 252200; www.visitoxfordandoxfordshire.com

Royal Shakespeare Theatre ✉ Waterside, CV37 6BB; www.rsc.org.uk 🚹 Theater tours ($)

Anne Hathaway's Cottage, just west of Stratford, was the childhood home of Shakespeare's wife

York

Two thousand years of English history are written across the face of York. Within the old city's walls, and within sight and sound of the magnificent York Minster cathedral, narrow, cobbled streets, ancient remains, medieval buildings, historic churches and award-winning museums sit happily alongside modern stores, restaurants and hotels.

York, although a city, is a small town at heart. It began life as a riverside encampment established by an ancient British tribe, the Brigantes. In turn, the Brigantes were usurped in AD 71 by Roman invaders who made York their empire's northern European capital. Anglo-Saxons, who established York as a center of early Christianity, followed the Romans. In AD 867, the settlement was captured by the Danes – the plundering Vikings of romantic history.

In subsequent centuries York fell under the control of the Normans, who laid the first substantial foundations of the present minster and built the original city walls. During the 16th and 17th centuries, religious and dynastic struggles kept the city in the national forefront, at a time when poverty, plague and famine often made ordinary life harsh and terrible. As a major religious center, York suffered significantly as the monasteries were suppressed and church-owned houses in the city were seized and sold on to rich merchants under orders from the reigning monarch – King Henry VIII.

The more enterprising world of the 18th and 19th centuries and the emergence of York as the railroad capital of northern England made the city a fashionable commercial center, one that was only lightly touched by the more brutal aspects of the Industrial Revolution. Today visitors walk on hallowed ground that has supported more than 2,000 years of human achievement, as well as misery.

Sightseeing in York

Many parts of central York are pedestrian-only, and though crowds may throng the narrow streets, people have precedence over vehicles. In the nicest areas of old York there is no stream of roaring traffic pinning you to the sidewalk. You go with the flow, but there is no rush-hour element even during the busiest times of day.

The exterior of York Minster, northern Europe's largest Gothic cathedral

York's flavor can be captured via a York City Sightseeing open-top double-decker bus or on a bicycle or a riverboat. The inner city can be explored on one of numerous walking tours, led by local experts. Or you can take an evening "ghost walk," complete with an entertaining guide and actors making impromptu, phantom appearances in dark alleys.

You could also explore on your own. Central York is not large, and you're never far from the next fascinating building, museum or attraction. Few houses in York rise above two or three stories, and the sun finds its way into hidden corners, lighting the upper parts of old buildings. Take time as you stroll to appreciate the colorful facades and architectural features, like Stonegate's

little red devil above the corner with Coffee Yard Lane.

The many different people who colonized York left an engaging but confusing legacy of local words. The word "bar" means gate and refers to the magnificent stone gateways, such as Bootham Bar and Monk Bar, that punctuate the city walls. On the other hand, the Viking word "gate," as in Stonegate and Petergate, means street.

Walk part of the city walls for a superb overview of York. Try the section from Monk Bar (location of the fascinating Richard III Museum), at the north end of Goodramgate, to Bootham Bar at the west end of High Petergate. The views of York Minster along this stretch of the city walls are outstanding. Visit such main attractions as York Minster and

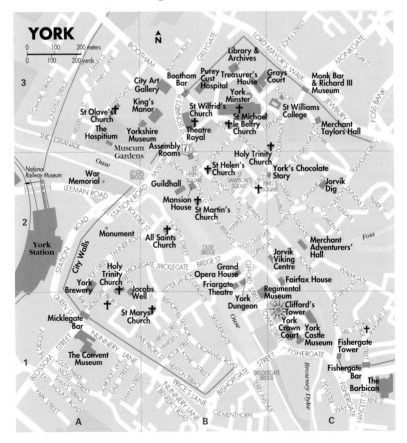

JORVIK Viking Centre, but do not neglect other sights – like the hands-on archeological DIG in St. Saviour's Church and The York Dungeon on Clifford Street, both great fun for children. (Save money on entry to key attractions with the York Pass, available from the Visitor Information Centre.) Enjoy the talented street entertainers and the many festivals and events staged here each year.

Shopping in Old York

Shopping in York is fun. Streets such as Stonegate and The Shambles are overflowing with specialty stores, including antiques shops, art and craft galleries, bookstores, jewelers, tea blenders and boutiques. Every major chain store is represented in the main shopping areas of Coney Street, St. Mary's Square and Parliament Street.

A huge variety of eateries will tempt you, from traditional English tea and coffee houses – such as Bettys Café Tea Rooms in St. Helen's Square and The Earl Grey Tea Rooms in The Shambles – to numerous restaurants, offering a choice of dining experiences. Authentic English pubs include Stonegate's Ye Old Starre Inne and the 15th-century Black Swan, on Peasholme Green.

York is essentially English at heart, but its northern regional identity makes it very different from London and southern England. Expect friendliness and helpfulness from locals, along with the matter-of-fact approach for which Yorkshire people are famous. You will be given facts not fiction and guidance rather than gossip to help you get the best out of England's heartland.

Minster

The Old English word "Minster" was used in medieval England as a variant of the word "monastery." It was sometimes used to describe the church attached to a monastery, which was used for worship by the monks. Through time the word became associated with certain cathedral churches, like York Minster.

Essential Information

Tourist Information

York Visitor Information Centre
1 Museum Street, YO1 7DT ☎ 01904 550099;
www.visityork.org

Urban Transportation

York railroad station, Station Road, YO24 1AB (☎ 03457 225 333). The center of York is pedestrian-only. First buses operate in and around the center of the city (☎ 01904 883063; www.firstgroup.com). There are taxi stands at York railroad station and at Duncombe Place, near York Minster. To hire a taxi call Streamline Taxis (☎ 01904 656565).

Airport Information

Leeds Bradford International Airport (www.leedsbradfordairport.co.uk), 31 miles southwest, is a 45-minute drive from York. Manchester airport (☎ 0161 489 2636; www.manchesterairport.co.uk) is 56 miles southwest by road, but has direct train services to York; either way it's a travel time of 90 minutes.

Climate – average highs and lows for the month

Jan.	Feb.	Mar.	Apr.	May	Jun.	Jul.	Aug.	Sep.	Oct.	Nov.	Dec.
6°C	7°C	9°C	13°C	16°C	19°C	21°C	20°C	18°C	14°C	9°C	7°C
43°F	45°F	48°F	55°F	61°F	66°F	70°F	68°F	64°F	57°F	48°F	45°F
0°C	1°C	2°C	4°C	7°C	10°C	12°C	11°C	10°C	7°C	4°C	2°C
32°F	34°F	36°F	39°F	45°F	50°F	54°F	52°F	50°F	45°F	39°F	36°F

York Sights

Inside the paneled Merchant Adventurers' Hall

Fairfax House

This elegant house was lavishly decorated by Viscount Fairfax in 1759, subsequently neglected, and bought in 1980 by the York Civic Trust, which carried out an inspired restoration. Today, Fairfax House is one of the finest examples of an 18th-century town house in Britain. Enjoy the sumptuous plasterwork ceilings, rich damask hangings, elegant marble fireplaces and magnificent furnishings.

 C2 Castlegate, YO1 9RN 01904 655543; www.fairfaxhouse.co.uk Tue.–Sat. 10–5, Sun. 11–4. Last admission 30 minutes before closing. Mon.: guided tours only at 11 and 2. Closed Christmas and Jan.–early Feb. City center buses $

JORVIK Viking Centre

This very popular attraction reveals the archeological remains of Viking York, or Jorvik, unearthed here from 1976 to 1981. Deep underground, you're shuttled back in time 1,000 years to a reconstructed Viking street complete with thatched houses, lifelike figures and the evocative sounds and smells of everyday life.

Traveling in a "time capsule" back to the year AD 975, you "fly" across the city, over streets and yards, to discover how a Viking settlement of 10,000 people functioned on this very site.

 C2 Coppergate, YO1 9WT 01904 615505; www.jorvik-viking-centre.co.uk Daily 10–5, Apr.–Oct.; 10–4, rest of year. Opening times may vary during school vacations City center buses $$

Merchant Adventurers' Hall

This medieval guildhall is the finest of its kind to survive in Europe. Its brick and timber-framed exterior, the vast, open timberwork of the Great Hall and the interior paneling effortlessly transport visitors from the present into a convincing medieval environment. The hall was built from 1357 to 1361 by a religious fraternity that evolved into a merchants' guild, which survives today as a charitable organization and guardian of this outstanding building.

 C2 Fossgate, YO1 9XD 01904 654818; www.theyorkcompany.co.uk Mon.–Thu. 9–5, Fri.–Sat. 9–3:30, Sun. 11–4, Mar.–Oct.; Mon.–Thu. 10–4, Fri.–Sat. 10–3:30, rest of year City center buses $; audio tour included in admission

National Railway Museum

For travel enthusiasts young and old, this atmospheric museum – the world's largest – offers vivid insight into 300 years of transportation history. There are displays of more than 100 steam, diesel and electric locomotives, including a working replica of George Stephenson's famous 1829 *Rocket*; the wonderful *Mallard*, still the fastest steam engine in the world; the *Flying Scotsman* (undergoing restoration so not always on display), one of the world's most famous steam locomotives; and the only Shinkansen (Bullet Train) outside Japan.

 Off map at A2 Leeman Road, YO26 4XJ 01904 621261; www.nrm.org.uk Daily 10–6 Park & Ride 2; "Road Train" from Duncombe Place (next to York Minster) every 30 minutes, daily 11:15–4:15, Apr.–Oct. Restaurant and café Free; charge for events

York Castle Museum

This wonderful museum is housed in two former prisons. Behind its building's

York Minster seen from the medieval city walls

handsome neoclassical facade is an outstanding collection of exhibits illustrating the social history of York, and of Britain, over the past 400 years. Walkways lead past vivid and lifelike reconstructions of a Victorian street, lined with stores full of authentic contents. Allow several hours for this experience, which also includes a major World War I exhibit, plus a visit to the cell that once held highwayman Dick Turpin, and other topical temporary exhibitions.

⊞ C1 ✉ Eye of York, YO1 9RY ☎ 01904 687687; www.yorkcastlemuseum.org.uk 🕐 Daily 9:30–5 🚌 City center buses ♦ Café 💲 $$. Children (16 and under) free with paying adult

York Minster

York cathedral's present foundations were laid by the Normans in the 12th century and this is northern Europe's largest Gothic cathedral. A visit to the Minster is a historical as well as a religious experience; the walls are crowded with dramatic monuments and the architectural features are superb. Catch the cathedral choir here at Evensong (5:15 p.m. Tue.–Sat., 4 p.m. Sun.) or enjoy the accoustics at a summer concert.

Past the broad introductory nave is the central crossing, where north and south transepts, nave and choir all meet below the soaring vaulted roof of the central tower, 200 feet above. The choir is full of intricate design and ornamentation. At the east end of the church you will find the Lady Chapel and the great East Window – as big as a tennis court and the largest medieval stained-glass window in the world. Also visit the interactive displays in the Undercroft, and see the medieval glass up close in The Orb. In the Chapter House, look for the wickedly irreverent figures of priests and prelates among the carvings above the stalls. You can climb the 275 spiral steps of the great 234-foot tower, but only if you're fit and weather permits.

⊞ B3 ✉ Minster Yard, YO1 7JN ☎ 01904 557200;

www.yorkminster.org 🕐 Minster: Mon.–Sat. 9–5, Sun. 12:45–5. Hours may change according to church services 🚌 City center buses 💲 $$–$$$ 🚹 Free guided tours (Mon.–Sat.)

York's Chocolate Story

York became the chocolate-making capital of England in the 19th century when Quaker families Rowntree (who created the world renowned KitKat brand) and Terry (the Chocolate Orange) opened their factories in the city, alongside the Cravens (for boiled sweets). Explore the story of chocolate and its impact on the city at this lively visitor center, where you can watch expert chocolatiers at work, and even design your own chocolate bar.

⊞ C2 ✉ King's Square, YO1 7LD ☎ 01904 633482; www.yorkschocolatestory.com 🕐 Daily 10–6 🚌 City center buses ♦ Café 💲 $$

Yorkshire Museum and Gardens

This eclectic treasure-house includes some of the finest Roman, Viking, Anglo-Saxon and medieval artifacts in Europe. The 10-acre grounds feature fine gardens that contain York's oldest ruin, the Multangular Tower, part of fourth-century Roman fortifications.

The luminous Middleham Jewel, a 15th-century sapphire set within a gold pendant, engraved back and front, is a major exhibit. Also of interest is a collection of sea dragons from the Jurassic period. The museum building incorporates part of the ruins of medieval St. Mary's Abbey. This section, with its haunting reconstructions and medieval music, is a delight.

⊞ A3–B3 ✉ Museum Gardens, YO1 7FR ☎ 01904 687687; www.yorkshiremuseum.org.uk 🕐 Museum: daily 10–5. Gardens: daily 7:30–6 (open later from late Mar.–late Oct.) 🚌 City center buses 💲 $

Walk Through the Past

York's appeal stems largely from the survival of its central core of streets in their original form. While many cities and towns had their centers remodeled over the years, central York was spared wholesale change. Plans to demolish the city walls during the Victorian period were resisted, and within the precise boundaries of those restored walls the narrow streets and interlocking alleys and courtyards make up one of the best-preserved late medieval cities in Europe.

Many of York's old houses are not the original buildings; they have been rebuilt or restored over time. But their styles are medieval, and so venerable is the layout of central York that when you walk down Stonegate you follow the exact line of the Roman approach road to the imperial encampment of AD 71.

The most famous of York's ancient thoroughfares is The Shambles, a narrow street overhung by timber-framed houses. Its name derives from the butchers' shops and slaughterhouses once located here. The Shambles today is a delight. It typifies York's medieval character, but in times past this would have been a filthy, raucous, rough-and-ready place that would horrify modern sensibilities. Today it can be enjoyed for its quaintness, free of medieval realities. Don't miss bustling Newgate Market, with more than 80 stalls (open daily), between Parliament Street and The Shambles, where – within the rules of modern hygiene and legality – some of the liveliness of medieval times still survives.

To get the most out of old York, explore the interlocking alleys that connect the center. Wander at will with a city map, which will show you the main landmarks, but investigate the twists and turns of the numerous passages leading off Stonegate, Petergate, Davygate and Church Street. They'll land you unexpectedly in the bustle of St. Helen's Square, with its handsome Mansion House and Guildhall, or in King's Square, where old gravestones make up part of the paving. Brimming with charming little shops, cafés and restaurants, old York exudes unforgettable character.

The overhanging houses, so typical of The Shambles, are atmospheric at night

Czech Republic

Opposite: The Astronomical Clock in Prague was installed in the 15th century

Czech Republic

Since November 1989, the people of this landlocked country have been embracing change and finding their footing as a new republic. In that year, the Velvet Revolution saw Czechoslovakia throw out 40 years of Communist rule without firing a shot. In 1993, Czechs and Slovaks amicably split into the Czech Republic and Slovakia. Today, the Czech Republic is a successful member of the European Union.

Bohemia and Moravia

Most visitors head straight for Prague, but there is plenty to enjoy in the country's diverse landscapes. Locked between Poland, Germany, Slovakia and Austria, the republic takes in two regions: Bohemia, surrounded by mountains, and the easterly highlands of Moravia. Both regions are filled with historical and cultural wonders, and boast areas of extreme natural beauty. Bohemia is considered beer country, while Moravians tend to favor wine.

In southern Bohemia, such medieval towns as České Budějovice (home of Budějovický Budvar or Budweiser beer) and Český Krumlov, with its 13th-century castle (one of Europe's largest), recall a time when kings and nobles were eager to build in one of Europe's richest regions. To the west are spa towns, best known by their German names: Franzenbad (Františkovy Lázně), Karlsbad (Karlovy Vary) and Marienbad (Mariánské Lázně).

In Moravia, wedged between the western uplands and the eastern White Carpathian mountains, the city of Brno gives access to the Punkevní jeskyně (Punkva Caves).

Czech Culture

Despite the hijacking of the term "bohemian" by the West to mean "unconventional," the Czechs are generally rather reserved. Beyond this, though, is a friendliness and genuine interest in other cultures. Young Czechs often speak English, and are tuned in to Anglo-American pop culture. Love of arts and literature is also widespread. The late Václav Havel, the first post-Communist president, was better known among Czechs as a playwright.

Music has a special place in Czech life, too – from oompah-style brass bands to

A lovely way to explore Old Town Square in Prague

the classical tradition that produced such composers as Antonín Dvořák and Bedřich Smetana.

Generally speaking, most people who travel around the Czech Republic will be struck by the diversity of this small nation. As the republic embraces tourism, facilities for visitors continue to improve.

CZECH REPUBLIC

0   20   40   60   80km
0 10 20 30 40 50 miles

POLAND

N

Jeseník
Krnov
Šumperk
Opava
Ostrava
Karviná
Šternberk
Odra
D1
Frýdek-Místek
Olomouc
Nový Jičín
Punkevní jeskyně
Valašské Meziříčí
Kroměříž
Vsetín
Vyškov
D1
Zlín
Slavkov u Brna
Uherské Hradiště
D2
Hodonín
Mikulov
Břeclav
SLOVAK REPUBLIC

D   E

More Top Destinations in the Czech Republic

- ■ České Budějovice B1
- ■ Český Krumlov B1
- ■ Český ráj C3
- ■ Karlovy Vary A2
- ■ Krkonoše C3
- ■ Mariánské Lázně A2
- ■ Olomouc D2
- ■ Punkevní jeskyně D2
- ■ Šumava A1–B1
- ■ Telč C1
- ■ Vranov C1

Timeline

AD 872	The Přemysl Dynasty begins its 421-year rule of Bohemia.
929	"Good" King Wenceslas is assassinated by his brother, Boleslav, and made the country's patron saint.
1346	Devout Charles IV, Holy Roman Emperor, is crowned king of Bohemia and ushers in its Golden Age.
1415	Religious reformer Jan Hus is burned at the stake in Constance; four years later, in Prague, his supporters throw Catholic councillors from town hall windows and start the Hussite Wars.
1583	The Habsburg court moves to Prague.
1620	Battle of White Mountain. Bohemia's Protestants are defeated and the Czech lands are occupied by the Austrian Habsburgs.
1848	The Habsburgs suppress an uprising of Czech nationalism.
1914	Czechs are forced to fight for Austria–Hungary in World War I, but thousands desert to the Russians.
1918	With the defeat of Austria–Hungary, the new state of Czechoslovakia is proclaimed.
1938	Czechoslovakia is forced to hand over the Sudetenland to Hitler. The country is occupied by Germany the following year.
1945	Slovakia and the Czech lands are liberated by the Red Army and the United States; the Communist Party seizes power in 1948.
1968	The First Secretary, Alexander Dubček, introduces "socialism with a human face" in the reforms of the "Prague Spring;" in August, Soviet troops invade Czechoslovakia.
1989	"Velvet Revolution;" Václav Havel becomes president of Czechoslovakia.
1993	Czechoslovakia splits into the Czech and Slovak republics.
1999	Czech Republic becomes a NATO member.
2004	Czech Republic joins the European Union.
2009	Czech Republic holds the presidency of the European Union.
2011	Václav Havel, former president and leader of the 1989 Velvet Revolution, dies.
2013	The country holds its first direct, popular vote for the presidency, resulting in the election of Miloš Zeman.
2015	Plzeň hosts the European Capital of Culture.

The Velvet Revolution

On November 17, 1989, a week after the fall of the Berlin Wall, there was an officially sanctioned demonstration in Prague to mark the 50th anniverary of the Nazi suppression of Czech universities. It soon turned into a protest march against the Communist authorities, and was forcefully put down by riot police. A rumor began that the police had killed one demonstrator. In fact, it wasn't true, but the story was enough to fuel public anger. People poured into the streets night after night, watched by television viewers across the world. Former leader Alexander Dubček was brought back from obscurity in Bratislava to address the crowds. Human rights activist and writer Václav Havel headed a newly established Civic Forum, and on December 10 a new government was formed, with the Communists reduced to a minority. Less than three weeks later, Havel was installed as president.

St. Vitus' Cathedral (Katedrála sv Víta) towers over Prague's historic buildings and the Vltava river

Survival Guide

- Czech pronunciation is difficult, but worth mastering if only for place-names. Any attempt to speak Czech will be heartily appreciated, although many Czechs – particularly young city dwellers – may speak excellent English. The key is to stress the first syllable of a word. A grasp of German is also useful.

- The cuisine here is heavily meat-based – dumplings with pork and duck are popular dishes – and can be quite flavorful. Czechs claim to have the world's best beer, and the products of České Budějovice (Budweis) and Plzeň (Pilsen) are the most famous among a multitude of local varieties.

- It's worth looking through bookstores, as the illustrated books are a treat. For souvenirs, take home Bohemian crystal, porcelain, lacework, wooden toys and puppets, garnets and prints.

- Easter is as important a holiday as Christmas, and is marked by the traditional fertility ritual of boys whipping girls' legs with birch twigs.

- On St. Nicholas' Eve (December 5), trios in costume can be seen – St. Nicholas, an angel and a devil – walking the streets giving candy to good children and lumps of coal to "bad" ones. Christmas dinner is traditionally carp – sold live at street stalls to be eaten on Christmas Eve, fried, baked or cooked in a soup.

- Prague is even busier than usual from mid-May to early June, when it hosts the Prague Spring International Music Festival (☎ 257 314 040; www.festival.cz): Reserve accommodations several weeks in advance for this period.

- Public transportation (both buses and trains) is a good way of seeing the republic. Almost every town has a railroad station (*nádraží*), and side trips are cheap. The fast trains (*rychlík*) stop at major cities; local trains (*osobní vlak*) are slow, stop everywhere and usually have only second-class carriages.

- Outside of Prague, the Czech Republic still suffers from a shortage of quality hotels and hostels, although this is fast changing. Many historic hotels have been overhauled and new accommodations built. A sign saying *Zimmer frei* ("room available" in German) indicates a bed-and-breakfast in a private home.

Prague

Nothing will prepare you for the beauty of Prague. Its title of "Golden Prague" barely conveys the color and elegance of its historic center: painted medieval, baroque and Renaissance facades glinting pink and green and silver in the sun; a jumble of rust-red rooftops; turquoise domes and gray Gothic spires. Prague's buildings and streets span 1,000 years. Wandering the cobbled alleys becomes the highlight of any visit.

Compass Bearings

Central Prague is made up of four towns, joined together in 1784. On the west bank of the Vltava river are Hradčany and the Lesser Quarter (Malá Strana); on the east bank are the Old Town (Staré Město) and New Town (Nové Město). In the 19th century the Jewish ghetto, Josefov, was also incorporated into the Old Town. Beyond this core is a circle of suburbs, but the main historic sights are within the substantially traffic-free center.

Charles Bridge and Prague Castle

The two banks of the Vltava are connected by a series of 15 bridges, the oldest of which, the Charles Bridge (Karlův most, see pages 127 and 129), is a magnet for tourists, performers and

vendors. On the west bank, Hradčany, the area around Prague Castle (Pražský hrad, see pages 129–130) and its hill, is the major attraction. It includes (along with the castle), St. Vitus' Cathedral (Katedrála sv Víta), Golden Lane (Zlatá ulička), with tiny 16th-century houses originally occupied by gatekeepers; the Gothic Mihulka Powder Tower (Prašná

Nerudova

A steep street climbs from Malá Strana Square, in the Lesser Quarter, all the way up to Prague Castle. This street, Nerudova, was named after journalist and writer Jan Neruda. He wrote stories about daily life in 19th-century Prague, and was born at No. 47, near the top. Eighteenth-century houses line the street, identified by intricately crafted signs; numbers weren't introduced until the 1770s. Look for The Three Fiddles (No. 12), The Golden Cup (No. 16), The Green Lobster (No. 43) and Neruda's home, The Two Suns (No. 47).

věž Mihulka), where alchemists tried to create gold; and the palaces surrounding Hradčany Square (Hradčanské náměstí).

Old Town and New Town

Here, across the river, in the Old Town is the Old Town Square (Staroměstské náměstí), with the sprawling Old Town Hall (Staroměstská radnice; see page 130), the Church of St. Nicholas (Kostel svatého Mikuláše, see page 127) and the dark towers of Týn Church (Týnsky chrám). This is a popular place for street artists to perform. The real hub of the New Town (Nové Město) is Wenceslas Square (Václavské náměstí), a thriving boulevard and the focus of many anti-Communist protests during 1989.

PRAGUE

0   100   200 meters
0   100   200 yards

Ⓜ Metro

Letenské sady
Ikova vila
otkovy sady
Kramářova vila
Vltava
NÁBŘEŽÍ EDVARDA BENEŠE
ŠTEFANIKOV MOST
N
DVOŘÁKOVO NÁBŘEŽÍ
Ministerstvo dopravy
Strakova akademie
DVOŘÁKOVO NÁBŘEŽÍ
LANNOVA
NÁBŘEŽÍ EDVARDA BENEŠE
ilostranská
Ⓜ
Právnická fakulta UK
Ministerstvo obchodu a prumyslu
KLIMENTSKÁ
PETRSKÁ
FJFI CVUT
Židovské muzeum
PETRSKÉ NÁMĚSTÍ
ENSKÁ
JOSEFOV
BÍLKOVA
TRUHLÁŘSKÁ
ŽITNÁKSÁ
Ministerstvo financí
Rudolfinum
Umeleckoprumyslové muzeum v Praze
NA PORÍCÍ
janovy sady
ŠIROKÁ
OD Kotva
Náměstí Republiky Ⓜ
Masarykovo nádraží
Franz Kafka Museum
Staroměstská
Exposice Franze Kafky
Týnsky Chrám
Prašná brána
Masarykovo nádraží
HYBERNSKÁ
KARLŮV MOST
PLATNÉRSKÁ
Dum U Cerné Matky Boží
CELETNÁ
HYBERNSKÁ
RANA
Klementinum
Staroměstská radnice
Stavoské divadlo
NA PRÍKOPE
SENOVÁŽNÉ NÁMĚSTÍ
Lichtenštejský palác
KARLOVA
All Colours Theatre
Slovanský dum
Muzeum Bědřicha Smetany
STARÉ MĚSTO
Muzeum komunis
Vrchlického sady
Museum Kampa
Náprstkovo muzeum
Mucha museum
Hlavní Nádraží
Střelecký Ostrov
Můstek Ⓜ
Ⓜ Můstek
Hlavní Nádraží
MOST LEGIÍ
divadlo Bez Zábradli
Františkánská zahrada
divadlo Rokóko
Petschkuv palác
Státní opera Praha
Národní divadlo
divadlo Viola
divadlo Kalich
ABC divadlo
Muzeum Ⓜ
Palác Žofín
Národní Ⓜ třída
divadlo Komedie
Muzeum Ⓜ
Nová budova Národního muzea
Stará budova Národního muzea
Dětský Ostrov
NAVRÁTILOVA
Slovanský Ostrov
Novoměstská radnice
divadlo V Reznické
ŽITNÁ
Malostranská vodárna
Petržilkovská
MáNES
NOVÉ MĚSTO
Tancíčí dum
JIRÁSKŮV MOST
RESSLOVA
České vysoké ucení technické v Praze Fakul
JEČNÁ
Karlovo náměstí park
Muzeum A Dvořáka
I P Pavlova Ⓜ
Všeobecná fakultní nemocnice, areál U nemocn

C   D   E

Locals love their music – as Mozart found out, when he triumphed here after only moderate success in Vienna. Classical music seems to be everywhere in Prague, advertised in listings guides and on posters across the city. Tickets are reasonably priced and the performances can be superb.

Pražský hrad (castle) and the Malá Strana district

Czech Beer and Puppets

Restaurants and cafés fill up quickly in Prague, so it's a good idea to make reservations. You'll find a wide range of options as well as local cuisine, from American and Italian to Lebanese and Japanese. Don't leave the city without tasting at least one Czech beer. Some of Prague's own brews include Staropramen and U Fleků.

The best shopping is along elegant Pařížská Street in the Old Town, along the pedestrian-only street Na Příkopě and also along Celetná. There are some interesting souvenir shops on Karlova, near the Charles Bridge. If you're looking for souvenirs, puppets make ideal gifts – they're works of art, not just playthings. For a huge selection of books, try Palác knih Luxor (Palace of Books) at Václavské náměstí 41.

Essential Information

Tourist Information

Prague City Tourism ☎ 221 714 444; www.prague.eu
Main Office: Staroměstská radnice (Old Town Hall), Staroměstské náměstí 1; daily 9–7
Branches: Staré Město (Old Town), Rytířská 31; Mon.–Fri. 10–6
Malá Strana (Lesser Town), Malostranská mostecká věž (Lesser Town Bridge Tower); daily 10–6, Apr.–Oct.
Prague Airport Terminal 2; daily 8–8

Urban Transportation

Prague has three metro (subway) lines: A (green), B (yellow) and C (red). Stations are indicated by the letter "M" (marked in a red circle on the city map). Trains run frequently every day between 5 a.m. and midnight. Trams and buses are frequent (4:30 a.m. to midnight, with some night services). Buses run outside the city center. One ticket can be used for the metro, buses and trams. For information call ☎ 296 191 817 (daily 7 a.m.–9 p.m.; www.dpp.cz). Make sure a taxi has a meter registering the fare, or agree on a price before you get into the cab. Avoid taxi stands, especially near tourist spots or nightclubs. To hire a taxi call AAA Radio taxi (☎ 140 14).

Airport Information

Prague Airport (Václav Havel Airport Prague) (☎ 220 111 888; www.prg.aero) is 12.5 miles northwest of the city; bus Nos. 100 and 119 operate between the airport and central Prague. The Airport Express (AE) bus provides a direct service to Hlavní nádraží (Prague main train station).

Climate – average highs and lows for the month

	Jan.	Feb.	Mar.	Apr.	May	Jun.	Jul.	Aug.	Sep.	Oct.	Nov.	Dec.
	2°C	2°C	8°C	12°C	18°C	20°C	22°C	23°C	18°C	12°C	5°C	2°C
	36°F	36°F	46°F	54°F	64°F	68°F	72°F	73°F	64°F	54°F	41°F	36°F
	-4°C	-4°C	0°C	2°C	7°C	10°C	13°C	12°C	9°C	4°C	0°C	-2°C
	25°F	25°F	32°F	36°F	45°F	50°F	55°F	54°F	48°F	39°F	32°F	28°F

Prague Sights

Key to symbols

⊞ map coordinates refer to the Prague map on pages 124–125 Ⓤ admission charge: $$$ more than 110Kč, $$ 70Kč–110Kč, $ less than 70Kč

See page 5 for complete key to symbols

Josefov

Walls went up around Prague's Jewish community in 1254, in keeping with a church law dictating that Christians and Jews should live apart. The inhabitants of the ghetto suffered centuries of persecution. In 1389, 3,000 inhabitants were killed in a pogrom, and at regular intervals, kings passed laws forcing Jews to wear particular clothes or colors to identify them.

Even in the face of such vicious discrimination, the ghetto developed as a center of learning. In 1784 Joseph II abolished residence restrictions (the area was later named after him).

The ghetto survived until the end of the 19th century, when the area was cleared for residential housing, though many of the most important buildings were left standing. In the Starý židovský hřbitov (Old Jewish Cemetery), some 12,000 tombstones are crammed into

Sculptures line both sides of Charles Bridge

the small but powerfully moving space, now part of the Jewish Museum. Other museum holdings are scattered throughout the quarter. An exhibition in the Pinkasova synagoga (Pinkas Synagogue) remembers the 80,000 Czech and Moravian Jews who died in concentration camps in World War II.

The oldest building in the ghetto is the 13th-century Staronová synagoga (Old-New Synagogue), where legend has it the clay man, or Golem, created by Rabbi Löw in 1580 to serve and guard the ghetto, is still kept in the attic. The Rabbi had to return his creation to clay after it ran rampant through the streets. This and other synagogues around the cemetery survived World War II because of Hitler's perverse plan to create a museum dedicated to a vanished race. The synagogues (apart from the Old-New Synagogue) collectively form the Židovské muzeum (Jewish Museum) and can all be visited on one ticket.

⊞ C4 ✉ Jewish Museum: Information and Reservation Center, Maiselova 15; Old-New Synagogue: Červená 2 ☎ 222 317 191; www.jewishmuseum.cz Ⓞ Jewish Museum sites: Sun.–Fri. 9–6, Apr.–Oct.; 9–4:30, rest of year. Old-New Synagogue: Sun.–Fri. 9:30–6, Apr.–Oct.; 9–4:30, rest of year. Closed Jewish holidays Ⓜ Staroměstská 🚃 Tram 17, 18 🍴 Restaurant Ⓤ Jewish Museum $$$; Old-New Synagogue $$$

Karlův most

Karlův most (Charles Bridge) is more than just a river crossing. A walk across the 1,700-foot span takes you past 30 sculptures and musicians, and offers breathtaking views of the river and of the city's domes and looming spires. It was the work of Petr Parléř, who also created much of St. Vitus' Cathedral, and was built in 1357 to link the Old Town with the Lesser Quarter. Known until 1870 as the Stone or Prague Bridge, it has 16 sandstone arches but was originally quite plain. The first ornament, a bronze crucifix, was added in 1657. Over the following 60 years more statues were erected, evenly spaced

Kafka

Franz Kafka wrote two of the 20th century's most significant novels – *The Trial* and *The Castle* – but he died practically unknown, having made his friend, Max Brod, promise to destroy all his writings. It's only because Brod broke his promise that Kafka is read throughout the world today.

His tales of helpless individuals caught in the workings of massive bureaucracy were inspired by the overgrown Habsburg administration. They came to represent the menace and detachment of authority in general, and the term "Kafkaesque" was coined to describe a seemingly ordinary but surreal and dangerous world of systems with their own life and logic.

Kafka was born in Prague, and moved with his family from house to house around Old Town Square, where his father was a haberdasher. He studied law and worked as an insurance clerk, writing his stories by night. The city appears throughout his writings. *The Castle* was inspired by Prague Castle; his story *The Great Wall of China* was based on the "Hunger Wall" on Petřín Hill, built as part of a 14th-century job-creation scheme and funded by money expropriated from Jews. Kafka rented a house between 1916 and 1917 on Golden Lane (Zlatá ulička) at No. 22, but his health was poor and he died of tuberculosis at the age of 41. His grave can be seen at the New Jewish Cemetery (Židovské hřbitovy) in the Vinohrady district. He left behind a third, unfinished novel, *Amerika,* and many short stories.

The most famous, *Metamorphosis,* related the story of Gregor Samsa, who awakens to find himself transformed into a giant insect and to his family becomes an object first of horror, then of pity and finally of contempt. The theme of a bewildered victim of inexplicable events is characteristic of Kafka's style.

The author also recorded his wanderings around Prague, his relationship with his father and with Felice Bauer (to whom he was twice engaged), and his tortured nights of writing in his diaries, which also were posthumously published.

The Communist regime subsequently suppressed Kafka's work, but he is now acknowledged and honored in the city he once described as "a little old mother with sharp claws: she won't let go."

Cobbled Golden Lane is built into the castle; Franz Kafka stayed here between 1916 and 1917

Visitors in the vaulted Loreto Chapel

➕ B4 ✉ Malostranské náměstí ☏ Church: 257 534 215; www.stnicholas.cz 🕐 Daily 9–5, Mar.–Oct.; 9–4, rest of year. Tower: daily 10–10, Apr.–Sep.
Ⓜ Malostranská 🚋 Tram 12, 20, 22 💶 Church $$; tower $

Loretánská kaple

As part of its campaign to win worshipers back to Catholicism after the Reformation, the Church made much of the cult of the Virgin Mary, and the ornate Loretánská kaple (Loreto Chapel) is one result. It was built in 1626 around a replica of Mary's house, supposedly flown by angels from Nazareth to Loreto in Italy, and it soon became a site of pilgrimage. Don't miss the painting of St. Starosta, who grew a beard to repel a suitor and was crucified by her father.

➕ Off map at A4 ✉ Loretánské náměstí 7 ☏ 220 516 740; www.loreta.cz 🕐 Tue.–Sun. 9–12:15 and 1–4:30 🚋 Tram 22 💶 $$

along the parapets; they include St. John of Nepomuk (with the spangled halo), who was allegedly thrown from the bridge in 1393 after taking the side of the church in a dispute with the king. You can visit the fortified towers at each end of the bridge – the Old Town Bridge Tower and Lesser Town Bridge Tower.

➕ C3 ✉ Staré Město/Malá Strana 🕐 Old Town Bridge Tower: daily 10–10, May–Sep.; 10–7, Apr. and Oct.; 10–6, Mar.; 10–5, rest of year. Lesser Town Bridge Tower: daily 10–6, Apr.–Oct. Ⓜ Staroměstská 🚋 Tram 12, 17, 18, 20, 22

Kostel svatého Mikuláše

Mozart played the 2,500-pipe organ here in 1787; he couldn't have chosen a more grandiose setting than the Kostel svatého Mikuláše (St. Nicholas' Church). It was constructed in the 18th century and is considered the city's best example of baroque style. The church is a frenzy of decoration: pink-and-green mock-marble pillars; a 16,146-square-foot fresco; a formidable copper statue of St. Nicholas; and huge sculptures of the four church fathers, including St. Cyril killing the devil.

Petřín

Woods and orchards cover this hill on the city's western bank, and a funicular railway (*lanová dráha na Petřín*) takes passengers up and down. The carriages were installed in 1891, the year that the Petřínská rozhledna (Petřín Lookout Tower) was built at the top. Steps (299 of them) lead to the viewing platform.

➕ A3 ✉ Petřín Lookout Tower: Petřínské sady. Funicular railway: Újezd ☏ 257 320 112; www. muzeumprahy.cz 🕐 Lookout Tower: daily 10–10, May–Aug.; daily 10–8 in Sep.; daily 10–7 in Apr.; daily 10–6 in Oct.; Sat.–Sun. 10–5, rest of year. Funicular: daily 9 a.m.–11:30 p.m., Apr.–Oct. (to 11:20 p.m., rest of year) 🚋 Tram 6, 9, 12, 20, 22 (then take funicular) 💶 Tower $$; funicular $

Pražský hrad

Looming over the city and the river, Pražský hrad (Prague Castle – a UNESCO World Heritage Site) has been a symbol of Czech authority since the first fortress was built on this high, rocky site in the ninth century. The name refers to a complex of palaces, courtyards, churches and streets, all spread across the hill known as

Cafés in the square under the Astronomical Clock

Hradčany. A flight of broad steps climbs to the castle, a mixture of styles spanning 450 years of restoration and guarded by a series of courtyards. At the entrance to the outer courtyard, two soldiers stand at attention under some rather grotesque statues of the Titans. The guard is changed every hour on the hour (🕐 daily 5 a.m.–midnight, Apr.–Oct.; 6 a.m.–11 p.m., rest of year). In the second courtyard are the castle's art gallery and information center.

Finally, you reach the third courtyard and Katedrála sv Víta (St. Vitus' Cathedral), which took 600 years to complete – it was only finished in 1929. Starý královský palác (Old Royal Palace), to the right, is a maze of rooms centered around the 15th-century Vladislav Hall, where mounted knights would trot down the Riders' Staircase to take part in indoor jousting matches.

➕ A4 ✉ Hradčany ☎ 224 372 423; www.hrad.cz 🕐 Castle precincts: daily 5 a.m.–midnight, Apr.–Oct.; 6 a.m.–11 p.m., rest of year. Castle sights: daily 9–6, Apr.–Oct.; 9–4, rest of year. Castle gardens: daily 10–9, Jun.–Jul.; 10–8 in Aug.; 10–7 in May and Sep.; 10–6 in Apr. and Oct. 🚇 Hradčanská or Malostranská 🚊 Tram 12, 18, 20, 22 🍴 Lví dvůr, see page 471 ✋ Admission is by combined-entry ticket only which covers all of the sights $$$; gardens free ℹ Tours in English ($$$)

Staroměstská radnice

Since a merchant's house was earmarked for the city council in 1338, the Staroměstská radnice (Old Town Hall) has gradually expanded and taken over a row of houses.

A tower and chapel were added to the original buildings; features range from the original carved facade to the 19th-century house known as "At the Cock." Its main attraction, and what the crowds gather to see, is the huge, 15th-century Astronomical Clock, which gives the month, season, zodiac signs, course of the sun and Christian holidays. On the hour (9–9) a skeleton appears and chimes the bell, followed by a parade of the Twelve Apostles and, finally, a crowing gilded cock.

➕ D4 ✉ Staroměstské náměstí 1 ☎ 236 002 629; www.staromestskaradnicepraha.cz 🕐 Mon. 11–6, Tue.–Sun. 9–6 🚇 Staroměstská 🚊 Tram 17, 18 ✋ $$

Šternberský palác

In an alley off Hradčany Square is Šternberský palác (Sternberg Palace), a town house built for Count Sternberg in 1698, with a fine collection of Old Masters. Highlights include *The Feast of the Rosary*, by German Renaissance painter and engraver Albrecht Dürer, and *Adam and Eve*, by artist and woodcut-designer Lucas Cranach the Elder, both housed on the first floor.

➕ A4 ✉ Hradčanské náměstí 15 ☎ 224 301 122; www.ngprague.cz 🕐 Tue.–Sun. 10–6 🚇 Hradčanská 🚊 Tram 22 🍴 Café ✋ $$

Strahovský klášter

The baroque spires of Strahovský klášter (Strahov Monastery) dominate the hilltop west of Hradčany: the name means "to watch over" and it has guarded this site since the 12th century. Library halls store more than 130,000 books and manuscripts.

➕ Off map at A4 ✉ Strahovské nádvoří 1 ☎ 233 107 711; www.strahovskyklaster.cz 🕐 Daily 9–noon and 1–5 🚇 Malostranská 🚊 Tram 22 🍴 Peklo ("Hell") restaurant (below ground) ✋ $$

Excursion to Kutná Hora

When silver and copper ore deposits were found on this hill 40 miles southeast of Prague, a town shot up virtually overnight, taking the appropriate name of Kutná Hora, which suggests "miners' mountain." That was in the late 13th century, and soon a royal mint was set up, hammering out the silver coin known as *pražské groše* in its workshops. Also constructed was a royal palace known as the Italian Court, a reference to the Florentine advisers of King Wenceslas II (1283–1305). The town flourished on its mining proceeds and by the 14th century was the country's

The Italian Court was once a royal palace

most important center after Prague. Kutná Hora even managed to recover after being taken over by one force after another during the Hussite Wars. But by the end of the 16th century the mountain was all mined out and the town fell into decay, suffering the final blow with a disastrous fire in 1770.

The handsome Cathedral of St. Barbara was paid for by miners and dedicated to their patron saint. For its design they turned to the prestigious architect of Prague's St. Vitus' Cathedral, Petr Parléř, who rose to the occasion with distinctive tent-like spires and flying buttresses.

Sculptures line Barborská ulice, a street leading to an impressive 15th-century house built for a profiteer who ran an illegal private mining operation. It's now the Mining Museum, and behind it is the medieval mine itself, consisting of 820 feet of tunnels; a horse-drawn winch at the entrance drew out the bags of ore. The royal mint is gone (although it is still possible to make out its outline); parts of the Italian Court – including the chapel, adorned with art nouveau frescoes – can be visited also. Kutná Hora is a UNESCO World Heritage Site. Some 2 miles north of town in Sedlec is the spooky *kostnice,* a chapel decorated with human bones, that was originally owned by Cistercian monks. During the 19th century its 40,000 human bones were put to artistic use by František Rint, who made them into bells and other items.

Contact Prague City Tourism (see page 126).

For an organized tour of Kutná Hora, contact:

Martin Tour ✉ Štěpánská 61, 110 00 Praha 1 ☎ 224 212 473; www.martintour.cz

For more information contact: **Informační centrum Kutná Hora** ✉ Palackého náměstí 377, Kutná Hora ☎ 327 512 378; www.kutnahora.cz

Denmark

Opposite: Designed in 1913, Copenhagen's famous *The Little Mermaid (Den Lille Havfrue)* statue in the harbor area is the most popular expression of Hans Christian Andersen's fairy-tale world

Denmark

Denmark was the cradle of ancient Scandinavia. When you talk of the first Vikings you talk of Danes. It was from this fragmented mosaic of peninsulas and islands between mainland Europe and the Swedish-Norwegian landmass that those consummate seamen first struck out in search of plunder and new territory to conquer. Denmark is the smallest of the four Scandinavian nations, and yet the Danes have succeeded in making their country one of the most advanced and progressive in the world.

Danish Archipelago

The Kingdom of Denmark is just over 200 miles long, and the Jutland (Jylland) peninsula (the primary landmass) is only 75 miles wide. Nowhere in Denmark is much higher than 100 feet above sea level, and the country's highest point, Yding Skovhøj in central Jutland, only rises to 567 feet. Jutland's narrow southern border is with

Germany, Denmark's only land frontier; its west coast adjoins the North Sea.

East of Jutland, and with barely a sliver of water in between, is Denmark's second-largest island, Funen (Fyn). East of Funen is Zealand (Sjælland), the largest island. Its northeastern tip is about 40 miles from the Swedish coast and home to the capital, Copenhagen (København), itself only a short drive or train journey across the Øresund bridge (see page 136) to Sweden. Zealand and Funen lie like natural fortresses across the Kattegat, the sea separating Denmark from Sweden. This position across the entrance to the Baltic Sea, to the south, has always placed the country at the maritime heart of northern Europe.

Houses on Bornholm, an island east of the mainland

The Jutland Peninsula

Copenhagen is the magnet for visitors, but the rest of this disparate and fascinating country has much to offer. Far western Jutland has an invigorating coastal landscape of long, sandy beaches backed by broad dunes and moorland. This landscape is repeated in north Jutland beyond the dividing waters of the Limfjord and all the way to the Skagen peninsula, the birdlike beak of land that thrusts into the sea at Denmark's northern tip. In north Jutland, outside the city of Aalborg, are evocative traces of Scandinavia's Viking culture at the archeological site of Lindholm Høje, a remarkable Viking burial ground of nearly 700 excavated graves, many marked by stones in the shape of long ships.

The heathland of the west coast of central Jutland gives way in the east to a fertile, undulating countryside of small farms and woodland, interspersed with country towns and pretty villages. On the east coast is Århus, a sophisticated and historic university city and Denmark's second largest. Here you will find the mighty Århus Cathedral and the intriguing Den Gamle By, the Old Town and its dozens of restored, timber-framed buildings. South of Århus is a

great stretch of woodland where you can enjoy peace and quiet along walking, bicycling and horseback riding trails. Southwest of Århus is the town of Billund, overshadowed by Denmark's famous Legoland Billund, the country's most visited attraction outside of Copenhagen. Beyond all the plastic bricks is the farming country of south Jutland, which claims to be Denmark's oldest region with such fascinating towns and villages as Ribe, the oldest town in Denmark, established in the eighth century AD, with its handsome cathedral, cobbled streets and gabled houses. The little village of Møgeltønder, in the far southwest of the country, has

More Top Destinations in Denmark (see map page 134)	
■ Århus B2	■ Louisiana C2
■ Bornholm C4	■ Møgeltønder A1
■ Egeskov B1	■ Møn C1
■ Frederiksborg C2	■ Nyborg B2
■ Køge C2	■ Ribe A2
■ Kronborg Slot, Helsingør C2	■ Roskilde C2
	■ Skagen B4
■ Legoland Billund A2	
■ Lindholm Høje B3	

a superb frescoed church and some charming thatched houses.

Country of Islands

More than 400 islands are scattered around Denmark's coasts and out across the Kattegat and the Baltic Sea. About 100 islands are inhabited. Funen (Fyn) is hailed as the "Garden of Denmark," a term probably first used by author Hans Christian Andersen (see page 151) because of its rich alluvial soils, a legacy of the glacial debris left by retreating ice sheets. The capital of Funen is Odense, birthplace of Andersen.

Funen has a gentle rural nature, its lush farmland complemented by a pleasant southern coastline and by good beaches on the peaceful island of Langeland, off the southeast coast. Funen is connected to Denmark's largest island, Zealand, by a typically Danish feat of remarkable civil engineering. The 11-mile-long Storebælt (Great Belt) rail and road fixed-link bridge island hops, via Sprogø island, across the Store Bælt channel. The project took nine years to complete and the first rail passengers crossed the rail bridge in 1997, followed in 1998 by cars on the road link.

The ferry connection, used by visitors prior to 1998, was more romantic, but Scandinavian efficiency triumphed with a tunnel and bridge combination. A similar joint Danish-Swedish project, linking Copenhagen to Malmö across an artificial island built in the middle of the Øresund, was completed in 2000, laying the foundations for a new cultural and economic region.

Historic Zealand

Copenhagen may dominate Zealand, but the whole island is a treasure-house of Danish history. North Zealand has much to offer in terms of historic buildings: the lakeside setting of Frederiksborg Castle (Frederiksborg Slot), Denmark's magnificent Renaissance castle; and Elsinore Castle (Kronborg Slot) at Helsingør, thought to be the setting for Shakespeare's *Hamlet*, overlooking the Øresund and the Swedish coast.

Just west of Copenhagen is Roskilde, Denmark's medieval capital, with a splendid cathedral housing the decorated crypts of 38 Danish kings and queens. In southern Zealand is the city of Køge, whose medieval center survives; at Trelleborg, near Slagelse on the west coast where the new rail bridge slices across the Great Belt, are the remains of the finest Viking ring fort in Denmark. There are six circular forts in

Little villages nestle amid lush greenery on the coastline of Denmark

Traditional painted houses in Odense, birthplace of Hans Christian Andersen, on the island of Funen

Denmark and Sweden called Trelleborgs – all named for this one, which was excavated first, between 1936 and 1941.

Finally, just off the south coast of Zealand are the islands of Møn, Falster and Lolland, Denmark's third-largest island, after Zealand and Funen, all linked to the main islands by bridges. Of these, Møn is the most interesting because of its green hills and chalk cliffs, a landscape in startling contrast to Denmark's almost uniform flatness.

Exploring Denmark

Denmark is one of the most accessible European countries. Its compact size and the smooth transition from island to island that modern engineering has accomplished makes exploring various regions by car an easy option once you are clear of Copenhagen's urban center.

This compactness makes traveling by public transportation almost as convenient. Fast, comfortable trains can whisk you from Zealand to Funen, and then on to Jutland, in a few hours. The efficient and extensive rail network offers stiff competition to long-distance bus services in Denmark, although buses are less expensive than trains.

Denmark's climate is typical of a maritime environment, and the low elevation means there are no great extremes of temperature. Summers are pleasantly mild, but there can be wet spells; in winter snow is likely at times, but much less so than in the other Scandinavian countries.

In matters of food and drink Denmark remains engagingly Scandinavian. Danes relish the same hearty sandwich feast, here called the *smørrebrød*, that you find in Norway and Sweden, complete with its garnished mixes of delicious meat and seafood. Beer is a Danish specialty, and the famous Danish breweries of Carlsberg and Tuborg produce some of the most popular brews in the world.

You will find that Danes are generally helpful, friendly and speak good English. In rural areas and in provincial cities such as Odense, people are unfailingly polite, but in Copenhagen there may be a sharper edge to people's attitudes. At times you may detect an apparent reserve on the part of Danish people. It is not a negative sentiment; the Danes are supremely accomplished, and beneath the reserve is a fierce national pride in their country.

Timeline

4000 BC	Neolithic settlers begin developing a farming economy.
500 BC to AD 500	Iron Age people trade from Jutland and Funen.
AD 793	Danish Vikings raid England's east coast and penetrate deep into mainland Europe along the northern rivers.
circa 925	Gorm the Old becomes first king of a united Denmark.
1167	The founding of Copenhagen by Absalon, Bishop of Roskilde.
1588	Christian IV becomes king of Denmark and promotes the construction of great Renaissance buildings, particularly in the city of Copenhagen.
1611–60	Periodic wars with Sweden.
1814	Union with Norway ends after 278 years.
1849	New constitution abolishes absolute monarchy, establishing a two-chamber parliament.
1914–18	Denmark is neutral during World War I.
1940	Denmark is invaded by the German army in spite of its declared neutrality; the Danish Resistance carries out a vigorous campaign against Germany.
1945	Denmark is liberated. A postwar reconstruction program begins.
1949	Denmark joins NATO.
1973	Denmark joins the European Economic Community.
1998	Opening of the fixed-link rail and road bridge across the Store Bælt (Great Belt) Channel.
2000	Road and rail link opens to Malmö in Sweden.
2004	Prince Frederik marries Australian Mary Donaldson.
2009	Copenhagen hosts the United Nations summit on climate change.
2011	Go-ahead given to build an underwater tunnel between Lolland Island and the German island of Fehmarn.
2012	Queen Margrethe II celebrates 40 years on the Danish throne.
2014	Copenhagen hosts the Eurovision Song Contest.

A Talented Royal Lady

Denmark's current queen, Margrethe II, was born in 1940. She was the eldest daughter of King Frederik IX, who had no sons. After a favorable 1953 referendum, the Danish constitution, which allowed only for a male heir to the throne, was amended to enable female succession. Margrethe became queen at the age of 32, after Frederik's death in 1972. She is Denmark's first female monarch since the 15th century. Queen Margrethe qualified as an archeologist after studying at Copenhagen, Århus, Cambridge and Paris. She is a talented artist, who has illustrated an edition of J. R. R. Tolkien's fantasy *The Lord of the Rings* and designed stamps for the Danish postal service and theatrical costumes and stage settings for the Danish Royal Theatre. An accomplished linguist, Queen Margrethe has translated the work of the French novelist Simone de Beauvoir, a task in which she worked with her husband and consort, French-born Prince Henrik.

Survival Guide

■ If you drive or cycle through Denmark, ask the tourist office for details about the "Marguerite Route," which is a series of linked routes (2,170 miles long) along quieter roads that wind through the most scenic parts of the country. Distinctive signs display a daisy (marguerite) motif on a brown background. A map is available from VisitDenmark.

■ The Copenhagen Card, valid for 24, 48, 72 or 120 hours, costs 359/499/589/779 DKr (half-price for 10–16 year olds, up to two children under 10 years free with a paying adult). It entitles you to travel by train, bus, harbor bus or metro, entry into more than 72 museums and attractions, and car rental, restaurants and shopping discounts in the city. Buy the Copenhagen Card online at www.copenhagencard.com.

■ Danes celebrate Midsummer's Eve (*Sankt Hans*) on June 23. Bonfires are lit throughout the country on the longest day of the year.

■ In Denmark *morgenmad* is the word for breakfast, *frokost* is lunch. *Smørrebrød*, the tasty Scandinavian open-faced sandwich with a choice of toppings, including cheese, salami, smoked salmon and egg, remains a lunchtime favorite; but try *frikadeller*, fried meat or fish patties with salad and potatoes; or dip into a *koldt bord*, a buffet-style selection. For main meals, enjoy *kogt torsk*, poached cod in mustard sauce, or old-fashioned *Skipperlabskovs*, Danish stew.

■ Danish pastries are called *wienerbrød* and come in all shapes and flavors.

■ Amber is a Danish specialty, the "Danish gold." The Amber Specialist (28 Frederiksberggade, Copenhagen, ☎ 33 11 88 03) is the place to look in Copenhagen, but you will find distinctive amber jewelry in stores throughout the country. If you're

A soldier outside Amalienborg Palace, Copenhagen

looking for Danish glass, porcelain and silverware, there are several shops on and leading off Strøget and also the Royal Copenhagen flagship store (Amagertorv 6, Copenhagen, ☎ 33 13 71 81; www.royalcopenhagen.com).

■ Denmark, like Sweden, is noted for its distinctive furnishing designs. The style known as "Danish Modern" is a classic merging of the functional with the aesthetic. Visit Illums Bolighus (Amagertorv 10, Copenhagen, ☎ 33 14 19 41) store for some of the finest examples.

■ Unlike some of the northern Scandinavian countries, Denmark has a relaxed approach to the sale of liquor. You can buy wines, spirits and beers in grocery stores.

■ Traditionally formal, Danes have become more relaxed about what to wear when eating out. Nowadays, stylish, casual clothes, especially during the summer are acceptable for dining at most Danish restaurants.

Denmark

Copenhagen

Copenhagen (København) is where the European experience becomes Scandinavian. This is a magnificent, vibrant city, far more a "Wonderful Wonderful Copenhagen" than even the Danny Kaye song implies. It is a city of towers and steeples that are elegant as well as monumental. It is a city that draws you in along pedestrian-only streets that lead in and out of delightful squares. It is a city with fine museums and attractions, restaurants, cafés and entertainment that place it among the finest of European capitals.

Copenhagen originated, like so many other Scandinavian towns and cities, as a small fishing village, its occupants taking advantage of the sheltered waters around Slotsholmen Island, the island that is now home to the Danish National Parliament (Folketing), and the Christiansborg Palace (Christiansborg Slot, see page 143). By the 12th century Slotsholmen had been fortified in keeping with the settlement's growing commercial status, a status signified by its name, Kømandshavn, "port of the merchants," later amended to København. By the middle of the 15th century, Copenhagen was the recognized capital of Denmark.

The city's status was enhanced by the construction of many fine buildings during the reign of Christian IV of Denmark (1588–1648) in the 16th and 17th centuries, and by the 19th century Copenhagen had emerged as a major European capital. Development continued during the 20th and 21st centuries, and today Copenhagen stands as a mature and hugely successful city.

First Impressions

The initial impression visitors have of Copenhagen is of a city overpowered by traffic. To reach the central City Hall Square (Rådhuspladsen) from Copenhagen's central railroad station (Hovedbanegården), visitors pass Tivoli and then negotiate busy downtown streets. Hans Christian Andersen Boulevard, a broad thoroughfare, is as far removed from Andersen's fairy-tale world as can be imagined. Keep your eyes open for cyclists as well as cars. The broad expanse of City Hall Square, a relaxed, traffic-free environment, leads to a refreshing world of lively streets, colorful squares and hidden corners, where pedestrians are the priority.

There is a lot to see in Copenhagen. Most attractions, including Rosenborg Castle (Rosenborg Slot, see page 145) and the National Museum (Nationalmuseet; see page 144), are based around the Old Town. The furthest sight is *Den Lille Havfrue* (*The Little Mermaid*), on the waterfront.

Getting around is easy, however, if you take advantage of the various guided walking tours that are available, or pick up a map from the tourist office. Other sightseeing tours go by bus and by harbor or canal boats. Copenhagen's bus service is extremely efficient, complemented by a system of electric S-trains and a metro (subway). The electric 11A bus takes in many of the city's main sights. However, exploring the city on foot or by bicycle (free rental in summer), is a pleasure.

Strøget and Beyond
Start at City Hall Square. Look up at the Nordea building, where you will see a bronze weathervane featuring a girl who appears on her bicycle in fine weather and with an umbrella when it rains.

The sequence of streets known collectively as Strøget (the Promenade) begins at Rådhuspladsen (City Hall Square), at narrow Frederiksberggade. Amid the many stores and restaurants, side streets lead to quaint antiques shops and specialty outlets.

City on the Water's Edge
At the far end of Strøget, cross the large, bustling square of Kongens Nytorv (New Royal Market) to reach Nyhavn (New Harbor), the old harbor inlet, now a picturesque area with trendy restaurants. Visit Amalienborg Plads (Amalienborg Square, see page 143), then head east to waterside Larsens Plads; from this square a pleasant walk north takes you to the city's symbol, *Den Lille Havfrue* (*The Little Mermaid*). Opposite the statue is the Operaen (Opera House).

Nearby is the Frihedsmuseet (Museum of Danish Resistance), a celebration of resistance against the Nazis.

Essential Information

Tourist Information
Copenhagen Visitor Center
Vesterbrogade 4A ☎ 70 22 24 42;
www.visitcopenhagen.com

Urban Transportation
Copenhagen's railroad station is København H/ Central Station on Bernstorffsgade. For information call ☎ 70 13 14 15 (free service phones at all stations); www.dsb.dk. The train system consists of S-trains (about 10 lines; trains every four to 20 minutes, depending on line). Copenhagen has good bus routes leaving from Rådhuspladsen. For information call ☎ 36 13 14 15; www.moviatrafik.dk/dinrejse/ tourist. There is a 24-hour driverless metro (light rail) system (M1 and M2). For information call ☎ 70 15 16 15; intl.m.dk.

Taxis have fixed rates. Call Taxa 4X35
☎ 35 35 35 35; www.taxa.dk.

Airport Information
Copenhagen Airport (☎ 32 31 32 31 24 hours; www.cph.dk) is at Kastrup, 6 miles south of the city center. Trains run between København H/Central Station and Terminal 3 daily every 10 minutes during the day (travel time 13 minutes, plus five minutes on the free shuttle bus that runs every 15 minutes to or from other terminals). Metro line M2 trains run every four to six minutes from 5 a.m. to midnight, and every 15 to 20 minutes during the night, (travel time 14 minutes). Buses serve the airport; the 5A can be caught from Copenhagen Central Station, City Hall and Nørreport.

Climate – average highs and lows for the month

Jan.	Feb.	Mar.	Apr.	May	Jun.	Jul.	Aug.	Sep.	Oct.	Nov.	Dec.
3°C	3°C	5°C	10°C	15°C	19°C	20°C	20°C	16°C	11°C	7°C	4°C
37°F	37°F	41°F	50°F	59°F	66°F	68°F	68°F	61°F	52°F	45°F	39°F
-2°C	-2°C	0°C	2°C	7°C	11°C	13°C	12°C	10°C	7°C	3°C	0°C
28°F	28°F	32°F	36°F	45°F	52°F	55°F	54°F	50°F	45°F	37°F	32°F

Copenhagen Sights

Amalienborg Plads

The royal heart of Copenhagen is the octagonal Amalienborg Plads (Amalienborg Square), with a statue of King Frederik V at its center, rococo palaces on four sides, and broad avenues leading off the other four. The Danish royal family spends most of the fall and winter in the palaces. The square has a rather detached atmosphere except during the changing of the guard, daily at noon when the Queen is in residence.

On the northwest corner of the square is Christian VIII's Palace, containing the Amalienborgmuseet (Amalienborg Museum), with royal memorabilia and a sequence of reconstructed private rooms that illustrate what life was like for the royal Glücksburg family between the 1860s and the 1970s.

➕ D3 ✉ Amalienborg Plads ☎ Museum: 33 12 21 86; www.kongernessamling.dk 🕐 Museum: daily 10–4, May–Oct.; Tue.–Sun. 11–4, rest of year. Christian VIII's Palace: tours in English available by advance reservations only 🚇 Kongens Nytorv 🚌 1A, 20E, 26, 350S 💷 Museum $$

Christiansborg Slot

The monumental complex that makes up Christiansborg Slot (Christiansborg Palace) dominates the whole island of Slotsholmen. It presents a rather stern face to the city approaching across the encircling canal from Strøget and Højbro Plads. A visit to this complex may take a whole day. The vast west wing houses the Danish Parliament (Folketinget), the Supreme Court and the Prime Minister's Office, built between 1907 and 1928.

Here too, are the lavishly decorated Kongelige Repræsentationslokaler (Royal Reception Rooms).

Below the palace are the preserved Ruinerne (Ruins) of Bishop Absalon's Castle, dating from 1167, and its successor, Copenhagen Castle. Museums around the royal riding grounds include Museet Kongelige Stalde og Kareter (Royal Stable and Carriages Museum), the Teatermuseet (Theater Museum) and the Tøjhusmuseet (Royal Danish Arsenal Museum). The Kongernes Lapidarium (Lapidarium of Kings), next to the Tøjhusmuseet, displays statues from the gardens and buildings of some royal palaces within its vaulted interior.

The Christiansborg Slotskirke (Palace Chapel), built in 1826, is used on all royal and state occasions.

Christiansborg Slot ➕ C2 ✉ Christiansborg Slotsplads ☎ 33 92 64 92; www.christiansborg.dk 💷 Combined ticket for Royal Reception Rooms, Ruins and Stables $$$ (valid for one month) 🚇 Kongens Nytorv or Nørrebro 🚌 1A, 2A, 26, 40, 66, 350S

Folketinget ➕ C2 ☎ 33 37 32 21; www.thedanish pariament.dk 🚶 Guided tours in English Mon.–Fri. 1 p.m., Jul.–Sep.; Sun. 1 p.m., rest of year 💷 Free

Kongelige Repræsentationslokaler ☎ 33 92 64 92 🕐 Daily 10–5, May–Sep.; Tue.–Sun. 10–5, rest of year 💷 $$$ 🚶 Guided tours in English daily at 3 p.m.

Ruinerne ☎ 33 92 64 92 🕐 Daily 10–5, May–Sep.; Tue.–Sun. 10–5, rest of year 💷 $

Museet Kongelige Stalde og Kareter ☎ 33 40 26 76; www.kongehuset.dk 🕐 Daily 1:30–4, May–Sep.; Tue.–Sun. 1:30–4, rest of year 💷 $

Teatermuseet ☎ 33 11 51 76 🕐 Tue.–Thu. 11–3, Sat.–Sun. 1–4 💷 $

Tøjhusmuseet ✉ Tøjhusgade 3 ☎ 33 11 60 37; www.natmus.dk 🕐 Tue.–Sun. noon–6 💷 Free

Kongernes Lapidarium ✉ Frederiksholms Kanal 29 ☎ 33 92 64 92 🕐 Daily 10–5, May–Sep.; Tue.–Sun. 10–5, rest of year 🍴 Café 💷 $$

Christiansborg Slotskirke 🕐 Tue.–Sun. 10–5, Easter, Jul. and mid-Oct.; Sun. 10–5, rest of year 💷 Free

Dansk Jødisk Museum

Designed by Daniel Libeskind and built within the 17th-century Royal Boathouse on Slotsholmen, the Danish Jewish Museum is both an architectural eye-opener and a fascinating exploration of the Jewish community's experience in Denmark over 400 years.

🕇 C2 ✉ Proviantpassagen 6 ☎ 33 11 22 18; www.jewmus.dk ⏰ Tue.–Sun. 10–5, Jun.–Aug.; Tue.–Fri. 1–4, Sat.–Sun. noon–5, rest of year ⓜ Kongens Nytorv 🚌 1A, 2A, 6A, 11, 12, 15, 26, 29, 33, 40, 66 💶 Free; some exhibitions $$

Den Blå Planet

Northern Europe's latest, and largest, state-of-the-art aquarium, Den Blå Planet (The Blue Planet) opened at Kastrup Havn, near Copenhagen Airport in 2013. The enormous steel-clad building, inspired by a whirlpool, contains 53 aquariums, including five giant tanks that re-create the world's great oceans and rivers. Birds and butterflies add to the experience in the Amazon area, while sharks, sea turtles and rays patrol the wrap-around Great Ocean tank. Be prepared for long lines on weekends and during school vacations.

🕇 Off map at D1 ✉ Jacob Fortlingsvej 1, 2770, Kastrup ☎ 44 22 22 44; www.denblaaplanet.dk ⏰ Daily 10–6 (until 9 p.m. Mon.) ⓜ Kastrup 🚌 5A 🍴 Restaurant 💶 $$$ 🛈 Tours

Inside Marmorkirken, or the Marble Church

Marmorkirken

With its great dome, Frederiks Kirke (Frederick's Church), known universally as Marmorkirken (Marble Church), seems out of place in a Copenhagen of slender steeples and towers. The church was begun in 1749 as a final flourish to the nearby Amalienborg Palace, but was not completed until 1894. Modeled on St. Peter's in Rome, its dome measures almost 100 feet in diameter.

The nave is circular and surrounded by a circular walkway, above which is a whispering gallery with superb acoustics. A tour of the tower is available (Saturday and Sunday, $$) subject to services. The paneled frescoes on the inside of the dome are glowingly painted and gilded.

🕇 D4 ✉ Frederiksgade 4 ☎ 33 15 01 44; www.marmorkirken.dk ⏰ Church: Mon.–Thu. and Sat. 10–5 (also Wed. 5–6:30 p.m.), Fri. and Sun. noon–4 ⓜ Kongens Nytorv 🚌 A1, 15 💶 Church free; Dome $ 🛈 Concerts of religious music Wed. 4:30 p.m. Dome tours: daily at 1 and 3 p.m., mid-Jun. to Aug.; Sat.–Sun. at 1 and 3, rest of year

Nationalmuseet

Copenhagen's Nationalmuseet (National Museum) is one of the finest of its kind in Europe. Particular draws are the burial possessions of two Bronze Age bog people and a collection of *lur* (horn instruments used for ceremony and communication). Other major collections cover the Middle Ages and the Renaissance, Egyptian and classical antiquities, and human cultures. There is a children's museum and a theater. You can also visit the Victorian Home at nearby Frederiksholms Kanal.

🕇 B2 ✉ Ny Vestergade 10 ☎ 33 13 44 11; www.natmus.dk ⏰ Museum: Tue.–Sun. 10–5. Victorian Home: Sat. 2 p.m., Jun.–Sep. ⓜ S-train København H 🚌 1A, 2A, 11A 🍴 Restaurant and café 💶 Free; Victorian Home $

Ny Carlsberg Glyptotek

A winter garden with huge palm trees is the unexpected focal point of the Ny (New) Carlsberg Glyptotek, one of the country's finest art museums. Highlights are the Etruscan collection, one of the largest outside Italy, and French sculpture (including a Rodin collection) and paintings by Paul Gauguin.

B1 Dantes Plads 7 33 41 81 41; www.glyptoteket.dk Tue.–Sun. 11–6 (also Thu. 6–10 p.m.) København H 1A, 2A, 9A, 11A, 40, 60 Museum café $$$ (free on Tue.)

Rosenborg Slot

The early 17th-century Rosenborg Slot (Rosenborg Castle) is an outstanding example of Renaissance architecture and style; it stands at the edge of the lovely Kongens Have (King's Gardens).

The lavishly decorated rooms reflect the regal styles of Danish monarchs from Christian IV to Frederick IV. There are superb marbled ceilings, late 17th-century Dutch tapestries, gilded mirrors, silver lions, gold and enamelware, and beautiful ceiling paintings.

The Royal Treasury is in the castle basement; here the Danish Crown Jewels and other royal treasures sparkle.

C4 Øster Voldgade 4A 33 15 32 86; www. rosenborgslot.dk Daily 10–5, Jun.–Aug.; 10–4, May and Sep.–Oct.; Tue.–Sun. 10–2 (Royal Treasury also Tue.–Sun. 11–4), Jan.–Apr. and Nov.–Dec. Nørreport 14, 42, 43, 150S, 173E, 184, 185, 350S Restaurant $$$

Rundetårn

The Rundetårn (Round Tower) is a must for anyone fit enough to trek up the covered, cobbled ramp that winds its way for 685 feet and through seven and a half turns to the top of the 114-foot landmark. Peter the Great of Russia is said to have ridden his horse up the ramp while the Czarina followed in a horse-drawn carriage. Today, everybody walks; keep to the outside for the easiest angle. From the top there are marvelous views of Copenhagen's red-tiled roofs and far-flung outskirts. The Round Tower dates from 1642 and was built by Christian IV as an observatory. It still functions as such and the public has access to the astronomical telescope.

B3 Købmagergade 52A 33 73 03 73; www.rundetaarn.dk Tower: daily 10–8, late May–late Sep.; 10–6, rest of year (10–9 Tue. and Wed., mid-Oct to mid-Mar.). Observatory: dependent on astronomical activity Nørreport 5A, 6A, 11A, 14, 42, 150S, 173E, 184, 185, 350S $

Statens Museum for Kunst

A huge number of works are on display at the Statens Museum for Kunst (National Gallery). International and Danish art from the 13th century to 1900 includes superb 17th-century Dutch paintings by Pieter Bruegel, Rembrandt, Jacob Jordaens and Jacob van Ruisdael; 19th-century Danish painting is represented by Golden Age artists such as Christoffer Eckersberg and Christen Købke, and by the Skagen painters, Theodor Philipsen and the Funen Painters.

Twentieth-century art, displayed in the old building, includes works by Henri Matisse (*Odalisque*), Max Ernst, the CoBrA Group (*Springtime* by Asger Jorn), Georges Braque and Pablo Picasso, as well as other modern works.

C4 Sølvgade 48–50 33 74 84 94; www.smk.dk Tue.–Sun. 10–5 (also Wed. 5–8 p.m.) Nørreport, Østerport or Kongens Nytorv 6A, 14, 26, 40, 42, 43, 184, 185, 150S, 173E Café Free; special exhibitions $$$

Tivoli

At the heart of the city, Tivoli is given over to entertainment: flower gardens, lakes, theater, concert hall, carnival rides including a roller coaster, amusements, and, above all, people-watching.

There is an entrance fee, and separate charges for carnival rides and indoor attractions (you can buy a pass). Tivoli is never dull; it is lit brilliantly at night and there are shows and major rock concerts during the summer.

B1 Vesterbrogade 3 33 15 10 01; www.tivoli.dk Mon.–Fri. 11–11, Sat.–Sun. 11 a.m.–midnight, Apr.–Sep., 2 weeks mid-Oct., and mid-Nov. to Dec. (closed Dec. 24 and 25) S-train København H 5A, 10, 11A, 15, 26, 30, 40, 66, 250S 38 food outlets $$$

Odense

Odense radiates a persuasive charm. Even factory chimneys on the outskirts of the city are gaily painted, and the surviving medieval buildings of the Old Town are enchanting. Above all, this city makes a refreshing change from the urban bustle of Copenhagen. Odense's wealth of museums and attractions is worthy of a city several times its size. This important regional capital and university town retains its provincial charm, and is celebrated as the birthplace of Hans Christian Andersen and the great composer Carl Nielsen.

The Modern City

You will relax when you arrive at Odense's railroad station, on Østre Stationsvej. Street life is busy here and the traffic is just as heavy as in any city, but directly across the road is Kongens Have, the old Royal Park. The park provides a peaceful introduction to Odense and takes you along tree-shaded paths past the Odense Theater and Brandts 13 (see page 148) into the heart of the city.

The center of Odense is at Flakhaven, a pedestrian-only area in front of the red-brick Town Hall (Rådhus), in a mixture of architectural styles, the interior of which can be seen on a guided tour. The friendly and helpful VisitOdense (Odense tourist office) is to the left of the Town Hall.

All buses leave from stops near the Town Hall, but you will have little need of public transportation unless you travel outside the city. Most attractions are just a short walk from the center, and it is easy to find your way around. From Flakhaven, turn left along the street Vestergade, which takes you into the pleasant, pedestrian-only heart of modern Odense. Here you will find a variety of stores, including top fashion boutiques. Visit Inspiration Zinck (Vestergade 82–84, ☎ 66 12 96 93) for the best in Danish design and handicrafts. Step down the adjoining street of Jernbanegade to Målet bar and restaurantfor a *smørrebrød*, Denmark's delicious lunchtime snack, the ubiquitous open sandwich consisting of a piece of rye bread with a portion of sliced meat or fish and loaded with different garnishes.

The Old Town

Going east from the Town Hall takes you across the traffic-laden street Thomas B. Thriges Gade and into Odense's Old Town. Here in Hans Jensens Stræde is the Hans Christian Andersen Musem (entrance on Bangs Boder, see page 149), amid a little complex of cobbled streets and doll-like houses that was once the poor quarter of the city. Nearby is the Carl Nielsen Museum (see pages 148–149), which adjoins the Odense Koncerthus (Odense

Concert Hall; Claus Bergs Gade 9, ☎ 66 14 78 00), home of the Odense Symfoniorkester. But the best of Old Odense is a couple of streets away, where the medieval thoroughfares of Overgade and Nedergade retain many of their detailed, interesting old buildings.

Pause at the entrance to Nedergade and look down the side street leading down to the river. This is Paaskestræde, location of the Old Poor House, with its rippled red-tile roof and scalloped cornice above the first floor. Hans Christian Andersen went to school here, and the wording on the wall is his touching comment: "Here I went with my wooden shoes to the poor school."

The combination of old and new is what makes Odense such a delight. The city's human scale, its sense of healthy provincialism and its vigorous regional culture are all enhanced by the international cachet of Hans Christian Andersen and Carl Nielsen. What you will find refreshing is that the locals have retained a friendly, unaffected nature in the face of all this.

Essential Information

Tourist Information
VisitOdense
Rådhuset, Vestergade 2 ☎ 63 75 75 20;
www.visitodense.com

Urban Transportation
Odense's railroad station (Odense Banegård Center) on Østre Stationsvej (☎ 70 13 14 15; for English press 3) is a 10-minute walk from the city center, where most of Odense's main attractions are located. For bus information, call ☎ 63 11 22 00; www.fynbus.dk. The pink

city buses are free. For taxis, call Taxafyn ☎ 66 15 44 15.

Airport Information
Odense Airport operates only domestic flights and charter flights to southern Europe. The nearest airport serving the U.K. and northern Europe is Billund Airport, on Jutland ☎ 76 50 50 50; www.billund-airport.com; Mon.–Fri. 8–5. There are no bus connections between Billund Airport and Odense. Call the airport for information or visit www.rejseplanen.dk.

Climate – average highs and lows for the month

Jan.	Feb.	Mar.	Apr.	May	Jun.	Jul.	Aug.	Sep.	Oct.	Nov.	Dec.
2°C	3°C	9°C	14°C	19°C	22°C	25°C	24°C	20°C	14°C	7°C	4°C
36°F	37°F	48°F	57°F	66°F	72°F	77°F	75°F	68°F	57°F	45°F	39°F
-3°C	-2°C	2°C	5°C	9°C	13°C	15°C	15°C	12°C	6°C	2°C	-1°C
27°F	28°F	36°F	41°F	48°F	55°F	59°F	59°F	54°F	43°F	36°F	30°F

Denmark

Odense Sights

Brandts 13

In 2013, the Fyns Kunstmuseum (Funen Art Museum) merged with Brandts Museum of Photographic Art. As well as acquiring a new name, the collection's elegant Classical building received a new area for changing exhibitions of Danish and international art.

Most of the works are by Danish artists from the 17th century to the present day. Highlights include Jens Juel's vivid self-portrait and P. S. Krøyer's *Italian Field Workers*, with its interesting preponderance of left-handed men – a little art puzzle. H. A. Brendekild's big painting *Outworn*, with its prostrate worker in a vast, flat field, portrays the hard life of peasant workers in old Funen. By contrast, a real charmer is Gustava Emilie Grüner's *Group Portrait of the Family Leunbach*, with its cheerful, inviting faces. The museum also has some fine sculptures and a permanent collection of contemporary abstract art, including examples from the Danish CoBrA movement (1935–60).

➕ B2 ✉ Jernbanegade 13 ☎ 65 51 46 01; www.brandts.dk ⊙ Wed. and Fri.–Sun. 10–5, Thu. 12–9 🅿 $$

Carl Nielsen Museet

Already blessed with Hans Christian Andersen, Odense also has Denmark's most famous composer, Carl August Nielsen, as another native son. Nielsen was born in 1865 at nearby Nørre Lyndelse and began his musical career as a trumpeter in a local band. His most famous works are his six symphonies, his opera *Saul and David* and choral works such as *Springtime on Funen*.

The Carl Nielsen Museum is a restful place housed in an extension of the Odense Koncerthus (Concert Hall).

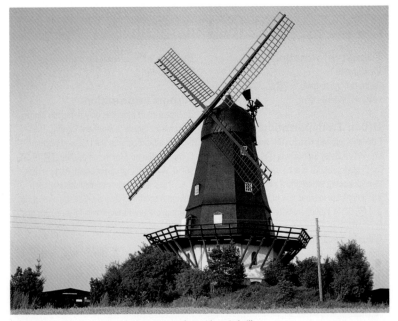

Den Fynske Landsby is an open-air museum, complete with a windmill

It tells the story of his life through displays of artifacts. Stop at key points, don earphones and drift away, listening to Nielsen's music. His wife, Anne Marie Broderson, was a sculptor, and there are displays of her work here to admire.

➕ B3 ✉ Claus Bergs Gade 11 ☎ 65 51 46 01; www.museum.odense.dk 🕐 Thu.–Fri. 3–7, Sat.–Sun. 11–3, Jan.–Apr.; Wed.–Sun. 11–3, May–Aug.; Thu.–Fri. 3–7, Sat.–Sun. 11–3, Sep.–Dec. Also 4–9 p.m. during performances by Odense Symphony Orchestra 🎫 Free

Danmarks Jernbanemuseum

Denmark's Railway Museum is ideally located next to Odense railroad station and is the biggest museum of its kind in Scandinavia. Small boys will be in heaven here. The museum features a reconstructed early 19th-century station and locomotives, including luxurious royal carriages. Add to this a model train collection, trips on a mini train and a section dedicated to ferries and you might not even get out of the station.

➕ B3 ✉ Dannebrogsgade 24 ☎ 66 13 66 30; www.jernbanemuseum.dk 🕐 Daily 10–4 🍴 Café 🍽 $$–$$$ 🚂 Steam-train trips during school vacations

Den Fynske Landsby

The open-air museum of Den Fynske Landsby (The Funen Village) gives an insight into rural life on the island of Funen during the 18th and 19th centuries. Around 30 thatched, timber-framed buildings are arranged like a farming village, with duck pond, smithy, water mill and windmill.

Imaginative tableaux detail the contrasting lives of a poor and a well-off 19th-century villager. In summer, visitors can watch harvesting, beer brewing and craftwork conducted as part of daily life by actors dressed as villagers, and from mid-July to mid-August the Hans Christian Andersen Players enact one of the famous fairy tales on the open-air stage.

➕ Off map at B1 ✉ Sejerskovvej 20 ☎ 65 51 46 01;

www.museum.odense.dk 🕐 Daily 10–6, Jul. to mid-Aug.; Tue.–Sun. 10–5, Apr.–Jun. and mid-Aug. to mid-Oct. 🍴 Restaurant 🍽 $$$ 🚩 Living history events in summer

H.C. Andersens Hus

Worth a visit, the H.C. Andersens Hus (Hans Christian Andersen Museum) brings to life the story and works of Odense's most famous son. The museum describes Andersen's extraordinary life and the intensity of character that shaped his work, tracing his development from humble beginnings to worldwide fame as a best-selling author. Particularly atmospheric is a reconstruction of the study at his last apartment using only artifacts that belonged to the author.

Exhibitions throughout the museum show other aspects of the man, such as his artistic talent. The writer's childhood home is at Munkemøllstræde 3–5 in the center of a charming complex of old single-story houses, once considered the "poor quarter" of Odense.

➕ B2 ✉ Bangs Boder 29 ☎ 65 51 46 01; www.museum.odense.dk 🕐 Daily 10–5, Jul.–Aug.; Tue.–Sun. 10–4, rest of year 🍽 $$$ (includes entry to Hans Christian Andersen's childhood home)

Møntergården

Housed in a marvelous old building, with red-brick, red-timber framing and a red-tiled roof, Møntergården tells the story of Odense's past with special emphasis on the Stone Age and the Viking era. Behind the main building is a lovely yard and on one side of the yard is a series of preserved domestic interiors from the 17th and 18th centuries right up to the 1950s.

➕ C2 ✉ Overgade 48 ☎ 65 51 46 01; www.museum.odense.dk 🕐 Tue.–Sun. 10–4, Sep.–early Feb.; Tue.–Sun. 10–4 (also Wed. 7–9 p.m.) mid-Feb. to Aug. 🍽 $$

Sankt Knuds Kirke

The elegant Gothic style of Sankt Knuds Kirke (St. Canute's Cathedral), Funen's cathedral, reflects the importance of early medieval Odense and the homage paid to King Knud (Canute). Knud, with his brother Benedikt (Benedict) and 17 retainers, was slaughtered here on July 10, 1086 – having taken refuge in the church – by Jutland farmers in a rather drastic protest against royal taxes (see below). The church has some impressive artifacts, not the least of which are its splendid rococo pulpit and altarpiece, a dazzling wood triptych with exquisite carvings and gold leaf that is one of the finest pieces of religious art in northern Europe. In the atmospheric crypt are two reliquaries containing the alleged skeletons of Knud and Benedikt, endearing somehow in their gaunt way.

➕ B2 ✉ Klosterbakken 2 ☎ 66 12 03 92; www. odense-domkirke.dk 🕐 Mon.–Sat. 10–5, Sun. 10–4, Apr.–Oct.; Mon.–Sat. 10–4, Sun. 12–4, rest of year 💰 Free

Tidens Samling

For a museum with a difference, Tidens Samling (Time Collection) is hard to beat. It displays a series of eight set-piece interiors from various periods from 1900 to the 1980s, each one crammed full of authentic artifacts and stylish furnishings. The result is delightful – a unique look at changing domestic style and fashions in dress. One of the many charming aspects of the Time Collection is that you are able to step into the displays, relax in the chairs, have a good poke through the drawers or, if it takes your fancy, do a bit of sock-mending. There is even a period-style coffee bar. Period fashion shows and temporary exhibitions with a cultural theme are sometimes staged. The museum is on the third floor (there is an elevator).

➕ A2 ✉ Farvegården 7, 3 sal ☎ 65 91 19 42; www.tidenssamling.dk 🕐 Mon.–Sat. 10–4, first Sun. of month 11–3 🍴 Café 💰 $$

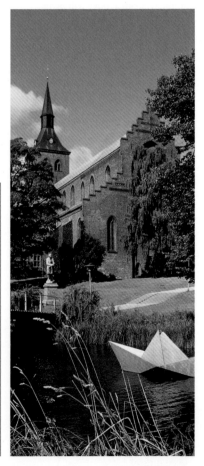

The Gothic cathedral of Sankt Knuds Kirke

The Martyred King

The violent death of the 11th-century Danish King Knud (Canute), a descendant of Canute, one-time king of England, did Odense a favor. The king and his brother, Benedikt, were slaughtered in Odense's old Church of St. Alban's on July 10, 1086, by Jutland peasant farmers angered by excessive taxes levied by the king to finance war with England. Fourteen years later Pope Paschalis II canonized the king as St. Knud the Holy. In an ironic twist, Benedictine monks from England settled in Odense and successfully promoted the town as a place of pilgrimage to the murdered ruler.

The reputed skeletons of Knud and Benedikt can still be seen in Sankt Knuds Kirke (see pages 149–150).

Hans Christian Andersen

Odense's most famous son left his native city at an early age, yet Odense is still associated with Hans Christian Andersen. From quite humble beginnings – his mother was a washerwoman and his father was a shoemaker – Andersen's astonishingly fertile imagination and creativity led him on extensive travels throughout Europe and established him as Denmark's major literary figure. He was born in 1805 in Odense, but it is not certain in which location. By the age of seven Andersen was inspired after visiting the theater in Odense; by 14 he was in Copenhagen, where he tried unsuccessfully to join the Royal Theater Company.

Andersen was a man of complex sensitivities whose relationships were profound and often difficult, although he was never short of friends and benefactors. He was essentially a poet and dramatist, and his early works reflect this. He had the urge to travel, and his first, self-published book was about a journey he made on foot through Denmark. In 1835 he published *Fairy Tales, Told for Children*. Plays, novels and travel accounts followed, along with a continuing output of the fairy tales that were to make his name.

Andersen's fairy tales were far more profound than mere fantasy, however charming. He was a powerful moralist, an intensely humane man who understood the human condition and injected into his stories remarkable life lessons. Famous and popular tales such as *The Emperor's New Clothes, The Little Mermaid, The Ugly Duckling, The Tinder Box* and *The Nightingale* have entered the consciousness of generations of readers worldwide, for their literary elegance as much as their theatricality.

Andersen remained an intense and sometimes troubled man throughout his life. He was a friend and associate of kings and of the famous. He never married, though he was deeply in love at times, not least with the Swedish opera soprano Jenny Lind. He died at 70 in 1875, in a friend's house near Copenhagen. In the Denmark of his day Andersen was criticized and diminished for what was seen as his absorption with the wider European world. As always with genius, however, his work transcended time. In Odense the spirit of this remarkable man is vividly present, at the Hans Christian Andersen Museum (see page 149) and also in quieter corners of the Old Town.

Hans Christian Andersen reads his story *The Angel* to a sick child

Finland

Opposite: A sauna house at the edge of a forested lake near Jyväskylä

Finland

Finland, one of the world's great survivors, is a small nation that has had to contend with harsh nature and belligerent neighbors in an often hostile northern European world. For centuries Finland was trapped between the aggressive ambitions of Sweden and Russia, and then in the 20th century between the Eastern and Western protagonists of the Cold War.

The country's emergence as a self-confident, modern nation, with its historic identity intact, is a celebration of steady nerve, political shrewdness and tenacity.

A tall-masted vessel moored in Helsinki harbor

Land of Forests and Lakes

Finland is bordered on the east by Russia, on the northwest by Sweden and on the north by Norway. Most of Finland is less than 600 feet high, and over 70 percent of the country supports coniferous spruce and pine. The northern areas are covered with peat bog, and there are almost 188,000 lakes and nearly 180,000 islands. All of Finland is a seemingly endless blanket of trees, water and wide skies.

The main "lake district" of Saimaa in the east is a paradise of woodland and navigable rivers and lakes, punctuated by rugged cliffs and a glittering mosaic of islands and lakeside towns and villages. Apart from the special nature of the Finnish landscape, the main cities and towns – Helsinki, Turku (Åbo), Tampere, Porvoo, Savonlinna, Oulu and Rovaniemi – have much to offer the visitor. They are as modern as any other European urban center, yet retain a deep-seated Finnish identity.

The Islands and Lapland

The mirror image of the inland water world is Finland's coastal region. Off Finland's southwestern coast is the Saaristomeri archipelago, with its thousands of islands and little rock islets known as "skerries." Farther out lie the Åland Islands (Åland Avenanmaa), stepping stones to Sweden. You can explore the archipelago by ferry or steamship, or on land, visit the beaches of Yyteri, to the north.

In northern Finland, in the great wilderness of Lapland, you can learn about the life and culture of the Sami (Lapp) people in Rovaniemi's Arctic Center (Arktikum). The adventurous can go white-water rafting on the Tornionjoki river, follow one of the numerous hiking routes or head into the mountains of the northwest, where Finland's highest peak, Haltitunturi, reaches 4,300 feet. Up here in this wilderness, the Sami tend their reindeer herds and pursue the ever-hopeful prospect for gold.

Traveling in Finland

Traveling around the country by car is a good way to see rural Finland. There are excellent road systems around Helsinki and between the main towns, but in rural areas some roads may be poor or even just dirt tracks.

Finland's state railroad, Valtion Rautatiet, serves all but the extreme north of the country, with the most frequent service in the south. There is an excellent bus service that runs

The view from the summit of Koli hill toward scattered small islands on Lake Pielinen

throughout the country, and the east–west network in central and southern Finland is especially efficient.

The Finnish climate is far more amiable than you might expect. In spite of being in the same latitude as Alaska and Siberia, Finland and the whole Scandinavian peninsula enjoy a much milder climate owing to the influence of the Gulf Stream. There can be warm dry spells in summer; the southeast area of Finland has the highest summer temperatures throughout the Scandinavian region.

The Finnish people have a well-developed sense of irony, which may emerge in the form of jovial self-disparagement, especially among the young. The Finns know when to keep quiet and may appear to be unwilling to talk very much. But throughout the country you will be welcomed, and helped, with courtesy and kindness.

More Top Destinations in Finland

- Åland Ahvenanmaa A1
- Helvetinjärven Kansallispuisto A1
- Lapland A2
- Loviisa B1
- Porvoo B1
- Rauma A1
- Rovaniemi B2
- Saimaa B1
- Savonlinna B1
- Tampere A1
- Turku A1
- Vaasa A2

Timeline

4000 BC	Sami peoples move into northern Finland from the east.
1600 BC	Development of Iron Age culture and emergence of the Finno-Ugric language.
1100	Finland is occupied by four tribal elements: the Sami in the north, Karelians in the east, Tavastians in the central lakes and Finns in the southwest.
1249	Swedish regent Birger Jarl establishes colonies in the southwest of Finland.
1290s	Invasions by Russia lead to Swedish–Russian conflicts.
1555	Finland is made a Swedish duchy.
1807	Czar Alexander I of Russia occupies Finland.
1906	Finland (although still part of the Russian Empire) is the first European nation to achieve universal suffrage.
1917	Finland declares its independence.
1919	Finland becomes a republic. Kaarlo Stahlberg is its first president.
1939–44	Finland declares neutrality but Russia invades; Finland declares itself a "co-belligerent" with Germany in resisting Russian attacks.
1992	The 1948 Treaty of Friendship, Cooperation and Mutual Assistance between Finland and Russia is dissolved.
1995	Finland becomes a member of the European Union.
2000	Tarja Halonen becomes the first female president of Finland.
2002	Finland adopts the euro as its national currency.
2010	Finland becomes the first country in the world to give its residents a legal right to broadband internet access.
2012	Sauli Niinisto of the National Coalition party becomes the first Conservative president since 1956.
2014	UNESCO awards Helsinki "City of Design" status.

A Bridge between East and West

Finland's 20th-century relationship with Russia has very often been misunderstood. The term "Finlandization" was used disparagingly by some to describe the country's carefully orchestrated policy toward its giant neighbor, but Finland's sensitive geographic position dictated this policy. For centuries, Russia competed with Sweden for domination over Finland. After 1807, Russian influence prevailed. Finland's declaration of independence in 1917 led to an uneasy relationship between the two countries, and resulted in bitter conflict during World War II. After the war, Finland was forced to tread a careful path between the Cold War policies of East and West. The Finnish politician who did the most to maintain national identity under these circumstances was Urho K. Kekkonen (president 1956–1981). Kekkonen's pragmatism and his careful balancing act between East and West earned him much criticism from Western politicians. But Finland remained essentially a Scandinavian country while maintaining "friendly coexistence" with Russia. Finland's rapid emergence, post-Cold War, as a democratic, pluralist and modern society is a testament to Kekkonen's strategy. It is said that he frequently conducted discussions with visiting Russian politicians in the relaxation of a traditional sauna.

Finland

Survival Guide

- Driving with dimmed headlights in the daytime is compulsory in Finland. When driving in rural Finland you will need to watch out for elk and reindeer on the roads.

- For Finnish and international fashion in Helsinki try Marimekko (www. marimekko.com), which has locations at Pohjoisesplanadi 33, the Itis shopping mall and the Kamppi mall complex. For exclusive silkwear look for Marja Kurki's scarfs in Stockmann department store, Aleksanterinkatu 52. For traditional jewelry and Finnish national clothing, you cannot beat Kalevala Koru, Pohjoisesplanadi 25–27 (www.kalevalajewelry.com).

- You will find that consumer goods are generally more expensive in Finland than in the rest of Europe, although prices are gradually starting to come down. Accommodations and restaurants also are more expensive.

- Many hotels have saunas, but most are electrically heated. The traditional Finnish "smoke" sauna is heated by a wood-burning stove and is said to be the real experience, an important cultural institution. For information on traditional saunas, contact the Finnish Sauna Society (Suomen Saunaseura), Vaskiniementie 10, FIN-00200 Helsinki ☎ 50 371 8178; www.sauna.fi.

- In Helsinki you will find numerous "grill kiosks," little huts selling fast food such as hamburgers, french fries, meat-filled pies and grilled sausages (*grillimakkara*). The kiosks are good for daytime snacks, but late at night they often attract rowdy revelers.

- On the weekend that falls between June 20 and 26 there are midsummer celebrations throughout the country. After the long nights of winter, Finns celebrate Midsummer's Day with gusto.

- The useful Helsinki Card (www. helsinkiexpert.com/helsinki_card) entitles you to entry to museums and

Elk can be a hazard for motorists in rural Finland

major sights, unlimited travel on local public transportation, a city sightseeing tour and a range of discounts. The cards are available for periods of 24 hours (€41), 48 hours (€51) and 72 hours (€61).

- There is a state monopoly on the sale of alcohol, apart from medium-strength beers, which can be bought in some grocery stores. Wine and spirits can be bought only in state-controlled outlets known as *Alko* (stores not open on Sunday). Restaurants usually serve alcohol.

- All public restrooms in Finland are generally clean and modern. Signs are *Naiset* for ladies and *Michet* for men.

Helsinki

Helsinki (sometimes referred to in Swedish as Helsingfors) will take your breath away. It does so quite literally in the frozen winter, but even then it can have days of glorious weather. In summer, the city will delight you even more with its stunning architecture and its blue Baltic waters.

City of the Sea

The best way to approach Helsinki is by sea. The Lutheran Cathedral (Tuomiokirkko) and the Uspenski Cathedral (Uspenskin katedraali) stand out against the skyline behind the handsome waterfront buildings that include the 19th-century City Hall (Kaupunki aula) and Presidential Palace (Presidentin linna). In front of them is Market Square (Kauppatori), with vendors selling items from fish to crafts.

You miss this introduction to the city if you arrive by plane, bus or train, but the early 20th-century railroad station is a striking example of Helsinki's architecture. Bus and railroad stations are close to the heart of things and only a few streets from Senate Square (Senaatintori, see page 162) and the bustle of Mannerheimintie, the city's main street.

Helsinki is easy to explore independently. Trams and buses serve all parts of the city, but the subway system is of little help to visitors.

The heart of summertime Helsinki is the tree-lined Esplanade (Eteläesplanadi)

that runs west from Market Square and South Harbor (Eteläsatama) to Mannerheimintie. There is a bandstand next to the Kappeli restaurant (see page 473), where you can sample Finnish specialties such as salmon soup (*lohikeitto*).

The streets bordering the Esplanade have many stylish boutiques, as well as colorful cafés and restaurants. Stop for

Uspenski Cathedral in Northern Harbor, Helsinki

Finlandssvenska

The form of Swedish spoken in Finland is *Finlandssvenska*, "Finland's Swedish." Today about six percent of Finnish residents speak Swedish exclusively, and everybody else has some knowledge. Swedish is a mandatory subject in schools. Most of Finland's signs and street names appear in Finnish and Swedish.

coffee and pastries in the Swedish Theater (Svenska Teatern) at the west end of the Esplanade.

Quiet Corners

For green spaces and seashore walks go south from the Esplanade, past the University Observatory and the Russian Embassy, to reach Kaivopuisto Park, at the far end encircled by the seashore road, Ehrenströmintie, where moored yachts enhance the views of numerous islands. Alternatively, go north from the square in front of the railroad station to Kaisaniemi Park and the University Botanical Gardens (Kasvitieteellinen Puutarha), and on to the tree-fringed sea inlets beyond. Wander along and up Mannerheimintie to see the monumental Parliament House (Eduskuntatalo) and

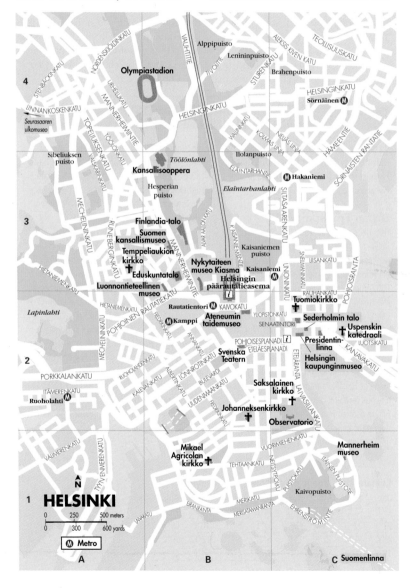

Finlandia Hall (Finlandiatalo), then go west to Temppeliaukio Church (Temppeliaukion Kirkko), a copper-domed church carved out of rock.

Despite Helsinki's reputation for long, dark winters, there is much to reward the visitor all year. Enjoy restaurants, listen to the music of Jean Sibelius in Finlandia Hall (☎ 09 402 41; www.finlandiatalo.fi) or attend a performance at the Finnish National Opera (☎ 09 4030 2211; www.opera.fi).

You will find fewer English speakers here than in other Scandinavian countries, but Helsinkians are eager to help visitors enjoy this cultured city.

"Smoke" Sauna

Sauna is a way of life for Finns. Apart from being healthy and relaxing, it's a social, cultural and, some say, almost religious practice.

A sauna is an insulated room that is traditionally heated by a wood-burning stove. In a "smoke" sauna, steam is generated by throwing water on the hot stones of the stove, and the correct mix of steam and heat, known as *löyly*, fills the room in which you sit naked. Sometimes pine needles are added to the water. Plunging into icy lakes or rolling in the snow between bouts of *löyly* are other options.

Essential Information

Tourist Information
Helsinki City Tourist & Convention Bureau
Pohjoisesplanadi 19 ☎ 09 3101 3300; www.visithelsinki.fi

Urban Transportation
Helsinki's railroad station is located on Kaivokatu. It is the terminus for main train services throughout the country and to Russia. For information ☎ 0600 41 902 (358 9 2319 2902 from outside Finland; www.vr.fi/en). Helsinki's bus, tram and subway network is operated by Helsingforsregionens trafik or HSL (Helsinki Region Transport; ☎ 09 4766 4000, Mon.–Fri. 7–7, Sat.–Sun. 9–5; www.hsl.fi). Tram 2 is a useful route for visitors to take as it passes the main sights, while Tram 4 passes many of Helsinki's most striking buildings. The city bus terminal is in the Kampii Mall, from where connections to the rest of Finland also depart. Main tram stops are on Kaivokatu. For information call Matkahuolto ☎ 0200 4000.

Helsinki has a small metro (subway) system serving mainly suburban areas. Stations have a sign marked "M." Taxis have a yellow dome light and are available when it is lit. There is a taxi stand at the railroad station. Call the Helsinki Taxi Center at ☎ 0100 0600.

Airport Information
Helsinki-Vantaa Airport is 12 miles north of the city. Finnair buses run to and from the airport to Helsinki railroad station (www.finnair.com/INT/GB/information-services/at-the-airport/transportation). The service is every 20 minutes, daily 5 a.m.–1:10 a.m., and the trip takes about 35 minutes. Slower, but less expensive, regular bus service No. 615 also runs between the airport and the city center (Rautatientori). At night, use bus No. 620 from downtown Helsinki. For 24-hour flight information call the service center ☎ 0200 14636; www.helsinki-vantaa.fi.

Climate – average highs and lows for the month

Jan.	Feb.	Mar.	Apr.	May	Jun.	Jul.	Aug.	Sep.	Oct.	Nov.	Dec.
-3°C	-3°C	1°C	7°C	14°C	18°C	21°C	19°C	13°C	7°C	2°C	-1°C
27°F	27°F	34°F	45°F	57°F	64°F	70°F	66°F	55°F	45°F	36°F	30°F
-9°C	-9°C	-5°C	0°C	5°C	9°C	12°C	10°C	6°C	2°C	-2°C	-7°C
16°F	16°F	23°F	32°F	41°F	48°F	54°F	50°F	43°F	36°F	28°F	19°F

Helsinki Sights

Ateneumin taidemuseo

The Ateneumin taidemuseo (Ateneum Art Museum) is housed in a handsome 19th-century building. Vincent van Gogh, Amedeo Modigliani and Paul Cézanne are represented, among many other international figures from the 19th century to the 1960s. In addition, a significant collection of Finnish art, from the 18th century to the mid-1960s, includes powerful works by realist painters Fanny Churberg and Albert Edelfelt, such as Edelfelt's gossiping group, *Women of Ruokalahti on the Church Hill*. Finland's master Akseli Gallen-Kallela dominates with works such as the seductive *Aino-taru*, the *Aino Myth* and the earthy *A New House*. Gallen-Kallela pupil Hugo Simberg's mildly disturbing and surrealistic *The Wounded Angel* is another highlight.

✚ B2 ✉ Kaivokatu 2 ☎ 02 9450 0401; www.ateneum.fi ◉ Tue. and Fri. 10–6, Wed.–Thu. 10–8, Sat.–Sun. 10–5 🚇 Kaisaniemi 🚌 All buses to Rautatientori Square bus terminus; tram 2, 3, 6, 9 🍴 Café 💷 $$$ (free 5–8 p.m. first Wed. of the month) 🅸 Guided tours in English. Reserve in advance

Helsingin kaupunginmuseo

The Helsingin kaupunginmuseo (Helsinki City Museum) is located in the Sofiankatu, one of the oldest streets in Helsinki. It has branches throughout the city, including the nearby Sederholmin talo (Sederholm House, see right). The main museum has an exhibition on Helsinki's history.

Within the museum, you can see historic films about Helsinki in the Kino Engel (movie theater). These are mostly in Finnish or Swedish, but on Saturday afternoons, from June to August, short films in English also are shown.

✚ C2 ✉ Sofiankatu 4 ☎ 09 3103 6630; www.helsinkicitymuseum.fi ◉ Mon.–Wed. and Fri. 9–5, Thu. 9–7, Sat.–Sun. 11–5 🚊 Tram 1, 2, 4/4T, 7A/B 💷 Free

Luonnontieteellinen museo

The venerable Luonnontieteellinen museo (Natural History Museum) is guarded by a very handsome bronze elk, just one of the animals in the museum's vast collection of mammals, birds, insects and minerals. The mammal collection is one of the best of its kind in Europe, showing exotic beasts and Finnish wildlife in their native habitats.

✚ B3 ✉ Pohjoinen Rautatiekatu 13 ☎ 09 1911; www.luomus.fi ◉ Tue.–Wed. and Fri. 9–4, Thu. 9–7, Sat.–Sun. 10–4, Sep.–May; Tue.–Sun. 10–5 (also Thu. 5–7 p.m.), rest of year 🚇 Kampi 🚌 24; tram 4, 7A, 10 🍴 Museum café 💷 $$ (free first Thu. of the month 4–6 p.m., Sep.–May; first Thu. of the month 3–5 p.m. rest of year)

Nykytaiteen museo Kiasma

The Nykytaiteen museo Kiasma (Museum of Contemporary Art Kiasma) is housed in a custom-designed building. Its bold postmodern style, by American architect Steven Holl, aroused some controversy when it opened in 1998. The changing exhibitions of conceptual art and often radical installations are at the forefront of European contemporary art and also are indicative of the sophistication of Finnish culture.

✚ B3 ✉ Mannerheiminaukio 2 ☎ 02 9450 0501; www.kiasma.fi ◉ Tue. 10–5, Wed.–Fri. 10–8:30, Sat. 10–6, Sun. 10–5 🚌 All buses to Rautatientori Square bus terminus; tram 4, 7A, 10 🍴 Museum café 💷 $$ (free first Fri. of the month 4–8:30 p.m.)

Sederholmin talo

The Sederholmin talo (Sederholm House) is said to be the city's oldest stone house (built in 1757) and is now home to the Children's Town in Sederholm House museum.The hands-on exhibits here encourage visitors of all ages to experience the social history of Helsinki through play

Finland

and first-hand experience of conditions in the past. Visit 18th-century shops and workshops, sit in a 1930s' classroom or a 1970s' home, unload cargo from a ship or help out at the cobbler's.

🞡 C2 ✉ Aleksanterinkatu 16–18 ☎ 09 3103 6529; www.hel.fi 🕓 Due to reopen during 2016 following renovation works 🚃 Tram 1, 3, 2, 4 🎫 Free

Senaatintori

Senaatintori (Senate Square) is the focus of Russian Imperial-style buildings. This form of architecture was encouraged by Tsar Alexander I in his bid to make Helsinki a stylistically eastern capital after it was annexed by Russia in 1809.

The square and its major buildings were designed by C. L. Engel. Helsinki's Lutheran Cathedral (Tuomiokirkko) dominates Senate Square and the city skyline. The cathedral, also by Engel and completed in 1852, is essentially Classical but has Byzantine elements. Its domes are copper-sheathed and gilded, the only accents in an otherwise blinding whiteness. The buildings that flank the square and cathedral include the Senate House, University Building and University Library. A new branch of the city museum is due to open on the square in 2016.

🞡 C2 ✉ Unioninkatu 29 ☎ Lutheran Cathedral: 09 2340 6120 🕓 Lutheran Cathedral: daily 9–6 (also 6 p.m.–midnight, Jun.–Aug.) 🚃 Tram 1, 2, 7A, 7B 🍴 Cafe Krypta, daily 11–5, Jun.–Aug. 🛈 Summer events; organ recitals Wed. at noon

Seurasaaren ulkomuseo

The Seurasaaren ulkomuseo (Seurasaari Open-Air Museum) is a collection of Finnish regional buildings from the 17th to the 20th century. On Seurasaari Island, it is easily reached from central Helsinki. Most of the 87 buildings on the site date from the 18th and 19th centuries and include a manor house, traditional farmhouses and a church.

🞡 Off map at A4 ✉ Seurasaari ☎ 09 4050 9660; www.nba.fi/en/museums 🕓 Buildings: daily 11–5, Jun.–Aug.; Mon.–Fri. 9–3, Sat.– Sun. 11–5, mid-May to May 31 and in early Sep. Park: daily, all year

🚌 24, then a 10-minute walk 🍴 Café 🎫 $$ (park free) 🛈 Guided tours in English daily at 3 p.m., Jun. to mid-Aug.

Suomen kansallismuseo

The Suomen kansallismuseo (National Museum of Finland), designed by architects Herman Gesellius, Armas Lindgren and Eliel Saarinen, dates from the early 20th century and is an excellent example of the art nouveau, or Jugend, style of architecture. The building is easily recognized by its tower and the entrance is "guarded" by a statue of a bear by artist Emil Wilkström.

Spread over four floors, there are exhibits on Finnish history and many artifacts, including a Stone Age sculpture of an elk's head from around 3000 BC. The throne of Alexander I is on display, from which he proclaimed Finnish "incorporation" with Russia in 1809.

🞡 B3 ✉ Mannerheimintie 34 ☎ 0 40 128 6469; www.nba.fi/en/nmf 🕓 Tue.–Sun. 11–6 🚃 Tram 4, 4T, 7A, 7B, 10 🍴 Museum restaurant 🎫 $$ (free Fri. 4–6 p.m.)

Suomenlinna

The historic sea fortress of Suomenlinna, a UNESCO World Heritage Site, is built on six interconnecting islands and was once dubbed the "Gibraltar of the North." First used by Sweden in 1748 under the name Sveaborg ("Sweden's Fortress"), the island was surrendered to Russia in 1808. It remained in Russian control until 1918, when newly independent Finland named it Suomenlinna ("Finland's Fortress").

The museums here include the Suomenlinna Museum, the Military Museum and the Customs Museum, as well as a Doll and Toy Museum.

🞡 C1 ✉ Suomenlinna ☎ Visitor Center: 02 9533 8410; www.suomenlinna.fi 🕓 Visitor Center: daily 10–6, May–Sep.; 10–4, rest of year ⛴ Ferries leave regularly from the eastern side of Market Square 🍴 Choice of restaurants and cafés 🎫 Site and Visitor Center free; other museums $$ 🛈 Guided tours ($$) in English daily at 11 a.m., 12:30 and 2:30 p.m., Jun.–Aug.; Sat.–Sun. at 1:30 p.m., rest of year

Imperial City: The Buildings of Helsinki

Helsinki has some of the finest buildings in northern Europe, with the architectural heart of the city being Senate Square. Here, in the early 19th century, Berlin-born Carl Ludvig Engel was commissioned to create a new Helsinki in neoclassic Russian Imperial style. On its high podium, the gleaming white Lutheran Cathedral (Tuomiokirkko) is the focus of the square. Leave the square at its northeastern corner and take a stroll up Snellmaninkatu a short distance to where the Bank of Finland (Suomen Pankki) faces the regal-looking House of Estates (Säätytalo), built in the Classical style with beautiful gilded Corinthian capitals.

Another great architectural theme in Helsinki is art nouveau, or Jugend as it is known in Finland. This style drew its motifs from Finnish culture and tradition; its materials are the timber and rough-faced granite of the country used in naturalistic ways. Jugend architecture is best seen in residential areas such as Eira, on the southern peninsula of the city, and on the little island to the east of the harbor, Katajanokka. The island is guarded by the magnificent Uspenski Cathedral (Uspenskin katedraali), the most impressive expression of orthodoxy you are likely to find in northern Europe.

Jugend architecture is characterized by turrets, castellated features and carved motifs. Yet the buildings remain elegant and restrained. Take a walk down Eira's streets of Huvilakatu and Laivurinkatu. On Laivurinkatu, look for No. 25, the Villa Johanna. Walk down Luotsikatu and Kauppiaankatu, a short distance east of the cathedral, where there are numerous examples of Jugend to compare with Senate Square's Classicism and with the city's more modern buildings. Finlandia Hall and the Museum of Contemporary Art Kiasma maintain Helsinki's international reputation for architectural excellence.

Helsinki's dramatic white Lutheran Cathedral (Tuomiokirkko) is the focal point on Senate Square

France

Opposite: The view across the water to Le-Mont St.-Michel

France

France is the largest country in western Europe, geographically one of the most diverse, and among the most beautiful. Its cities contain some of the greatest treasures in Europe; its countryside is prosperous and well tended. The French combine practicality with romance; they lead a stylish life, eat delicious food and bask in a pleasant climate.

Historically, France has developed the notion of equality for all and, while retaining its sense of tradition, remains a forward-looking country. Over the past half-century, for instance, the French have forged ahead in modern technology. France is a country of contrasts, making it a delight to explore.

France Today

France was among the first European countries to dispense with its monarchy. Apart from a couple of brief periods, it has been a republic almost as long as the United States. The French Revolution gave a tremendous sense of patriotism to all French men and women, which continues to the present day.

Despite the apparently never-ending political ups and downs, French people have a strong sense of national pride and

More Top Destinations in France

- Avignon D2
- Beaune D3
- Biarritz B2
- Bordeaux B2
- Carcassonne C1
- Carnac A4
- Château de Versailles C4
- Cirque de Gavarnie B1
- D-Day Beaches B4
- Grasse E2
- Grotte de Lascaux C2
- Honfleur C4
- Le Mont-St.-Michel B4
- Pont du Gard D2
- Rocamadour C2
- Sarlat C2
- Toulouse C2

France

Calais
Dunkerque
Boulogne-sur-Mer
Saint-Omer
A25 **Lille**
BELGIUM
GERMANY
Béthune
Lens Douai Valenciennes
A16 Arras
A2
Cambrai Maubeuge
Abbeville
Dieppe
Fécamp
Amiens A26 Saint-
Quentin
Charleville-
Mézières
LUXEMBOURG
A29
Havre
A29 Rouen
A16 A1 L'Oise
Laon
A34
Honfleur Beauvais Compiègne Soissons
Forbach
Sarreguemines
Caen A13 Pontoise
Chantilly **Reims** Verdun **Metz**
A13
Falaise
A28
Évreux Meaux A4 **Nancy** A4 Haguenau
A88 Argentan **PARIS** La Marne
Châlons-en-
Champagne Bar-le-Duc
ançon Chartres Château de
Versailles Melun A26 Saint-
Dizier
Saint-Dié-
des-Vosges **Strasbourg**
A11 Fontainebleau La Seine Troyes A35 Colmar
Le Mans Châteaudun A10 Étampes A5 Chaumont A31 Épinal
A6 Sens Mulhouse
La
che Vendôme
A28 **Orléans** Auxerre Langres Vesoul Belfort
Blois Gien A31 Montbéliard
Tours La Loire Avallon A6 **Dijon** A36
A85 Loches Cosne-Cours-
sur-Loire Beaune Dole **Besançon**
Chinon Vierzon
hâtellerault Bourges Autun Chalon-
sur-Saône Lons-le-Saunier **SWITZERLAND**
A10 Châteauroux A71 Nevers A6 A39
thenay Argenton-
sur-Creuse **Moulins**
Poitiers A20 Montluçon Mâcon Bourg-
en-Bresse Annemasse
Bellac La Loire A40 Chamonix-
Mont-Blanc
Guéret Vichy Villefranche-
sur-Saône Annecy 4810m
gnac **Limoges** Roanne Aix- A41 Mont Blanc
Angoulême A89 Clermont-
Ferrand A89 **Lyon** A43 les-Bains Chambéry
A89 1885m
Puy de
Sancy A72 Vienne **Grenoble** A41 A43
Brive-la-Gaillarde Tulle **Saint-
Étienne** Voiron **ITALY**
Grotte de
Lascaux Saint-Flour A49
Bergerac Sarlat Aurillac Le Puy-
en-Velay Privas A7 Valence Briançon
angon Rocamadour A75 Gap
Cahors A20 Figeac Massif Montélimar
A62 Agen Moissac Rodez Central Mende Digne-
les-Bains
Montauban Millau Alès Orange
Albi Pont du
Gard Avignon A51
Auch A68 **Nice** Menton
Castres **Nîmes** Manosque Grasse Monaco
Toulouse A9 Arles **Aix-en-
Provence** Antibes
Muret Béziers Martigues A8 Cannes
Tarbes A64 Carcassonne Sète **Marseille** Fréjus
Lourdes A61 Narbonne A57
Foix **Toulon**
Saint-Girons Golfe du Lion
n é e s A9
Cirque de
Gavarnie **ANDORRA** **Perpignan**

**MEDITERRANEAN
SEA**

C D E

Bastia

Corte

Ajaccio Corse

Porto-Vecchio

The Château d'Azay-le-Rideau is built on an island on the Indre river in the heart of the Loire Valley

unity; they are essentially one people and one country. Every town and village in France flies the flag (*tricolore*) with pride, and displays in its town hall a bust of Marianne, the beautiful woman who epitomizes the spirit of the country.

The French despair of their politicians, grumble at their government and taxation, and are quite capable of unruly demonstrations against the most surprising things, but *au fond*, at heart, they remain proud and devoted admirers of their country.

La belle France

La belle France – beautiful France – is indeed truly beautiful. Hexagonal in shape, each of its six sides acts as a natural boundary. The English Channel and the rolling Atlantic guard the west coast; the Pyrenees and Alps, the southwest and southeast borders; the Mediterranean laps along the southern coast; and the mighty Rhine river forms a barrier against Germany in the northeast. Within this area lies a huge variety of landscapes, with plains, arable flatlands, forested hills, vine- and olive-growing terraces, lush river valleys, inhospitable mountain massifs and a combined coastline stretching for almost 2,000 miles.

As you travel around France you'll notice how sparsely populated the land is compared to most other European countries. Miles go past without a sign of a town or village, yet the land is mostly cultivated, forested or tended in some way. France has always been an agricultural country, and today is the largest agricultural producer in the European Union.

Cities, Towns and Villages

In a country as geographically varied as France there is bound to be a diverse range of architecture, as styles evolved to suit the environment. In southern rural areas, the population lived in easily defensible communities and worked the fields daily, leaving a legacy of picturesque hilltop villages, with narrow streets for shelter against the fierce sun. In the mountains the design was dictated by the climate, and cozy wooden chalets evolved, with steep or flat roofs depending on the region.

The whole country in general enjoyed great prosperity during the 17th and 18th centuries, and in most of the major cities there are architectural reminders of this time, in the shape of churches, fine civic buildings, spacious squares and well-planned streets.

Before the French Revolution, the aristocracy spent several months a year on their estates and built fine fortified houses and beautiful châteaux in which they lived.

This wonderful mixture of styles still exists, and the French have been far more successful than some other European nations at preserving the historic centers of their towns. The second half of the 20th century saw some truly imaginative and innovative civic building projects in major cities, which you'll certainly notice.

The French Character

Other Europeans have a peculiar relationship with the French people, in which there may be more than a touch of envy. The French have much to boast about, and are rightly proud of their culture. As a result, they have gained a reputation with their neighbors for being arrogant. They are often accused of seeing themselves as decidedly superior to every other nation.

For years the French have been criticized and stereotyped for their attitude. But the minute a foreigner steps on French soil he or she is once more seduced: by the country, the overwhelming charm of the people, the way of life.

Lifestyle

The French strike a happy balance between the work-driven culture of northern Europeans and the wonderfully alluring, but sometimes frustratingly relaxed, southern European approach to life. This is a prosperous country with a high standard of living, where both men and women hold down prestigious and influential jobs in every sector. It also is a highly efficient country with an excellent infrastructure, making things very easy for visitors.

Public transportation is first-rate, with Europe's best and fastest train system. If you're driving, you'll find the roads fast and in good condition; the country's speeding and drunk-driving laws are strictly enforced.

Hotels are comfortable, restaurants provide good value, and tourism is a well-organized, thriving industry.

All this is augmented by the innate French sense of style, which is obvious the minute you arrive. This is evident in everything from the way produce is artfully stacked in market stalls to the sensible layout of an airport.

You'll find the French have a relaxed approach to most problems, but note that the wheels of daily life are oiled with a high level of politeness. Even if you don't speak the language, bear in mind that courtesy is extremely important in everyday dealings.

People work hard in France, but indulge in relaxation as well. In the evenings they enjoy themselves over a lengthy meal or sit for hours in cafés. French citizens have always backed their country's achievements in culture and

The Vieille Ville (Old Town) area of Nice in Provence

France

The national game of *boules* is taken very seriously by its devotees, and is fun to watch

the arts, so there's a lively arts scene everywhere. You'll also find that almost everyone has strong views on a wide range of artistic, political and economic events, which they're eager to share.

Religion

France is nominally a Catholic country, with the church separated from the state in 1905.

More than 80 percent of its 65 million inhabitants have been baptized into the Catholic church, although only a small percentage regularly attends services.

There are approximately 1 million Protestants, who for historical reasons tend to be more active churchgoers. Immigrants from France's former colonies make up a large proportion of the considerable number of Muslims, while the Jewish population in France never recovered its numbers after World War II.

Every large town has one or more churches with Sunday services.

Pastimes

The French take relaxation seriously. They enjoy sports, both as spectators and participants, with soccer the national favorite, closely followed by rugby. Cycling is popular with the Tour de France rolling through the streets around the country in July, watched by millions. Tennis and golf also are popular sports, both with good facilities for tourists, and you'll find challenging golf courses all over France. Resort areas offer a huge range of pastimes, from tennis to sailing to organized hiking.

With the Alps on their doorstep, many people ski, especially during early February when children are out of school and families head for the slopes. As well as the Alps, the Pyrenees and the Massif Central at Le Mont-Dore also are destinations for French skiers.

You may often see *boules* being played. This is a game where players attempt to surround a small target ball on the ground by throwing larger, heavier balls

Les Aiguilles (literally "The Needles") is a mountain range in Chamonix, a popular skiing area

from a specified distance. A game local to the Basque area is *pelota*, where two teams hit a ball against a wall.

Pleasures

Food and drink are among the national pleasures of France, and much time is spent shopping for and preparing food. Although modern life has taken its toll, fast food, frozen meals and "grazing" items are not considered mealtime options. If the French can't be bothered to cook, they can pick up fresh dishes from a *traiteur*, a type of delicatessen. Desserts are rarely homemade, bought instead from a *pâtisserie* (cake shop), ensuring the highest quality.

Every region has its own particular food specialties and these are taken so seriously that some foodstuffs have an *appellation controlée* label, similar to the labeling used for wine, meaning that the product must be from the area for which it is known. Well-known regional dishes include *pot au feu de la mer* (seafood

stew) from Brittany, *salade Niçoise* (Niçoise salad, made with fresh tuna, anchovies and eggs) from Provence and quiche Lorraine from the north.

French wines need no introduction, and visitors can enjoy winery visits and tastings in all the wine-producing areas. Champagne is kept for special occasions, while alongside wine, everyday drinks include many varieties of beer and the *pastis* family – an aniseed-flavored spirit diluted with water so it turns milky.

Material pleasures are important in France, where shopping is an art form. This is the country that produces cognac, internationally famous scents, and some of the world's most desirable clothes and accessories. Prices may vary little from those back home, but the satisfaction is great from buying luxuries in their native land.

Expect a wealth of experience and pleasure in France: natural beauty, historic cities and good value despite the relatively high cost of living.

Timeline

15,000 BC	Lascaux cave paintings; first works by tribal group in area now covered by modern France.
3000 BC	Carnac stones erected.
58 BC	Julius Caesar invades Gaul.
AD 500	Frankish King Clovis unites tribes to form France.
800	Charlemagne crowned first Holy Roman Emperor.
1431	Joan of Arc burned at the stake; resulting patriotism gives France national identity.
1763	France loses North American possessions to England at end of Seven Years War.
1789	Start of French Revolution; monarchy overthrown and republic established.
1804	Napoleon proclaimed emperor; Napoleon defeated at Waterloo in 1815.
1889	Eiffel Tower, at the time the world's tallest man-made structure, built for Paris Exhibition; beginning of *belle époque* era.
1914–18	France allies with Britain, Russia and United States against Germany and Austro-Hungary to fight World War I.
1939–45	France swiftly defeated by Germans in World War II; Charles de Gaulle leads Free French Army from England.
1957	France is a founder member of European Economic Community.
1968	Student and Trade Union unrest almost bring down the government of President de Gaulle.
2003	The French government votes against military intervention in Iraq and takes no part in the coalition action.
2007	Nicolas Sarkozy is elected as the French President.
2010	The left's success in mid-term regional elections in May shows a slide in President Sarkozy's popularity.
2012	Socialist François Hollande is elected as the French President.
2014	France's March mayoral elections see a move to the right in protest at President Hollande's handling of the economy. Parisian's vote in their first female mayor, Anne Hidalgo.
2015	Millions of French people take to the streets in peaceful protest in defence of *liberté* (liberty) following deadly attacks at the offices of the *Charlie Hebdo* satirical magazine and a Jewish store in Paris.
September 2015	President Hollande announces that France will accept more than 20,000 Syrian refugees.

Impressionism

By the 1870s a group of Parisian artists had become increasingly bored with the traditional style of painting. They were obsessed with light and its effects; painting outside, they worked on several canvases at a time. Among these artists were Monet, Manet, Pissarro, Renoir, Dégas and Sisley. In 1874 they held their first public exhibition, where their work was ridiculed. One critic was scathing about Monet's painting *Impression of a Sunrise*, and so the name of the movement was born. Literary figures such as Zola and Flaubert supported Impressionism, feeling they could do with words what artists were doing with paint, and public opinion was gradually won over.

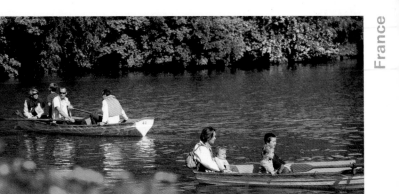

A sunny day can be spent in rowboats on the lake in the Bois de Boulogne, Paris

Survival Guide

■ Many French people speak some English and young people in particular are keen to practice their language skills. It's polite to master the phrase "*parlez-vous anglais?*" to use before asking a question.

■ Politeness is highly regarded in France, so preface requests with "*bonjour monsieur/madame*" (hello) and always say "*merci*" (thank you).

■ French people can be among the world's best dressed, with a casual style that's difficult to emulate.

■ Smoking is banned in all public buildings. This includes all cafés, bars and restaurants. However, smoking is still allowed on terraces attached to restaurants and bars, and smoking is still a popular habit with French people of all ages.

■ Make sure taxi meters are set at zero when starting a trip.

■ Restrooms in most places are generally modern, but in some rural areas the toilet may consist of two floor-level porcelain plaques, on which the user squats. This often flushes automatically at high pressure causing splashes, so watch out for your shoes.

■ Paris Pass offers free entry to more than 60 museums and monuments in the city plus a fast track entry to some attractions, free transport on metro and buses, a river cruise and a hop-on, hop-off bus tour. The pass is valid for 2, 4 or 6 consecutive days from the date of first use and costs €122, €182 and €219 correspondingly. See also www.parispass.com.

■ Parisians are notoriously inconsiderate drivers, giving little leeway to other road users, but elsewhere you'll encounter few problems. If you are driving long distances, use the toll (*péage*) highway system. It's faster and less crowded.

■ Sodas and soft drinks are very expensive in France; a beer (*bière*) often costs less than a Coke.

■ Ice water and ice in drinks is not served routinely in France. Ask for *des glaçons* if you want ice. Legally, restaurants are obliged to serve tap water if you ask for it.

■ French coffee is strong, so if you want a weaker cup ask for a *café américain*. Unless you ask for milk (*lait*) or cream (*crème*), it will always be served black (*noir*).

Paris

It's hard to be indifferent to historic, hectic, elegant Paris. With all its moods, this is a city that can exhilarate you, exasperate you and leave you speechless with wonder, but it won't leave you cold. Paris is beautiful no matter when you visit: the quality of light ranges from crystalline brilliance to mellow gold; distant sounds mingle with bustling main streets; and with each season a new scent blows in to announce its arrival.

Getting Your Bearings

It would take months to explore all of Paris, so resign yourself to the idea that you're not going to be able to see everything on just one trip to this great city. Some people prefer to familiarize themselves with the city by wandering the different neighborhoods; others will try to see as many attractions as possible. Consider which style best suits you and then plan ahead.

You will probably be surprised by the compressed scale of the city; the 2.2 million inhabitants of inner Paris all live within an area bounded by the 21-mile boulevard Périphérique that encircles the city. Even so, be prepared to walk considerable distances, even within the museums, some of which are on a grand scale.

Your first stop should be at one of the seven city tourist offices, the main office being at rue des Pyramides (open daily). Here you can get excellent maps, leaflets and information on excursions and events. Ask about tourist passes, which may reduce entry fees into the city's many museums and attractions and offer discounts on eating and shopping.

Tours and Excursions

Taking a city tour is an excellent way to get your bearings. Most tours cover the main sights on either side of the Seine river and take about two hours. An alternative is to take a bus run by Paris

L'Open Tour (www.parislopentour. com), a choice of four routes that cover the city center, Bastille-Bercy, St.-Germain and Montmartre with stops along the way, allowing you to get on and off to do your own sightseeing. Tickets are valid for one, two or three days, and there's English commentary. You may want to take a tour outside Paris; obvious choices are the fabulous

Palace of Versailles built for Louis XIV, or the old royal hunting lodge of Fontainebleau and its surrounding forest, a favorite retreat of the kings of France. If you'll be spending your entire stay in Paris, consider taking a day trip to the châteaux of the Loire Valley, Chartres and its fine cathedral, or to the magical island of Le Mont-St.-Michel in Normandy.

Parisian Neighborhoods

Most Parisians mentally split their city into two neat halves – Left Bank (Rive Gauche) and Right Bank (Rive Droite) – with the sinuous curve of the Seine dividing them. Traditionally, the Right Bank has stood for order and elegance, typified by the monumental architecture running from the Louvre up to the Arc de Triomphe; while the Left

A sightseeing boat heads toward Pont Notre Dame, soon to pass the cathedral on the Île de la Cité

Bank is an altogether more raffish place. This is too simplistic, however. Paris, in fact, is a series of extremely individual *quartiers* (districts), each with its own personality, style and charm.

Riverbanks and Bridges

More than 30 bridges crisscross the Seine, and the banks, known as *quais*, offer lovely views of the city. The best stretch of riverside for walking lies between the Pont de la Concorde (Concorde Bridge), leading to the place de la Concorde, and the Pont de Sully (Sully Bridge), at the eastern end of the Île St.-Louis. Browse in the *bouquinistes* (secondhand booksellers') stalls that line the riverbank, or simply revel in the subtly blended colors of sky, river, trees and stone. Several companies operate cruises on the Seine, an ideal way to enjoy the river.

Parisians

As inhabitants of a capital city, Parisians are surprisingly able to combine the inevitable pace of big-city life with the ability to switch off and spend hours strolling, window-shopping or endlessly chatting in a café. This is the quintessential image of the chic Parisian. To get a good taste of another side of life in the city, however, you should visit a neighborhood market: Food shopping is a serious business.

One characteristic you will notice is how much people seem to read: There are countless bookstores, and métro (subway) commuters seem to always have their noses in a book. Your overall impression may be that the pace of life here is hurried, and the people can seem brusque, but they can also be charming, particularly to those who love their city.

Shopping

The selection in the stores makes shopping irresistible for some. Haute couture stores cluster mainly around the Faubourg St.-Honoré and avenue Montaigne, with boutiques selling ready-to-wear (*prêt-à-porter*) designer outfits. Paris has a number of department stores; the best known are Galeries Lafayette and Printemps, on the monumental boulevard Haussmann. Both buildings are an architectural tour de force and purveyors of high-quality merchandise.

Visit some of the covered shopping arcades, built in the 18th and early 19th centuries; Galerie Colbert and Galerie Vivienne are among the most attractive. Food stores are a must. Head for the ultramodern emporium of Fauchon, 26 place de la Madeleine; Androuët, 134 rue Mouffetard, the ultimate cheese shop; and Lionel Poilâne, 8 rue du Cherche-Midi, Paris' most famous baker.

Essential Information

Tourist Information
Office de Tourisme et des Congrès de Paris (Paris Convention and Visitors Bureau)
25 rue des Pyramides (daily); Anvers/ Montmartre (daily); Gare du Nord (daily); Gare du Lyon (Mon.–Sat.); Gare de l'Est (Mon.–Sat.).
www.parisinfo.com (Note: no phone service)

Urban Transportation
The easiest way to get around Paris is by the métro (subway), which runs Mon.–Thu. 5:30 a.m.– 1:15 a.m., Fri.–Sat. 5:30 a.m.–2:15 a.m. Métro maps (free) are available at métro stations. The RER (Réseau Express Régional), a suburban express train, connects with the métro inside Paris. Tickets are available singly or in *carnets* (books) of 10; they are available at the stations and from tobacconists *(tabacs)* and must be validated before boarding. Keep your ticket, as there are heavy fines for travelers without tickets. The Paris Visite card, valid for 1, 2, 3 or 5 consecutive days, is interchangeable with the métro, bus and SNCF (main line) trains within the Île-de-France. Buses run daily 6:30 a.m.–8:30 p.m. (some routes until 5:30 a.m.); tickets are interchangeable with the subway. For transportation information in English, phone ☎ 32 46 (toll call) from within France or ☎ 33 8 92 69 32 46 from outside France; www.ratp.info. A tourist bus, the Balabus, operates on Sundays and holidays noon–8 p.m.

from Apr. through Sep.; stops are marked "Balabus (Bb)." Taxis can be hailed on the street or from stands around the city. From early Feb. to early Jan. you can take the Batobus (☎ 0825 050 101; www.batobus. com); this boat runs between the Eiffel Tower and the Jardin des Plantes daily 10–9:30 every 20 minutes, May–early Sep.; Mon.–Thu. 10–7, Fri.–Sun. 10–9:30 every 20 minutes, Apr.; Mon.–Thu. 10–5, Fri.–Sun 10–7 every 25 minutes, rest of year.

Airport Information
Paris has two international airports, Roissy-Charles-de-Gaulle and Orly (both aiports ☎ 3950 within France; 33 1 70 36 39 50 from outside France; www.aeroportsde paris.fr). Most U.S. visitors arrive at CDG. It is 14 miles north of Paris; taxis are available at both terminals (terminal 2 serves Air France only). Roissybus buses run every 15–30 minutes, daily 5:15 a.m.–12.30 a.m. into central Paris, and RER trains every 12–15 minutes daily 4:50 a.m.–11:50 p.m. (travel time 45 minutes; buses may replace some trains). Orlybus buses (for Roissybus and Orlybus ☎ 32 46 within France; 33 8 92 69 32 46 from outside France) run from Orly, 8 miles south of Paris into the center, every 15 minutes, 6 a.m.–12:30 a.m. Bus transfers to RER trains leave every 20–28 minutes, daily 5:12 a.m.–00.27 a.m.

Climate – average highs and lows for the month

Jan.	Feb.	Mar.	Apr.	May	Jun.	Jul.	Aug.	Sep.	Oct.	Nov.	Dec.
2°C	3°C	9°C	14°C	19°C	22°C	25°C	24°C	20°C	14°C	7°C	4°C
36°F	37°F	48°F	57°F	66°F	72°F	77°F	75°F	68°F	57°F	45°F	39°F
-3°C	-2°C	2°C	5°C	9°C	13°C	15°C	15°C	12°C	6°C	2°C	-1°C
27°F	28°F	36°F	41°F	48°F	55°F	59°F	59°F	54°F	43°F	36°F	30°F

France

Paris Sights

Arc de Triomphe

At the western tip of the Champs-Élysées, the Arc de Triomphe is a splendid starting point for a day's sightseeing. Commissioned by Napoleon, the 164-foot-high Arc is now dedicated to the Unknown Soldier of World War I; the eternal flame burns beneath. Twelve avenues radiate from it, giving the surrounding square its original name of place de l'Étoile (the star); today it's called place Charles-de-Gaulle, in memory of the famous general. There are 284 steps to the top of the arch, and no elevator.

➕ A3 ✉ place Charles-de-Gaulle ☎ 01 55 37 73 77; www.monuments-nationaux.fr ⏰ Daily 10 a.m.– 11 p.m., Apr.–Sep.; 10 a.m.–10:30 p.m., rest of year. Last admission 45 minutes before closing Ⓜ Métro/RER Charles de Gaulle-Étoile 💷 $$

Cathédrale Notre-Dame

The great Gothic Cathédrale Notre-Dame (Cathedral of Our Lady), built between 1163 and 1345, stands on the Île de la Cité, the oldest part of Paris. The outside elevation is as impressive as the lofty interior; admire the twin towers, buttresses and facade.

Arrive early to climb one of the towers, and to view the paintings and the rose window at each end of the transept.

➕ D2 ✉ 6 place du Parvis de Notre-Dame ☎ Cathedral: 01 42 34 56 10; www.cathedraledeparis.com. Towers: 01 53 40 60 80; www.monuments-nationaux.fr ⏰ Mon.–Fri. 8–6:45, Sat.–Sun. 8–7:15 (no visits during religious services). Towers: Sun.–Thu. 10–6:30, Fri.–Sat. 10 a.m.–11 p.m., Jul.–Aug.; daily 10–6:30, Apr.–Jun. and in Sep.; daily 10–5:30, rest of year. Last admission 45 minutes before closing Ⓜ Cité; RER Châtelet or St.-Michel Notre-Dame 💷 Cathedral free; Tower $$ ℹ Organ recitals Sun. and Mon. at noon. Guided tours in English Wed.–Thu. at 2 p.m., Sat. at 2:30 p.m. (free)

Centre National d'Art et de Culture Georges-Pompidou

This controversial 1970s-built art center quickly earned the nickname "the refinery in the center of the city," due to its similarity to an oil refinery. The architectural team of Richard Rogers and Renzo Piano designed it as the first postmodernist public building to show its structural elements on the outside.

It's home to a movie theater, library and exhibition space, and the Musée National d'Art Moderne (National Modern Art Museum), which displays art from 1905 to the present day, including work by Salvador Dalí, Pablo Picasso's early Cubist *Femme Assise dans un Fauteuil*, and pop art by Andy Warhol.

The Arc de Triomphe is a symbol of the city and those who climb to the top can enjoy far-reaching views

D3 ✉ place Georges Pompidou ☎ 01 44 78 12 33; www.centrepompidou.fr 🕐 Wed.–Mon. 11–10 (museum and exhibitions close at 9 p.m. but Galeries 1, 2 and the Level 6 exhibition close at 11 p.m. Thu.). Ticket counter closes an hour before galleries 🚇 Hôtel de Ville or Rambuteau; RER Châtelet-Les-Halles 🍴 Restaurant 🎫 Center $; Musée $$–$$$ (free first Sun. of the month)

Champs-Élysées

The stately and much-loved Champs-Élysées (Heavenly Fields) runs from the place de la Concorde (see page 184) up to the Arc de Triomphe, and divides neatly into two sections, with the Rond-Point standing at the halfway mark. The lower section is bordered with grass and chestnut trees, behind which stand the Grand and Petit Palais, both devoted to the arts. Along the upper section from bustling Rond-Point are stores, offices, movie theaters and sidewalk cafés.

B3 ✉ avenue des Champs-Élysées 🚇 Concorde, Champs-Élysées-Clémenceau, Franklin D. Roosevelt, George V or Charles de Gaulle-Étoile 🍴 Le Cinq, see page 474

Cité des Sciences et de l'Industrie

On the northeast edge of Paris stands a modern park, La Villette, now housing Cité des Sciences et de l'Industrie (City of Sciences and Industry) and Cité de la Musique (City of Music). If time is short, visit the main exhibition, Explora, focusing on life, natural resources and technological development. Go to the Géode, a movie theater with a hemispheric screen; tour L'Argonaute, a real submarine from the 1950s; or let the kids enjoy interactive games in the Cité des Enfants (Children's City). Nearby the Cité de la Musique complex is devoted to music; it houses the Musée de la Musique (Music Museum), and the sparkling and futuristic Philharmonie de Paris, designed by Jean Nouvel and inaugurated in 2015.

Cité des Sciences et de l'Industrie 🏢 Off map at E4 ✉ 30 avenue Corentin Cariou ☎ 01 40 05 80 00; www.cite-sciences.fr 🕐 Tue.–Sun. 10–6 (also Sun.

The glowing interior of the church of Ste.-Chapelle

6–7 p.m.); L'Argonaute closes an hour before the museum 🚇 Porte de la Villette 🍴 Restaurant 🎫 Individual attractions $$ (multiattraction ticket $$$) Cité de la Musique ✉ 221 avenue Jean-Jaurès ☎ 01 44 84 44 84; www.citedelamusique.fr 🕐 Music Museum: Tue.–Sat. noon–6, Sun. 10–6 🚇 Porte de Pantin 🍴 Restaurant 🎫 Concert Hall free; Music Museum $$

Conciergerie et Ste.-Chapelle

The Conciergerie, so called because it was administered by a "concierge" or governor, gained a sinister reputation during the 1790s, when Marie Antoinette, queen of France, and the infamous revolutionary Robespierre were imprisoned here. It is the only remaining part of the royal complex on the Île de la Cité, a superb Gothic building with twin round entrance towers and a distinctive roofline. Inside, its huge vaulted hall is the highlight, along with reconstructed prison cells.

Nearby stands Ste.-Chapelle, commissioned by Louis IX in 1245 to house the Crown of Thorns and a fragment of the True Cross. Built as two chapels, the upper was reserved for the royal family. Slender pillars divide the 13th-century, 50-foot-high stained-glass windows showing scenes from the Old and New testaments.

Conciergerie 🏢 D2 ✉ 2 boulevard de Palais ☎ 01 53 40 60 80; www.monuments-nationaux.fr

The Cathédrale Notre-Dame is one of the world's greatest churches

🕐 Daily 9:30–6. Last admission 30 minutes before closing 🚇 Cité; RER St.-Michel Notre-Dame 💰 $$$. Combined ticket with Ste.-Chapelle ($$$). Tours for visitors without a reservation, daily 11:15 a.m. and 4:15 p.m. operate on a first come, first served basis ☎ 01 44 54 19 30 (tour reservations)

Ste.-Chapelle ✉ 4 boulevard du Palais ☎ 01 53 40 60 80; www.monuments-nationaux.fr 🕐 Daily 9:30–6, Mar.–Oct.; 9–5, Nov.–Feb. (also Wed. 6–9:15, mid-May to Sep.). Last admission 30 minutes before closing 🚇 Cité; RER St.-Michel Notre-Dame 💰 $$; combined ticket with Conciergerie $$$ ℹ Audio guide ($), guided tours for visitors without reservation, daily 11:15 a.m. and 4 p.m. Security (overseen by the National Police) will confiscate any sharp metal objects

Île de la Cité

One of the loveliest parts of Paris, the Île de la Cité is the ancient heart of the city; in medieval times it was the monarch's capital and a religious and intellectual center. Among its pretty streets and squares you'll find famous monuments, including Notre-Dame (see page 178) and Ste.-Chapelle (see pages 179–180), as well as impressive civic buildings. ✚ D2 ✉ Île de la Cité 🚇 Cité

Île St.-Louis

Pont St.-Louis will lead you straight from the Île de la Cité onto the Île St.-Louis, ideal for a peaceful stroll, a light lunch and some expensive shopping. Once two islands, this largely residential area was developed in the 17th century, when most of its lovely streets and houses were built. ✚ D2 ✉ Île St.-Louis 🚇 Pont Marie

Jardin des Tuileries

The Jardin des Tuileries (Tuileries Gardens) is a good place to recharge your batteries after the rigors of a visit to the Louvre. Designed by Le Nôtre, it's an excellent example of a 17th-century formal garden, its long central *allée* (alley) carrying the eye from the Louvre buildings and fountains to the expanse of the place de la Concorde. ✚ C3 ✉ place de la Concorde ☎ 01 40 20 90 43 🕐 Daily 7:30–7:30, Oct.–Mar.; 7 a.m.–9 p.m., Apr.–May and Sep.; 7 a.m.–11 p.m., Jun.–Aug. 🚇 Concorde or Tuileries 💰 Free

Le Marais et place des Vosges

For many people, le Marais is the loveliest part of Paris. Its charm lies in the combination of architecture, atmosphere, the crowds that wander its streets, and its restaurants and shops. In the early 17th century Henri IV launched development by building the place des Vosges, Paris' oldest square. Its brick-and-stone facades, arcades and central garden make it one of the world's most beautiful examples of city planning. Surrounding it are fine mansions built along streets that form an

The French Revolution

All over Paris there are reminders of France's 1789 Revolution, when the monarchy was swept away and equal rights for all citizens were established under the law. America's own Revolutionary War served as the catalyst for events in France.

By the end of Europe's Seven Years War in 1763, France had lost all its North American possessions. Louis XVI of France, thirsting for revenge, was happy to offer arms and troops to help American colonists during their struggle against the English. These soldiers came home inspired by the American ideals of liberty and equality, taking what was, in France, an intellectually led and tiny movement to a larger grass-roots level.

France had enjoyed a Golden Age during the 17th and much of the 18th centuries; power became centralized in the hands of the monarchy, the country prospered and Paris became a center of art and sophistication. But this was at the expense of most of the population, whose standard of living dropped lower and lower. Meanwhile the nobility, deprived of any real political power, threw itself into a reckless and hedonistic lifestyle. The divide between the rich and the poor grew ever wider; time was ripe for republican ideas to bear fruit.

In 1789, the Third Estate, representing some 96 percent of France's commoners, declared itself a National Assembly and demanded social and constitutional reform. On July 14, a Parisian mob attacked Les Invalides to procure arms then stormed the Bastille prison, a hated symbol of royal power. Matters moved quickly, and within weeks France was in the grip of revolution as peasants across the country rose in revolt against the nobility and clergy.

In August, the Declaration of the Rights of Man was signed and the cry "*Liberté, égalité, fraternité*" (liberty, equality, brotherhood) was heard all over France. These high ideals soon degenerated into a bloodbath resulting in more than 40,000 people being executed. This period, aptly known as the "Terror," was halted only by Napoleon's rise to power.

The excesses of royalty who built Versailles while peasants starved led to the Revolution

enclave of superb domestic architecture. The area has excellent museums, among them the Carnavalet Museum, Picasso Museum and Victor Hugo's House.

Musée Picasso 🛗 D2 ✉ 5 rue de Thorigny ☎ 01 85 56 00 36; www.musee-picasso.fr ⏰ Tue.–Fri. 11:30–6 (to 9 every third Fri. of the month), Sat. and Sun. 9:30–6 🚇 St. Paul; RER Châtelet-Les Halles 🍴 Café 👤 Guided tours in English Thu. 3 p.m. and Sat. 11 a.m.

Maison de Victor Hugo 🛗 E2 ✉ 6 place des Vosges ☎ 01 42 72 10 16 ⏰ Tue.–Sun. 10–6. Last admission at 5:40 p.m. 🚇 Bastille or St.-Paul 💵 Free (charge for exhibitions 🎧 Audio guide $$

Montmartre

Over-commercialized and crammed with tourists, Montmartre still draws thousands of visitors daily. The neighborhood, once famous for its 40 or more windmills, gained a bohemian reputation in the late 19th century when artists and writers moved in, among them Pierre-Auguste Renoir, who portrayed the area in some of his liveliest and most popular paintings. Later came a new wave of talent, when Montmartre became home to Pablo Picasso and fellow Cubist painters. The place du Tertre is the hub of the quarter; nearby is the Basilique du Sacré-Cœur (Sacred Heart Basilica), an ornate 19th-century church built of brilliant white stone, whose domes are a familiar landmark on the skyline of the city.

🛗 C4 ✉ Montmartre ☎ Basilique du Sacré-Cœur: 01 53 41 89 00; Welcome Center: 01 53 41 89 09; www.sacre-coeur-montmartre.com ⏰ Basilique du Sacré-Cœur: daily 6 a.m.–10:30 p.m.; last admission at 10:15 p.m. Crypt and dome: daily 8:30–8, May–Sep.; 9–5, rest of year 🚇 Anvers, Abbesses or Lamarck-Caulaincourt 💵 Basilique du Sacré-Cœur free; crypt and dome $$

Musée d'Art Moderne de la Ville de Paris

The Musée d'Art Moderne begins where the Musée d'Orsay (see pages 183–184) leaves, with collections leading from Fauvism and Cubism through Surrealism to the abstract art of today. Don't miss the Salle Dufy (the Dufy Room) with *La Fée Electricité (The Electricity Fairy)*, a wraparound vista created by Raoul Dufy in 1937.

🛗 A3 ✉ 11 avenue du Président Wilson ☎ 01 53 67 40 00; www.mam.paris.fr ⏰ Tue.–Sun. 10–6 (also Thu. 6–9). Last admission 45 minutes before closing 🚇 Alma-Marceau or Iéna 💵 Free

Musée Carnavalet

The Musée Carnavalet (Carnavalet Museum) combines a chance to see the interior of one of the finest houses in the Marais (see pages 180 and 182) with an introduction to the history of Paris itself. Built in 1540 and remodeled in the 17th century, this beautiful Renaissance mansion was the home of Madame de Sévigné, a famous hostess and literary figure during the reign of Louis XIV. Allow time to study the models showing

The 20th-century Pyramide contrasts sharply with the 18th-century architecture of the Musée du Louvre

Paris' development, as well as the reconstructed rooms and objets d'art.

🟩 D2 ✉ Public access via 16 rue des Francs-Bourgeois ☎ 01 44 59 58 58; www.carnavalet.paris.fr 🕙 Tue.–Sun. 10–6. Ticket office closes 5:30 p.m. Last admission 30 minutes before closing 🚇 St.-Paul or Chemin Vert 🎟 Free; temporary exhibitions $

Musée du Louvre

The Musée du Louvre (Louvre Museum) started life as a palace in the 1190s. Demolished, rebuilt and extended over the centuries, this vast royal residence on the Seine assumed its present form by the 18th century, when the court of Louis XIV moved to the palace at Versailles. The Revolutionary government of 1793 transformed it into a museum to house the royal collections, which were augmented by subsequent donations and purchases.

In the 1980s President François Mitterrand launched the "Grand Louvre" project to renovate and extend the existing museum space. Chinese-born U.S. architect I. M. Pei was commissioned to design a new entrance in the Cour Napoléon. Below his stunning glass Pyramide lies a vast new foyer giving access to the main museum areas, named Richelieu, Denon and Sully. The Louvre seems confusing on arrival, but signage is excellent. It is best to plan your visit and go early.

The museum is divided into eight departments, ranging from Egyptian, Greek, Etruscan, Roman and Oriental antiquities through a huge painting collection, to sculpture, objets d'art, prints and drawings. Most visitors head straight for the famous pieces, with Leonardo da Vinci's enigmatic and mysterious *Mona Lisa* topping the list (now in a prominent position in the Salle de la Joconde, room 6 in the Denon Wing). Another great work of art to admire is the *Virgin of the Rocks*, also by Da Vinci, a work in better shape and just as representative of his genius. The Louvre also has wonderful paintings by Georges de la Tour, the 17th-century French painter of candlelit night scenes. Take time, too, for Jan Vermeer's light-infused *Lacemaker*; Veronese's *Marriage Feast at Cana*, the largest work in the Louvre and full of fascinating detail; and Raphael's *Beautiful Gardener*, one of the sweetest of all his paintings of the Virgin Mary.

Two classical sculptures draw the crowds: the *Winged Victory of Samothrace*, a second-century BC marble figure, full of movement and tension and standing at the top of a grand staircase; and the *Venus de Milo*, a Hellenistic figure of the goddess Aphrodite from the fourth century BC. Contrast these two with Michelangelo's *Slaves*, sculpted almost 2,000 years later but clearly inspired by Classical work.

🟩 C3 ✉ rue de Rivoli (main entrance: Pyramide, Cour Napoléon) ☎ 01 40 20 53 17; www.louvre.fr 🕙 Main museum and collections: Mon., Thu. and Sat.–Sun. 9–6, Wed. and Fri. 9 a.m.–9:45 p.m. Napoleon Hall: Wed.–Mon. 9 a.m.–10 p.m. 🚇 Palais-Royal Musée du Louvre 🍴 Restaurants 🎟 $$ (free first Sun. of the month Oct.–Mar. and Jul. 14 – does not include Salle Napoleon); temporary exhibitions $$; combined tickets for permanent collection and temporary exhibitions $$$ ℹ Self-guiding audio tours ($$) and guided tours ($$) in English are available daily 11:15 a.m. and 2 p.m. (☎ 01 40 20 52 63). Sections may be closed; check ahead of your visit

Musée d'Orsay

The architecturally controversial Musée d'Orsay (Orsay Museum) was opened in 1986 in the old railroad station, the Gare d'Orsay. Whatever your view, the art collection inside cannot fail to impress. The whole field of visual arts – painting, sculpture, architecture and design – from 1848 to 1914 is represented.

The major draw is the Impressionist and Postimpressionist collection. Here hangs Edouard Manet's *Olympia*, a portrait of a naked prostitute that caused a sensation when it was painted in 1863. Also in the gallery is a series of countryside scenes by Alfred Sisley and Camille Pissarro. You'll find world-famous paintings such as Manet's *Déjeuner sur l'Herbe*, and Claude Monet's radiant images of Rouen Cathedral and his water gardens at Giverny. Here, too, are James Abbott McNeill Whistler's portrait of his mother, examples by Renoir, and Edgar Degas' little dancers.

➕ C2 ✉ 1 rue de la Légion d'Honneur ☎ 01 40 49 48 14; www.musee-orsay.fr 🕔 Tue.–Wed. and Fri.–Sun. 9:30–6, Thu. 9:30 a.m.–9:45 p.m. 🚇 Solférino; RER Musée d'Orsay 🍴 Restaurant and snack bar 💲 $$ (reduced fee after 4:30 p.m. Tue.–Wed., Fri.–Sun. and after 6 p.m. Thu.; free first Sun. of the month); combined ticket with Musée de l'Orangerie or Musée Rodin ($$$) 🎧 Guided tours in English ($$); contact the museum for details. Audiotape ($$) available in English.

Musée du quai Branly

Housed in an innovative and elevated glass structure set around trees and vegetation, this museum is a center of excellence for non-Western arts, with collections from cultures throughout Africa, the Americas, Asia and Oceania.

➕ A3 ✉ 37 quai Branly 75007 ☎ 01 56 61 70 00; www.quaibranly.fr 🕔 Tue.–Wed. and Sun. 11–7, Thu.–Sat. 11–9 🚇 Ecole Militaire or Alma-Marceau 🚌 42 🍴 Restaurant and café 💲 $$; free first Sun. of the month 🎧 Downloadable audio guides available

Place de la Concorde

Nothing better epitomizes the wealth, self-confidence and flair of 18th-century France than the place de la Concorde, scene of Louis XVI's execution in 1793. From this elegant square there are sweeping views up the Champs-Élysées (see page 179) and down to the Louvre (see page 183), and from the Madeleine to the Assemblée Nationale across the river. The octagonal square is decorated with statues, while in the center rises a slender 3,000-year-old Egyptian obelisk, flanked by two fountains.

➕ B3 ✉ place de la Concorde 🚇 Concorde

Quartier Latin and vicinity

The area around the Sorbonne, Paris' ancient university, has long been known as Le Quartier Latin (The Latin Quarter) because until the 1789 Revolution, Latin was the language spoken by students. Cross the boulevard to admire the Jardin du Luxembourg (Luxembourg Garden), then move on to the Panthéon, where great Frenchmen, including Voltaire and Victor Hugo, are buried.

Jardin du Luxembourg ➕ C2 ✉ rue de Medicis/rue de Vaugirard ☎ Website only: www.senat.fr/visite/jardin 🕔 Daily, opens 7:30 a.m. (Mar.–Oct. then 15 minutes later each fortnight thereafter) and closes 4:30–9:30 p.m. 🚇 Odéon; RER Luxembourg

Panthéon ➕ D2 ✉ place du Panthéon ☎ 01 44 32 18 00; www.monuments-nationaux.fr 🕔 Daily 10–6:30, Apr.–Sep.; 10–6, rest of year. Last admission 45 minutes before closing 🚇 Cardinal-Lemoine or Jussieu; RER Luxembourg 💲 $$

Tour Eiffel

When it was built by engineer Gustave Eiffel in 1889, the Tour Eiffel (Eiffel Tower) was, at almost 1,000 feet, the world's tallest man-made structure. Part of the World Exhibition, it became a familiar symbol of Paris. You can take an elevator to each of its three levels. Mail a letter from the first-floor post office and the postmark will be "Paris Tour Eiffel."

➕ A2 ✉ Champ de Mars ☎ 08 92 70 12 39 (toll call); www.toureiffel.paris 🕔 Daily 9 a.m.–midnight, mid-Jun. to Aug. (final elevator to top floor at 11 p.m., steps close at midnight); 9:30 a.m.–11 p.m., rest of year (final elevator for top floor 10:30 p.m., steps close at 6:30 p.m.). Last admission 30 minutes before closing 🍴 Two restaurants and Champagne bar 🚇 Bir-Hakeim; RER Champ de Mars Tour Eiffel 💲 Elevator: 2nd floor $$; top floor $$$; Staircase: 2nd floor $$

What's On Where

Brochures published weekly and monthly help you track down evening entertainment in Paris. English-language publications include *Where Paris*, *Gogoparis* and *Time Out* (monthly) and the weekly *Pariscope*, which has an English section. These list an enormous selection of entertainment, including temporary events, shows and festivals. You can find them at tourist offices and many English-language bookstores.

Eating and Drinking in Paris

Your hotel will probably provide you with breakfast (normally at an extra charge), usually consisting of fruit juice, freshly baked baguettes and a selection of croissants and *viennoiseries* (assorted pastries). However, a basic Continental breakfast can be purchased at most street cafés for a fraction of the price charged in many hotels, and usually with a genuine Parisian atmosphere.

Main Meals
Lunch is generally served from midday until 2:30, and dinner from 7:30 until after 10. If you want either earlier, head for a brasserie, where you'll get simple, freshly cooked meals, and drinks and snacks throughout the day. Bistros are more modest than restaurants, although not always cheaper. You'll get the best value anywhere by choosing from the menu (often called *la formule*), where there's a choice of three or four courses for a fixed price. Some noted restaurants also serve what they term a *menu gastronomique*, which will include small portions of many of the famous house specialties, an excellent way to sample a wide range of dishes. If you order water, you'll probably get bottled mineral water (still or carbonated), for which you'll be charged. Wine can be fairly expensive, but all restaurants serve their own house wine in bottles and carafes, which is often good value. A typical meal will include a starter, frequently some type of salad; a main course with vegetables; and cheese, followed by the dessert.

Snacks, Fast Food and Picnics
If you want a light lunch head for the cafés, which usually have tables outside when the weather's nice. They serve sandwiches and other snacks, and hot, cold and alcoholic drinks. A popular lunch place in Paris is the *bar à huîtres* (oyster bar), where other seafood also is available, or an internet café where you can have a snack or a drink while you surf the net. There also are plenty of burger joints, as well as the *boulangerie* (bakery), where you can get a variety of savory pastries to take out. For those with a sweet tooth, a *pâtisserie* (cake shop) is the place for a mouthwatering range of cakes and pastries. Summer weather may tempt you to plan a picnic: you can put together a wonderful feast at any of the many food markets that are scattered throughout the city.

French *pâtisseries* are famous for their beautifully crafted cakes and delicate pastries

Lyon

France's second-largest city, once a hub on a vital trade route, has much to offer. It's a fascinating place where history and tradition, excellent civic facilities and architectural merit combine with commercial importance to give a real big-city feel on a very human level.

The City and the Presqu'Île

Lyon's sprawl may be daunting if this is your first visit, but the city's major tourist attractions are in a surprisingly compact area. Public transportation is excellent, so it should take little time for you to get your bearings.

Lyon's name is derived from the Latin *Lugdunum*, the capital of Roman Gaul, which was founded at the top of the hill called Fourvière in 43 BC, from where the settlement spread to above the confluence of two great rivers known today as the Rhône and the Saône. After Rome fell, the medieval town gradually established itself, spreading out slowly to occupy the narrow spit of land immediately above the rivers' junction. This became known as the Presqu'Île (the isthmus), and here the city grew in the 17th and 18th centuries; it was only later that it expanded farther to the north and east. For visitors, the main sights are almost all either along the west bank of the Saône river or on the Presqu'Île, the oldest parts of the city.

Exploring Lyon

Most visitors use the métro system, or subway, to travel around. Although it will get you from place to place effortlessly, you'll get a better sense of the city's layout if you set out on foot, and walking can actually be quicker. The hill of Fourvière (see pages 189–190) is a useful landmark; if it's on your left you're heading north, right and you're walking south. For orientation purposes remember that the Saône is the river immediately below Fourvière, while the Rhône lies on the other side of the Presqu'Île. Lyon is remarkably hilly, especially the climb up Fourvière and the slopes of the Croix-Rousse district (see pages 189 and 193), so a trip to these places probably merits the short métro or bus ride.

The tourist office offers an excellent one-, two- or three-day pass called the Lyon City Card (www.lyoncitycard. com). This moderately priced ticket gives you unlimited travel on the bus, trolley bus, tram and métro network, a river cruise (April through October), admission to Lyon's best museums, a guided tour, a self-guiding audio tour of the Fourvière Basilica, access to the observatory, a performance at the Théâtre le Guignol and discount entrances to the aquarium and several other sights, as well as literature to help you make the most of your stay.

The Lyonnais – with their reputation for common sense, wit and kindness – are helpful and friendly, and are usually happy to assist strangers.

Enjoying the Sights

Lyon, like so many historic cities, really needs to be explored at leisure. Get a flavor of the city by wandering through its picturesque neighborhoods, sit in cafés, pause in the lovely squares and linger on the bridges to admire the river scene. If pressed for time, consider taking a tour. The tourist office can provide details for both bus and walking tours, and cruises run during summer.

This prosperous city is well endowed with museums, some of which are remarkably esoteric. If you're an avid old-film fan, period automobile fanatic or if medical history or the discovery of electricity rivets you – you'll not be disappointed. Lyon also has many child-friendly attractions, including a museum of automation history, a puppet museum and a huge and well-presented natural history museum.

La Cuisine

Ask any French citizen what he or she thinks is Lyon's main attraction and the answer will probably be "la cuisine" (the food). This is a city where eating is taken very seriously indeed. There are hundreds of restaurants, ranging from very simple, family-run places to world-class establishments, and then there is the wine.

North of Lyon, miles of famous vineyards produce quality reds and

A view of Lyon from Notre-Dame de Fourvière

whites, with names to excite a wine lover – Mâcon, Pouilly, Fleurie and Beaujolais, to name but a few. Wine enthusiasts may consider an excursion to the wine country; the tourist office can help with this.

Souvenirs of Silk

Lyon has all the shopping you would expect from a city of its size and importance. The most fashionable stores lie in and around rue Président Edouard Herriot, and in the streets near place Bellecour and place des Terreaux, on the Presqu'Île. All the big international names are here, from jewelers, fashion designers and interior decorators to the best of shoe, leather, china and glass stores. The modern city center, around Part-Dieu railroad station, is home to downtown malls and chain stores, and there also are branches of France's top

department stores, such as Galeries Lafayette. Lyon has its own specialties, with silk topping the list, and you'll find lovely silk goods to take home. Silk has been produced in Lyon for hundreds of years and the history and craft can be seen still in workshops in Passage Thiaffait as well as on the slopes of the Croix-Rousse (see pages 189 and 193).

On the Town

Lyon has plenty to offer in the way of evening entertainment. Opera, ballet, classical concerts, theater, jazz, rock and movies all thrive, with constantly changing programs; listings are available from the tourist office. There are dozens of bars playing live music; cabaret restaurants; nightclubs and floor shows; discos and karaoke bars; English, Irish and Australian pubs; a casino – the list goes on and on.

Essential Information

Tourist Information

Office du Tourisme et des Congrès du Grand Lyon (Lyon Convention and Visitors Bureau) place Bellecour ☎ 04 72 77 69 69; www.lyon-france.com

Urban Transportation

Central Lyon has an extensive bus, trolley bus, tram and métro (subway) system. The métro runs daily 5 a.m.–12:25 a.m. Transportation maps are available from station service booths and tourist offices. Métro stations are marked with an "M" on the city map. Tickets, single (valid for one or two hours' travel) or in *carnets* (books) of 10, are interchangeable between the métro, bus and tram systems. A one-day travel pass (Ticket Liberté 1 Jour) gives

unlimited access to the transportation system and is good value. For information ☎ 04 26 10 12 12 (toll call); www.tcl.fr. Validate tickets before boarding. Taxis can be hailed or called. Try Allo Taxi ☎ 04 78 28 23 23; www.allotaxi. fr. Lyon Prestige Limo (www.lyonprestigelimo. com) offers chauffeur-driven tourist routes.

Airport Information

Lyon-Saint Exupéry Airport (☎ 08 26 80 08 26, toll call; or 33 426 00 70 07 outside France; www.lyonaeroports.com) is 13 miles from the city. Rhonexpress runs a tram service between the airport and Part-Dieu train station, 5 a.m.–midnight (travel time 30 minutes), ☎ 08 26 00 17 18; www.rhonexpress.fr.

Climate – average highs and lows for the month

Jan.	Feb.	Mar.	Apr.	May	Jun.	Jul.	Aug.	Sep.	Oct.	Nov.	Dec.
5°C	8°C	12°C	14°C	20°C	23°C	27°C	26°C	22°C	17°C	10°C	7°C
41°F	46°F	54°F	57°F	68°F	73°F	81°F	79°F	72°F	63°F	50°F	45°F
0°C	1°C	3°C	5°C	10°C	14°C	17°C	16°C	12°C	8°C	4°C	2°C
32°F	34°F	37°F	41°F	50°F	57°F	63°F	61°F	54°F	46°F	39°F	36°F

Lyon Sights

Key to symbols

➕ map coordinates refer to the Lyon map on page 186 💶 admission charge: $$$ more than €12, $$ €5–€12, $ less than €5

See page 5 for complete key to symbols

Cathédrale St.-Jean

Post-Roman Lyon grew up around the site of the Cathédrale St.-Jean (St. John's Cathedral), a serene building with a flamboyant Gothic facade, flanked by a Romanesque 11th-century choir school. Much of the interior dates from the 14th and 15th centuries. The rose windows in the transept date to the 1200s.

Due to renovation work, some parts of the cathedral are not accessible, however, the cathedral is open for worship.

➕ A3/B3 ✉ place St.-Jean ☎ Cathedral: 04 78 81 48 81; www.cathedrale-lyon.cef.fr 🕐 Cathedral: Mon.–Fri. 8:15–7:45, Sat. 8:15–7, Sun. 8–7 🚇 Vieux Lyon 💶 Free

Centre d'Histoire de la Résistance et de la Déportation

World War II saw a highly organized, fearless and active resistance movement in Lyon, so it's fitting that the city should have created the fascinating Centre d'Histoire de la Résistance et de la Déportation (Center of the History of the Resistance and Deportation) here. Permanent and temporary displays, documents, audiovisual guides and videos commemorate the past as well as educate the young.

➕ Off map at C1 ✉ 14 avenue Berthelot ☎ 04 78 72 23 11; www.chrd.lyon.fr 🕐 Wed.–Sun. 10–6 (ticket office closes 5:30) 🚇 Jean Macé 🚌 C4, C7, C12, C14, 35; tram T2 (Centre Berthelot) 💶 $

Croix-Rousse

The slopes of the Croix-Rousse (Red Cross) area rise at the north end of the Presqu'Île, the neck of land between the Saône and Rhône rivers.

This area was mainly occupied by religious institutions before the French Revolution, but these were dissolved in 1789, leaving the area open to redevelopment by the silk industry. Today it is a UNESCO World Heritage Site and one of the liveliest areas of Lyon.

➕ Off map at B4 ✉ Croix-Rousse 🚇 Croix-Rousse 🍴 Le Comptoir du Vin, see page 475 ℹ You can arrange a guided tour at the tourist office

Fourvière

One of your first impressions upon arriving in Lyon will be the hill of Fourvière, the site of Roman *Lugdunum*,

The Roman Catholic Cathédrale St.-Jean stands at the center of the old city of Lyon

with its amphitheaters (France's oldest, begun in 15 BC), a second-century *odeum* (a small, roofed theater) and remains of a craft district.

The hill rises above the Saône river, topped by the ornate mass of the 19th-century Basilique Notre-Dame de Fourvière and what appears to be a scaled-down copy of the Eiffel Tower – actually the Tour Metallique (Metal Tower), also called Tour Paufique after the architect, built in 1894 and now a radio and television transmitter.

Take the funicular to the top and enjoy the fabulous views across the city.

✚ A3 ✉ Roman theaters: 6 rue de l'Antiquaille, Fourvière ☎ 04 72 38 49 30 (for information about the site) or 04 72 57 15 40 (for information about concerts); www.musees-gallo-romains.com ◷ Daily 7 a.m.–9 p.m., mid-Apr. to mid-Sep.; 7–7, rest of year 🚇 Vieux Lyon then Fourvière funicular 🍴 Jérémy Galvan, Têtedoie, see page 475 💳 Free

Maison des Canuts

The Silk-weavers' House is a museum-cum-workshop devoted to the history of silk and silk-weavers (*canuts*) in the heart of the Red Cross area.

Here you can enjoy an informative video, browse through old machinery displays and watch silk-weaving demonstrations on traditional looms. On a clear day you can enjoy wonderful views right across to the Alps.

✚ Off map at B4 ✉ 10–12 rue d'Ivry ☎ 04 78 28 62 04; www.maisondescanuts.com ◷ Guided tours only Mon.–Sat. 11 a.m. and 3:30 p.m. 🚇 Croix-Rousse 🚌 2, 33, 45, C13 🍴 Le Comptoir du Vin, see page 475 💳 $$

Musée des Beaux-Arts

The elegant building of the Musée des Beaux-Arts (Museum of Fine Arts) dominates one side of the spacious place des Terreaux, with the impressive Hôtel de Ville (Town Hall) at right angles to it.

The building was formerly the Benedictine convent of St.-Pierre, rebuilt between 1659 and 1685, and it opened as a museum in 1803. The museum has exhibits from Egypt and the ancient

world, and interesting collections of pottery, porcelain, glass and sculpture.

Track down the Lalique glass display or paintings by Bacon, Degas, Dürer, Gauguin, Monet, Picasso, Rubens and Veronese.

In the entrance foyer Pietro Perugino's *Ascension of Christ* is a fitting introduction to what's in store.

✚ B4 ✉ 20 place des Terreaux ☎ 04 72 10 17 40; www.mba-lyon.fr ◷ Wed.–Thu. and Sat.–Mon. 10–6, Fri. 10:30–6 (some galleries close during lunch between 12:30 and 2) 🚇 Hôtel de Ville 🚌 S1, C3, C5, S6, 9, S12, C13, C14, C18, 19, 171 🍴 Museum restaurant 💳 $$ 🛈 Audio guide free

Musées Gadagne

The Musées Gadagne (Gadagne Museum) consists of two museums, the Musée d'Histoire de Lyon (Lyon Historical Museum) and the Musée des Marionnette du Monde (Museum of Puppets of the World). Both are housed in the 15th-century Hôtel de Gadagne, one of Old Lyon's stateliest Renaissance mansions. The building has undergone extensive renovation work.

The history museum galleries display over 80,000 objects explaining Lyon's long and fascinating history.

✚ A3 ✉ 1 place du Petit Collège ☎ 04 78 42 03 61; www.gadagne.musees.lyon.fr ◷ Wed.–Sun. 11–6:30 🚇 Vieux Lyon 🚌 S1, C3, C14, 19, 31, 40 🍴 Café 💳 $$

Musée Gallo-Romain de Fourvière

Housed in an innovative underground building designed by B. H. Zehrfuss, the 17-room Musée Gallo-Romain de Fourvière displays fascinating objects found in Lyon.

Highlights include the "Claudius Tablet," part of a bronze tablet inscribed with a speech given by Emperor Claudius to the Senate in AD 48, and the Circus Mosaic, which vividly portrays a chariot race.

✚ A2 ✉ 17 rue Cléberg ☎ 04 72 38 49 30; www.musees-gallo-romains.com ◷ Tue.–Sun. 10–6 🚇 Vieux Lyon then Fourvière funicular 💳 $; exhibitions $$ 🛈 Audio guide free

Musée des Tissus et Musée des Arts Décoratifs

The Musée des Tissus (Fabric Museum) is appropriately located in Lyon – home of some of the most beautiful silk and innovative production methods the industry has seen. An impressive 18th-century mansion houses the collection, which has fabrics from all over the world, dating from as early as the fifth century.

The Far Eastern silks and embroideries are exquisite, but the Lyon silk and costumes steal the show. These intricate pieces – including designs by Philippe de Lassalle – are still stunningly vivid. Also exhibited are articles of clothing, featuring Mariano Fortuny's Greek-influenced gowns, as wearable today as they were in the 1920s.

The Musée des Arts Décoratifs (Museum of Decorative Arts) displays examples of all types of French craftsmanship in chronological order.

➕ B1 ✉ 30–34 rue de la Charité ☎ 04 78 38 42 00; www.museedestissus.com ⏰ Both museums: Tue.–Sun. 10–5:30 Ⓜ Ampère Victor Hugo 🚍 S1 💵 $$ (includes both museums)

Parc de la Tête d'Or

Rose lovers should visit the superb 259-acre Parc de la Tête d'Or (Golden Head Park), home of Lyon's botanical gardens, which are beautifully landscaped around a lake.

The *roseraie* (rose garden) has more than 60,000 bushes and 350 varieties, all thriving and filling the summer air with an overwhelming scent.

➕ Off map at C4 ✉ place Général-Leclerc ☎ 04 72 82 35 00 ⏰ Daily 6 a.m.–11 p.m., Apr.–Sep.; daily 6 a.m.–9 p.m., rest of year 🚍 C1, C2, C4, C5, C26, 27, 38, 70 Ⓜ Masséna, then short walk 💵 Free

Place Bellecour

The sweeping expanse of the place Bellecour – the old place Royale – is one of Europe's biggest squares.

In the center is a bronze equestrian statue of Louis XIV. Elsewhere within the park are meandering gravel paths and large shady trees, making this a splendid oasis of calm in the heart of the busy Presqu'Île.

➕ B2 ✉ place Bellecour Ⓜ place Bellecour

Vieux Lyon

Until the 1960s, Vieux Lyon (Old Lyon) was a run-down, derelict area. Happily, both the French government and the city of Lyon stepped in with the funds to save this historic quarter, the largest Renaissance-era urban area in France and a UNESCO World Heritage Site.

Here the medieval cathedral town grew and prospered as an international trade and banking center. Rich merchants and bankers built superb, ornately detailed houses along the narrow streets that included the St.-Paul, St.-Jean and St.-Georges neighborhoods. They still stand today, rescued and restored, with their spick-and-span mullioned windows, vaulted walkways, towers and galleries. Many streets are linked by the passages known as *traboules*, which wind through courtyards and under other buildings; the name is derived from the Latin words *trans ambulare*, meaning "to walk through."

Today Old Lyon hums with new life; there are studios, boutiques, bars and restaurants, thronged in summer with both locals and visitors.

➕ A2 ✉ Vieux Lyon Ⓜ Vieux Lyon 🍴 Jérémy Galvan, Têtedoie, see page 475 ℹ Guided walking tours available with audiocassette or English-speaking guides. Apply at the tourist office

An equestrian statue of Louis XIV in place Bellecour

La Cuisine Lyonnaise

Lyon is said to have more restaurants per capita than any other city in the world; no wonder that even other French people will admit, "*on mange bien à Lyon*" ("you eat well in Lyon").

Geography helps: The city stands at an agricultural crossroads, benefiting from prime beef from Charolles, excellent wines from Beaujolais and superb dairy products from the Dauphiné. The commercial fruit and vegetable gardens of France supply the freshest ingredients, and better *boulangers* (bakers) and *pâtissiers* (cake-makers) than the Lyonnais are hard to find. Here you can spend happy hours practicing the art of *lèche-vitrines*, literally "licking the windows," but in reality window-shopping for food. Have a look in the *boucheries* (butchers), *traiteurs* (delicatessens) like you've never seen before, and *épiceries* (grocer shops) piled high with olive oil, vinegar, honey and jam. Afterward, go to the morning markets (except Monday) on the quai St.-Antoine along the river and drool over the gleaming vegetables, glistening fish and mounds of fruit. Then you can find a restaurant and eat – *bon appetit!*

Lyon has a long tradition of professional kitchens being managed by women, a legacy from times when all restaurants were family-run and *Maman* (mother) did the cooking. Such restaurants, known as *bouchons*, still exist, and are usually small and friendly, with visible kitchens. You can count on authentic Lyonnaise dishes accompanied by straightforward wines, which are served in small jugs called *pots*, holding a standard amount. Some restaurants are renowned, and it's often necessary to book ahead to secure a table.

What should you eat? The cooking is classic French, with quality ingredients, subtle sauces, properly aged meat and perfectly ripe cheeses. *Boudin blanc*, a veal sausage, is a specialty, as are *quenelles*, lighter-than-air poached fish dumplings served with Lyon's classic crayfish-based *sauce Nantua*. Tripe, pigs' feet and brains may not be what you're used to, but don't rule them out. *Pommes Lyonnaises* (potatoes fried with onions) are eaten worldwide, but try *gratin dauphinois* (a satisfying dish of potatoes baked in butter, cream, garlic and mustard) as well.

Leave room for a dessert, such as a luscious fruit tart; *île flottante*, a dish with floating islands of meringue on a custard lake; sinful chocolate mousse; or the simplicity of *fromage blanc* – a fresh cream cheese eaten with sugar and cream, or tasty *crêpes* with different flavorings.

Fruit and vegetable markets supply Lyon's many restaurants with excellent fresh produce

Lyon and the Silk Tradition

Nearly 5,000 years ago the Chinese discovered that the cocoon of an insignificant moth, *Bombyx mori,* could be gently unraveled in a continuous thread and woven to produce a light and luxurious fabric. This fabric is silk, still one of the softest and most desirable of all textiles.

Silk thread made its way overland from China to Europe by the 12th century, and by the 1600s Lyon had become the center for European silk textile production. (The silkworm also came to Europe and is now a domesticated insect with a ravenous appetite for mulberry leaves, which grow well in southern France and elsewhere.) The industry thrived, producing sophisticated weaves to supply France's rich and demanding upper classes. Sumptuous designs in dazzling colors were achieved on hand looms; silk damask, patterned silks and brocades, and figured silk velvets poured out of the workshops of Lyon.

In 1804, Joseph-Marie Jacquard invented the mechanical loom, which enabled patterns to be programed using a punch-card system. These very large looms were moved from the Old Town into special buildings designed to accommodate their size in the Croix-Rousse (Red Cross) area (see page 189). The silkweavers *(canuts)*, who also moved, were paid an abysmally low price for each pattern, with the middleman scooping the profits. Social unrest finally erupted in 1831, after a three-year struggle by the *canuts* to get better pay and conditions.

By 1870 the industry had recovered and Lyon silk was considered to be among the best fabrics in the world. The creation of artificial silk and other man-made fibers in the 20th century brought an end to large-scale silk production. Numbers of Lyon's 30,000 weavers dwindled, and today there are only a handful of workshops where people still weave manually; hand-woven weaves are in high demand and are used to help restore the interiors of France's historic buildings.

If you're interested, follow the silk trail in Lyon, from the Old Town to the slopes of the Red Cross district, where you can visit silk workshops and working hand looms. Be sure not to miss the Fabric Museum (Musée des Tissus, see page 191), keeping in mind that the most a skilled worker could hope to weave was three to four inches a day.

Ties, scarves and colorful fabrics make excellent souvenirs to take back home (see page 188).

Healthy silk worms and their cocoons are essential in the production of high-quality fabric

Nice

Nice, France's fifth-largest city and its biggest tourist resort, is perfectly situated on the sweeping Bay of Angels (Baie des Anges). With hills as its backdrop, it is blessed with gorgeous surroundings, a superb climate, a historic past and friendly people. Until 1860 Nice belonged to the County of Savoy, which became part of Italy in 1870, and to this day both the way of life and the inhabitants seem to combine Italian charm and flair tempered with a strong dash of Gallic sophistication.

The City

The Greeks built their settlement on the hills above the bay, and 300 years later the Romans settled here. The modern city stands on the same spot and has spread down to the flat land along the sea. Sheltered to the east and west by substantial promontories, and with the Maritime Alps to the north, Nice has its own microclimate, with mild winters and perfect summers. Over the centuries city planners have taken advantage of these conditions, resulting in one of the most graceful and flower-filled cities in Europe – the average Frenchperson's retirement-home fantasy. In recent years, Nice has marketed itself as a convention center and vacation hotspot. It has more museums than any other French city outside of Paris, including the new Musée National du Sport (National Museum of Sport). A ticket that gives entry to all Nice municipal museums costs €20 and is valid for seven days (www.nicetourisme.com).

Getting Around

Nice is a big city, with several districts – each of which you'll want to experience. The best way to orient yourself is to take a bus or taxi to an area, then explore on foot. Start with the atmospheric and picturesque Old Town (Vieille Ville, see page 198), which you'll probably want to visit more than once.

The seafront stretches nearly 4 miles west of the Old Town, with the famous promenade des Anglais running along much of it. Behind the promenade and situated around the place Masséna is the commercial and business center, punctuated by peaceful gardens. The upscale residential suburb of Cimiez lies on the hill behind the old port and is home to excellent museums. As you explore, notice how the ambience varies, from the earthy gaiety in the streets of the Old Town to the haute couture you'll find along the Promenade des Anglais. You can see the different parts

NICE

0   250   500 meters
0   250   500 yards

N

BOULEVARD DE CESSOL

Cathédral Orthodox Russ St.-Nicolas

AVENUE PRIMEROSE

VOIE PIERRE MATHIS

BOULEVARD FRANCOIS GROSSO

Parc Naturel Departemental d'Estienne d'Orves

BOULEVARD DE LA MADELEINE

AVE DE LA BORNALA

GROSSO

Musée des Beaux Arts

Jardin Botanique, Parc Floral Phoenix, Musée des Arts Asiatiques

RUE DE FRANCE

PROMENADE

A   B

of Nice in style by hiring a *calèche* (horse-drawn carriage), or by taking the tourist train around the old quarter.

Flavors of the South

The French- and Italian-influenced cuisine of Nice is complemented by the sunny flavors of southern France. Look for fish and seafood. Vegetable dishes include *ratatouille* (Mediterranean vegetable stew), which was created here. Also try *mesclun*, a bitter selection of wild leaves. *Estocaficada* is a Niçois dish made from dried Norwegian cod and tomatoes.

The area produces several wines including Château de Bellet (only 100,000 bottles each year). The main wine from the region, often offered as house wine in restaurants and cafés, is Côtes de Provence AOC.

Local Wares and Souvenirs

Nice combines the temptations of big-city chain stores and designer outlets with local markets, antiques shops and souvenir stores. Department stores and big-name labels are found around place Masséna, while local products are sold in the Old Town. Traditional cotton

France

goods, scents from around Grasse, oils and wines make lovely gifts, but the best souvenirs from Nice are traditional carved figurines, known as *santons*.

Carnaval

Nice has dynamic theaters, concert halls and an opera, as well as movie theaters, nightclubs, a casino and cabaret restaurants, live-music bars and discos. Enjoy the local festivals, popular all year. The biggest and most colorful is the *Nice Carnaval et Bataille de Fleurs* (Nice Carnival and Battle of Flowers; www.nivecarneval.com) in February, which draws huge crowds.

Beaches

Nice has some public beaches, but to spend a day in the sun as the Niçois do, go to one of the city's 15 private beaches (open April through October). A fee is payable, but included in the fee is use of an outdoor lounge chair and sun-shade umbrella, changing rooms, freshwater showers, a range of activities and access to a private bar/restaurant.

The beaches are covered in pebbles here, not sand. Topless sunbathing is accepted on the French Riviera though it's falling out of fashion with the younger generation.

Essential Information

Tourist Information

Office de Tourisme et des Congrès de Nice (Nice Convention and Visitors Bureau)
5 Promenade des Anglais;
www.nicetourisme.com
SNCF railroad station, avenue Thiers, Terminal 1 and Terminal 2, Aéroport Nice-Côte d'Azur, Promenade de Paillon
Tourist information line ☎ 08 92 70 74 07 (24 hours)

Urban Transportation

Ligne d'Azur operates all over the city; maps are available from 1 rue d'Italie (☎ 08 10 06 10 06; www.lignedazur.com ◑ Mon.–Fri. 7:30–7, Sat. 9:30–6); ✉ boulevard Jean Juarès ◑ Mon.–Fri. 8–7 or from tourist offices. Buy your ticket – SOLO, Multi or Pass 1 Jour (valid for 1 day), Pass 7 Jours (valid for 7 days) or books of tickets valid for different numbers of days – at a kiosk before you board; don't forget to validate your ticket. Only SOLO (single journey ticket) and Pass 1 Jour are

available for sale on board. Buses run until around 8 p.m. with limited night service. The Nice tram system links the city center with the northern suburbs. Ticket prices are the same as for the bus. Taxis can be found at city-center cab stands (Esplanade Masséna, Promenade des Anglais and place Garibaldi are convenient), or call Taxi Riviéra (☎ 04 93 13 78 78; www.taxis-riviera.fr).

Airport Information

Aéroport Nice-Côte d'Azur (☎ 08 20 42 33 33 for inquiries in English; www.nice.aeroport.fr) is west of the city. International flights generally leave from Terminal 1; Paris and other French destinations are served by Terminal 2. Shuttle bus services from both terminals, linking the airport to the city center, are 98 (to main bus station and city center every 20 minutes 5:49 a.m.–11:45 p.m.) and 99 (to train station, every 30 minutes from 7:53 a.m. to 8:53 p.m.). Taxis are at airport exits, and take about 20 minutes to reach the city.

Climate – average highs and lows for the month

Jan.	Feb.	Mar.	Apr.	May	Jun.	Jul.	Aug.	Sep.	Oct.	Nov.	Dec.
13°C	13°C	14°C	17°C	20°C	24°C	25°C	27°C	24°C	20°C	17°C	13°C
55°F	55°F	57°F	63°F	68°F	75°F	77°F	81°F	75°F	68°F	63°F	55°F
5°C	6°C	8°C	9°C	13°C	17°C	19°C	20°C	17°C	13°C	9°C	6°C
41°F	43°F	46°F	48°F	55°F	63°F	66°F	68°F	63°F	55°F	48°F	43°F

Nice Sights

> **Key to symbols**
> ➕ map coordinates refer to the Nice map on pages 194–195 💵 admission charge: $$$ more than €12, $$ €5–€12, $ less than €5
> See page 5 for complete key to symbols

Cathédrale Orthodoxe Russe St.-Nicolas

The Cathédrale Orthodoxe Russe St.-Nicolas (St. Nicholas' Russian Orthodox Cathedral) is an exuberant pink-and-gray church with six green-and-gold onion-shaped cupolas and an ornate exterior.

Tzar Nicolas II built it from 1903 to 1912 for the Russian nobility in Nice, a city they favored for its climate.

➕ B2 ✉ avenue Nicolas II ☎ 04 93 96 88 02; www.cathedrale-russe-nice.fr 🕐 Due to re-open during 2016. Closed to visitors during services 🚌 17, 27, 64, 75 💵 Free ⓘ Respectful dress required

Cimiez

Cimiez is a residential area packed with attractions, including the Matisse Museum, a 16th-century Franciscan church and monastery, a small museum and cloister devoted to St. Francis, and the cemetery where artists Henri Matisse and Raoul Dufy are buried.

A Roman site has been excavated here, revealing the remains of an amphitheater and public baths. The attached museum holds the treasures uncovered.

Franciscan Church, Monastery and Museum

➕ D4 ✉ place du Monastère ☎ 04 93 81 00 04 🕐 Church: Thu.–Mon. 9–6. Monastery and Museum: Mon.–Sat. 10–noon and 3–5:30 🚌 17, 25 💵 Free ⓘ Concerts in monastery cloisters in Aug.

Musée d'Archéologique Nice–Cimiez

➕ D4 ✉ 160 avenue des Arènes de Cimiez ☎ 04 93 81 59 57; www.nice.fr 🕐 Wed.–Mon. 10–6 🚌 15, 17, 22, 25 💵 $$ (combined ticket with other science museums); $$$ (all municipal museums ticket)

Jardin des Arènes de Cimiez ➕ D4 ✉ avenue des Arènes 🕐 Daily dawn–dusk 🚌 15, 17, 22, 25 💵 Free

This Genoese-style villa houses the Musée Matisse

Musée d'Art Moderne et d'Art Contemporain (MAMAC)

The Museum of Modern and Contemporary Art, or MAMAC, is an impressive museum constructed of four gray marble towers linked by glass walkways. The collection, founded by Nice artist Yves Klein, includes New Realism, Minimalism and Pop Art, with works by Roy Lichtenstein and Andy Warhol. Look for Klein's innovative *Mur du Feu* (*Wall of Fire*).

➕ D2 ✉ place Yves Klein, Promenade des Arts ☎ 04 97 13 42 01; www.mamac-nice.org 🕐 Tue.–Sun. 10–6 🚌 8, 38, 81, 100; tram 1 (Garibaldi) 🍴 Café 💵 $$ (combined ticket with other contemporary art museums); $$$ (all municipal museums ticket)

Musée des Arts Asiatiques

Japanese architect Kenzo Tange designed the glass-and-marble building that houses a collection of exquisite arts and objects from Asia.

➕ Off map at A1 ✉ 405 Promenade des Anglais ☎ 04 92 29 37 00; www.arts-asiatiques.com 🕐 Wed.–Mon. 10–6, early May to mid-Oct.; 10–5, rest of year 🚌 9, 10, 23 💵 Free

Musée Matisse

The whole range of artworks covering the working life of this remarkable artist forms the collection, along with personal possessions and photos.

Bequeathed to the city by Henri Matisse (and then his heirs), it traces the artist's evolution through Impressionism and Fauvism. The artworks are housed in a 17th-century Genoese-style villa with a stunning modern extension.

🔵 D4 ✉ 164 avenue des Arènes de Cimiez ☎ 04 93 81 08 08; www.musee-matisse-nice.org 🕐 Wed.– Mon. 10–6 🍴 Café/restaurant 🚌 15, 17, 22, 25 💳 $$ (combined ticket with other contemporary art museums); $$$ (all municipal museums ticket) 🔖 Guided tours $$ ☎ 04 93 53 40 53

Musée National Marc Chagall

The Marc Chagall National Museum is a dramatic modern gallery that houses Chagall's donations to the city and is the world's most important single collection of his work. The 17 canvases that make up the Biblical Message were painted between 1954 and 1967 and depict the artist's interpretation of the Bible's story. Other rooms display the 39 gouaches, 105 etchings and copper plates, and 200 sketches that Chagall used to help create the finished pieces.

🔵 D3 ✉ avenue Dr. Ménard ☎ 04 93 53 87 20; www.musees-nationaux-alpesmaritimes.fr 🕐 Wed.–Mon. 10–6, May–Oct.; 10–5, rest of year 🚌 15 💳 $$

Place Masséna and Promenade de Paillon

The Niçois regard the elegant, arcaded place Masséna as the heart of their city. Around the square, with its sparkling fountain representing the planets, are broad boulevards and gardens. A long stretch of manicured gardens known as the Promenade de Paillon links place Masséna and the sea with the Théâtre National de Nice and has become a new outdoor focus for the town.

🔵 D1 ✉ Promenade des Anglais 🕐 Gardens: 7 a.m.–11 p.m. Apr.–Sep.; 7 a.m.–9 p.m., rest of year 🚌 3, 4, 7, 8, 10, 11, 14, 17, 22, 27, 38, 52, 59, 70, 94, 98, 100, 217, 230; tram Masséna 💳 Gardens free

Promenade des Anglais

Early in the 19th century the English discovered that France's sheltered Mediterranean coast had mild winters, and soon they flocked here in large numbers. Afternoon strolls were fashionable, but the rocky, 6-foot-wide path along the shore was hardly suitable for gentle walks. In 1820 the Reverend Lewis Way organized the construction of a sweeping promenade, planted with palm trees and decked with flowers. The locals soon called it the Promenade des Anglais (the Englishmen's Walk). Today a busy highway cuts between the sea and the ornate exteriors of the *belle époque* luxury hotels. Even amid the sprawl of ugly concrete apartment blocks, the palms, flowers and strolling crowds and views remain unchanged.

🔵 B1 ✉ Promenade des Anglais 🚌 8, 11, 52, 59, 60, 62, 70, 94 🔖 *Nice Carnaval et Bataille de Fleurs* (Feb.); *Fête Nationale* fireworks display (Jul. 14); *Les Soirées estivales*, music evenings (Jul. and Aug.)

Vieille Ville

Until the 1970s Nice's Vieille Ville (Old Town) was a decaying slum, but today it's one of the liveliest neighborhoods in the city, with shops, bars, fine old houses, baroque churches and 17th- and 18th-century civic buildings. The cours Saleya is the hub of the quarter, an elongated square that is the home of Nice's fresh produce and markets.

🔵 D1 🕐 Fruit and vegetable markets: Tue.–Sun. morning. Antiques market: Mon. Flower market: Tue.– Sat. all day, Sun. morning. All located on cours Saleya 🚌 Any bus for the Gare Routière; tram Opéra–Vieille Ville and Cathedral–Vieille Ville

Lido Plage is near the Promenade des Anglais

Parks, Gardens, Trees and Flowers

Many Mediterranean cities have lovely *parcs* (parks) and *jardins* (gardens), but none more so than Nice, and every street is decked with tubs, planters and window boxes filled with colorful flowers.

Formal parks lie within the city center, forming a green oasis for locals and visitors; the newly reopened Promenade de Paillon (see page 198), incorporating several once separate smaller parks, is the best example. Also in the city center, the wooded Parc du Château features winding paths and cascading water. The wilder Jardin des Arènes de Cimiez (see page 197) is a beautifully tended olive grove, the wind rustling the silver-gray foliage on the shapely trees.

Lovely, aromatic Aleppo pine trees, planted in 1866, abound in the Parc Forestier du Mont-Boron; they line almost 7 miles of trails that are edged with wild carnations and tiny orchids. Views from this park are spectacular: to the east is St.-Jean Cap Ferrat, and to the west is Nice's own Bay of Angels.

Avid gardeners should head for Nice's Jardin Botanique (Botanic Garden) at the west side of Nice, which has a comprehensive collection of Mediterranean flora as well as some tropical plants. The Parc Floral Phoenix is another garden attraction focusing on tropical plants and fruit trees. A vast greenhouse, one of the largest in Europe, dominates the 17-acre site and is packed with numerous exotic and rare orchids among other delights. There also is an aviary and beautifully colored butterflies.

Most of Nice's trees and flowers are common to all Mediterranean countries, where this vegetation thrives in lime-rich, sandy or poor soil, can withstand months of summer heat and drought, and can endure an occasional wet or cold spell in winter. Olives, palms and pines are native; citrus trees, bougainvillea, mimosa, gerbera and many succulents have been introduced. Roses love Mediterranean conditions, which is why you'll see bigger and brighter ones here than anywhere else.

If you're in the countryside – nature's own glorious garden – in April, May or June, you'll find spreads of wildflowers to rival any city park.

Detail of a fountain in Promenade de Paillon, the green artery in downtown Nice

France

Strasbourg

Strasbourg's tiny historic center, circled by arms of the Ill river, could easily lull a visitor into thinking that there was little more to the city than picturesque streets, a breathtakingly beautiful cathedral and a huge number of restaurants. But beyond its medieval core lie grandiose 19th-century civic buildings, an ancient university and the gleaming buildings housing European institutions, since Strasbourg is the seat of the European Parliament.

It's a prosperous, cosmopolitan city, a beguiling blend of ancient and modern, Teutonic and French.

A Visitor's Strasbourg

For tourists, modern everyday Strasbourg need not intrude upon enjoyment of the old city. Aim to stay within the old, mostly pedestrian quarter; it's a delightful place to walk around, with an impressive choice of hotels, bars and restaurants.

There's a large presence of European parliamentary officials, many of whom speak English, and the range of English-language tourist literature is excellent.

Strasbourg's appeal lies in its combination of history, architecture and culture. First impressions are of a very German city, the timbered houses and cobbled streets reminiscent of villages across the Rhine river, a little to the east. But the atmosphere is definitely French, with the style and way of life that it implies. Lying so near the German border, however, Strasbourg is a favorite destination for day and weekend visits, and you'll see and hear many Germans.

Exploring the City

Undoubtedly, it's best to explore Strasbourg on foot. Apart from visiting the wonderful cathedral, museums and fine churches, most visitors spend time simply strolling the streets. You'll find hidden corners and buildings waiting to be photographed around every turn, so take your time. Water plays a large part in the city's layout; the center is encircled by water, divided into different channels and crossed by graceful bridges. Old mills and fortifications along the river bear witness to the city's

The medieval Ponts-Couverts, a fortified bridge in the heart of old Strasbourg

historic importance, while the mighty Rhine, the German border, lies only a stone's throw away.

If you're interested in architecture, you could follow one of several marked routes through the heart of the old city center (see Petite France, page 204). The tram can be useful for saving your legs, and taxis are easily available. There's also the peaceful boat trip around the center (see page 205).

Eat, Drink and Enjoy

The Strasbourg and Alsace area is one of the few regions in Europe that produces both notable wines and beers, and it also is home to some of the finest cooking in France. There are strong German influences here, giving the cuisine a different character from typical French fare. The popular French dish *choucroute*, for instance, is really the same thing as sauerkraut.

But don't be fooled. There's much more to the cuisine in Strasbourg than German cooking; you'll find Italian, Chinese, Lebanese, Tex-Mex, Moroccan and others. Don't overlook the opportunity to try some real Strasbourg specialties (see page 476). Stop in a *winstub*, a small family-run restaurant often housed in a historic building, where you'll be able to sample the best of local cooking and flavors in a cozy setting with a friendly atmosphere.

Alsace produces some notable wines, mainly whites, which are similar in character to the best of German wines. They are traditionally labeled with the name of the grape rather than the place of origin. Riesling, Gewürztraminer, Pinot Blanc and Muscat are all reliable varieties to look for. Beer also is big in Alsace, the home of Heineken and Kronenbourg. Other smaller local breweries produce excellent beer.

Evening Diversions

Strasbourg has a rich cultural life, with its own orchestra participating at the renowned International Music Festival in June; in late September through early October there's the annual *Musica* (www.festivalmusica.org), a festival of contemporary music. Opera, theater, jazz and dance performances are held year-round and are widely advertised. In summer, most tourists are drawn to the nightly folklore displays of music and dance held in some of the old city's most picturesque squares.

Malls and Markets

Shopping in Strasbourg is a real pleasure, with an excellent choice of designer names, jewelers, antiques shops and international bookstores clustered around the center of the old city. Across the river, the Place des Halles (www.placedeshalles.com) is a fair-sized shopping mall housing France's familiar chain stores.

The weekly farmer's market takes place on Saturday mornings on rue de la Douane, where stalls of fresh produce, cheese and meat jostle with inexpensive and cheerful clothes and household goods. Souvenir shops sell Alsatian handicrafts; pottery, lace and carved wood are worth looking at. Strasbourg is famous for its colorful Christmas market, *Christkindelsmärik*, first held in 1570 in the cathedral (www.noel. strasbourg.eu). Each year, from late November to late December, the festive market attracts shoppers from across Europe (see page 203).

Essential Information

Tourist Information

Office de Tourisme de Strasbourg (Strasbourg Tourist Office)
17 place de la Cathédrale
☎ 03 88 52 28 28;
place de la Gare
Parc de l'Etoile
www.otstrasbourg.fr

Urban Transportation

Buy tickets for the trams from machines located at stops, and validate them before boarding. Outer Strasbourg is served by an efficient bus service, which you can use to visit the European institutions. The Trio ticket is valid for one day across the public transportation network for up to three people. Transportation maps are available at the railroad station and the tourist office (for information call Compagnie des Transports Strasbourgeois ☎ 33 88 77 70 70; www.cts-strasbourg.eu). Taxis are reasonably priced; find them at the station, place Kléber or place Gutenberg, or call Taxi 13 ☎ 03 88 36 13 13; www.taxi13.fr.

Airport Information

Strasbourg-Entzheim International Airport (☎ 03 88 64 67 67; www.strasbourg.aeroport. fr). operates flight connections to most major European cities, and is 10 minutes south of the city by car. A train service links the central train station to the airport. Trains run every 15 minutes Mon.–Fri. 5:20 a.m.–10 p.m., Sat. 7:55 a.m.–8:55 p.m. and Sun 7:55 a.m.–9:55 p.m.

Climate – average highs and lows for the month

Jan.	Feb.	Mar.	Apr.	May	Jun.	Jul.	Aug.	Sep.	Oct.	Nov.	Dec.
4°C	5°C	10°C	15°C	19°C	22°C	24°C	24°C	20°C	14°C	8°C	4°C
39°F	41°F	50°F	59°F	66°F	72°F	75°F	75°F	68°F	57°F	46°F	39°F
-2°C	-2°C	1°C	5°C	9°C	12°C	14°C	13°C	10°C	6°C	2°C	0°C
28°F	28°F	34°F	41°F	48°F	54°F	57°F	55°F	50°F	43°F	36°F	32°F

Strasbourg Sights

The red sandstone facade of the cathedral

Cathédrale Notre-Dame

A superb example of Gothic architecture, the Cathédrale Notre-Dame (Cathedral of Our Lady) dominates old Strasbourg, its single steeple soaring to 466 feet. Imposing by day, the cathedral is a striking sight by night when it is beautifully lit.

Built between 1176 and 1439, the cathedral stands in a cobbled square on the site of an earlier basilica. A team of masons from Chartres worked on it in the 13th century, creating superb statuary and a harmonious interior, subtly lit by fine stained-glass windows. The main facade, a riot of sinuous, graceful biblical figures and saints, was completed half a century later. A platform constructed in the late 14th century to connect the two towers is reached by 332 stairs.

The astronomical clock in the south transept is a huge timepiece with a planetary dial constructed in the 1540s. Its automated figures perform daily at 12:30 (see below), when the Apostles appear, a cock crows and beats its wings, and the seven ages of man can be seen.

The cathedral's loveliest sculpture is the *Pilier des Anges* (*Pillar of the Angels*), a wondrously carved pillar entwined with the four evangelists and trumpeting angels, all heralding the Last Judgment.

➕ B2 ✉ place de la Cathédrale ☎ 03 88 21 43 34; www.cathedrale-strasbourg.fr 🕓 Cathedral: daily 7–11:20 and 12:40–7. Platform: daily 9:30–8, Apr.–Sep.; daily 10–6, rest of year. Cathedral closed during Mass 🚋 Tram A, B, C, D, F 💶 Cathedral free; platform $; clock $ (free Sun.) – ticket holders enter by porte St.-Michel. A video is shown Mon.–Sat. 11:45 a.m. before clock performs ℹ Daily allocation of clock tickets on sale 9:30–11:20 a.m.

Les Grandes Places

Strasbourg is scattered with *grandes places* (large squares). The main three – place Kléber, place Gutenberg and place de la Cathédrale – are all within a five-minute walk of each other. The cathedral square, with its cobblestones and timber-framed houses, is distinctly medieval; 18th-century place Kléber has an elegant spaciousness; and attractive Renaissance-style place Gutenberg nicely bridges the architectural time gap. From late November through December, all three squares are the backdrop for Strasbourg's famous *Christkindelsmärik* (Market of the Child Jesus), a month-long street market dating from 1570.

➕ B2 ✉ place Kléber, place Gutenberg, place de la Cathédrale 🚋 Tram A, B, C, D, F ℹ *Christkindelsmärik*, last week in Nov. through Dec.

Musée Alsacien

If you have time to visit only one museum in Strasbourg, it should be the Musée Alsacien (Alsatian Museum), housed in a disorderly canalside building. Not only does it offer a chance to see the interior courtyards and inside of a 15th-century house, but it's crammed with displays illustrating traditional Alsatian life. Look for the votive pictures – naive religious paintings commissioned as prayer and thanks to God, and illustrating farm animals, children and loved ones.

➕ B1 ✉ 23–25 quai St.-Nicolas ☎ 03 88 52 50 01;

France

www.musees.strasbourg.eu ⏰ Wed.–Mon. 10–6
🚌 10; tram A, D 💳 $$, 1-day ticket for nine museums in Strasbourg $$, 3-day ticket $$$ (free to all first Sun. of the month)

Musée Archéologique

Strasbourg is proud of the Musée Archéologique (Archeological Museum), one of the most important museums of its kind in France. Imaginatively laid out, it's housed in the basement of the Palais Rohan (Rohan Palace) and takes visitors through the history of Alsace from 600,000 BC to AD 800. There are interesting prehistoric sections, but more appealing are the reminders of everyday life in Roman Gaul.

➕ C2 ✉ 2 place du Château ☎ 03 88 52 50 00; www.musees.strasbourg.eu ⏰ Wed.–Mon. 10–6 🚋 Tram A, B, C, D, F 💳 $$, 1-day ticket for nine museums in Strasbourg $$, 3-day ticket $$$ (free to all first Sun. of the month)

Musée d'Art Moderne et Contemporain (MAMCS)

The Musée d'Art Moderne et Contemporain (Modern and Contemporary Art Museum) is an airy building across the water from the Old Town. It covers painting and sculpture from 1870 to the present day. The room devoted to Gustave Doré gives a fine introduction to his many works of art.

➕ Off map at A2 ✉ 1 place Hans-Jean Arp ☎ 03 88 23 31 31; www.musees.strasbourg.eu ⏰ Tue.–Sun. 10–6 🚌 4, 10; tram B, F 🍴 Museum restaurant 💳 $$, 1-day ticket for nine museums in Strasbourg $$, 3-day ticket $$$ (free to all first Sun. of the month)

Musée des Beaux-Arts

The elegant first-floor rooms of the Palais Rohan (Rohan Palace) house the Musée des Beaux-Arts (Fine Arts Museum), a comprehensive provincial collection covering European paintings from the Middle Ages to 1870. Memling's *Polyptych of Earthly Vanity and Heavenly Redemption* steals the show, although the museum is justly proud of *La belle Strasbourgeoise*, by Nicolas de Largillière – a portrait of an enigmatic local lady. The ground floor of this same Renaissance building is home to the Musée des Arts Décoratifs (Decorative Arts Museum) and the Musée Archéologique (see left).

➕ C2 ✉ 2 place du Château ☎ 03 88 88 50 68; www.musees.strasbourg.eu ⏰ Wed.–Mon. 10–6 🚋 Tram A, B, C, D, F 💳 $$, 1-day ticket for nine museums in Strasbourg $$, 3-day ticket $$$ (free to all first Sun. of the month)

Musée des Arts Décoratifs ➕ C2 ✉ 2 place du Château ☎ 03 88 52 50 08; www.musees.strasbourg. eu ⏰ Wed.–Mon. 10–6 🚋 Tram A, B, C, D, F 💳 $$, 1-day ticket for nine museums in Strasbourg $$, 3-day ticket $$$ (free to all first Sun. of the month)

Musée de l'Œuvre Notre-Dame

The Musée de l'Œuvre Notre-Dame (Museum of the Works of Our Lady) occupies a building used from the 14th to 16th centuries for cathedral maintenance. In addition to the rambling warren of fine rooms and staircases, there are courtyards, one of which is planted with medicinal herbs and plants similar to a 13th-century garden. Some of the cathedral's most precious sculptures are kept here, including examples of 14th-century Gothic sculpture. The streamlined *Seven Wise Virgins* is a highlight, as is the group of singularly unintimidating lions from the cathedral's main facade.

➕ B1 ✉ 3 place du Château ☎ 03 88 52 50 00; www.musees.strasbourg.eu ⏰ Tue.–Sun. 10–6 🚋 Tram A, B, C, D, F 💳 $$, 1-day ticket for nine museums in Strasbourg $$, 3-day ticket $$$ (free to all first Sun. of the month)

Petite France

On the banks of the Ill river, at the west end of the town's historic center, cobbled streets of picturesque Little France are lined with medieval and Renaissance timbered houses, shaded by ancient trees. The area got its name in the 16th century, when sufferers of syphilis were isolated here, to keep them well away from "worthier" citizens.

➕ A1 ✉ place Benjamin-Zix 🚌 15; tram A, B, D, F 🍴 Le Baeckeoffe d'Alsace, see page 476

A Day in Strasbourg

You awake early in the morning, and your time in this wonderful old city is limited. Here's what to do: Spend an hour or so strolling around the historic center, visiting one of the daily produce markets, taking some photos in the morning light and nibbling on something delicious from one of the tempting *pâtisseries* (cake) shops. Around mid-morning head for the Ill river, near the Palais Rohan, and buy your ticket for one of the 70-minute boat tours of Strasbourg. On the tour you can sit back and listen to the English commentary about the city's history and important monuments. The tour circles the central island, passing churches, fine buildings and flower-hung, timber-framed houses before heading upstream to give you a glimpse of the modernistic glass-and-steel palaces housing the buildings connected with the European Union.

Head next for the cathedral, timing your visit so that you'll be there at 12:30, when the marvelous astronomical clock (see page 203) swings into action. For lunch there is a wide choice of pretty outdoor eating places serving local specialties, such as *tarte flambée* (onion tart).

If you enjoy museums, the afternoon's the time for checking out two of the best. At the top of the list is the Alsatian Museum (Musée Alsacien, see pages 203–204), closely followed by the Gothic treasures in the Museum of the Works of Our Lady (Musée de l'Œuvre Notre-Dame, see page 204). After this, you may be ready for a drink at a sidewalk café.

Evenings in Strasbourg feature a special dinner in one of the dozens of superb restaurants; be sure to eat a local dish, or follow the set menu, which is bound to be good. Afterward you can go to the movies (in English), a concert, enjoy a folklore display or simply stroll through the atmospheric old streets and have a nightcap at a music bar. For night owls, there are discos and clubs that stay open into the early hours.

🛈 Boat tours leave from the landing stage near the Palais Rohan, on two different tours, daily. There are many departures daily between 9:30 a.m. and 9:15 p.m. in July and August, and several departures between 9:45 a.m. and 5 p.m. in December. There are few sailings in January and February. Call Batorama (☎ 03 88 84 13 13; www.batorama.fr) for details 💲 \$\$–\$\$\$. Consult the tourist office about the 3-day inclusive "Strasbourg Pass" and for evening events

This half-timbered house is characteristic of the older houses in the center of the city

Germany

Opposite: Pleasure craft on the Mosel river at Cochem

Germany

Germany

Germany is not easily summed up. Before 1871 there was no single, unified German state: The area was made up of several territories, loosely knit together in alliance. Their local languages and loyalties still have first claim on many Germans' hearts.

After World War II, the country was split between two opposing powers: the West, whose territory was known as the Federal Republic of Germany; and the Soviets, who created the German Democratic Republic (GDR). In 1989, faced with popular protests and a retreating Soviet authority, the GDR's government opened the Berlin Wall, which had divided the city's eastern and western zones since 1961.

A year later the country was reunited, and a new Germany was born. But within its unified political boundaries this is still a nation of diversity, where the people and cultures vary as dramatically as the landscapes.

Traveling in Germany

Germany's 16 federal states (*Bundesländer*) extend from the tail of Denmark south to the Swiss and Austrian Alps; the Netherlands, Belgium, Luxembourg and France border on the

More Top Destinations in Germany

- Bamberg C2
- Berchtesgaden D1
- Bodensee C1
- Dresden D3
- Freiburg im Breisgau B1
- Goslar C3
- Hamburg C4
- Heidelberg B2
- Lübeck C5
- Mecklenburgische Seenplatte D4
- Regensburg D2
- Rheintal B3
- Sächsische Schweiz D3
- Trier B2
- Tübingen B2
- Ulm C1

DENMARK

BALTIC SEA

POLAND

CZECH REPUBLIC

AUSTRIA

SWITZERLAND

Flensburg
Schleswig
Kieler Bucht
Puttgarden
Kiel
A7
Heide
Brunsbüttel
A23
Neumünster
Itzehoe
A21
A27
Cuxhaven
Bremerhaven
Stade
A7
Lübeck
A1
A20
Wismar
Güstrow
Mecklenburger Bucht
Stralsund
Rostock
A20
Bad Doberan
Sassnitz
Rügen
Greifswald
Schwerin
Waren (Müritz)
Neubrandenburg
A19
Hamburg
A24
Parchim
Mecklenburgische Seenplatte
Neustrelitz
A20
Prenzlau
A39
Lüneburg
Ludwigslust
Idenburg
Bremen
Soltau
Uelzen
Wittenberge
Elbe
Neuruppin
Eberswalde
A11
Oder
A1
Salzwedel
A24
Nienburg (Weser)
Celle
Stendal
Brandenburg an der Havel
BERLIN
Frankfurt (Oder)
Weser
Hannover
Wolfsburg
A10
A12
A2
Braunschweig
A2
Potsdam
Treuenbrietzen
A13
Lübben (Spreewald)
Guben
rford
A2
Hildesheim
Wolfenbüttel
Magdeburg
Hamelu
Salzgitter
A9
Lutherstadt Wittenberg
Luckau
Cottbus
Bielefeld
Goslar
Halberstadt
Dessau-Rosslau
A15
Gütersloh
A7
Harz
Quedlinburg
Elbe
Lauchhammer
Paderborn
Northeim
A14
Lippstadt
Göttingen
Nordhausen
Halle (Saale)
A13
Bautzen
A38
Leipzig
Meissen
Görlitz
Kassel
Mühlhausen/Thüringen
Naumburg (Saale)
Colditz
Dresden
Neisse
Eisenach
Gotha
Erfurt
Weimar
Freiberg
Sächsische Schweiz
Zittau
Marburg
A4
Arnstadt
Jena
Gera
Chemnitz
A5
Alsfeld
Thüringer Wald
A71
Saale
Zwickau
Erzgebirge
Giessen
Fulda
Bad Neustadt an der Saale
A9
A72
Plauen
etzlar
A66
Bad Kissingen
Coburg
Hof
rankfurt m Main
Schweinfurt
A73
Bayreuth
Offenbach am Main
Aschaffenburg
Bamberg
Weiden in der Oberpfalz
Wiesbaden
inz
Darmstadt
A3
Würzburg
A9
Michelstadt
Odenwald
A7
Erlangen
Amberg
orms
Mannheim
Bad Mergentheim
Fürth
Nürnberg
Heidelberg
Ansbach
A93
Heilbronn
Dinkelsbühl
Fränkische Alb
A3
Regensburg
Karlsruhe
Schwäbisch Hall
Eichstätt
Donau
A8
Pforzheim
Nördlingen
Ingolstadt
aden-aden
Stuttgart
A92
Passau
Tübingen
A7
A9
Lech
Isar
Landshut
Reutlingen
A8
udenstadt
Ulm
Dachau
A94
A81
Hechingen
Augsburg
München (Munich)
berg
A96
Burghausen
Villingen
Donau
Kempten (Allgäu)
Rosenheim
Chiemsee
A95
A8
Berchtesgaden
Überlingen
Oberammergau
Bodensee
Konstanz
Füssen
Garmisch-Partenkirchen
2713m *Watzmann-Mittelspitze*
Lindau (Bodensee)
Lech
Mittenwald
2962m *Zugspitze*

C

D

E

west, Poland and the Czech Republic on the east. Each state has enough of interest to warrant a vacation in its own right, and Germans are themselves often tourists in their own country.

Traveling in Germany – by automobile or by public transportation – is not a problem, despite the country's size. The road network here is excellent, from the highways (*Autobahnen*) to minor roads.

The biggest culture shock to drivers is likely to be the speed of traffic. There is no official upper limit on some sections of German highways, and many drivers ignore, and drive in excess of, the recommended 130 k.p.h., the equivalent of which is 80 m.p.h. Driving etiquette is taken seriously, though: You can be stopped and fined for swearing or making rude gestures.

Taking the train is a convenient way to cover large areas. The quickest and most comfortable trains are the high-speed InterCityExpress (ICE) trains, and the somewhat slower InterCity (IC) and EuroCity (EC) trains linking major centers. Even the InterRegio (IR) trains connecting smaller towns are quite fast.

The North and the Baltic

Northern Germany has a maritime character. Schleswig-Holstein, a state Germans and Danes have often fought over, is made up of two former dukedoms and shares the coastline with Lower Saxony. Together they take in a shore ranging from the fjords and hills of the Baltic coast to wind-lashed North Sea beaches. Inland, the countryside is rolling farmland and peat bogs; offshore, the East Frisian, North Frisian and Baltic islands are favorite summer destinations, with beaches and brisk sea air. The inhabitants of coastal Friesland have their own culture and language.

Northern Germany's cities were a force to be reckoned with in the Middle Ages. In the interests of trade and power, they banded together to form the Hanseatic League, a federation of trading towns and seaports that monopolized trade between the North and Baltic seas. The league's merchants made huge fortunes and had impressive houses and churches built in seaports such as Hamburg, Lübeck and Bremen.

Some of their legacies have survived – or at least have been rebuilt after the heavy bombing raids of World War II. The Gothic/Renaissance architecture of Bremen's Town Hall and Lübeck's Music Academy, both converted from merchant homes, still suggest the affluence and style of the region's medieval heyday.

Lower Saxony has many features that are quintessentially German. Its historic center, Hannover, is a thriving commercial city; towns such as Celle, Brunswick, Hildesheim and Wolfenbüttel, the latter with its painted, half-timbered facades, have been partly restored after wartime damage.

The winter-sports resort of Goslar, once a silver- and lead-mining town, has picture-book streets and squares lined with Gothic, Renaissance and baroque buildings, some inscribed with gold lettering, others featuring curving, sinuous slate roofs. To the east are the Harz Mountains, on the old East–West border, where witches are said to celebrate their Sabbath on *Walpurgisnacht*, the eve of May Day.

The Rhine

The great 765-mile Rhine flows from the Swiss Alps across the western regions of Germany, through the ancient city of Koblenz and the former seat of West German government, Bonn, and through the industrial country of the Ruhr toward Rotterdam. Its valleys and those of its tributaries, the Mosel, Main, Nahe and Neckar, have been wine-producing (mainly white wines) areas since Roman times. Castles with fairy-tale Gothic towers loom over the river, built for their powerful princes' protection and profit, which was gleaned from tolls on passing river traffic.

Gilded statuary sits at the center of a pond in the grounds of Schloss Linderhof, built for Ludwig II

On the Lorelei rock, above a twisting Rhine gorge, the beautiful siren Lorelei is said to lure sailors to their death with her enchanting song. This is a myth-laden part of the country, and a river cruise is a popular way of seeing it.

The East

More than 20 years after German reunification, some parts of the old East Germany are still blighted to some degree by industrial decay, unemployment and depopulation. Many other parts, though, are booming and have regained much of their pre-War and pre-division cachet. Among the winners are Baltic seacoast islands, resorts and cities that can trace their upscale lineage back to the days of the Kaisers (19th century) and the Hanseatic League.

These include places like Rügen, Germany's largest island; the tiny resort of Heiligendamm, and former Hanseatic powerhouses like Rostock, Wismar and Stralsund. Inland from the seacoast, aristocratic towns like Schwerin and Güstrow, national parks, and the many hundreds of lakes in the state of Mecklenburg-Lower Pomerania, exert a magnetic pull on vacationers.

One of eastern Germany's highlights is Dresden, which re-created itself after devastation by more than 2,000 Allied bombers in 1945. Fine 18th-century buildings surround its Brühlsche Terrace, an elevated section on the bank of the Elbe river, and the nearby baroque Zwinger pavilions house a marvelous collection of museums. Leipzig, the famous medieval university town, also is worth visiting, with its pedestrian-only center and attractive gardens and squares.

Weimar, once the home of the poet and dramatist Johann Wolfgang von Goethe, composer Franz Liszt and philosopher Friedrich Nietzsche, has a core of lovely historic buildings, parks and boulevards.

The gentle hills and red-roofed villages of the Thüringian Forest form a stretch of popular walking country. This attractive region has a flourishing industry of family-run lodgings and restaurants to attract visitors.

The gilded clockface on the exterior of the Altes Rathaus (Old Town Hall) on Marienplatz in Munich

The Black Forest and Bavaria

Two states make up southern Germany: Baden-Württemberg in the southwest and Bavaria in the southeast. As the name suggests, Baden-Württemberg is itself made up of two distinct areas: mainly Catholic Baden, where the inhabitants are said to be amiable and easy-going, and traditionally Protestant Württemberg (Swabia), where the work ethic is strongly established and the Swabian dialect is spoken.

Lovers of the outdoors flock to the Black Forest (Schwarzwald), a swath of highlands reaching over 4,800 feet and encompassing attractive villages, lush valleys, orchards and meadows, as well as woods. Clock-making has been a successful industry here since the 1660s, and cuckoo clocks are on sale at every gift shop. The other notable local product is Black Forest cake – the authentic and superior original is called Schwarzwälder Kirschtorte.

East of the Black Forest there is an impressive range of limestone cliffs and hills known as the Swabian Jura, where castles peer down at the Danube

(Donau) river as it begins its long journey to the sea. Pleasant resorts surround the "Swabian Ocean," Lake Constance (Bodensee), which straddles the German-Austrian-Swiss border. The Neckar river flows through Swabia's vineyards and past romantic Heidelberg, where students and tourists really do raise huge beer tankards over tavern tables, as they did in Sigmund Romberg's operetta The Student Prince.

Clichés also come true in southern Bavaria. Here the people are characterized by their detractors as loud and brash, and by their admirers as humorous, warm and fun-loving. People are often seen dressed in traditional leather trousers (Lederhosen) or embroidered dresses, and are primarily Catholic and conservative: the standard daily greeting here is "Grüss Gott," or "God's greeting."

Between the Bavarian capital, Munich (München), and the magnificent Alpine peaks lie the wooded hills, pretty villages, lakes and castles that attract so many visitors from all over the world to this part of the country. The spectacular

Deutsche Alpenstrasse (German Alpine Road) takes in the mountain scenery and passes the theatrical 19th-century castles of Linderhof, Herrenchiemsee and Neuschwanstein.

Northern Bavaria has its own character. In fact, not everyone here appreciates being labeled "Bavarian." This is the region known as Franconia (Franken), and its main city is Nuremberg (Nürnberg). Architecture and art come into their own here. During the late Middle Ages and early Renaissance, artists such as Lucas Cranach and Albrecht Dürer were prominent in Germany, and Nuremberg's wonderful German National Museum displays some of their best work. A more sinister aspect of the city's past is recalled in the giant stadium and Hall of Congress, built for Hitler's mass rallies, and preserved as chilling memorials to that era.

The hugely popular Romantische Strasse (Romantic Road), running from ancient Würzburg and the Franconian wine country all the way to the Alps, 255 miles south, links several unspoiled medieval towns. On the way, it passes Rothenburg ob der Tauber, one of the loveliest old towns in Germany.

Also along this route are the old walled, half-timbered town of Dinkelsbühl and the wonderful Renaissance city of Augsburg.

Spa Towns

Health and fitness are national preoccupations, apparent in the German love of soccer, skiing and tennis, and in the spa towns that thrive all over the country. At these spas Germans reap the benefits of the medicinal waters and enjoy the other facilities, which can include mud baths, saunas and steam treatments.

Germany's oldest casino is one of the features of Baden-Baden, a celebrated spa town with graceful 19th-century hotels. Other spas also are worth investigating. Bad Ems, in the Rhineland's picturesque Lahn valley, was 19th-century ruler Kaiser Wilhelm's personal favorite. A steam train travels from Bad Doberan, near Rostock in eastern Germany, to the country's oldest seaside resort, Ostseebad Heiligendamm, founded in 1793. Bad Kissingen, Bavaria's most popular spa, is on the banks of the Saale river.

A view of Freiburg in the Black Forest region

Timeline

800–700 BC	Celtic tribes settle around the Rhineland.
AD 9	The Roman Empire is defeated in its campaign to conquer Germania east of the Rhine.
AD 800	Franks overrun the territory; Charlemagne, the Frankish king, is crowned Emperor of the West.
1241	Hamburg and Lübeck form an alliance, from which the Hanseatic League federation of trading cities evolved.
1273	Rudolf of Habsburg is elected king, founding the 600-year Habsburg dynasty.
1517	Martin Luther precipitates the Reformation.
1740	Frederick the Great is crowned king of Prussia.
1871	Franco-Prussian War ends with states united under the Prussian King and German Kaiser Wilhelm and chancellor, Otto von Bismarck.
1914–19	Habsburg claims to the Balkans lead to World War I; the Treaty of Versailles demands huge war reparations and surrender of territories from defeated Germany.
1930	The Nazis gain power in elections.
1933	Adolf Hitler is made chancellor; under Hitler's dictatorship, millions of Jews and minorities are persecuted and killed.
1939	Hitler invades Poland; Britain and France declare war on Germany.
1945	Allied forces enter Berlin; Hitler kills himself.
1949	Western occupying powers create the Federal Republic of Germany; Russia forms the German Democratic Republic.
1961	The Berlin Wall is built.
1989	Radical political change in East Germany leads to the opening of the Berlin Wall and jubilation on the streets.
1990	East and West Germany reunite.
1999	Government moves to Berlin. Parliament meets in the newly refurbished, glass-domed Reichstag.
2005	Angela Merkel is elected as the first woman Chancellor.
2009	Celebrations mark the 20th anniversary of the fall of the Berlin Wall.
2011	Compulsory military service is abolished.
2014	Germany's soccer team wins the 2014 World Cup in Brazil.
September 2015	The Prime Minister, Angela Merkel, announces that Germany will accept thousands of Syrian refugees.

Mad King Ludwig

Ludwig II of Bavaria lost all interest in running his kingdom after it was drawn first into war and then into the German Empire by the Prussian Chancellor, Otto von Bismarck. The late 19th-century ruler was left with nothing to do so he amused himself by having three flamboyant castles built – Herrenchiemsee, Linderhof and Neuschwanstein. Ludwig found other ways to spend his money, too, supporting Richard Wagner while he wrote his operas, but eventually he ran out of cash altogether. This, and his eccentric manner, made him an increasing liability to the Bavarian government. Its ministers plotted with Ludwig's uncle Luitpold to depose him and certify him insane. Only days later, Ludwig and his doctor drowned in the Starnberger See, a boating lake near Munich – whether by accident or design, no one knows.

Survival Guide

- Formality is important to Germans. Don't address people by their first names unless invited to; always use *Herr* (Sir) or *Frau* (Madam) at first.
- Job titles are used frequently in social exchange; doctors, for example, are addressed as *Frau Doktor* or *Herr Doktor*.
- Local dishes, particularly in southern Bavaria, use the classic German ingredients of sauerkraut (pickled cabbage), *Wurst* (sausage), dumplings, pork and potatoes. German cooking (*Gutbürgerliche Küche*) can be sampled at a *Gasthaus*, a restaurant serving simple meals.
- German wine is mainly white. *Tafelwein* is table wine, less expensive and harsher than the quality wines; *Deutscher Tafelwein* is guaranteed to be wholly German, rather than a mix of different countries' grapes. *Qualitätswein* is the better product, from a specified range of vineyards. Some of the best grapes are Riesling, the fruity Müller-Thurgau and the spicy Gewürztraminer.
- Brewing is big business in Germany. *Bock* is a strong beer, light or dark, popular in Bavaria; *Weissbier* is pale wheat beer; and *Malz*, an unfermented black malt beer.
- *Imbiss* (snack) stands are found everywhere and sell fast food.
- Stores in cities are usually open from 9 or 9:30 a.m. until 7 or 8 p.m., sometimes until 10 p.m. A few close on Saturday afternoons; most stores are closed on Sunday.
- Germany has a long tradition of toymaking, particularly china dolls and the famous Steiff teddy bears.
- Beer and wine festivals take place all over the country. Munich's *Oktoberfest* (September/October) is the best known, and the *Weinfeste*, celebrations held in the Rhine-Mosel area also are worth attending.
- Dinkelsbühl's 10-day *Kinderzeche* festival (July), recalls the Thirty Years War, when local children persuaded Swedish soldiers not to ransack their town. It features plays, a pageant and the *Knabenbataillon* (boys' battalion) in 18th-century military garb.
- The music of Richard Wagner is performed in the summer *Bayreuther Festspiele* (Bayreuth Festival), northeast of Nuremberg near the composer's former home. Tickets are snapped up a year in advance, and must be reserved online or by mail; for information and an application form contact Bayreuther Festspiele, Kartenbüro, Postfach 100262, 95402 Bayreuth, Germany, ☎ 0921 7878-780; www.bayreuther-festspiele. de. If you want to order a ticket for the first time, you must request an application form or complete an online application. All orders must be received by October 20.

The Berliner chocolate shop inside the huge KaDeWe department store in Berlin

Berlin

Berlin has had its highs and its lows, but while not everything in today's Berlin is idyllic, there's no doubt that this time is one of the highs. As a visitor here, you'll encounter a city that's going places, that's filled with a vibrant creative energy, and that holds a natural place as one of Europe's great capitals.

For nearly 30 years Berlin was, for all intents and purposes, two cities. Tourists posed on the Western side of the Berlin Wall, and those who crossed the East–West boundary at Checkpoint Charlie did so with the trepidation of travelers visiting another planet.

Then, in 1989, Berlin changed virtually overnight. The wall has all but vanished; Checkpoint Charlie is a museum; and the No Man's Land that lay between the two zones is now the site of a new complex of offices, stores and hotels.

Berlin Flavors

There are many restaurants and cafés in Berlin, serving every imaginable kind of food. The most popular restaurant areas are around Savignyplatz and Hardenbergstrasse and on Ku'damm (Kurfürstendamm), and all buzz late into the night. Berlin has a larger Turkish community than any other city outside Turkey, and many live in the old quarter of Kreuzberg, where inexpensive Turkish meals are served in dozens of restaurants, especially in the neighborhood of Kottbusser Tor. Oranienstrasse, one of Kreuzberg's main streets, reflects the area's Turkish character – even more so the farther east you go.

Kaffee und Kuchen (coffee and cakes) is an institution, usually indulged at about 4 p.m., but it doesn't come cheap. The café that started it all – Café Kranzler, which opened in 1835 – still operates on Ku'damm.

Heavy, hearty German food can be sampled all over the city, in restaurants or in a tavern (*Kneipe*). There are more than 4,000 taverns, many offering *Hackepeter* (meatloaf), *Aal grün* (eel in parsley sauce) and *Soleier* (pickled eggs). If you find the traditional fare daunting, try the lighter new German cuisine (*neue Deutsche Küche*).

Beer is, of course, a favorite beverage. One popular custom is to have a light beer with a *Schnaps* chaser; another German preference is *Berliner Weisse mit Schuss*, light wheat beer that is turned pink with a dash of raspberry syrup or turned green with some extract of woodruff.

Music and Cabaret

There are cabaret clubs all over the city as well as folk, jazz and other music venues. To find out what is on, consult listings available from tourist offices, or the English-language Berlin magazine *ExBerliner* (www.exberliner.com).

The Berlin Philharmonic has its home at the Philharmonie, in the Kulturforum (see page 220), a large complex of concert halls and museums near Potsdamer Platz. The Berlin Symphony Orchestra performs at the Philharmonie and in the 19th-century Konzerthaus

Berlin (Berlin Concert House), on Gendarmenmarkt. Berlin's oldest opera house (built 1743) is the Staatsoper (State Opera), a fine neoclassical concert hall on Unter den Linden – its glittering list of past directors includes big names such as Felix Mendelssohn Bartholdy. Its completion, after several years of major building works, reveals an opera house for the 21st century.

Store of the West

One of Europe's biggest department stores is Berlin's KaDeWe (Kaufhaus des

Westens, or Store of the West), on Tauentzienstrasse. A branch of Galeries Lafayette is on Friedrichstrasse, near designer shops on the same street, and the Europa-Center complex has 99 stores, cafés and bars.

Berlin porcelain makes a perfect souvenir. It has been produced here since 1763, when the Royal Porcelain Manufactory opened (KPM, Wegelystrasse 1; tours, in German, Sat. 3 p.m. Call to book ☎ 030 390 090).

Street markets flourish in Berlin; on weekends try Strasse des 17. Juni, Tiergarten, Am Zeughaus or John F.-Kennedy-Platz, and the popular Saturday-morning Winterfeldtmarkt on Winterfeldtplatz is a lively affair.

Berlin Classicism

Sculptor, painter, set designer and architect Karl Friedrich Schinkel (1781–1841) left his mark all over Berlin. After designing the Prussians' military medal, the Iron Cross, he was commissioned to create a series of civic buildings, including the National Theater, the Old Museum on Museum Island and St. Nicholas' Church in Potsdam. He mixed his own Romantic tastes with the royally approved Classical style to form "Berlin Classicism," and gave his undivided attention to every detail, right down to the doorknobs. Despite his involvement in the movement, Schinkel moved away from Classicism in later life.

Essential Information

Tourist Information
Visit Berlin
Service Center ☎ 030 25 00 23 33, 00 49 30 25 00 23 33 (from abroad); www.visitberlin.de
Berlin Tourist Information offices
☎ 030 25 00 25
Hauptbahnhof (Central Station), Floor 0, North entrance, Europa Platz 1, daily 8 a.m.–10 p.m.
Neues Kranzler Eck Passage, Kurfürstendamm 22, Mon.–Sat. 9:30–8
Brandenburger Tor (Brandenburg Gate) South Wing, Pariser Platz, daily 9:30–7, Apr.–Oct.; 9:30–6, rest of year
At Berlin Airports: Tegel, daily 8 a.m.–9 p.m.; Schönefeld Terminal A, daily 8–8

Urban Transportation
There are two city rail networks: the U-Bahn (subway) and the city S-Bahn (railroad). Tickets are interchangeable. U-Bahn stations are identified by a white "U" on a blue background (often a circle), and S-Bahn stations by a white "S" in a green circle. Buy tickets (valid for all transportation) in the station foyer; validate them in the machine on the platform. Trains run daily 5 a.m.–12:30 a.m. and all through the night Fri.–Sat. Bus route 100 runs through the center from Bahnhof Zoo (Zoo station) in the west to Unter den Linden in the east. The long-distance bus terminal is the ZOB, at the Congress Center (Messegelände). Information on all Berlin transportation is available from BVG ☎ 030 19 449; www.bvg.de; for the S-Bahn, ☎ 030 297 43 333; www.s-bahn-berlin.de. For taxis call ☎ 26 10 26 or 20 20 20 or at city stands.

Airport Information
Berlin has two airports, Tegel and Schönefeld. The new Berlin Brandenburg Airport, should be open by 2018. For information on airports ☎ 030 609 11150; www.berlin-airport.de.

Climate – average highs and lows for the month

Jan.	Feb.	Mar.	Apr.	May	Jun.	Jul.	Aug.	Sep.	Oct.	Nov.	Dec.
2°C	3°C	8°C	12°C	18°C	21°C	23°C	23°C	18°C	13°C	7°C	3°C
36°F	37°F	46°F	54°F	64°F	70°F	73°F	73°F	64°F	55°F	45°F	37°F
-3°C	-3°C	0°C	2°C	7°C	11°C	13°C	13°C	10°C	5°C	2°C	-1°C
27°F	27°F	32°F	36°F	45°F	52°F	55°F	55°F	50°F	41°F	36°F	30°F

Berlin Sights

Key to symbols
➕ map coordinates refer to the Berlin map on pages 216–217 💷 admission charge: $$$ more than €10, $$ €3–€10, $ less than €3
See page 5 for complete key to symbols

Alexanderplatz

Germany's largest square, and known to Berliners as "Alex," was the heart of the old city and the center of former East Berlin. Two old buildings have survived: the Rotes Rathaus (Red City Hall), built from 1861 to 1869 in Italian Renaissance style; and the St. Marienkirche (St. Mary's Church), built from 1270 to 1340 and Berlin's second-oldest parish church.

At the center of the square, the iconic Fernsehturm, a 1,207-foot television tower, has a revolving restaurant and a viewing platform at the top.

➕ E3 ✉ Alexanderplatz ☎ Fernsehturm: 030 2475 75875; www.tv-turm.de. St. Marienkirche: 2475 9510; www.marienkirche-berlin.de ◷ Fernsehturm: daily 9 a.m.–midnight, Mar.–Oct.; 10 a.m.–midnight, rest of year. St. Marienkirche: daily 10–8, Apr.–Sep.; 10–6, rest of year ◉ U-Bahn/S-Bahn to Alexanderplatz 🚌 100, 200, 248, N2, N42, TXL; tram M2, M4, M5, M6 🍴 Restaurant in Fernsehturm 💷 Fernsehturm $$$; St. Marienkirche: free ℹ St. Marienkirche: guided tours by appointment (☎ 030 247 595 10)

Bauhaus-Archiv

After World War I Walter Gropius founded an architectural movement in Weimar known as "form follows function," stressing function above beauty and encouraging collaboration between art and industry.

The Bauhaus (Building House) school's theory influenced 20th-century design, but was closed in Berlin by the Nazis in 1933. The Gropius-designed Bauhaus-Archiv (Bauhaus Archive), built between 1976 and 1979, shows the style and explains the aims of the Bauhaus artists.

➕ C2 ✉ Klingelhöferstrasse 14 ☎ 030 254 0020; www.bauhaus.de ◷ Wed.–Mon. 10–5 ◉ U-Bahn

The Brandenburg Gate on Pariser Platz

to Nollendorfplatz 🚌 100, 106, 187, M29 🍴 Café on site 💷 $$

Berliner Dom

Berliner Dom, Berlin's Protestant Cathedral, completed in 1905, is a monument to imperial wealth and power, and contains approximately 90 sarcophagi and some tombs of the royal Hohenzollern dynasty in its vault.

➕ E3 ✉ Am Lustgarten ☎ 030 202 69119; www.berlinerdom.de ◷ Mon.–Sat. 9–8, Sun. noon–8, Apr.–Sep.; Mon.–Sat. 9–7, Sun. noon–7, rest of year ◉ U-Bahn/S-Bahn to Alexanderplatz; S-Bahn to Hackescher Markt 🚌 100, 200, N2; tram M4, M5, M6 🍴 Restaurants and cafés nearby 💷 $$ ℹ Guided tours Mon.–Sat. 10:15, 11, 12:30, 1:30, 2:30 and 3:30, Sun. noon, 1 and 2

Brandenburger Tor

Built from 1788 to 1791 as an "arch of peace," the Brandenburger Tor (Brandenburg Gate) was modeled after the entrance to the Acropolis temple in Athens. A sculpture of the goddess Victory and her chariot, added to the top of the gate between 1789 and 1793, was stolen by Napoleon in 1806. After it was returned, Karl Friedrich Schinkel added a triumphal wreath and iron cross to the goddess' staff. During the East–West split, it stood in the area known as No Man's Land. Now a symbol of reconciliation, the city's historic landmark is a key tourist destination.

✚ D3 ✉ Pariser Platz 🚇 U-Bahn/S-Bahn to Brandenburger Tor 🚌 100

Denkmal für die Ermordeten Jüden Europas

A powerful and moving monument to the 6 million Jews who were victims of the Nazis, the somber Memorial for the Murdered Jews of Europe – also known as the Holocaust-Denkmal (Holocaust Memorial) – occupies a rectangular space covering 2 square miles, filled with 2,711 gray concrete stelae of varying heights. The maze looks from a distance like a vast field of headstones. In an underground information center, the Holocaust's terrible human cost is carefully documented.

✚ D2 ✉ Cora-Berliner-Strasse 1 ☎ 030 263 94336; www.stiftung-denkmal.de ⏰ Memorial open permanently; Information Center Tue.–Sun. 10–8, Apr.–Sep.; 10–7 rest of year 🚇 U-Bahn/S-Bahn to Brandenburger Tor 🚌 100, 200, M85, TXL 💳 Free

Kaiser-Wilhelm-Gedächtniskirche

The Kaiser-Wilhelm-Gedächtniskirche (Kaiser William Memorial Church) is worth visiting as a memorial to the devastation of World War II. The 19th-century Romanesque hall was all that remained of Kaiser Wilhelm II's church after the 1945 air raids; it has been left as it was, and an octagonal chapel and hexagonal blue stained-glass tower were added to it from 1957 to 1963. Inside, the church displays a cross of nails donated by Coventry, in Britain – another city devastated by bombs.

✚ B2 ✉ Breitscheidplatz ☎ 030 218 5023; www. gedaechtniskirche-berlin.de ⏰ Church: daily 9–7; guided tours start in the Memorial Hall in the Ruined Tower: Mon.–Sat. at 1:15, 2 and 3. Mon., Fri. and Sat. also at 10:15, 11 and noon 🚇 U-Bahn/S-Bahn to Zoologischer Garten; U-Bahn to Kurfürstendamm 🚌 M19, M29, M46, X9, X10, X34, 100, 109, 145, 200, 204, 245 💳 Free

Kulturforum

World-class museums, art galleries and concert halls cluster in modernist buildings edging Potsdamer Platz. Highlights include the Gemäldegalerie (Picture Gallery) displaying European masterpieces from the 13th to the 18th centuries; the Kunstgewerbemuseum (Museum of Decorative Arts) and the Kupferstichkabinett (Museum of Prints and Drawings). The Neue Nationalgalerie is closed until 2020. Music lovers shouldn't miss the Philharmonie and Kammermusiksaal (Philharmonic and Chamber Music Hall), home to the Berlin Philharmonic Orchestra and Musikinstrumenten-Museum (MIM; Museum of Musical Instruments).

✚ C2 ✉ Gemäldegalerie, Kunstgewerbemuseum, Kupferstichkabinett: Mattäikirchplatz. Philharmonie: Herbert-von-Karajanstrasse 1. Musikinstrumenten-Museum (MIM): Ben-Gurion-Strasse ☎ Gemäldegalerie: 030 266 424242; www.smb. museum. MIM: 030 254 81178; www.sim.spk-berlin.de ⏰ Gemäldegalerie: Tue., Wed. and Fri. 10–6, Thu. 10–8, Sat.–Sun. 11–6. Kunstgewerbemuseum, Kupferstichkabinett: Tue.–Fri. 10–6, Sat.–Sun. 11–6. MIM: Tue.–Fri. 9–5, Thu. 9–8, Sat.–Sun. 10–5 🚇 U-Bahn/S-Bahn to Potsdamer Platz; S-Bahn S1, S2, S25 to Potsdamer Platz 🚌 M29, M41, M48, M85, 200 🍴 Cafés on site 💳 Kulturforum area ticket $$$, 3-day Museum Pass Berlin $$$

Museum Haus am Checkpoint Charlie

The crossing point of the Berlin Wall, known as Haus am Checkpoint Charlie (House at Checkpoint Charlie), is now a tourist attraction. The Eastern border guards' hut was taken down and moved to the Deutsches Historisches Museum on Unter den Linden (see page 221).

Displays at the site's Mauermuseum illustrate the effects of the wall and some escape attempts. A video on the history of the wall includes a look at the graffiti artists who decorated the Western side.

✚ D2 ✉ Friedrichstrasse 43–45 ☎ 030 253 7250; www.mauermuseum.de ⏰ Mauermuseum: daily 9 a.m.–10 p.m. 🍴 Café on site 🚇 U-Bahn to Kochstrasse 🚌 M29 💳 $$$

Museumsinsel

The first of a group of five imposing museum buildings was begun on an island in the Spree river in 1830. In 1841, Frederick William IV designated the area a "sanctuary for art and science." Ravaged by war and the East–West divide, work on the restoration of the museum complex is expected to continue until 2025–26. The Alte Nationalgalerie (Old National Gallery), modeled on the Acropolis in Athens, displays 19th-century German art and French Impressionist paintings. The baroque Bode Museum is renowned for its sculpture collection and Byzantine art. The Neues Museum (New Museum) displays 6,000 years of human history; its showstopper is a bust of Egyptian Queen Nefertiti. Reconstruction continues on the neoclassical Altes Museum (Old Museum), housing Greek and Roman antiquities, and on the monumental Pergamonmuseum, which attracts over a million visitors a year (the Pergamon Altar is closed until 2019).

➕ E3 ✉ Museumsinsel, Am Lustgarten/Bodestrasse ☎ 030 2090 5577; www.smb.museum 🕐 Tue., Wed. and Fri.–Sun. 10–6, Thu. 10–8 🚇 U-Bahn/S-Bahn to Friedrichstrasse; S-Bahn to Hackescher Markt; U-Bahn to Weinmeisterstrasse/Gipsstrasse 🚌 100, 200, TXL; tram M4, M5, M6 to Hackescher Markt; M1, 12 to Am Kupfergraben 🍴 Cafés on site 🎟 $$$

Schloss Charlottenburg

When work started on the Schloss Charlottenburg (Charlottenburg Palace) in 1695, it was designed as a rural home for Sophie-Charlotte, wife of the future King Fredrick I of Prussia. Over the next 100 years it grew into a sprawling palace with royal apartments, dazzling rooms such as the White Hall and Golden Gallery, and gardens in formal French and landscaped English style.

➕ A3 ✉ Spandauer Damm 10–22 ☎ 0331 969 4200; www.spsg.de 🕐 Tue.–Sun. 10–6., Apr.–Oct.; 10–5, rest of year 🚇 U-Bahn to Richard-Wagner-Platz or Sophie-Charlotte-Platz; S-Bahn to Westend 🚌 M45, 109, 309, X21 🍴 Café on site 🎟 Combination ticket for all buildings $$$

Tiergarten

Once a well-stocked hunting ground, the Tiergarten (Animal Garden) is a 524-acre park in the center of the city, with woodlands, lakes and waterways, gardens and a network of walking and cycling paths. Landscaping first began in 1818. The park is divided by the Strasse des 17. Juni, where the 1873 Siegessäule (victory column) commemorates Prussian successes against Denmark, Austria and France.

➕ C2 ✉ Around Strasse des 17. Juni 🚇 S-Bahn to Tiergarten 🚌 100, 123, 200, 248, 341, TXL

Topographie des Terrors

The grim Topographie des Terrors (Topography of Terror) occupies the site of the former Nazi secret police headquarters. Photographs trace the emergence of Nazism, and a nearby viewing platform overlooks the enormous Regierungsviertel (Government Quarter), where the Third Reich had its administrative offices.

➕ D2 ✉ Niederkirchnerstrasse 8 ☎ 030 254 509-50; www.topographie.de 🕐 Daily 10–8 🚇 U-Bahn to Potsdamer Platz or Kochstrasse; S-Bahn to Anhalter Bahnhof or Potsdamer Platz 🚌 M29, M41 🍴 Café on site 🎟 Free

Unter den Linden

Unter den Linden (Under the Lime Trees) was laid out in 1648 as a route to Tiergarten. It runs from the Brandenburg Gate to Museum Island and the river, and is lined with baroque and neoclassical buildings. The 1695 Zeughaus (Arsenal) houses the Deutsches Historisches Museum (German History Museum). An equestrian statue of Frederick the Great at the eastern end was turned by the Communist regime to ride toward the East rather than the West.

➕ D3 ✉ Deutches Historisches Museum: Unter den Linden 2 ☎ Museum: 030 2030 4444; www.dhm.de 🕐 Museum: daily 10–6 🚇 U-Bahn to Französische Strasse, Hausvogteiplatz or Friedrichstrasse; S-Bahn to Hackescher Markt or Friedrichstrasse 🚌 100, 200, TXL 🎟 Museum $$

The Berlin Wall

On August 13, 1961, shortly after East German leader Walter Ulbricht had stated that there was "no intention of building a wall," the German Democratic Republic began work on an "Anti-Fascist Protection Wall." Relations between the Eastern and Western sectors of Berlin had never been easy. The Soviets closed off their access routes in 1948, so supplies had to be flown in from the West in a year-long airlift. There had been popular protests against the Soviet authorities, and a steady exodus of East Berliners to the West. Finally the Eastern government decided to mark its boundary with bricks and barbed wire.

The border was based on a 1920 map of Berlin, and this was the course taken by the wall without regard for any houses or streets that might be in the way. The houses on Bernauer Strasse (Bernauer Street), which happened to be on the route, became part of the barrier, and their exits were bricked up. Residents tried to jump to freedom from the upper windows; 20 people were shot down. One guard took a last opportunity to leap over the temporary barbed wire entanglement when the wall was under construction. Those who didn't make it across were cut off from the West and from their friends and families as the 70 miles of 12-foot-high barricade took shape.

After the escape of 30 people through a tunnel from a bakery cellar in 1964, a large part of Bernauer Street was demolished, and a No Man's Land, or "death strip," was created, guarded by dogs and 302 watchtowers, and wide enough for tanks and vehicles to patrol. Booby traps were sunk into the Teltow canal, at the point where the border crossed the Spree river, after Günter Litfin was shot trying to swim his way to the West, on August 24, 1961. As the restrictions increased, the escapes grew more daring. One steamship's crew got the captain drunk and shut him in his cabin before sailing to the western bank. A homemade hot-air balloon was used to float over the wall. But the risks were very high: 239 people were killed in these attempts, including 25 guards.

At 9:15 p.m. on November 9, 1989, under pressure from an increasingly impatient crowd, border guards finally lifted the barriers and let Easterners cross the border freely for the first time for more than 40 years. Fittingly, the first to cross the divide were residents of Bernauer Street.

Souvenir pieces of the Berlin Wall that were gathered after its destruction in 1989

An Excursion to Potsdam

Visits to several palaces can be combined on a trip to Potsdam, southwest of Berlin. The setting for the 1945 Potsdam Conference, at which Allied leaders redrew the European map, was Cecilienhof Palace (Schloss Cecilienhof), a 1916 mock-Tudor building now partly used as a hotel.

It was built for Kaiser Wilhelm II; although his nation was two years into a war with Britain, the Kaiser chose to have it built in the style of an English country house. Those of the imperial Hohenzollern family not in exile lived here until 1945. The conference hall, delegates' studies and the reception rooms used by Churchill, Truman and Stalin are unchanged and can all be seen.

The palace that really draws crowds to Potsdam is the Sanssouci Palace (Schloss Sanssouci). This summer retreat was where Frederick the Great could enjoy life "without care" (*sans souci*).

A green dome tops the single-story, yellow rococo facade; inside, the richly furnished rooms are full of artworks and ornaments. Sanssouci Park has lovely gardens, an 18th-century Chinese teahouse and the third Potsdam palace: Frederick's New Palace (Neues Palais), with its vast marble hall and indoor grotto beautifully decorated with shells.

The town of Potsdam also is worth seeing. St. Nicholas' Church (Nikolaikirche) is one of Karl Friedrich Schinkel's classical monuments. In the Old Town, sculptures of rearing horses mark the site of the former royal stables, and the 17th-century Marstall building is now a movie museum. Built in 1732, the New Town became the focus of Potsdam's exiled French Huguenot (Protestant) community. Some of the original redbrick, gabled houses survive in what became known as the Dutch Quarter, as it was home to the many Dutch construction workers.

🕿 Cecilienhof Palace, Sanssouci Palace and New Palace: 0331 969 4200; www.spsg.de

🕐 Cecilienhof and Sanssouci palaces: Tue.–Sun. 10–6, Apr.–Oct.; 10–5, rest of year. Sanssouci Park: daily dawn–dusk. New Palace: Wed.–Mon. 10–6, Apr.–Oct.; 10–5, rest of year 🚌 612, 614, 650, 695 or the S-Bahn (Potsdam Stadt) from Berlin to Potsdam; from there bus 605, 606, 695 to Neues Palais. Tour operators in Berlin offer day trips by bus (inquire at the tourist office) 🎟 Cecilienhof Palace $$; Sanssouci Palace $$$ (guided tour only); New Palace $$

The Neues Palais (New Palace) was built for Frederick II on the western side of Sanssouci Park

Cologne

The skyline of Cologne (Köln) is dominated by the 515-foot-tall twin spires of the Cathedral that soar above the Rhine, reminders of its past glory as a center of pilgrimage and the biggest city in medieval Germany. Despite the destruction of most of its central core through heavy bombing during World War II, the city has retained and restored considerable evidence of its long and distinguished past. Today Cologne is thriving again, in business, trade, the arts and education, and its inhabitants' renowned sense of fun adds to the character that makes it one of Germany's most attractive cities.

Old Town

Cologne's Old Town (Altstadt) forms a vast semicircle on the west bank of the Rhine (Rhein) river, hemmed in by the Ring, a long boulevard that changes names along its route. The Old Town extends along the line of the former city fortifications and passes the old city gates of Eigelsteintor, Hahnentor and St. Severinstor.

Within this area, the Cathedral (Dom, see page 227) is the main attraction and, in fact, the most visited monument in Germany. The railroad station and a group of major museums are within easy reach of it.

Passenger barges on the Rhine near the cathedral

The Gothic-Renaissance Town Hall (Rathaus, see page 228) stands at the heart of the Old Town, just south of Alter Markt (Old Market Square); to the east, toward the river, is the 12th-century church of Gross St. Martin (see page 227), one of 12 wonderful pre-Gothic churches still standing in the city. These sights form the old core.

Head across the river via the bridges Deutzer Brücke (90 feet wide) or Hohenzollern Brücke for a look back at an unrivaled view of historic Cologne.

Cafés and Taverns

There are 24 breweries here, more than in any other German city. All produce the refreshing local beer, *Kölsch*, which is light and clear and served in tall, slim glasses. (*Kölsch* is also the name of the dialect spoken by natives of Cologne.) Beer halls, known in the local dialect as *Weetschaften*, also serve food at very reasonable prices. Specialties at these establishments include rolls with cheese (*Halve Hahn*) or rye bread with black sausage (*Kölsche Kaviar*).

You will find plenty of restaurants in the historic center, ranging from the traditional *Gasthaus* (tavern) to trendy bistros, and the range of cuisines includes Japanese, French, Burmese, Chinese, Turkish and East European. Wine bars and cellars are another source of refreshment, serving some of the excellent wines from the Rhine valley. There are many cafés in which to stop for the ubiquitious *Kaffee und Kuchen* (coffee and cakes).

Karneval and Concerts

To see Cologne at its most boisterous, come to the city before Easter for Carnival (*Karneval*) week. Precise dates change every year, but the celebrations and fun always reach a peak before Ash Wednesday, in time for the abstinence of Lent.

On the Thursday before the seventh Sunday prior to Easter, the festival begins in a morning ceremony at Old

Market Square, and everyone gears up for the three "Crazy Days" *(Tolle Tage)* – Thursday, Sunday and Monday.

There are costume balls at night, and more informal revelry on the streets and in the taverns. On Sunday there's a procession of floats, and on Rose Monday a spectacular parade provides the lively and colorful climax.

For the rest of the year, there is a choice of calmer entertainment at the city's main cultural centers. Concerts are performed at the Philharmonie, beside the Wallraf-Richartz/Ludwig museums building, which is located on Bischofsgartenstrasse.

Other concerts take place regularly in the city's churches and are usually free. Opera is staged at the Opernhaus. Cologne has a famous puppet theater – the Puppenspiele – but dialogue is in the local *Kölsch* dialect.

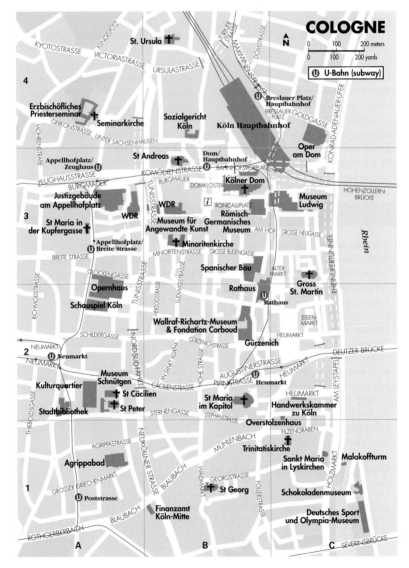

COLOGNE

0 100 200 meters
0 100 200 yards

Ⓤ U-Bahn (subway)

4

Kyotostrasse
Klingelpütz
Victoriastrasse
Ursulastrasse
St. Ursula

Turiner Strasse
Maximinenstrasse
Domstrasse

Ⓤ Breslauer Platz/ Hauptbahnhof
Breslauer Platz
Goldgasse

Erzbischöfliches Priesterseminar
Gereonstrasse
Seminarkirche
Unter Sachsenhausen
Sozialgericht Köln
Köln Hauptbahnhof
Oper am Dom

Konrad-Adenauer-Ufer

Mohrenstrasse
Zeughausstrasse
Appellhofplatz/ Zeughaus Ⓤ
St Andreas
Komödienstrasse
Burgmauer
Dom/ Hauptbahnhof
Bahnhofsvorplatz
Kölner Dom

Hohenzollern-Brücke

Justizgebäude am Appellhofplatz
Burgmauer
Domkloster

3

St Maria in der Kupfergasse
WDR
Tunisstrasse
WDR
Museum für Angewandte Kunst
ℹ Roncalliplatz
Römisch-Germanisches Museum
Am Hof
Grosse Neugasse
Museum Ludwig

Appellhofplatz/ Breite Strasse Ⓤ
Breite Strasse
Glockengasse
Minoritenstrasse
Minoritenkirche
Grosse Budengasse

Richmodstrasse
Opernhaus
Schauspiel Köln
Tunisstrasse
Herzogstrasse
Ludwigstrasse
Spanischer Bau
Alter Markt
Rathaus
Gross St. Martin
Rheinufertunnel
Rhein

Ⓤ Rathaus

Schildergasse
Nord-Süd-Fahrt
Wallraf-Richartz-Museum & Fondation Corboud
Gürzenichstrasse
Gürzenich
Heumarkt
Eisen-Markt

Deutzer Brücke

2

Ⓤ Neumarkt
Neumarkt
Neumarkt
Kulturquartier
Museum Schnütgen
An Sankt Agatha
Cäcilienstrasse
Augustinerstrasse
Ⓤ Heumarkt
Pipinstrasse Heumarkt
Heumarkt
Am Leystapel

Thieboldsgasse
Stadtbibliothek
St Cäcilien
St Peter
Sternengasse
St Maria im Kapitol
Stephanstrasse
Handwerkskammer zu Köln

Overstolzenhaus
Filzengraben

Agrippastrasse
Neuköllner Strasse
Blaubach
Mühlenbach
Trinitatiskirche
Sankt Maria in Lyskirchen
Holzmarkt
Malakoffturm

1

Agrippabad
Grosser Griechenmarkt
Georgstrasse
St Georg
Folerstrasse
Schokoladenmuseum

Ⓤ Poststrasse
Finanzamt Köln-Mitte
Deutsches Sport und Olympia-Museum

Rothgerberbach
Blaubach

Severinsbrücke

A
B
C

Listings for movies, theater and concerts are published in the magazines *Kölner Illustrierte, StadtRevue* and *Köln-Magazin.*

Nightclubs and discos are concentrated on the streets around Gross St. Martin; in the St. Severin quarter, Südstadt; and in the university quarter – the Kwartier Lateng, in the southwest part of the city.

Eau de Cologne

Probably the most appropriate souvenir to take home from Cologne is a bottle of the world's most famous fragrance, *eau de Cologne*, first distilled from flower blossoms by an Italian immigrant in the 18th century and intended as an aphrodisiac. Known here as *Kölnisch Wasser*, it's made by about 20 local businesses, including one of the originals, Farina, which has been in operation since 1709. Stores all over the city sell it, but the Old Town is the best place to browse around for gifts.

An all-day market takes place each Friday in the Old Market Square. On spring weekends, during April and May, the same square is completely taken over by hundreds of flower stalls. Wine markets set up in New Market to sell their wares in May and late June. Just before Lent Cologne celebrates *Karneval* (Carnival), and all shops close during the "Crazy Days."

Crazy Days

On the first of the *Tolle Tage* (Crazy Days) of Carnival, a procession takes place based on the local legend of Jan and Griet. Jan von Werth worked for a farmer and was very much in love with Griet, who refused him, hoping to find a wealthy husband. In desperation, Jan went off to fight in the Thirty Years War. However, he came back many years later as a highly honored hero who went on to become a general.

Essential Information

Tourist Information

KölnTourismus (Cologne Tourist Office)
Kardinal-Höffner-Platz 1, in front of the cathedral ☎ 0221 346430; www.koeln tourismus.de; www.cologne-tourism.com

Urban Transportation

Cologne has an integrated transportation system. Trams travel through the Old Town, some above ground (east–west lines), some underground (north–south lines). U-Bahn (subway) stations are identified by a white "U" on a blue background. Tickets are sold individually or for groups of up to five people (valid 9 a.m.–3 a.m.); you can also buy a 7-day

travel card. The bus and railroad stations are next to the Cathedral. Information is available from Cologne transportation company, KVB ☎ 0180 650 4030; www.kvb-koeln.de. For a taxi, call TAXI RUF Köln ☎ 0221 2882.

Airport Information

Köln Bonn Airport (www.koeln-bonn-airport. de) is approximatley 20 minutes by taxi from the city center. Suburban (S-Bahn) trains operate from the airport to the city center, and InterCity Express (ICE) trains take passengers to destinations across Germany. Call for flight information ☎ 02203 40 4001 (24 hours).

Climate – average highs and lows for the month

Jan.	Feb.	Mar.	Apr.	May	Jun.	Jul.	Aug.	Sep.	Oct.	Nov.	Dec.
3°C	4°C	10°C	14°C	19°C	22°C	24°C	24°C	20°C	14°C	8°C	3°C
37°F	39°F	50°F	57°F	66°F	72°F	75°F	75°F	68°F	57°F	46°F	37°F
-2°C	-2°C	0°C	4°C	8°C	12°C	14°C	13°C	10°C	6°C	3°C	0°C
28°F	28°F	32°F	39°F	46°F	54°F	57°F	55°F	50°F	43°F	37°F	32°F

Cologne Sights

Detail of reliquary busts in St. Ursula's church

Gross St. Martin

From its consecration in 1172 until the 19th century, the church of Gross St. Martin was the most distinctive feature of Cologne's skyline. Its tower, with four turrets at the corners, makes an interesting contrast to the lacy stonework of the spires.

Originally this was a monastery church, built for Benedictine monks from Ireland and Scotland.

➕ C3 ✉ An Gross St. Martin ☎ 0221 277 94747 🕐 Tue.–Fri. 10–noon and 2–5, Sun. 2–4 🚇 Lines 5, 12, 16, 18 to Dom/Hbf 🚊 Tram 1, 7, 9 to Heumarkt 🍴 Pfaffen Brauerei Max Päffgen, nearby at Heumarkt, see page 477 🎟 $

Kölner Dom

It took more than 600 years to complete the Kölner Dom (Cathedral), a Gothic masterpiece that incorporated all of the original architects' plans. The purpose of the project (begun in 1248) was to provide a grand setting for the relics of the Three Magi, which were snatched from Milan and kept here in a golden shrine. The final result is majestic, with intricately worked masonry serving to lighten the great mass of the facade and the two 515-foot spires, which, at the time that they were built, were the tallest structures in the world.

The golden shrine is the main focus of the interior, but there are many other treasures. In the south ambulatory chapel, the altarpiece of the *Adoration of the Magi* is a superb work by Stefan Lochner, one of the 15th-century artists of the Cologne School.

In the north chapel is the 11th-century Gero Crucifix. One of the church's most inspiring features is the stained glass, ranging from the 13th-century Bible Window in the ambulatory to the Bavarian windows in the nave, donated by King Ludwig I in the 19th century.

➕ B3 ✉ Am Hof ☎ Cathedral: 0221 9258 4730; www.koelner-dom.de 🕐 Cathedral: daily 6 a.m.–9 p.m., May–Oct.; 6 a.m.–7:30 p.m., Nov.–Apr. Treasure Chamber: daily 10–6. Tower: daily 9–6, May–Sep.; 9–5, Mar.–Apr. and Oct.; 9–4, rest of year 🚇 Lines 5, 12, 16, 18 to Dom/Hbf 🍴 Brauhaus Sion, see page 477 🎟 Cathedral free (guided tours $$); Treasure Chamber $$; Tower $

Museum für Angewandte Kunst

Founded in 1888, the Museum für Angewandte Kunst (Museum of Applied Art), known as the MAKK, has an exquisite collection of European arts and crafts dating from medieval to contemporary times. Paintings and sculptures, fashion and textiles, porcelain and art nouveau jewelry are highlights.

➕ B3 ✉ An der Rechtschule ☎ 0221 2212 3860; www.museenkoeln.de/museum-fuer-angewandte-kunst 🕐 Tue.–Sun. 11–5 (also 11–10 first Thu. of the month) 🚇 Lines 5, 12, 16, 18 to Dom/Hbf 🍴 Café 🎟 $$

Museum Ludwig

Many great 20th-century artists are represented in the Ludwig Museum, among them Otto Dix and Max Ernst; the section on Pop Art has works by Andy Warhol and Roy Lichtenstein.

➕ C3 ✉ Heinrich-Böll-Platz ☎ 0221 221 26165; www.museum-ludwig.de 🕐 Tue.–Sun. 10–6 (also 10–10 first Thu. of the month) 🚇 U-Bahn to Hauptbahnhof 🍴 Café 🎟 $$$

Museum Schnütgen

Some fine medieval religious art and furnishings can be seen at the Schnütgen Museum, which occupies the deconsecrated church of St. Cäcilien (St. Cecilia).

Among the treasures here are original carvings from the cathedral altar. The carved *memento mori* (reminders of mortality) are chilling depictions of human bodies in a state of decay.

✚ A2 ✉ Cäcilienstrasse 29 ☎ 0221 2213 1355; www.museum-schnuetgen.de ⏰ Tue., Wed. and Fri.–Sun. 10–6, Thu. 10–8 (also 10–10 first Thu. of the month) 🚇 Lines 1, 3, 4, 18 to Neumarkt 🚋 Tram 1, 3, 4, 9, 16, 18 to Neumarkt 🍴 Brauhaus Sion, see page 477 💳 $$ ℹ Guided tours; audio guide

Rathaus

The Rathaus (Town Hall) is a Cologne landmark at the heart of the Old Town. A flamboyant, octagonal, 15th-century tower tops off the 14th-century main body of the building. The Renaissance loggia (porch) was added sometime in the 1570s.

Under a glass pyramid in front of the hall is a 12th-century Jewish bathhouse, the *Mikwe*. There was once a ghetto on this land, where the city's Jewish community lived until they were expelled in 1424.

✚ B2 ✉ Rathausplatz ☎ 0221 221 23332 ⏰ Mon.–Thu. 9–3, Fri. 8–noon 🚇 Lines 5, 12, 16, 18 to Dom/Hbf; 5 to Rathaus 🚋 Tram 1, 7, 9 to Neumarkt 🍴 Restaurant in Ratskeller ℹ Contact Tourist Office to book guided tours (see page 226)

Römisch-Germanisches Museum

For hundreds of years Cologne was under Roman rule; city status was granted in AD 50 by Emperor Claudius. The Römisch-Germanisches Museum (Roman-Germanic Museum) depicts daily life in the Roman Empire through locally excavated items.

The main exhibit is the impressive 230-foot Dionysus Mosaic, once part of a third-century Roman villa: it features Dionysus, god of wine, indulging in drunken revelry. An older exhibit is the 49-foot-high tomb of a legionnaire called Poblicius, who died about AD 40.

There's an interesting display of third- and fourth-century glass designs from Cologne, as well as jewelry found at Frankish burial sites.

✚ B3 ✉ Roncalliplatz 4 ☎ 0221 2212 4438; www.museenkoeln.de/roemisch-germanisches-museum ⏰ Tue.–Sun. 10–5 (also 10–10 first Thu. of the month) 🚇 Lines 5, 12, 16, 18 to Dom/Hbf 💳 $$ ℹ Admission and hours may vary for exhibitions. Guided tours available

St. Ursula

To the north of the city center is the Romanesque church of St. Ursula, named for the daughter of a fourth-century king of Britain, who was said to have been killed in the city by Huns, along with her 11,000 virgin companions. The popularity of the cult of St. Ursula contributed to the city's development as a center of pilgrimage, and she appears in the Cologne coat of arms. The church sacristan can provide visitor access to the baroque Goldene Kammer (Golden Chamber).

✚ B4 ✉ Ursulaplatz 30 ☎ 0221 133 400 ⏰ Mon.–Sat. 10 a.m.–noon and 3–5, Sun. 3–4:30 🚇 Lines 5, 12, 16, 18 to Dom/Hbf 💳 $

Wallraf-Richartz-Museum & Fondation Corboud

Cologne's major collection of German and international art is housed in this impressive museum, with works through the 19th century displayed here. Also at the Wallraf-Richartz you can study the work produced in Cologne in the 15th century, when this city was at the forefront of artistic development. In particular, make time to look for the triptychs by the artist known as the Master of St. Bartholomew, whose interesting, brightly colored paintings resemble carvings.

✚ B2 ✉ Obenmarspforten ☎ 0221 2212 1119; www.wallraf.museum ⏰ Tue.–Sun. 10–6 (also Tue. 10–9) 🚇 Lines 5, 12, 16, 18 to Dom/Hbf 💳 $$ ℹ Special exhibitions

An Excursion to Bergischer Dom

Bergischer Dom (Altenberger Dom), about 11 miles northeast of Cologne, is set on the Dhünn river in the woods of the hilly country called Bergisches Land. The original church of this former Cistercian monastery was built using stone from the manor of the Count of Berg, who left it to the monks after moving his headquarters elsewhere in 1133. It took a little more than 100 years to finish building the present monastery, which was begun in 1259 – only seven years after work had started on the cathedral in Cologne (which took more than six centuries to complete). In medieval times it was a stopping-off place for pilgrims on the way to Santiago de Compostela in Spain.

The end result is one of Germany's best examples of 13th-century Gothic style: no elaborate embellishments and no tower, but a marvelous sense of space and light, enhanced by the simple, silvery stained-glass windows in the chancel. The west window representing *Das Himmlische Jerusalem (Holy Jerusalem)* is the biggest stained-glass window in the country. You will find tombs of the past counts, princes and abbots of Berg in the north transept.

During the Napoleonic Wars in the late 18th and early 19th centuries, the church fell into disuse and disrepair. Luckily, King Frederick William IV took an interest in its restoration, and it was opened to worshipers on the condition – decreed by the king – that both Catholics and Protestants could attend. This holds true today, and on Sundays both Catholic and Protestant congregations attend services. The outbuildings house various restaurants; at any of these, you can ask for the key to the oldest standing part of the monastery, the 13th-century Markuskapelle (chapel). An exquisite feature of the complex is the choir surrounded by chapels, viewed most rewardingly from the slope east of the monastery.

It takes an hour to reach Bergischer Dom from Cologne's center: The underground trams (U-Bahn lines 4, 15, 16, 18, 19) take you to Wiener Platz for a connection with bus 434.

Guided excursions from Cologne can be arranged by the Cologne Tourist Office (KölnTourismus, see page 226) 🅾 Daily 8–6. No visits during services and concerts 🛈 For information about free guided tours ☎ 02202 30008; www.altenbergerdom.de

Fine stonework dominates the light, airy interior of Bergischer Dom

Munich

The capital of Bavaria, just an hour from the Alps, is one of Germany's most appealing and popular cities. Although Munich (München) is the country's third-largest city, with a cosmopolitan society and culture, it has retained a village-like atmosphere with parks, a pedestrian-only center and an easygoing feel. Even on the briefest German tour, Munich is a city not to be missed.

Munich on Foot

Central Munich is compact and attractive and the easiest way to explore is on foot. Long pedestrian-only streets (Kaufingerstrasse and Neuhauser Strasse) run from the main railroad station and from Karlstor, one of the city gates, to Marienplatz, the square at the heart of the Old Town. Here you can watch the mechanical characters of the carillon (*Glockenspiel*) at the front of the Neues Rathaus (New Town Hall, see page 234) and visit the twin-towered cathedral. To the north of the square is the tree-lined Maximilianstrasse, which leads to the Bavarian Parliament building and the Residenz (palace, see page 236). Great art collections – the Alte Pinakothek (Old Picture Gallery, see page 233), the Neue Pinakothek (New Picture Gallery, see page 234) and the Pinakothek der Moderne (Modern Art Picture Gallery, see page 236) – are northwest of the city center; to the south are the history museum and, on an island in the Isar river, one of the world's foremost museums of science and technology, the Deutsches Museum (German Museum, see page 233).

Bavarian Eateries

There are many restaurants and cafés in Munich, and its large foreign population ensures a wide range of cuisines. At specifically Bavarian cafés, the Munich *Weisswürste* (white veal sausage with parsley) is a staple. This delicacy is usually eaten before noon. Meals are generally early in Munich, as people start work at 7 or 8 a.m. Lunch can begin at 11:30 but is often substantial, and the "lunch hour" can last until 2 p.m. Dinner is served between 6:30 and 11 p.m., but locals tend to stick to a light supper (*Abendbrot*). The Schwabing district, north of the city center, is a busy area of sidewalk cafés and taverns. Snack bars (*Lokal* or *Schnellimbiss*) and even butcher shops (*Metzgereien*) sell tasty meatloaf and sausages all day.

Music and Film

Munich is a major European cultural center, with thriving movie and publishing industries and a proud musical tradition. Three symphony orchestras are based here, and the Residenz provides an impressive venue – either in the concert hall or, in summer, in the courtyard. Opera and ballet are staged at the Bavarian State Opera, where the July Opera Festival is the highlight of the city's calendar. The main cultural center is the modern Gasteig, home of the Munich Philharmonic Orchestra; students from the Richard Strauss Conservatory give free lunchtime or early-evening recitals in the Small Concert Hall during the week. The annual International Film Festival takes place across the city in late June and early July – the high point of a series of festivals devoted to the movies.

Munich tends to shut down early, but Schwabing has many cabarets, theaters

MUNICH

| 0 | 100 | 200 meters |
| 0 | 100 | 200 yards |

Ⓤ U-Bahn (subway)

N

SCHELLINGSTRASSE

GESCHWISTER-SCHOLL-PLATZ

eue akothek

Universität Ⓤ

Salinenhof

KAULBACHSTRASSE

AMALIENSTRASSE

LUDWIGSTRASSE

Ludwigskirche ✝

Schwabinger Bach

Englischer Garten

OETTINGENSTRASSE

EMIL-RIEDEL-STRASSE

Museum Brandhorst

Bayerische Staatsbibliothek

Eisbach

akothek r Moderne

TÜRKENSTRASSE

Staatsarchiv München

OSKAR-VON-MILLER-RING

VON-DER-TANN-STRASSE

Haus der Kunst

Archäologische Staatssammlung

WIDENMAYERSTRASSE

MARIA-THERESIA-STRASSE

NNER ASSE

Prinz-Carl-Palais

FRANZ-JOSEPH-STRAUSS-RING

Dichtergarten

Deutsches Theatermuseum

Hofgarten

PRINZREGENTENSTRASSE

Bayerisches Nationalmuseum

Galerie Schack

ODEONSPLATZ

Ⓤ Odeonsplatz

START

OETTINGENSTRASSE

PLATZ VOR DER FELDHERRNHALLE

Bayerische Staatskanzlei

LIEBIGSTRASSE

END

LATZ

Residenz

RESIDENZSTRASSE

Sankt-Anna-Pfarrkirche ✝

PRINZREGENTEN STRASSE

Villa Stuck

MARSTALLPLATZ

KARL-SCHARNAGL-RING

SANKT-ANNA-STRASSE

STERNSTRASSE

WIDENMAYERSTRASSE

MAFFEISTRASSE

Nationaltheater

MAX-JOSEPH-PLATZ

PERUSASTRASSE

Ⓤ Lehel

MARIA-THERESIA-STRASSE

Frauenkirche

FRAUENPLATZ

KAUFINGERSTRASSE

ALTER HOF

MAXIMILIANSTRASSE

Maximiliansanlagen

Maximiliananlagen

ℹ Neues Rathaus

Hofbräuhaus

THOMAS-WIMMER-RING

Schwindinsel

Bayerischer Landtag

MARIENPLATZ

MAXIMILIANSTRASSE

Staatliches Museum für Völkerkunde

MAXIMILIANSBRÜCKE

Ⓤ

UBERGRABEN

Marienplatz Ⓤ

Spielzeugmuseum

MAFFRANCKSTRASSE

Max-Weber-Platz

Sankt Peterskirche ✝

HEILIGGEIST ✝

TAL

HACKENSTRASSE

Haus des Alpinismus

ℹ

Viktualienmarkt

FRAUENSTRASSE

Isartor

Isar

Sankt Nikolai ✝

INNERE WIENER STRASSE

SANKT-JAKOBS-PLATZ

Münchner Stadtmuseum

RUMFORDSTRASSE

ZWEIBRÜCKENSTRASSE

STEINSDORFSTRASSE

Auf der Insel

PREYSINGSTRASSE

BLUMENSTRASSE

KLENZESTRASSE

BAADERSTRASSE

GÄRTNER-PLATZ

Klosterkirche Herz Jesu ✝

Europäisches Patentamt

Müllersches Volksbad

Kulturzentrum am Gasteig

ROSENHEIMER STRASSE

KELLERSTRASSE

SEDANSTRASSE

FRAUNHOFERSTRASSE

Fraunhoferstrasse

ERHARDTSTRASSE

CORNELIUSBRÜCKE

Deutsches Museum

ZEPPELINSTRASSE

ICKSTATTSTRASSE

Ⓤ Rosenheimer Platz

HOCHSTRASSE

PRABLSTRASSE

C

D

E

and live music venues ranging from rock to folk and jazz, including Jazzclub Unterfahrt at Einsteinstrasse 42.

Boutiques and Markets

There's good window-shopping all over the old center, especially along Neuhauser Strasse and Kaufingerstrasse. Maximilianstrasse is a browser's paradise, lined with designer boutiques, art galleries and jewelers. More stores abound in the arcades and lanes leading off Residenzstrasse. Antiques and secondhand stores are concentrated in the student area of Schwabing, and Bavarian crafts are sold in the streets that run off Max-Joseph-Platz.

Munich's open-air Viktualienmarkt, with its formidable vendors and fresh goods ranging from local cheese to Alpine flowers, sets up south of Marienplatz every day except late Saturday afternoon and Sunday.

City of Monks

Munich's city emblem is the *Münchner Kindl*, or "little monk," recalling its origins as a monastic settlement. The first recorded mention of *Munichen*, or "the home of monks," was in AD 777. The city itself was founded nearly 400 years later by Henry the Lion, Duke of Saxony.

Essential Information

Tourist Information

München Tourismusamt
(Munich Tourist Office)
Sendlinger Strasse 1
☎ 089 23 39 65 00;
www.muenchen.de
Hauptbahnhof, Bahnhofplatz 2
Neues Rathaus (New City Hall), Marienplatz

Urban Transportation

A U-Bahn (subway) and S-Bahn (suburban) train network covers the city center and beyond. U-Bahn stations are identified by a white "U" on a blue background, and S-Bahn stations by a white "S" on a green background. Trains run daily 5 a.m.–1 a.m. Buy tickets from machines at Münchner Verkehrs und Tarifverbund (MVV) stations, MVV sales desks, newsstands and on buses and trams. Purchase tickets individually, in strips or for 1 or 3 days: multiple tickets are valid for buses and trams, too. Validate your ticket in the machine as you board, except for tickets bought from machines on trams (these will stamp automatically). One ticket is good for up to four bus/tram or two train stops; two tickets for additional stops. For MVV information ☎ 089 41 42 43 44; hotline: 0800 344 22 66 00; www.mvv-muenchen.de (Mon.–Fri. 7–5). Taxi stands can be found all over the city. Call Taxi-München ☎ 089 21610 or 089 19410, or IsarFunk Taxizentrale ☎ 089 45 05 40.

Airport Information

The international airport, Flughafen München Franz Josef Strauss (www.munich-airport.de), is 19 miles northeast of the city center. S-Bahn trains (lines 1 and 8) run 3:18 a.m.–12:38 a.m. to the main railroad station (Hauptbahnhof), a 40-minute trip; airport buses run to the station from the North Terminal daily 6:20 a.m.–9:40 p.m., a 45-minute trip. For flight information ☎ 089 97 500.

Climate – average highs and lows for the month

Jan.	Feb.	Mar.	Apr.	May	Jun.	Jul.	Aug.	Sep.	Oct.	Nov.	Dec.
2°C	3°C	9°C	14°C	19°C	22°C	25°C	24°C	20°C	14°C	7°C	4°C
36°F	37°F	48°F	57°F	66°F	72°F	77°F	75°F	68°F	57°F	45°F	39°F
-3°C	-2°C	2°C	5°C	9°C	13°C	15°C	15°C	12°C	6°C	2°C	-1°C
27°F	28°F	36°F	41°F	48°F	55°F	59°F	59°F	54°F	43°F	36°F	30°F

Munich Sights

Alte Pinakothek

The huge Alte Pinakothek (Old Picture Gallery), built in 1836 to store the expanding royal art collection, exhibits about 700 paintings chosen from its collection of 14th- to 18th-century art. Among the treasures are works by Albrecht Dürer, Raphael, Rembrandt and the world's best collection of work by Peter Paul Rubens.

Ongoing renovations (until 2019) may cause disruption but extensive areas of the museum will remain open.

⊞ B4 ✉ Barer Strasse 27, door on Theresienstrasse ☎ 089 23 80 52 16; www.pinakothek.de 🕐 Tue. 10–8, Wed.–Sun. 10–6 🚇 U-Bahn to Königsplatz 🚌 100; tram 27 🎫 $$ ($ on Sun.)

Asamkirche

The tiny Asamkirche (Asam Church) is a fine example of baroque architecture. Built as a private chapel (1733–46) by two architect and sculptor brothers Egid Quirin Asam and Cosmas Damian Asam, it is dedicated to St. John Nepomuk. Squeezed in between two houses, the heavily decorated interior includes the Asams' frescoes, stucco and gilding.

⊞ B2 ✉ Sendlinger Strasse 32 ☎ 089 2368 7989 🕐 Daily 9–5:30 🚇 U-Bahn to Sendlinger Tor; S-Bahn to Marienplatz 🚌 Tram 16, 17, 18, 27 🎫 Free

BMW Museum

This stylishly revamped museum is now five times bigger than before and celebrates nine decades of BMW technology and expertise. There are plenty of vehicles to see, of course, along with themed areas and displays relating to automobile design, media design and architecture. A central route leads visitors along a historical time line.

⊞ Off map at A4 ✉ Am Olympiapark 2 ☎ 089 1250 16001; www.bmw-welt.com 🕐 Tue.–Sun. and public holidays 10–6 🚇 U-Bahn to Olympiazentrum or Petuelring 🚌 50; tram 27 🍴 Café and restaurants on site 🎫 $$$ ℹ Guided tours, audio guide

Deutsches Museum

One of the biggest science and technology museums in the world, the German Museum has more than 100,000 items on display, and deals with everything from lightning demonstrations to space travel to hydraulics to the first German submarine. Audiovisual displays and hands-on exhibits add to the fun.

⊞ D1 ✉ Museumsinsel 1 ☎ 089 21 79-1; www.deutsches-museum.de 🕐 Daily 9–5; closed some holidays 🚇 U-Bahn to Fraunhoferstrasse; S-Bahn to Isartor 🚌 132; tram 16, 18 🍴 Café on site 🎫 $$ ℹ Guided tours; audio guide

Englischer Garten

The landscaped park Englischer Garten (English Garden) was created in 1789. Today it is busy with street entertainers and people boating and relaxing. Boats can be rented at the Kleinhesseloher See and there is a beer garden, the Seehaus, near the lake. Enjoy good city views from the circular "temple," the *monopteros*; other attractions include the Chinesischer Turm (Chinese Tower). In summer, surfers ride the waves on the Eisbach river that runs through the park.

⊞ D4 ✉ Northeast Munich 🕐 Daily 24 hours 🚇 U-Bahn to Universität or Giselastrasse 🚌 54, 154

Englischer Garten offers surprising sports options

to Chinesischer Turm; tram 18 to Tivolistrasse 🍴 Beer gardens, cafés and restaurants

Frauenkirche

Munich's twin-towered cathedral (Church of Our Dear Lady) was built between 1468 and 1488, but was left without a roof. In 1524 its Italian Renaissance, green onion domes were "temporarily" added – and have been there ever since. Near the entrance is a footprint in the floor, said to be that of the devil, who stamped with glee thinking that the architect had forgotten to put in the windows. In fact, the windows can't be seen from where the devil was standing – but they are there. The south tower can be climbed.

✚ C2 ✉ Frauenplatz 1 ☎ 089 29 00 82-0; www.muenchner-dom.de 🕐 Church: Sat.–Thu. 7–7 (also Thu. 7–8:30 p.m.), Fri. 7–6 🚇 U-Bahn/S-Bahn to Marienplatz 🚌 52, 132; tram 19 🎫 Church free

Haus der Kunst

Opened by the Nazis in 1937 as "Haus der Deutschen Kunst" (House of German Art) the large white columned building was immediately mocked by its detractors as "Weisswurststallee" (White Sausage Boulevard). The gallery was part of Hitler's campaign against modern so-called *entartete Künstler* (degenerate artists). Today the Haus der Kunst shows sophisticated thematic exhibitions and retrospectives.

✚ D3 ✉ Prinzregentenstrasse 1 ☎ 089 211 27-113; www.hausderkunst.de 🕐 Daily 10–8 (also Thu. 8–10 p.m.) for exhibitions only; closing times are extended for special exhibitions 🚇 U-Bahn to Odeonsplatz or Lehel 🚌 100; tram 18 🍴 Café in gallery 🎫 $$$; exhibition admission varies

Lenbachhaus

Built in 1887 as the home of aristocratic painter Franz von Lenbach, the Lenbachhaus is now an art gallery. It shows the progression of art in Munich from the 15th and 16th centuries to the 19th-century Romantics. Highlights of the collection are works by the Munich Expressionists, the so-called *Blaue Reiter*

(Blue Rider) group of the 20th century, with more than 90 abstract paintings and 900 other works by Wassily Kandinsky – the world's largest assemblage of his art.

The spectacular new wing with its dramatic atrium reflects this world-class museum's continuing acquisition of international contemporary art.

✚ A4 ✉ Luisenstrasse 33 ☎ 089 2333 2000; www.lenbachhaus.de 🕐 Wed.–Sun. 10–6, Tue. 10–9 🚇 U-Bahn U2, U8 to Königsplatz 🚌 100; tram 27 to Karolinenplatz 🍴 Café 🎫 $$$

Neue Pinakothek

Across the street from the Renaissance-style Alte Pinakothek (Old Picture Gallery, see page 233) is the Neue Pinakothek (New Picture Gallery), a modern building featuring art from the late 18th to the 20th centuries.

It has examples of the French and German Impressionists, Romantic and rococo paintings, and the art nouveau style known in Germany as *Jugendstil*.

✚ B4 ✉ Barer Strasse 27, entrance on Theresienstrasse ☎ 089 23 80 51 95; www.pinakothek.de 🕐 Wed.–Mon. 10–6 (also Wed. 6–10 p.m.) 🚇 U-Bahn U2 to Königsplatz 🚌 Tram 27 to Pinakotheken 🍴 Café 🎫 $$$ ($ on Sun.)

Neues Rathaus

A forest of neo-Gothic turrets, towers, spurs and gargoyles, the 19th-century Neues Rathaus (New Town Hall) sprawls around six courtyards on the north side of Marienplatz.

On its central tower is a 43-bell clock (*Glockenspiel*), which comes to life every day at 11 a.m. (also at noon and 5 p.m., Mar.–Oct.) as life-size figures from Munich's history come dancing out to its four melodies. The *Schäfflertanz*, a dance which celebrates the end of the plague in 1517, is performed by dancers in the city streets every seven years (the next is due in 2019).

✚ C2 ✉ Marienplatz 8 ☎ 089 23 300 🕐 Tower: daily 10–7, May–Oct.; Mon.–Fri. 10–5, rest of year 🚇 U-Bahn/S-Bahn to Marienplatz 🚌 52, 132 🍴 Ratskeller, see page 478 🎫 Tower $

Hofbräuhaus

Wilhelm V, Duke of Bavaria, founded Munich's Hofbräu brewery in 1589 to brew a dark ale more to his liking than the local beer. At this time, beer was a drink restricted to the Bavarian upper classes: they had made it their own preserve after losing their vineyards in a series of severe winters. In 1828, the brewery became an inn, and the delights of its beer were made accessible to all townspeople.

The huge beer hall and its tree-shaded courtyard have been the scene of political upheaval and violence in modern history. The Nazi party held its early mass meetings here, and a fight that became known as the Battle of the Hofbräuhaus broke out during one of Adolf Hitler's speeches.

Nowadays, there is nothing sinister about the hall's fame: tourists flock to the long benches, listen to the Bavarian brass bands and drink beer served by traditionally dressed waitresses. They no longer practice the customary quality test for *Bock* beer, though, which is probably just as well. The test apparently consisted of drinkers sitting at one of the Hofbräuhaus' beer-soaked benches and consuming *Bock* beer for hours at a time, staying put even while nature took its course. If, at the end of the session, they stuck to the benches when they tried to get up, the beer was reckoned to be thick enough and ready to sell.

The Hofbräuhaus is the city's most popular beer hall and fills up very quickly, especially during the world-famous, 16-day *Oktoberfest*, a beer festival that traditionally ends on the first Sunday in October. Barbecues, processions and music all play their part in this annual jamboree, but beer is the main ingredient.

If the Hofbräuhaus is too crowded, there are other options all over town, plus numerous beer gardens where you are allowed to bring your own food. The *Oktoberfest* action takes place on the fairground at Theresienwiese, west of the city center.

Whether you choose to drink at the Hofbräuhaus or elsewhere, make sure you don't sit at the regulars' table *(Stammtisch)*. You'll soon know you've made this mistake if the waitress refuses to take your order!

Musicians perform traditional Bavarian music in Munich's Hofbräuhaus (beer hall)

Germany

A detail of the ceiling in the fabulous Residenz

Odeonsplatz

This regal square was laid out for Ludwig I early in the 19th century and marks the beginning of Ludwigstrasse and Prinzregentenstrasse. The Feldherrnhalle (Military Commanders' Hall) was added as a tribute to the Bavarian army, and is guarded by two marble lions. Overlooking Odeonsplatz is the lovely baroque, golden-stone Theatinerkirche, the church where members of the ruling Wittelsbach family were laid to rest. The gardens of Hofgarten are next to the square.

✚ C3 🚇 U-Bahn to Odeonsplatz 🚌 100 🍴 Halali, see page 478

Olympiapark

The park built for the 1972 Summer Olympics has become a focus for joggers, strollers and swimmers, sporting and music events. Its television tower, the 995-foot-high Olympiaturm has a platform and revolving restaurant with Alpine views. The Rock Museum, on the platform, features memorabilia from famous rock groups. A tour train takes visitors around Olympic Lake; Olympic Hill, made of wartime debris; and the Olympic Village. You also can visit the Olympiastadion (Olympic stadium).

✚ Off map at A4 ✉ Spiridon-Louis-Ring 21 ☎ 089 30 67-0; www.olympiapark.de 🕐 Olympiapark: daily 9–6, Apr.–May 15 and Sep. 16–Nov. 6; 9–8, May 16–Sep. 15; 11–4, rest of year. Olympiaturm: daily 9 a.m.–midnight (last admission at 11:30 p.m.) 🚇 U-Bahn to Olympiazentrum 🚌 50, 60, 173, 175, 177, 178; tram 20, 21, 27 🍴 Revolving restaurant, Olympiaturm 🎫 Olympiapark free; Olympiastadion $$; Olympiaturm $$

Pinakothek der Moderne

This is one of the most important contemporary art museums in Germany. The building, innovative in design and architecture, displays 20th- and 21st-century art.

✚ B4 ✉ Barer Strasse 40 ☎ 089 2 38 05 3-60; www.pinakothek.de 🕐 Tue.–Sun. 10–6, Thu. 10–8 🚇 U-Bahn to Königsplatz 🚌 100, 154; tram 27 🎫 $$$ (Sun. $)

Residenz

The 112 rooms of the Wittelsbach dynasty's dazzling palace are a treasure trove of artworks, ornaments, furnishings and statues. Highlights include the vaulted Antiquarium, built between 1568 and 1571; the rococo Cuvilliés Theater; the crown jewels in the Treasury; and the Ahnengalerie (Ancestral Portrait Gallery).

✚ C3 ✉ Residenzstrasse 1/Max-Joseph-Platz 3 ☎ 089 29 06 71; www.residenz-muenchen.de 🕐 Daily 9–6, Apr. to mid-Oct.; 10–5, rest of year 🚇 U-Bahn to Odeonsplatz; U-Bahn/S-Bahn to Marienplatz 🚌 100 to Odeonsplatz; tram 19 to Nationaltheater 🍴 Spatenhaus an der Oper, see page 478 🎫 $$$

Schloss Nymphenburg

For centuries the mighty Wittelsbach family ruled Bavaria. Schloss Nymphenburg (Nymphenburg Palace) was built as their summer villa by Agostino Barelli between 1664 and 1674, and later generations of Wittelsbachs added to his creation. In the central section is the Schönheitsgalerie, or Gallery of Beauties – 36 paintings of beautiful women produced between 1827 and 1850 for Ludwig I. The former palace stables house the Marstallmuseum, a museum of porcelain and a collection of state carriages and sleighs, and in the 1734 Amalienburg hunting lodge there is a Hall of Mirrors.

✚ Off map at A4 ☎ 089 17 90 8-0; www.schloss-nymphenburg.de 🕐 Palace: daily 9–6, Apr. to mid-Oct.; 10–4, rest of year. Gardens: daily dawn–dusk 🚇 U-Bahn to Rotkreuzplatz 🚌 51; tram 12, 17 🎫 $$$

A Walk Along Prinzregentenstrasse

This grand boulevard runs east from the 17th-century Court Garden (Hofgarten), with its beautiful fountains and Renaissance arcades. A startling modern addition, the steel-and-glass Neue Staatskanzlei, houses the Bavarian State Chancellery. Prinzregentenstrasse was laid out at the end of the 19th century and named for Prince Luitpold, who ruled as regent after his nephew, Ludwig II, had been declared mad and deposed.

Today it takes visitors through one of the city's main museum and gallery quarters. Running past the southern end of the English Garden (see pages 233–234), the boulevard first reaches the Haus der Kunst (House of Art, see page 234), formerly a gallery of Nazi-approved art. It exhibits the kind of work the Nazis had condemned.

Next door is the Bavarian National Museum (Bayerisches Nationalmuseum), in an early 20th-century building incorporating different architectural styles.

The next notable monument is the former Prussian Embassy, now the Galerie Schack (Prinzregentenstrasse 9), named for one of the 19th century's great patrons of the arts, Count Schack. His own collection of paintings is represented by such artists as Franz von Lenbach and Arnold Böcklin, who relied on the count for their livelihoods. The gallery is open Wednesday–Sunday 10–6.

Prinzregentenstrasse continues across the Isar river and past the *Angel of Peace (Friedensengel)*, a golden monument to peace, erected to commemorate the end of the Franco-Prussian War. Nowadays citizens gather on New Year's Day to enjoy fireworks displays and the view of Munich. Farther along, past Europaplatz, is the Villa Stuck (Prinzregentenstrasse 60), a 19th-century house built in a mix of styles by artist Franz von Stuck. Von Stuck was part of the 1890s *avant-garde* school known as the Munich Secession, and his own work is displayed inside. There also are exhibitions by such modern artists as Brian Jungen from Canada. For guided tours in English ☎ 089 45 55 51–0. The boulevard continues east to the Prinzregententheater (☎ 089 21 85 28 99), which stages drama, concerts and musicals. It was designed in 1900–01 to emulate the neoclassic Wagner Festival Theater in Bayreuth and sits on Prinzregentenplatz 12, where there is a U-Bahn station; trains travel back to Odeonsplatz and the Hofgarten. For the walking route, consult the city map on pages 230–231.

The Diana Temple stands at the heart of the Hofgarten (Court Garden); musicians often entertain visitors here

Greece

Opposite: The narrow streets and old white-painted houses that are typical of the Pláka area in Athens

Greece

Subconsciously, we all feel we have a stake in Greece. The language, political systems, values and ethics of the Western world are inextricably connected to this country's ancient civilization. Visitors often arrive with high expectations and romantic notions, snippets of myths, history and hearsay mingled in their minds. However, the country and its people have endured economic strife in recent years and face yet more difficult times ahead in order to realise a level of political and economic stability.

The Land

Greece's landscape is as dramatic as the people who inhabit it. There are about 200 inhabited islands in Greece, scattered on three sides of the mainland. Some are lush and studded with pine and eucalyptus, and others are arid or mountainous. Most are blessed with idyllic sand beaches and picturesque villages, and many have superb ancient sites, Frankish castles or Venetian fortifications.

You could spend years discovering them all, so spare at least a few days to visit one or two. Greek islands are a vital part of the country and have bedazzled travelers for centuries. There are regular ferry services to the main islands in summer, but services to more remote islands are less regular and can be challenging – though worth the effort – to organize. Check the website www.gtp.gr, which lists monthly ferry routes.

Much of mainland Greece is very mountainous. The slopes of Olympus and Parnassus are carpeted with wildflowers in spring, offering superb vistas and rewarding hiking, as do the eerie and stony landscapes of the Máni, a region of rugged mountains and isolated villages, and the steep-sided gorges and wild coastline of Crete.

Public transportation, especially by bus, is usually regular and reliable in mainland towns.

If you prefer to be more independent, car rental is simple to arrange. If you do rent a car, be prepared for some poorly surfaced roads, and avoid driving in cities and some of the larger rural towns if possible.

Traditional Culture

Greece has one of Europe's most vigorous cultures, perpetuated through architecture, crafts, music and dance. Traditional customs permeate everyday life, despite the growing impact of Western consumer values. If you can, see traditional dancing and listen to the music – the real thing is often easier to find in rural areas.

As in many other Mediterranean countries, much of life is lived in the full gaze of the public eye, hence the strolling crowds and packed cafés.

The worldwide recession sparked riots in Athens in the last few years.

The Greeks and You

Tourism is not a slick operation in Greece; everything works, things eventually happen, but not necessarily with streamlined efficiency. So relax, slow down and you'll get much more out of your trip.

The Greeks have been dealing with foreign incursions for centuries, so they took the late 20th-century tourist influx in their stride. The classical Greek tradition of hospitality to strangers is still strong, which makes for a relaxed attitude toward visitors, particularly when you go off the beaten track.

Greek is the official language, but English is widely spoken, though in remote areas it is likely that only Greek will be understood.

Hospitality often takes the form of innumerable personal questions, among which "How much do you earn?" is usually near the top of the list. Don't be offended, as this is considered an acceptable and friendly exchange. If someone offers you something – a drink, some fruit, a flower – accept it graciously, as the donor is acting out a tradition that goes back thousands of years.

Greeks have a strong code of honor, which makes Greece a safe country to visit. It's highly unlikely you'll be cheated in any way, and you can still safely walk most streets at night without worrying.

Society has changed beyond recognition in the last 40 years, and young Greeks are far more emancipated than their parents. Female virtue – especially in rural areas – is still held in high regard. As a consequence young Greek males may occasionally pester foreign girls in the often mistaken belief that they will respond more readily to their advances.

There's still a large rural class in Greece, and outside cities and tourist areas you'll see black-garbed figures laboring in tiny fields. This traditional way of farming has been going on for centuries, a lifestyle that is a million miles from that of city dwellers.

More Top Destinations in Greece (see map page 240)

- Chaniá B1
- Delfoí B2
- Ídra B2
- Kefalloniá A2
- Léros C2
- Máni A1
- Metéora A3
- Mikonos B2
- Monemvassía B1
- Mykínes B2
- Náxos C2
- Óros Píndos A3
- Samothráki B3
- Skópelos B2
- Thíra/Santorini B1

Timeline

776–700 BC	City-states established; first Olympic Games.
499–400 BC	Persian Wars; Golden Age of classical Greek culture; Peloponnesian Wars against Sparta.
336–323 BC	Alexander the Great conquers the known world.
146 BC	Greece becomes a Roman province.
AD 394	Christianity established throughout the Roman Empire; the Olympic Games finish and the Delphic Oracle is closed.
476–1453	Greece ruled from Constantinople; fall of Constantinople in 1453; Greece ruled by Turks for next 400 years.
1821–29	Greek War of Independence; Greece becomes an independent modern state.
1917–18	Greece sides with Allies in World War I.
1920–23	Greece continues a misjudged war against Turkey, ending in defeat.
1940–44	Axis occupation during World War II.
1945–60	Many Greeks emigrate to the United States and Australia; others flood into Athens from the countryside.
1974	Conflict with Turkey over Cyprus; situation remains tense into the 21st century.
1975	Tourist boom begins.
1981	Greece joins the European Economic Community; community funding catapults much of the country into mainstream Europe.
1996	Macedonian claims by former Yugoslavs seen as implicit threat to northern Greek region of Macedonia.
2001	Greece adopts the euro as its new national currency.
2004	Athens hosts the 2004 Olympic Games.
2009	George Papandreou of the PASOK party is elected as Prime Minister.
2010–2014	Widespread protest marches take place against austerity measures to deal with the country's deepening and ongoing debt crisis.
January 2015	Alexis Tsipras, of the radical left-wing SYRIZA Party, is elected Prime Minister. Greece's deepening debt crisis leads to the country needing an emergency financial bailout worth billions of dollars in order to function economically and to stay in the Eurozone.
August 2015	Prime Minister Alexis Tsipras resigns. Refugees and migrants fleeing Syria's war zone reach Greek Islands by sea from Turkey.

The Golden Age of Classical Greece

The peace following the defeat of the Persians in the fifth century BC marked the start of a cultural, artistic and intellectual blossoming for Athens and the other city-states. Much of what truly epitomizes "the glory that was Greece" dates from this era. The great architectural triumphs, the start of drama and comedy, and the first steps in philosophical thought can all be traced to Athens at this time. The Acropolis took the form whose remains are seen today, decorated by Pheidias' sublime marbles, and subtly harmonious temples were built everywhere. The names Sophocles, Euripides, Aristophanes, Socrates and Plato are familiar worldwide; it's worth remembering that they lived and worked in this tiny state in the eastern Mediterranean more than 2,500 years ago.

Survival Guide

■ Athens is best avoided during the sweltering summer months, when temperatures can soar above 90°F, noise levels are high around the clock, and the ever-present pollution is at its worst.

■ Head for restaurants and tavernas where the locals eat; the food will be good. If you don't understand the menu in a taverna you may be invited into the kitchen for a look – choose what you want and point!

■ In some areas of Greece there is an enduring belief that hot food harms the stomach, and food may therefore be served lukewarm. However, the preference for hot food is normally accommodated.

■ Remember to *never* flush toilet tissue down the toilet – it goes in the basket provided. You'll flood the bathroom if you put paper down the narrow pipes. The only exceptions are modern, luxury hotels. Public restrooms are few and far between, and many of them leave much to be desired. Carry your own toilet paper as it is not always available.

■ Greeks prefer to be cool and comfortable rather than stylish, but usually don't wear shorts in the city. It's respectful to cover bare shoulders and upper arms when visiting churches or religious establishments. Topless and nude sunbathing are widely but discreetly practiced.

■ Taxis outside main cities are fairly inexpensive, but in Athens drivers may hike rates for foreign visitors. Ask what the destination fare is before getting into a taxi or compare fares before deciding which one you'll use. On arrival by ferry or plane, if you already have a hotel reserved, resist being talked into going to another hotel.

■ Don't rent a scooter; more tourists have accidents on them than by any other means.

Guarding the Tomb of the Unknown Soldier, Athens

■ At important sites you may be approached by guides wanting to be paid for their services; some are good, others barely speak English. If you want guide service, use an official one or take a tour.

■ There's a plethora of attractive, handmade items to buy in Greek stores and markets. Most prices are fixed, but you can try a little gentle haggling in markets.

■ Be careful after it rains, when marble-surfaced walkways in Athens become very slippery. Also look out for unmarked holes on sidewalks, especially in poorly lit areas at night.

Athens

Athens is one of the Mediterranean's great cities, boasting some of the world's most treasured relics; it's also noisy, crowded, traffic clogged and polluted, with sprawling, unattractive suburbs. Summertime heat and the lack of shady spots can be oppressive, but the city is exhilarating, fascinating and stimulating, as much for its past as its present. Enjoy it for the colorful place it is.

Tackling Athens

You'll probably spend most of your visit in Athens' tiny historical center. Base yourself near Syntagma Square (Platéia Syntagmatos, see page 250) or Pláka (see page 250), which are a short walk from most of the main tourist sights. Plan your day carefully; get an early start to avoid the heat of the afternoon.

If you need information or advice, you will find that most people connected with tourism speak English, ranging from a few words to polished and idiomatic speech.

Moving around the historic center on foot is easy, but is occasionally challenging at busy street crossings. Be aware that where there are no traffic lights local drivers rarely take note of pedestrian crossings; wait for a clear gap in the traffic before crossing. In the last few years there has been an expanding pedestrianization program in the center.

City buses and trolley buses are often packed and may be delayed by traffic jams. Taxis are convenient for excursions out of the city, as is the greatly improved metro (subway) system. The main road systems into the city have also been improved.

Athenian Flavors
Sitting at a shady café table, lingering over a gargantuan lunch, munching sunflower seeds, melon, pistachios and

pine nuts, or eating ice cream as you stroll on balmy evenings are true Athenian pleasures.

In a country where hospitality to strangers is one of the bedrock rules of society, it's not surprising that eating and drinking socially play an important role. Eating establishments are known as *estiatorio* (restaurants) or tavernas (less expensive, simpler and often family run). Greek food is delicious and healthy – fresh salads with feta cheese and olives, fantastic *mezédhes* (hors d'oeuvres), grilled meats, moussakas, and tasty stews and vegetables, perhaps washed down with one of the increasingly good selections of Greek wines. Dessert is normally fresh local fruit; if you want something sweeter, head for a *zaharoplastío*, a café serving the honey-soaked pastries much loved by the Greeks.

Festivals and Theater
Athens has theater, movies, dance, galleries and nightlife; everything changes rapidly, so pick up a free copy of one of the English-language newspapers to find out schedules.

In summer, the main tourist attraction is the Hellenic Festival (www. greekfestival.gr/en/), which runs from June through September. The festival offers a wonderful program of excellent cultural events, although it's most famous for classical Greek theater, some taking place at the Odeon of Herodes Atticus on the slopes of the Acropolis.

The Greek Alphabet
At first it may be daunting to see Greek script everywhere, but it won't be a major inconvenience. All street signs are in both Greek and Roman letters, as are signs to museums and most restaurants and shops. Public transportation is usually displayed in Greek. However, you'll get the hang of deciphering Greek letters and you'll feel a real sense of achievement when you do.

Ceramics and Honey

There's a wide range of shopping in Athens, from international labels to traditional Greek products. In Kolonáki and on and around Ermoú Street, the most fashionable retail areas of the city, you'll find familiar merchandise.

Ethnic buys are another matter, with much to hunt down around Pláka and its vicinity. Leather and woolen goods, ceramics and tapestries, felt slippers, olive oil, honey and pistachio nuts are all excellent buys. For something that bit more special, check out jewelry or religious stores; Greece has a long tradition of gold craftsmanship, and traditional icons are still made.

Keep a look out for Athens' *períptera* (kiosks) – much more than newsstands, they sell everything from snacks and

A view of Lycabettus Hill from the Acropolis, Athens
Opposite: The Acropolis Museum, Athens

drinks to bus tickets, simple medicines and telephone cards. In central Athens you will find that some *períptera* open 24 hours a day.

Essential Information

Tourist Information

Tsoha 24, Ambelokipi ☎ 210 870 7000;
www.visitgreece.gr
At the Acropolis ☎ 210 331 0529

Urban Transportation

The metro (subway) system is being expanded, but it's a long-term project and for now the easiest way to get around Athens is to walk or take one of the numerous yellow taxis. Taxis are hailed on the street and often shared; you pay for your segment of the trip, so check the meter when you get in. Alternatively, your hotel can arrange a taxi for you. Buses, trolley buses and the metro (subway) operate daily 5:30 a.m.–midnight (Fri.–Sat. metro operates until 2 a.m.); tickets are available at kiosks and are interchangeable with metro tickets, which can be bought at stations. Validate bus and trolley bus tickets on board, and metro tickets at entrances to platforms. The Athens Urban Transport Organization's (OASA) website, www.oasa.gr, is useful for finding bus, trolley bus and metro routes.

Airport Information

Athens International Airport (Eleftherios Venizelos) is at Spáta, 17 miles east of Athens (☎ 210 353 0000; www.aia.gr). The metro line 3 linking the airport to the city is the easiest way into Athens. There are four 24-hour express bus lines, connecting the airport with Athens and Piréas: the X93 to the Kifíssos Coach Station, X95 to Syntagma Square, X96 to Piréas and X97 to the Dafni metro station. Tickets cost €5 one way. For details see the airport's website: www.aia.gr.

Climate – average highs and lows for the month

Jan.	Feb.	Mar.	Apr.	May	Jun.	Jul.	Aug.	Sep.	Oct.	Nov.	Dec.
13°C	13°C	15°C	19°C	24°C	30°C	31°C	32°C	28°C	23°C	17°C	14°C
55°F	55°F	59°F	66°F	75°F	86°F	88°F	90°F	82°F	73°F	63°F	57°F
6°C	6°C	7°C	11°C	15°C	20°C	22°C	22°C	19°C	15°C	11°C	8°C
43°F	43°F	45°F	52°F	59°F	68°F	72°F	72°F	66°F	59°F	52°F	46°F

Greece

Athens Sights

> **Key to symbols**
> ➕ map coordinates refer to the Athens map on
> pages 244–245 💳 admission charge:
> $$$ more than €10, $$ €5–€10, $ less than €5
> See page 5 for complete key to symbols

Agorá

The stately civic center and marketplace
of ancient Athens is at the foot of the
Acropolis, to which it was once linked
by the Panathenaic Way.

Today, the site is an atmospheric
jumble of tree-shaded ruins, and you'll
need to use your imagination to
visualize how much of it looked in its
glorious heyday. However, dominating
one end is the virtually reconstructed,
fifth-century BC Doric temple known
as the Thieío.

Opposite, the two-story Stoá Attálou,
a second-century BC arcade, has been
restored by the American School of
Archeology to give an idea of the glory
of these ancient public buildings.
It contains a museum with displays of
archeological finds from in and around
the site.

➕ B2 ✉ Adrianou or Theorias ☎ 210 321 0185
🕐 Daily 8–3 🚇 Thiseío or Monastiráki 💳 $$$

Akrópoli

The Akrópoli (Acropolis) should top
your sightseeing list. This naturally
defensible rock was the sacred focal
point of ancient Athens. What you see
today dates mainly from the fifth
century BC, an era of peace and
prosperity thought of as the true
"Golden Age" of Greece.

You reach the summit through the
Propylaia, a magnificent stepped
gateway, with the graceful little temple
of Athena Nike to your right. Ahead
rises the great Doric temple of the
Parthenón, one of the world's most
beautiful buildings; built using no
perpendicular lines, its columns actually
taper, giving the whole structure a
feeling of lightness. It was decorated by
Athenian sculptors and dedicated to the
goddess Athena Parthenos, whose statue
by the sculptor Pheidias stood inside.

To the left of the Parthenón stands the
Erechtheion, shrine to Athena and
Poseidon, and said to be the place where
the goddess created the first olive tree.
The roof of the south portico is
supported by six caryatids, stately
maidens dressed in pleated tunics.

At the foot of the Acropolis you can
see two Roman theaters, and visit the
Acropolis Museum (see page 250).

Looking toward the Acropolis on its rocky setting, as the sun sets across the city

➕ C2 ✉ Akrópoli ☎ 210 321 0219;
www.acropolisofathens.gr 🕐 Daily 8–8. Last
admission 7:30 p.m. Ⓜ Akrópoli 💵 $$$

Ethnikó Archaiologikó Mouseío

For lovers of Classical art the Ethnikó
Archaiologikó Mouseío (National
Archeological Museum) is one of the
world's top sights. This vast and varied
collection covers all the finest art from
ancient Greece, with the added bonus of
an exceptional Egyptian collection.

The best approach is to concentrate on
only the prime examples. Head first for
the treasures from the royal tombs at
Mycenae, dating from 1500 BC; they
include exquisite gold funerary masks,
necklaces and filigree flowers. Next,
take in the sixth-century BC *kouros*,
vibrant statues of nude male athletes;
Aristodikos' superbly tactile athlete is
one of the finest ever carved. Move on to
admire the huge statue of Poseidon and
the little jockey urging on his horse,
both found in the sea off Cape
Artemision on the island of Evvoia in
1927. There's also a stunning bronze
by the famous sculptor Praxiteles in
room 28.

Upstairs you'll find frescoes from
Santorini (Thíra), buried 3,500 years ago
during a volcanic eruption, showing
riverside scenes. Rooms 49–56 house the
pottery collections; look for the rare
lekythoi (white-ground clayware), and
the exquisite red and black Attic vases.

➕ C4 ✉ 44 Patission ☎ 210 821 7724;
www.namuseum.gr 🕐 Daily 8–8 Ⓜ Omónoia 🚌 2,
3, 11, 13, 15, 022, 224, 226 🍴 Café in museum 💵 $$

Ethnikós Kípos

The green and somber Ethnikós Kípos
(National Gardens) provide a wonderful
oasis of cool off noisy Leóforos Amalias.
Laid out in the 19th century by Queen
Amalia, wife of King Otto, this is a true
southern Mediterranean garden – no
colorful flowerbeds, but deep shade and
sylvan green. With plenty of cafés, the
gardens are a good place for lunch.
Within the grounds is a botanical

museum with samples of all the gardens'
plants, many of them rare.

➕ D2 ✉ Amalias 🏛 Museum: 210 721 1178
🕐 Daily dawn to 30 minutes before dusk (museum:
Tue.–Sun. 9–3) Ⓜ Syntagma 🚌 1, 2, 4, 11, 12, 022,
025, 026

Goulandris Mouseío Kykladikís Téchnis

The beautifully presented Goulandris
Mouseío Kykladikís Téchnis (Museum
of Cycladic Art) was established in 1986
and houses a superb collection of
prehistoric artifacts from around the
Aegean islands. The collection, once the
private property of the shipowning
Goulandris family, dates from the
Cycladic civilization, which flourished
on the Greek islands from 3000 until
2000 BC. The marble figures displayed
could be taken for 20th-century work,
elegant and minimalist, yet full of
powerful feeling.

➕ D2 ✉ 4 Neophytou Douka ☎ 210 722 8321;
www.cycladic.gr 🕐 Mon., Wed. and Fri.–Sat. 10–5,
Thu. 10–8, Sun. 11–5 Ⓜ Syntagma or Evangelismós
🚌 3, 7, 13, 224, 235 🍴 Café in museum 💵 $$

Lykavittós and Kolonáki

From Kolonáki Square, the hub of one
of Athens' most fashionable shopping
areas, the slopes of Lykavittós
(Lycabettus Hill) rise steeply to the
912-foot-high summit, one of the city's
great vantage points. You can walk up or
take the funicular for panoramic views
over the city, from the Acropolis down
to the sea at Piréas. Get there for sunset,
and visit the whitewashed chapel of
Agios Giorgios (St. George), which
crowns the top of the hill.

➕ D2–D3 ✉ Kolonáki 🕐 Funicular: daily
9 a.m.–midnight (times may vary) 🚌 022, 060
🍴 Terrace restaurant at top 💵 $$ (funicular)

Monastiráki

This bustling area surrounds
Monastiráki Square, named for a former
monastery on this site. Today the
square's focal point is the 18th-century
Tzistarakis Mosque, a relic of Turkish

rule, which houses the Keramiki Silogi (Museum of Greek Ceramics). Most people head straight for Monastiráki's famous flea market, selling anything from clothes and kebabs to icons and CDs. Sunday is the big day here.

➕ B2 ✉ Monastiráki ☎ Museum of Greek Ceramics: 210 324 2066 ⏱ Market open daily, but largest on Sun. Museum: Wed.–Mon. 9–2:30 🚇 Monastiráki 🎟 $ (free to all some Sun. in winter)

Naós tou Olympíou Diós and Pýli Adrianoú

Along with the Tower of the Winds in the Roman Agora, Naós tou Olympíou Diós and Pýli Adrianoú (Temple of Olympian Zeus and Hadrian's Arch) are Athens' most impressive Roman legacy. Both of these structures were completed around AD 130 by the Emperor Hadrian; the temple as a shrine to this paramount Roman god, and the arch to mark the boundary between the old Greek city and Hadrian's new one. Fifteen massive columns remain of what was once the largest temple in Greece.

➕ C1 ✉ 2 Vasilissis Olgas ☎ 210 922 6330 ⏱ Daily 8–3 🚇 Akrópoli 🚌 1, 4, 11, 040, 057 🎟 $

Piréas

Piréas is a town in its own right, although it's only five stops on the subway from Athens' city center. It's a noisy, bustling port, one of the biggest in the Mediterranean, and many of the interisland boats leave from its harbor. Piréas boasts a magnificent cathedral, rebuilt after World War II; a fine archeological museum with some striking exhibits; and Greece's national naval museum.

Come here on a Sunday for a leisurely browse in the flea market.

➕ Off map at A2 🚇 Piréas

Pláka

Visitors return time and again to the pretty Pláka neighborhood, at the foot of the Acropolis. The maze of colorful narrow streets, flower-bedecked squares and huge range of stores and tavernas may be touristy, but they also radiate timeless charm. Bustling Kidhathineon and Adrianoú, the main thoroughfares, teem with noisy street life and are lined with mainly 19th-century, colorfully painted houses.

Don't miss the dazzling white alleys that make up Anafiotika, on the northern slopes of the Acropolis. This area was built in the 1840s by masons from the Cycladic islands, and it still retains a village atmosphere.

➕ C2 ✉ Pláka 🚇 Syntagma or Monastiráki 🚌 9, 11, 15, 025, 026

Plateía Syntágmatos

Noisy, crowded, Plateía Syntágmatos (Constitution Square) is at the heart of modern Athens, where you'll find a variety of hotels, offices, banks, restaurants and myriad jostling Athenians. The neoclassic edifice at the top is the Voulí (Parliament Building), which was once the royal palace. In front of it is the Tomb of the Unknown Soldier, patrolled around the clock by the Evzones, a guard of honor whose dress uniform features a short pleated kilt and pom-poms on their shoes.

The central area is pleasantly pedestrianized, with several cafés.

➕ C2 ✉ Syntágmatos 🚇 Syntagma 🚌 1, 2, 4, 5, 022, 025, 026 ⓘ Changing of the guard at varied times Mon.–Fri., at 11 a.m. on Sun.

Acropolis Museum

The stunning Mouséio Akrópolis, built at a cost of €130 million, opened in June 2009. The interior of the long-awaited yet controversially modern building is phenomenal with its superbly designed galleries, subtle lighting and spectacular views of the Acropolis. The museum exhibits some 4,000 interesting artifacts.

➕ C1 ✉ Dionysiou Areopagitou 15 ☎ 210 900 0900; www.theacropolismuseum.gr ⏱ Mon. 8–4, Tue.–Thu. and Sat.–Sun. 8–8, Fri. 8 a.m.–10 p.m. Last admission 7:30 p.m. Closed public holidays 🚇 Akrópoli 🎟 $$

An Excursion To Delphi

The sacred site of Delphi (Delfoí), 93 miles northwest of Athens, is the obvious choice for a day trip. The greatest shrine of the ancient Greek world, the center of their earth, lies in an unrivaled position below the great peaks of Mount Parnassós. Dedicated to the god Apollo, in ancient times Delphi was independent – belonging to no state – so enemies could worship there together. It was famed for its oracle, which gave enigmatic and prophetic advice through the medium of a priestess.

In return for this, petitioners brought gifts and erected treasure-houses to hold them; ancient writers referred to the marble and precious stones of the sanctuary. For centuries, pilgrims trudged through the mountains to bathe in the sacred Castalian spring and worship here, but in the fourth century Christianity triumphed and the last oracle slipped away. Below the site, olive groves spread down to the sea, the ground is carpeted with flowers and the sky is full of birds.

The French excavated Delphi in the 1890s, and today it lies on a series of terraces below Parnassós. The paved Sacred Way leads past treasure-houses – one has been sensitively reconstructed – to the remains of the Temple of Apollo. Six columns still stand, giving an idea of the ancient ruin's former size and grandeur.

Up the hill you'll find the 5,000-seat theater and the marvelously evocative and well-preserved athletic stadium, set amid pine trees. To visit the ruins of the Sanctuary of Athena, you will need to leave the main site and cross the modern road. Use the columns of the fourth-century BC Tholos, undoubtedly the most photographed of all Delphi's wonders, as your guide.

The adjacent museum contains the finds from Delphi, some of the finest in Greece. Sculptures from the Temple of Apollo, two superb examples of archaic *koroi* (statues), ivory, jewelry and pottery are all here. The highlight of the collection is the striking bronze sculpture of a charioteer, which dates from 478 BC and is an artistic and technical masterpiece.

➕ See page 240, B2 ✉ Delphi ☎ 226 508 2312 or 226 508 2346 🕐 Daily 8–7. Museum 8–8
💲💲 ℹ A guided excursion is the easiest way to visit Delphi

Excursion Operators Chat Tours (✉ 9 Xenofontos Street, off Amalias Avenue ☎ 210 323 0827; www.chatours.gr) is an experienced tour operator in Athens

The Sacred Way leads past this well-reconstructed Treasury building at Delphi

Hungary

Opposite: Hősök tere (Heroes' Square), Budapest, with statues of the ancient leaders who founded Hungary

Hungary

Hungary is situated at the heart of Europe. Surrounded by Austria, Slovakia, Ukraine, Romania, Serbia, Croatia and Slovenia, it has absorbed the cultures of such peoples and conquerors as the Romans, Magyars, Turks and Habsburgs. Its majestic capital, Budapest, sits on the broad Danube river, which has brought trade and settlers through the country on its course from southern Germany to the Black Sea.

For centuries Hungary has been a nation in flux, its territories gaining or diminishing through much invasion, occupation and liberation.

It is today undergoing yet further change after emerging from more than 40 years of life behind the Iron Curtain and transitioning to a modern democracy and member of the European Union.

Landscape of History

Northern, western and southern Hungary are different worlds. In the north, beyond the architecturally beautiful capital of Budapest and the industrial city of Miskolc, are the uplands and their wide, rolling, forested hills. The vineyards in this region produce the famous Tokay (Tokaj) and Bull's Blood (Egri Bikavér), the "wine of kings and king of wines."

In the west there continue to be strong links with Western European culture. The rich farmlands are punctuated with historic towns that have many examples of both fine Renaissance and ornate baroque buildings.

In the south and east the landscape changes completely. Vast, flat grasslands form the *puszta* of the Great Plain (Alföld), dotted with farmsteads are presided over by the regional capital, Debrecen. In the far south, the medieval city of Pécs, provincial capital of the county of Baranya, preserves many relics of its 143 years under Turkish rule.

Making Contact

The Hungarian language, distantly related to Finnish and Estonian, can be daunting for visitors. English may be spoken in the main tourist areas, but German is more frequently used. When you find a common language, however, you will discover that Hungarians are courteous and generous, but formal.

Hungary is a multiethnic nation, and despite its close proximity to the Balkan region, it considers itself to be West European.

Hungarian Heritage

Hungarians have strong folk traditions and customs, especially when it comes to music and dance. You can enjoy them at a dance house (*táncház*); there are several in Budapest. Bands usually include bagpipes, cimbalom (a stringed instrument) and a hurdy-gurdy, and the dancing is fast and furious.

In Kiskunság National Park, between the Danube and the Tisza rivers, a horse-drawn buggy takes visitors to see farmsteads, long-horned cattle and curly-horned Podokan sheep. There also are displays at Hortobágy National Park – Hungary's first national park – with its endless grasslands.

In the Cserhát hills of the north, the village of Hollókő sits at the foot of a 13th-century castle. The village is home to the Palóc people, who speak a distinct regional dialect and wear colorful embroidered costumes and elaborate headdresses. For another insight into

Hungary's heritage, visit the famous Király thermal baths in Budapest and enjoy the luxury of a Turkish-style bath or massage.

More Top Destinations in Hungary

- Balatonfüred B2
- Bugac-Puszta C2
- Eger D3
- Fertőd A2
- Gödöllő C2
- Hollókő C3
- Hortobágyi Nemzeti Park D2
- Kecskemét C2
- Mátra C3
- Pécs B1
- Sopron A3
- Szabadtéri Néprajzi Múzeum C2
- Szentendre C2
- Tihany B2
- Tokaj D3
- Visegrád C3

Timeline

13 BC	The Roman province of Pannonia is established on the west bank of the Danube; nomadic tribes occupy the east.
AD 896	Seven Magyar tribes cross the Carpathian Mountains and invade the Hungarian plains.
1000	King Stephen is crowned and makes Hungary a centralized, Christian state.
1443	King Matthias I, considered the greatest Hungarian king, is born in Cluj-Napoca, in modern-day Romania.
1526	The Turkish army of Sultan Suleiman I defeats the Hungarians at Mohács.
1686	Habsburg troops recapture Buda, on the west bank of the Danube (later united with Pest, on the east).
1896	The Great Exposition celebrates the 1,000th anniversary of the Magyar Conquest.
1919	Hungary briefly becomes a Bolshevik republic.
1920	Under the Treaty of Trianon, Hungary loses two-thirds of its territory to Czechoslovakia, Yugoslavia and Romania.
1939	Hungary enters World War II as a German ally.
1944	German occupation; most Jews are deported to concentration camps.
1948	Communists take power.
1956	Rebellion against Communist rule is crushed by Soviet troops.
1989	Hungary opens its borders to Austria and the Iron Curtain begins to lift.
1990	Free elections are won by a center-right coalition.
1999	Hungary officially joins NATO.
2004	Hungary joins the European Union.
2006	Danube floods to record levels.
2010	Pécs is the European Capital of Culture.
2011	Celebrations mark the 200th anniversary of the birth of composer Franz Liszt.
2014	Center-right Prime Minister Viktor Orban wins reelection in a vote dominated by right-wing parties.
2015	Hungary's European border crossings come under pressure as thousands of Syrian refugees and migrants try to cross Europe.

The Good Old Days

Hungary enjoyed two "golden ages" – one in the 15th century and another in the 19th. Under 15th-century ruler King Matthias, the son of a Transylvanian general, the nation expanded its borders and established its court in Vienna. Matthias patronized some of Europe's most brilliant scholars, and employed the best Italian artists to work on his palace in Visegrád. Ruins were unearthed here in the 1930s. His reign became a byword for good government. When he died, say Hungarians, justice died with him. The man known as "the greatest Hungarian" ushered in a second age of achievement. In the 19th century Count István Széchenyi modernized the country, laying surfaced roads, introducing steamships and founding an academy of sciences. He also linked Buda and Pest with the Chain Bridge, and stopped the regular cycle of floods around the Tisza river by building dams that regulated its flow.

Survival Guide

- Hungary is not a place to visit if you are on a strict diet. Its best-known export, *gulyás* (goulash), is a soup made with beef, onions, potatoes, paprika, tomatoes, garlic and caraway seeds. Salami is a familiar item, as is *lecso*, a mix of peppers, tomatoes, onions and bacon fried in pork fat. Pastries also are specialties, sold in the *cukrászda* (pastry shop). Try *palacsinta*, thin pancakes filled with all manner of goodies, from poppy seeds to chocolate to curd cheese.

- Rural Hungarians produce and sell beautifully crafted items such as embroidered blouses and carved wood furniture. Buy these in city stores, at national parks and from street sellers like the costumed Transylvanian (Romanian) Hungarians.

- Wine is another good Hungarian buy, sold by dealers in the main vineyards, such as Eger. The vineyards on the slopes of Lake Balaton are delightful and many give tastings in their barrel-lined cellars.

- Go to street markets in the main towns and cities, such as the popular morning flea market on the southwest outskirts of Pécs. This is one of the biggest open-air markets in the country, selling antiques, crafts and food. On Sundays it also sells livestock, and the place is packed with country people.

- Some of the most fascinating ethnic communities have inevitably become big tourist magnets. Hollókő is filled with visitors for the August Palóc Festival and for Easter – an important celebration everywhere, marked with processions, egg-painting and a water-splashing ceremony.

- Summer festivals attract crowds to Pécs and Sopron in June, and on St. Stephen's Day on August 20. There are fireworks, fairs and processions all over Hungary.

- The state railroad, Hungarian Railways (operating passenger trains as MÁV-Start), travels all over the country, though the service is being reduced in rural areas. Special Eurail One Country tourist passes offer unlimited use of the network for 3 to 8 days: contact MÁV-Start (BH-1426 Budapest, P.O. Box 56 ☎ 06 40 49 49 49; 1 444 4499 from outside Hungary; www.mav-start.hu).

- Accommodations are not limited to city hotels. The Danube bend, a spectacular deep gorge north of Budapest, is lined with attractive towns where many private homes offer rooms. The resorts around Lake Balaton are another option.

- For overnight stays on the Great Plain, try the Hortobágy Club Hotel in Hortobágy National Park (BH-4071 Hortobágy-Máta; ☎ 52 369 020; www.hortusnaturaehotels.hu) or the Sarlóspuszta Club Hotel near Dabas (BH-2375 Tatárszentgyörgy-Sarlóspuszta ☎ 29 319 118; www.sarlospuszta.hu).

Detail of the entrance of National Széchényi Library

Hungary

Budapest

Until the 19th century, two communities faced each other across the Danube. Royal, medieval Buda, with its majestic architecture, stood on the hilly western bank; and modern Pest, a flat area of busy boulevards, was on the east bank. Then the Chain Bridge (Széchenyi lánchíd) was built and Budapest, "Queen of the Danube," was created, linking the green uplands behind Buda, and the flat fields of the Great Plain beyond Pest.

Crossing the Divide

The best place to get a feel for the capital's character and history is at Buda. Here you will find the oldest and grandest architecture, museums and galleries, and cafés and bars. You can survey the whole city from Gellért Hill (Gellért-hegy, see page 261), and visit Castle Hill (Várhegy), a renovated medieval quarter which is reached by funicular railroad from the Buda end of Chain Bridge (Budavári Sikló). This is where you'll find the Buda Castle (Budai Vár, see page 261) and the Fisherman's Bastion (Halászbástya, see page 262).

Pest has a much more contemporary feel; its main landmark is the neo-Gothic parliament building (Országház, see pages 263–264) on the riverbank. Also worth visiting are the Hungarian State Opera House (Magyar Állami Operaház, see page 262) and the Hungarian National Museum (Magyar Nemzeti Múzeum, see page 263). Between the riverbanks is tranquil Margaret Island (Margit-sziget), named after St. Margaret, a medieval nun of royal birth.

Local Flavors

In the late 19th and early 20th centuries Budapest ranked with Vienna and Paris as part of European café society, drawing artists and intellectuals to its great coffeehouses. At the end of World War II, few of these hubs of creative life remained. The Café Restaurant New York, at (Erzsébet körút 9–11, ☎ 1 886 6111; www.newyorkcafe.hu) manages to preserve the aura of those days.

Traditionally, Hungarian meals rely on the staples of spices, meat and cream and include intriguing specialties such as *túrós csusza* (pasta with cheese curd and sour cream). Since 1989 the range of international restaurant options has increased immeasurably.

Budapest at Night

The main home of opera and ballet is the Hungarian State Opera House (Magyar Állami Operaház, Andrássy út 22, ☎ 1 81 47 100; www.opera.hu), a massive neo-Renaissance confection. Classical concerts occasionally take place in the Academy of Music (Zeneakadémia, Liszt Ferenc tér 8, ☎ 1 462 4600; www.zeneakademia.hu). There are many clubs, rock venues, bars and discos. Since the mid-1990s Hungary has been included in the mainstream of European pop and rock. There are several English-language websites with entertainment listings, as well as the popular monthly magazine *Budapest Panorama* (www.budapestpanorama.com).

Halászbástya (Fisherman's Bastion) in Budapest

Shopping

Pedestrian-only Váci utca, on the Pest side of the river, is the perfect place to begin shopping trips as well as other main boulevards in central Pest. In Buda, there's an excellent browsing area around Móricz Zsigmond körtér.

A well-known flea market (Ecseri) sets up daily (mornings on Sunday) at Nagykőrösi út 156 (☎ 030 365 5708; www.ecseri.hu). It's also a pleasure to wander among the stalls of the renovated Nagy-vásárcsarnok (Central Market Hall) on Vámház körút 1–3 (☎ 1 366 3300; www.piaconline.hu). The market is open all day Monday to Saturday until 2 p.m.

Essential Information

Tourist Information

Budapestinfo (Tourism Office of Budapest)
Sütő utca 2 ☎ 1 438 8080 (all offices)
www.budapestinfo.hu
Deak Ferenc tér, Sütő utca 2 (daily 8–8)
Liszt Ferenc tér 11 (Mon.–Fri. 10–6)
Budapest Liszt Ferenc International Airport:
Terminal 2A and Terminal 2B, daily 8–8

Urban Transportation

Metro (subway) lines are color coded: yellow (M1), red (M2), blue (M3) and green (M4). Buy tickets from the counter *(pénztár)* until 8 p.m., then from the section called *forgalmi ugyelét*. Trains run daily 4:30 a.m.–11 p.m. Buses with red or black numbers and no letter stop all over the city; avoid the express buses, which have a letter "E." Trams and trolley buses also have an extensive network and run daily 4:30 a.m.–11 p.m. Tickets are available from transport terminals, metro stations, vending machines or newsstands. For public transportation information ☎ (36) 1 3-255-255; www.bkv.hu. Metro stations are marked with an "M" on the city map. Make sure that taxis display a sign and the meter is on and running. The biggest city taxi company is Fötaxi (☎ 1 222 2222; www.fotaxi.hu).

Airport Information

Budapest's Ferenc Liszt International Airport is 12 miles southeast of the center: Terminal 2A serves flights within the European Union's Common Schengen border, while Terminal 2B serves other international flights. For flight details ☎ 090 181 818; general information; ☎ 1 296 7000; www.bud.hu. The cheapest way to reach the center is by bus 200E, which runs from both terminals and to the Kőbánya-Kispet metro station. Airport minibuses depart regularly; go to the Airport Minibus Service desk or book at www.airportshuttle.hu.

Climate – average highs and lows for the month

Jan.	Feb.	Mar.	Apr.	May	Jun.	Jul.	Aug.	Sep.	Oct.	Nov.	Dec.
2°C	4°C	10°C	15°C	22°C	24°C	26°C	26°C	22°C	15°C	7°C	3°C
36°F	39°F	50°F	59°F	72°F	75°F	79°F	79°F	72°F	59°F	45°F	37°F
-4°C	-3°C	1°C	5°C	10°C	14°C	15°C	15°C	11°C	6°C	1°C	-3°C
25°F	27°F	34°F	41°F	50°F	57°F	59°F	59°F	52°F	43°F	34°F	27°F

Budapest Sights

Key to symbols

➕ map coordinates refer to the Budapest map on pages 258–259 💵 admission charge: $$$ more than Ft1,000, $$ Ft600–Ft1,000, $ less than Ft600 See page 5 for complete key to symbols

Budai Vár

A UNESCO World Heritage Site, Budai Vár (Buda Castle) looks down over the Danube from the southern end of Várhegy (Castle Hill). Little is left of the earliest castle, built in the 13th century under Béla IV.

What remains is in the underground passages and cellars, now part of the Budapesti Történeti Múzeum (Budapest History Museum), in Wing E, which displays Roman, medieval and more recent finds, and has an excellent collection of historical paintings and prints. The castle was rebuilt in the second half of the 20th century with a neoclassical dome.

The Magyar Nemzeti Galéria (Hungarian National Gallery) collection of Hungarian art is housed in Buildings A, B, C and D, under the dome. A walk from here through a peaceful garden square and past the lovely Matthias Fountain takes you to the West Wing (F) and the Országos Széchényi Könyvtár (National Széchényi Library), which stores some 2 million books.

There are several statues outside the palace, including Prince Eugene of Savoy, who routed the Turkish armies; King Matthias, in the west courtyard; and a mythical bird called the Turul.

➕ B2 ✉ Várhegy 🚌 For all attractions: 5, 16, 16a, 78, 116; tram 18, 19, 41; funicular from west end of Chain Bridge

Budapesti Történeti Múzeum ✉ Szent György tér 2 ☎ 1 487 8800; www.btm.hu 🕐 Tue.–Sun. 10–6, Mar.–Oct.; Tue.–Sun. 10–4, rest of year 💵 $$$

Magyar Nemzeti Galéria ☎ 1 201 9082; www.mng.hu 🕐 Tue.–Sun. 10–6 🍴 Gallery café 💵 $$ (free on public holidays) ❗ Guided tours (book in advance)

Országos Széchényi Könyvtár ☎ 1 224 3700; www.oszk.hu 🕐 General collection Tue.–Sat. 10–9 💵 $

Gellért-hegy

Bishop Gellért failed to convert the pagan Magyars to Christianity; legend has it they stuck him in a barrel and threw him into the river from this 771-foot-high limestone cliff. His statue stands at the bottom of Gellért-hegy (Gellért Hill).

At the top is the Citadella (Citadel), a stronghold built after the 1848–49 War of Independence to watch over the restive citizens. Inside the fortifications are a war museum, an exhibition, hotel and restaurant. The Szabadság szobor (Freedom Monument), also at the top, was erected by the Russians in 1947. Before the fall of Communism, the monument featured a Soviet soldier as well as the now lone woman brandishing a palm leaf.

➕ B1 ✉ Between Erzsébet híd (Elizabeth Bridge) and Szabadság híd (Freedom Bridge) 🚌 7; tram 47, 49 🍴 Panorama, see page 479

Matthias Fountain on the north wall of Buda Castle

The columned entrance to Magyar Nemzeti Múzeum

Halászbástya

Halászbástya (Fisherman's Bastion) is one of the city's greatest tourist draws: a fairy-tale, seven-towered rampart in pale stone wedged into the eastern rim of Castle Hill. The architect, Frigyes Schulek, designed the fortress as part of the city's millennial celebrations of Magyar nationhood in 1896.

This is the perfect place to enjoy some great river views, and to browse the souvenir stalls and shops.

➕ A3 ✉ Szentháromság tér, Várhegy ☎ No phone; www.fishermansbastion.com 🕓 Daily 9 a.m.–11 p.m., Apr.–Sep. 🚌 16, Várbusz (Castle Bus) from Moszkva tér 💳 $ 🍴 Alabárdos, see page 479

Hősök tere

At the end of the grand Andrássy út and at the entrance to Városliget (City Park) is magnificent Hősök tere (Heroes' Square), which was designed to mark the city's 1896 millennial celebrations. On either side of the square are the Műcsarnok (Palace of Arts) and the Szépművészeti Múzeum (Museum of Fine Arts, closed for renovation until 2018); between these two buildings is a monument to Hungarian successes. Perched on a 118-foot-high column is the Archangel Gabriel; guarding the foot of the column are statues of the seven

fierce and triumphant Magyar chiefs, with Árpád, their leader, in the center. They are flanked by colonnades bearing the figures of Fame, Knowledge, Peace and War; between the columns there are more Hungarian icons, including King Stephen (who would later be sainted).

➕ D4 ✉ Andrássy út 🚇 Hősök tere

Iparművészeti Múzeum

The striking green-tiled roof and building of the Iparművészeti Múzeum (Museum of Applied Art) is worth a look in its own right. A fine example of art nouveau architecture, it dates from the end of the 19th century. The museum's collections include furniture, metalwork, ceramics and glassware, reflecting the different periods of its 140-year history. There also is an impressive array of Ottoman Turkish carpets, jewelry, bookbinding and leatherwork. The building itself is the star here though, providing dozens of glimpses of intricate masonry, tiling and glazing.

➕ D1 ✉ Üllöi útca 33–37 ☎ 1 456 5107; www.imm.hu 🕓 Tue.–Sun. 10–6 🚇 M3 Corvin-negyed 🚋 Tram 4, 6 💳 $$$

Magyar Állami Operaház

The Magyar Állami Operaház (Hungarian State Opera House) building has beautiful marble-work, gold leaf and frescoes. Opened in 1884, it celebrates the musical world with statues of Beethoven, Mozart, Verdi and Wagner on the stone cornice of the front terrace. Pride of place goes to Hungarians Franz Liszt and opera composer Ferenc Erkel, whose statues flank the entrance.

Inside the building an enormous bronze chandelier hangs over the auditorium, which is decorated with dazzling frescoes of the Greek gods by Károly Lotz.

➕ C3 ✉ Andrássy út 22; tours begin at Hajós utca entrance ☎ 1 353 0170 (box office) or 1 332 8197 (tours); www.operavisit.hu 🕓 Tours daily at 3 and 4 (duration 45 minutes) 🚇 Opera 🚋 4 🍴 Művész Kávéház, see page 479 💳 Tour $$$

Spires and turrets characterize the Országház, the parliament building

Magyar Nemzeti Múzeum

Five collections form the Magyar Nemzeti Múzeum (Hungarian National Museum), Hungary's largest museum, covering an area of 861,111 square feet. They include Roman artifacts, medieval and modern displays, a numismatic collection and historical portraits. The prize among the exhibits is the mantle from St. Stephen's 11th-century crown. The crown jewels were recovered from Nazi sympathizers at the end of World War II and found their way to the United States. President Jimmy Carter ordered their return in 1978. The crown and other regalia are at the Hungarian Parliament Building (Országház, see right). Other curiosities are the inscribed brick from a 13th-century monk's tomb and the tent of a Turkish commander taken at the siege of Vienna in 1683.

✚ C2 ✉ Múzeum körút 14–16 ☎ 1 327 7773; www.mnm.hu ⊘ Tue.–Sun. 10–6 🚇 Astoria or Kálvin tér 🚌 9, 15; tram 47, 49 🍽 Café 💷 $$$ ❙ Tours (book in advance)

Mátyás-templom

Fifteenth-century King Matthias was married twice in the Mátyás-templom (Matthias Church), which had already been in existence for two centuries. It later served the Turks as a mosque, and was remodeled in the 19th century in striking neo-Gothic style. Medieval touches have been reproduced in the interior, along with dramatic features such as the soaring 262-foot spire. The tombs of 12th-century monarch Béla III and his wife, Anne of Châtillon, are in the Trinity Chapel near the main door.

✚ A3 ✉ Szentháromság tér 2 ☎ 1 489 0716; www. matyas-templom.hu ⊘ Religious visits: daily 6 a.m.–8 p.m.; tourists generally Mon.–Fri. 9–5, Sat. 9–1, Sun. 1–5 🚌 16 💷 Religious visits free; tourists $$

Nagy Zsinagóga

Budapest's Great Synagogue marks the site of the former Jewish quarter and is one of the largest Jewish houses of worship in the world. It's home to the city's excellent Jewish Museum, as well as a Holocaust Memorial.

✚ C2 ✉ Dohány ut 2–8 ☎ 1 343-0420; www.dohanystreetsynagogue.hu ⊘ Sun.–Thu. 10–5:30, Fri. 10–4, Apr.–Oct.; early closing rest of year 🚇 Astoria 💷 $$$ ❙ Call ahead for guided tours

Országház

Bristling with neo-Gothic spires and turrets, the Országház (parliament building) sits on the eastern bank of the Danube, and covers an enormous 200,000 square feet. Its red dome is 315 feet high and rises above a 16-sided hall between the upper and lower houses of parliament.

✚ B3 ✉ Kossuth Lajos tér 1–3 ☎ 1 441 4904; www.parlament.hu ⊘ Guided tours in English daily at

10, noon, 1, 2, and 3 (subject to parliamentary sessions)
🎫 Kossuth tér 🚇 15; tram 2; trolley bus 70, 78
💵 $$$ (tickets available from the visitor center or in advance online) ⓘ Long lines for tours in summer

Széchenyi Gyógyfürdő és Uszoda
This sprawling complex of 15 indoor and three outdoor pools, plus thermal baths and steam rooms, is the most popular and accessible for visitors of Budapest's many public baths. The bathing complex dates from the early 20th century, but it was thoroughly modernized in 1999 and is clean and safe. The location is within Budapest's large City Park (Városliget).
➕ E4 ✉ Állatkerti Körút 9–11 ☎ 1 363 3210
🕐 Pools: daily 6 a.m.–10 p.m. Thermal baths: daily 6 a.m.–7 p.m. 🎫 Széchenyi fürdő 🚇 Trolley bus 72 💵 $$$

Szent István Bazilika
Budapest's biggest church, Szent István Bazilika (St. Stephen's Basilica), took 55 years to finish, and its dazzling interior includes 90 pounds of 24-carat gold. Transylvanian and Hungarian heroes are represented by 88 statues, and the most cherished item – the mummified right hand of St. Stephen – displayed in a glass case. The 315-foot-high dome provides views of the city.
➕ C3 ✉ Svent István tér 33 ☎ 1 338 2151 (tours); www.bazilika.biz 🕐 Church: Mon.–Fri. 9–5, Sat. 9–1, Sun. 1–5. Chapel: Mon.–Sat. 9–5, Sun. 1–5, Apr.–Oct.; Mon.–Sat. 10–4, Sun. 1–5, rest of year. Dome: daily 10–5:30, Apr.–Oct. Tours in English (Mon.–Sat. 10–3)
🎫 Bajcsy-Zsilinsky út or Deák tér, Arany János utca 🚇 15; trolley bus 70, 72, 78 💵 Free; dome $; tour $$$

Városliget
Beyond the boulevards of Pest is Városliget (City Park). It was laid out in the 18th century and has acquired several extras over the years. The oddest is Vajdahunyad vára (Vajdahunyad Castle), built for the 1896 World Exhibition and based on a Transylvanian fortress. Inside the walls is the Magyar Mezőgazdasági Múzeum (Hungarian Agricultural Museum). The Állatkert

(zoo) is another favorite, as is the Fővárosi Nagycirkusz (circus).

In the southeast corner are the Közlekedési Múzeum (Museum of Transportation) and the Petőfi Csarnok youth center, hosting pop concerts in summer. The hall contains the Repüléstörténeti Múzeum (Aviation Museum), with the space capsule flown by the first Hungarian cosmonaut.

Magyar Mezőgazdasági Múzeum ➕ E4
✉ Vajdahunyad vára ☎ 1 363 1117;
www.mmgm.hu 🕐 Tue.–Sun. 10–5, Apr.–Oct.;
Tue.–Sun. 10–4 (also Sat.–Sun. 4–5), rest of year
🎫 Széchenyi fürdő 🚇 Trolley bus 72, 75, 79
🍴 Gundel, see page 479 💵 $$

Állatkert ➕ D4 ✉ Állatkerti Körút 6–12 ☎ 1 273 4900; www.zoobudapest.com 🕐 Mon.–Thu. 9–6:30, Fri.–Sun. 9–7, May–Aug.; daily 9–4, Nov.–Feb.; Mon.–Thu. 9–5, Fri.–Sun. 9–5:30, Mar. and Oct.; Mon.–Thu. 9–5:30, Fri.–Sun. 9–6, rest of year
🎫 Széchenyi fürdő 🚇 Trolley bus 72, 75, 79
🍴 Gundel, see page 479 💵 $$$

Fővárosi Nagycirkusz ➕ E4 ✉ Állatkerti út 12
☎ 1 343 8300; www.fnc.hu 🕐 Mar.–Aug. Call or check website for details 🎫 Széchenyi fürdő
🚇 Trolley bus 70, 72, 75, 79 🍴 Gundel, see page 479
💵 $$$

Közlekedési Múzeum ➕ E4 ✉ Városligeti körút 11
☎ 1 273 3840; www.mmkm.hu 🕐 Tue.–Sun. 10–5 (also Sat.–Sun. 5–6), May–Sep.; Tue.–Sun. 10–4 (also Sat.–Sun. 4–5), rest of year 🎫 Széchenyi fürdő
🚇 Trolley bus 75, 79 🍴 Gundel, see page 479 💵 $$

Petőfi Csarnok/Repüléstörténeti Múzeum ➕ E4
✉ Zichy Mihály utca 14–16 ☎ 1 273 3840;
www.mmkm.hu 🕐 Tue.–Fri. 10–5, Sat.–Sun. 10–6,
May–Oct. 🎫 Széchenyi fürdő 🚇 Trolley bus 72, 75, 79 🍴 Gundel, see page 479 💵 $

The Danube Esplanade
Running alongside the river on the Pest bank, between Chain Bridge (Széchenyi lánchíd) and Elizabeth Bridge (Erzsébet híd), is the broad, tree-lined Danube Esplanade (Duna-korzó). In the 19th century, this was the most fashionable place to be seen. The elaborate Pesti Vigadó (Pest Concert Hall) is a legacy of that era, and still a venue for classical music concerts.

Excursion to Esztergom

Hungary's largest cathedral towers over the stunning scenery of the
Danube Bend at Esztergom, former royal city and the birthplace of King
Stephen I (975–1038). There has been a settlement here, guarding the
western approach to the gorge, since Roman times. Medieval Esztergom
was destroyed by the Turks in 1543, but the city rose again, and it now
boasts a center full of ornate baroque buildings.

The cathedral (*bazilika*) is by far the most imposing: It is 328 feet from
the floor to the top of its huge, glittering dome, which is visible for miles
around. It includes one of the world's biggest paintings – an altarpiece
based on the work of 16th-century Italian artist Titian. The white marble
altar itself was designed in 1519 and made by expert craftsmen from
Florence, Italy.

Among other treasures are the impressive Renaissance interior of the
Bakócz Chapel, dedicated to Archbishop Tomás Bakócz, and a gold and
enamel Gothic cross, studded with pearls and precious stones, known as
the Calvary of Matthias Corvinus. The dome offers a spectacular view over
Esztergom and its surroundings.

The present version of the cathedral was begun in the 1820s: Hungarian
composer Franz Liszt celebrated its reconsecration in 1856 with a Mass.
Long before this second lease of life, Esztergom was the seat of the
Hungarian Primate – head of the nation's Catholic Church – and an
important royal base. King Stephen was crowned in a church on the site
in AD 1000, and the remains of a royal palace are housed in the Castle
Museum (Vár Múzeum) next door.

Two other museums are worth a visit. The Museum of Christian Art
(Keresztény Múzeum) has a superb collection of medieval religious
paintings and works by Italian artists such as Duccio di Buoninsegna,
Lorenzo di Credi and Giovanni di Paolo. The Danube Museum (Duna
Múzeum) features displays that clearly illustrate (despite Hungarian-only
captions) the role of the river and its effects on the life of the town.

Esztergom is 41 miles north of Budapest. To travel by bus, take metro M3 to Árpád híd, then the
Vólanbusz intercity bus (line 800) direct to Esztergom (www.volanbusz.hu).

In summer, boats leave from Vigadó tér landing stage (journey time 70 minutes). Contact Mahart
☎ 1 484 4013; www.mahartpassnave.hu.

There is a regular service from Nyugati (Western) railroad station.

Hungary's largest cathedral, begun in the 1820s, dominates Esztergom

Ireland

Opposite: Giant's Head in County Antrim, with Dunluce Castle in the background

Ireland

Ireland

People long for Ireland in a way that they pine for few other countries. Call it romantic, call it sentimental, but there is something about this remarkable country that tugs at the heartstrings of even those who have no Irish blood.

The beauty of the country, its powerful Gaelic traditions and the irrepressibly romantic and creative nature of the Irish people underscore this potent appeal.

This is a country that is not without problems, however, and its political and religious divide has had far-reaching, universal impact.

Mists of Time

Ireland claims with pride that it was a "land of saints and scholars" when the rest of Europe was deep in the Dark Ages. It is often described as a Celtic country, with all the myth-making that goes along with that term.

The Celts are seen as being a distinctive lost race of Iron Age people who, in the face of first Roman and then Anglo-Saxon aggression, retreated into Scotland, Ireland, Wales and Cornwall in England, from which they passed down the cultural values of their time. They did not call themselves Celts, and the term may be only a convenient label, but what is certain is that the influence

of the earliest Bronze Age and Iron Age cultures survives on the peripheries of the British Isles. This is especially true in Ireland, where the Gaelic language, still heard today and experiencing a revival, is its greatest expression.

There are thousands of prehistoric sites in Ireland, including megalithic tombs, stone circles and cairns littering the countryside: on the remote western seaboard, on the Beara Peninsula, in County Kerry, and at exceptional places such as the Brù na Bòinne burial complex, in County Meath, north of Dublin. Together with evidence of primitive dwellings such as *crannógs* (island settlements) and ring forts, Ireland's heritage is everywhere to be seen. Even where they are ruinous and vestigial, these ancient sites are hauntingly evocative.

You will find within the same landscape the music, poetry, wit and drama of Ireland that have been enshrined in hundreds of films, songs, dances and stories. A sense of the past is intense here; it has shaped Ireland in a seminal way, for better or for worse.

From Dublin to Kerry

Dublin is the boisterous heart of Ireland, the "family home." It should not be missed, of course, but Dublin will only whet your appetite for the rest of the country. Save time to explore other areas for the essential Irish experience. South of the capital lie the Wicklow Mountains, with the popular Glendalough at their heart – half religious site, wholly spectacular from a scenic point of view.

Farther south lies the fascinating Viking town of Wexford, from where the long, rambling southern coast of Ireland runs through endless great bays toward the distant west (and the most spectacular scenery).

The western coast stretches for nearly 180 miles from north to south, but measures much more if all the many sinuous indentations, bays, river

IRELAND

N

NORTH
ATLANTIC
OCEAN

Malin
Head
Giant's
Causeway
Rathlin
Island
Ballycastle
Lough
Foyle
Coleraine
Rathmullan
Letterkenny
Dungloe
N13
**Londonderry/
Derry**
A26
Ballymena
N14
NORTHERN
Antrim
A2
Ardara
Ballybofey
Strabane
IRELAND
Bangor
N15
Cookstown
Lough
Neagh
M2
Donegal
Omagh
Titanic Belfast
Ballyshannon
A32
M1
BELFAST
Erris
Head
Donegal
Bay
Bundoran
Lough
Erne
Armagh
Bangor
Enniskillen
A1
Sligo
N16
Monaghan
Clones
Newry
Mourne
Mts
Newcastle
Ballina
Collooney
Castleblayney
N2
Swinford
Boyle
Cavan
Carrickmacross
Dundalk
Castlebar
N5
N3
764m
Croagh▲
Patrick
Carrick
on Shannon
Longford
Brú na Bóinne
(Newgrange)
Drogheda
Westport
N17
Claremorris
Kells
Lough
Mask
Cong
Roscommon
Lough
Ree
N4
Navan
Skerries
Clifden
Tuam
Mullingar
Trim
M1
Lough
Corrib
Athlone
REPUBLIC OF
Lucan
DUBLIN
Galway
Ballinasloe
M6
M4
Dún Laoghaire
Galway Bay
Tullamore
IRELAND
Bog of
Allen
Kildare
Naas
Bray
Oileáin Árann
(Aran Islands)
The
Burren
Loughrea
Birr
Port
Laoise
M7
Athy
Glendalough
N11
Wicklow
Lough
Derg
M18
Roscrea
Carlow
Rathdrum
Ennis
Nenagh
M7
Durrow
M9
Arklow
Kilrush
Bunratty
Limerick
Thurles
Kilkenny
M11
Gorey
Adare
N24
Rock of
Cashel
M8
Ballybunion
N21
Tipperary
Cashel
New
Ross
N11
Wexford
Listowel
Abbeyfeale
Cahir
Carrick
on-Suir
N25
Dunganstown
Rosslare
An Daingean
(Dingle)
Tralee
N20
Clonmel
Waterford
Harbour
Slea
Head
Castleisland
Mallow
Lismore
Tramore
Carnsore
Point
Killorglin
Killarney
Blackwater
Fermoy
Dungarvan
Glenbeigh
1039m▲
N25
Cahirciveen
Iveragh
Peninsula
Kenmare
N22
Blarney
Castle
Blarney
Youghal
Waterville
Macroom
Cork
Cobh
Beara
Peninsula
Bandon
Kinsale
Bantry
Clonakilty
Mizen
Head
Skibbereen

0 20 40 60 80 100km
0 10 20 30 40 50 60 miles

A

B

C

mouths, peninsulas and islands are taken into account.

Try to visit the far southwest. Take in the charming historic city of Kilkenny on the way; and visit Cork, the Irish Republic's second largest city, where you can kiss the nearby Blarney Stone.

Heading to the West

Beyond Cork lies the Beara Peninsula. The bigger Iveragh peninsula is part of County Kerry to the north, land of the mountains of Macgillycuddy's Reeks. The town of Killarney, with its scenic lakes, is the gateway to the romantic Dingle peninsula (Corca Dhuibhne) and County Clare. County Clare's southern half is mundane, but becomes spectacular the farther north you go, past the huge, echoing Cliffs of Moher and into the limestone country of the Burren, with its karst landscape (natural limestone pavement), dramatic stone burial chambers and hill forts.

Fishing boats moored in the harbor at An Daingean (Dingle) in County Kerry

In the pubs of Clare you are likely to encounter the foot-tapping essence of Irish music and song, in an environment that preserves the best of the past with energy, vitality and lyricism.

Off Clare's northwestern coast are the stunning Aran Islands (Oileáin Árann), the magic names of Inishmore (Inis Móir), Inishmaan (Inis Meáin) and Inisheer (Inis Óirr) resonating with all things Irish.

Beyond Clare is Galway Bay and Galway City (known as "The City of the Tribes"), the latter a lively, unfailingly charming place on the threshold of the Gaeltacht, the major area of Gaelic-speaking Ireland. Here, the mountains of Connemara and the broad waters of Lough Corrib and Lough Mask match an astonishing coastline of raw, rocky wilderness that lies to either side of the romantic town of Clifden.

Inland, Ireland also has much to offer. The heart of the country is a green bowl of rich farmland, of lakes, rivers and isolated ranges of rounded hills. Landlocked Ireland is outshone by the stupendous coastline of the far west, but it is a charming country full of character

and tradition, where you will hear talk of horses and history and where lakes and rivers throng with fish.

Traveling North

Farther north is the remote county of Mayo, where you can follow the pilgrims' route up the Holy Mountain of Croagh Patrick, if you feel fit enough for the grueling four-hour clamber over rough rocks to the place where St. Patrick is said to have banished the snakes. Beyond Mayo are Sligo and Donegal, and golden beaches and tumbling Atlantic surf. Lakes and remote peninsulas enhance north Donegal, where the coast turns east toward the beautiful City of Derry (Londonderry), gateway to Northern Ireland, and Antrim, Armagh, Down, Londonderry, Fermanagh and Tyrone – the six (of a total of nine) counties of Ulster known as Northern Ireland.

This British-ruled area was riven for decades by sectarian violence, but the Good Friday Agreement of 1998 began the slow process of peace. Ulster's image has suffered from "the Troubles" (the resumption of political violence since

The unusual "organ-pipe" cliffs of the Giant's Causeway, County Antrim

1969), yet the beauty of its coast and countryside is of classic Irish quality.

The Giant's Causeway, on County Antrim's north coast, is Northern Ireland's most famous landmark, an astonishing landscape of perfectly formed hexagonal rock sections. Farther east lies the seaside town of Ballycastle, beyond which are the towering cliffs of Fair Head and then the green and peaceful Glens of Antrim.

South of Antrim lies Belfast, Northern Ireland's capital, a city that in the past has shown a grim face but is now welcoming a new generation of tourists. Belfast has rediscovered its waterfront and invested in redevelopment. Victoria Square is now a contemporary shopping center, the old Gasworks site has been replaced with hotels and offices, and redevelopment of the Titanic Quarter on Queen's Island has quickened its pace. All this new building has brought an exciting dynamic to the city.

The Gaelic Lifestyle

In Dublin you will find museums, stores, theaters and restaurants to match those anywhere else in Europe, all suffused by the richness of Irish culture and by a modern sophistication.

In parts of rural Ireland things are different. You may come across an easygoing attitude, a relaxed approach reflecting the fact that the Irish have been around for a long time and often see no reason to rush things. At the same time, you may find yourself swept off your feet in places like beautiful Galway City, where a vigorous student population adds a contemporary note to the Gaelic culture that most young people continue to embrace.

If you travel through Ireland, you will find the Irish a particularly hospitable and friendly people. Often, if you ask a local for the way to a nearby site or place in town, you will be taken there rather than given directions.

The Irish are fired by an all-consuming curiosity and have an almost total lack of pretension. They are a people whose history has often been terrible, bleak and unforgiving. Yet they have survived as the inheritors of a bewitching country that lies off the western edge of Continental Europe but is also an integral part of it.

Timeline

circa 3000 BC	Neolithic burial chambers constructed at Brù na Bòinne.
circa 500 BC	Celtic tribes arrive from Europe.
AD 430	St. Patrick brings Christianity to Ireland.
circa 795	Vikings found Dublin, Waterford, Wexford and Limerick.
1170	Powerful Anglo-Irish hegemony established in Ireland.
circa 1610	Large areas of Ulster are confiscated by the English Crown.
1845–51	The Great Famine; a million Irish people die and a million emigrate, chiefly to America.
1916	Easter Rising.
1921	Anglo-Irish Treaty partitions Ireland into the Irish Free State and Northern Ireland, which remains under British rule.
1948	Irish Free State is declared a republic.
1969	Beginning of "the Troubles" in Northern Ireland.
1972	Republic of Ireland joins the European Economic Community.
1985	The Anglo-Irish Agreement promises cooperation on Northern Ireland's future.
1994	Main paramilitary groups in Northern Ireland call a ceasefire.
1997–2007	Ireland enjoys rapid economic growth, known as the "Celtic Tiger."
1998	Good Friday Agreement paves the way for a Northern Ireland Assembly. Sporadic violence continues.
2007	Devolved government returns to Northern Ireland with an historic power-sharing agreement.
2008–10	The global financial crisis causes Ireland's booming property bubble to burst, resulting in a bailout by the EU/IMF in 2010.
2011	Enda Kenny, of Fina Gael, is voted *Taioseach* (Prime Minister).
2011	Queen Elizabeth II and the Duke of Edinburgh make an historic state visit to the Republic of Ireland. This is the first such visit by a British monarch since 1911.

Divided Ireland

Ireland has been a divided country for centuries. The reasons are complex and lie in historical developments over hundreds of years. The largest part of modern Ireland is the Republic of Ireland, Poblacht na h' Eireann – mainly Roman Catholic, with a small minority of Protestants and a strong Irish Gaelic culture and identity. After years of economic stagnation the nation enjoyed a period of great success and modernization. This ended in 2008 when the global economic crisis took effect. It will be a long time until the "Celtic Tiger" roars again. Six counties in the province of Ulster in the northern part of Ireland are called Northern Ireland, and remain part of the United Kingdom. Its majority Protestant community is traditionally Unionist and wishes to maintain the union between Great Britain and Northern Ireland. The smaller, but substantial, Catholic community is traditionally Republican and wishes to break the union with Great Britain and establish an all-Ireland republic. The political differences and the lack of civil rights for Northern Ireland Catholics gave rise to some 30 years of violent conflict. Through the peace process, the 1998 Good Friday Agreement created a devolved legislative Assembly for Northern Ireland and a framework for multiparty power-sharing. Violence was largely eliminated, and following a temporary reversion to direct British rule, the Northern Ireland Assembly reconvened in 2007 and continues to strive for peace.

Survival Guide

■ If you visit the city of Dublin in the early spring, try to be there on March 17, St. Patrick's Day, when the city celebrates with song and dance, culminating in a parade, all-night parties and fireworks displays.

■ If you're interested in shopping for Celtic crafts, don't miss the Kilkenny Design Centre in Kilkenny. This is the city's finest showcase for stylish Irish housewares, glass, books, fashion and jewelry. The upstairs restaurant serves delicious homestyle food.

■ Ireland is rapidly modernizing its road system, but there are still some poor public roads, especially in rural parts of the country and the further west you travel. Here, roads are narrower, so passing oncoming traffic (vehicles and animals) requires patience.

■ One of the best ways to learn a little about the complexities of Irish politics is to take a tour. Coiste Political Tours provides walking tours of Belfast's historical and political sites, led by ex-prisoners, and Blue Badge Guides take visitors on tours of Derry City and the Bogside. In Dublin, there are tours covering the Great Famine, the 1916 Easter Rising, the War of Independence and Partition.

■ Be aware that there is a no-smoking policy throughout the Republic of Ireland in all public places.

■ Visit the local pubs in rural Ireland, especially in County Clare, where in towns like Ennis you will find some of the greatest Irish music of all and the wholehearted Irish *craic* (good times, enjoyment and fun).

■ Visit popular places such as Glendalough in County Wicklow, Killarney in County Kerry and the Cliffs of Moher in County Clare outside of peak season (July and August). Glendalough, especially, can become jammed with traffic.

■ Enjoy the beautiful and often remote beaches of Ireland's west coast, but

A statue of James Joyce at Dublin's Merrion Hotel

take great care if you go swimming. The tides are very strong here and there can be unexpected sea currents.

■ Irish road signs began to appear in both Gaelic and English in the Republic of Ireland shortly after partition and today they must appear in both languages by law, the Irish first in italics with the English underneath. In the Gaeltacht (Irish-speaking) areas only the Irish name is written.

■ Ireland's Roman Catholic churches are extremely important places to the communities they serve, and you'll usually find someone praying if you visit. Be as discreet as possible when walking around church interiors, especially in front of the altar. Please refrain from taking photographs during Mass and other services.

Dublin

All roads seem to lead to Dublin; it is a homecoming city where the visitor will feel as welcome as the Irish do. Dublin is celebrated today as one of Europe's most vibrant, colorful cities. It is a rich distillation of all things Irish – music, conversation and laughter amid the city's lively streets, buzzing pubs and magnificent Georgian buildings.

Finding Your Way

The Dublin tourist office is located in the handsome old church of St. Andrew's, just west of Trinity College in the city center. Here you can obtain information about guided summer walking tours.

Central Dublin is a reasonably easy place to explore on foot. The main museums and notable buildings are concentrated in south Dublin, but there are must-see attractions across the River Liffey in north Dublin.

A good starting point is the famous O'Connell Bridge. Take time to adjust to the breezy pace of it all. To the north is O'Connell Street, one of the broadest streets in Europe. Lively shopping streets such as Abbey Street Lower and Earl Street North lead off to either side.

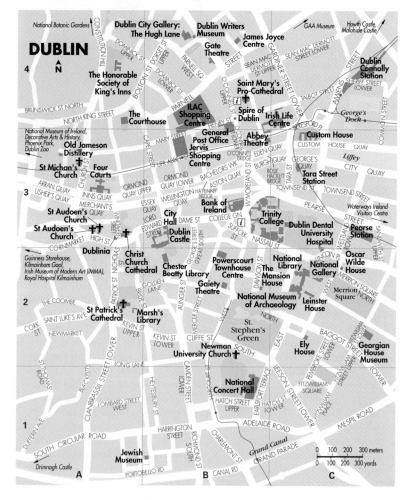

On Earl Street you will find a statue of James Joyce, Ireland's most famous writer and chronicler of Dublin life. Go down Earl Street and then turn left onto Marlborough Street to visit St. Mary's Pro-Cathedral, a magnificent neoclassical building.

Opposite Earl Street is the busy and revitalized Henry Street, with the huge ILAC and Jervis shopping centers and the adjoining fruit and vegetable market on Moore Street. This whole area leading down to Smithfield Village has been the subject of much renovation work. The men and women who work the stalls are famous for their lively Joycean banter.

On O'Connell Street, just before Henry Street, is the General Post Office. This is a landmark site of the 1916 Easter Rising, when Irish nationalists mounted an uprising against British rule and occupied the building. Opposite is the dramatic Monument of Light, a stainless-steel needle unveiled in 2002. At the north end of O'Connell Street, by the Parnell Monument, is Parnell Square, home to Dublin City Gallery: The Hugh Lane (see pages 277 and 279) and the Dublin Writers Museum (see page 279).

The Heart of Dublin

South of O'Connell Bridge is the buzzing heart of Dublin. From the south side of the bridge, walk down Westmoreland Street to College Green, a concentration of traffic that initially detracts from the stupendous buildings that surround it. Admire the neoclassical splendor of the Bank of Ireland and the elegant entrance to Trinity College (see page 280), through which you can escape to the crowded but relaxing college campus.

Otherwise, cross College Green to the south and then continue past the works for the Cross City Luas. This is the original spot for the statue of Molly Malone, heroine of the famous "Cockles and Mussels" refrain. The statue has been moved to Suffolk Street (until 2017) for the duration of the works.

Ahead lies pedestrian-only Grafton Street, with interesting stores and delightful side streets, plus a variety of street performers. Stop at Bewley's Oriental Café, a Dublin institution. Head east and make for Leinster House, seat of Irish government, and to the National Museum of Archaeology (see page 280) and the National Gallery (see page 280).

Beyond these lie the 18th-century Georgian splendors of Merrion Square and Fitzwilliam Street. Alternatively, go west from Grafton Street along store-lined Wicklow Street, then on to Dublin Castle (see page 277) and Christ Church Cathedral (see page 277); or head back north across Dame Street and into lively Temple Bar, the rejuvenated old riverside district that is the exciting focus of Dublin by night.

Vary your Dublin experiences. Enjoy Temple Bar's restaurants and lively

A view along the sun-drenched River Liffey toward the Ha'penny Bridge and Bachelors Walk area of Dublin

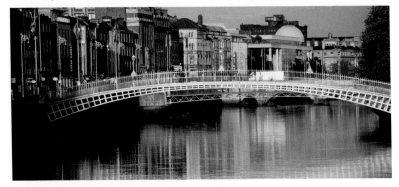

lanes, visit St. Patrick's Cathedral on Patrick Street or the rejuvenated Docklands district. Cross the Liffey via the modern Samuel Beckett and Sean O'Casey bridges and book theater tickets for the Bord Gáis Energy Theatre on the south side. Enjoy outstanding drama at Dublin's Abbey Theatre on Abbey Street, or classic Irish entertainment at the Olympia on Dame Street. Above all, visit Dublin's famous pubs (see page 281) for great music and chat. There is a quicker, sharper edge to the Irish here, as befits a busy, cosmopolitan city.

The Ha'penny Bridge

Dublin's famous Ha'penny Bridge, over the River Liffey, is best reached from Temple Bar by going down the narrow Merchant's Arch – look closely for the symbols of nearby stores carved into the street.

The bridge dates from 1816 and is made of cast iron; its elegant arches are lit up at night. It was officially named the Wellington Bridge after the British Duke of Wellington, but gained its popular name from the half-penny toll once charged for crossing it.

Essential Information

Tourist Information

Discover Ireland Information Office
14 Upper O'Connell Street ☎ 01 850 230330; www.visitdublin.com.

Visit Dublin
Suffolk Street ☎ 01 890 324 583; www.visitdublin.com. Also at Terminal 1 and Terminal 2, Dublin Airport

Urban Transportation

Dublin has two main railroad stations: Heuston Station, Kingsbridge, and Connolly Station, Amiens Street. The Dublin Area Rapid Transit (DART) railroad line runs north to Malahide and Howth, and south to Greystones. Connolly Station, Pearse Station and Tara Street Station are city-center stops. For intercity train information call ☎ 01850 366 222; www.irishrail.ie. For DART call ☎ 01 703 3504; www.dublin.ie//transport/dart.htm. The LUAS Green Line tram system (St. Stephen's Green to Bride's Glen) and Red Line (Connolly and The Point to Tallaght and Saggart) bring passengers from the suburbs into the city center. For LUAS call ☎ 01 850 300 604; www.luas.ie. There is a good citywide bus service run by Dublin Bus (Bus Átha Cliath), 59 Upper O'Connell Street (☎ 01 873 4222; www.dublinbus.ie); buses daily 7 a.m.–11:30 p.m. (some begin earlier). Nitelink service Fri.–Sat. midnight–4 a.m. The Leap card is a prepaid smartcard for use on public transportation in Dublin, Cork and Galway, and is available to buy at places displaying the Payzone logo or online at www.leapcard.ie. Countrywide services leave from the main bus station, Busáras, on Amiens Street (www.buseireann.ie). Dublin taxis are on stands at O'Connell Street, St. Stephen's Green, College Green and Dame Street, or phone Global Taxis (☎ 01 872 7272) or Blue Cabs (☎ 01 02 2222).

Airport Information

Dublin Airport (www.dublinairport.com) is 7 miles north of the city. Aircoach runs a bus service to the city center every 15 minutes, 24 hours a day; the trip takes 30 minutes (☎ 01 844 7118; www.aircoach.ie). The Dublin Bus Airlink (No. 747) runs to/from Busáras and the railroad stations.

Climate – average highs and lows for the month

Jan.	Feb.	Mar.	Apr.	May	Jun.	Jul.	Aug.	Sep.	Oct.	Nov.	Dec.
8°C	8°C	9°C	11°C	14°C	17°C	19°C	18°C	16°C	13°C	10°C	8°C
46°F	46°F	48°F	52°F	57°F	63°F	66°F	64°F	61°F	55°F	50°F	46°F
3°C	3°C	4°C	5°C	7°C	10°C	12°C	12°C	10°C	8°C	5°C	4°C
37°F	37°F	39°F	41°F	45°F	50°F	54°F	54°F	50°F	46°F	41°F	39°F

Dublin Sights

Key to symbols
⊕ map coordinates refer to the Dublin map on page 274 🎟 admission charge: $$$ more than €7, $$ €4–€7, $ less than €4
See page 5 for complete key to symbols

The State Drawing Room in Dublin Castle

Christ Church Cathedral

Dublin's great cathedral was originally founded around 1030 under Dunan, its first bishop. The building dates from the 12th century, but much of it is now a 19th-century Gothic Revival renovation.

The oldest remaining parts of the cathedral include the late 13th-century transepts and crypt, one of the largest medieval crypts in Europe, measuring 175 feet long. Rough stone pillars support the weight of the huge building above; the atmosphere is dense with age. Monuments and artifacts lie half hidden in niches, and include battered statues of English kings and oddities such as a mummified cat and a rat.

Linked to the cathedral by a covered stone bridge is Synod Hall, where the interactive Dublinia exhibition explores Dublin's Viking and medieval history.

Christ Church Cathedral ⊕ A3 ✉ Christchurch Place ☎ 01 677 8099; www.christchurchcathedral.ie ◷ Mon.–Sat. 9–7, Sun. 12:30–2:30 and 4:30–7, Jun.–Sep.; Mon.–Sat. 9–6, Sun. 12:30–2:30 and 4:30–6, Mar.–May; Mon.–Sat. 9–5, Sun. 12:30–2:30, rest of year 🚌 49, 49A, 54A, 123 🍴 Café 🎟 $$ ℹ Guided tours (all include belfry) Mon.–Fri. at 11 a.m., 12:10, 2, 3 and 4 p.m. ($$); belfry only tours Sat. 11:30, 1:15, Sun. 1:15 ($$)

Dublinia ⊕ A3 ✉ St. Michael's Hill ☎ 01 679 4611; www.dublinia.ie ◷ Daily 10–6:30, Mar.–Sep.; 10–5:30, rest of year. Last admission 1 hour before closing 🚌 49, 49A, 54A, 123 🍴 Cathedral café 🎟 $$

Dublin Castle

Dublin Castle was built by King John in 1204 on the site of a former Gaelic ring fort and Viking fortress. Today only one of the medieval towers remains, the rest destroyed by fire in the 17th century. Most of what can be seen today dates from the 18th century, including the opulent state apartment rooms. However, restoration work in the 1980s uncovered 10th-century Viking defences (Medieval Undercroft), a reminder of Dublin's Viking heritage.

The state apartments open to the public include St. Patrick's Hall, the Throne Room, the State Drawing Room and the Picture Gallery, all of which have sumptuous decorations and furnishings. The castle's Chapel Royal is a glorious neo-Gothic indulgence dating from 1814. Its exterior bristles with pointed Gothic motifs and 90 or so carved heads of historical figures. The interior has lavish plaster vaulting and superb carved oak galleries. Within the castle grounds are the Revenue Museum and the Chester Beatty Library (free) with its fascinating collection from around the world.

⊕ B3 ✉ Dame Street ☎ 01 645 8813; www.dublincastle.ie ◷ Mon.–Sat.10–4:45, Sun. and public holidays 12–4:45 🚌 49, 56A, 77, 77A, 123 🍴 Restaurant and café 🎟 $$$ ℹ Guided tours only. State apartments may be closed for official functions

Dublin City Gallery: The Hugh Lane

The Hugh Lane gallery is located in Charlemont House, an elegant, limestone Georgian mansion. The

James Joyce

Ireland's most controversial novelist, James Joyce, was one of world literature's most important figures. Joyce was an innovator of the highest order, a writer of dazzling intellect.

He was born in 1882 into a Dublin Catholic family of some gentility, although poverty overtook the family while Joyce was in his teens. He was educated at Ireland's leading Jesuit school and then at Catholic University College in Dublin.

Joyce rebelled early against the tenets of his class and religion and against Ireland's prevailing politics and culture, both of which he felt were too "nationalistic." He left Ireland in 1904 with Nora Barnacle, who became his lifelong partner. After a visit in 1912, Joyce never returned to Ireland and remained in Europe until his death in Zurich in 1941.

Joyce wrote several books of poetry and novels; his most famous novels were *Ulysses* and *Finnegans Wake*. *Ulysses* was a monumental work, an allegorical saga describing the daylong wandering of its central character, Leopold Bloom, through the streets of Dublin. The novel developed new literary forms in its exploration and use of language and in its epic structure. It was published in Paris in 1922 but was banned for obscenity in Britain and in the United States until 1936. *Finnegans Wake* was published in 1939 and carried the "stream of consciousness" style of writing to revolutionary limits.

Joyce is a national hero in Ireland, something that would have amused this complex and essentially solitary man. The James Joyce Centre is at No. 35 North Great George's Street in north Dublin (www.jamesjoyce.ie, open Tue.–Sat. 10–5, Sun. 12–5, $$). Each year on June 16, Dublin celebrates Bloomsday, during which there are guided walks, readings and numerous events based on Leopold Bloom's progress through the Dublin of *Ulysses*. Visits to famous Dublin pubs play a lively part in the festivities; participants dress in Edwardian clothes from the period featured in the novel and readings and other celebrations of *Ulysses* are staged.

Cafe Ulysses at the James Joyce Centre has a Parisian atmosphere

collection, bequeathed by Hugh Lane in 1908, features 19th- and 20th-century Irish and international painters, including Claude Monet, Edouard Manet and Edgar Degas. There are several outstanding works, including Renoir's *Les Parapluies*. Notable Irish artists include Jack B. Yeats, and there are contemporary Irish works and exhibitions, often of daring conceptual art. The gallery also has a fine collection of stained glass. An extension houses a collection of Sean Scully paintings donated by the artist. Francis Bacon's studio was gifted to the gallery in 1998, painstakingly removed from its London home and reconstructed here.

The interior of Kilmainham Gaol

🔼 B4 ✉ Charlemont House, Parnell Square North ☎ 01 222 5564; www.hughlane.ie 🕐 Tue.–Thu. 10–6, Fri.–Sat. 10–5, Sun. 11–5 🚇 DART Connolly Station (15-minute walk) 🚌 7, 11, 13, 16, 38, 40, 46A, 123; LUAS Abbey Street 🍴 Gallery café 💷 Free

Dublin Writers Museum

Literary Dublin in all its glory is represented by this engrossing museum's large collection of documents, artifacts, portraits and memorabilia of famous Irish writers, including Oscar Wilde and Samuel Beckett. The museum is housed in a fine, 18th-century Georgian property – look for well-preserved period detail such as the stuccowork downstairs. The colonnaded main salon, which is now the Gallery of Writers, has busts, paintings, a decorative ceiling and various boisterous friezes. Next door are The Writers' Centre, while Chapter One, one of Dublin's best regarded eateries, is located below the museum.

🔼 B4 ✉ 18 Parnell Square North ☎ 01 872 2077; www.visitdublin.com 🕐 Mon.–Sat. 10–4:45, Sun. 11–4:45 🚇 DART Connolly Station (15-minute walk) 🚌 7, 11, 13, 16, 38, 40, 46A, 123 🍴 Museum coffee shop; Chapter One restaurant (see page 480) in basement (separate entrance) 💷 $$$ ℹ️ Self-guiding audio tour lasts about 40 minutes

Guinness Storehouse

Dublin without Guinness is like the earth without air. You can sample Guinness in its creamy, lip-smacking originality in the city's multitude of pubs (see page 281), but to reach the heart of things visit the enlightening and entertaining Guinness Storehouse, located in an original hop store at the brewery. Admission includes a pint of the famous stout in the Gravity Bar.

🔼 Off map at A2 ✉ St. James's Gate ☎ 01 408 4800; www.guinness-storehouse.com 🕐 Daily 9:30–7, Jul.–Aug.; 9:30–5, rest of year 🚊 LUAS St. James's Hospital 🚌 123 🍴 Bars and restaurant 💷 $$$

Kilmainham Gaol

The notorious Kilmainham Gaol (prison) has been the scene of great misery. Kilmainham opened in 1796 and until 1924, when it closed, just about every famous name in the struggle for Irish independence and statehood was a "guest" at one time, including Robert Emmet, Charles Stewart Parnell and Eamon DeValera. Fourteen leaders of the 1916 Easter Rising were executed in the prison yard. Explore the gloomy cells and chilly corridors. Guided tours give a graphic picture of Irish history.

🔼 Off map at A2 ✉ Inchicore Road ☎ 01 453 5984; www.heritageireland.ie 🕐 Daily 9:30–6, Apr.–Sep.; Mon.–Sat. 9:30–5:30, Sun. 10–6, rest of year. Last tour begins 1 hour before closing 🚌 13, 40, 69; LUAS Suir Road 🍴 Tearoom 💷 $$ (includes guided tour)

National Gallery

Ireland's national art collection eschews quantity for quality, and this fine building holds works that represent all major schools of European art. Restoration of the historic wings of the gallery is ongoing. However, the European Masterpieces collection in the Millennium Wing will stay open as well as a rotating exhibition of highlights plucked from the European collection. Painters represented include Francisco de Goya and Caravaggio, Thomas Gainsborough and J. M. W. Turner, and Irish artists Frederick William Burton, Jack B. Yeats and Sir John Lavery.

✚ C2 ✉ Merrion Square; entrance via Millennium Wing on Clare Street only ☎ 01 661 5133; www. nationalgallery.ie ◉ Mon.–Sat. 9:30–5:30 (also Thu. 5:30–8:30), Sun. 11–5:30. Last admission 15 minutes before closing Ⓠ DART Pearse Station (5-minute walk) 🚌 4, 7, 8, 39A, 47A 🍴 Café 🅿 Free; charge for some exhibitions ℹ Self-guiding audio tours, free

National Museum of Archaeology

Part of the National Museum of Ireland, this museum occupies some grand buildings that date from the 1890s. Together with the National Library opposite, the complex forms the approach to Leinster House, the seat of the Irish Government. Exhibits dating from 7000 BC onward include examples of Celtic and medieval art and the finest collection of prehistoric gold artifacts in Europe. Highlights of the collection include the Tara Brooch, the Cross of Cong, the Ardagh Chalice and Viking discoveries from Dublin itself.

✚ C2 ✉ Kildare Street ☎ 01 677 7444; www.museum.ie ◉ Tue.–Sat. 10–5, Sun. 2–5 Ⓠ DART Pearse Station 🚌 4, 5, 7, 7A, 8, 13A, 39A, 44, 45, 46A, 48A; LUAS St. Stephen's Green 🍴 Café 🅿 Free; guided tours $

St. Stephen's Green

Delightful St. Stephen's Green has been a public park since 1664, when Dublin Corporation set aside 22 acres of open ground, albeit for use by its well-to-do citizens. Access was by payment only until 1880, when the park was made free to all. There are statues and busts of famous Irish men and women, including James Joyce, Robert Emmet, Constance Markiewicz and Sir Arthur Guinness.

The park is surrounded by some of the finest buildings in Dublin. They include the Shelbourne Hotel, the Royal College of Surgeons and the Roman Catholic University Church.

✚ B2 ✉ St. Stephen's Green ☎ 01 475 7816; www.ststephensgreenpark.ie ◉ Mon.–Sat. 7:30–dusk, Sun. 9:30–dusk 🚌 All city center buses; LUAS St. Stephen's Green

Trinity College

Dublin's Trinity College is an outstanding architectural and cultural oasis at the heart of a busy city. It was founded in 1592 on the site of an Augustinian monastery, but all of the present buildings date from after 1700. Enter the complex from College Green, between statues of poet Oliver Goldsmith and orator Edmund Burke, and then go through the Corinthian facade of the Palladian Regent House. This leads into cobbled Parliament Square, lined with grand buildings and dominated by a tall campanile.

Trinity's Old Library and its Long Room contain some outstanding artifacts, including the ninth-century *Book of Kells*, an illuminated manuscript of the four gospels of the New Testament. The "Turning Darkness into Light" exhibition in the Old Library leads you up to the *Book of Kells*. It offers a historical perspective on the manuscripts, allowing greater understanding of the work.

Campus ✚ B3 ✉ College Green ☎ 01 896 1000; www.tcd.ie ◉ Daily 🚌 All cross-city buses 🅿 Free ℹ Walking tours (30 minutes long) depart from inside the Front Gate daily from 10:15, year round. Last tour at 3:40 Mon.–Sat., at 3 Sun. 🅿 $$$

Old Library ✉ College Green ◉ Mon.–Sat. 9:30–5, Sun. 9:30–4:30, May–Sep.; Mon.–Sat. 9:30–5, Sun. noon–4:30, rest of year. Closed 10 days from late Dec. to early Jan. 🚌 All cross-city buses 🅿 $$$

Dublin's Pubs

Irish pubs are fueled by good drink, but they are rooted in the gregarious nature of the Irish, and in lively gossip. Many pubs also are outstanding folk music venues, inevitable in a country so well suited to such spontaneous music.

A local favorite is the Brazen Head, at 20 Lower Bridge Street, hailed as the oldest pub in Dublin. Davy Byrnes, on Duke Street, just off busy Grafton Street, is associated with James Joyces' *Ulysses*, as it was here that the book's main protaganist, Leopold Bloom, stopped for refreshment. For Victorian authenticity try the Stag's Head, on Dame Court, with its stained-glass windows and wood paneling. Very popular with Dubliners in the 1890s, the pub was another favorite of author James Joyce.

You can hear great Irish music with your Guinness in some of the busy Temple Bar pubs like Oliver St. John Gogarty's, on the corner of Fleet and Anglesea streets.

One of the best Dublin music pubs is O'Donoghue's, on Merrion Row, down from St. Stephen's Green. This was the favored haunt of the Dubliners folk group in its 1960s heyday, and the city's best folk musicians regularly raise the roof here.

Other good traditional pubs are Doheny & Nesbitt on Lower Baggott Street; McDaid's on Harry Street, just off Grafton Street; O'Neill's, on Suffolk Street, opposite the tourist information office; and old-fashioned Mulligan's on Poolbeg Street, a last outpost of Joycean Dublin amid the chilly lifelessness of modern office blocks. South of St. Stephen's Green at the corner of Camden Street Upper and Harcourt Road is The Bleeding Horse, formerly a blacksmith's shop and a church; it is a warren of little rooms called "snugs."

If you want a more modern vibe, try Café en Seine on Dawson Street, where a trendy, sophisticated crowd drinks in extravagant surroundings. For a fusion of old and new, try the Chop House Gastro Pub on Lansdowne Road. For a down-to-earth atmosphere, visit the Foggy Dew on Fownes Street, with music memorabilia behind the bar, a laid-back, young crowd and regular live music.

At the heart of Dublin's lively nightlife scene is the Temple Bar area

Italy

Opposite: Santa Maria della Salute, Venice, illuminated at night

Italy

Few countries have as much to offer as Italy, with its warm and passionate people, varied and beautiful landscape, a rich artistic, historic and cultural heritage, some of the world's best food and wine, and a stylish and relaxed philosophy on life.

Italy has something for everyone, whether the visitor is seeking great cities, tiny villages, idyllic countryside or beautiful beaches.

Bell' Italia

Of all European countries, Italy is the one to which many travelers return time and again, their love affair blossoming with each trip. Whether your visit is a chance opportunity or the dream of a lifetime, Italy will fulfill and exceed your expectations, capture your heart and senses, and leave you longing to return.

From the Alps in the north, through the prosperous and fertile heartland to the stark beauty of the deep south, Italy is blessed with some of the world's most beguiling landscapes. The northern half features Tuscany's classic olive, vine and cypress-studded rolling countryside; the dramatic peaks of the Dolomites (Dolomiti); pine-clad white cliffs and turquoise seas; and the eerie loveliness of mist-laden mornings in the great river valleys. The south is equally lovely, with an arid and fierce beauty during the

More Top Destinations in Italy

- Agrigento C1
- Amalfi Coast D2
- Assisi C4
- Cinque Terre B4
- Dolomiti C5
- Gargano Peninsula D3
- Lago di Garda B5
- Mantova B4
- Ravenna C4
- San Gimignano B4
- Siena B4
- Urbino C4
- Verona B5
- Vicenza C5

long hot summers, when the intense color of the sea offsets the bleached ocher of the mountains.

Most of Italy is mountainous, the long spine of the Apennines (Apennini) running almost from top to bottom and stretching virtually from coast to coast. Some hilly areas are immensely fertile, as in Tuscany and Umbria in central Italy, while in other places, such as Basilicata and Calabria in the south, the combination of altitude and extreme climate can make the land unproductive.

The largest area of flatland is the great plain of the Po river valley in the north, which extends down the eastern seaboard, an agriculturally rich and productive swath. Much of upland Italy is wooded, and there is a wide variety of indigenous plants.

Diverse Regions

Until 1870 Italy was a collection of separate and disparate states with a complex history, which does much to explain the diversity of people and attitudes. Camillo Cavour (statesman and first prime minister of a united Italy) remarked after unification in 1860, "We have made Italy, now we must make Italians." This aim still seems to await fruition, such is the gulf between the different regions. Italy has been a republic since 1946, the 20 regions (regioni) enjoying a large degree of self-government; some, such as Sicily and Sardinia, are semiautonomous.

Italians would be the first to agree that there is no such thing as "an Italian." Ask an Italian where he or she is from and the answer will be "from Tuscany", or Rome, or Naples, or Sicily, but rarely "from Italy." Primary loyalties are firmly local and regional. The Italian character, attitudes, outlook and prejudices have been formed by the native region, not by the country as a whole. So the fiery Sicilians are light years away from the Milanese and their urbane efficiency,

the cool and rational Tuscans or the abrasive Romans.

Language has also played a part. Modern Italian, rich, elegant and musical, derives from Tuscan, a medieval dialect used by Dante and Petrarch and firmly based on Latin. But throughout Italy there are some 1,500 diverse dialects, which were in daily use until widespread literacy and access to television. There are still some elderly people who have difficulty speaking modern Italian, although mass media are rapidly weakening dialects.

The considerable geographic differences between the north and south have produced another element of regionalism – a very real economic and cultural divide between the halves of the country. The cooler, more fertile north is richer, more advanced and more successful than the arid and impoverished south.

The People

All Italians do seem to share the same attitude toward life, one that is instantly apparent to foreigners. Life is for living, for enjoying, for savoring. There's always time to pause to chat, time for kindness, time to laugh; passions run high but anger is quickly over and forgotten. Watch the way Italians treat children or the elderly, without condescension but with respect for their age. Problems are solved with little fuss on a personal level, although the labyrinth of Italian bureaucracy might drive visitors crazy.

Despite having one of the world's lowest national birthrates, family ties are exceptionally close, with children often living with their parents into their 30s, and elderly people are still mainly cared for at home. The mother's role is pivotal; Italian men, it is said, search for a woman who lives up to their mother.

If you want to attract the opposite sex, you have to do your best to look good.

Opposite: Siena's narrow winding streets seen from the town's 14th-century campanile (bell tower)

This helps explain the importance of the *bella figura*, literally "beautiful form," but meaning infinitely more. Italians have an innate sense of style, and it matters greatly that their clothes, cars and other personal possessions are stylish and contemporary.

Bella figura dictates that these must all be admired, and what better way to display them than during that fine Italian tradition, the *passeggiata*? This nightly outdoor perambulation occurs in every village, town and city, when citizens exit en masse from their homes, strolling through the streets, exchanging news and gossip, but above all admiring and hoping to be admired in return.

Landscapes and Townscapes

A rich historical and cultural past has shaped the townscapes in Italy. Cities, towns and villages are crammed with fine buildings, churches and works of art, a legacy of pre-Unification days. But over the past century, and notably since World War II, there has been huge development and growth in urban areas, with unattractive spreads of industrial buildings and blocks of soulless

The evening stroll around Piazza Rotonda, Rome

apartments on the outskirts of countless towns. Every town still retains its central piazza, with civic buildings and a church grouped around or near it.

In many rural areas, people have traditionally lived in villages rather than on the land they work, traveling daily to the fields, so in some areas isolated country farmhouses are rare. There has sometimes been a huge gulf between the urban and rural populations, possibly due to the very early development of Italian towns.

The middle class was a late arrival in Italy and only really emerged during the great economic boom of the 1950s and 1960s. Even now there are agricultural workers and small shareholders working the land as it has been worked for centuries, while their cousins may be employed in high-tech industries.

Exploring Italy

Despite the enduring financial woes affecting the country as a whole, as well as other parts of Europe, Italy has a comfortable standard of living, making traveling easy and pleasurable. Tourism is a major industry, so you'll find English widely spoken in city hotels and restaurants, although less so away from the main tourist areas.

Italian engineering prowess has produced an excellent road network, with both toll roads and good highways. Minor roads are often unpaved. Italians drive fast and aggressively but mostly safely; once you're accustomed to the style of driving you should have no problems. All major cities have an airport, with frequent internal flights. Trains are cheap and punctual, although cross-country routes can be slow and complicated; it's safer to stick to the intercity services. Buses connect even the smallest villages.

Italian hotels are rated and inspected by regional authorities; regardless of the price range, they are spotlessly clean. Bathtubs are rare except in deluxe establishments, and showers frequently

A *traghetto* (ferry) crossing the Grand Canal in Venice; it's customary to stand

dribble when turned on; water is precious in many parts of the country. Air-conditioning is becoming more widespread but is by no means universal, and buildings can be stifling in summer. Laws govern the date when public places turn their heat on or off.

Culinary Traditions
Italian cooking is regional and simple, relying on the superb quality of the ingredients, and you'll find wonderful dishes wherever you go. In a country where frozen food is only now becoming widespread, menus are dictated by the seasons, with a rich variety of dishes punctuating the different months.

The various types of restaurant can be confusing. The terms *ristorante, osteria* and *trattoria* are fairly interchangeable; *tavola calda* and *pizzeria* imply something a bit more humble. Lunch has traditionally been the main meal, but there is a trend toward making dinner the extravaganza. The evening menu often consists of *antipasto* (hors d'oeuvre), the first course (*primo*) of pasta, soup or rice, the meat or fish second course (*secondo*) with its accompanying *contorni* (vegetables) or *insalata* (salad), followed by *formaggio*,

dolce or *frutta* (cheese, dessert or fruit). If a meal this size seems a bit daunting, choose just a couple of courses.

The perfect accompaniment to Italian food is a locally produced wine. *Denominazione d'Origine Controllata* (DOC) is a method of classification that guarantees the origin of the wine, and that it has been made following the guidelines for a particular area. However, it is no indication of quality.

Pastimes
The favorite Italian pastimes are probably eating, drinking and talking; preferably all together. Immensely sociable people, they tend to relax en masse, making group activities of every type very popular. Soccer is the national sport, and despite the national team's early defeat in the 2014 World Cup tournament, Italy is still among Europe's most successful soccer nations, ranking in the top 16 in 2015. Many Italians are passionate about soccer.

Deeply traditional, Italians prefer their pleasures to be family-oriented; a Sunday drive, a day at the beach or a gentle stroll, accompanied by a nonstop stream of chatter, constitute most people's idea of leisure.

Timeline

3000–1800 BC	First traces of migratory peoples in peninsula.
700–300 BC	Etruscan federation exists alongside Roman republic.
264–146 BC	Punic Wars against Carthage.
AD 200–400	Decline of Roman Empire.
550–770	Peninsula fragmented with different areas under Byzantine, Papal, Lombard and Frankish influence.
1300–1400	Emergence of the city-states in north; Renaissance era.
1500–1848	Fragmentation of peninsula under foreign domination.
1848–61	Struggle for unification, with brief republic established in 1848; kingdom of Italy proclaimed in 1861.
1870	Rome and the Papal States become part of a unified Italy.
1890	Emergence of Fasci Siciliani movement to help the poor and exploited – which was to evolve into the Mafia.
1915–18	Italy sides with Allies during World War I.
1940	Italy enters World War II on Axis side.
1943	Fall of Mussolini and armistice with Allies; Mussolini reinstated by Germany as head of puppet republic; Rome liberated in 1944.
1946	Italian Republic established.
1957	Treaty of Rome; Italy becomes a founding member of European Economic Community, now called the European Union.
1985–2000	Corruption is rife, but Italy flourishes as desire for political and institutional reform grows.
2009	An earthquake decimates L'Aquila in the Abruzzo region.
2011	Prime Minister Silvio Berlusconi steps down in midst of scandal; technocrat government, led by Mario Monti, is put in place.
2013	Pope Benedict XVI abdicates, the first pope to do so since 1415. Cardinal Jorge Mario Bergoglio of Argentina, the first Jesuit pope and the first pope from the Americas, is elected as Francis I.
2014	Matteo Renzi, Secretary of the Democratic Party, becomes Prime Minister. He promises electoral reform.
2015	Sergio Matarella, Matteo Renzi's nomination, is elected President of the Italian Republic.

The Etruscans

For centuries historians have questioned exactly who the Etruscans were. This enigmatic race preceded the Romans and were at the height of their power from 800 to 400 BC. They formed a confederacy of 12 cities, built towns, passed laws, traded overseas and believed firmly in an afterlife. A lively and imaginative people, they also had highly developed cultural, political and social systems. The Romans, admirers of Etruscan culture, absorbed much of it as they rose to power. By the third century BC the Romans had virtually assimilated the entire nation, along with much of its language, customs and religious beliefs. Today only the monuments remain, particularly those to the Etruscan dead. Wonderful finds have been made in these tombs – jewelry, vases, sculpture and frescoes. They are preserved in museums all over ancient Etruria, the name given to the area they inhabited. You can visit Etruscan sites at Tarquinia and Cerveteri, both a short distance north of Rome, and see the finest Etruscan collection in the world at the Museo Nazionale Etrusco di Villa Giulia in Rome (see page 298).

People viewing paintings displayed on a street stall in Rome

Survival Guide

- The fashion-conscious Italians spend much time and thought on looking good. Dressing appropriately means no shorts in cities. If you do show too much leg or arm, you won't be allowed to enter churches.
- Inevitably, Italy's star attractions in Rome, Venice, Florence and other major cities become packed during the hot summer. Get out early to avoid the main rush or, better still, visit in the late fall or winter when it's quieter and cooler.
- Nowadays, many of the stores and major sights in larger cities throughout the country stay open all day, but in rural towns everything closes from around 12:30 until 4:30 or 5, while in high summer most of the population eats a large lunch and has a siesta. Plan your day around this, remembering that most museums, churches, galleries and stores will all be closed for several hours too.
- Italians love their wine, which they drink with meals, but they disapprove of people who drink to excess.
- It is typical to go out to eat lunch from around 12:30 to about 2:30, and dinner at around 7:30 or 8.

- Vegetarians will find plenty of choices in most restaurants. As for children, Italians genuinely love them, and most restaurants – even upscale ones – welcome them. Italian coffee is extremely strong, so if you want it weaker just ask for a *caffè americano*.
- Bars are much more than the name suggests. They are open from dawn until midnight or later, and offer coffee, tea, soda, snacks and pastries, as well as alcohol. All bars have restrooms.
- Many Italians are enthusiastic smokers, but smoking is prohibited in all public places, including bars, cafés and restaurants. The law is generally well observed.
- One of the joys of Italy is shopping in local stores and at the colorful street markets. However, Italian shopping habits are slowly changing and out-of-town shopping centers are becoming more common. All shop and market prices are fixed.
- Facilities for visitors with disabilities are improving, but are not yet as good as those back home. If you need help it's best to check ahead with local tourist offices and with hotels and sights themselves.

Rome

There's almost too much to Rome (Roma); too much history, too much art, too much noise, confusion, traffic.

This is an overwhelming city in every way, with splendors and frustrations in equal measure. Nowhere else in the world will your senses be assaulted by such a glorious mélange of ancient, medieval, Renaissance, baroque and modern sights.

Expectations run high, and every visitor comes with preconceptions of sun-filled days of *dolce vita* and romantic strolls through ancient streets. Put them aside, take it slow, accept Rome not as you think it should be, but as it is, and you'll discover a city that is virtually impossible to describe.

Mapping the City

It's a good idea to stay as centrally located as you can, but avoid the unwholesome area around the central railroad station, Stazione Termini, and keep in mind that few areas of the city offer peace and quiet.

You'll quickly realize that Rome has no discernible center, although Piazza Venezia, dominated by the vast, wedding cake-like monument of Victor Emmanuel II, is a good place to orient yourself. From here, the Via del Corso stretches north, and to the south lies the Forum (Foro Romano, see page 297), the heart of classical Rome.

Between the Corso and the Tiber (Tevere) river lies the *centro storico*, or historic center, a maze of medieval streets and Renaissance squares and one of the city's most beguiling areas.

On the other side of the Corso are Rome's most elegant shopping streets, more sun-dappled piazzas, some lovely green spaces and the Via Vittorio Veneto, with its luxury hotels and galaxy of upscale cafés.

Across the river lies Trastevere, filled with charming streets and squares and noted for its excellent restaurants.

To the north is Vatican City (Città del Vaticano, see page 299), home of the Pope and St. Peter's Basilica (Basilica di San Pietro, see page 296).

Seeing the Sights

It would take months to see all of Rome, so before you arrive, decide where your priorities lie. It's a mistake to rush out, exhausted from travel, and see the Vatican on your first day; instead wander around the back streets or linger over a cup of coffee before you plunge into serious sightseeing. If you're not a sightseer, enjoy the street life and the stylish stores and restaurants.

It's best to tackle the highlights early in the day, before the crowds and heat intensify and while you're still fresh. Make a point of resting during the early afternoon; most stores and attractions are closed then anyway, and you can venture out again refreshed and relaxed in the late afternoon.

If time is short and you want to see a lot, think about taking a tour; your hotel will be able to advise you.

Other options include walking tours with local experts to explore off-the-beaten-track areas, or a boat trip on the Tiber river.

Peace and Quiet

Tranquility is in short supply in Rome, but there are moments when it seems within reach. In addition to the Villa Borghese (see page 301), other green spaces exist around the city, where the roar of the traffic is at least muted.

One of the best is the Palatine Hill (Palatino, see page 297) above the Forum, a good place to picnic after a morning's sightseeing, with scattered ruins, cypresses and wildflowers. The Botanical Garden (Giardino Botanico) in Trastevere provides cool shade amid the 7,000 species of plants, while the park Colle Oppio, with its strolling mothers and babies, is a good bet after a morning at the Colosseum.

Roman Cuisine

Romans enjoy dining out, and there are plenty of restaurants to choose from. Trastevere and the streets around Piazza Navona are packed with eateries; as always in Italy, look for places that locals patronize.

Roman specialties center around the less attractive parts of animals, such as offal, brains and tripe, but staples like grilled meat and the delicious *saltimbocca alla Romana* (veal scaloppine cooked with prosciutto and sage) are easy to find. Pasta dishes include spicy *rigatoni all'amatriciana* (pasta with bacon, chili and tomato), and the delicious and familiar *spaghetti alla carbonara*, made with bacon, egg and fettuccine. Artichokes are a great Roman specialty, eaten either deep fried or raw; look also for asparagus in early summer. Pizzas are excellent too.

Desserts are simple, but Roman ice cream is mouthwatering, and it's worth forgoing restaurant desserts and opting instead for a *gelateria*.

Local wines come from the hills outside Rome, in an area known as the Castelli Romani; Frascati is the best known. You'll also find wines from all over Italy, as well as herbal aperitifs and liqueurs.

Boutiques and Markets

Shopping can be a pleasure in self-indulgent Rome, where there is a superb range of luxurious silk, linens, leather and accessories. Shoes, bags, handmade evening wear and exquisite china and porcelain are found in the very chic stores clustered around the Via Condotti and the Via Frattina, just off the Piazza di Spagna. You'll find moderately priced shops along the Via del Corso and the Via Nazionale; knitwear and sweaters are good buys.

Rome also has several department stores, including the upscale La Rinascente in Galleria Sordi off the Corso and Piazza Fiume; Upim and OVS are inexpensive chain stores with plenty of surprisingly stylish buys.

If you enjoy markets, head for the popular daily food and vegetable market in the lovely Campo dei Fiori, or the many smaller street markets dotted around the city.

Nightlife

Romans consider having a meal in a restaurant the pinnacle of evening

Roman Fountains

Lovely fountains are scattered around Rome, and their beauty will stick in your mind when much else has faded. They provide cool places for a few minutes of rest, and the soothing sound of splashing water somehow manages to make itself heard over the noise of Rome's frenetic traffic. Be sure to pause at the Fontana delle Naiadi in Piazza della Repubblica, with its bronze nymphs; the dolphin-decorated Fontana del Tritone in Piazza Barberini; and the charming tortoise fountain, the Fontana delle Tartarughe, in Piazza Mattei.

The city's most famous fountain is the Fontana di Trevi in the small Piazza di Trevi (see page 297). This awesome baroque masterpiece of carved figures flanking the central figure of Neptune is the most photographed fountain in Rome.

entertainment, but there are many other options and events going on. Pick up a copy of *Trovaroma* or go online at www.trova-roma.com for information on where to go and what to do in Rome.

There are plenty of music bars and discos to satisfy music lovers. Opera is a good option, either at the Teatro dell'Opera or outdoors in summer at the Terme di Caracalla.

Rome has a clutch of movie theaters showing films in their original language. Concerts and recitals are frequently held in the city's churches.

Essential Information

Tourist Information

Call Centre ☎ 06 0608 (for all offices)
Daily 9:30–7 (English speaking)
Fiumicino Airport: International arrivals, Terminal 3
Ostia Lido: Lungomare Paolo Toscanelli
Castel Sant'Angelo: Piazza Pia
Ciampino airport: arrivals hall
Minghetti: Via Marco Minghetti
Navona: Piazza delle Cinque Lune
Nazionale: Via Nazionale, near Palazzo delle Esposizioni
Termini: Termini Railway Station. Inside station at Binario 24 (Platform 24)
Tiburtina: Tiburtina Station Information Point
www.turismoroma.it or www.060608.it

Urban Transportation

Public transportation in Rome consists of red-gray, orange or green buses and trams and a two-line metro (subway) system. Metro stations are marked on the Rome city map by the letter "M" in a red circle. Bus tickets must be purchased from machines before boarding, or from shops and newsstands displaying an ATAC or COTRAL sticker. They are valid for multiple bus trips plus one metro trip within a 100-minute period, and must be validated at the rear of the vehicle when boarding. The *Biglietto Integrato Giornaliero* (BIG) is valid for a day's unlimited travel on buses, trams, the metro and the suburban train service.

A weekly pass, the *Carta Integrata Settimanale*, also is available. Taxis are white, and park next to the stands with a blue-and-white sign; they do not stop on the street. Call a taxi from Radio Taxi (☎ 06 3570); the meter will start running straight after your call. Be sure that the meter is set at zero if you begin your ride at the taxi stand. Do not get in a "private" taxi, especially at the airports.

Airport Information

Rome has two airports (http://www.adr.it): Leonardo da Vinci, at Fiumicino (west of the city); and Ciampino, south of Rome, for charter flights and low-cost carriers. The easiest link from Leonardo da Vinci to the city center is by train to Stazione Termini (the central railroad station); trains leave every 30 minutes between 6:23 a.m. and 11:53 p.m., and 17:53 and 22:53; every 15 minutes between 12:53 and 17:53 (precise times may vary). Buses also run to Termini and Tiburtina stations (check Terravision online at www.terravision.eu); note there are no night bus services. Tickets cost €8 return. Travel time is 70 minutes, with four stops. Taxis cost a fixed €48 to central Rome. Only take official white or yellow taxis with meters, numbers and names. Ciampino is also served by the Terravision bus company; buses leave from outside the terminal every 20 minutes until midnight. Return fare €8, journey time 40 minutes; www.terravision.eu.

Climate – average highs and lows for the month

Jan.	Feb.	Mar.	Apr.	May	Jun.	Jul.	Aug.	Sep.	Oct.	Nov.	Dec.
13°C	14°C	16°C	19°C	23°C	27°C	31°C	31°C	27°C	23°C	18°C	14°C
55°F	57°F	61°F	66°F	73°F	81°F	88°F	88°F	81°F	73°F	64°F	57°F
3°C	4°C	7°C	8°C	12°C	15°C	18°C	18°C	14°C	11°C	9°C	5°C
37°F	39°F	45°F	46°F	54°F	59°F	64°F	64°F	57°F	52°F	48°F	41°F

Rome Sights

Italy

> **Key to symbols**
> ✚ map coordinates refer to the Rome map on pages 292–293 🅱 admission charge: $$$ more than €8, $$ €4–€8, $ less than €4
> See page 5 for complete key to symbols

Basilica di San Pietro

The spiritual heart of Catholicism, the Basilica di San Pietro (St. Peter's Basilica) stands on the site of the saint's burial place.

This is architectural grandeur on a triumphant scale, from the sweeping colonnades branching from the magnificent facade to the soaring dome above the twisted columns of Giovanni Bernini's High Altar *baldacchino*.

There's much that dates from 1506 to 1626, when Donato di Angelo Bramante and Bernini were the basilica's principal architects.

Near the end of his life, Michelangelo designed the dome, from which there are superb views; inside you can see the sublime *Pietà*, one of his earliest works. The right nave contains a bronze statue of St. Peter, his right foot worn away by pilgrims' caresses. Other artists who

worked on the decoration of this exquisite basilica include Antonio Canova and Pietro da Cortona.

✚ A3 ✉ Piazza San Pietro, Città del Vaticano ☎ 06 6988 3462; www.vatican.va 🕐 Daily 7–7, Apr.–Sep.; 7–6:30, rest of year. Dome: daily 8–6, Apr.–Sep.; 8–5, rest of year 🚇 Ottaviano 🚌 62 to Piazza San Pietro; 23, 32, 49, 81, 271, 590, 982, 990 to Piazza del Risorgimento 🅱 Admission free ($$ for elevator to terrace and steps to dome)

Colosseo

The massive Colosseo (Colosseum) dates from AD 72, and the design has never been bettered. This is a functional stadium that once seated 55,000; its sophisticated "backstage" facilities allowed the arena to be flooded for mock sea battles. Most ancient entertainment featured animals, slaves and gladiators, but few Christians were martyred here.

During the Middle Ages the Colosseum was a source of building stone, which explains the missing sections.

✚ D2 ✉ Piazza del Colosseo, Via dei Fori Imperiali ☎ 06 700 5469; 06 3996 7700 or www.coopculture.it for advance reservations 🕐 Daily 8:30 a.m. to 1 hour before dusk 🚇 Colosseo 🚌 3, 60, 81, 84, 85, 87, 117, 175, 186, 271, 571, 810 🅱 $$$ (includes Palatino and Foro Romano; valid 48 hours)

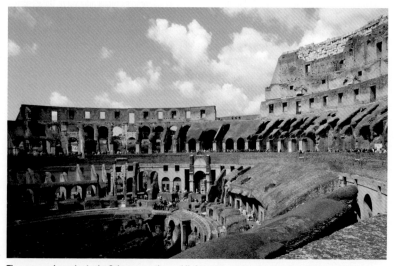

The arena and arcades in the Colosseum – the world's largest surviving structure from Roman antiquity

Fontana di Trevi

Among Rome's delightful fountains, none is more famous than the Fontana di Trevi (Trevi Fountain), a baroque creation tucked into a tiny piazza. There's been a fountain here since Roman times; the present example dates from 1732 and takes its name from the three roads – *tre vie* – that converged here. With your back to the fountain throw two coins over your shoulder into the water; legend claims that the first coin grants a wish, the second guarantees that you will return to Rome.
➕ C3 ✉ Piazza di Trevi ⓢ Spagna or Barbarini
🚌 52, 53, 61, 62, 63, 71, 80, 85, 160, 492, 850

Foro Romano e Monte Palatino

Heart of the Roman Empire, the Foro Romano (Roman Forum) contained all of the ancient city's most important political, religious and municipal buildings. Today it's a romantic jumble of tumbled columns and walls set amid cypresses and wildflowers. Spend time here, tracking down the second-century Arch of Septimius Severus, the Temple of Antoninus and Faustina (AD 141), the stately columns of the fourth-century Portico of the Dei Consentes, and the House of the Vestal Virgins, home of the guardians of the sacred fire. On the Palatino (Palatine Hill), overlooking the Roman Forum, there are ruins of the homes of rich Romans and emperors.
➕ D2 ✉ Via dei Fori Imperiali, Largo Romolo e Remo 1 ☎ 06 3996 7700 ⏰ Daily 8:30 a.m. to 1 hour before dusk ⓢ Colosseo 🚌 40, 60, 63, 70, 75, 81, 85, 87, 95, 117, 160, 170, 186, 175, 271, 571, 628, 716 💶 $$$ (includes Foro Romano, Colosseo and Palatino; valid 48 hours)

Galleria Borghese

The Galleria Borghese (Borghese Gallery), housed in the 17th-century summer palace of Cardinal Scipione Borghese, is a treasure-house of sculpture, mainly collected by the cardinal. He greatly admired Giovanni Bernini, whose works dominate – the *David* is said to be a self-portrait.

Look for Antonio Canova's *Paolina Borghese*; this beautiful little minx was Napoleon's sister, married off to a later Borghese. Stunning paintings include Caravaggio's *Boy with a Fruit Basket*.
➕ D4 ✉ Villa Borghese, Piazzale del Museo Borghese 5 ☎ 06 32810; www.galleriaborghese.it
⏰ Tue.–Sun. 8:30–7:30 ⓢ Spagna 🚌 5, 19, 52, 53, 63, 86, 88, 92, 95, 116, 204, 217, 231, 360, 490, 491, 495, 630, 910, 926 🍽 Museum/gallery restaurant
💶 $$$ (advance reservations necessary ☎ 06 328 10, Mon.–Fri. 9–6, Sat. 9–1, or online at www.tosc.it)

Musei Capitolini

The two *palazzi* housing the great classical collection of the Musei Capitolini (Capitoline Museums) are set on either side of a square designed by Michelangelo. Look for the *Dying Gaul* and the tautly muscled *Discobolus* (Discus Thrower). Bronzes include the famous fifth-century BC *Capitoline Wolf Suckling Romulus* and *Remus* and, finest of all, the superb equestrian statue of *Marcus Aurelius*. Paintings include major works by Titian, Paolo Veronese, Van Dyck and Caravaggio.
➕ C2 ✉ Piazza del Campidoglio 1 ☎ 060608; www.museicapitolini.org ⏰ Tue.–Sun. 9–8
ⓢ Colosseo 🚌 40, 63, 70, 81, 87, 95, 160, 170, 271, 628, 630, 716 💶 $$$

Musei Vaticani

The Vatican Museums make up the world's largest museum complex, with around a dozen self-contained museums in 1,400 rooms. It would take days to see it all, so plan your visit to pick out some highlights. However, do not miss the Cappella Sistina (Sistine Chapel), with world-renowned frescoes by Michelangelo covering the ceiling and the altar wall, showing scenes from the Old Testament, and the powerful *Last Judgment*. The Stanze di Raffaello (Raphael Rooms), among the artist's masterpieces, were started in 1508. Classical sculpture, an Egyptian collection and modern religious art are among the other features at this venue.
➕ A3 ✉ Viale Vaticano 100, Città del Vaticano

☎ 06 6988 4676; www.museivaticani.va ⏰ Mon.–
Sat. 9–6, (last ticket 4 p.m.). Also last Sun. of month
9–2 (last ticket 12:30 p.m.). Closed major religious
holidays 🚇 Ottaviano, Cipro-Musei Vaticani 🚌 49
(to front of museums), 32, 81, 982 to Piazza del
Risorgimento or 492, 990 to Via Leone IV, both 5
minutes' walk 💶 $$$; free to all last Sun. of the month
ℹ Vatican tickets available online at http://
biglietteriamusei.vatican.va/musei/tickets

Museo d'Arte Contemporanea di Roma (MACRO)

An imaginative conversion of a former
brewery houses the Rome Museum of
Contemporary Art. The original building
was extended with a 108,000-square-
foot purpose-built area, large enough for
multimedia installations by cutting-edge
young artists as well as established
international names. The permanent
collection concentrates on Italian
modern artists from the 1960s on, while
changing exhibitions highlight the work
of Italian and world artists.

✚ E4 ✉ Via Nizza 131 (corner of Via Cagliari)
☎ 06 6710 70400; www.museomacro.org ⏰ Tue.–Fri.
and Sun. 11–7, Sat. 11–10 🚌 38, 90 💶 $$$

Museo Nazionale Etrusco di Villa Giulia

Visit this enlightening museum to learn
more about the Etruscans (see page
290). The collection is housed in a late
Renaissance villa; its architects included
Michelangelo. Highlights are the
Castellani exhibits and fine Greek vases.
Be sure to see the Sarcofago degli Sposi,
sixth-century BC figures of a reclining
married couple, and the terra-cotta
Hercules and Apollo.

✚ C4 ✉ Piazzale di Villa Giulia 9 ☎ 06 322 6571;
www.villagiulia.beniculturali.it ⏰ Tue.–Sat. 8 a.m.–
6 p.m. 🚇 Flaminio 🚌 3, 19, 30,52, 926 💶 $$$

Pantheon

The superb Pantheon, erected between
AD 118 and AD 128 and still in use today,
gives a better idea of the splendor of
ancient Rome than any other surviving
monument. Built as a temple, it became
a Christian church in AD 609 and now

The interior of the Pantheon, seen from the doorway

houses Raphael's tomb and those of two
Italian kings. Its dome was the largest
ever built before the introduction of
reinforced concrete in the 20th century.

✚ C3 ✉ Piazza della Rotonda ☎ 06 6830 0230;
www.pantheonroma.com ⏰ Mon.–Sat. 8:30–7:30,
Sun. 9–6:30, holidays 9–1 🚇 Spagna 🚌 64, 70, 81,
86, 87, 90, 119, 170 and all services to Largo di Torre
Argentina 💶 Free

Piazza Navona

Piazza Navona owes its shape to the
Roman racetrack that once stood here.
Pope Innocent X, who commissioned
Giovanni Bernini to design the focal
point, the Fountain of the Four Rivers,
rebuilt the piazza in 1644. The 17th-
century church of Sant'Agnese is a good
example of Francesco Borromini's work.

✚ C3 ✉ Piazza Navona 🚇 Spagna 🚌 30, 56, 60

Piazza di Spagna e Scalinata della Trinità dei Monti

The Scalinata della Trinità dei Monti
(Spanish Steps), situated at the heart of
Rome's trendiest shopping area and
curving gracefully up from Piazza di
Spagna to the church of Trinità dei
Monti, attract myriad visitors. The steps,
built in 1723, get their name from the

The Vatican

The Città del Vaticano is a focus of universal admiration, though it has had its detractors. Thomas Paine, the English-born American revolutionary, writer and inventor, once said it "is a dagger through the heart of Italy." Even so, it remains perhaps the world's greatest monument to art and beauty. The Vatican, an area covering about 109 acres around the Basilica of St. Peter (Basilica di San Pietro), in the heart of Rome, is the world's smallest independent sovereign state. Until Italian unification in 1870, the Papacy had held territory covering a large part of central Italy, known as the Papal States. These became part of the new united Italy, and the Pope, Pius IX, retreated to the Vatican, a virtual prisoner, but in 1929 the Lateran Treaty brought the Vatican State into existence.

The Pope, as well as being head of the Catholic church, is also Europe's only absolute monarch, ruling over the 200-plus inhabitants of the Vatican. In March 2013 Cardinal Bergoglio, Archbishop of Buenos Aires, was elected Pope (Francis I) following the surprise abdication of Benedict XVI. The Argentinian son of Italian immigrants, he grew up in Buenos Aires and became a Jesuit priest. Francis I, despite his steady rise to high office and prominence, has maintained a modest lifestyle and preaches a simple message of love and hope. Many of the world's Catholics are hopeful that this Pontificate will see the Church return to Christianity's basic tenets and teaching.

The Pope has been defended by the Swiss Guard since 1506. Their distinctive, colorful striped red, yellow and blue dress uniform, said to have been designed by Michelangelo, is instantly recognizable. The 90 members are Swiss, young men recruited between the ages of 19 and 25, from Switzerland's four Catholic cantons. They are Swiss rather than Roman because it was unthinkable that the army of the Church of Rome should take up arms against Romans in defence of the Papacy.

The Pope gives a weekly general audience on Wednesdays at 11 a.m. in the Papal Audience Chamber, and very occasionally in the Basilica of St. Peter or in the piazza. These occasions, for up to 7,000 people, are open to everyone and tickets are free. The Pope also gives a blessing from the windows of his rooms overlooking the piazza on Sundays at midday.

Audience tickets are available by writing to Prefettura della Casa Pontificia, 00120 Città del Vaticano, online at www. papalaudience.org or by visiting the office through the bronze doors in the right-hand colonnade of Piazza San Pietro, open daily 8–6.

The Biblioteca Vaticano (Vatican Library) holds more than 1.5 million books

Excursion to Tivoli

Most visitors to Rome seize the chance to escape the city by taking an excursion to Tivoli, a small town in a lovely wooded location 19 miles northeast of Rome. Its main attractions are the gardens of the Villa d'Este, among the world's most beautiful, and the vast Classical site of Villa Adriana (Hadrian's Villa), about 4 miles southwest of Tivoli.

It's easy to make an independent trip to Tivoli, either by train from the central railroad station, Stazione Termini, then local bus, or by bus from central Rome. There are guided excursions from the city, while an English-speaking guide tells you all you need to know.

Villa d'Este

The Villa d'Este is famous not so much for the villa itself, built by Cardinal Ippolito d'Este in 1550, but for the stunning gardens, terraces and fountains that belong to it. The main attractions are two Giovanni Bernini fountains, the elegant Fontana di Biccierone and the Fontana dei Draghi, and the breathtaking Avenue of a Hundred Fountains (Viale delle Cento Fontane), a wooded walkway. Nearby lies the lovely Villa Gregoriana, where a pair of waterfalls cascades into a deep-cut gorge.

Villa Adriana

Many prosperous Romans built retirement villas at Tivoli, and in AD 125 the Emperor Hadrian embarked on the construction of his own. The villa and its gardens grew and grew, eventually covering as much ground as Imperial Rome itself. The site is vast and romantic, and you'll need a map to make sense of it all. Don't miss the Maritime Theater (Teatro Marittimo), a colonnaded palace on an island in the middle of a lake.

Villa d'Este ➕ Off map ✉ Piazza Trento 5 ☎ Toll-free in Italy 199 766166 or 00 39 041 271 9036; www.villadestetivoli.info 🕐 Tue.–Sun. 8:30 to 1 hour before dusk. Last admission 1 hour before closing 🚌 COTRAL bus from metro station Ponte Mammolo (Line B) 🚆 Train to Tivoli 🍴 Refreshments available in gardens 💶 $$$

Villa Gregoriana ✉ Piazza Tempio di Vesta ☎ 0774 332650; www.villagregoriana.it 🕐 Tue.–Sun. 10–6:30, Apr.–Oct.; Tue.–Sun. 10–4, Nov.–Dec. and Mar.; Jan. and Feb. by appointment only 💶 $$

Villa Adriana ✉ Via di Villa Adriana 204 ☎ 06 3996 7900 for reservations; www.villaadriana-beniculturali.it 🕐 Daily 9 a.m. to 1 hour before dusk 🚌 COTRAL bus from metro station Ponte Mammolo (Line B) to Tivoli, then local bus Tivoli Piazza Garibaldi to Villa Adriana 🚆 Train to Tivoli 🍴 Refreshments at villa site 💶 $$

The Avenue of a Hundred Fountains in the gardens at Villa d'Este piazza, which once housed the Spanish Embassy. The eccentric-looking "sunken boat" fountain dates from 1627, while on the right of the steps (at No. 26) is the Museo Keats-Shelley, in the lodgings where poet John Keats died in 1821.

✚ C3 ✉ Piazza di Spagna 26 ☎ Museo Keats-Shelley: 06 678 4235; www.keats-shelley-house.org 🕐 Museum: Mon.–Sat. 10–1 and 2–6 🚇 Spagna 🚌 116, 117, 119, 590 🎟 Museum $$

San Clemente
No church in Rome gives a better idea of history than San Clemente, a multilayered structure whose newest part dates from the 12th century. In its dim interior, the apse mosaics glitter above the marble panels of the choir screen and pulpits. From here, descend to the fourth-century lower church, with its ghostly traces of 8th- to 11th-century frescoes, before plunging deeper to examine the fine altar of the Roman Mithraic temple (the Mithraic cult was most popular in Rome from 67 BC to the late second century).

✚ E2 ✉ Via Labicana 95 ☎ 06 7740 0021; www.basilicasanclemente.com 🕐 Mon.–Sat. 9–12:30 and 3–6, Sun. 12–6 🚌 3, 85, 87, 117, 186, 571, 810, 850 🎟 Church free; Temple $$$

Santa Maria Maggiore
Mass has been said daily in Santa Maria Maggiore (St. Mary the Major) since the fifth century, when it was built on a site marked by a summer snowfall, as predicted by the Virgin when she

appeared before the reigning Pope. The mosaics in the nave date from the fifth century, those in the apse from the 13th century. The gilding on the ceiling reputedly comes from the first gold to arrive from the New World.

✚ E2 ✉ Piazza di Santa Maria Maggiore 42 ☎ 06 698 86800 🕐 Daily 7–7, Apr.–Sep.; 7–6:30, rest of year 🚇 Cavour, Termini 🚌 5, 16, 75, 84, 105, 360, 590, 649 🎟 Free

Santa Maria in Trastevere
The facade of Santa Maria in Trastevere, with its lustrous 12th-century mosaics, overlooks an atmospheric fountained piazza. The charming portico, added in 1702, leads to an interior with nave columns that once supported Roman buildings. The 12th-century, Byzantine-style mosaics of the apse represent the glorification of the Virgin.

✚ B2 ✉ Piazza Santa Maria in Trastevere ☎ 06 581 4802 🕐 Daily 7:30 a.m.–9 p.m (may close 12:30–3:30 in winter) 🚌 H, 23, 44, 75, 170, 181, 280, 630, 780

Via Appia Antica
A short bus ride from central Rome takes you to the Via Appia Antica (Old Appian Way), built in 4 BC to link Rome with Brindisi in southern Italy. Here, Spartacus and his men were executed, and St. Paul marched to prison. This cobbled way, shaded by pine trees, is lined with monuments and tombs; you can visit the catacombs, with their mementos of early Christian life.

✚ Off map at E1 ✉ Catacombe di San Sebastiano: Via Appia Antica 136 ☎ 06 785 0350; www.catacombe.org 🕐 Catacombs: Mon.–Sat. 10–4:30 🚌 118, 218, 660 🎟 $$$

Villa Borghese
If you long for some cool green grass, head for the extensive grounds of the Villa Borghese gardens, central Rome's largest park, an oasis of verdant lawns, umbrella pines, lakes and fountains. The adjoining Pincio Gardens offer views across the rooftops to St. Peter's.

✚ C4 ✉ Porta Pinciana 🕐 Daily dawn–dusk 🚇 Flaminio, Spagna 🚌 52, 53, 88, 116, 120, 150, 490

The beautiful apse of Santa Maria in Trastevere

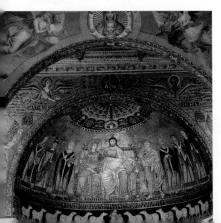

Italy

Florence

More than 6 million tourists visit Florence (Firenze) annually, the capital of Tuscany, which has a resident population of about 500,000. Visitors come with high expectations of beauty, stunning art and history. Sadly, they can be so overwhelmed by heat, crowds, noise and cultural overload that the city fails to live up to expectations. When touring Florence, planning pays off.

Choose the time you visit carefully. If art and architecture are the main purpose of your trip, try to come off-season, when Florence is quieter and the heat in this largely non-air-conditioned city won't wipe you out. Be prepared for crowds, time gallery visits for early and late in the day,

FLORENCE

0   250   500 meters
0   250   500 yards

Museo
San Marc
Basilica di
San Marco
PIAZZA
SAN MAR

4

N

VIA VALFONDA
VIA FAENZA
VIA GUELFA
VIA SAN GALLO

Stazione di
Santa Maria Novella

PIAZZA DELLA STAZIONE

PIAZZA DEL
MERCATO
CENTRALE

Mercato
Centrale

Galleria
dell'Accademia

VIA NAZIONALE
VIA DE' GINORI
VIA CAVOUR
VIA RICASOLI

PIAZZA DELLA STAZIONE

PIAZZA
DELL'UNITÀ
D'ITALIA

PIAZZA DI
SAN LORENZO

Cappelle
Medicee

Palazzo
Medici
Riccardi

Basilica
Santa Maria
Novella

VIA DE' PUCCI
VIA DE' GORI

Basilica di
San Lorenzo

Museo
dell'Ope
del Duon

VIA DELLA SCALA

PIAZZA
SANTA
MARIA
NOVELLA

PIAZZA SAN
GIOVANNI

Duomo

3

VIA DE' CERRETANI

Battistero

Chiesa di
Ognissanti

BORGO OGNISSANTI

VIA PALAZZUOLO

Campanile
di Giotto

PIAZZA DEL
DUOMO

PIAZZA
OGNISSANTI

LUNGARNO AMERIGO VESPUCCI

PONTE AMERIGO
VESPUCCI

VIA DE' FOSSI

VIA DEGLI STROZZI

PIAZZA DELLA
REPUBBLICA

VIA DEL CORSO
VIA DEL CALZAIUOLI

Badia
Fiorentina

PIAZZA
CARLO
GOLDONI

VIA DELLA VIGNA NUOVA

Arno

LUNGARNO SODERINI

Basilica di
Santa Trinita

VIA DE' TORNABUONI

VIA PORTA ROSSA

VIA DELLA CONDOTTA

PONTE ALLA
CARRAIA

LUNGARNO CORSINI

PIAZZA DELLA
SIGNORIA

PIAZZA
SAN FIRENZE

2

BORGO SAN FREDIANO

LUNGARNO GUICCIARDINI

PIAZZA DEL LIMBO

Palazzo
Vecchio

LUNGARNO DEGLI ACCIAIOLI

VIA SANTO SPIRITO

PONTE
SANTA TRINITA

Galleria
degli Uffizi

Basilica di
Santa Maria
del Carmine

Museo
Galileo

PONTE
VECCHIO

TUNGARNO GENERALE DI

Basilica di
Santa Maria del
Santo Spirito

VIA DE' GUICCIARDINI

LUNGARNO TORRIGIANI

PIAZZA
SANTO
SPIRITO

VIA MAGGIO

VIA DE' BARDI

Chiesa di
Santa Felicita

VIA DELLA CHIESA

COSTA SAN GIORGIO

1

VIA DE' SERRAGLI

PIAZZA
DE' PITTI

Giardino
Torrigiani

VIA ROMANA

Palazzo
Pitti

Forte di
Belvedere

Giardino di Boboli

Giardino Bard

A   B   C

and check opening times for museums and churches before you visit to avoid disappointment. Reserve accommodations before you come, and don't plan to use Florence as a base for touring the rest of Tuscany.

Florence and Florentines

Florentines are Tuscans – generally restrained and rational, and less given to

fiery displays. They also are more reserved. Accustomed to huge numbers of visitors, they do not go out of their way to befriend tourists but are courteous and professional in their everyday dealings.

Florence at first glance is not as instantly appealing as Rome or Venice – let it grow on you and experience it as a living city, not merely as a vast treasure-house of art. Get away from the major sights and their crowds of sightseers, and explore the quieter areas, with atmospheric streets and traditional activities. Vary the artistic glories with a bit of hedonism, and take time to relax.

The best way to see Florence is on foot. Most of the main attractions are clustered together in the largely pedestrian central core, making walking easier (but watch out for enthusiastic scooter riders).

Eating in Tuscany

There are all types of restaurants in Florence, from fast-food joints to world-class establishments. Many are specifically aimed at tourists and have prominently displayed fixed-price (but mediocre) menus. To ensure a memorable meal, eat where the Italians themselves eat and be prepared to pay somewhat high prices. For a simple lunch, try a slice of fresh-baked pizza to go or a quick snack in a *vinaio* or *fiaschetteria*, traditional wine bars.

Food markets are particularly tempting, where you can put together the makings of a picnic – bread, salami, cheese, fruit and a bottle of wine. Tuscan food is simple and excellent, centered around basic ingredients such as olive oil, fresh vegetables and meat, with plenty of soups, superb pork dishes, grilled meats and vegetables. Bean dishes are especially popular (Tuscans are fondly nicknamed *mangiafagioli*, or "bean-eaters"). The most famous wine is Chianti, a delicious red wine, but look also for Brunello di Montalcino, a superb red from Tuscany.

Pucci, Gucci and More

Intriguing stores, markets and boutiques are scattered throughout the center of Florence. Shoes and leather goods are famous, as are fine china, exquisite bed and table linen, and jewelry. Designer-label fans can visit Pucci and Gucci on their home ground; other tempting gifts include glazed majolica pottery, marbled paper, prints and antiques.

Via de'Tornabuoni and surrounding streets house the most elegant stores; less expensive fashion is found around Piazza della Repubblica and Via dei Calzaiuoli, while jewelers line the Ponte Vecchio. There are many leather factory outlets near Santa Croce. Be sure to spend time browsing in a market; you'll find tempting food in the Mercato Centrale. Most stores will ship to the United States.

Festivals Galore

A summer visit is likely to coincide with one of the cultural festivals, the *Estate Fiesolana* or the *Maggio Musicale Fiorentino*, which run from May through August, with concerts, opera and ballet – often outdoors in an historic setting.

Excursions

Even if your time in Tuscany is limited, try to fit in an excursion outside Florence, viewing the timeless landscape en route to another of the region's superb historic towns. Possibilities include Pisa, Siena, San Gimignano and the wine country of Chianti, all easily reached by tour bus or public transportation. Nearer still lies Fiesole, a picturesque hill town just above Florence, the perfect escape from noise and heat.

Essential Information

Tourist Information

Via Cavour 1r ☎ 055 290 832; Piazza della Stazione 5 ☎ 055 212 245; Loggia del Bigallo, Piazza San Giovanni ☎ 055 288496; Aeroporto Amerigo Vespucci, Peretola (arrivals hall) ☎ 055 315874; www.firenzeturismo.it

Urban Transportation

Buses, both regular and electric, run from Santa Maria Novella station all over town. Buy tickets (€1.20) before boarding: passes are available from machines and tobacconists and are valid for unlimited trips within a period of 90 minutes; 24-hour (€5), 3-day (€12) and 7-day passes (€18), or an electronic Carta Agile (10 or 20 90-minute tickets), also are available. Maps and timetables can be found at the ATAF office (✉ Piazza della Stazione

☎ 800 424500 toll free; www.ataf.net). Stamp tickets, as you board, in the orange box on the bus. Hail taxis at central locations, or call Radio Taxi Cotafi (☎ 055 4390) or Radio Taxi Socata (☎ 055 4242).

Airport Information

Most visitors arrive and leave from Pisa's Galileo Galilei Airport (☎ 050 849 111; 050 849 300 for flight information; www.pisa-airport.com), connected to Florence's Santa Maria Novella railroad station by bus or train services; travel time approximately 1 hour. Some railroad services are direct, others require a connection at Pisa Centrale. Florence Airport (Amerigo Vespucci Airport) is at Peretola (☎ 055 306 1300; www.aeroporto.firenze.it), 4 miles outside the city.

Climate – average highs and lows for the month

Jan.	Feb.	Mar.	Apr.	May	Jun.	Jul.	Aug.	Sep.	Oct.	Nov.	Dec.
10°C	12°C	15°C	18°C	23°C	27°C	31°C	30°C	26°C	21°C	14°C	10°C
50°F	54°F	59°F	64°F	73°F	81°F	88°F	86°F	79°F	70°F	57°F	50°F
1°C	2°C	5°C	7°C	11°C	14°C	17°C	17°C	14°C	10°C	5°C	2°C
34°F	36°F	41°F	45°F	52°F	57°F	63°F	63°F	57°F	50°F	41°F	36°F

Florence Sights

Cappelle Medicee

The beautiful Cappelle Medicee (Medici Chapels) were built as the mausoleum for Florence's most powerful family.

The Sagrestia Nuova, built by Michelangelo between 1520 and 1534, contains some of his most powerful sculptures. Carvings of reclining figures representing *Night* and *Day* and *Dawn* and *Dusk* decorate the tombs of Lorenzo, duke of Urbino, and Guiliano, duke of Nemours. The fluid lines are a perfect foil for the austerity of the architecture.

➕ C3 ✉ Piazza Madonna degli Aldobrandini 6
☎ 055 294 883; www.polomuseale.firenze.it 🕐 Daily
8:15 a.m.–1:50 p.m. Closed first, third and fifth Mon.,
and second and fourth Sun. of the month 🚌 14, 22,
31, 23, 71, C1 🈺 $$

Duomo, Battistero e Campanile di Giotto

The Gothic Duomo (Cathedral) of Santa Maria del Fiore, the first domed structure erected in Europe since Roman times, was built between 1296 and 1436. Its austere interior, with a Paolo Uccello fresco, leads to the 463 steps to the top of Brunelleschi's Cupola (Dome).

The chief draw of the 11th-century marble Battistero (Baptistery) is the three sets of bronze doors, with their Old Testament scenes. Andrea Pisano cast the south pair in 1326, and they inspired Lorenzo Ghiberti to design the doors at the north and east in the 1400s.

The Campanile (Bell Tower), designed by Giotto, was built between 1334 and 1359. Its marble walls are decorated with superb relief sculptures. The 280-foot, 414-step climb offers lovely, if vertiginous, views over Florence.

➕ C3 ✉ Piazza del Duomo 🚇 Duomo and
Campanile: 055 230 2885; www.operaduomo.firenze.it
🕐 Duomo: Mon.–Wed. and Fri. 10–5, Sat. 10–4:45,
Sun. 1:30–4:45 (closes Thu. at 4:30 p.m., Jan.–Apr. and
Nov.–Dec.; 4 p.m. May and Oct.). Cupola: Mon.–Fri.
8:30–7, Sat. 8:30–5:40. Battistero: Mon.–Sat. 11:15–7
(first Sat. of the month 8:30–2), Sun. 8:30–2.
Campanile: daily 8:30–7:30 🚌 23, 71, C1, C2
🈺 Duomo free; Cupola, Campanile, Battistero $$

Galleria dell'Accademia

Founded as an art school in 1784, the Galleria dell'Accademia (Academy Gallery) today houses the world's most important collection of Michelangelo sculptures, as well as works by other artists. The main attraction is his *David*, a huge and technically perfect nude male figure, possibly the most famous in the history of sculpture. More moving by far are the other sculptures by the artist, particularly the four *Prisoners*, the figures struggling to break free from their block of marble.

➕ D4 ✉ Via Ricasoli 58–60 ☎ 055 238 8609;
www.polomuseale.firenze.it. Advance booking
(advisable) ☎ 055 294883; www.b-ticket.com
🕐 Tue.–Sun. 8:15–6:50 🚌 1, 7, 10, 20, C1 🈺 $$

The frescoes decorating the Cupola of the Duomo were created by Giorgio Vasari and Federico Zuccari

Galleria degli Uffizi

Arguably the world's greatest collection of Renaissance paintings, the Galleria degli Uffizi (Gallery of the Offices) is housed in an elegant arcaded building designed by Vasari as administrative offices – hence the name.

Here, in chronological order, are paintings representing the greatest names in art, among them Giotto, Paolo Uccello, Botticelli, Piero della Francesca, Leonardo da Vinci, Michelangelo, Raphael and Caravaggio. Many of the stunning artworks date from the 12th to 17th centuries.

Come early or late to avoid waiting in the longest lines, though the surprisingly small rooms are likely to be thronged with visitors.

C2 ✉ Loggiato degli Uffizi 6 ☎ 055 238 8651; 055 294 883 for reservations or book online at www.b-ticket.com; www.polomuseale.firenze.it ⏰ Tue.–Sun. 8:15–6:50 (occasionally stays open later in summer) 🚌 C1, C2 🍴 Café in gallery 💷 $$

Museo Nazionale del Bargello

Surrounding a courtyard, in a building dating from 1255, the Museo Nazionale del Bargello (National Bargello Museum) houses Italy's finest collection of Renaissance sculpture. The first floor has works by Michelangelo, Benvenuto Cellini, the flamboyant Giambologna and other late Renaissance artists, but the vaulted second-floor hall contains the museum's masterpieces. Here are Donatello's bronze of a vulnerable *David*, his exquisite *St. George,* and the superb Baptistery door reliefs showing *The Sacrifice of Isaac* by Lorenzo Ghiberti and Brunelleschi, made for a competition in 1401.

Upstairs you will find a collection of bright enameled terra-cottas by the della Robbia family.

D2 ✉ Via del Proconsolo 4 ☎ 055 294883 (advance booking); www.polomuseale.firenze.it ⏰ Daily 8:15 a.m.–1:50 p.m. Closed first, third and fifth Sun., and second and fourth Mon. of the month 🚌 23, 71, C1, C2 💷 $$

Museo di San Marco

Rebuilt in 1437, the convent attached to the church of San Marco, decorated by Fra Angelico, is one of Florence's loveliest treasures. It's a peaceful religious house, where each monk's cell is adorned with a tiny fresco to aid prayer. The pilgrim's hall contains many paintings by Fra Angelico and his school, and additional works are on display in the cloisters and on the stairs, notably the radiant *Annunciation.*

D4 ✉ Piazza San Marco 3 ☎ 055 294883 (advance booking); www.polomuseale.firenze.it ⏰ Mon.–Fri. 8:15–1:50, Sat.–Sun. 8:15–4:50. Closed first, third and fifth Sun., and second and fourth Mon. of the month. Closed Jan. 6, Easter, Apr. 25, Jun. 2, Aug. 15, Nov. 1 and Dec. 8 and 26 🚌 7, 10, 11, 25, 32, C1 💷 $$

Ponte Vecchio

This most photographed Florentine bridge, the Ponte Vecchio (Old Bridge), was built in 1345 to replace an earlier one. It has been lined with exclusive goldsmiths and jewelers' shops since 1593. Above it runs a corridor used by members of the Medici family to travel from the Pitti Palace to the Uffizi. The sole bridge across the Arno river in Florence not destroyed by the Germans in World War II, the Ponte Vecchio also survived the floods in 1966.

C2 ✉ Ponte Vecchio 🚌 C3, D

Santa Croce

This huge Franciscan church was built in 1294, but was badly damaged by the 1966 floods. Today it contains superb early frescoes telling the story of the Santa Croce (Holy Cross). Michelangelo is buried here, along with Ghiberti, Machiavelli and Galileo Galilei.

In the serene cloisters is a museum featuring Cimabue's famous *Crucifix*, and the Cappella dei Pazzi (Pazzi Chapel) by Brunelleschi.

E2 ✉ Piazza Santa Croce 16 ☎ 055 246 6105; www.santacroceopera.it ⏰ Mon.–Sat. 9:30–5, Sun. 2–5 🚌 14, 23, 71, C3 💷 $$ (includes entry to adjoining Museo dell'Opera di Santa Croce)

A Day in Florence

Many Florentines start working by 8 a.m., when food stores also open. Since many people live in centrally located apartments, visitors have the chance to see the neighborhoods waking up. Housewives go to market early, children walk to school and people pause for a quick bar breakfast on their way to work.

For the tourist in Florence an early start makes sense. Head straight for major sights such as the Galleria degli Uffizi, Galleria dell'Accademia, Duomo or Palazzo Pitti (Pitti Palace) while you're still fresh and before the big tour groups arrive. Most of the museums open at 8:30 a.m. and the churches earlier, so it's feasible to pop into a specially noted church first thing.

Pause mid-morning for a drink and a rest, but bear in mind that some attractions shut for several hours in the middle of the day, as do stores. It's a good idea to follow the siesta habit – a leisurely lunch and a quiet hour or so digesting all you've seen will leave you fresh for more touring in the late afternoon. Early evening is a popular time for Florentines to shop, and a good opportunity for you to track down that must-have leather bag, beautiful fabric, silk tie or marbled paper souvenir.

Florentines are back at work and out on the streets again some time after 4:30, looking rested, relaxed and ready for the rest of the day and evening. By 6:30 the town is thronged with well-dressed crowds, strolling, meeting friends and wholeheartedly enjoying the evening *passeggiata* through the streets of their beautiful city. Crowds thin out and shops close around 8:30, when people head home or to a restaurant for dinner, and there's a break before the evening's activities.

Florence has plenty of nightlife to choose from, with a wealth of cultural offerings such as theater, opera and classical music, movies, and numerous discos and bars with live music. The streets are busy well into the early hours – especially in the height of summer – with locals and foreigners alike enjoying the balmy night air.

Detail from *Madonna with Child and Angels* c.1455, by Fra Filippo Lippi, in the Uffizi Gallery

Naples

Vibrant, noisy, crumbling Naples (Napoli), the capital of southern Italy and one of Europe's most beautifully located cities, is light years removed in atmosphere from the prosperous north. The city epitomizes southern Italy: confusing, passionate, dirty and charming, redolent with a rich and complicated history that has physically shaped it and emotionally shaped its residents. Naples can feel alien and intimidating, but also inspires fierce loyalty as visitors are quickly won over by its exuberance, way of life, attractions and, above all, its people.

Shops on the narrrow Via San Gregorio Armeno

The people of southern Italy are generally charming, warm and enthusiastic, and Neapolitans are no exception. They live at what appears to be a fever pitch of excitement and noise, which you'll notice on the street. You'll find people eager to help, and anxious for you to enjoy Naples. Authorities have encouraged citizens to welcome tourists, and have succeeded admirably.

Getting Around

Central Naples is best tackled on foot, as the traffic is so horrendous that any form of transportation can be excruciatingly slow. Much of what you'll want to see is walkable, and sights are grouped together in different areas, so take a bus or cable car to your general destination and then walk. Wandering around is an essential and fascinating part of the Naples experience, as the street life is lively and beguiling – but stick to well-frequented areas.

You'll want to travel down the coast to Pompeii and the Sorrento peninsula; both can be reached by train.

The best way to appreciate the beauty of Naples' spectacular setting on the bay is from the sea; you could combine a visit to the Sorrento peninsula with a boat trip to Sorrento or to the ravishing islands of Capri and Ischia.

Safety in Naples

The city authorities have done much to clean up Naples in every way, making it a much safer and more attractive city to visit. However, it is still wise to avoid the labyrinthine back streets, the docks and, at night, the railroad station. Avoid carrying a lot of cash, and be aware of pickpockets, particularly in crowded tourist areas.

Be careful when crossing the street: Neapolitan drivers often ignore pedestrian crossings, and unless you step off the sidewalk you could be stranded for what seems like hours. Scooters appear to come out of nowhere, and they frequently use the sidewalks or go against the direction of traffic.

Mediterranean Flavors

Neapolitan cooking ranks among the best in Italy, with a strong emphasis on the freshest fish and seafood, and local fruit and vegetables from the fertile volcanic soil of the hinterland. Flavors are intense, and the combination of ingredients unusual and interesting. There are pasta dishes with shellfish, grilled fish of all varieties, mozzarella cheese dripping with freshness, and numerous salamis, as well as some excellent local prosciutto.

Naples is the home of thin, tasty and crisp pizzas; they are always baked in wood-fired ovens, and can be eaten as a snack or light meal. Neapolitan cakes and pastries are famous and best enjoyed from a *pasticceria* (a specialist pastry and cake shop). Try honeyed *stuffoli*, iced chocolate *mustaccioli, zeppola* (doughnuts) and *sfogliatelle* filled with ricotta cheese. Don't miss out on the fantastic ice cream. Local wines to try are Lacrima Christi and Greco di Tufo. Be sure to sample Limoncello, a lemon-flavored liqueur, or delicious *mirtillo* (bilberry) and *finocchietto* (fennel) liqueurs.

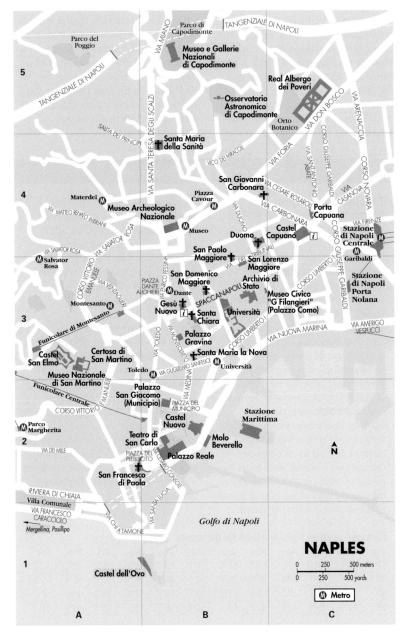

NAPLES

| 0 | 250 | 500 meters |
| 0 | 250 | 500 yards |

Ⓜ Metro

Shopping and Nightlife

Naples' upscale stores are clustered along the Via Toledo and the Via Chiaia, where you'll find outlets for Italy's top designers, as well as local stores selling fine leather goods, fashion and knitwear. Jewelers abound near Via San Biagio; the traditional best buys in Naples are coral necklaces, bracelets, earrings and cameo brooches. If you like antiques, head for Via Domenico Morelli, where stores specialize in 18th-century furniture and paintings.

Traditional nativity figurines are still made in the historic area around San Biagio, along with decorated masks and elaborately dressed dolls. Galleria Vanvitelli, in the Vomero district, is a useful shopping center, while downtown, you'll find a branch of the department store La Rinascente, and the Galleria Umberto I, an architecturally splendid early 20th-century mall.

If you like opera and classical music, a performance in the wonderful San Carlo opera house, the oldest working theater in Europe, should be high on your list. Traditional Neapolitan music is easy to find, and even the least tourist-oriented restaurants generally have musicians ambling through their premises serenading diners.

Essential Information

Tourist Information

Piazza del Gesù Nuovo 7 ☎ 081 551 2701
Via San Carlo 9 ☎ 081 402 394;
www.inaples.it

Urban Transportation

Neapolitan traffic makes any form of transportation slow, so it's best to walk if it's feasible. Longer distances can be covered by metro (subway), bus and *funiculari* (cable cars), all of which are slow. There are two types of *Giranapoli* tickets, valid for either 90 minutes or all day; they are interchangeable between buses, cable cars and the metro, and obtainable from tobacconists or newsstands. They must be validated in the special machines onboard buses; before boarding cable cars; and at the entrance to metro platforms. To travel around the bay, use the Circumvesuviana railroad, which leaves from the railroad station on Corso Garibaldi every half-hour and takes an hour to reach Sorrento, its farthest point. You also can travel to

Sorrento by ferry or hydrofoil from the Mergellina or Molo Beverello docks; the same companies also serve Capri, Ischia and the other islands (www.caremar.it, www.alilauro.it, www.snav.it). There are taxi stands throughout the city, or you can call a cab (☎ 081 88 88 or book online at www.consorziotaxinapoli.it).

Airport Information

Naples' Capodichino Airport ☎ 081 789 6111 (for flight information please see carriers' websites or go to www.portal.gesac.it, the main airport website), with internal and European flights, is northwest of the city center. The airport "Alibus" (☎ 0800 639 525, toll-free within Italy; www.anm.it) buses run at 20-minute intervals to Piazza Municipio via Piazza Garibaldi, daily 6:30 a.m.–11:30 p.m. Tickets cost €3. ANM route 35 links the airport with the central station every 30 minutes (contact details the same as Alibus).

Climate – average highs and lows for the month

Jan.	Feb.	Mar.	Apr.	May	Jun.	Jul.	Aug.	Sep.	Oct.	Nov.	Dec.
12°C	13°C	15°C	18°C	22°C	26°C	29°C	29°C	26°C	22°C	17°C	13°C
54°F	55°F	59°F	64°F	72°F	79°F	84°F	84°F	79°F	72°F	63°F	55°F
4°C	5°C	7°C	9°C	13°C	17°C	19°C	19°C	17°C	13°C	8°C	5°C
39°F	41°F	45°F	48°F	55°F	63°F	66°F	66°F	63°F	55°F	46°F	41°F

Naples

Naples Sights

```
Key to symbols
⊞ map coordinates refer to the Naples map on
page 309 ⛴ admission charge: $$$ more than €8,
$$ €4–€8, $ less than €4
See page 5 for complete key to symbols
```

Castel Nuovo

The five massive towers of the 15th-century Castel Nuovo (New Castle) dominate the Naples waterfront. A magnificent Renaissance gateway accesses the central courtyard, which is surrounded by buildings housing the Museo Civico (Civic Museum), the Gothic Sala dei Baroni (Barons' Hall) and the Cappella Palatina (Palatine Chapel), the only surviving part of a 13th-century building.

Nearby is the 17th-century Palazzo Reale (Royal Palace) and the San Carlo opera house.

⊞ B2 ✉ Piazza Municipio ☎ 081 7955 877; www.museincampania.it ⏱ Mon.–Sat. 9–7 🚌 R2, R3; tram 1, C24 ⛴ $$

Castel dell'Ovo

Encircled by the sea, the Castel dell'Ovo (Egg Castle), Naples' oldest castle, was built between the 9th and 16th centuries. Once run down, it is now restored and used for cultural events.

⊞ B1 ✉ Borgo Marinaro ☎ 081 2400 055 ⏱ Mon.–Sat. 9–6, Sun. 10 a.m.–2 p.m. 🚌 R3, 140; tram 1 ⛴ Free

Certosa di San Martino

Visible from all over Naples is the hilltop complex of the Certosa di San Martino (St. Martin's Charterhouse), constructed mainly between the 16th and 18th centuries.

Highlights include the sumptuous baroque church, the arcaded Chiostro Grande (Main Cloister) and the lavish Quarto del Priore (Prior's Quarters).

Don't miss the exhibition of *presepi* (crib figures), a charming collection of figures and everyday objects fashioned for Christmas cribs in the 19th century, in the Museo Nazionale di San Martino (San Martino National Museum).

⊞ A3 ✉ Largo San Martino 5 ☎ 081 229 4568;

Pompeii

The 20,000 inhabitants of Roman Pompeii enjoyed a civilized lifestyle in their prosperous city, with fine civic amenities, temples, public baths, and housing suitable for every taste and pocket. The one drawback was Pompeii's location on the slopes of Vesuvius, an active volcano. In AD 79 its worst eruption occurred, engulfing the city and many of its inhabitants in a thick layer of pumice and volcanic ash. For nearly 1,700 years Pompeii remained buried, perfectly preserved beneath a hard layer of volcanic debris. About 1750 it was rediscovered, excavations started, and gradually the ruins emerged. It's a complete small city that can be explored like any other, wandering the streets and visiting the sites that appeal. It has the main features of every Roman city – the forum, two theaters, an amphitheater, a sports stadium and symmetrical streets laid out in a grid pattern.

Start at the forum and walk through the paved streets, looking into houses and shops. Track down the covered market, the bakery, the laundry and the numerous taverns, some advertising bargain prices on the outside walls. The House of the Vetii, with its lovely garden and frescoed dining room, is a highlight, as is the House of the Tragic Poet, whose owners had a portrait mosaic of their dog displayed by the front door with "cave canem" (beware of the dog) carefully inscribed at the entry.

⊞ See page 285, D2 ✉ Pompeii ☎ 081 857 5347 or 081 857 5347; www.pompeiiturismo.it ⏱ Daily 8:30–7:30, Apr.–Oct.; 8:30–5, rest of year 🚂 Circumvesuviana or Trenitalia train to Pompeii Scavi station. Trenitalia–Pompeii (stop at Villa dei Misteri) 🚌 SITA Napoli–Salerno (stop at Piazza Esedra); CSTP No. 4 Salerno 🍴 Self-service restaurant and bar outside forum ⛴ $$$ ⓘ Last admission 90 minutes before closing

Naples' waterfront gem, Mergellina, lies at the foot of Posillipo Hill

www.polomusealenapoli.beniculturali.it ⏰ Thu.–Tue. 8:30–7:30 🚇 Montesanto, Centrale or Chiai to Vomero 🚌 V1 💷 $$ (price may differ due to temporary exhibitions)

Mergellina
This picturesque waterfront area, traditionally the fishermen's quarter, is a delightful place to stroll. Fishing boats and island ferries still operate here.
➕ Off map at A1 ✉ Mergellina 🚇 Mergellina 🚌 C4, C16, R3

Museo Archeologico Nazionale
The Museo Archeologico Nazionale (National Archeological Museum) houses one of the world's most important collections of Classical sculpture, as well as mosaics, gems, glass, silver and Egyptian antiquities.

Finds from Pompeii are here; don't miss the graceful fresco portrayal of Flora. The *Farnese Hercules* and *Farnese Bull* are equally impressive; the *Bull* is the largest Classical sculptural group to have survived, dating from 200 BC.

Allow two or three hours for your visit to do the museum justice.
➕ B4 ✉ Piazza Museo Nazionale 19 ☎ 081 442 2149; www.cir.campania.beniculturali.it/

museoarcheologiconazionale ⏰ Wed.–Mon. 9–7:30 🚌 C57, R4 💷 $$; $$$ during exhibitions

Museo e Gallerie Nazionali di Capodimonte
Built in the 18th century as a palace and museum, and surrounded by a wooded park, Capodimonte has been restored and rearranged. Don't miss Masaccio's *Crucifixion*, which is the star of the Renaissance painting collection, and the majolica and porcelain exhibits, much of it made by the Capodimonte factory.
➕ B5 ✉ Parco di Capodimonte, Via Miano 2 ☎ 081 749 9111; www.cir.campania.beniculturali.it/ museodicapodimonte ⏰ Museum: daily 8:30–7:30; Park: daily 8–1 hour before closing 🚌 C63; metro line 2 to Cavour and then bus M2, 178, 201 💷 Museum $$; park free

Spaccanapoli
Spaccanapoli is the name of the string of atmospheric, traffic-free streets slicing through Naples' historic core, following the line of what was the Roman city's main artery. Its length is lined with monuments that trace the city's story – medieval, Renaissance and baroque *palazzi*, churches and civic buildings.
➕ B3 ✉ Via Benedetto Croce, Via San Biagio dei Librai

Excursion to Capri

A favorite with the Roman emperors, Capri has been a tourist hot spot for many years. This tiny island, with its lovely scenery and crystal-clear waters, now welcomes more than 2 million visitors annually.

You can travel from Naples' Mergellina or Molo Beverello docks by ferry or hydrofoil, a trip that takes between 50 and 90 minutes. Spectacular views open up back to the city and across to Mount Vesuvius as you approach the hills of the Sorrento peninsula, with the island of Capri lying off its tip. Boats dock at Marina Grande, the island's main harbor.

The charm of Capri lies in the combination of lovely scenery, picturesque villages and a holiday atmosphere. The two main settlements are Anacapri and Capri; their whitewashed houses and narrow, winding streets are crammed with boutiques, outdoor cafés and lively fish restaurants. There are boat trips to Capri's most famous sight, the Grotta Azzurra (Blue Grotto), a spectacular sea cave filled with glorious refracted turquoise light. Another highlight is the beautiful Villa San Michele in Anacapri. Built in the late 19th century by Swedish physician Axel Munthe, this dreamlike villa is filled with Classical statues. There also is a peaceful green garden, and from its shady pergola you can enjoy some of the island's loveliest views.

Walk to the ruins of Villa Jovis, Emperor Tiberius' clifftop villa, from which he allegedly threw his enemies into the sea. Or stroll to a lookout above the Faraglioni, a cluster of offshore rocks, for beautiful sea views.

Capri 🚏 See page 285, C2 ☎ Tourist offices: Banchina del Porto, Marina Grande ☎ 081 837 0634; Piazza Umberto I, Capri ☎ 081 837 0686; Via G. Orlandi 59, Anacapri ☎ 081 837 1524; www.capritourism.com 🚌 From Marina Grande to Marina Piccola, Capri and Anacapri 🚢 Ferry operator: Caremar from Molo Beverello, Naples: www.caremar.it (ticket sales and information online only). Hydrofoil operators: Caremar, from Molo Beverello: www.caremar.it (ticket sales and information online only); SNAV, from Mergellina (☎ 081 428 5555; www.snav.it). Alilauro (☎ 081 497 2238; www.alilauro.it) and Metro del Mare (www.metròdelmare.it) also operate services to the islands and points in the Bay of Naples

Blue Grotto ☎ 081 837 7714; www.motoscafisticapri.com 🕐 Daily 9–1 hour before dusk 🚢 From Marina Grande 💲$$$

Villa San Michele, Anacapri ☎ 081 837 1401; www.villasanmichele.eu 🕐 Daily 9–6, May–Sep.; 9:30–5 in Apr. and Oct.; 9–4:30 in Mar.; 9–3:30, rest of year 🚌 From Capri 💲$$

Villa Jovis ☎ 081 837 4549 🕐 Wed.–Mon. 9–1 in first half of month, Mar.–Nov.; Mon.–Sat. 9–1 in second half of each month, Mar.–Nov. 🚌 From Capri 💲$

Large boats and sailing craft at Marina Grande, Capri, on the Bay of Naples

Venice

No matter how many pictures or films you've seen, nothing can prepare you for the impact of the real Venice (Venezia), one of the world's most captivating cities. Whether it's sparkling in late spring sunshine or shrouded in winter mist, it will enchant you in every way.

Tackling Venice

When you first arrive in Venice, don't head straight for the main sights (which will invariably be packed); take time to get a feel for the city, either from the vantage point of a ferry or by strolling the streets and squares.

As for accommodations, luxury hotels lining the Grand Canal (Canal Grande) are clearly the optimum choice, but there are many with great charm elsewhere. The *sestieri* (city areas) of Dorsoduro, San Marco, Castello and San Polo are among the nicest parts of the city to stay. Avoid the area around the train station, which is noisy and less attractive and under no circumstances should you stay in Mestre, which is an industrial sprawl across the causeway on the mainland.

Accept that you will do a great deal of tiring walking around the city, and come prepared with comfortable shoes. Make a point of working out your daily itinerary; shortcuts across the city save valuable time. Main routes are clearly marked along the streets by yellow signs.

There are numerous tour options; if time is short these can be helpful, and you'll have the benefit of English-speaking guides.

Venetian Glass, Velvet Slippers

The city's main fashion and leather stores cluster along the Calle dei Fabbri, the Frezzeria and the so-called Mercerie, a district made up of the streets connecting Piazza San Marco with the Rialto area.

Glass is a true Venetian specialty, made for centuries on the island of Murano. Marbled paper, made here for centuries, is another good buy, and Venetian masks make wonderful souvenirs. Other typical products are velvet slippers in jewel-bright colors or a real gondolier's hat; you'll find one at Emilio Ceccato, near the Rialto.

Festivals

Carnival lasts for the 10 days before *martedì grasso* (Shrove Tuesday), the start of Lent, when thousands of people wearing costumes parade the city streets.

The summer sees several ancient festivals, most notably the feast of *La Sensa*, when the mayor and his entourage sail out into the lagoon in the state barge and enact a symbolic

VENICE

0   100   200 meters
0   100   200 yards

Ⓥ Vaporetti (boat)

N

San Michele

Canale delle Fondamente

anta Maria ssunta

Santi Giovanni e Paolo

CAMPO SANTI GIOVANNI E PAOLO

San Francesco della Vigna

Santa Maria ormosa

CAMPO SANTA MARIA FORMOSA

Palazzo Grimani

Scuola di San Giorgio degli Schiavoni

Fondazione Querini Stampalia

Chiesa di S Zaccaria

San Giorgio dei Greci

Basilica di San Marco

PONTE DEI SOSPIRI

CAMPO BANDIERA E MORO

Chiesa di San Giovanni in Bragora

Palazzo Ducale

Chiesa di Santa Maria della Pieta

Museo Navale

Bacino S Marco

San Giorgio Maggiore

San Giorgio Maggiore

Teatro Verde

D   E

Gondolas
The shiny black gondola – symbol of Venice – is a shallow-draft vessel propelled by a single oarsman, the gondolier, who stands at the back of the boat. A ride in a gondola is a great Venetian experience for many visitors, but it is expensive and normally follows a set route. Be sure to ascertain what you're getting before you set out.

marriage to the waters. This is followed in July by the *Festa del Redentore*, a thanksgiving festival for deliverence from the plague.

During the *Regata Storica* in September, there are races of spectacular decorated craft, manned by crews in period dress down the Grand Canal.

Essential Information

Tourist Information
Call center ☎ 041 2424 (for all information)
Palazzina dei Santi, Giardini ex Reale
San Marco 71f
Aeroporto Marco Polo
Stazione Santa Lucia
www.veneziaunica.it; www.turismovenezia.it

Urban Transportation
If you arrive by car, you must leave the vehicle in one of the parking lots on the outskirts of the city. The parking at Piazzale Roma is the nearest to the city center. Venice's public transportation system is operated by ACTV (office at Piazzale Roma, ☎ 041 2424; www. actv.it) and uses two types of boats – *vaporetti* (big and slow) and *motoscafi* (small and fast). All are numbered on the front of the boat and follow set routes. *Vaporetti* boats leave from *pontile* (floating docks), which are clearly marked with service numbers and a route map. As the same numbers head in two directions, check that you are going the right way before you board. Tickets (€7), valid for 1 hour, can be bought at the *pontile* or at shops showing the ACTV sticker. Save money by buying 24-, 48-, 72-hour and 7-day tickets (€20, €30, €40 and €60 respectively). All tickets must be scanned by the iMob reader before boarding. There is a limited night service on most routes. *Vaporetti* stops are marked on the Venice city map with a "V." *Taxi motoscafi* (water taxis) are fast and expensive; they can be hailed on various canals, or call ☎ 041 522 2303; www.motoscafivenezia.it. Gondolas can penetrate even the narrowest canals, but are very expensive. As there are only four bridges over the Grand Canal, the seven *traghetti* (ferries) crossing at various points are useful. These ferries are old gondolas and are marked by green signs. Pay as you board and watch your balance, as it is customary to stand.

Airport Information
Venice's Marco Polo airport (☎ 041 260 9260; www.veniceairport.com) is 5 miles from the city center on the northern edge of the lagoon, and handles both domestic and international flights. For city connections take an ATVO shuttle bus (www.atvo.it) or ACTV bus No. 5 from the terminal to the Piazzale Roma at the edge of the city, where the road ends, and then connect with your hotel by *vaporetto* (water bus). The transfer takes 20 minutes by ATVO bus and 25 minutes by ACTV bus; ACTV tickets (€3) must be purchased from the office inside the airport arrivals terminal before boarding; buy ATVO tickets (€7) either inside the terminal or from the machines at the bus stop. An *Alilaguna* (boat) leaves from the dock outside the terminal for San Marco and the Lido; transfer time is around 50 minutes (www.alilaguna.it). The fastest way to reach the city is by water taxi; they leave from the dock outside the terminal and take 20 minutes to reach the center, but are expensive.

Climate – average highs and lows for the month

Jan.	Feb.	Mar.	Apr.	May	Jun.	Jul.	Aug.	Sep.	Oct.	Nov.	Dec.
5°C	8°C	12°C	17°C	21°C	24°C	27°C	26°C	23°C	18°C	12°C	8°C
41°F	46°F	54°F	63°F	70°F	75°F	81°F	79°F	73°F	64°F	54°F	46°F
0°C	2°C	5°C	9°C	13°C	17°C	19°C	18°C	16°C	12°C	7°C	3°C
32°F	36°F	41°F	48°F	55°F	63°F	66°F	64°F	61°F	54°F	45°F	37°F

Venice Sights

Basilica di San Marco

The Basilica di San Marco (St. Mark's Basilica) is a fusion of western and Byzantine styles and is connected to the Doge's Palace. Dating from 1094, it stands on the site of the ninth-century basilica built to house the body of St. Mark.

On entering, admire the facade carvings, then proceed inside to take in the glittering mosaics and ornate marble pavements; the gem-encrusted altar screen, the Pala d'Oro, a masterpiece of Gothic-Byzantine goldsmith art; and the third-century bronze horses, which once adorned the facade.

D2 ✉ Piazza San Marco 1 ☎ 041 270 8311; www.basilicasanmarco.it ⏰ Mon.–Sat. 9:45–5, Sun. 2–5, Easter–Oct.; Mon.–Sat. 9:45–5, Sun. 2–4, rest of year 🚌 1, 2, 4.1, 4.2, 5.2, N ∎ Basilica free; Loggia $$; Pala d'Oro $

Ca' d'Oro

The facade of the Ca' d'Oro (House of Gold), so called because it was once gilded, is a perfect example of the finest Venetian-Byzantine architecture.

Behind the facade is a beguiling small museum with an impressive *St. Sebastian* by Andrea Mantegna and a lovely *Madonna* by Giovanni Bellini, as well as sculptural fragments, bronzes and tapestries. All pieces are arranged in rooms around the *palazzo's* central *portego*, or inner courtyard.

C4 ✉ Calle di Ca' d'Oro 3932, off Strada Nova ☎ 041 522 2349, reservations: 041 520 0345; www.cadoro.org; www.polomuseale.venezia.beniculturali.it ⏰ Tue.–Sun. 8:15–7:15, Mon. 8:15–2 🚌 1 ∎ $$$

Campanile

The graceful Campanile, Venice's tallest building, is just over 100 years old. The original bell tower, reputedly built in AD 912, collapsed in 1902, killing no one and leaving St. Mark's unscathed. A cry of *"Dov'era e com'era"* ("where it was and how it was") went up, and 10 years later a replica was completed. Take the elevator up for superb views – on a clear day you can see as far as the Alps.

D2 ✉ Piazza San Marco ☎ 041 522 4064 ⏰ Daily 9–9, Jul.–Sep.; 9–7, Apr.–Jun. and in Oct.; 9:30–3:45, rest of year. Closed 3 weeks in Jan. 🚌 1, 2, 4.1, 4.2, 5.1, 5.2, N ∎ $$$

Canal Grande

The allure of the Canal Grande (Grand Canal), Venice's magical highway, never

The beautiful loggia of the Ca' d'Oro (House of Gold) overlooks the Grand Canal

seems to fade. Almost 4 miles long, with an average depth of 16 feet, it divides Venice in two and is crossed by four bridges. The canal is lined with palaces and churches, built over the course of 500 years.

By day many boats chug up and down the canal; at night it epitomizes romance, with reflected lights twinkling on the water. Take a No. 1 or No. 2 water bus (*vaporetto*) from stops on the Grand Canal.

🚌 B2, B4, C2, C3, C4 🚏 1, 2, N

Collezione Peggy Guggenheim

American heiress Peggy Guggenheim's modern art collection (on public view since 1951) is installed in her 18th-century *palazzo* on the Grand Canal. Here you'll find works by Pablo Picasso and Salvador Dalí and fine examples of paintings by Jackson Pollock and Mark Rothko. The garden makes a wonderful background for some Henry Moore sculptures and Marino Marini's *Angel of the Citadel*.

🚌 C2 ✉ Palazzo Venier dei Leoni, Dorsoduro 701 ☎ 041 240 5411; www.guggenheim-venice.it 🕐 Wed.–Mon. 10–6 🚏 1, 2 💰 $$$

Gallerie dell'Accademia

Allow plenty of time to admire the masterpieces in the Gallerie dell'Accademia (Academy Galleries), the finest collection of Venetian painting in the world. Arranged chronologically, the gallery's 24 rooms contain masterpieces such as Giorgio Giorgione's enigmatic *Tempest*, Giovanni Bellini's luminous *Virgins*, and superb works by Mantegna. Don't miss the dramatic *Translation of the Body of St. Mark* by Jacopo Tintoretto and Paolo Veronese's sumptuous *Feast in the House of Levi*.

Among other highlights are two cycles of paintings; *The Miracle of the True Cross* had several contributors, while the *Life of St. Ursula* is by Vittore Carpaccio.

🚌 B2 ✉ Campo della Carità 1050 ☎ 041 522 2247, reservations: 041 520 0345; www.gallerieaccademia. org; www.polomuseale.venezia.beniculturali.it

🕐 Tue.–Sun. 8:15–7:15, Mon. 8:15–2. Last admission 45 minutes before closing 🚏 1, 2 💰 $$$

Palazzo Ducale

The huge Gothic complex of the Palazzo Ducale (Ducal Palace) was the seat of Venice's government, where the Council of Ten met, ambassadors were received and the Doge (Duke) held councils of state. The present building dates from the 15th century, with later alterations following two fires in the 1500s.

The marked route leads through rooms to the vast Sala del Maggior Consiglio (Great Council Chamber), dominated by Jacopo Tintoretto's *Paradiso*, the world's largest oil painting.

The famous Ponte dei Sospiri (Bridge of Sighs) spans a canal to the right of the *palazzo's* waterfront facade.

🚌 D2 ✉ Piazzetta San Marco ☎ 041 271 5911; www.visitmuve.it 🕐 Daily 8:30–7, Apr.–Oct. (last admission at 6 p.m.); 8:30–5:30, rest of year 🚏 1, 2, 4.1, 4.2, 5.1, 5.2 💰 $$$. A Museum Pass giving access to all Musei Civici (Civic Museums) is the best value

Piazza San Marco

The only piazza in Venice (all the others are officially *campi*) is thronged around the clock with strolling and chattering crowds. Go early or late to avoid the worst crush, and marvel at the harmony of this wonderful open space.

Highlights here are the 15th-century Torre dell'Orologio (Clock Tower) and its zodiac clock, the graceful architecture of the Libreria Sansoviniana (Sansoviniana Library), and the two columns near the waterfront, topped by the lion of St. Mark and St. Theodore with his crocodile emblem.

🚌 D2 ✉ Piazza San Marco 🚏 1, 2, 4.1, 4.2, 5.1, 5.2, N

Punta della Dogana

The Punta della Dogana (Custom's House Point) contains warehouses built between 1677 and 1682; customs officials once operated from the buildings. In 2007 François Pinhault, a wealthy collector, leased the neglected buildings and spent €20 million on their

The Sala del Maggior Consiglio (Great Council Chamber) in the Palazzo Ducale

restoration and conversion into a contemporary art space. The superb interior is a fitting backdrop to showcase cutting-edge 21st-century art, which reflects Pinhault's own taste.

✚ C2 ✉ Campo di Salute, Dorsoduro 2 ☎ 199 112 112 (within Italy), (U1139) 041 271 9031 from U.S.; www.palazzograssi.it ⊙ Wed.–Mon. 10–7 🚏 1, 2 🚌 $$$

Rialto

Throughout the Middle Ages the Rialto was Europe's financial and banking center; the name had the same connotations as does Wall Street now. Today, you can admire the bridge and browse in Venice's food markets, one of the city's great sights. Wander through the fruit and vegetable stalls, but leave time to enjoy the scents and sights of the fish market, full of the day's catch.

✚ C3 ✉ Rialto 🚏 1, 2

San Giorgio Maggiore

To visit the superb Palladian church of San Giorgio Maggiore (St. George the Great), whose serene bulk dominates the view of St. Mark's Basin, you must take a water bus across the canal of St. Mark's

to St. George's Island. Built by Andrea Palladio in 1559, the church embodies order, grace and harmony. Take the elevator up the campanile (bell tower) to enjoy extensive views across to the Doge's Palace and the Campanile of San Marco.

✚ D1 ✉ Campo San Giorgio, Isola di San Giórgio Maggiore ☎ 041 522 7827 ⊙ Daily 9:30–12:30 and 2:30–6, May–Sep.; 9:30–12:30 and 2:30–5, rest of year. Closed during services 🚏 2 🚌 Free; $$ (elevator to campanile)

Santa Maria dei Miracoli

The jewel-like church of Santa Maria dei Miracoli (Our Lady of the Miracles) was built around 1480 to house an image of the Madonna credited with reviving a man who spent half-an-hour at the bottom of the Giudecca canal. Pietro Lombardo, who adorned the face of his church with colored marble and porphyry rock, created the harmonious interior as a frame for fine sculpture and beautiful carvings.

✚ D3 ✉ Campo dei Miracoli ☎ 041 275 0462 ⊙ Mon.–Sat. 10–5 🚏 1, 2 🚌 $ or $$$ "Chorus Pass" for entry to Venice's minor churches (www.chorusvenezia.org)

The church of Santi Giovanni e Paolo

Santa Maria della Salute

During the 1630 plague the Senate promised to build a church in honor of the Virgin if she would save the city. The pestilence passed, an architect was commissioned and the great dome of Santa Maria della Salute (Our Lady of Health and Salvation) rose at the entrance to the Grand Canal. An outstanding skyline feature, the interior has fine sculptures and paintings.

➕ C2 ✉ Campo della Salute 1 ☎ 041 241 1018 🕐 Daily 9–noon and 3–5:30 🚌 1

Santa Maria Gloriosa dei Frari

Santa Maria Gloriosa dei Frari (Glorious Virgin Mary of the Brothers), a lofty Franciscan church, is the final resting place of Titian and the composer Claudio Monteverdi. Built as a preaching church about 1250, it contains Titian's great *Assumption*, hung over the high altar, and his *Madonna of Ca' Pesaro*. Best of all in the right transept of the church is Giovanni Bellini's *Madonna and Child with Saints* tryptych, considered to be one of the world's finest paintings.

➕ B3 ✉ Campo dei Frari ☎ 041 272 8611; www.chorusvenezia.org; www.basilicadeifrari.it (Italian only) 🕐 Mon.–Sat. 9–6, Sun. 1–6 🚌 1, 2 💲 (accepts multi-church "Chorus Pass" ticket $$$)

Santi Giovanni e Paolo

More than 20 of Venice's doges are buried in the Gothic church of Santi Giovanni e Paolo (St. John and St. Paul),

rising majestically on one side of its *campo* (square). The square's focal point is the great equestrian statue of Bartolomeo Colleoni, a 15th-century Venetian army officer who left his wealth to the Republic in return for a monument. The 13th-century church contains many tombs, their monuments representing the best of Venetian medieval sculpture, and some lovely paintings, including Giovanni Bellini's *St. Vincent Ferrer*.

➕ D3 ✉ Campo SS Giovanni e Paolo ☎ 041 523 5913; www.basilicasantigiovanniepaolo.it 🕐 Mon.–Sat. 9–6, Sun. 12–6; closed during services 🚌 4.1, 4.2 💲 $

Scuola di San Giorgio degli Schiavoni

Carpaccio painted one of the city's most delightful picture cycles between 1502 and 1508 for the headquarters of Venice's Dalmatian, or Slavic, community – the Scuola di San Giorgio degli Schiavoni (School of St. George of the Slavs). He used Dalmatia's patron saints, St. George, St. Tryphon and St. Jerome, as his inspiration. Highlights are *St. George Slaying the Dragon* and *St. Augustine in his Study*, with his dog.

➕ E3 ✉ Calle dei Furlani 3259/a ☎ 041 522 8828 🕐 Mon. 2:45–6, Tue.–Sat. 9:15–1 and 2:45–6, Sun. 9:15–1 🚌 1, 2, 5.2 💲 $$

Scuola Grande di San Rocco

In 1564 the brotherhood of St. Roche ran a competition to choose an artist to decorate the walls of the Scuola Grande di San Rocco (Grand Meeting Halls of the Confraternity of St. Roche). Tintoretto (real name Jacopo Robusti) won, and spent 23 years working on a stupendous cycle of 54 paintings, including the wonderful *Crucifixion*. New Testament scenes line the walls of the ground floor's main hall. The many works on the staircase are by other artists.

➕ B3 ✉ Campo San Rocco ☎ 041 523 4864; www.scuolagrandesanrocco.it 🕐 Daily 9:30–5:30 🚌 1, 2 💲 $$$

The Lagoon Islands

You can spend a delightful day exploring some of the islands in the lagoon. Most visitors opt for Murano, famous for its glass; Burano, with its lace-making; or Torcello, a virtually uninhabited island with an ancient cathedral and church. Guided excursions run to all three, but a more flexible option is to take the No. 12 boat, which leaves from the Fondamenta Nuove and takes around 40 to 50 minutes to reach Burano and (with a shuttle boat) Torcello.

Murano: Venetian glass has been made here since 1291, when the furnaces were moved away from the city to avoid the constant danger of fire. A visit to the fascinating Museo del Vetro (Glass Museum) will give you an idea of glassblowers' skills through the ages. Murano also has two exquisite churches: San Pietro Martire, which contains a glowing altarpiece by Giovanni Bellini; and Santi Maria e Donato, a beautiful 12th-century basilica with a colonnaded exterior apse and fine mosaics on its walls and floor.

Burano: Here, colorful canalside houses, narrow streets and sun-splashed squares are as picturesque as anything in Venice itself. This is still a fishing community, with a robust workaday atmosphere, and you'll see moored fishing boats and nets drying in the sun. Local women have always been skilled lace-makers, and you can admire the fragility of their exquisite work in the Lace Museum (Museo del Merletto).

Torcello: This is one of the most evocative and magical places in Venice. The sleepy island, with its overgrown canals and green fields, was the lagoon's first settled area, and once had fine buildings and palaces. A combination of the build up of silt and outbreaks of malaria caused its 12th-century decline. Today the only remaining signs of its past importance are the Cathedral of Santa Maria Assunta and the adjacent church, Santa Fosca. The cathedral's main glories are two 12th-century mosaics, which completely cover the apse and the opposite rear wall. High above the seventh-century altar is a lovely depiction of the Byzantine Madonna and Child, its poignant beauty highlighted by the simple gold background, while the graphic *Judgment* scenes make a telling contrast. The campanile (tower) is solid and square. The nearby church of Santa Fosca, with its arcaded porch, is lovely in its own way.

Modern glassware is still made on the island of Murano

Luxembourg

Opposite: Medieval tranquility on the Alzette river in the district of Grund, Luxembourg City

Luxembourg

Luxembourg lies at the heart of the European landmass. It is a minuscule country, measuring 51 miles from north to south and a mere 32 miles from east to west. Belgium lies to the north and west, France to the south and Germany to the east. Because of its attractive financial laws and constitutional stability, it has become a center of European politics and finance.

And despite a rather turbulent history, Luxembourg retains its independence and sovereignty; it is a true survivor of the Continent's stormy past.

Luxembourg Landscapes
Luxembourg is a Grand Duchy, the only one in the world, with the city of Luxembourg as its main focus, although its rural areas are remarkably varied for such a small country.

They include part of the delightful Ardennes region, the hilly area that lies across the northern third of Luxembourg

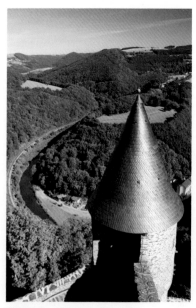

and extends into Belgium. The Ardennes have a distinctive landscape of forested plateaus sliced through by deep valleys that are drained by beautiful rivers. Fairy-tale castles crown wooded bluffs. At Vianden, a medieval castle, one of the Grand Duchy's finest historic sites, dominates the landscape. The equally magnificent Bourscheid Castle stands guard above the winding Sûre and Wark rivers. At Clervaux, the castle is matched in impact by the red-roofed Benedictine Clervaux Abbey, which stands amid the wooded heights above the beautiful town.

At the southern edge of the Ardennes, in the area where the hills meet the flatter, more fertile land known as Le Cour du Bon Pays, or "The Good Land," lies the picturesque little town of Diekirch. Only a short distance southwest is Ettelbrück, where there is a monument to General George S. Patton Jr. and the General Patton Memorial Museum containing many personal items from his life.

The most southerly part of Luxembourg is the country's economic powerhouse. Here in the "Good Land" are farms and orchards, forests and even more castles. In fact, the lovely valley of the Eisch river is known as the Vallée des Sept Châteaux (Valley of the Seven Castles).

Farther south from the city of Luxembourg is Les Terres Rouges, or

More Top Destinations in Luxembourg (see map page 325)
- Abbaye d'Echternach C2
- Abbaye St.-Maurice et St.-Maur B4
- Château de Bourscheid B3
- Diekirch B3
- Esch-sur-Sûre A3
- Grevenmacher C2
- Mondorf-les-Bains B1
- Vallée du Müllerthal B2–C2
- Vallée des Sept Châteaux A2–B2
- Vianden B3

The view from Château de Bourscheid

"The Land of the Red Rocks" around the towns of Dudelange and Pétange, home to much of the country's industry.

East of here is Mondorf-les-Bains, a fashionable spa town on the edge of the famous Moselle region. This area, running north to south along the border with Germany, is Luxembourg's wine-growing district, which has a heritage of more than 2,000 years.

Exploring the Country

You will find Luxembourgers are very cosmopolitan and friendly, and a large percentage of them speak English. The Grand Duchy has an excellent road system and distances are short between the many towns and villages, making independent travel a good option. There also are numerous day trips organized from the city of Luxembourg.

Timeline

AD 963	Count Siegfried of the Ardennes builds a castle called the Lützelburg ("Little Castle") on the Bock promontory.
1354	Luxembourg becomes a duchy.
1447	The Duchy of Luxembourg comes under the rule of the Habsburgs through marriage.
1542	The city of Luxembourg is captured by the French.
1554	The Spanish capture the city of Luxembourg.
1713	Under the terms of the Treaty of Utrecht, Luxembourg is controlled by the Kingdom of the Netherlands.
1815	Congress of Vienna establishes Luxembourg as a Grand Duchy within The Netherlands under the rule of the German Confederation.
1839	Under the terms of the Treaty of London, the western part of the Grand Duchy is ceded to Belgium: The rest of the Duchy becomes an independent state.
1867	Under the terms of the Second Treaty of London, Luxembourg's status as an independent and neutral state is affirmed.
1914	Germany occupies Luxembourg in World War I.
1940	Germany invades Luxembourg again in World War II.
1944	American troops liberate Luxembourg; Germany launches its "Ardennes Offensive." The Battle of the Bulge follows.
1945	Luxembourg becomes a member of the United Nations.
1948	Luxembourg joins Belgium and the Netherlands in forming Benelux, a trading and economic union.
1949	Luxembourg abandons neutrality and joins NATO.
1958	Luxembourg becomes a founding member of the European Economic Community (now known as the European Union).
1992	Luxembourg ratifies the Maastricht Treaty.
1994	City of Luxembourg declared a World Heritage Site by UNESCO.
1999	Luxembourg adopts the euro as the national currency.
2009	The Cabinet announces a relaxation of banking secrecy laws to help cut global tax evasion.
2015	World Bank announces Luxembourg has the world's second highest GDP after Qatar.

Luxembourg: the Great Survivor

Luxembourg, with its long history at the heart of Europe, has secured a major part in the working of the European Union. The country today is a constitutional monarchy ruled by HRH Grand Duke Henri, who heads a Cabinet of 12 ministers appointed from an elected Chamber of Deputies. Consensus politics is used in Luxembourg's government, and coalitions of more than one party usually hold power. On the international front, Luxembourg is home to, among others, the General Secretariat of the European Parliament, the European Court of Justice, the Court of Auditors, the European Bank of Investment, the Plenary Hall of the European Parliament and several Directorates of the European Commision – all of which are based in the city of Luxembourg's Centre Européen (European Center).

Sidewalk cafés amid the downtown bustle of the city of Luxembourg

Survival Guide

■ The *Schueberfouer* (☎ 4796-4294; www.fouer.lu), one of Europe's largest city fairs, takes place for nearly three weeks from mid-August to early September.

■ Most shops in the city of Luxembourg are closed on Monday until noon and may close Tuesday through Friday between noon and 2 p.m., but often stay open until 8 p.m. on Thursdays.

■ There are numerous stores in the Gare district of the city of Luxembourg, especially on avenue de la Liberté.

■ Enjoy an evening in the Grund district. There are lovely areas, good bars and restaurants, and a different ambience from the city center, which is known as the Ville area.

■ Earthenware bird whistles (*peckvillerchers*) are a popular present given on Easter Monday, when their sound fills the air.

■ The city of Luxembourg has many designer shops, such as Hermès, Dolce & Gabbana, Armani, Louis Vuitton and Claudia Sträter along Grande-Rue and rue Philippe II. There also are tempting treats in Leonidas, the renowned Belgian chocolatiers.

■ Typical Luxembourg souvenirs include cast iron from the Mersch foundry, in the heart of the Grand

Duchy. Designs incorporate castles and coats of arms. Authentic Luxembourg porcelain and earthenware are produced by Villeroy & Boch (330 rue du Rollingergrund, Luxembourg City ☎ 46 82 12 78; www.villeroy-boch.com; factory shop ◉ Mon.–Fri. 9:30–7, Sun. 9:30–6).

■ If you travel in the Moselle wine-producing region, enjoy some of Luxembourg's dry white and sparkling vintages, such as the subtle Rivaner; Pinot Blanc to go with fish dishes; or the strong Pinot Gris to complement a meal of *judd mat gaardebounen* (roast, smoked pork).

■ Children will love the Jardin des Papillons (exotic butterfly garden; route de Trèves, Grevenmacher ☎ 75 85 39; www.papillons.lu ◉ Daily 9:30–5, Apr.–Oct. ✋ $$$). Youngsters also will enjoy Parc Merveilleux (route de Mondorf, Bettembourg ☎ 51 10 48-1; www.parc-merveilleux.lu ◉ Daily 9:30–6, early Apr. to mid-Oct. ✋ $$$), at the southern tip of Luxembourg, where there are attractions from fairy-tale tableaux and exotic birds and reptiles to children's animal enclosures and children's games of all types.

City of Luxembourg

The city of Luxembourg is known as the landlocked "Gibraltar of the North" because of its once-fortified location. It is set above the cliffs that flank the canyon-like valleys of the Alzette and Pétrusse rivers. Today, the city of Luxembourg is more fairy tale than fortress. The old city, especially, is a pleasing mix of the past and present. Its elegant towers, spires and turrets, and its walls of golden sandstone helped win Luxembourg the UNESCO designation of World Heritage Site in 1994.

The steep-sided plateau on which Luxembourg stands explains its origins. The Romans first set up camp here. They had one eye on military control and the other on the advantages of a strategic trading position at the crossroads of northern Europe. In AD 963, Count Siegfried of the Ardennes built a castle on the narrow Bock promontory above the Alzette river.

Over the next 900 years, Luxembourg evolved into one of the mightiest fortifications in Europe. In 1867, the terms of the 1839 Treaty of London were applied, and Luxembourg became a neutral state. The military fortress was dismantled and the encircling walls were replaced by wide outer boulevards.

Ville and Gare

The several distinct areas of the city of Luxembourg are the city center, known as *Ville*, perched on the high plateau above the Pétrusse and Alzette river valleys; and the more modern district, known as *Gare*, south of the river. The two are connected by bridges across the Pétrusse valley; the main ones are the pont Adolphe and the pont Viaduc, the latter known locally as Passerelle. Below the cliffs lies Grund, the main part of the city's valley settlements.

The area around the railroad station is emphatically modern. Buses leave regularly from outside the station and take you to place E.-Hamilius, on the western side of Ville. From here a short walk east along rue de la Poste leads to the central square of place d'Armes.

At the east end of place d'Armes is the handsome City Hall (Palais Municipal, or Cercle). Nearby in place Guillaume II is the Luxembourg City Tourist Office. Ask here for details on guided tours and the LuxembourgCard, which is good for one, two or three days and costs €13, €20 and €28 respectively. Two- and three-day cards must be used within two weeks and give free entry to more than 70 museums and attractions, plus reductions to 10 other sites and free use of public transportation in the Grand Duchy (www.visitluxembourg.com/en/luxembourg-card).

The maze-like streets of the Old Town (Vieille Ville, see page 332) and the complex of steps and terraces that connect plateau and valley floor make Luxembourg a very walkable place.

Conversation and Music

The place d'Armes is a public space shaded by lime trees. In summer it is filled with the chairs and tables of the surrounding restaurants and cafés, where you can enjoy the hum of relaxed conversation and the music of regular concerts on the nearby bandstand.

All around the place d'Armes are the city's pedestrian-only shopping streets. To the north is Grande-Rue, known locally as Groussgaass, the city's main shopping street. Here, and in the

---

A Lift in Luxembourg

You can reach the riverside Grund district in the Alzette valley by public elevator from place du St.-Esprit, near the intersection with boulevard F. D.-Roosevelt. Look for the glass-fronted elevator shelter in the corner of the place du St.-Esprit. The elevator takes you to a tunnel that emerges at montée du Grund.

adjoining streets of rue Phillipe II and rue des Capucins, are fashion boutiques, as well as good restaurants and cafés. Stop for coffee at Namur, on the corner of Grande-Rue and rue des Capucins. At the east end of Grande-Rue look for the fountain known as Hämmelsmarsch, "The March of the Sheep."

Exploring Historic Luxembourg

To reach historic Luxembourg, leave the southeast corner of place d'Armes, where a covered passage leads between bookshops and into the large place Guillaume II. A colorful flower and vegetable market is held here on Wednesdays and Saturdays.

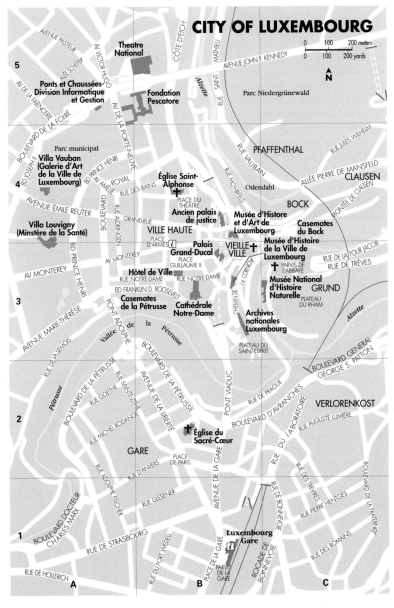

CITY OF LUXEMBOURG

Theatre National

Ponts et Chaussées-
Division Informatique
et Gestion

Fondation
Pescatore

Parc Niedergrünewald

PFAFFENTHAL

CLAUSEN

Parc municipal

Villa Vauban
(Galerie d'Art
de la Ville de
Luxembourg)

Église Saint-
Alphonse

Odendahl

BOCK

Ancien palais
de justice

Musée d'Histoire
et d'Art de
Luxembourg

Casemates
du Bock

Villa Louvigny
(Minstère de la Santé)

VILLE HAUTE

Palais
Grand-Ducal

VIEILLE
VILLE

Musée d'Histoire
de la Ville de
Luxembourg

Hôtel de Ville

PARVIS DE
L'ABBAYE

Casemates
de la Pétrusse

Cathédrale
Notre-Dame

Musée National
d'Histoire
Naturelle

GRUND

Archives
nationales
Luxembourg

PLATEAU DU
SAINT-ESPRIT

VERLORENKOST

Église du
Sacré-Cœur

GARE

PLACE
DE PARIS

Luxembourg
Gare

From here you can quickly reach the Palais Grand-Ducal (see page 332) on rue du Marché-aux-Herbes.

Behind the palace lies the Old Town. Look for rue de l'Eau, with its cluster of restaurants known as Îlot Gastronomique. Then head down rue Sigefroi to the stunning viewpoint of the Bock, above the Alzette valley.

From here you can see the famous pont Grande-Duchesse Charlotte, known as the Red Bridge because of its color. It connects the city center plateau with the Kirchberg plateau and the ultramodern European Center (Centre Européen), home of numerous European Union institutions (see page 326).

Visit the famous Bock Casemates (see page 331), the maze of underground tunnels in the cliffs, and then walk the Chemin de la Corniche, the terrace that leads south above the Alzette valley.

Discover the valley district of Grund, a riverside haven of well-preserved old houses, restaurants and taverns. From here you can turn left and wander along the paths and terraced lanes of the Alzette to reach the 17th-century riverside church of St. John (Saint-Jean Baptiste), with its rich baroque altar and famous Black Madonna statue.

The city center (Ville) is more relaxed than other European cities, although city life is sophisticated in its restrained way. Fine music can be enjoyed at the city's Grand Théâtre de la Ville de Luxembourg, Philharmonie Luxembourg and Music Conservatory. The top fashion stores of Grande-Rue speak for themselves, and Ville restaurants are excellent.

Essential Information

Tourist Information
Luxembourg National Tourist Office
68–70 boulevard de la Pétrusse ☎ 42 82 82 20; www.ont.lu or www.visitluxembourg.com
Luxembourg City Tourist Office
30 place Guillaume II, Luxembourg City ☎ 22 28 09; www.lcto.lu

Urban Transportation
Buses are the only form of public transportation in the city of Luxembourg. Visitors will probably require the service only between the airport or the railroad station and the city terminus at place E.-Hamilius as the city is largely pedestrian-only and most places are within walking distance. A flat fare of €2 is valid for 2 hours or you can buy a pack of 10 tickets for €16. Buses run daily from 5 a.m.–midnight. For information ☎ 47 96 29 75; www.vdl.lu/mobilite/autobus.html. Taxis are expensive, but can be hired by calling City Taxis Centrale ☎ 48 00 58; www.citytaxis.lu.

Airport Information
Luxembourg's Findel Airport (☎ 2464-0; www.lux-airport.lu) is located 4 miles east of the city of Luxembourg. Public bus No. 16 runs every 10–15 minutes (30 minutes on Sundays) between the airport and the city center and railroad station (journey time is 25 minutes, fare €2, plus €2 for baggage, which can be refused during peak periods if too bulky). Taxis between the airport and city are expensive (around €30) ☎ 48 00 58; www.citytaxis.lu.

Climate – average highs and lows for the month

Jan.	Feb.	Mar.	Apr.	May	Jun.	Jul.	Aug.	Sep.	Oct.	Nov.	Dec.
3°C	4°C	9°C	14°C	18°C	21°C	23°C	22°C	19°C	13°C	7°C	4°C
37°F	39°F	48°F	57°F	64°F	70°F	73°F	72°F	66°F	55°F	45°F	39°F
-2°C	0°C	2°C	4°C	8°C	11°C	13°C	12°C	10°C	6°C	3°C	0°C
28°F	32°F	36°F	39°F	46°F	52°F	55°F	54°F	50°F	43°F	37°F	32°F

City of Luxembourg Sights

Key to symbols

⊞ map coordinates refer to the Luxembourg map on page 329 💷 admission charge: $$$ more than €4, $$ €2–€4, $ less than €2

See page 5 for complete key to symbols

The steeples of Cathédrale Notre-Dame

Casemates de la Pétrusse

The great cliffs of the Pétrusse and Alzette valleys are honeycombed with tunnels, stairways and chambers called the Casemates, hollowed out of rock during the 17th and 18th centuries. Originally the network of Casemates measured over 14 miles and accommodated thousands of soldiers. There was room for the stabling of their horses, and for all the garrison supply services.

Today about 10 miles of the Casemates survive. Two sections, the Casemates du Bock (Bock Casemates) and the Casemates de la Pétrusse (Pétrusse Casemates), are open to the public in summer (see also Fortress Luxembourg, page 333).

Casemates du Bock ⊞ C4 ⊠ montée de Clausen ☎ 22 28 09 (4796-2709 for guided tours) ◐ Daily 10–5, Mar.–Oct. 🚌 7, 9 💷 $$
Casemates de la Pétrusse ⊞ A3 ⊠ place de la Constitution ☎ 22 28 09 (4796-2709 for guided tours) ◐ Daily 11–4, Jun.–early Sep.; Wed.–Sun. 11–4, Apr.–May 🚌 All city center buses 💷 $$

Cathédrale Notre-Dame

The steeples of the 17th-century Cathédrale Notre-Dame (Cathedral of Our Lady) form a striking part of the city's skyline. Inside, the high altar is a shrine to Our Lady, "Comforter of the Afflicted." Stone steps lead to the crypt; at the rear, two bronze lions guard the barred entrance to the burial chamber of the grand-ducal family. A sarcophagus lies in a dark blue marble setting.

⊞ B3 ⊠ rue Notre-Dame ☎ 46 20 23 ◐ Mon.–Sat. 10–noon and 2–5:30, Sun. 2–5:30, except during services 🚌 No buses in city center 💷 Free

Musée d'Histoire de la Ville de Luxembourg

A late 1990s restoration of the Musée d'Histoire de la Ville de Luxembourg (Luxembourg City History Museum) has created a superb must-see venue. Take care in some rooms where sunken channels containing hidden lighting run around the edges of the room. The museum is located in four old 17th-, 18th- and 19th-century, six-story town houses. This is a sophisticated, interactive museum; visitors are given a card to operate audiovisual displays and touch screens that explain the city's history from the 10th century to the present day. Follow the room numbers counterclockwise, and do not miss a trip in the glass elevator that rises through many layers of history as well as architecture.

⊞ B3 ⊠ 14 rue du St.-Esprit ☎ 47 96 45 00; www.mhvl.lu ◐ Tue.–Sun. 10–6 (also Thu. 6–8 p.m.) 🚌 No buses in city center 🍴 Café 💷 $$$

Musée National d'Histoire Naturelle

The Musée National d'Histoire Naturelle (National Museum of Natural History),

The magnificent Palace of the Grand Dukes is on a city street

or Natur Musée (Nature Museum), is tucked away in the Grund area, below the cliffs.

The museum is housed in the old Hospice of St. John, later a women's prison, and the building's splendid entrance survives. It features interactive activities of a geological and geographical nature, plus information on local flora and fauna, and landscapes.

✚ C3 ✉ 24 rue Münster ☎ 46 22 40-1; www.mnhn.lu ◷ Tue.–Sun. 10–6 🚌 6, 23 🍴 Café
🍷 $$$

Palais Grand-Ducal

The Palais Grand-Ducal (Palace of the Grand Dukes), the official residence of Grand Duke Henri of Luxembourg, is on rue du Marché-aux-Herbes. The building is a much-renovated and extended replacement of a medieval town hall, which was destroyed in a fire in 1554. The 16th-century Spanish rulers of Luxembourg rebuilt it 20 years after the fire, and you can see the architectural influences of southern Spain in its Renaissance facade.

The interiors are exquisite, especially the Main Hall, the King's Room and the Banqueting Hall.

✚ B3 ✉ 17 rue du Marché-aux-Herbes ◷ Guided tours run Mon.–Fri. 2:30–5, Sat. 10–11, mid-Jul. to early Sep. English-language tours only Mon.–Fri. 4:30. Contact the Luxembourg City Tourist Office for details (☎ 22 28 09) 🚌 No buses in city center 🍷 $$$

Vieille Ville

The city of Luxembourg Vieille Ville (Old Town) lies between the rear of the Palais Grand-Ducal and the Bock promontory. The area of the Old Town is small, lying within narrow streets and squares such as rue de l'Eau, rue de la Loge, rue du Rost and the Marché aux Poissons (Fish Market).

The feeling of medieval Luxembourg is palpable here, although today's fine streets and buildings hardly reflect the din and dirt of those days. The market was once the heart of the community outside the castle walls.

Down rue Sigefroi from the Marché aux Poissons is Église Saint-Michel (St. Michael's Church; open daily 10–5, except during religious functions; admission free). It is the oldest church in the city and is built on the site of the 10th-century castle church, but its oldest surviving parts date from the 17th century. The church's baroque altar is superb, and there is a wonderfully vivid carved oak pietà.

✚ B3

Villa Vauban (Galerie d'Art de la Ville de Luxembourg)

The elegant Villa Vauban (Luxembourg City Art Gallery) stands in City Park, on the foundation of the former Vauban Fort. The gallery has an excellent permanent collection of the works of Dutch and Flemish masters and of later European painters, and hosts many temporary exhibitions.

✚ A4 ✉ 18 avenue Emile Reuter
☎ 47 96 49 00; www.villavauban.lu
◷ Mon., Wed.–Thu. and Sat.–Sun. 10–6, Fri. 10–9
🚌 1, 2, 3, 7 🍷 $$$

Fortress Luxembourg

The history of the city of Luxembourg as a medieval fortress is fascinating. Ringed by impregnable cliffs on every side but the west, it was easy to secure the western approach by building a defensive wall. The narrow and rocky Bock promontory offered the first natural fortification.

It was here on this narrow shelf, 300 feet above the Alzette valley, that prehistoric settlers may have established a camp. The Romans built their own fortifications on the Bock and called it Castellum Lucilinburhuc. Then, in AD 963, Count Siegfried of the Ardennes built his castle and linked it to the main plateau by a drawbridge. This Lützelburg, the "Little Castle," gave the city and the country its present name.

By 1050 a defensive western wall nearly 30 feet high, with numerous towers and gateways, protected the castle and the community that was growing around it to the west. Soldiers and knights were billeted within Siegfried's fort, while traders and artists began to settle outside of its walls. This then gave the first impression of an upper and a lower city area, until the 12th century when stone ramparts were built to define the whole city.

In 1554 a massive explosion of stored gunpowder destroyed much of the settlement. New fortifications were built during a period of Spanish rule. They included excavation of the Pétrusse Casemates (Casemates de la Pétrusse, see page 331); the Bock Bastion; and the ramparts known today as the Corniche and dubbed the "Balcony of Europe" because of the spectacular views.

In the late 17th century Vauban, the French military engineer, reshaped and extended the ramparts. In the 18th century the Austrians extended them once more and excavated the Bock Casemates (Casemates du Bock, see page 331). Such was the strategic importance of Luxembourg as a fortification that all buildings on the Bourbon Plateau, where Gare (the modern town) now stands, were built of wood so that they could be quickly destroyed before an attack on the fortress, thus robbing the enemy of any cover.

On May 11, 1867, Luxembourg became an independent state. As part of the agreement, and after nearly a thousand years, the city's fortifications were dismantled or destroyed. At that time, the fortress walls enclosed an area to the west that was larger than the city.

What remains today are the Casemates, the retaining walls of the cliffs and ruins concentrated on the cliff edges, all adding to the city's already spectacular position. City boulevards and parkland lie where great walls and towers once protected the western approach.

The Bock Casemates above the Alzette river and alongside St. John's Church in the Grund

The Netherlands

Opposite: This historic windmill in Zaanse Schans outdoor museum is one of several on the site

The Netherlands

The Netherlands is a country where freedom has come with responsibility and hard work. It is a country where the word "land" means something special – a valuable resource won from the sea. For, in literal terms, when you walk on dry land in The Netherlands, your head is barely above sea level in some places, and well below it in others. Amsterdam itself is 10 feet below sea level.

Dutch Icons

To the outside world, the enduring image of The Netherlands is of a land unremittingly flat, crisscrossed by canals and dotted with windmills. Popular imagination conjures up pictures of clogs, cheese and swaths of brightly colored tulips. Then there is Amsterdam, the lively, lovely and evocative capital, seen by many as a slightly wicked city.

The Netherlands is, of course, a far more complex and fascinating entity than such assumptions imply. Although the country is often known as Holland, this name actually only relates to the country's heavily populated western

Buildings along Prinsengracht Canal, Amsterdam

provinces of Noord (North) and Zuid (South) Holland. These provinces contain the main cities, such as Amsterdam, Rotterdam and The Hague (Den Haag), known collectively as the Randstad, or "Ring Town."

Compared with this heavily urbanized area, The Netherlands' other provinces offer the visitor a remarkably diverse landscape and regional cultures that will correct any misconception that the country is homogeneous.

Land from the Sea

The Netherlands is a small country, just over 15,500 square miles in area. Its eastern neighbor, Germany, is nine times larger. To the south lies Belgium, once part of the United Provinces of The Netherlands (see page 50) but an independent nation since 1830. To the north and west of The Netherlands lies the North Sea, and it is with this near neighbor that the Dutch have their most pressing relationship. You will not be too aware of the sea in Amsterdam or The Hague. You will need to go north to Noord-Holland and Friesland, or south to Zeeland, to fully appreciate the astonishing control over their watery environment that the Dutch have engineered.

For the definitive story of land reclamation, visit the fascinating Zuiderzeemuseum in Enkhuizen or travel across the Afsluitdijk, a 20-mile dam that seals the great inland lake of IJsselmeer and connects Noord-Holland to Friesland.

You could go south to Zeeland, a glittering mosaic of water within a vast web of land. There you'll want to visit the Delta Expo at Neeltje Jans to learn about the Delta Plan, a massive engineering program. This system of huge dams and movable barriers was built after the storm-driven North Sea breached the existing dykes during a high spring tide in 1953, killed more than 1,800 people and devastated the countryside.

Exploring Inland

Beyond these water lands – and beyond
the great dunes and beaches of the
North Sea coast, and the neon-bright
lights of downtown Amsterdam – lie the
delights of the landlocked Netherlands.

In the south, Limburg is known as the
Dutch "hill country." In the province
of Noord-Brabant, the De Kempen
region's landscape of sandy heath and
woodland is a very different image from
that of the "flat" Holland most people
envision. You can explore Gelderland
meadows and orchards; the serene

More Top Destinations in The Netherlands

- Arnhem B2
- De Hoge Veluwe B2
- Delta Expo A2
- Edam B3
- Enkhuizen B3
- Haarlem B3
- Het Loo B3
- Heusden B2
- Keukenhof B3
- Maastricht B1
- Orvelte C3
- Scheveningen A2
- Utrecht B2
- Zwolle C3

THE NETHERLANDS

De Magere Brug (The Skinny Bridge) over the Amstel opens to allow a barge to pass through

villages and waterways of Overijssel; and the moorlands and flower-filled bogs of Drenthe, so beloved by Vincent van Gogh. They all add to the variety of rural Netherlands. In the north country in Groningen, the quintessential Dutch images of windmills, clogs and flat green landscapes reassert themselves. In neighboring Friesland you will find another country altogether, a province with its own language and distinctive cultural heritage.

Reaching these districts is not difficult since the public transportation system in The Netherlands is efficient and generally inexpensive. Most places are within a three-hour train ride of Amsterdam.

Excellent bus services run between cities, and there is an extensive bus network linking towns and villages in the provinces.

Driving in rural areas is convenient and reasonably straightforward, but in urban areas it can be stressful. Regular ferry services connect the mainland with the islands farther afield.

The Dutch

Generally speaking, the Dutch people are self-confident and accomplished, qualities that have evolved from their history and surroundings. Although they could easily boast of the way in which their environment has been mastered, they are refreshingly modest and restrained. Once the ice is broken, however, people are enthusiastic and friendly, and show tolerance and mutual respect for others.

Pancakes and Beer

Contemporary Dutch cuisine, especially fish dishes, is fast reversing the view that Dutch food is dull. In larger cities – especially in Amsterdam and The Hague – Holland's colonial past has left a fine tradition of Indonesian cooking. Most hotels have plentiful buffet breakfasts, including smoked meats, pickled herring and a variety of cheeses. For a traditional lunch try *erwtensoep*, a satisfying soup of peas and pork, accompanied by a hunk of crusty bread; or *uitsmijter*, an open sandwich of ham with cheese, topped (molasses) or *poedersuiker* (powdered sugar). If you're on the move, street stalls also serve a smaller type of pancake, *poffertjes*.

Beer is the most popular drink. Dutch beers tend to be lighter, although you will know that you are drinking something substantial when you sample *Pils* in a Dutch "brown café" – a traditional bar. An excellent and popular light beer is Grolsch, often drunk with meals as a replacement for wine. Heavier Belgian beers also are available, as is *jenever*, a grain spirit. *Oude jenever* is the sweetest; *jonge* is for the stronger palate. These and vintage gins and liqueurs can be enjoyed in a *proeflokaal*, or "tasting house."

Porcelain and Jewelry

Some stores in Holland are closed all day Sunday and on Monday morning, but many open every day, and stores in the larger cities usually stay open late one night a week. Cities such as Amsterdam and The Hague have a variety of international clothing stores, but the real shopping experience is in the antiques and craft districts, looking for such Dutch specialties as jewelry and porcelain. In the provinces, look around and you will find some excellent regional buys.

with a fried egg. For dinner have a *hutspot* stew of vegetables, smoked bacon and meat; or *stampott*, mashed potatoes and vegetables with smoked sausage or bacon. For more exotic experiences, eat Indonesian specialties, especially *rijsttafel* ("rice table"), or any of several dozen other spiced, sauced, tangy, exquisite dishes. For sweets try *pannekoek*, pancakes with *stroop*

Blue-and-white Delft ceramics are known throughout the world

Timeline

AD 50	Iron Age Frisian and Batavi tribes settle in present-day Netherlands.
8th century	The Frankish Empire rules the Low Countries.
12th century	Herring fishermen settle at the mouth of the Amstel river, later site of Amsterdam.
1519	Charles V is crowned Holy Roman Emperor; the Low Countries come under Habsburg rule.
1566–67	Repression by Spain leads to lengthy struggle against Spanish control.
1579	Formation of Republic of the United Provinces of The Netherlands.
1602	Formation of United East India Company; "Golden Age" of Amsterdam as an affluent world trading center lasts for most of the 17th century.
1815	Northern and southern Netherlands become a united kingdom after fall of Napoleon.
1831	Southern Netherlands becomes independent as Belgium.
1914–18	The Netherlands remains neutral during World War I.
1940	Germany invades The Netherlands; Amsterdam liberated in 1945.
1947	Formation of Benelux Trade Treaty between Belgium, The Netherlands and Luxembourg.
1957	The Netherlands signs up as a founding member of the European Economic Community.
1980	Queen Beatrix is crowned.
2002	The Netherlands adopts the euro as its official currency.
2004	Queen Mother Juliana, who ruled for 32 years from 1948, dies at the age of 92.
2010	Dissolution of the Netherlands Antilles. Caribbean islands of Bonaire, Sint Eustatius and Saba become special municipalities of the Netherlands. The islands are also collectively referred to as the BES islands.
2011	Law change whereby only Dutch citizens are allowed to frequent Amsterdam's Cannabis "coffee shops."
2013	Queen Beatrix abdicates on April 30, 2013. The successor to the throne is her son, crowned King Willem-Alexander of Orange.

Tulips

Tulips are a universal symbol of the country. They also are part of the Dutch flower trade, which accounts for 60 percent of the world market in exported flowers. In the 17th century the importation of tulip bulbs from Turkey led to "tulip mania;" during the 1630s, single bulbs sold for thousands of florins. The tulip has been a major focus of Dutch flower growing since, although carnations, roses and chrysanthemums outsell tulips today. The great floral explosion is in late April, when the fields just inland from the west coast are vibrant with color. Visit the 79-acre Keukenhof Gardens at Lisse, north of Leiden, for floral extravaganzas from about mid-March to late May.

Tulips at Keukenhof Gardens; this 79-acre park is situated between The Hague and Amsterdam

Survival Guide

- Large cities have regulated routes for pedestrians, cyclists, trams and automobiles. Next to the sidewalk there may be a bicycle lane. Always remember that bicycles approach silently, and always check to your left. Beyond the cycle lane you may find a second sidewalk, then a tram track, then the main thoroughfare for buses and automobiles. This sequence is the same on both sides of the road. Remember that trams also approach quietly from the left.

- There are few public restrooms, and those that exist are not known for their cleanliness. Railroad and bus stations, restaurants and the bigger cafés have public bathrooms with attendants. You are expected to pay about 20–50 cents to use them.

- Eating out in The Netherlands is considered a fashion event as much as an eating experience. The Dutch tend to dress up a little when going out for a meal, although attitudes have become more relaxed.

- You may tip for good restaurant service. Always tell the waiter or waitress that you're tipping them, and the amount; don't leave a cash tip on the table when you leave.

- You may be tempted to sample raw herring. Follow local custom: Dip the herring in a bowl of diced onions, hold it by its tail, tip your head back, and savor.

- For tasty snacks, try the always-available *patat* (french fries) with mayonnaise or spicy sauce dips; *kroketten*, small rolls of meat filling covered in bread crumbs and fried; and pickled herring or smoked eel. *Broodjes* are baguettes filled with smoked sausage, spicy meat and delicious cheeses.

- If you buy a present in a shop, especially chocolates, tell the assistant that it is a present and it will often be carefully wrapped in gift paper.

- If you buy Delftware porcelain, make sure the trade name has a D, and buy from reputable outlets only.

Amsterdam

Amsterdam's past, canals and decorative buildings have all combined to make it one of the most exciting and seductive capitals in western Europe.

The city began life in the 12th century, when fishermen built a dam across the mouth of the Amstel river and settled nearby in wooden houses. Amsterdam developed on reclaimed land around a network of canals. By the end of the 17th century the city was the world's leading commercial port, its success based on entrepreneurial skills.

For most of the 18th century Amsterdam prospered – until its ships lost command of the seas to England. The city became the capital of The Netherlands in 1813. During World

War II, Amsterdam was occupied by the Germans. Since then its history has been characterized by consolidation, urban maturity and social liberalism – influences that have produced the vigorous and tolerant city of today.

First Impressions

Most visitors arrive by train at Amsterdam's Centraal Station, a smoothly run modern complex within a handsome 1880s neoclassic building. A helpful tourist information office (see Essential Information, page 344) is just outside the train station.

In front of the station is busy Stationsplein, a mix of tramline, bus track, bicycle lane and pedestrian concourse, with added passenger traffic heading to the subway station (45 feet underground). Straight ahead lies Damrak; watch out for traffic on this very busy street, and always wait patiently for the green light to show at pedestrian crossings.

A Cultural and Liberal City

Amsterdam's liberal traditions are apparent in the notorious Red Light District (De Wallen), located mainly between Warmoesstraat and Oudezijds Achterburgwal. Be advised – do not take photographs of prostitutes' booths. Be on the lookout for pickpockets.

The city also is notorious for its "coffee shops," where hashish and marijuana sold for personal use is tolerated by the authorities, but strictly only for Dutch citizens, after a controversial law change in 2011. *Eetcafés*, on the other hand, are conventional cafés where coffee is served. "Brown cafés" (*bruine cafés*) are traditional bars where liquor is sold.

All this alternative culture is a minor aspect of the larger Amsterdam, a sophisticated city and a working community. There are peaceful canals and shaded, cobbled streets lined with narrow gabled houses. It's a flower-filled

Supporting the City

Amsterdam is built on hundreds of thousands of pilings that have been driven through the surface layers of soft peat to rest soundly on hard sand. The 17th-century Royal Palace (Koninklijk Paleis, see page 346) on the Dam rests on 13,659 wooden pilings. Concrete pilings sunk to 65 feet have replaced the original ones.

city of exhilarating art museums, glorious civic buildings, medieval churches, quality stores, superb restaurants and entertaining street life.

Getting to Know Amsterdam

Purchase one of the "I amsterdam" cards (valid for one, two or three days) for admission to more than 20 museums, the Holland Casino, use of the tram, bus and subway system and a canal tour, a guided tour of a diamond factory, a 25 percent reduction on city attractions and restaurants, plus other benefits. For a taste of the city's canal culture, take a

trip on a Museum Line boat. Two routes stop near the major museums and you get up to a 50 percent discount on entry to them. Walking tours show you the city's architecture, history, art and special neighborhoods.

Amsterdam is a rewarding city to explore by foot. Enjoy street theater on Leidseplein, or walk in the footsteps of Rembrandt through the Jewish Quarter. The major shopping street of Kalverstraat leads to the busy open space of Spui, or try wandering down to the daily Bloemenmarkt (Flower Market) along the Singel canal.

Essential Information

Tourist Information

VVV Amsterdam Tourist Office
Stationsplein 10 (opposite Centraal Station entrance)
VVV Amsterdam/Ticketshop Leidseplein, Leidseplein 26
Holland Tourist Information (HTI), Amsterdam Airport Schiphol (arrival hall 2)
For general tourist information:
☎ 020 702 6000; www.holland.com, www.iamsterdam.com

Urban Transportation

Trains run from Centraal Station (central railroad station), Stationsplein. GVB Amsterdam is the public transportation authority. Amsterdam's metro (subway) mainly serves suburban areas, but also a few important points in the city center. Metro stations are marked with an "M" on the city map. There is a station and information desk at Centraal Station. For information on all public transportation within The Netherlands

☎ 0900 9292 (Mon.–Fri. 6 a.m.–midnight, Sat.–Sun. 7 a.m.–midnight); www.gvb.nl or www.9292.nl. Taxis are expensive, but can be picked up at the stands at Amsterdam Airport Schiphol, Centraal Station, Dam and Leidseplein. You also can call Taxicentrale (☎ 020 777 7777, 24-hour service; www.tcataxi.nl).

Airport Information

Amsterdam Airport Schiphol (☎ 0900 0141, or 020 794 0800 from outside The Netherlands; www.schiphol.com) is 11 miles southwest of the city. Fast trains run from a station at the airport to Amsterdam's Centraal Station; the trip takes 15 to 20 minutes. Trains depart every 15 minutes daily from 4 a.m.–12:30 a.m., on the hour 1 a.m.–5:40 a.m. Buses run regularly to Amsterdam from Schiphol Plaza. Arrival hall 2 has post offices, banks, shops and a Holland Tourist Information office.

Climate – average highs and lows for the month

Jan.	Feb.	Mar.	Apr.	May	Jun.	Jul.	Aug.	Sep.	Oct.	Nov.	Dec.
5°C	5°C	9°C	11°C	15°C	18°C	20°C	21°C	18°C	13°C	9°C	7°C
41°F	41°F	48°F	52°F	59°F	64°F	68°F	70°F	64°F	55°F	48°F	45°F
1°C	0°C	3°C	5°C	8°C	11°C	13°C	13°C	10°C	8°C	4°C	2°C
34°F	32°F	37°F	41°F	46°F	52°F	55°F	55°F	50°F	46°F	39°F	36°F

Amsterdam Sights

Amsterdam Museum

Amsterdam's story is well told in the Amsterdam Museum. Once a monastery, and then a city orphanage for four centuries, the museum is now an elegant complex of bright and airy rooms. Highlights include a model of a Dutch East India sailing ship and the silver drinking horn of the medieval Guild of St. George.

To the right of the entrance is the glass doorway into Schuttersgalerij. This was once an open street and is now the Civic Guards Gallery, with group portraits of 17th-century city militiamen.

🛑 B3 ✉ Entrances: Kalverstraat 92 or Nieuwezijds Voorburgwal 357 ☎ 020 523 1822; www.amsterdammuseum.nl ⏰ Daily 10–5 🚋 Tram 1, 2, 4, 5, 9, 14, 16, 24, 25 🍴 Museum café 🏛 $$$

Anne Frank Huis

No matter how often you have heard the Anne Frank story, a visit to Het Achterhuis, "The Secret Annex," is unforgettable. Here, in the Anne Frank Huis (Anne Frank House), the Frank family and their friends lived secretly in Nazi-occupied Amsterdam until their arrest just months before the Liberation. The only one to survive the horrors of the concentration camps was Anne's father, Otto. The lively, passionate diary kept by Anne during her years in hiding was later published to worldwide acclaim. The museum has absorbing displays and multimedia installations, but the Secret Annex is the heart of it all. The stark emptiness intensifies the experience. From every corner Anne Frank bears witness on behalf of millions of Nazi victims. After your visit, a walk through the peaceful, reflective Jordaan district is recommended.

🛑 B3 ✉ Prinsengracht 267 ☎ 020 556 7105; www.annefrank.org ⏰ Sun.–Fri. 9–9, Sat. 9 a.m.–10 p.m., Apr.–Oct. (also 9–10 p.m., Jul.–Aug.); Sun.–Fri. 9–7, Sat. 9–9, Nov.–Mar. Last admission 30 minutes before closing. Closed Yom Kippur 🚌 21, 170, 172, 174; tram 13, 14, 17 🚏 Museum Line stop 🍴 Museum café 🏛 $$

Begijnhof

Amsterdam's secluded Begijnhof (Béguinage) is an outstanding example of a medieval almshouse community. It was built in the 14th century to accommodate Béguines, a group of pious single women of the Catholic faith, who chose to live a religious and charitable life but without the stricture of holy vows.

The Béguines were later ostracized because of their faith, and today the discreet facade of the Béguinage's once

Regent's Chamber, Amsterdam Museum

The tomb of Michiel de Ruyter, a renowned 17th-century admiral, in the Nieuwe Kerk

clandestine Catholic church masks a haunting little Italianate chapel. Opposite is the original church that was transferred to the city's Protestant community in the late 16th century.

In the south corner of the Begijnhof is the 15th-century Houten Huys, one of Amsterdam's oldest houses, wooden-fronted and steeply gabled. Today's Begijnhof still accommodates single women of modest means.

☩ B2 ✉ Access via a gateway at Gedempte Begijnensloot (9–5) and then via the gate at Spui (after 5 p.m.) ☎ 020 622 1918 ⏲ Chapel: Tue.–Fri. 9–6:30, Sat.–Sun. 9–6, Mon. 1–6:30 🚊 Tram 1, 2, 5 🎟 Free

Nieuwe Kerk

The 17th-century Nieuwe Kerk (New Church) was new only in its original form, as compared with the more venerable Oude Kerk (Old Church). The New Church is a fine counterpoint to Dam square's Koninklijk Paleis (Royal Palace), with its beautifully decorated rooms.

Today the church is used for major art exhibitions. There are a dozen or more side chapels and a magnificent vaulted roof. The fine organ and the pulpit are permanent features. In 2013, the new monarch, King Willem-Alexander of Orange, was crowned here.

☩ B3 ✉ Dam 34–38 ☎ 020 638 6909; www.nieuwekerk.nl ⏲ Fri.–Wed. 10–6, Thu. 10–10 🚊 Tram 1, 2, 4, 5, 9, 14, 16, 24, 25 🍴 Café 🎟 $$

Oude Kerk

The Oude Kerk (Old Church) is the oldest building in Amsterdam. The church stands on the banks of the Oudezijds Voorburgwal canal in the heart of the Red Light District. Its glorious stained-glass windows, featuring Lambert van Noorts' *Annunciation* and *The Visit of Mary to Elizabeth*, look down on prostitutes' booths in the narrow Enge Kerksteeg, much as they might have done in medieval times. A triple nave and high-vaulted roof give a sense of added spaciousness to the dramatically bare interior of the Old Church. A poignant feature is the gravestone of Rembrandt's wife Saskia van Uylenburgh, set below the choir organ.

☩ C3 ✉ Oudekerksplein 23 ☎ 020 625 8284; www.oudekerk.nl ⏲ Mon.–Sat. 10–6, Sun. 1–5:30 🚇 Centraal Station or Nieuwmarkt 🚊 Tram 4, 9, 14,

16, 24, 25 🍺 $$ (may be more expensive for concerts and exhibitions) 🎫 Art exhibitions and music recitals at various times

Rijksmuseum

The Rijksmuseum (National Museum) contains some of the world's greatest works of Dutch art. The building dates from 1885 and was designed by Pierre Cuypers. Its neo-Gothic facade is something of a mirror image to Cuypers' Centraal Station.

In April 2013, the Rijksmuseum completed an extensive 10-year program of renovation that came close to being a veritable reconstruction of the building, with the aim of setting up the museum to fulfill its key role in Dutch cultural life through the 21st century. This means that a considerable part of the vast collection will once again be displayed throughout the museum, and visitors will no longer be teased with a glimpse of the finest pieces in the restricted space of the Philips Wing. Galleries will certainly include such highlights as Johannes Vermeer's *The Kitchenmaid*, a masterpiece of complementary colors; Rembrandt's *The Nightwatch*; and dazzling displays of sculpture, Delftware, silverware, furniture, dolls' houses and historical artifacts from the Dutch Golden Age.
➕ B1 ✉ Jan Luijkenstraat 1 ☎ 020 674 7000; www.rijksmuseum.nl 🕐 Daily 9–5 🚊 Tram 2, 5 🚌 Museum Line stop 🍽 Café Cobra, Museumplein (discount for museum ticket-holders) 🍺 $$$ 🎫 Audio tour available

Van Gogh Museum

To view the finest and largest collection of Vincent van Gogh's paintings, visit the Van Gogh Museum, where the artist's works (200 paintings and nearly 500 drawings) chart his intense and ultimately tragic life. The collection takes you through his early period, when he was a missionary in the Belgian coal fields; pieces include such dark social commentary as the Dutch peasants of *The Potato Eaters*. His later Parisian work reflects the influence of the Impressionists, but it is the paintings inspired by his life at Arles, in sunny Provence (France), that exhilarate with their fiery yellows and oranges. The most famous works are the iconic *Sunflowers* series. Conversely, *The Garden of St. Paul's Hospital*, painted at St.-Rémy mental asylum the year before Van Gogh's death, is a heartrending evocation of a dejected figure. But the sum of the Van Gogh Museum, the painter's legacy of outstanding work, is uplifting. There are other works by such contemporaries of Van Gogh as Toulouse-Lautrec, Gauguin and Redon.
➕ B1 ✉ Paulus Potterstraat 7 ☎ 020 570 5200; www.vangoghmuseum.nl 🕐 Daily 9–6 (also Fri. 6–10 p.m.) 🚊 Tram 2, 3, 5, 12 🚌 Museum Line stop 🍽 Museum restaurant 🍺 $$$ (more for special exhibitions) 🎫 Audio tour ($)

Vondelpark

Vondelpark, Amsterdam's principal park, is named for 17th-century playwright Joost van den Vondel. The park starts as a green avenue that leads southwest from a busy corner on Stadhouderskade, just south of Leidseplein. Soon it opens into a broad green space peppered with trees and interspersed with ornamental lakes and linked waterways. There are children's playgrounds, a sweetly scented rose garden, teahouses and a bandstand.
➕ A1 ✉ Stadhouderskade 🕐 Daily dawn–dusk 🚊 Tram 1, 2, 3, 5, 12 🚌 Museum Line stop 🍽 t' Blauwe Theehuis ("The Blue Teahouse"), by the lake 🎫 Open-air theater and concerts during summer

Wheatfield with Crows in the Van Gogh Museum

Amsterdam's Canals

So many northern European capitals claim the title "Venice of the North" that the sobriquet has become devalued. Some say there is no substitute for the real thing, but perhaps Amsterdam has the strongest claim to the title. While the city lacks Venice's romantic splendor, there is a restrained beauty about Amsterdam's canals (*grachten*) and their attendant buildings.

The finest canals are west of the city center, beyond the bustling main streets of Damrak and Nieuwezijds Voorburgwal, both of which once were canals. A stroll along side streets from Nieuwezijds Voorburgwal and across Spuistraat brings you to the great waterways of Singel, Herengracht, Keizersgracht and Prinsengracht.

Herengracht

Herengracht is the finest canal of the *grachtengordel*, the ring or girdle of canals that were built in the early 17th century to defend the city. The name Herengracht translates into English as "Gentlemen's Canal," a sign of contemporary male ascendancy. This was the district where the wealthiest Amsterdam merchant families built themselves handsome canalside mansions notable for their superb ornate gables. The houses were designed to be tall and narrow because of limited space.

Take a stroll down Herengracht to appreciate it all. You can start from the canal's northern end at its intersection with Brouwersgracht. The Brouwersgracht (Brewery Canal) is the short stretch of canal that links Herengracht to Singel canal at Haarlemmer Sluis, one of the 40 or so sluices that are opened each night to flush clean water through the canal system. Haarlemmer Sluis can be reached from Centraal Station by walking northwest along Prins Hendrikkade for about 300 yards and then turning left. Cross the wide sluice bridge. (There is a superb cheese shop, Kaasland de Roompot, on the opposite corner.) Go left, then turn right along Brouwersgracht to reach the tree-shaded bridges at the intersection with Herengracht.

Walk south, then east for a mile of scenic history to where Herengracht meets the Amstel river. You can stroll down either side of the great canal and cross over bridges to get the best views of the handsome canalside houses. Herengracht 168, formerly the Theatermuseum, and the exquisite Bartolotti House next door are particularly impressive. The latter is a 17th-century Renaissance mansion built by the head of the Bartolotti Bank. Enjoy the *Gouden Bocht*, which translates as "Golden Bay" or "Bend," between Leidsestraat and Vijzelstraat – note the decorative double-fronted houses along the elegant curve of the canal.

The curve is an engaging motif amid Amsterdam's general flatness – in the decorativeness of house gables, the elegant bridges, the sweep of railings, even in the curved handlebars of the wonderful old upright bicycles still favored by Amsterdammers. There are said to be 700,000 bicycles in the city, and it seems that everybody cycles in Amsterdam. Elderly *dames* and *heren* (ladies and gentlemen) cruise past to the tinkling of bells. And stylishly dressed young people skim along with a wary eye on the tourists' uncertain bid to run across the street in front of them.

Connections

Explore Prinsengracht (Princes' Canal) and Keizersgracht (Emperors' Canal), as well as the main canals, and don't neglect the connecting waterways. There's Leidsegracht on the Golden Bend, or the peaceful, leafy Egelantiersgracht near the Anne Frank House (Anne Frank Huis, see page 345) that takes you into the quiet heart of the Jordaan district. Sidestep between Herengracht and Singel into enchanting streets such as Gasthuismolensteeg or Oude Spiegelstraat, where craft and antiques shops and boutiques rub shoulders with delightful little cafés and restaurants. And try a nighttime walk along the great canals, when many of the finest houses are floodlit and the numerous bridges twinkle with lights.

In summer the canals become venues for concerts by the water, rowing regattas, Chinese dragon boat races and various other events. Amsterdam is many things to many people, but the city's fascinating network of canals will always be the enduring motif of this very special city. For the walking route, see the city map on pages 342–343.

Above left to right: A tour in an open-topped pleasure craft along Amsterdam's canals; Blauwburgwal is a canal in the peaceful Jordaan district

The Hague

The Hague (Den Haag), third-largest city in The Netherlands, is justly proud of its status as the political and royal capital of this beautiful country and as a focus of international affairs. Although it lacks the fast pace and excitement of Amsterdam, a sense of well-being and security underpins the rich cultural and political heritage.

The city's name derives from Gravenhage, which means "the Count's hedge", and the city's official name is still 's-Gravenhage. In the 13th century the Count of Holland built a hunting lodge among sand dunes – this is where

The Hague's historic center, the Binnenhof (Inner Court), now stands. The settlement that developed around the lodge was the Count's "hedge," sheltering him against the outside world.

In the 16th century the States General of the United Netherlands met at The Hague, and since then the city has been the seat of Dutch government. The Hague Convention of 1907, which formulated laws governing warfare worldwide, gave this city international status. The 1913 opening of the Peace Palace (Vredespaleis, see page 354) further enhanced The Hague's standing, and it is today considered a center of international diplomacy and business.

THE HAGUE

The Permanent Court of Arbitration and the International Court of Justice are located at the Peace Palace; numerous embassies, ministries and headquarters of international organizations also have their offices here.

In 1980 the royal residency was relocated from Utrecht to The Hague, and is home to newly sworn-in King Willem-Alexander and Queen Maxima.

Arrival

The Hague's main railroad station, Den Haag Centraal Station, is primarily used by trains for which the city is the final destination. Most through trains stop also at the Hollands Spoor station south of the city center. A short walk southwest from Centraal Station leads to the heart of The Hague, where the Binnenhof and several museums cluster around a graceful little lake, Hofvijver.

Guided bus, cycling and walking tours of the city are offered during summer, as well as self-guiding itineraries. Among these tours, available from the tourist information center between Centraal Station and the Binnenhof, are a walk discovering the city's lost Jewish Quarter; an introduction to the "Royal Miles" in and around the city; and coast-to-city cycling routes.

On Your Own

Exploring The Hague on your own on foot can be a very satisfying experience. The oldest section centers on the Hofvijver, the "Court Pond." On its south side the Hofvijver laps against the walls of the Binnenhof (see page 353) and the Mauritshuis (see page354), which houses The Hague's outstanding art collection. Its northern side is lined with trees and is backed by the elegant 18th-century street Lange Vijverberg.

From the Hofvijver you can stroll north beneath the lime trees on the wide avenue Lange Voorhout. A colorful arts and antiques market is held here on Thursdays and Sundays from early May to late September.

Continue past the grand facade of the Hotel des Indes to reach Denneweg, a charming street with a Parisian flavor and a host of interesting antiques and craft galleries, delicatessens, popular restaurants and cafés, and distinctive fashion boutiques.

Quickening Pace

West of the Hofvijver and the Binnenhof lies the bustling open area of the Buitenhof, where the pace quickens to that of a busy city.

Beyond the Buitenhof is The Hague's commercial and shopping district and the pedestrian-only streets that lead to the Kerkplein (Church Square) and the hexagonal-towered Grote Kerk

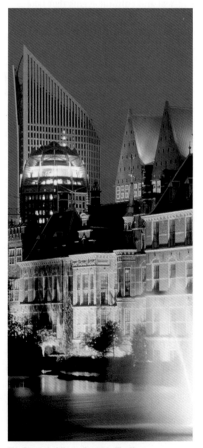

The Binnenhof (Inner Court) in The Hague

(Great Church). The Wednesday market that used to be a feature here has been moved to nearby Hofweg.

North of the church is the Hofkwartier, one of the oldest areas of The Hague. There are quite a few specialty shops, restaurants and cafés here. Be sure to stroll along onto Hoogstraat (Palace Promenade) and on into Noordeinde, one of The Hague's most attractive streets. Along here you will find a marvelous selection of art galleries, antiques shops and fashion boutiques, restaurants and the Paleis Noordeinde (Royal Palace).

Enjoy this fine city by filling your day with activities involving the arts and history and then seek out the numerous musical and cultural events that take place in the summer.

A short ride on tram 1, 9 or 11, or bus 14, 22 or 23 will take you to the coast and the popular resort of Scheveningen (proper pronunciation of the name Scheveningen is the sign of a true local; try "Shravin-eeng-e" and you might get by). You can break the journey halfway at the miniature "town" of Madurodam, a favorite with children.

In addition to Scheveningen's superb beach and promenade, the numerous attractions include the Holland Casino, the Muzee Scheveningen and a pier.

Hooigracht
Several ring canals were built around The Hague during the 17th century. Although many of them have been filled in, you can walk east from Denneweg to reach the serene little stretch of surviving canal, Hooigracht, its leafy banks lined with elegant and attractive old buildings.

Essential Information

Tourist Information
Tourist information centers are known as VVV (Vereniging Voor Vreemdelingenverkeer)
VVV, in the Central Library, Spui 68
☎ 0900 340 3505
www.denhaag.com
VVV, Informatiepunt Scheveningen, Gevers Deynootweg 990–58 ☎ 0900 340 3505;
www.denhaag.com

Urban Transportation
Den Haag has an excellent transportation system, HTM (www.htm.net), with tramlines serving The Hague, Scheveningen, Kijkduin and neighboring Voorburg, Rijswijk, Wassenaar, Wateringen, Leidschendam, Delft and Nootdorp. For information and tickets for buses and trams inquire at the tourist information centers, or call ☎ 0900 9292; www.journeyplanner.9292.nl. Taxi stands are located at the railroad stations and throughout the city. To call a taxi try HTMC ☎ 070 390 7722 or book online at www.htmc.nl.

Airport Information
Amsterdam Airport Schiphol (see page 344) serves The Hague. Trains for The Hague leave the airport at regular intervals (travel time 30 minutes). Trains from the airport stop first at Station Hollands Spoor, south of the city center. If you are going to the city center, stay on the train until Centraal Station.

Climate – average highs and lows for the month

Jan.	Feb.	Mar.	Apr.	May	Jun.	Jul.	Aug.	Sep.	Oct.	Nov.	Dec.
5°C	5°C	9°C	11°C	15°C	18°C	20°C	21°C	18°C	14°C	9°C	7°C
41°F	41°F	48°F	52°F	59°F	64°F	68°F	70°F	64°F	57°F	48°F	45°F
1°C	0°C	3°C	5°C	8°C	12°C	14°C	13°C	11°C	9°C	4°C	3°C
34°F	32°F	37°F	41°F	46°F	54°F	57°F	55°F	52°F	48°F	39°F	37°F

The Hague Sights

Binnenhof

The Binnenhof (Inner Court) of the original lodge of the Counts of Holland is the oldest part of The Hague and is where all matters political have taken place for centuries – and do still today.

The turreted Ridderzaal (Knights' Hall), where medieval guests were received, stands at the heart of a central square; behind it is the Dutch parliament building.

The main room is the Knights' Hall, restored in 1900 to its medieval glory, with coats of arms, Dutch provincial flags, stained glass and artifacts. Ceremonies, including *Prinsjesdag*, the day of the reigning monarch's speech to the Dutch parliament, are held here.

There are guided tours of the Knights' Hall and the two chambers of parliament when they are not in use. Tours are in Dutch only with an English-language tour on Sundays at 2.

➕ C2 ✉ Binnenhof 8a ☎ 070 757 0200
🖲 Mon.–Sat. 10–4, Sun. 11–4 🚌 4, 5, 22; tram 10, 16, 17 🖲 $$$ (exhibition free) 🚹 Last tour at 3:45 p.m. (subject to demand). Reservations recommended. May be closed to the public on other occasions

Gemeentemuseum Den Haag

The Gemeentemuseum Den Haag (The Hague Municipal Museum) has collections of musical instruments and ceramics, including Delftware and The Hague silverware. The art collection includes works by Pablo Picasso and Claude Monet, and there is a large collection of paintings and drawings by the 20th-century Dutch painter Piet Mondrian. The fashion department features exhibitions of Dutch and international fashion, including an exhibition showcasing the opulent and fantastic "Romantic Fashions."

Major visiting exhibitions can include dramatic works by Damien Hirst and large canvases by Mark Rothko.

➕ A3 ✉ Stadhouderslaan 41 ☎ 070 338 1111; www.gemeentemuseum.nl 🖲 Tue.–Sun. 11–5
🚌 24; tram 17 🍽 Museum café 🖲 $$$

Haags Historisch Museum

Haags Historisch Museum (The Hague Historical Museum) is very much a Dutch institution; there are no English translations to supplement the Dutch labeling of the paintings. But a visit is rewarding, especially to see such big paintings as Jan van Goyen's *View of The Hague*. In the attic there is a permanent exhibition illustrating the history of The Hague; look for the explanatory panels that are translated in English.

➕ C2 ✉ Korte Vijverberg 7 ☎ 070 364 6940; www.haagshistorischmuseum.nl 🖲 Tue.–Fri. 10–5, Sat.–Sun. noon–5 🚌 22, 24; tram 1, 9, 16, 17 🖲 $$$

The Binnenhof is the complex where The Hague had its beginnings

Mauritshuis

The original Mauritshuis (Maurits' House) was built as a private home in the 17th century by Johan Maurits van Nassau-Siegen and was carefully reconstructed after a disastrous fire in 1704. It is home to the Royal Cabinet of Paintings, an outstanding collection of Dutch art which includes Johannes Vermeer's *Girl with a Pearl Earring* and the crowning glory, Rembrandt van Rijn's famous *The Anatomy Lesson of Doctor Nicolaes Tulp*.

✠ C2 ✉ Korte Vijverberg 8 ☎ 070 302 3456; www.mauritshuis.nl ⏰ Tue.–Wed. and Fri.–Sun. 10–6, Thu. 10–8, Mon. 1–6 🚌 4, 5, 22; tram 1, 16, 17 💶 $$$

De Mesdag Collectie

Hendrik Willem Mesdag was a leading figure in the art world of The Hague during the 19th century.

Famous for his *Panorama Mesdag* (a cylinder-shaped painting of coastal resort Scheveningen in 1881), Mesdag was himself a painter and an avid collector of other artists' works, especially of the Barbizon School of French painters, including Jean-François Millet, Jean-Baptiste Camille Corot and

Mauritshuis (left) and the Peace Palace

Gustave Courbet. Their works – along with those of Mesdag's and other members of The Hague School – grace the museum, built as an annex to Mesdag's house.

✠ B2 ✉ Laan van Meerdervoort 7f ☎ 070 362 1434; www.demesdagcollectie.nl ⏰ Wed.–Sun. noon–5 🚌 24; tram 1, 17 💶 $$

Museum de Gevangenpoort

A guided tour of the Museum de Gevangenpoort (Prisoner's Gate Museum) is great fun, but is not for the fainthearted. The Prisoner's Gate Museum was The Hague's notorious incarceration place for offenders for hundreds of years. Stark interrogation rooms, a debtors' chamber and a torture room give a gruesome picture of medieval justice. The Dutch treat the whole thing with humor.

The tour commentary is mostly in Dutch, but information sheets in other languages are available and the excellent guides here will answer questions in English.

✠ B2 ✉ Buitenhof 33 ☎ 070 346 0861; www.gevangenpoort.nl ⏰ Tue.–Fri. 10–5, Sat.–Sun. noon–5 🚌 4, 5, 22; tram 1, 9, 16, 17 💶 $$$ ℹ️ Tours Mon.–Fri. hourly from 10:45–4:45, Sat.–Sun. hourly from 12:45–4:45; extra tours Jul.–Aug.

Vredespaleis

The Vredespaleis (Peace Palace) is an awe-inspiring building symbolizing the power of statehood. Scottish philanthropist Andrew Carnegie, who made his fortune in America, paid for its Gothic splendor in the early 20th century. The Vredespaleis' exquisite furnishings and artifacts were donated by nations around the world.

A guided tour of the building includes a visit to the International Court of Justice. Due to security control, you must wait outside at the palace gates for the hourly tour to begin.

✠ B2 ✉ Carnegieplein 2 ☎ 070 302 4137; www.vredespaleis.nl ⏰ Visit by guided tour only 🚌 24; tram 1, 10 💶 $$ ℹ️ Tours require advance reservation and times are subject to change

Delft

Fine ceramics and architecture are the main features of Delft. The ceramics have been exported worldwide, but Delft's buildings remain much as they were when immortalized on canvas by Johannes Vermeer, a native of the city. The Vermeer Centrum, Voldersgracht 21, takes you into the painter's 17th-century world.

There are organized motorcoach trips to Delft from The Hague, and seats can be reserved through tourist information centers (see page 352). The town is only 20 minutes from The Hague via tram 1, and takes even less time by train. Tram and train both arrive at a two-lane highway, but a few steps along cobbled lanes transport you into a delightful medieval world enclosed by tranquil canals. Delft centers on an imposing main square, the Markt, where there are numerous stores, cafés and restaurants.

Delft is a popular tourist destination, and in summer the Markt can be especially crowded. Explore farther afield; follow the canalside street of Oosteinde from behind the New Church (Nieuwe Kerk) to reach the medieval city gate of Oostport. Visit the splendid Gothic Old Church (Oude Kerk), at the head of the lovely street of Oude Delft. View it from the Peperstraat Bridge, three bridges to the south on Oude Delft, to fully appreciate its remarkable leaning tower. Close to the Old Church is the Prinsenhof Museum (Museum Het Prinsenhof). This former convent became the palace of William of Orange during the Dutch war of liberation from Spain. William did not live to enjoy the fruits of victory; he was assassinated here in 1584. The museum has exhibits from that revolutionary struggle, along with tapestries, pottery, silver and paintings.

Many stores on the Markt sell Delft china. The Koninklijke Porceleyne Fles, a factory involved in producing Delftware since the 17th century, is at Rotterdamsweg 196 (☎ 015 251 2030; www.royaldelft.com) and has tours.

✉ Kerkstraat 3 ☎ 0900 5151 555 or 015 215 4051; www.delft.nl

Canals thread through the pretty streets of Delft just as they did in medieval times

Norway

Opposite: The Geirangerfjord on Norway's west coast is a UNESCO World Heritage Site

Norway

Norway forms the edge of Europe's most northerly landmass, with land borders to Finland, Sweden and Russia, and where sea and mountains have merged to produce one of the world's most breathtaking and dramatic landscapes.

This is a country whose forebears, the Vikings, helped shape the history of northern Europe. The Vikings once controlled half of Britain, and sent mariners as far west as Newfoundland and as far south as the Strait of Gibraltar, as well as establishing some cities in the Republic of Ireland.

It is this vigorous and resourceful national character, reflected in Viking tradition, that still exemplifies modern Norway. This is a nation that has mastered an inhospitable, though beautiful landscape, without despoiling it, becoming a leading oil and gas producer in the hostile environment of the North Sea.

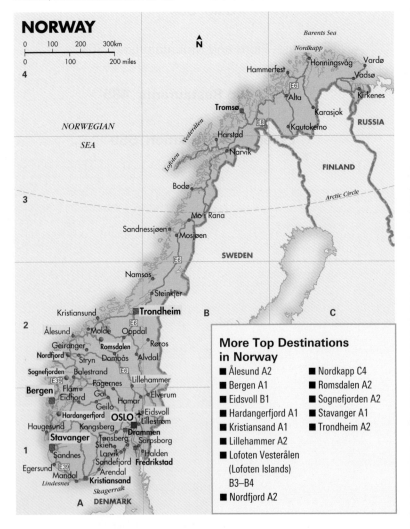

More Top Destinations in Norway

- Ålesund A2
- Bergen A1
- Eidsvoll B1
- Hardangerfjord A1
- Kristiansand A1
- Lillehammer A2
- Lofoten Vesterålen (Lofoten Islands) B3–B4
- Nordfjord A2
- Nordkapp C4
- Romsdalen A2
- Sognefjorden A2
- Stavanger A1
- Trondheim A2

Landscape

Norway's spectacular landscape is dominated by intervening seas – the Barents Sea to the north, the Norwegian Sea to the west, the North Sea to the southwest and the Skagerrak inlet farther south. The corrugated coastline measures nearly 13,600 miles, including fjords and the country's 150,000 offshore islands. This scattered mosaic of islands – the "Skerry Guard" – is Norway's natural sea defense. The islands break the onslaught of the ocean, creating the country's sheltered seaways to the north and south and protecting the gateways to the fjords.

Norway is shaped like a Viking club, narrowing in the north and with a broad base in the south. The country's mountain system runs from northeast to southwest and reaches its greatest height at Galdhøppigen, at 8,100 feet, in the Jotunheimen National Park.

The mountains separate the rugged western seaboard, known as the Vestlandet, from the gentler eastern region, the Øslandet.

The broad southwestern half of the country is known as Sørlandet, the South Country. Here, on the coastal fringe and around Oslo, is lowland Norway, where the sheltered coast is a favorite vacation destination for Norwegian families – a landscape of mellow woods and fields and tranquil blue waters. On the southern tip of Sørlandet is the sunny town of Kristiansand, with its flock of offshore islands. Southwest along the coast is Mandal, where attractive beaches catch the best of the summer sun; nearby is the promontory of Lindesnes, where a *fyr* (lighthouse) marks Norway's southernmost point.

Then the coast turns to the northwest, twisting through a rugged landscape of rocky headlands and deeply indented fjords, past the pleasant town of Egersund and finally through rich farming country to Stavanger and the open west.

Fjordland

Norway's famous Fjordland begins at Stavanger. Stretching for more than 375 miles is one of the most spectacular landscapes and seascapes in the world. In the Ryfylke area, east of Stavanger, lies the stunning Lysefjord, with its flat-topped and sheer-sided Pulpit Rock. Farther north is the mighty Hardangerfjord, with its massive cliffs, and the silver-white waterfalls of Skykkjedalsfoss and Vøringfoss, set off by snowcapped mountains.

Even farther north into Hordaland lies fascinating Bergen, against a setting of islands and mountains. Bergen is the starting point for boat journeys to the north along the coastal islands and into the 127-mile-long and 4,291-foot-deep Sognefjord, the deepest and longest fjord in Norway and second longest in the world. Its side fjords twist between towering cliffs and penetrate as far as Flåm and Gudvangen, at the head of Nærøyfjord (the narrowest fjord in Europe), and to Fjærland, below the southernmost edge of the great Jostedalsbreen glacier (the largest glacier in continental Europe, covering an area of 188 square miles).

Along Sognefjord are lovely villages such as Balestrand. Throughout the area, ancient pagoda-like stave churches survive at settlements such as Vik, Kaupanger and Urnes. Inland to the east lies the mountain range of Jotunheimen, known as the "Land of the Giants."

The Northern Fjords

Beyond the Sognefjord lies Nordfjord and then the county, or *fylke*, of Møre og Romsdal. The coastal town of Ålesund is renowned for its art nouveau architecture of turrets, towers and medieval motifs. Inland is the Geirangerfjord and its magnificent waterfalls. From Ålesund, spectacular roads lead over the mountains to the town of Åndalsnes and the Romsdalsfjord. Along the coast farther north is the Atlantic Road, a highway

A bronze statuary group by Norway's favorite
sculptor, Skule Waksvik

linking a chain of islands. Northeast
from here lies Trollheimen, the
mountainous "Home of the Trolls," and
then comes the great expanse of
Trondheimsfjorden and Trondheim
itself – once called Nidaros – the ancient
capital of Norway.

Beyond Trondheim is the narrowing
edge of Norway's northwestern
seaboard, fertile coastal lands backed
by barren mountains that reach into
Nordland and to the Arctic Circle. At
Narvik, you look out across the waters
of Vestfjorden to the spectacular Lofoten
Islands – including Austvågøy, Gimsøy,
Vestvågøy and Flakstadøy – before
continuing north to Tromsø, known as
"The Paris of the North." You then go
on through Finnmark, the land of the
Sami people and of the midnight sun, to
the Arctic island of Honningsvåg and
Nordkapp (North Cape), the symbolic
northern end of Europe.

Traveling in Norway

Norway is a pleasant country in which
to travel, but to enjoy this magnificent
land you should be selective about how
and where to explore. Roads are well
maintained throughout. Good driving
skills are required, however, where

roads are narrow and twisting and
where they pass through long tunnels.

Norway's public transportation system
is excellent. This is a country that copes
with some of the most difficult winter
conditions in Europe. Only in severe
conditions are train services to the
northwest likely to be curtailed. Buses
serve more remote villages throughout
the north and west.

Travel by boat is a way of life in
Norway, especially on the western
seaboard. There is no finer way of
touring Fjordland than by boat.

Most of Norway has a comparatively
mild, wet, maritime climate, as it is
influenced by the Gulf Stream. The west
coast and mountains have high rainfall
even in midsummer. But there can be
long spells of fair weather, when
Fjordland is glorious. In eastern and
southeastern Norway, summers can be
warm and dry. Winter in the higher
elevations is cold and extremely snowy,
creating excellent skiing conditions at
Norway's winter resorts. In the far north
the weather conditions border on the
subarctic. The Norwegians are
philosophical about their weather,
preferring to think of it as invigorating.

The Norwegians

Norway, as a constitutional monarchy,
is extremely well run. The moderate
Labor Party dominated government
from the 1930s to 1981 when coalition
governments began to be the norm, with
its ministers being elected through a
system of proportional representation.
The Norwegians are a level-headed,
open, courteous and generous people.
Only in busy Oslo does an occasional
impatience with visitors emerge.

The people share the Scandinavian
tendency toward self-effacement, but
they are understandably proud of their
success at shaping a modern nation out
of such a wild landscape.

Wooden houses on the small island of Omaholmen,
amid Hardangerfjord's striking scenery

Timeline

2000–1000 BC	Early neolithic and Bronze Age people leave numerous rock carvings throughout Scandinavia.
AD 787	Viking expansion begins with increased expeditions to Britain and northern Europe.
870	Vikings settle in Iceland.
1000	Christianity is introduced to Norway; Lief Eriksson reaches the coast of Labrador.
1070	Bergen is founded on the southwest coast of Norway.
1262	Iceland finally accepts rule of Norwegian kingdom after long and bloody conflict.
circa 1300	Oslo becomes capital of Norway.
1350	The Black Death kills over half of Norway's population.
1397	Union of the Three Crowns of Denmark, Sweden and Norway signed at Kalmar.
1536	Norway is reduced to a "province" of Denmark and remains so for nearly 300 years.
1814	The country is forced into union with Sweden.
1905	Norway breaks the union with Sweden and Prince Carl of Denmark is invited to become king of the independent nation.
1911	Norwegian Roald Amundsen reaches the South Pole.
1914–18	Norway remains neutral during World War I.
1925	City of Christiana reverts to its original name of Oslo.
1940	Invasion of Norway by Germany, in spite of Norway's declaration of neutrality.
1945	German troops surrender; Norway becomes one of the founders of the United Nations.
1949	Norway becomes a founding member of NATO.
1970s	Oil and gas extraction from Norwegian sector of North Sea boosts Norway's economy.
1994	In a referendum, Norwegians reject membership of the European Union.
2005	Norway celebrates 100 years of independence.
2008	Stavanger is European Capital of Culture for 2008.
2011	July 22, 2011. Two sequential acts of terrorism are carried out by a Norwegian right-wing extremist: A bomb in Oslo leaves eight people dead and 209 people injured; two hours later, on the island of Utøya, 69 young people are killed and 110 people are injured.

The Viking Settlers

History has painted the Vikings as aggressive, anarchic sea raiders, but this view has changed somewhat in recent times. The restless voyaging that took the Vikings around the coast of Britain and into the deep estuaries of northern France led to bloody conflict. There seems no question that the Vikings plundered and destroyed. But modern theory argues that a desire for new territory made them settlers in foreign lands more often than just violent raiders. In later, more stable times, the Vikings' commercial success was just as powerful as their military ferocity had been.

Sunset among the cliffs of Nordkapp (North Cape), Magerøya Island

Survival Guide

- Mid-June to mid-August is the national vacation period, and many Norwegians escape the cities and towns and head for the fjords, mountains and countryside. This summer period can be a good time to visit Oslo.

- During the peak summer vacation season, North Cape (Nordkapp), Europe's northernmost viewpoint, and its approaches are very busy with traffic and visitors.

- When driving in Norway, dimmed headlights must be kept on at all times, even during daylight hours.

- Because of Norway's strict control on the sale of alcohol, you will have difficulty buying wines and spirits outside of larger towns. You cannot buy alcohol (except beer) from supermarkets. Special state-controlled Vinmonopolet outlets are the only liquor stores, and they are very expensive. You must be at least 18 to buy wine and beer and 20 to buy spirits. Most restaurants are licensed; you may be able to buy beer in some grocery stores.

- Norwegians are catching up with international fashion and trends, but there is more interest in good-quality outdoor clothing. For something to wear that's thoroughly Norwegian try the Oslo Sweater Shop at the Radisson SAS Scandinavia Hotel (✉ Tullinsgate 5, ☎ 22 11 29 22; www.sweater.no) or the Clarion Royal Christiania Hotel (✉ Skippergaten/Biskop Gunnerus' gate 3, ☎ 22 42 42 25). Other souvenirs include ceramics, pewter, glass, wooden troll figures, enamel jewelry and woven wall hangings.

- You can eat very well in Norway, especially in Oslo and the larger towns. Norwegians are experts at buffets, the ideal lunch experience, often with elaborate fish specialties. Smoked salmon and trout, and lamb dishes such as *fenalår* (smoked leg of lamb) are delicious, or try reindeer or elk for a taste of mountain Norway.

- Overall, prices are higher here than elsewhere in Europe, with some things about 30 percent more expensive. Several passes and discount programs offer reduced prices at hotels (contact your local travel agent for information). If you're on a budget, watch for Lavpris (low-price) food stores.

Oslo

Oslo is a small, modern city of great character, but without the grandeur of many larger European capitals. Its spacious suburbs, forests and parks, all within sight and sound of the sea, give the city great vistas. It has outstanding art galleries and maritime museums, music venues, cafés, restaurants and fashionable boutiques. Yet there is always that inescapable feeling that wide-open spaces are not too far away.

Oslo Through History

Oslo was founded in 1000, but its progress to capital city was checkered. It was significant only as a fjord settlement during the Viking age. In the 11th century, the Norwegian King Harald Hardråde chose to make Oslo a rival to the northern capital of Trondheim. Oslo's fortunes rose and fell thereafter.

It was devastated by plague, and in the 17th century, following a disastrous fire and while under Danish rule, the settlement was rebuilt to the west of its original site and renamed Christiana, after the Danish King Christian IV.

Christiana became the capital of Norway in 1814. Throughout the 19th century the profitable timber trade and the economic advantages of union with Sweden increased its prosperity. By 1905, when Norway broke with the union, Christiana was a mature city economically and politically, and by 1925 the country was confident enough to reinstate the traditional name of Oslo.

The story of Oslo in the final decades of the 20th century was one of rapid modernization, as much on cultural as on social, political and economic terms. Wealth from the oil industry, the internationalization of Norwegian culture and a growing Norwegian self-confidence transformed the city into the vibrant capital that it is today.

The City's Stage

The most impressive way to arrive in Oslo is by sea. Viewed from the narrow neck of the Oslofjorden, the city's buildings are set against a backdrop of serene peninsulas and wooded hills. The hills are dotted with houses and accented by the exciting, new white Holmenkollen ski jump.

Arrival by train, however, brings you to Jernbanetorget, the big open space in front of Oslo's central railroad station. This is not the most attractive part of the city, but a short walk along

---

Nobel Peace Prize

The Nobel Peace Prize has been awarded in Oslo Rådhuset (Oslo City Hall) since 1990. The award was founded at the end of the 19th century by Swedish inventor and industrialist Alfred Bernhard Nobel (1833–96). The Peace Prize winner is decided on criteria in Nobel's will citing "the person(s) who shall have done the most or the best work for brotherhood between nations…" The ceremony takes place each year on December 10, the anniversary of Nobel's death. Famous recipients include Marie Curie (1911), Martin Luther King (1964), Mother Teresa (1979), Nelson Mandela (1993), Jimmy Carter (2002), Barack Obama (2009), Lin Xiaobo (2010) and the Organization for the Prohibition of Chemical Weapons (OPCW) 2013.

Vigeland Park, Oslo, has 227 sculptures

Karl Johans Gate (the city's main street) takes you quickly to Oslo Cathedral (Oslo Domkirke) and the busy open space of Stortorget, with its colorful flower market.

A few steps farther on is the Parliament (Stortinget). Before it lies the open space of Eidsvollsplass, the busy city center, alive with action in summer. Its pond becomes a skating rink in winter.

To the northwest of Eidsvollsplass is the neoclassic Nationaltheatret (National Theater), where statues of Norwegian dramatists Bjørnstjerne Bjørnson and Henrik Ibsen stand guard. Farther northwest is tree-lined Slottsparken, which encompasses the unfenced and accessible Slottsparken (Royal Park) and the Kongelige Slott (Royal Palace) within its bounds.

To the south of the National Theater, down busy Olav V's Gate or Roald Amundsen Gate, lies Oslo Rådhus (Oslo City Hall) and the open space of Rådhusplassen. Adjoining this square is Rådhusbrygge (City Hall Pier) and the local ferryboat dock on Pipervika inlet.

The ferry to the Bygdøy peninsula operates at this dock from April through September.

Exploring Oslo

Central Oslo is easily explored on foot, but you should become familiar with the transportation system so you can take one of the many day trips within easy reach. Public transportation is very efficient and easily understood; travel on city trams is a relaxing experience in itself. Visit the outlying Bygdøy peninsula, with its clutch of outstanding museums (see page 367 and page 368), or Frognerparken (Frogner Park) and Vigelandsparken (Vigeland Park), Norway's most visited attraction (see page 368).

Oslo's main street, Karl Johans Gate, is full of stores of all kinds, including David-Andersen AS at No. 20 (☎ 24 14 88 00; www.david-andersen.no), Scandinavia's largest jewelry store. The Paléet shopping mall has a mix of fashion boutiques and restaurants. Stop for coffee and pastries at the Grand Café (see page 486) at the Grand Hotel, one of Henrik Ibsen's former haunts.

A short distance north of the Royal Palace is the busy shopping street of Hegdehaugsveien and its continuation, Bogstadveien. Down at the harbor, on the western side of Pipervika inlet in the converted shipyard buildings, is Aker Brygge, a modern complex with numerous stores, restaurants, cafés and entertainment venues. The area's attractive waterside setting adds to the character.

Eating out in Oslo offers a variety of local and international cuisine. Try traditional restaurants such as the excellent Engebret Café (see page 486) on Bankplassen, where you can enjoy Norwegian specialties. Feast on excellent music too, in the Oslo Konserthus on Munkedamsveien, a little to the north of Aker Brygge.

The Oslo experience is a relaxed one, because of the compactness of the city center and because of the ease with which you can reach the outlying attractions and surrounding countryside. The openness of the city is reflected in the people, who are brisk but friendly in their attitude. English is a second language, especially to younger Norwegians, and you are never far away from advice and guidance to help you make the most of your stay.

Essential Information

Oslo Visitor Centre
VisitOSLO
In Ø (Østbanehallen) by Oslo Central Station and Jernbanetorget
☎ 81 53 05 55;
www.visitoslo.com

Urban Transportation
Oslo's main railroad station is Sentralstasjon (Central Station), known as Oslo S. Oslo has an efficient bus and tram network. The bus terminal is next to Oslo Sentralstasjon. Six tramlines run east to west. The city also has a subway system, called the T-bane, with six lines running east to west identified by a "T" sign. Its main intersection is at Stortinget Station. For further information contact Ruter at Jerbanetorget 1, by Oslo S (Mon.–Fri. 7 a.m.–8 p.m., Sat.–Sun. 8–6); for travel outside Oslo visit www.ruter.no). Taxis are available from Oslo Taxi (☎ 02323).

Airport Information
Oslo Airport (☎ 06400 within Norway; www.osl.no) is located at Gardermoen, 31 miles north of the city. An Airport Express Train (FlyToget; www.flytoget.no) runs between the airport and Oslo S (Central Station) every 10 minutes; the trip takes 19 to 22 minutes, however there are no night services. Regular train services stop at the airport and take less than 30 minutes to reach the main railroad station, Oslo S. The SAS Airport Express buses (☎ 40 00 11 66 within Norway; www.flybussen.no/oslo) run every 20 minutes between the airport and the Radisson SAS Scandinavia Hotel (journey time 50 minutes) via the Oslo Bussterminal (Oslo Bus Station; travel time 40 minutes).

Climate – average highs and lows for the month

Jan.	Feb.	Mar.	Apr.	May	Jun.	Jul.	Aug.	Sep.	Oct.	Nov.	Dec.
0°C	0°C	4°C	9°C	16°C	19°C	22°C	20°C	16°C	9°C	4°C	0°C
32°F	32°F	39°F	48°F	61°F	66°F	72°F	68°F	61°F	48°F	39°F	32°F
-7°C	-7°C	-3°C	1°C	7°C	10°C	12°C	12°C	7°C	3°C	-2°C	-5°C
19°F	19°F	27°F	34°F	45°F	50°F	54°F	54°F	45°F	37°F	28°F	23°F

Oslo Sights

Akershus slott og festning

Akershus slott (Akershus castle) stands on a rocky height on the harbor inlet of Pipervika. It was founded in 1299 as a royal residence, but by the end of the 17th century it had been transformed into the powerful *festning* (fortress).

The Norges Hjemmefrontmuseum (Norwegian Resistance Museum) here is a compelling record of Norway's experiences in World War II, when the Nazi occupation headquarters were at Akershus. Also of interest is the Forsvarsmuseet (Armed Forces Museum).

Slott ➕ B1 ✉ Oslo mil/Akershus ☎ 23 09 35 53; www.visitoslo.com 🕐 Mon.–Sat. 10–4, Sun. 12–4, May–Aug.; Sat.–Sun. 12–4, Thu. guided tour only (in English) at 1, rest of year. Closed during official engagements 🚇 Stortinget 🚊 Tram 12 🍴 Engebret Café, see page 486 💳 $$$

Festning ✉ Oslo mil/Akershus ☎ 23 09 39 82; www.visitoslo.com 🕐 Outdoor area: daily 6 a.m.–9 p.m.; Information Center: Mon.–Tue. and Thu.–Fri. 10–5, Wed. 10–7, Sat.–Sun. 11–5, May–Aug. 🚇 Stortinget 🚊 Tram 12 🍴 Engebret Café, see page 486 💳 Free guided tours

Norges Hjemmefrontmuseum ✉ Oslo mil/Akershus ☎ 23 09 31 38 🕐 Mon.–Fri. 10–5, Sat.–Sun. 11–4, Jun.–Aug.; Mon.–Fri. 10–4, Sat.–Sun. 11–4, rest of year 🚇 Stortinget 🚊 Tram 12 💳 $$

Forsvarsmuseet ☎ 23 09 35 82 🕐 Mon.–Fri. 10–5, Sat.–Sun. 11–5, May–Aug.; Tue.–Fri. 11–4, Sat.–Sun. 11–5, rest of year. Closed Easter and Whit Sat.–Sun. 💳 Free

Frammuseet

The centerpiece of the Frammuseet (Fram Museum) is the preserved Arctic exploration vessel *Fram*, with a bow like a battering ram and a hull as solid as a castle wall. The *Fram* was launched in 1892 and was used by Norwegian explorers Fridtjof Nansen, Otto Sverdrup and Roald Amundsen in polar expeditions. Go aboard the vessel to see its sturdiness and get a sense of the tough and difficult life that its crew led.

➕ A1 ✉ Bygdøynesveien 36, Bygdøynes ☎ 23 28 29 50; www.frammuseum.no 🕐 Daily 9–6, Jun.–Aug.; 10–5 in May and Sep.; 10–4, rest of year 🚌 30 🚢 Bygdøynes Boat 91, from Rådhusbrygge 3 (Apr.–Sep.) 💳 $$$

Kon-Tiki museet

The Kon-Tiki museet (Kon-Tiki Museum) is a colorful celebration of Norwegian adventurer Thor Heyerdahl's amazing voyages.

This museum complements the general maritime themes of the adjacent Fram Museum and the Norwegian Maritime Museum (see page 368). Heyerdahl's ethos of adventure, linked to environmentalism and international cooperation, is vividly expressed. The *Kon-Tiki* balsa wood raft of his 1947 Pacific crossing and the papyrus vessel *Ra II* of his 1970 Atlantic crossing both reflect the Norwegian genius for maritime exploration.

➕ A1 ✉ Bygdøynesveien 36, Bygdøynes ☎ 23 08 67 67; www.kon-tiki.no 🕐 Daily 9:30–6, Jun.–Aug.; 10–5, Mar.–May and in Sep.; 10–4, rest of year 🚌 30 🚢 Bygdøynes Boat 91, from Rådhusbrygge 3 (Apr.–Sep.) 💳 $$$

Munch-museet

The Munch-museet (Munch Museum) is a celebration of Norway's famous artist. World-famous cultural icon, Edvard Munch's *The Scream*, is on display here. One of two versions, the other is in the National Gallery (see page 368).

Munch produced a huge body of work, and the Munch Museum holds nearly 28,000 pieces including paintings and sculptures, some of the artist's tools and many of Munch's sketch books. All of the items provide an insight into the artist's complex personality.

➕ C2 ✉ Tøyengata 53 ☎ 23 49 35 00; www.munch.museum.no 🕐 Daily 10–5, Jun.–Aug.;

Wed.–Mon. 11–5, rest of year 🔲 Tøyen 🔲 20
🍽 Café 💲 $$$ (free entry with Oslopass) 🚹 Guided
tours (free) in English daily at 1, Jul.–Aug.

Nasjonalgalleriet
Oslo's Nasjonalgalleriet (National
Gallery) has works by painters such as
Georges Braque and Pablo Picasso, but
its main collection is of work from 1800
up to 1950 by Norwegian masters such
as Christian Krohg, Johan Christian
Dahl, Thomas Fearnley and Edvard
Munch. Highlights include Krohg's
lively portrait *Oda Krohg, the Painter*, a
charming rendition of artist Oda Krohg
in vivid red and blue clothes. The
Romantic Fjordland paintings of Johan
Christian Dahl and Thomas Fearnley
will entice you to visit the fjords. Look
on the top floor for Ernst Josephson's
The Spanish Blacksmiths. The room
devoted to Munch shows some classic
masterpieces, including a version of
The Scream, the powerful *Dance of Life*,
the sensual *Day After* and the most
ravishing *Madonna*.

➕ B2 ✉ Universitetsgata 13 ☎ 21 98 20 00;
www.nasjonalmuseet.no/en 🕐 Tue.–Fri. 10–6 (also
Thu. 6–7 p.m.), Sat.–Sun. 11–5 🔲 Nationaltheatret
🚌 Buses to Nationaltheatret; tram 11, 13, 17, 18, 19
🍽 Café 💲 $$

Norsk Folkemuseum
The Norsk Folkemuseum (Norwegian
Folk Museum) gives an excellent
portrayal of Norway's folk culture. The
museum includes a lovely parklike area
consisting of 155 traditional buildings
and some reconstructed 19th-century
village streets.

The main buildings display crafts,
folk costumes and examples of rural
interiors. There also is an exhibition on
the culture of the Sami, the indigenous
people of northern Scandinavia.

➕ A1 ✉ Museumsveien 10, Bygdøynes ☎ 22 12
37 00; www.norskfolkemuseum.no 🕐 Daily 10–6,
mid-May to mid-Sep.; Mon.–Fri. 11–3, Sat.–Sun. 11–4,
rest of year 🔲 30 🚢 Bygdøynes Boat 91, from
Rådhusbrygge 3 (Apr.–Sep.) 🍽 Café 💲 $$$ (less
expensive mid-Sep. to mid-May)

Norsk Maritimt Museum
The Norsk Maritimt Museum
(Norwegian Maritime Museum), located
on the tip of the Bygdøy peninsula,
overlooks the calm waters of the
Oslofjorden. In the main hall Norwegian
artist Christian Krogh's great marine
painting, *Leiv Eriksson's Discovery of
America*, sets the scene for exhibits on
all things to do with shipping and the
sea. The basement theater shows a video
on Norway's great maritime history. On
the main floor is an escape boat, secretly
(and daringly) made from rough
planking scratched together by
Norwegian sailors while imprisoned by
the Germans aboard ships in West Africa
during World War II.

➕ A1 ✉ Bygdøynesveien 37, Bygdøynes ☎ 24 11
41 50; www.marmuseum.no 🕐 Daily 10–6, mid-May
to Aug; Tue.–Fri. 10–3, Sat.–Sun. 10–4, rest of year
🔲 30 🚢 Bygdøynes Boat 91, from Rådhusbrygge 3
(Apr.–Sep.) 🍽 Cafés 💲 $$$ 🚹 Audio tours

Den Norske Opera & Ballett
The massive, white building, designed
by the Norwegian company Snøhetta,
has captured several awards for its
contemporary architecture. Looking like
an iceberg at the very end of the Oslo
fjord, it's a "must see."

➕ C1 ✉ Kirsten Flagstad plass 1 ☎ 21 42 21 21;
www.operaen.no 🕐 Guided tours in English Wed.
and Sun. at 1, Sat. at noon 🔲 Oslo-S 💲 $$$

Vigelandsparken
One of Norway's most visited
attractions, Vigelandsparken (Vigeland
Park) represents the life's work of the
Norwegian sculptor Gustav Vigeland
(1869–1943) and is the world's largest
sculpture park accomplished by a single
artist. At the southern end of the park
the Vigeland-museet (Vigeland
Museum) displays much of his work.

➕ A3 ✉ Off Kirkeveien. Museum: Nobels gate 32
☎ 23 49 37 00; www.vigeland.museum.no 🕐 Daily
24 hours. Museum: Tue.–Sun. 10–5, Jun.–Aug.;
Tue.–Sun. noon–4, rest of year 🔲 Majorstuen 🔲 20;
tram 12 🍽 Café 💲 Park: free; Museum: $$$
(free entry with Oslopass)

Fjord and Mountain Line

Most visitors to Norway go to the western fjords during their stay. Even if your time is limited you can still make the famous "Norway in a nutshell" journey by train, bus and boat through some of the most magnificent scenery in western Norway. The trip can be completed in one to three days, depending on how much time you have available. It starts from Oslo, Bergen or Voss aboard the scenic Bergen Railway, the 292-mile rail link between Oslo and Bergen, northern Europe's highest railroad, rising at one point to 4,009 feet.

At Myrdal you'll transfer to the famous Flåmsbana (Flåm Railway), one of the high points of the tour. The stylish train, with its comfortable accommodations, takes 55 minutes to travel 12.5 miles down the wild Flåm valley, affording views of some of the most magnificent mountain scenery in Norway.

At Flåm (pronounced Flum) there is time to eat and to wander around before continuing the trip by boat on the Aurlandsfjord and into the Nærøyfjord, the narrowest fjord in Europe and on the UNESCO World Heritage List. Surrounded by mountains up to 5,900 feet high, the boat glides past small traditional farms clinging to the mountainsides. You will see goats grazing along the edge of the fjord and, if you're lucky, seals lying on rocks before the boat docks at Gudvangen.

The next stage of the trip is the bus ride up Stalheimskleiva (the steepest road in northern Europe – not passable October through April). Through 13 dramatic hairpin bends, offering views of the spectacular waterfalls Stalheimfossen and Sivlefossen, you'll arrive at the Stalheim Hotel, where there is a short stop before the trip carries on to Voss. From Voss you can continue your exploration by train to Bergen or Oslo for the last leg of one of the world's great round trips.

The "Norway in a nutshell" tour can be booked through Fjord Tours, Strømgaten 4, 5015 Bergen (☎ 81 56 82 22; www.fjordtours.com) or Rail Europe (☎ 08448 484 064; general reservations team; www.raileurope.com/us).

Tumbling in several steep cascades, a waterfall crashes into Sognefjord in fjord country

Portugal

Opposite: Colorful boats in the fishing village of Sesimbra, south of Lisbon

Portugal

Portugal, lying on the western edge of the Continent and overshadowed by Spain, its larger neighbor to the east, was for many years considered the poor relation of southwestern Europe.

Political turmoil and poverty have long hindered development, but after joining the European Union in 1986, billions of dollars have poured into the country, helping to modernize its economy.

The Land

For travelers who knew Portugal a few decades ago, some things have changed beyond recognition; others remain stubbornly the same. In rural areas Portugal is still old-fashioned and underdeveloped, a real bonus for visitors seeking something a little different from mainstream European travel.

The country is small, geographically diverse and beautiful. Stretching 350 miles from north to south, it is packed with mountains, river valleys, flat dry plains, rolling forested hills and a truly beautiful coastline. Portugal borders the Atlantic, and weather conditions can range from hot and sunny to stormy and wet. In the northern Trás-os-Montes region, winter temperatures drop well below freezing; in summer, it is not uncommon for the thermometer to top 100 degrees Fahrenheit.

The Algarve, a popular vacation area on the southern coast that's often visited by northern Europeans, enjoys a Mediterranean climate, and the vegetation is subtropical. On the whole, summers are warm and dry, winters mild and wet, although it can be cold in the mountains. Mainland Portugal's highest mountain is the imposing, granite Torre, in the wilds of the Serra da Estrela, which rises above 6,500 feet. The Tagus (Tejo) river divides the country roughly in half. The Tagus and two other important rivers, the Douro and the Guadiana, rise in Spain, and Portugal must share their waters with its bigger neighbor, a factor which sometimes leads to difficulties in supply and environmental problems.

Portuguese Empire

It's easy to forget that Portugal was once at the head of a powerful empire. Beginning in the early 15th century, Portuguese explorers pushed far into the unknown, challenging the traditional view that the world ended somewhere west of Gibraltar. Madeira and the Azores were the first to be discovered, and these islands remain part of Portugal. Portuguese ships rounded the

More Top Destinations in Portugal (see map page 373)

- Alcobaça B3
- Batalha B3
- Braga B4
- Bragança C4
- Castelo de Vide B2
- Chaves B4
- Coimbra B3
- Douro B4
- Évora B2
- Fátima B3
- Guimarães B4
- Monsanto C3
- Óbidos A2
- Parque Nacional da Peneda-Gerês B4
- Sagres B1
- Serra de Monchique B1
- Silves B1
- Tomar B3
- Torres Vedras A2

View over Lisbon from Esplanada da Igreja da Graça

Cape of Good Hope in 1488, and in 1497 Vasco da Gama reached Calicut, India. By 1560, Portugal had claimed Brazil and had an empire stretching east as far as Japan, with missionary and trading posts in Africa, India, Malaysia, Macau and Timor.

Despite strong rivalry between Portugal and Spain over discoveries in the Americas, the 16th century was a Golden Age, with spices, slaves and gold making Portugal hugely rich. But the voyages and maintenance of an overseas empire were extremely costly, and the

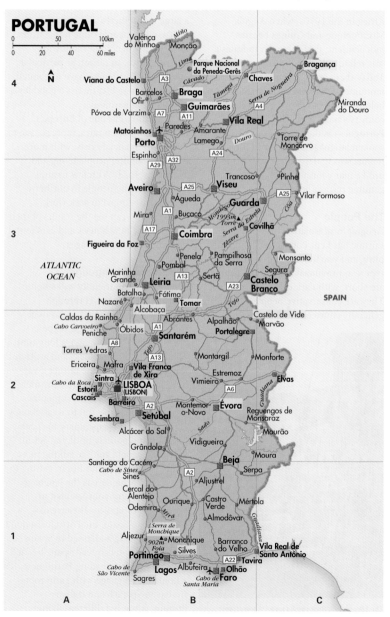

PORTUGAL

home economy was worsening. By 1580, Philip II of Spain had claimed the throne, becoming Philip I of Portugal the following year. Within 100 years, many of the overseas possessions had fallen to the English and Dutch.

The legacy of the empire still exists, however. Portugal extricated itself from Africa in the 1970s, when Angola, Mozambique and Guinea became independent; East Timor in Indonesia was relinquished at the same time. Today there are buildings, churches and monuments wherever the Portuguese held power, but language became the country's most important legacy. Portuguese is the seventh most widely spoken language in the world. Brazil retains strong ties with Portugal and, unlike many former colonies, there is genuine respect between the countries.

The People

Geographical isolation from most of Europe has kept Portuguese bloodlines pure, and you'll notice a definite racial type – in provincial areas, most people are short, with dark eyes, skin and hair. They are conservative people who are generally courteous and respectful.

The Elevador da Bica climbs up a Lisbon street

Northerners, with a harsher climate and historically poorer living conditions, tend to be less easygoing than people in the south, and more religious. Even so, the Catholic church continues to hold great sway everywhere.

Approximately 40 percent of the population still lives in rural areas, with a large urban increase occurring in the 1970s, when people came home from former African colonies following independence. In Lisbon in particular, many Afro-Portuguese have integrated into Portuguese life; there's a good level of interracial harmony.

The country has one of Europe's highest emigration rates, more so due to the recent financial crisis, with more than four million people living and working abroad. With few natural resources, many people in northern Portugal are forced to seek work overseas; you can see the results of their labors in the new houses and cars found in even the poorest villages.

Society and Language

Being polite and friendly will smooth your path as you travel through Portugal. The Portuguese tend to be welcoming and unhurried, so be prepared for things to take a long time. There are traditional ideas and attitudes toward women, and the farther away from major towns you travel the more obvious this becomes. It's sometimes considered disrespectful to wear skimpy clothing, and it is customary to speak formally and politely until you get to know the people you are talking to.

One of the major hurdles in getting to know the Portuguese is the language barrier. Don't try your Spanish in Portugal. Despite – or because of – proximity to Spain, the Portuguese don't appreciate being addressed in Spanish. However, if you can read Spanish you'll have no problem reading Portuguese. It's a Romance language with Latin roots, similar to Spanish and Italian. Pronunciation is a different matter

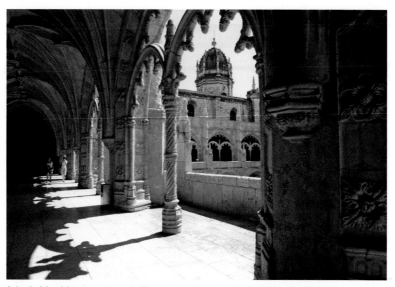

A detail of the elaborate carving at the Mosteiro dos Jerónimos in the Belém district of Lisbon

altogether, however, and spoken Portuguese, with its sibilants, nasal vowels and guttural consonants, can sound like Russian and Slavic languages.

The Portuguese are excellent linguists; you'll find English spoken in major tourist areas, and in the countryside among the younger generation. Do try to tackle one or two words; your efforts will be appreciated and faces will light up when you try to communicate.

Changing Portugal

Since Portugal joined the European Union in 1986, huge changes have occcured. Once one of the poorest countries in Western Europe, Portugal had one of the highest economic growth rates in the 1990s. While unemployment plummeted, the cost was a widening gap between rich and poor, noticeable wherever you travel.

The enlargement of the EU since 2004, however, poses several challenges. As countries farther east in Europe have swelled the ranks, Portugal lost its advange of relatively cheap labor costs, and a high proportion of national earnings comes from overseas – a global

market that becomes ever more challenging. Agriculture in Portugal is still relatively unproductive due to lack of investment and the difficulty of using modern methods and large equipment on much of the terrain. Education levels are low by European standards, with a surprising percentage of the population having literacy problems.

By 2014 Portugal had dropped to 20th in the GDP (Gross Domestic Product) table of European countries. As the world financial crisis broke in 2008, economic growth stalled at 0 percent and as yet it has failed to recover, with GDP growth of only 0.05% in 2014. However, Portugal does export large amounts of certain products including cork, tomato paste and wine. It also earns through foreign tourism, an industry that continues to develop. Portugal has become a much-loved holiday destination for many Europeans. For visitors, the blend of old and new is alluring. Investment in infrastructure through the early 2000s has improved the visitor experience, while the rustic way of life is still evident away from the major cities and towns.

Timeline

1000 BC to AD 400	Occupation by Phoenicians, Carthaginians, Iberians, Celts, Romans and Visigoths.
AD 713	Moors control most of the country and remain in power for 400 years.
1179	Pope recognizes Kingdom of Portugal.
1255	Afonso III makes Lisbon the capital of Portugal.
1480–1500s	Age of Discovery.
1488	Bartolomeu Dias rounds Cape of Good Hope.
1580	End of Golden Age with invasion by Philip II of Spain, who declares himself Philip I of Portugal.
1668	Treaty of Lisbon recognizes Portuguese independence.
1755	Lisbon earthquake.
1910	Portuguese monarchy overthrown and replaced by republic.
1916–18	Portugal joins Allies in World War I.
1933	Estado Novo (New State) established. Falls in 1974.
1939–45	Portugal neutral throughout World War II.
1960s	Portuguese colony of Goa occupied by India; local nationalist uprisings in Angola, Guinea and Mozambique.
1976	New constitution drawn up after the fall of the Estado Novo.
1986	Portugal admitted to European Union; start of period of huge economic growth and social reform.
2001	Porto is named European Capital of Culture for 2001.
2004	Portuguese Prime Minister José Manuel Barroso is appointed President of the European Union.
2005–2006	Portugal's driest summer on record brings drought and forest fires.
2006	Social Democrat Aníbal Cavaco Silva wins the presidential elections.
2008–2011	The Portuguese economy struggles on the verge of collapse as EU enlargement and the world credit crisis take their toll.
2011	Aníbel Cavaco Silva is reelected as President.
2012	Portugal receives EU/IMF bailout package as economy in crisis. Growing numbers of professionals begin to emigrate.
2014	Portugal exits the Economic Adjustment Program imposed as part of the EU/IMF bailout package, as it continues to meet its repayment schedule.

Prince Henry the Navigator

The impetus for the great Portuguese "Age of Discovery" of the late 15th century came from the son of João I, Prince Henry, who was born in 1394. He can be credited with transforming Portugal into a great maritime power whose success was based on a scientific approach to exploration, navigation and cartography. At his base in the Algarve, Henry gathered together accomplished shipbuilders, sailors, navigators, instrument makers and astronomers, encouraging them to prepare for long voyages into the unknown. A new type of ship, the highly successful caravel, was designed: a speedy vessel that made the great voyages possible. Motivated by religion as well as commerce, Henry's ships sailed ever farther south, rounding Cape Bojador in West Africa, then thought to be the end of the world, in 1434. By Henry's death in 1460, the Portuguese had reached Sierra Leone, and the known world had become a far bigger place.

Survival Guide

- The Portuguese are committed wine drinkers. Generally, when you order house wine in restaurants you'll get something very drinkable, even though it may appear in an earthenware jug in rustic eateries.
- Water available everywhere is safe to drink, although sometimes it may taste less than delicious. Avoid tap water in the Algarve during the summer and drink bottled water instead, to be on the safe side. It is readily available.
- In more rural areas, the modest Portuguese are often shocked by scanty clothes, especially men without shirts, except at the beach. If you are wearing a sleeveless top, take along a scarf to cover your shoulders as needed, particularly if you visit churches. Do not enter while a service is in progress.
- Take care when driving in Portugal. The accident rate here is one of the highest in Western Europe.
- Telephone calls from your hotel room are expensive, but Portugal's telephone system is state of the art. The on-street "Credifone," which accepts credit cards and plastic phone cards, offers an easy way to connect. You can buy the phone cards from street kiosks.
- Be prepared for Portugal to be different from its neighbor, Spain. Despite their proximity, the two countries are very different.
- In cafés and restaurants, meals often start with a selection of appetizers, which arrive automatically to your table and are added to your bill if you eat them. Simply send them back if you do not wish to enjoy them.
- Try not to let any apparent grime or shabbiness in some cities affect you; look for the positive qualities, such as elaborate period architecture.
- Don't be surprised by the sometimes startling amount of garbage you'll see in rural areas.
- It is increasingly easy to find luxury accommodations and excellent service away from major tourist centers, with the opening of a large number of spas, fine country hotels and boutique-style bed-and-breakfast places.
- Portuguese food is traditionally rustic and served in hearty portions. Some dishes require an adventurous spirit, alternatively you can enjoy roasted meats, grilled fish and chicken in most restaurants.
- Leave small change in a bar; tipping is not expected, but 5–10 percent is an adequate tip for good service.
- *Pousadas* offer many interesting accommodations options when traveling in Portugal. These are state-owned but privately run, deluxe establishments located in historic or beautiful places such as former monasteries, palaces and castles. Advance reservations are highly recommended.

Shoppers and diners at the café terraces in Rua Augusta in La Baixa district, Lisbon

Lisbon

Lisbon (Lisboa) is a beguiling city. It has a great past and, economic woes aside, a promising future. Its backstreets may easily strike the visitor as old-fashioned and crumbling, but these elements add to its charm. Look for the positive: the port city's vigor and life; its great colonial past; the atmospheric old trams; and the evocative sights, sounds and scents – laundry flapping in the wind, shoeshine men hawking their trade, the melancholy strains of *fado* music, the aroma of roasting coffee and chestnuts.

Most sights of interest are within walking distance of downtown, with the exception of the glorious attractions of suburban Belém (see page 384), to the west of the old city, a train, bus or tram ride away.

Lisbon Flavors and *Bacalhau*

Lisbon has restaurants at every price level, with the emphasis on traditional Portuguese cooking, although fast-food outlets are easy to find too. Breakfast consists of cakes and pastries, and hotels may offer a Continental-style breakfast buffet. Lunch is more substantial than in other European cities.

Heavy soups are popular, and salads, although sometimes limited in their

ingredients, are readily available, as is freshly squeezed orange juice. Lisbon inhabitants eat a lot of fish and seafood, including *bacalhau* (dried, salted codfish), and the warming winter stews are excellent.

The Lisbon Earthquake

On All Saints' Day (November 1), 1755, the Lisbon earthquake struck. Churches were packed for this major feast day, and thousands of lighted candles toppled during the tremors, starting fires that were as destructive as the quake. A massive tidal wave followed, swallowing Lisbon's fleet and flooding the already-destroyed lower city. During the aftermath hospitals opened, prices were fixed and a tax levied to cover rebuilding costs, including the lower city, today known as the Baixa district. Although Lisbon largely recovered, 1755 marked the end of its role as Europe's leading port city.

Lisbon

You may be surprised at the number of pastry and cake shops; the Portuguese are notoriously sweet-toothed, and Lisbon has many tempting, old-fashioned shops selling traditional specialties like the delicious *pastéis de Belém* (pastries filled with custard). Portugal makes very good red and white wine, national and foreign beers are everywhere, and all the usual spirits and aperitifs are available. It is known for the fortified wine, port.

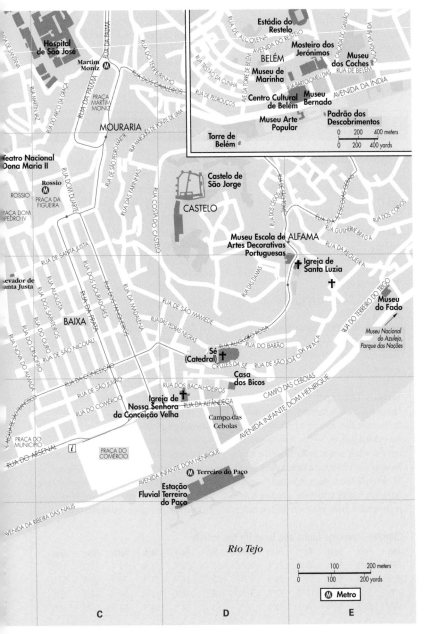

Souvenirs from Lisbon

Shopping is great fun in Lisbon and Portuguese crafts can be found. The area known as the Chiado, in downtown Lisbon, is the most fashionable shopping district, with streets lined with many classy clothing and jewelry boutiques.

Carpets from Arraiolos or the porcelain made by Vista Alegre (www.myvista alegre.com), linen and cotton sheets and tablecloths are all Portuguese specialties, as are the lovely glazed tiles, *azulejos*, which are made to order.

Film, Music and *Fado*

Lisbon offers a variety of music, theater, ballet and movies. Films are all shown in their original language with subtitles. *Fado*, a unique style of Portuguese music, is heard at its best in Lisbon and should be experienced. Its origins lie in history, a mix of Moorish and African elements, and can be described as a kind of operetta. The best place to hear it is at a *fado* house in the Upper Town of Lisbon (Bairro Alto, see page 381), or in the Alfama district.

Essential Information

Tourist Information

Turismo de Lisboa (Lisbon Tourist Office)
Welcome Center, Praça do Comércio
☎ 210 312 810
Santa Apolónia (railway station)
☎ 218 821 606
Lisbon International Airport (arrivals)
☎ 218 450 660
Jerónimos Monastery Quiosque
☎ 213 658 435
Palácio Foz, Praça dos Restauradores
☎ 213 463 314
Youth Tourist Office, Rua Jardim do Regedor
☎ 213 472 134
www.visitlisboa.com or
www.askmelisboa.com

Urban Transportation

Lisbon has a metro (subway) system, buses, trams, funiculars and ferries. Metro stations are marked with an "M" on the city map. A one-day travel card is available for the whole network. For visitors, the Lisboa Card, valid for 24, 48 or 72 hours, gives unlimited travel and free entry into 26 attractions. Zapping is a replenishable electronic card, valid on buses,

metro and ferries, or you can buy bus and tram tickets when boarding, and metro tickets from a machine or office at the metro station. The modern tram 15E is a useful line. For information on the whole network consult www.transporteslisboa.pt. Ferry tickets are available from offices at the ferry stations; a ferry trip is recommended as part of your sightseeing. Prepaid taxi vouchers to various zones and destinations are available online and at three tourist information centers – the airport, Lisboa Welcome Center and Palácio Foz. There are taxi stands on the Rossio and the Praça da Figueira, or you can call a cab (☎ 217 932 756 and 218 119 000).

Airport Information

Lisbon Airport (☎ 218 413 500 or 800 201 201, toll free within Portugal, for flight information, or online at www.ana.pt) is about 4 miles (a 20-minute drive, longer at peak times) north of the downtown area. The metro links the airport with downtown 6:30 a.m.–1 a.m. The Aero-Bus shuttle service leaves every 20 minutes daily 7 a.m.–11:20 p.m. from outside the terminal to downtown Lisbon.

Climate – average highs and lows for the month

Jan.	Feb.	Mar.	Apr.	May	Jun.	Jul.	Aug.	Sep.	Oct.	Nov.	Dec.
13°C	15°C	17°C	19°C	21°C	25°C	28°C	29°C	27°C	21°C	18°C	14°C
55°F	59°F	63°F	66°F	70°F	77°F	82°F	84°F	81°F	70°F	64°F	57°F
8°C	9°C	10°C	12°C	12°C	15°C	18°C	18°C	17°C	14°C	10°C	9°C
46°F	48°F	50°F	54°F	54°F	59°F	64°F	64°F	63°F	57°F	50°F	48°F

Lisbon Sights

Key to symbols
➕ map coordinates refer to the Lisbon map
on pages 378–379 💷 admission charge:
$$$ more than €7:50, $$ €4–€7:50, $ less than €4
See page 5 for complete key to symbols

Bairro Alto

The Bairro Alto (Upper Town) is one of
the five areas that constitute Lisbon's
historic center and the atmospheric
streets and squares tumble down slopes
to the Baixa (the Lower Town) below.
At night it's one of the city's liveliest
quarters, where in *fado* houses you can
hear melancholic Portuguese songs.

The Elevador de Santa Justa, a
wonderfully clunky elevator built in
1902, takes people from the Baixa up to
the Chiado and Bairro Alto.

➕ A3 ✉ Area on slopes to west of Baixa
🚇 Restauradores, Baixa-Chiado 🚌 758, 773; tram 28E

Baixa and Rossio

Rossio Square, properly known as Praça
Dom Pedro IV, and the grid of streets
forming the Baixa district will repeatedly
draw you back. The Teatro Nacional
(National Theater) and a soaring column
topped by a statue of Dom Pedro IV
dominate the spacious Rossio, which is
lined with stores and cafés. The square
has an ancient history and was the
dramatic scene of Inquisition burnings
in the 16th century.

Between Rossio and the waterfront lies
the Baixa, a perfect example of rational
18th-century planning, erected at the
Marquês de Pombal's instigation after
the 1755 earthquake (see panel, page
378). The orderly streets are lined with
lovely old stores, modern chain stores,
gracious buildings and tiled facades.

➕ C3, B4 ✉ Praça Dom Pedro IV and streets between
it and Praça do Comércio 🚇 Baixa-Chiado, Rossio
🚌 All services to Rossio and Praça do Comércio

Castelo de São Jorge

Visible from many parts of Lisbon, the
Castelo de São Jorge (St. George's
Castle) stands on the site of the earliest
settlement. Fortified sucessively by the
Romans, Visigoths and Moors, it was
besieged in 1147 by Afonso Henriques
and his Christian army and finally fell
after 17 weeks – a turning point in the
struggle to evict the Moors from
Portugal. The Moorish battlements still
stand, offering superb views over the
rooftops to the river. Today, extensive
restoration within the main structure
has made a verdant, cool oasis, with
terraces, pools and fountains.

The Periscópio-Torre de Ulisses
observation tower offers 360-degree
views of the city. The Alfama district
around the palace is worth exploring.

➕ D4 ✉ Rua Santa Cruz do Castelo ☎ 218 800 620;
www.castelodesaojorge.pt 🕐 Castle: daily 9–9,
Mar.–Oct.; 9–6, rest of year. Last admission 30 minutes
before closing. Periscópio: daily 10–5 🚌 737; tram 28E
💷 $$$ 🛈 Free guided tours daily at 1 and 4 p.m.

You can see the Tagus river beyond Lisbon's rooftops from the Castelo de São Jorge

Mosteiro dos Jerónimos

The stunning architectural ensemble of the Mosteiro dos Jerónimos (Jerónimos Monastery), a UNESCO World Heritage Site, stands on the site of an earlier chapel, visited by Portuguese explorers before their great voyages.

Building began on the present church in 1501 to celebrate Vasco da Gama's successful voyage to the Indies. It took almost 100 years to complete and, as a result, the church and adjoining cloisters are a glorious mix of Gothic, Renaissance and Manueline styles.

Pause first at the magnificent south door. Its intricate carving includes the figure of Henry the Navigator; the west door, equally splendid, features Manuel I, who started the construction. The soaring interior contains the simple tomb of Vasco da Gama, a contrast to the surrounding riot of stonework. The cloisters are equally elaborately carved, a combination of delicacy and strength.

🔀 See map inset 🖂 Praça do Império ☎ 213 620 034; www.mosteirojeronimos.pt 🕐 Tue.–Sun. 10–6:30, May–Sep.; 10–5:30, rest of year. Last admission 30 minutes before closing 🚃 Train: Belém 🚌 28, 714, 727, 729, 751; tram 15E 🚉 Belém 💲 $$$; free first Sun. of the month

Museu Calouste Gulbenkian

Portugal's greatest museum, the Museu Calouste Gulbenkian (Calouste Gulbenkian Museum) was financed by a bequest from the Armenian magnate, whose private collection makes up the bulk of the exhibits. It consists of two sections: European art and artifacts, and Oriental and ancient pieces. The museum is not vast, but everything it contains is of the highest quality.

Most visitors are particularly enthralled by the Lalique jewelry and glass, distinctive art deco pieces displayed in a darkened room.

🔀 Off map at A5 🖂 Avenida de Berna 45A ☎ 217 823 000; www.museu.gulbenkian.pt 🕐 Tue.–Sun. 10–6 (last entry at 5:30) 🚇 S. Sebastião or Praça de Espanha 🚌 713, 716, 742, 746, 756 🍴 Restaurant and café 💲 $$; free to all Sun. ℹ Audio guide ($$)

Museu de Marinha

The Museu de Marinha (Maritime Museum) is one of the best of its kind in Europe. It's a huge collection, with full-size boats, royal barges, paintings, uniforms and archaic navigational instruments. Most evocative, perhaps, is the attractive wooden statue of the Archangel Raphael, said to have accompanied Vasco da Gama on his epic voyage to the Indies in 1497.

🔀 See map inset 🖂 Praça do Império ☎ 213 620 019; www.museu.marinha.pt 🕐 Tue.–Sun. 10–6, May–Sep.; 10–5, rest of year 🚃 Train: Belém 🚌 714, 727, 729, 751; tram 15E 💲 $$; free first Sun. of the month

Museu Nacional do Azulejo

Throughout Lisbon and Portugal you'll notice the exquisite tiles, or *azulejos*, adorning the walls of countless buildings. The Museu Nacional do Azulejo (National Tile Museum) traces the history of the painted glazed tile, which has been used in Portugal since the 15th century. You can see how the art developed from simple early tiles to complex, multicolored examples. Blue and white has predominated since Chinese porcelain arrived in Europe; the wonderful tiled view of Lisbon, made in 1738, is a fine example.

🔀 Off map at E3 🖂 Rua da Madre de Deus 4 ☎ 218 100 340; www.museudoazulejo.pt 🕐 Tue.–Sun. 10–6. Last entry 30 minutes before closing 🚌 718, 742, 759, 794 🍴 Café 💲 $$; free first Sun. of the month ℹ Audio guide (free)

Padrão dos Descobrimentos

The eye-catching white mass of the Padrão dos Descobrimentos (Monument to the Discoveries) soars up from the water's edge at Belém, serving as a reminder of Portugal's great maritime past. It was erected in 1960 to mark the 500th anniversary of the death of Henry the Navigator, and has an angular front and curving form that represents a ship's prow and sails. Figures crowd the prow, led by Henry, who holds a ship. An elevator rises more than 435 feet to the top, offering panoramic views. Below, a

Lisbon Life

Everyday life in Lisbon, a relatively small and atmospheric city, is far more relaxed than in other European capital cities. The day starts around 7:30 a.m., when commuters are on the move and children make their way to school. Trams, the subway and buses are all crowded. Some people travel to town on the ferries that crisscross the Tagus. Many grab breakfast in a bar before work. Breakfast is usually coffee, with one of the cloyingly sweet pastries so loved by the Portuguese.

Lunch in Lisbon is taken seriously, and many people eat a full meal rather than a snack, although they eat it fast, often standing at a bar counter. Workers also use the lunch hour to shop for food or browse in stores. At the end of the afternoon, commuters head home but will often reemerge later to meet friends for a drink or more tea or coffee and cakes. Midweek evenings are often spent at home, although in the summertime the streets will be thronged for a few hours as people stroll around and chat outside.

Weekends are a different matter; people head for the Upper Town to eat and drink before going to concerts, movies or the theater, while young Portuguese enjoy the old district's waterfront clubs.

Saturday and Sunday are popular shopping days when crowds flock to huge malls on the outskirts of the city, which stay open late. Sundays, too, are high points for soccer fans, with the big matches attracting large crowds. Lisbon is blessed by its proximity to a beautiful coastline, and it's easy in summer to drive or catch a train to the coast for a day at the beach and dinner in an excellent fish restaurant. In midsummer, an outing to the cool green countryside around Sintra (see page 385), some 20 miles away, is another pleasant weekend option.

The exterior of the Teatro São Carlos in Lisbon's Chiado district

detailed mosaic map traces the Portuguese voyages of exploration.

✚ See map inset ✉ Avenida de Brasília ☎ 213 031 950; www.padraodosdescobrimentos.pt ⏰ Daily 10–7, Mar.–Sep.; 10–6, rest of year. Last admission 30 minutes before closing 🚈 Train: Belém 🚌 714, 727, 729, 751; tram 15E 🎟 $$ (temporary exhibitions free)

Parque das Nações

The Parque das Nações (Park of the Nations), constructed for the Expo '98, is used for trade fairs and exhibitions. Striking buildings, moorings, landscaped gardens, street cafés and restaurants front the Tagus river. From the water rises the Oceanário (Oceanarium). This state-of-the-art aquarium is one of Europe's largest. It features a vast central tank, surrounded by four others representing the main oceans. Marine mammals and seabirds thrive, as well as fish, underwater creatures and vegetation, making this one of Lisbon's most impressive sights.

✚ Off map at E3 ✉ Parque das Nações ☎ 218 917 000 (Oceanarium); www.portaldasnacoes.pt or www.oceanario.pt ⏰ Oceanarium: daily 10–8, Apr.–Oct.; 10–7, rest of year. Last admission 1 hour before closing 🚈 Oriente 🚌 400, 705, 708, 725, 744, 759, 782, 794 🎟 Park free; Oceanarium $$$

Praça do Comércio

One side of the spacious Praça do Comércio (Commercial Square) opens on the water, emphasizing its original purpose as an imposing gateway to the city from the sea. To experience its original perspective, take the short ferry trip from the Terreiro do Paço (Palace Square) river station across the Tagus to the suburb of Barreiro. The vista of the square and the triumphal arch leading to the streets of the Baixa opens up to buildings, churches and monuments, giving a flavor of the city's past.

✚ C2 ✉ Praça do Comércio 🚈 Terreiro do Paço 🚌 All buses to Praça do Comércio; tram 15E ⛴ Terreiro do Paço for ferries to Cacilhas

Sé

Construction of the Sé (Cathedral) started in 1150, soon after the expulsion of the Moors. It was the city's first church, a solid and harmonious Romanesque edifice. Its two massive towers are a prominent city landmark. It largely escaped damage in the 1755 earthquake, making it a symbol of Lisbon's history. Inside, be sure to see the font where St. Anthony of Padua was baptized.

✚ D3 ✉ Largo da Sé ☎ 218 866 752 ⏰ Church: Tue.–Sat. 9–7, Sun.–Mon. 9–5. Cloister: Mon.–Sat. 10–6:30, Apr.–Oct.; Mon.–Sat. 10–5, rest of year. Museum: Mon.–Sat. 10–5 🚈 Terreiro do Paço or Baixa-Chiado 🚌 737; tram 12E, 28E 🎟 Museum and cloister $

Torre de Belém

In the nearby suburb of Belém, the Torre de Belém (Belém Tower) rises beside the Tagus river. This exquisite stone tower is a symbol of Portugal's maritime past. Built between 1515 and 1520, it was designed by Francisco de Arruda, a Portuguese architect whose earlier Moroccan travels influenced his style. His work shows delightful Moorish elements – little domes topping the battlements, corner towers, and arcaded windows and loggias. Built as a bastion against pirate attack, it later served as a prison, and has been designated a World Heritage Site by UNESCO.

✚ See map inset ✉ Avenida de Brasília ☎ 213 620 034; www.torrebelem.pt ⏰ Tue.–Sun. 10–6:30, May–Sep.; 10–5:30, rest of year. Last admission 30 minutes before closing 🚈 Train: Belém 🚌 714, 727, 729, 751; tram 15E 🎟 $$; free first Sun. of the month

Visitors enjoy the views from the shady loggia of the Torre de Belém

Sintra

By far the most popular day trip from Lisbon is to beautiful Sintra, a small town packed with delights, set in lush and mountainous country some 20 miles northwest of Lisbon. Once there, the attractions are scattered over a wide area, so it makes sense to take a tour or rent a car and drive from the city. Alternatively, take the train from Lisbon and make use of the efficient Sintra buses which cover the main sites. Most tour operators include a detour to Cabo da Roca, the Continent's westernmost point.

For more than 500 years Sintra was the summer resort of Portuguese kings – a legacy that is apparent in the town's two astounding palaces (www.parquesdesintra.pt). The National Palace (Palácio Nacional) was first built by João I in the 15th century and remained in use until the end of the 19th century.

Architecturally imposing, it's nevertheless a muddle of mainly Gothic and Manueline styles. The interior is worth exploring. Note the superb ceramic tiles, as well as the elaborately decorated ceilings: one is painted with gold-collared swans and another with magpies.

The other main palace is the Pena National Palace (Palácio Nacional da Pena), built in the 1840s by Ferdinand of Saxe-Coburg-Gotha, husband of Queen Maria II. It's a creation rivaling the best of Disney, complete with towers, turrets and battlements. Inside is a riot of flamboyant furniture, wall hangings and paintings, including a whole room of nudes. Nearby is the eighth-century Castelo dos Mouros, a ruined Moorish stronghold.

The other outstanding attractions in Sintra are its gardens and parks. The warm, damp climate is ideal for a profusion of exotic trees, shrubs and roses, and you'll see everything from rhododendrons and camellias to tree ferns and palms. The Pena Gardens, below the Pena National Palace, are lovely, with lakes and mock temples. But the highlight is the Monserrate Gardens, west of Sintra. Two Englishmen laid out the gardens between 1790 and 1860, and they ramble over 74 acres.

Around Sintra lies the Parque Natural Sintra-Cascais (www.cm-cascais.pt), an area stretching from the mountains of Sintra down to the dramatic Atlantic coastline at Guincho.

Tour Operators

Cityrama-Grayline ✉ Avenida João XXI 7BE ☎ 213 191 090 (within Portugal), 800 472 5946 (US/CA toll free); www.grayline.com/lisbon or www.cityrama.pt

Lisboasightseeing ✉ Rua Pascoal de Melo 3 ☎ 976 086 536; www.lisboasightseeing.com

Inside Lisbon ✉ Avenida Forças Armadas 95 ☎ 968 412 612, 1 646 257 4042 (from US); www.insidelisbon.com

Diana Tours ✉ Campo Grande 30B ☎ 217 998 540; www.dianatours.pt

The Palácio Nacional da Pena is a storybook castle with turrets and towers

Porto

Porto, Portugal's second-largest city with about 200,000 residents and about 1.7 million in the greater Porto area, lies on the steep north bank of the Douro river, a few miles from its outlet on the Atlantic. The city suburbs sprawl down to the coast. Many visitors encounter Porto on their way up the beautiful Douro valley. The city also is known for its association with port wine, which has been shipped from the suburb of Vila Nova de Gaia since the 17th century. It has long been referred to as "Oporto," a name never used by the Portuguese and now declining in use elsewhere.

Development of Porto

Founded in pre-Roman times, the city of Porto gave its name to the country, and was the birthplace of Prince Henry the Navigator, son of João I of Portugal and Philippa of Lancaster, granddaughter of Edward III of England, in 1394. Traditionally liberal, its residents have always had a strong rebellious streak, which goes well with the city's industrious and down-to-earth image.

Porto is a refreshing antidote to the faded elegance of Lisbon – a bustling, no-nonsense city lying at the center of Portugal's most important economic area, its layout inextricably entwined with the history of the port trade. Grandiose buildings testify to its 18th- and 19th-century wealth, but the true spirit of the city lies in the maze of narrow streets below the cathedral, the old docks and the waterfront houses. Areas throughout the city are decorated with blue-and-white *azulejos* (glazed ceramic tiles).

Suggested Itineraries

Two or three days should be sufficient to see the main sights of Porto. Nearly everything of interest is within a short walk or bus ride from the city center. The streets are steep and hilly, so wear comfortable shoes.

If you're on your way up the Douro valley, make time to visit the port lodges in Vila Nova de Gaia (see page 390), Porto's main tourist attraction. If you've got more time, the city can be neatly divided into cultural itineraries, focusing on medieval, baroque and neoclassic monuments and churches. And for a state-of-the-art attraction, Porto now boasts a world-class arts center, the Casa da Música (www.casadamusica.com).

The heart of modern Porto centers around Avenida dos Aliados, a broad avenue with the monumental town hall at one end and the Praça da Liberdade, a transportation hub, at the other. This stretch is a good place to people-watch. The main shopping areas are east and north of this avenue. You can use the river to help orient yourself to the city.

Porto Flavors

The people of Porto have traditionally been known as *tripeiros*, or "tripe-eaters," allegedly because they sacrificed all their meat except the tripe to their army during a legendary battle – an historic indicator that, until recent years, refined cooking wasn't a priority. That said, hearty food still dominates. Expect plenty of fish with the much-beloved *bacalhau* (dried, salted codfish) and super-sweet desserts on every menu at any time of the day. On the other hand, a glass of smooth, silky and subtle port – drunk on its native soil – may convert even the most inveterate port-hater.

An especially atmospheric place to dine is beside the river at Ribeira (see page 389), in the heart of the oldest part of Porto. Until the early 1990s it was run-down and decayed, but most of the area has now been given a face-lift, and it is filled with dozens of good, lively restaurants, cafés and bars under the medieval arches, with tremendous tourist appeal.

Crafts and Shopping

Porto is the place to track down northern handicraft specialties, fine port, locally made shoes and traditional gold filigree jewelry from the villages of the Minho.

The city's wonderfully old-fashioned stores, many of which still retain their early 20th-century facades and details, are worth a visit even if you're not buying. Highlights include the Lello and Irmão bookstore on Rua das Carmelitas, with its superb double staircase and somber wooden paneling, and Cardoso Cabeleireiro on Rua do Bonjardim, a shop specializing in wigs and toupees. Similar stores cluster together in Porto, so you'll find streets packed with hardware stores, seed merchants, jewelers and linen stores. Marques Soares (www.marquessoares.pt), a chic department store on Rua das Carmelitas, carries exquisite leather goods.

Excursions and Entertainment

There are several marine operators that run cruises on the Douro river, varying

The Igreja and Torre dos Clérigos tower over Porto

in price and ranging from a week-long trip up the river on a luxury cruiser taking in the sights along the riverbank, to shorter trips of a couple of hours puttering around the lower reaches in a reproduction of a *rabelo*, the glorious old boats once used to carry barrels of port downstream from the vineyards. Sections of the 19th-century narrow-gauge railway still operate in the Douro valley – this is a fun way to do a little exploring. Tour operators also run bus trips in, around and out of Porto; Porto Tours (☎ 222 000 045; www.portotours.com) is a reliable operator with English-speaking guides. Alternatively, tickets may be bought at the tourist office. Be sure to visit the port lodges in Vila Nova de Gaia, an essential stop on any Porto visit.

For evening entertainment, locals attend theaters, concerts and the movies, although many people prefer to while away the hours of warm, balmy evenings at a terrace café or simply strolling along the riverbank.

Essential Information

Tourist Information
Turismo do Porto (Porto Tourism)
Casa da Camâra, Terreiro da Sé
☎ 223 393 472; www.visitporto.travel
Rua Clube dos Fenianos 25
☎ 223 393 472; www.portoturismo.pt
Also informaton kiosks at: Campanhã Railway Station (all year); Praça da Ribeira (May–Oct.)

Urban Transportation
The Sociedade de Transportes Colectivos do Porto (STCP) issues a Mapa de Transportes showing both day and nighttime bus, tram and metro routes (available from tourist offices). Pay as you get on the bus or the tram. A 1- or 3-day "Andante" card is valid on the city's tram and metro system (www.metrodoporto.pt). Porto Tourism issues a Porto Card, valid for 1, 2 or 3 days, which offers unlimited use of public transportation as well as free entrance to many attractions. Taxis are inexpensive; there is an additional charge to cross the river to Gaia. For bus information ☎ 226 158 158 or 808 200 166; www.stcp.pt.

Airport Information
Francisco Sá Carneiro International Airport (☎ 229 432 400 or 800 201 201 within Portugal, toll free; www.ana.pt) is 12 miles northwest of central Porto. Porto metro line E (☎ 808 20 50 60; www.metrodoporto.pt) links the airport with Trinidade station in the city; trains run from 6 a.m.–1 a.m. every 20 or 30 minutes; travel time is 35 minutes. Bus services 601 and 602 also serve the airport.

Climate – average highs and lows for the month

Jan.	Feb.	Mar.	Apr.	May	Jun.	Jul.	Aug.	Sep.	Oct.	Nov.	Dec.
13°C	13°C	15°C	17°C	18°C	22°C	23°C	23°C	23°C	19°C	17°C	14°C
55°F	55°F	59°F	63°F	64°F	72°F	73°F	73°F	73°F	66°F	63°F	57°F
6°C	7°C	7°C	9°C	10°C	13°C	14°C	14°C	14°C	12°C	8°C	7°C
43°F	45°F	45°F	48°F	50°F	55°F	57°F	57°F	57°F	54°F	46°F	45°F

Porto Sights

Key to symbols
➕ map coordinates refer to the Porto map on page 387 💷 admission charge:
$$$ more than €7:50, $$ €4–€7:50, $ less than €4
See page 5 for complete key to symbols

Igreja e Torre dos Clérigos

The soaring Torre dos Clérigos (Tower of Clérigos), attached to an 18th-century granite church (Igreja dos Clérigos), affords fine city views. Nicolau Nasoni designed the oval church, with its elaborately festooned facade of swags and garlands, in the 1730s.

➕ B3 ✉ Rua São Felipe de Nery ☎ 222 001 729; www.torredosclerigos.pt 🕐 Church and tower: daily 9–7, Apr.–Sep.; 9–6, rest of year. Last admission 30 minutes before closing 🚇 D line: São Bento 🚌 All Praça da Liberdade services 💷 Church free; Tower $

Jardins do Palácio de Cristal

At the Jardins do Palácio de Cristal (Crystal Palace Gardens), a lime tree-lined avenue leads from pools and fountains past magnolias, camellias and rhododendrons to rose gardens and terraces high above the river, and offers one of the best vantage points in Porto.

➕ Off map at A3 ✉ Rua de Dom Manuel II ☎ 225 320 080 🕐 Daily 8 a.m.–9 p.m., Apr.–Sep.; 8–7, rest of year 🚌 200, 201, 207, 302,303, 501 🍴 Café

Museu Nacional Soares dos Reis

The Soares dos Reis National Museum, named after the 19th-century sculptor, is Porto's most important museum. Housed in an impressive 1795 neoclassic edifice, it was occupied in the 1800s during the Peninsular War by first the French and then the English. The museum features works by dos Reis, with fine exhibits of glass and porcelain; look for pieces from the famous Vista Alegre factory.

➕ Off map at A3 ✉ Rua Dom Manuel II 44 ☎ 223 393 770; www.museusoaresdosreis.pt 🕐 Wed.–Sun. 10–6, Tue. 2–6. Last admission 30 minutes before closing 🚌 200, 201, 207, 208, 302, 303, 501, 507, 601 🍴 Café 💷 $$; free first Sun. of the month

Museu Romântico da Quinta da Macieirinha

For an insight into how the prosperous bourgeois of Porto lived in the 19th century, visit the Museu Romântico da Quinta da Macieirinha (Romantic Museum) in a pretty villa overlooking the river. Admire the furniture and paintings; many of the furnishings have connections with the last king of Piedmont, who lived here in exile.

➕ Off map at A3 ✉ Rua de Entrequintas 220 ☎ 226 057 000 🕐 Mon.–Sat. 10–5:30, Sun. 10 a.m.–12:30 p.m. and 2–5:30. Last admission 30 minutes before closing 🚌 200, 201, 207, 208, 302, 303, 501, 507, 601 💷 $; free Sat.–Sun.

Ponte Dom Luís I

Five bridges span the Douro river, all built high above the water over the river gorge. The most impressive of these is the Ponte Dom Luís I (Luis I Bridge), a striking bi-level iron construction designed by Théophile Seyring (one of Gustave Eiffel's collaborators) and dating from 1886.

➕ C1 ✉ Ponte Dom Luís I 🚇 D line: São Bento 🚌 900, 901, 906

Praça da Ribeira

The waterfront Ribeira Square is the focal point of the Ribeira district, by far the most atmospheric area of Porto and designated a UNESCO World Heritage Site. Many of the buildings were erected between 1776 and 1782.

The Casa do Infante (House of the Prince), Prince Henry the Navigator's reputed birthplace, was originally built in the 1350s as a customs house for the poor but was altered many times during the next few centuries, the interior courtyard being the oldest part of the structure. The building sits on the foundations of a Roman original, proving the longevity of a settlement and a community on this part of the river.

Casa do Infante ➕ B1 ✉ Rua da Alfândega 10, Ribeira ☎ 222 060 435 🕐 Museum: Tue.–Sun. 10–1 and 2–5:30. Last admission 5 p.m. 🚇 D line: São Bento 🚌 500, 900, 901, 906 💷 $; free Sat.–Sun.

Sé

Porto's magnificent Sé (Cathedral) stands high above the slopes leading to the river. Built in the 12th century as a fortress church, it was extensively altered in the 1700s in the baroque style, although the vast silver altarpiece in the north transept dates from the mid-16th century.

The two-story cloisters have solid granite lines enlivened with beautiful tiles, and there are good views over the town. A museum in the treasury houses archeological finds from pre-Roman to Gothic times, plus liturgical objects from the 15th to 19th centuries.

➕ C2 ✉ Terreiro da Sé ☎ 222 059 028 ⏰ Church: Daily 9 a.m.–12:30 p.m. and 2:30–7, Apr.–Sep.; daily 9 a.m.–12:30 p.m. and 2:30–6, rest of year. Cloisters and Museum: Daily 9 a.m.–12:15 p.m. and 2:30–6:30, Apr.–Sep.; 9 a.m.–12:15 p.m. and 2:30–5:30, rest of year 🚇 D line: São Bento 🚌 207, 303, 400, 500, 900, 901, 904, 905, 906, ZH 💵 Church free; Cloisters $$

Vila Nova de Gaia

A separate municipality, Vila Nova de Gaia lies across the Douro river from Porto itself. Its name is synonymous with port, for until 1987 all Portuguese port had to be matured here to be so named. The riverside slopes are dominated by the the port warehouses, or lodges. There are many opportunities for free tours and to buy port; the white aperitif variety is hard to find abroad.

High above the river is the old monastery of Serra do Pilar, now the "House of the Northern Patrimony." Visit the circular cloister and take a guided tour of the dome. A cable car links the quayside to a station, Jardim do Morro, offering access to Serra do Pilar and fine views of the Porto skyline.

➕ Off map at C1 ✉ Largo de Aviz, Vila Nova de Gaia ⏰ Most lodges open Mon.–Fri. 10–noon and 2–6 (also Sat. in summer) 🚇 D line: Jardim do Morro 🚌 900, 901, 906

Serro do Pilar ✉ 4430 Vila Nova de Gaia ☎ 932 528 579 ⏰ Tue.–Sun. 9–7, Jul.–Aug. (closes 6:30, Mar.–Jun. and Oct.; 5:30, Nov.–Feb. 💵 $$

Cable car ☎ 223 741 440; www.gaiacablecar.com ⏰ Daily 10–8, late Apr.–late Sep.; 10–7, late Mar.–late Apr. and late Sep.–late Oct.; 10–6, rest of year 💵 $$

World of Discoveries

This new interactive theme-park type attraction brings the Portuguese exploration of the New World to life. Costumed staff help put you in the mood to visit the time of Henry the Navigator and the lands he discovered, plus a re-created sailing vessel shows you how he traveled. There are 20 themed areas to visit.

➕ Off map at A3 ✉ rua de Miragaia 106 ☎ 220 439 770; www.worldofdiscoveries.com ⏰ Mon.–Fri. 10–6, Sat.–Sun. 10–7 🚌 1, 500 💵 $$$

The cathedral cloisters are lined with blue-and-white *azulejos* **(glazed ceramic tiles)**

Port Wine

Port, one of Portugal's glories, is drunk all over the world, as an aperitif and a digestive aid. In the 18th century, its production area was the world's first demarcated wine zone, helping to make port one of the few wines with a flavor that has remained untouched for centuries. Be sure to try it in Porto, a city more associated with port than any other.

Port is a fortified wine, which means that brandy is added to the grapes during the production process. This both "fortifies" the wine, making it stronger, and halts the fermentation process, leaving half the natural grape sugar in the wine. These two factors give port its strength, sweetness and smoothness; its complex flavors come from the soil and climate where the grapes are grown.

To people accustomed to the lush vineyards of other countries, those in the upper Douro valley, which produce port, are a revelation. It's a stony, barren area, a microclimatic zone where temperatures reach extremes of heat and cold. The soil is a thin layer on top of schist, and the vine roots must force their way through the rock, sometimes as much as 20 feet, to find water. The Portuguese insist, probably rightly, that these conditions are what gives port its unique character.

The vineyards grow on steep terraces, so much of the harvesting is done by hand, and until recently the grapes were still even trodden by foot. (Treading the grapes by foot enables the flavor to be released without crushing the grape seed, which would add a bitter taste to the port.) Today more than 90 percent are crushed and fermented at a controlled temperature, sometime between mid-September and mid-October. The new wine is stored upriver in a lodge or *armazém*, to clear until the following spring. In March it's ready for transportation. Following strict tradition, until as recently as 1987 it could not be called port unless the maturation had taken place in Vila Nova de Gaia, across the Douro from Porto. Increasingly, as is now allowed, it is matured on site due to space consideration and transportation costs.

Port comes in several varieties: white, a semi-sweet light wine; ruby, a clear, intense red; tawny, which is older and more complex; and vintage and late bottled vintage port. Vintage port is aged in the bottle and comes from grapes from a single year; late bottled is matured for up to four years before further maturing after bottling.

Barrels of port are stored at Solar do Vinho do Porto (Port Wine Rooms) in the Romantic Museum

Spain

Opposite: Casa Batlló designed by Gaudí is in the L'Eixample district of Barcelona

Spain

Spain is a country of diverse landscapes, climates, peoples and cultures, forged over the centuries into a political unity. Physically separated from the rest of Europe by the Pyrenees mountain chain, Spain also found itself isolated internationally during General Francisco Franco's dictatorship (1939–75). Since Franco's death, however, and with the restoration of its parliamentary monarchy (currently King Felipe VI and Queen Letizia), Spain has regained its place politically, economically and culturally within Europe.

But despite the rate of progress, many aspects of Spanish life remain untouched, and Spain retains much of its traditional character.

Spain Today

Spain's long and checkered history peaked in the Golden Age of the 16th century, when it was one of the most influential nations of the world. It had immense power across Europe and possessed many overseas colonies. The following centuries saw a gradual decline and increasing isolation from the rest of Europe, culminating in the bitter Civil War (1936–39) and Franco's long dictatorship.

In Spain today, political, cultural, artistic and sporting life flourishes, along with national confidence. Madrid (1992), Santiago de Compostela (2000), and Salamanca (2002) have all held the title of Cultural Capital of Europe, with San Sebastían holding the title in 2016. The world sailing competition, the Americas Cup, was hosted by Valencia in 2007 and 2010, and the soccer teams, Real Madrid and F.C. Barcelona are among the most successful in Europe.

The country, however, has been truly battered by the global financial crisis.

From Pyrenees to Portugal

One of Europe's most mountainous countries, Spain occupies much of the Iberian peninsula, stretching southwest from the Pyrenees. Much of the land area is covered by the mighty Meseta, a little-populated agricultural plateau surrounded by long mountain ranges. These ranges stretch from the Sierra Nevada in the south to the Cordillera Cantábrica in the north, and give Spain

More Top Destinations in Spain

- Burgos C4
- Córdoba B2
- Costa Brava E3
- Costa de la Luz A1
- Costa Verde B4
- Granada C1
- León B4
- Monestir de Poblet E3
- Pamplona/Iruña D4
- Parque Nacional de Picos de Europa B4
- Peñíscola D3
- Ronda B1
- Salamanca B3
- Segovia C3
- Sierra de Montserrat E3
- Zaragoza D3

Spain

A passionate flamenco display in Madrid

Such diversity is echoed in Spain's climate, which varies from the mild, wet weather of the northern Atlantic coast to the typical Mediterranean hot, dry summers and mild, wet winters in the south. Winter inland can be very cold.

The island groups of the Balearics (Mallorca, Menorca, Ibiza and small Formentera) and the Canaries (including Gran Canaria, Tenerife, Lanzarote and the tiny La Gomera) have their own geographical and climatic characteristics.

Diversities of Spain

Regional differences are reflected in the Spanish people, their looks, their character, their attitudes and, above all, their cuisine. The 800 years of Moorish occupation, the eventual unification of a number of small kingdoms, and the power and wealth of 16th-century colonial Spain have aided the evolution of diverse provincial characteristics.

The concept of centralized power is alien to many Spaniards, and regionalism is very strong in Spain. It has its base in the peninsula's linguistic groups: Galician, spoken in the northwest; Basque, another northern language; Castilian, also known as Spanish; and Catalan, based in the northeast, with Valencian and Mallorcan variations of this. These are all co-official languages in Spain.

In 1977, when the present constitution was established, various regional groups were provided for through the establishment of 17 autonomous governments. The Basque Country and Catalonia are the two regions in Spain having the most autonomy – both have powerful nationalist movements which are pushing for independence.

Spanish Characters

There are physical differences between Spaniards from different parts of the peninsula. With a population of 47 million, there's room for diversity; contrary to popular belief, not all

an average altitude of 2,100 feet. The highest mainland peak is the 11,414-foot Mulhacén in the Sierra Nevada, although Mount Teide on the Canary island of Tenerife is nearly 1,000 feet higher.

The mild, moist Atlantic coast of the Costa Verde in the north contrasts with the sun-baked Mediterranean beaches of the southern Costa del Sol. The grandeur of the Pyrenees is more than rivaled by the dramatic peaks of the Asturian mountains on Spain's northern coast, which some consider the most beautiful region in Spain. East of Asturias the Ebro valley slashes southeast toward the Mediterranean, where it bisects the coastal plain southwest of Barcelona.

The fertile gardens of Murcia and the agricultural flatlands of the Guadalquivir yield harvests rivaled only by the tourist crop drawn from the golden sands of the Mediterranean beaches.

The Mediterranean coast ends on the northern shore of the Straits of Gibraltar, only 9 miles from Africa.

Spaniards are dark-eyed and olive-skinned. The Moorish genetic legacy is strongest in Andalucia, where many are delicate-featured and dark, personifying the Spanish stereotype.

Spaniards are sometimes thought of as an exuberant, passionate and light-hearted people, much like the Italians, but nothing could be further from the truth. They are certainly passionate, but there's a strong streak of self-control and melancholy in the national character. History has given them loyalty and tolerance. Kindness to children and respect for the elderly are the norm.

Young Spaniards enjoy a freedom and lifestyle their grandparents could never have imagined, yet society is still in a state of flux, and there are huge contrasts between different regions, towns and rural areas. But wherever you go you'll find the same level of hospitality and friendliness, particularly if you speak a little Spanish. English is widely spoken along the Mediterranean coast and by hotel staff in big cities, but very rarely elsewhere.

Cities, Towns and Villages

For visitors the three great cities are Madrid, Barcelona and Seville, but in Spanish eyes the industrial centers of Valencia and Bilbao are of equal importance, and the inhabitants of each region claim their capital as the most beautiful in Spain.

Andalucia, with the architectural treasures of Granada and Córdoba, is rich in Moorish history.

The region of Castille has Christian castles built during the struggle to oust the Moors.

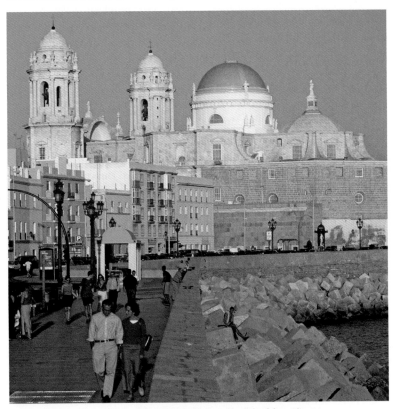

A view along the seafront to Cádiz's cathedral, bathed in the golden light of the setting sun

The Mediterranean coast has many remains from centuries of Roman occupation, while the Atlantic port of Cádiz boasts 2,000 years of maritime history. Rural Spain continues largely unchanged; agriculture is more mechanized with the inevitable introduction of some modern harvesting equipment, but the way and pace of life are still deeply rooted in the past.

As in other European countries, however, the young are abandoning rural villages in favor of city life, and now more than 75 percent of Spain's population lives in urban areas.

Spanish Lifestyle

Daily life in Spain differs in one major way from other southern European countries; mealtimes are very late. Breakfast in hotels is served from around 7:30 until 9:30 or 10. Most Spaniards rise early and eat little first thing, so they are ready for a snack around 11. This delays lunch until at least 2 p.m., and dinner is often around 9:30 p.m. or later.

An early start means you can take advantage of the cool mornings, vital in a country where air-conditioning is not universal. Virtually everything – stores, offices, churches and museums – closes from 1:30 or 2 p.m. until 4 or 5, and most people sleep or take a break after lunch for an hour on the weekends, during the fabled siesta.

This break in the day bypasses the worst heat and leaves people ready to stay up late and enjoy the cooler evening air. It's a pleasure to sit at a café or restaurant table until 1 or 2 a.m. as the nightlife continues all around.

You'll find that most entertainment begins very late, around 10 p.m., and clubs don't get going until the early hours of the morning. Along the Mediterranean coast things are more geared toward visitors, and you may be able to have dinner soon after 8:30 p.m.

Spain is traditionally a Catholic country. When you visit churches, cover the tops of your arms and shoulders and avoid wearing shorts. The local fiestas held in towns and villages are always in honor of the Virgin or some favorite local saint, and if you get the chance to watch one, you will see how religion plays an integral part in everyday life.

Traveling in Spain

The economic boom of the last few decades may have stalled but the country's infrastructure is excellent. Spain has a very good network of well-marked toll roads and highways. Spaniards drive fast but safely, and you should have no problems if you rent a car. Public transportation is good, with a choice of internal flights, fast and punctual trains, and long-distance buses going to even the most remote corners.

Hotels are graded and inspected by the government, so you are guaranteed a clean and adequate room no matter how little you pay. Try to spend at least a few nights at one of the *paradores*. These are state-owned hotels in historic buildings such as castles and monasteries, often furnished with antiques and offering a high standard of comfort and service.

Spanish Passions

Spaniards throw themselves whole-heartedly into leisure pursuits and sporting events. Their most famous and controversial spectator event is bullfighting, although support for this has dwindled considerably in recent years and it is now illegal in Catalonia. Soccer is a national passion; huge crowds follow the fortunes of teams such as Real Madrid and F.C. Barcelona.

Spain has some of Europe's finest golf courses, chiefly along the Mediterranean coast, where you'll also find excellent marinas and watersports facilities, as well as untouched wilderness areas. Young people travel from all over Europe to experience Spain's club scene, at its most frenetic on the island of Ibiza.

Moorish-style decoration on a house in Alicante

Timeline

15,000–12,000 BC	Caves at Altamira painted; earliest sign of habitation.
218–210 BC	Rome begins conquest of Iberian peninsula.
AD 411	Visigoths invade and establish powerful kingdom at Toledo.
711	Moors defeat Visigoths and begin period of occupation.
1478–79	Spanish Inquisition against Jews, Moors and Protestants.
1492	Christopher Columbus discovers the New World.
1519	Spanish conquistadors move across America.
1588	Spanish Armada is sent against Protestant England; fleet destroyed and maritime preeminence lost.
1704	British capture Gibraltar.
1808–14	Peninsular War (War of Independence) sees expulsion of French and defeat of Napoleon.
1898	Philippines and Cuba rebel against Spanish rule; the United States occupies Puerto Rico; end of Spanish Empire.
1914–18	Spain remains neutral in World War I.
1936–39	Spanish Civil War; General Francisco Franco leads Nationalist troops from Morocco against Republicans.
1939	Franco becomes head of state; Spain enters period of isolation and remains neutral throughout World War II.
1955	Spain joins United Nations.
1975	Death of Franco; Juan Carlos becomes king.
1986	Spain joins the European Economic Commmunity (later known as the European Union).
1992	Barcelona hosts Olympic Games; Madrid declared Cultural Capital of Europe; Seville is the venue for Expo '92.
2004	Madrid suffers horrifying terrorist attack resulting in 191 deaths.
2004–2008	Spanish Socialist Worker's Party, led by Zapatero, wins general election in 2004. Zapatero reelected in 2008.
2010	Catalonia becomes the first Spanish region to ban bullfighting.
2012	Right-of-center Partido Popular, led by Mariano Rajoy, wins general election in the wake of widespread alarm over the stalled economy.
2014	King Juan Carlos abdicates. In June 2014, at parliamentary chambers, Crown Prince Felipe is proclaimed the new king.

The Moorish Occupation

In AD 711 a faction of the ruling Visigoth tribe in Spain went to Islamic Africa to seek help with some domestic political problems. They returned with an army of 7,000; after victory at Cádiz, the Moors encountered little resistance in taking over all but a small strip of northern Spain over the next 30 years. Their tactics were a blend of intelligent strategy and diplomacy; they never demanded religious subordination, as long as Christians paid taxes. Beginning in AD 744, however, resistance against the invaders spread south from the small, unoccupied northern territory, fueled by the legend of St. James the Moorslayer. El Cid succeeded in capturing Toledo from the Moors in 1085, and despite some setbacks, a coalition of Christian armies was finally victorious at the Battle of Navas de Tolosa in 1212, the last great battle between Moors and Christians. The Moorish occupation left important legacies, however – they brought mathematics, papermaking, oranges, spices and rice to Spain.

The seafront promenade at L'Estartit on the Costa Brava

Survival Guide

- English is not widely spoken, even in large cities. Keep in mind that the Spanish you may have learned in high school differs in accent, pronunciation and some vocabulary from that spoken in Spain. In Barcelona, Catalan is widely spoken alongside Castilian.

- It's best not to discuss politics, since Spaniards are very proud and the subject could be sensitive.

- Public restrooms are few except in museums, but it's acceptable to use the facilities in a bar; leave a small tip on the counter or stop and have a cup of coffee while you're there.

- Inebriation is frowned on in Spain; the Spanish drink alcohol regularly, but in moderation.

- The Spanish are formal and polite; it is best to ask, in Spanish, if the person you're addressing speaks English before you start to speak, and shake hands with the person at the end of your conversation.

- Water is a precious commodity in many parts of Spain; you may find that hotel bathrooms have a shower rather than a tub. Shower pressure is generally low.

- You can safely drink the water throughout Spain, although you may prefer to drink bottled mineral water, which is inexpensive and served chilled. Ice is not generally served in drinks unless you ask.

- Throughout Spain, and especially along the Mediterranean coast, bars specialize in *tapas*, delicious selections of hot or cold savory mouthfuls served with drinks. Be sure to try some of the dozens available: fish, cured ham, stewed peppers, salads, *tortilla*, (a thick, Spanish omelet) anchovies, local almonds, olives. A few little dishes will make a delicious lunch.

- All large cities have shopping malls, usually located away from the town center; downtown department stores; and a range of antiques stores, designer boutiques, local craft and souvenir shops, gourmet food stores, and clothing and bric-a-brac markets.

- Prices in Spain are comparable to those found in the rest of Europe; meals can be a little cheaper than in other parts of Europe.

- Try to arrange your trip so that it coincides with one of the major local festivals. Spain has some of the most colorful and exotic celebrations in Europe.

Spain

Madrid

Unlike most European capital cities, Madrid did not evolve as the nation's capital. It was chosen. In 1561, Philip II settled the court permanently in Madrid, as much for its position in the center of Spain as for political reasons. Today Madrid is fascinating, noisy, vibrant and chaotic – a city of great wealth and grueling poverty, but still the country's financial capital.

Like so much of Spain, Madrid's spirit is elusive and diffused, and will surprise you repeatedly. Plan to stay in the city center, so you can easily reach your hotel in the middle of the day, when many museums and monuments are closed for the siesta. The best way to tackle sightseeing is to concentrate on one section at a time. There are three historical areas of interest in the vicinity of the city's main plaza, Puerta del Sol (see page 408); Old Madrid (Viejo Madrid), centering on the Plaza Mayor (see page 408); the Western Quarter (Madrid de los Asturias), by the Palacio Real (see page 407); and Bourbon Madrid, the heart of which is the sweeping avenues and sparkling

fountains around the Prado Museum (Museo Nacional del Prado, see page 406). A tourist bus (*bus turístico*; www.madridcitytour.es) links all three, allowing passengers to get on and off at will. Tickets are valid for one or two days, and there's English commentary. Turismo de Madrid organizes walking and bicycling tours in the city. Bookings should be made at the tourist office in Plaza Mayor 27 (☎91 454 4410; www. esmadrid.com). There also is an efficient subway system. Take along an English–Spanish dictionary, as English is not widely spoken here.

Dining Out

Local specialties include tripe, but many regional restaurants feature traditional dishes from all over Spain. The cuisine of the Basque country and Galicia, with its emphasis on seafood, is very good, or you could try a Latin-American restaurant, where even the meat is imported from Argentina. Fast-food outlets abound and offer hamburgers, *tortillas* or even paella to go.

Most restaurants have a good value, fixed-price lunch menu Monday through Friday which will include a first and second course, a dessert and a drink. Madrid has many bars where you'll find everything from tea and coffee to beer, champagne and exotic cocktails. In summer, bar life moves onto the sidewalks, with hundreds of outdoor venues (*terrazas*) crowded until dawn.

Malls and Markets

The central department stores, such as El Corte Inglés, are clustered in the commercial area around the Puerta del Sol and the Gran Vía. If you're looking for malls, the large Príncipe Pio occupies an attractive 19th-century station near the Royal Palace; the ABC Serrano, between Serrano and Castellana in the city center, is smaller and more upscale.

The most fashionable shopping area is the Salamanca district around the streets of Calle de Serrano and Goya, where you'll find expensive stores. Madrid is a good place for Spanish souvenirs, and there are many antiques stores – the Salamanca district alone has more than 50. Visit the Rastro flea market on Sunday morning and public holidays or visit the Mercado San Miguel for gourmet produce.

Evening Entertainment

Classical music, opera and theater thrive in Madrid, and the tourist office publishes an excellent monthly listings guide, *es Madrid*. It is available from tourist offices and hotels, or online at www.esmadrid.com. You might enjoy a *zarzuela* performance, a traditional form of musical, combining elements of opera, vaudeville and melodrama. Jazz is very popular, or, if you're looking for flamenco, there are several clubs (*tablaos*) where it is staged. Madrid has an exceptional nightclub scene and a number of movie theaters.

Essential Information

Tourist Information

Oficinas de Información Turística (Tourist Information Offices)

Plaza Mayor 27, Aeropuerto de Madrid-Barájas (airport), Terminals 2 and 4;
Plaza de Colón (underground passage); information points on Paseo del Prado and by the Atocha railroad station; for all offices contact ☎ 91 454 4410
www.esmadrid.com
http://turismomadrid.es
www.descubremadrid.com

SATE (Foreign Tourist Assistance Service)

The tourist police with translators available to help visitors in trouble and to report a crime Calle Leganitos 19 (near Plaza de España)
☎ 90 210 2112 (24-hours)

Urban Transportation

Getting around Madrid is simple on the metro (subway) and bus systems. Metro stations are marked on the Madrid city map by the letter "M" on a blue background inside a red diamond. The metro has 13 lines and runs daily 6 a.m.–1:30 a.m. Purchase tickets from machines or ticket offices in the stations. Go online at www.metromadrid.es for timetable and fare prices information only. The Metrobús ticket, valid for 10 trips on the metro and bus systems, is available from metro stations, tobacconists *(estancos)* and Municipal Transport Company (EMT) booths at some bus stops. Buses run daily 6 a.m.–midnight, with a limited, infrequent, all-night service. Pay the driver or stamp your pass in the machine when you board. Taxis are plentiful and can be hailed on the street. To call a taxi dial Tele-Taxi (☎ 91 371 2131).

Airport Information

Adolfo Suárez Madrid Barájas Airport (☎ 90 240 4704 or 91 321 1000) is 8 miles northeast of the city center, about a 30-minute drive. Express buses run every 20 minutes between the airport and Atocha railroad station – timetables are available online at www.emtmadrid.es. There is a metro (subway) line from the airport (with two stops, one for Terminals 1, 2, and 3, and another for Terminal 4) to Nuevos Ministerios (metro station of the same name). A train service links Terminal 4 with Chamartín, Atocha and other central city stations.

Climate – average highs and lows for the month

Jan.	Feb.	Mar.	Apr.	May	Jun.	Jul.	Aug.	Sep.	Oct.	Nov.	Dec.
9°C	12°C	15°C	18°C	21°C	27°C	32°C	31°C	26°C	19°C	13°C	10°C
48°F	54°F	59°F	64°F	70°F	81°F	90°F	88°F	79°F	66°F	55°F	50°F
1°C	2°C	4°C	6°C	9°C	14°C	17°C	17°C	13°C	9°C	4°C	2°C
34°F	36°F	39°F	43°F	48°F	57°F	63°F	63°F	55°F	48°F	39°F	36°F

Madrid Sights

Estadio Santiago Bernabéu

Home to the hugely successful soccer team Real Madrid, this vast stadium is a mecca for fans of Spanish soccer. Visitors can see the club's proudly displayed prestigious cups and trophies, and can also enjoy a stadium tour which includes a visit to the changing rooms and a special panoramic viewing terrace.

✚ Off map at D4 ✉ Avenida Concha Espina 1 ☎ 91 398 4370 ◷ Museum and Stadium tour: Mon.–Sat. 10–7, Sun. 10:30–6 (or 5 hours before kick-off on match days). Tours last 90 minutes ▣ Santiago Bernabéu ▤ 14, 27, 40, 43, 120, 126, 147, 150 ▓ $$$

Monasterio de las Descalzas Reales

The oddly named Convent of the Royal Barefoot Nuns was founded in 1557 as a convent for aristocratic ladies seeking the religious life. They and their families funded the decoration of 33 chapels with treasures by mainly Spanish artists.

✚ C2 ✉ Plaza de las Descalzas Reales 3 ☎ 91 454 8800 ◷ Tue.–Sat. 10–2 and 4–6:30, Sun. 10–3 ▣ Sol, Callao or Ópera ▓ $$ ℹ Guided visits only

Museo Arqueológico Nacional (MAN)

Spain's superb National Archaeology Museum contains more than 1,300,000 fascinating archeological artifacts from Spain and around the world. Highlights include the *Dama de Elche*, an Iberian female bust which dates from the 4th or 5th centuries BC, along with Greek and Roman treasures and Visigothic votive crowns made of gold inset with jewels.

✚ D3 ✉ Calle de Serrano 13 ☎ 91 577 7912; www.man.es ◷ Tue.–Sat. 9:30–8, Sun and public holidays, 9:30–3 ▣ Serrano or Goya ▤ 1, 9, 19, 51, 74 ▮ Café ▓ $$ ℹ Guided visits available

Eye-catching glass elevators scale the exterior of the Queen Sofía National Art Center

Museo Nacional Centro de Arte Reina Sofía

The spectacular Museo Nacional Centro de Arte Reina Sofía (Queen Sofía National Art Center) is housed in the former Hospital de San Carlos. Exterior glass elevators whisk you up to the permanent exhibitions. Visitors flock to Pablo Picasso's *Guernica*. When it was commissioned, his only instruction was to paint a big picture; this black-and-white composition has become a symbol of antiwar sentiment.

Other highlights in the museum include paintings by Salvador Dalí and Joan Miró.

✚ D1 ✉ Calle Santa Isabel 52 ☎ 91 774 1000; www.museoreinasofia.es ◷ Mon. and Wed.–Sat. 10–9, Sun. 10–7; closed on public holidays ▣ Atocha ▮ Café and restaurant ▓ $$$; senior citizens and under 18s free (free to all Mon. and Wed.–Sat. 7 p.m.–9 p.m., Sun. 1:30 p.m.–7 p.m.)

The Museo del Prado displays its collection of Spanish art to great effect in its large, well-lit rooms

Museo Nacional del Prado

The Prado Museum, with its unrivaled collection of Spanish paintings, is among the world's finest. Once the royal collection, the Prado represents the personal taste of the Spanish monarchs, with a noticeable emphasis on religious and courtly paintings. Space limitations allow only about 1,300 of the 22,000 works to be displayed; get an up-to-date floor plan as you arrive. Some works, particularly those by Diego Velázquez attract huge crowds.

Highlights include Velázquez's *Las Meninas,* often described as "the finest painting in the world." Goya's work occupies many rooms; look for his *Majas,* two paintings thought to be of the Duchess of Alba, one demure and clothed, the other sensuously naked. His *pinturas negras,* the dark pictures, stand in stark contrast; disturbing and pessimistic, they represent the apocalyptic vision of a man on the edge of madness. The Spanish monarchs were fascinated by the surreal work of Hiëronymous Bosch; his *Garden of Earthly Delights,* with its wealth of weird detail, is one of his finest works.
🔁 D1 ✉ Paseo del Prado ☎ 91 330 2800;

www.museodelprado.es 🕐 Mon.–Sat. 10–8, Sun. 10–7 🚇 Banco de España or Atocha 🍴 Café 🎟 $$$ (free Tue.–Sat. 6–8 p.m., Sun. 5–7 p.m and all day on certain national holidays. Under 18s free)

Museo de la Real Academia de Bellas Artes de San Fernando

Art lovers will enjoy the peaceful Real Academia de Bellas Artes de San Fernando (Royal Academy of Fine Arts), founded in the 18th century to emulate art venues in Paris and London. The academy has some fine paintings by Francisco Goya and a good Diego Velázquez portrait of Philip IV. The highlight is *Spring* by Italian artist Giuseppe Arcimboldo, a portrait in which the sitter's features are entirely composed of fruit and vegetables.
🔁 C2 ✉ Calle Alcalá 13 ☎ 91 524 0864; www.realacademiabellasartessanfernando.com 🕐 Tue.–Sun. 10–3. Closed Aug. 🚇 Sol or Sevilla 🎟 $$ (senior citizens and under 18s free)

Museo Thyssen-Bornemisza

Acquired in 1993 for about $350 million, the art collection of the Museo Thyssen-Bornemisza (Thyssen-Bornemisza Museum) includes much of the best of Western art produced in the

The majestic Palacio Real (Royal Palace) was built in the 18th century

last 800 years. It contains around 2,000 works, all acquired since the 1920s by Baron Heinrich and his son, Baron Hans-Heinrich Thyssen-Bornemisza. The Carmen Thyssen-Bornemisza Collection was incorporated in 2004.

Western paintings from the 13th to 20th centuries are arranged chronologically, so start on the top floor and work down. Early portraits and Renaissance works are grouped together, followed by Dutch interiors. Nineteenth-century American paintings feature a portrait of George Washington's cook by Gilbert Stuart and a sea scene by Winslow Homer. The 20th century is well represented by Joan Miró, Salvador Dalí and Mark Rothko. Expressionist artists include German Otto Kirchner and Norwegian Edvard Munch.

🚼 D2 ✉ Paseo del Prado 8 ☎ 90 276 0511; www.museothyssen.org 🕐 Mon. noon–4 p.m., Tue.–Sun. 10–7. Temporary exhibitions until 9 p.m. on Sat. 🚇 Banco de España 🍴 Café and restaurant 🎟 $$$; free Mon. 12–4 p.m. Fee for some exhibitions

Palacio Real

The vast white bulk of the Palacio Real (Royal Palace) looks striking from the Campo del Moro, a peaceful garden behind the palace. After a fire destroyed the Moorish original, the palace was planned to be three times its existing size. In the 18th century, architect Francisco Sabatini began to rebuild and extend the palace. Funds ran out, and the present structure was completed in 1764. The palace was in full use until 1931, and is now occasionally used for state receptions. The entrance fee includes the Armory and the Royal Pharmacy.

The 1993 Cathedral of the Almudena nearby offers panoramic views from its vast dome; the Plaza de Oriente is a grand, café-lined square across the road, home to the Teatro Real (Opera Theater).

🚼 B2 ✉ Calle Bailén ☎ 91 454 8700; www. patrimonionacional.es 🕐 Daily 10–8, Apr.–Sep.; 10–6, rest of year. Closed during official events 🚇 Ópera 🎟 $$$ (free to E.U. citizens on Wed. and Thu. 4–6 p.m., Oct.–Mar.; Wed. and Thu. 6–8 p.m., rest of year)

Parque del Retiro

The Parque del Retiro was laid out in the 1630s as part of the French-style pleasure gardens surrounding the Buen Retiro Palace. The building itself was destroyed during the Napoleonic Wars. Today the park is bright with flowers. Many people head for the lake, with its

Relaxing under the shady parasols of a café in the stunning Plaza Mayor

statue of Alfonso XII; other attractions include the Palacio de Cristal (Crystal Palace), a 19th-century glass palace.

A wood, the Bosque de Recuerdo, was laid out in memory of victims of the 2004 bomb attack on Madrid.

🚩 E1 ✉ Main entrance: Plaza de la Independencia 🕐 Daily dawn–dusk 🚇 Retiro or Ibiza 💷 Free

Plaza Mayor

One of Europe's most dazzling squares, the present Plaza Mayor (Main Square) stands on the site of the medieval market, the Plaza del Arrabal (Outskirts Square), so called because it was outside the city walls. When Madrid became Spain's capital, Philip III ordered it to be rebuilt as the focal point. It was completed in 1620, although it took on its current form in the 18th century to designs by the celebrated architect Juan de Villaneuva. The plaza was used for fiestas, bullfights and proclamations, and was also the scene of executions during the later days of the Inquisition.

🚩 B2 ✉ Plaza Mayor 🚇 Sol

Plaza de Toros Monumental de las Ventas

Madrid's Las Ventas Bullring was opened in 1934, and for bullfighting aficionados it is the most important bullring in the world. A small museum, the Museo Taurino, is dedicated to the sport.

🚩 Off map at E3 ✉ Alcalá, 237 Plaza de las Ventas ☎ 913 562 200; www.las-ventas.com 🚇 Ventas 🕐 Bullring: guided tours in English daily 10–6 ($$$). For information ☎ 68 773 9032 or go online at www. lasventastour.com or at info@lasventastour.com

Museum: Mon.–Fri. 9:30–2:30, Sun. and public holidays, Mar.–Oct. 10 a.m.–1 p.m. (free) 💷 Tickets for bullfights $$$. Museum free

Plaza de la Villa

The three different, main stone buildings around this plaza (Town Square) coexist harmoniously. The Gothic Torre de los Lujanes (Lujanes Tower), a 15th-century structure, is balanced by the Casa de Cisneros, a restored 1537 Plateresque-style palace. The Casa Consistorial was the meeting place for the town council from 1640 until 2008.

🚩 B2 ✉ Plaza de la Villa 🕐 Buildings: guided tour ($$) Mon. at 5 p.m. 🚇 Sol or Ópera ℹ Reserve tours at Centro de Turismo, Plaza Mayor 27, or check online www.esmadrid.com

Puerta del Sol

Puerta del Sol has been a plaza since 1570, when the original gate was demolished. The headquarters of the regional government are housed on the south side, where a stone in the sidewalk marks Kilometer Zero, from which all distances in Spain are measured.

🚩 C2 ✉ Puerta del Sol 🚇 Sol

Real Jardín Botánico

Established in 1755, these beautiful botanic gardens display a wealth of exotic plants in elegantly manicured beds and handsome 18th- and 19th-century greenhouses. Shady nooks provide perfect picnic spots.

🚩 D1 ✉ Plaza de Murillo 2 ☎ 91 420 3017; www.rjb.csic.es 🚇 Atocha 🚌 10, 14, 27, 34, 37, 45 💷 $$ ℹ Guided visits available

Monasterio de El Escorial

Twenty-five miles northwest of Madrid, on the southern slopes of the Sierra da Guadarrama mountain range, stands the massive religious complex known as El Escorial, which can be visited on a day trip by train or tour bus. One of the most impressive monuments in Spain, the complex is easily accessible from Madrid and gives true insight into the extraordinary wealth and power of the 16th-century Spanish monarchy.

In 1557 the Spanish forces of Philip II defeated the French at St. Quentin. To give thanks to God, Philip conceived the idea of building a monastery dedicated to St. Lawrence (San Lorenzo), which would also serve as a royal palace and burial place. The vast complex was principally designed in 1584 by the architect Juan de Herrera, and it took 1,500 laborers to complete the work. It has more than 1,200 doors, 2,600 windows and 16 courtyards, and is nearly 670 feet long. The granite stone accentuates the severe lines of the building, which is built on a grid plan. The clear air has kept the stone and tiles pristine. Later Bourbon monarchs left their stamp on the palace through decoration, furnishings and pictures.

El Escorial Today

Philip II's modest private apartments contrast with his throne room. He lived in a suite of small rooms with direct access to the chapel.

Later Bourbon monarchs extended these impressive royal Habsburg apartments near the church to the third floor. You will find sumptuously painted ceilings, frescoes and a wonderful tapestry collection. A frescoed courtyard gives access to the marbled staircase leading down to the Royal Pantheon (Pantéon de los Reyes), where virtually all of the Spanish kings and queens from the time of Charles V onward are buried.

The church itself is on a monumental scale. Its 100-foot-high altarpiece with onyx, marble and jasper columns is punctuated by bronze sculptures. Move on to the equally opulent library, with its shelves made from rare types of wood, and with marble tables and ornate ceiling.

One of the highlights is the art museum. Among numerous paintings by Peter Paul Rubens, Titian and Jacopo Tintoretto are Rogíer van der Weyden's thought-provoking *Calvary* and the acidic angularity of El Greco's *Martyrdom of St. Maurice*.

✚ C3 ✉ El Escorial ☎ 91 890 5903 🕐 Tue.–Sun. 10–8, Apr.–Sep.; 10–6, rest of year. Closes for official events 🚉 Trains from Atocha, train line C8 (☎ 90 232 0320) 🚌 Autobuses Herranz (☎ 91 896 9028); buses 661 and 664 leave from the terminus at Madrid's Moncloa subway station 💵 $$$

The harmonious facade of El Escorial stretches for almost 670 feet

Barcelona

Barcelona, the capital of the autonomous Spanish region of Catalonia (Catalunya), is one of the Mediterranean's most vibrant cities. Catalonia is the most innovative and prosperous area of Spain, with a proud history, an independent spirit and a strong sense of identity.

In 1975, the then King Juan Carlos restored Catalonia's status as an autonomous region, which marked the beginning of Barcelona's renaissance. The pride and self-confidence engendered by a thriving economy and urban renewal culminated in the Barcelona Olympic Games of 1992. Since then, the city has continued to forge ahead. With its 2,000-year-old history, exhilarating atmosphere and superb architecture, it can't fail to please.

The City and Its People

Wherever you stay, the excellent public transportation system gives easy access to the entire city. For atmosphere, stay somewhere near the avenue La Rambla (see page 416) or in the old town, and thus within easy walking distance of many of the main sights and the waterfront. The architecturally interesting L'Eixample area is more spacious, with excellent shopping and restaurants, and there are plenty of hotels close to the beaches. Barcelonins are exceptionally helpful and polite, with an ability to combine efficiency with a relaxed Mediterranean attitude.

English is not widely spoken, although most hotel staff speak it adequately. There are two official languages in Catalonia: Spanish and Catalan, which are both Romance languages with Latin roots. Catalan is widely spoken, and street signs are exclusively in Catalan.

Barcelonan Themes

Since there's so much to see in Barcelona, concentrate on specific areas and themes. Spend a day on the waterfront taking in the Old Port

(Port Vell, see page 416) district, La Barceloneta (see page 413) and the ultra-modern Olympic Port (Port Olímpic). There's a choice of boat tours around the harbor and up the coast, which is the best way to admire the port.

Head for l'Eixample (see pages 413–414), the Passeig de Gràcia and the Sagrada Família (see page 416) to enjoy the fabulous Modernista architecture for which the city is renowned. Barcelona is blessed with two hills, Montjuïc and Tibidabo; each offers a refuge from the summer noise and heat and has magnificent views over the city.

Barcelona has more than 50 museums and galleries. The Maritime Museum, (MNAC), the Pedralbes Monastery, the F.C. Barça Museum (Museu F.C. Barcelona, see page 415), the Barcelona City History Museum (Museu d'Història de Barcelona, see page 415), the Picasso Museum (Museu Picasso, see page 415) and Joan Miró Foundation (Fundació Joan Miró, see page 414) cater to a wide range of interests, and are all fascinating.

If time is short, there are plenty of English-language guided tours and excursions that take in the main city sights by day and night, and also offer a chance to explore some of the other parts of Catalonia.

Gaudí

Antoni Gaudí was born in Barcelona in 1852, and lived and worked in the city throughout his life. His architectural vision was unique and flamboyant, and guided by the premise that there are no straight lines in nature, he designed some of Barcelona's most outstanding Modernist buildings. Curved lines, pinnacles, organically inspired stone and towers are his trademarks, seen at their best in the remarkable Holy Family Temple (Temple Expiatori de la Sagrada Família, see page 416). He was run over by a tram in 1926 and died, unrecognized, in hospital. When his body was identified, the people of Barcelona lined the streets for his funeral.

Parks and Pools

Barcelona is rich in relaxing parks. The Parc de la Ciutadella, near the Old Town and waterfront, is a haven of tranquility with shady trees, a lake and Spain's best zoo and is a great place for a picnic.

Other parks in the city include Parc Güell (see page 416), with its ceramic sculpture, and several green, flower-filled gardens on the slopes of Montjuïc. Good beaches are within easy reach, and the city also has excellent public swimming pools.

Where to Shop

Prosperous Barcelona is a great shopping center. You'll find serious shopping along the Passeig de Gràcia and on its surrounding streets, which have all the big fashion names, expensive antiques stores and enticing interior design outlets. The wide avenue of Diagonal is lined with upscale stores, while the Plaça de Catalunya has a large branch of the department store El Corte Inglés.

For Spanish souvenirs, try the stores in Portal de l'Àngel and La Rambla. For the latest fashions and interior design head to the Born area. Mercat dels Encants is an antiques and secondhand market held on the Plaça de les Glòries on Monday, Wednesday, Friday and Saturday (7–6).

Nightlife

Classical music, jazz, rock, dance, theater and movies are popular forms of entertainment; there are comprehensive

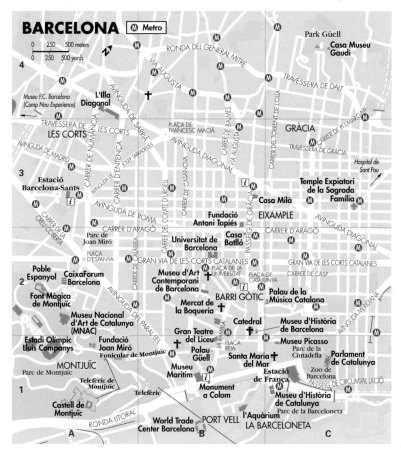

412

listings in the *Guía del Ocio* and *Time Out*, both available from newsstands. Dancing is very popular, and the club scene is one of the best in Spain, ranging from the elegant to the avant-garde. Nightlife reaches its peak around 2 a.m. and continues until dawn.

Barcelona has some superb festivals throughout the year, often featuring decorated floats, fireworks and processions of dragon and demon figures known as *capgrossos*, or "big heads." The biggest and best festival is La Mercè at the end of September.

The Three Graces fountain on Plaça Reial

Essential Information

Tourist Information
Barcelona Turisme (Barcelona Tourism)
Plaça de Catalunya 17-S
Plaça Sant Jaume
Estació Barcelona-Sants (railroad station)
Barcelona Airport (terminals 1 and 2B)
☎ For all inquiries: 93 285 3834
www.barcelonaturisme.com (also online shop)

Urban Transportation
Getting around is easy on the metro (subway) and bus systems. Metro stations are marked on the Barcelona city map by the letter "M" in a red circle. There are 11 color-coded lines on the metro; trains run Mon.–Thu. 5 a.m.–midnight, Fri. 5 a.m.–2 a.m., Sat. 24 hrs, Sun. 6 a.m.–midnight. The T10 ticket offers 10 rides on metro, trains and buses. Combination tourist tickets valid for 1, 2, 3, 4 or 5 days give unlimited use of the bus, tram, metro and urban trains; tickets and maps are available from metro stations. Validate tickets by stamping them at the turnstile before boarding trains, or on the bus or tram. Bus Turístic operates daily 9–8 (in summer), 9–7 (in winter)

and has two routes, plus a summer-only route, that take you close to Barcelona's main attractions. A cable car links La Barceloneta and Montjuïc, and there are two funiculars, serving Montjuïc and Tibidabo; the latter also is served by antique tram. Pick up a black-and-yellow taxi at a stand, hail one on the street, or call Radio Taxi (☎ 93 303 3033).

Airport Information
Barcelona International Airport (☎ 902 404 704) connects to most major European cities and is 11 miles southwest of the city center, about a 20-minute drive. A train connects to Estació Barcelona-Sants and Passeig de Gràcia station, daily 5:13 a.m.–11.14 p.m. (5:42 a.m.–11:38 p.m. from the airport); journey time 20 minutes. The Aerobús bus service departs from the Plaça de Catalunya from 5:30 a.m.–12:30 a.m. (A1 service for Terminal 1, A2 service for Terminal 2). Return services depart from Terminal 1 for the Plaça de Catalunya from 5:35 a.m.–1:35 a.m. (A1) and from Terminal 2 from 6 a.m.–1 a.m. (A2). Shuttle buses link the two airport terminals.

Climate – average highs and lows for the month

Jan.	Feb.	Mar.	Apr.	May	Jun.	Jul.	Aug.	Sep.	Oct.	Nov.	Dec.
13°C	14°C	15°C	17°C	21°C	24°C	28°C	28°C	25°C	21°C	17°C	14°C
55°F	57°F	59°F	63°F	70°F	75°F	82°F	82°F	77°F	70°F	63°F	57°F
5°C	6°C	8°C	10°C	12°C	17°C	20°C	20°C	19°C	13°C	9°C	8°C
41°F	43°F	46°F	50°F	54°F	63°F	68°F	68°F	66°F	55°F	48°F	46°F

Barcelona Sights

Key to symbols
🚩 map coordinates refer to the Barcelona map on page 411 💵 admission charge: $$$ more than €6, $$ €3–€6, $ less than €3
See page 5 for complete key to symbols

The Passion Facade of the Sagrada Família

La Barceloneta

The district of La Barceloneta (Little Barcelona) occupies a triangle of reclaimed land between the harbor and the sea. Developed in the 18th century to house seamen, fishermen and dockworkers, this delightful neighborhood retains its maritime atmosphere. This is a great place to eat at the many seafood restaurants.

🚩 C1 ✉ La Barceloneta 🚇 Barceloneta
🚌 17, 39, 45, 57, 64, D20

Barri Gòtic

A maze of narrow streets and squares make up this area, built within the old Roman walls when Barcelona was one of the richest and most important Mediterranean trading cities. At its heart the Barri Gòtic (Gothic Quarter) is centered around the Catedral and Plaça Sant Jaume. This plaza, once the power center of Catalonia's kings, is still the site of the city hall and buildings of the government of Catalonia. The Plaça del Rei, formerly the medieval marketplace, is said to be where King Ferdinand and Queen Isabella welcomed Christopher Columbus home from America in 1493. Nearby is the Plaça Reial, an arcaded square built in 1848. Gothic mansions line the streets, and you'll find museums, churches and plenty of bars and restaurants.

🚩 B2 ✉ Bounded by Rambla, Universitat, Laietana and Ferran 🚇 Jaume I 🚌 14, 17, 19, 45, 59, V19
🍴 Rasoterra, see page 489

Catedral

Nothing more strongly represents Barcelona's historic past than the great Catedral (Cathedral). It was built between the 13th and 15th centuries (with a 19th-century neo-Gothic facade), and the soaring space beneath the Catalan Gothic arches and numerous side chapels houses a wealth of treasures. The tranquil 14th-century cloister is beautiful.

🚩 B2 ✉ Plaça de la Seu ☎ 93 342 8262; www. catedralbcn.org 🕐 Church: daily 8 a.m.–12:45 p.m. and 5:45–7:30 p.m. Cloister 8:30 a.m.–12:30 p.m. and 5–7 p.m. Museum: 10 a.m.–12:30 p.m. and 5:45–7 p.m.
🚇 Jaume I 🚌 17, 19, 40, 45 💵 Cathedral $$ (Mon.–Sat. 1–5, Sun. 2–5), all other times for worship by donation; roof $; choir $; museum $

Eixample

Between 1860 and 1920 Barcelona expanded into a grid of uniform streets parallel to the sea, an area known as l'Eixample (the Extension). Today this is a residential, commercial and business district, divided in half by the Diagonal, a grand avenue cutting through the grid at a 45-degree angle.

An interesting example of innovative town planning, it contains Barcelona's finest Modernist buildings (see page 417). Some of the best are in the Passeig de Gràcia; look for No. 43, Gaudí's Casa

Ventilation chimneys on the roof of Casa Milà, also known as La Pedrera and designed by Antoni Gaudí

Batlló, with a mosaic facade and wavy roofline that represent St. George's dragon. The block at No. 92 is Casa Milà, known as La Pedrera, Gaudí's last secular work, built without one straight line or sharp corner (see page 417).

➕ C3 🚇 Diagonal, Catalunya or Passeig de Gràcia

Fundació Joan Miró

More than 10,000 vibrantly colored paintings, along with sculptures, tapestries and drawings, are gathered in the white, bright space of the Fundació Joan Miró (Joan Miró Foundation).

Born in Barcelona in 1893, Miró spent most of his life in the city before retiring to Mallorca in 1956. In 1971 he established the foundation to house the largest collection of his works and to promote contemporary art.

➕ A1 ✉ Avenida Miramar, Parc de Montjuïc
☎ 93 443 9470; www.fundaciomiro-bcn.org
🕐 Tue.–Sat. 10–8 (also Thu. 8–9:30 p.m.), Sun. 10–2:30, Jul.–Sep.; Tue.–Sat. 10–7 (also Thu. 7–9:30 p.m.), Sun. 10–2:30, rest of year 🚇 Espanya 🚌 55, 150; Montjuïc funicular from metro station Paral.lel
🍴 Café in museum 💶 $$$

Mercat de la Boquería

Make time to visit the glorious Mercat de la Boquería (Boquería Market), housed since the 1830s in a covered hall just off La Rambla. Memories of the

scents and colors of the fish, hams, freshly picked fruit and vegetables, and the babble of noise from the area will stay with you forever. At lunchtime, take advantage of the many snack bars.

➕ B2 ✉ Plaça de la Boqueria ☎ 93 318 2584
🕐 Mon.–Sat. 8 a.m.–8:30 p.m. Note: many stalls close earlier and fish stalls closed on Mon. 🚇 Liceu
🚌 14, 59, 91

Montjuïc

The green hill of Montjuïc, 698 feet high, dominates Barcelona's southern suburbs. It is a pleasant recreational area, dotted with gardens, museums and various sports facilities. The most impressive approach is through the monumental Plaça d'Espanya and the Font Màgica (Magic Fountain). The fountain stands below the pavilions, built for the 1929 International Exhibition on the avenue linking it to Plaça d'Espanya.

Also here is the 1992 Olympic complex, the Anella Olimpica.

➕ A1 ✉ Montjuïc 🕐 Font Màgica displays: Thu.–Sun. 9–11 p.m. (show finishes at 11:30 p.m.), Apr.–Sep.; Fri.–Sat. 7–8:30 p.m. (show finishes at 9 p.m.), rest of year. Closed six weeks in Jan. and Feb.
🚇 Subway to Paral.lel station, then funicular to Parc de Montjuïc and the *telefèric* cable car to Mirador and Castell; subway to Espanya for fountains 🚌 55, 150; all buses to Plaça d'Espanya for Font Màgica

Museu F.C. Barcelona (Camp Nou Experience)

F.C. Barcelona is one of the most popular and successful soccer teams in the world, with a massive international following. This museum celebrates the club's achievements with video footage of match highlights, displays of trophies and a visitor's book inscribed with the names of illustrious fans. A visit includes a tour of the Camp Nou stadium.

Off map at A4 Camp Nou, Avenida Aristides Maillol s/n 90 218 9900; www.fcbarcelona.com Mon.–Sat. 9:30–7:30, Sun. 10–2:30, Apr. to mid-Oct.; Mon.–Sat. 10:30–6:30, Sun. 10–2:30, rest of year. Hours reduced on match days Les Corts 54, H10 $$$

Museu d'Història de Barcelona

Barcelona's fascinating City History Museum covers more than two millennia of history. It is built above the subterranean ruins of Roman Barcino, where you can still walk along ancient roads rutted by cart wheels, and admire the faded remnants of original mosaics. Above ground, the visit continues in the magnificent Saló del Tinell, a Gothic throne room spanned by vast stone arches. This is where Isabella and Ferdinand received Columbus after his second transatlantic voyage. Adjoining the throne room is the Capella de Santa Àgata, a dainty Gothic chapel built in 1302, which is dedicated to St. Agatha.

B2–C2 Plaça del Rei s/n 93 256 21 00; http://.museuhistoria.bcn.cat Tue.–Sat. 10–7, Sun. 10–8 Jaume I or Liceu 45, 120, V17 $$ (free Sun. 3–8 p.m.)

Museu Nacional d'Art de Catalunya (MNAC)

The National Museum of Catalonian Art contains a vast collection, spanning more than a millennium. The highlight is the medieval art collection, one of the finest in the world. Catalan Romanesque art, with its solid rounded forms and stunning simplicity, is represented by sculpture and carving, gold, enamel and textiles. The outstanding treasures are the 11th- and 12th-century murals, from isolated country churches. The superb Gothic collection features ornately gilded paintings and altarpieces, while the Modernista section displays furnishings by Gaudí as well as artwork. These collections are compemented by the Thyssen-Bornemisza bequest of about 100 masterworks by Fra Angelico, Raphael and Titian, among others.

The rooftop terrace offers superb city views ($).

A2 Palau Nacional, Parc de Montjuïc 93 622 0376; www.mnac.cat Tue.–Sat. 10–8, Sun. 10–3, May–Sep.; Tue.–Sat. 10–6, Sun. 10–3, rest of year Espanya 13, 55, 150 Museum café and restaurant $$$ (free for seniors and free first Sun. of the month); guided tours by appointment

Museu Picasso

Pablo Picasso, born in Andalucia in 1881, lived in Barcelona from 1895 until 1904, and he held his first exhibition in the city in 1900. The Picasso Museum is the most important collection of his early works in Spain. Set in five splendid palaces, it also hosts temporary exhibitions.

C1 Calle Montcada 15–23 93 256 3000; www.museupicasso.bcn.cat Tue.–Sun. 10–8 Jaume I 17, 40, 45, 120, V17 Café $$ (free first Sun. of the month, and Thu. 7–9 p.m. in Jan. and Feb.) Guided tours Sun. at 11 a.m. by reservation

A series of unique tiles in Parc Güell by Jujol, one of Gaudí's main collaborators

Park Güell

Güell Park has architectural elements by
Antoni Gaudí scattered across its 50
acres. Planned as a residential
landscaped area by Gaudí's main
patrons, the Güell family, only the grand
entrance, the plaza, the paths and the
steps were completed. These are
interspersed with sculptures, fountains
and columns, many decorated with tiny
pieces of colorful broken ceramics
(*trencadís*). Inside the park is the Casa
Museu Gaudí (tel: 93 219 3811
www.casamuseugaudi.org; open daily
10–8, Mar.–Oct.; 10–6, rest of year; $$).
➕ C4 ✉ Calle Olot s/n ☎ 90 220 0302; www.
parkguell.cat ⏱ Daily 8 a.m.–9 p.m., May–early Sep.;
8–8, late Mar.–early May; 8:30-6:15, late Oct.–late Mar.
Ⓜ Vallcarca, Lesseps 🚌 24, 32, 92, H6 🎫 $$$
(admission fee is for the Monumental Area which
includes the most important elements by Gaudí; timed
ticket only); rest of park free

Poble Espanyol

The streets and squares of the Spanish
Village, built for the 1929 World
Exhibition, give a glimpse of the
country's many architectural styles.
Buildings range from the white houses
of Andalucia to the flat granite facades of
Galicia, and house workshops where
you'll find crafts and artifacts from all
over Spain. In summer, stores stay open
into the evening when there is also live
music and flamenco.
➕ A2 ✉ Avenida de Marquès de Comillas ☎ 93 508
6300 ⏱ Daily 9–8. Bars and clubs are open late
Ⓜ Espanya 🚌 13, 23, 150 🎫 $$$

Port Vell

The Port Vell (Old Port) district, once
run-down, was transformed for the 1992
Olympics. An integral part of the city
again, it is a busy recreation area, with a
modern marina and elegant bridges and
walkways connecting its attractions. The
centerpiece is Maremagnum, a shopping
and leisure center, with an aquarium with
a glass-walled "walk through" tunnel.
➕ B1 ✉ Port Vell Ⓜ Drassanes or Barceloneta
🚌 14, 59, 64, D20, H14, V17

La Rambla

La Rambla, Barcelona's most famous
street, runs from Plaça de Catalunya to
the waterfront. It's an exuberant
tree-lined promenade effectively joining
the old and new parts of the city. The
name Rambla is Arabic, from *ramla*,
"a torrent," a reminder that the street
follows an old watercourse. Here is the
Liceu opera house, restored after a fire
in 1994. From here head to the statue of
Christopher Columbus on a 164-foot
iron plinth near the waterfront; take the
elevator to an observation deck.
➕ B1–B2 ✉ La Rambla Ⓜ Catalunya, Drassanes or
Liceu 🚌 14, 59, 91

Santa Maria del Mar

Built between 1329 and 1384 at the
height of Barcelona's medieval prestige,
the beautiful Gothic church of Santa
Maria del Mar (Our Lady of the Sea) is
tucked away in the Ribera district. Its
stark, serene interior allows the elegant
architecture to speak for itself.
➕ C1 ✉ Plaça de Santa Maria ☎ 93 310 2390
⏱ Daily 9–1:30 and 4:30–8 Ⓜ Jaume I 🚌 45, 120,
V15, V17

Temple Expiatori de la Sagrada
Família

The famous Catalan Modernist architect
Antoni Gaudí worked on the Temple
Expiatori de la Sagrada Família
(Expiatory Temple to the Holy Family)
for over 40 years. He envisioned a vast
cathedral, with facades to show the
birth, death and resurrection of Christ,
and 18 towers to represent the Twelve
Apostles, the Four Evangelists, the
Virgin and Christ. At his death in 1926
only the Nativity Facade, the crypt and
one of the towers was complete. In 2010
Pope Benedict XVI consecrated the
as-yet-unfinished temple. The plan is to
finish this magnificent building by 2026.
➕ C3 ✉ Plaça de la Sagrada Família ☎ 93 513
2060; www.sagradafamilia.cat ⏱ Daily 9–8, Apr.–
Sep.; 9–7, Oct. and Mar.; 9–6, Nov.–Feb. Ⓜ Sagrada
Família 🚌 19, 33, 34, 43, 44, 50, 51, B20, B24 🎫 $$$;
guided tours $$ ℹ Reserve online to avoid lines

Modernista Highlights

At the turn of the 20th century, Barcelona's streets bloomed with extraordinary buildings created in the newly fashionable Modernista style. Chief among the style's proponents was Antoni Gaudí, but fellow architect, Domènech i Montaner, also created some iconic buildings. Most of the buildings are open to visit and have become top attractions.

Casa Milà (1906–1910)

Gaudí's creation, the Casa Milà, was quickly nicknamed "La Pedrera" (the stone quarry) for its creamy, undulating and apparently unfinished facade, which was quite unlike anything ever seen before. One of the apartments has been carefully restored, and the building is crowned by a rippling rooftop terrace. Summer nights see jazz concerts held on the roof.

🚇 B3 ✉ Carrer Provença 261–265 ☎ 90 220 2138; www.lapedrera.com

Casa Batlló (1904–1906)

The Casa Batlló is a fairy-tale mansion with a shimmering tiled facade and wrought-iron balconies of intricate delicacy. Inside, the staircase culminates in a curving, tiled roof which is said to resemble a dragon's scaly back. In summer there are concerts and cocktails on the terrace.

🚇 B2 ✉ Passeig de Gràcia 43 ☎ 93 216 0306; www.casabatllo.es

Palau Güell (1900–1914)

This mansion was Gaudí's first important commission for Eusebi Güell, who became the architect's most committed patron. Less playful than Gaudí's later designs, it displays his ingenuity with light and curves.

🚇 B1 ✉ Carrer Nou de la Rambla 88 ☎ 93 472 5775; http://palauguell.cat

Hospital de Sant Pau (1901–1930)

A masterpiece by Montaner, this renovated former hospital complex now has extravagantly decorated and graceful pavilions set in fine gardens. The pavilions were once linked by underground passages.

🚇 Off map at C3 ✉ Carrer Sant Antoni Maria Claret ☎ 93 556 5577; www.santpaubarcelona.org

Palau de la Música Catalana (1905–1908)

This sumptuous concert hall by Domènech i Montaner erupts from the dark streets of the medieval city centre. The main concert hall (pictured below) is lit by a vast stained-glass ceiling with an inverted dome, and dominated by a stage in which Valkyries erupt from the arch.

🚇 C2 ✉ Carrer Palau de la Música 4–6 ☎ 93 295 7200; www.palaudelamusica.org

Santiago de Compostela

Tucked away in the green fringes of Galicia, in northwest Spain, is the beautiful granite city of Santiago de Compostela – one of the great shrines of medieval Christendom. Millions of pilgrims braved hazardous journeys to worship at the shrine of St. James, the patron saint of Spain. People still come here on pilgrimages, especially during holy years, which occur when St. James' Day (July 25) falls on a Sunday.

Santiago is a perfect medieval city – a mix of religious and secular buildings, with an ancient and thriving university and a unique spiritual atmosphere. It is also home to the parliament of Galicia, which is an autonomous region, and there is a lively and prosperous modern town surrounding the central core.

Old Santiago

The historic heart is pedestrian-only and can be traversed on foot in less than a half-hour; everything you'll want to see lies within this small area. Santiago offers quality, not quantity, so most visitors find a stay of a few days ample.

The two main streets, Rúa do Franco and Rúa do Vilar, lead south from the cathedral square and are lined with bustling stores, bars and restaurants. Pick up a map at the tourist office; it's easy to lose your bearings.

Santiago Flavors

Galician cooking is delicious and relies on the excellent quality of local ingredients. Seafood and shellfish are extensively farmed in the *rias*, deeply indented coastal inlets, and are of superb quality. Regional specialties include *pulpo* (octopus) cooked in various ways; blood puddings and sausages; and *empanadas*, flat pies with a meat or fish filling. Local lamb and beef are particularly good. Santiago has many pastry shops, where you'll find wonderful cakes and cookies.

Galicia produces excellent wines, including the *albariños* from the D.O.

Baixas, and the lesser known, but much praised reds from the D.O. Ribeira Sacrá. If the weather's cold, try a cup of hot chocolate; thick enough to eat, it's some of the best in Spain.

Souvenirs and Entertainment

Santiago's streets are lined with stores selling all types of pilgrim souvenirs – medals, rosaries, key rings, holy pictures and statues, many decorated with the image of St. James and his scallop shell emblem. The traditional material for pilgrimage souvenirs is jet, polished and cut, or fashioned into the *figa*, a clenched-fist amulet. The guild of silversmiths, hugely important in the past, is still active and makes fine pieces.

This is a university town with a thriving cultural life, and there are year-round classical concerts, as well as the clubs frequented by students. You'll often hear bagpipes, Galicia's national instrument, played on the streets; this is a favorite way for students to make extra cash to pay their way through university.

Santiago Festivals

Santiago's biggest festival is on July 25, the Fiesta de Santiago (feast of St. James), when the city is packed with pilgrims, tourists and local people. The night before sees the Fuego del Apóstol (Apostle's Fire), a spectacular fireworks display in front of the cathedral (detail picture opposite). The feast itself represents a solemn Mass, with music, choirs and Galician bagpipes. The huge incense burner, the *botafumeiro*, is swung in the cathedral. The feast falls in the middle of Santiago's folklore festival, a two-week celebration of Galician culture, with street music, parades, concerts and markets. An international music festival is held in July and draws crowds from across Europe.

Essential Information

Tourist Information
Turismo de Santiago
Rúa do Vilar 63 ☎ 98 155 5129
Airport ☎ 98 189 7194;
Pilgrim Information office, Rúa do Vilar 1,
☎ 98 156 8846
www.santiagoturismo.com

Urban Transportation
Santiago's historic center is pedestrian-only; vehicular access is for taxis and delivery vehicles. It takes 15 to 20 minutes to walk from one end of the center to the other, and most sights and hotels are within this area. If you are staying outside the historic center, take a taxi to the edge of the old town and

then walk. Taxis can be found at stands outside the old city, or call Radio Taxi (24 hours) ☎ 98 156 9292). Eurotaxis (☎ 61 990 3024) operate wheelchair-adapted taxis.

Airport Information
Santiago-Lavacolla International Airport (☎ 902 404 704), with services to many European cities, is 7 miles east of the city, about a 15- to 30-minute drive. Buses into Santiago run every 30 minutes from the terminal, daily 7 a.m.–1 a.m. (travel time 30 minutes). Buses run from the bus station and several other central stops to the airport from 6 a.m.–midnight. Taxis also leave from the terminal.

Climate – average highs and lows for the month

Jan.	Feb.	Mar.	Apr.	May	Jun.	Jul.	Aug.	Sep.	Oct.	Nov.	Dec.
13°C	14°C	15°C	17°C	19°C	22°C	25°C	25°C	24°C	20°C	17°C	14°C
55°F	57°F	59°F	63°F	66°F	72°F	77°F	77°F	75°F	68°F	63°F	57°F
5°C	6°C	7°C	8°C	10°C	14°C	16°C	16°C	14°C	12°C	9°C	7°C
41°F	43°F	45°F	46°F	50°F	57°F	61°F	61°F	57°F	54°F	48°F	45°F

Santiago de Compostela Sights

Key to symbols

➕ map coordinates refer to the Santiago map on page 418 🎟 admission charge: $$$ more than €6, $$ €3–€6, $ less than €3

See page 5 for complete key to symbols

Barrio Antiguo

The Barrio Antiguo (Old Quarter) of Santiago is packed with beautiful, historic buildings. The main streets are lined with arcaded old granite houses in the traditional Galician style.

East of the cathedral, the spacious Praza da Quintana is surrounded by notable buildings, including the arcaded Casa da Conga (Canon's Residence). This faces a gracious flight of steps leading up to the 17th-century Casa da Parra (House of the Bunch of Grapes). On the third side is the austere facade of San Paio de Antealtares Monastery, founded in the ninth century. Opposite, the Puerta del Perdón (Door of Pardon) opens onto the east end of the cathedral – this is only used during holy years. On the cathedral's north side stands the huge complex of the Monasterio de San Martín Pinario, with its church and three cloisters. Behind the monastery lies the 17th-century Convento de San Francisco, commemorating a pilgrimage by St. Francis of Assisi in 1213. It is now a museum devoted to the Holy Land and incorporates a hotel.

➕ A2–B2 ✉ Barrio Antiguo

Catedral

The present Catedral (Cathedral) dates from the 11th to 13th centuries. The simple Romanesque lines of the interior provide a superb contrast to the ornate facade, added in 1750, at the cathedral's main entrance. Here stands the 12th-century triple doorway known as the Pórtico da Glória (Doorway of Glory), one of the sculptural marvels of Spain. Prophets and Apostles surround Christ the Savior and the Four Evangelists, all carved with exceptional imagination and fluidity. Behind the worn entrance pillar and the statue of St. James is a figure said to be Maestro Mateo, the cathedral's designer. It was customary to bump your head against his in the hope that some of his genius would rub off, but it's now protected.

You'll notice a pulley system high above the transept; this operates the *botafumeiro*, a monster incense burner used during major feasts, which requires eight men to swing it through a huge arc above the transept. The silverwork and gilded figures of the High Altar glitter under the lights of the candelabra.

➕ A2 ✉ Praza do Obradoiro ☎ 98 156 9327; www.catedraldesantiago.es 🕐 Daily 7 a.m.–8:30 p.m.; hours sometimes vary

Museo de las Peregrinacións

The Museo de las Peregrinacións (Pilgrimage Museum) tells the story of pilgrimage in general, and the Santiago pilgrimage in particular. Exhibits show how the cathedral and town grew around the apostle's tomb, how the routes west across Europe developed, what the pilgrims wore and how they traveled. There's a facsimile of the fascinating *Codex Calixtinus*, a 13th-century guide to the route, full of tips about travel and information about Santiago (the original is in the cathedral, but not on display). Look for the collection of souvenirs 14th-century pilgrims took home.

➕ B2 ✉ Praza das Praterías ☎ 98 156 6110; http://museos.xunta.es/es/peregrinacions 🕐 Tue.–Fri. 10–8, Sat. 10:30–1:30 and 5–8, Sun. 10:30–1:30 🎟 $

Museo do Pobo Galego

Santiago is more than a noted shrine, it's also one of the main towns in Galicia. The Museo do Pobo Galego (Museum of the Galician People), set in the old convent of San Domingo, explains

Galicia and the traditional way of life in this part of Spain. There are displays of pottery, costumes, tools, handicrafts and musical instruments, as well as exhibits on Galicia's dolmens, stone circles and hill forts. The museum's galleries encircle the 17th-century cloister; in one corner a superb staircase, with three intertwining flights of steps, rises through the building.

➕ B2 ✉ Rúa de San Domingo de Bonaval ☎ 981 583 620; www.museodopobo.es 🕐 Tue.–Sat. 10:30–2 and 4–7:30, Sun. 11–2 🍴 $$

Museo y Tesoro de la Catedral

The Museo y Tesoro de la Catedral (Cathedral Museum and Treasury) is housed around the magnificent 16th-century cloisters adjoining the cathedral. It also includes the Romanesque Old Cathedral (a crypt beneath the Pórtico da Glória) and the Chapel of San Fernando, which opens off the interior of the cathedral. In the latter you can see gem-encrusted gold crucifixes and statues still used for important feasts. The museum includes a fine collection of tapestries from the most prestigious workshops. The cloisters, a lovely blend of Castilian-Gothic and Renaissance architecture, are some of the largest in Spain. Stairs lead up to the gallery, completed in 1590, which offers a good vantage point over the cathedral square. The interesting building adjoining the left of the cathedral is the old Bishop's Palace.

➕ A2 ✉ Praza do Obradoiro ☎ 98 156 9327; www.catedraldesantiago.es 🕐 Daily 9–8, Apr.–Oct.; 10–8, Nov.–Mar. 🍴 $$

Praza do Obradoiro

The sweeping expanse of Praza do Obradoiro (Obradoiro Square), in front of the cathedral, is surrounded on its other sides by the Hostal Reyes Católicos (Hostel of the Catholic Monarchs), the Colegio de San Jerónimo (College of St. Jerome) and the Pazo de Raxoi, or Ayuntamiento (City Hall). The oldest building is the hostel (now the luxurious Hostal Reis Católicos, a *parador*, see page 489), originally founded by Ferdinand and Isabella as a pilgrims' lodging house. It has an elegantly plain facade centered by a superb Plateresque doorway. Inside, the building is laid out around four patios.

Across from the hostel is the college and its charming balcony, which dates mainly from the 17th century – although its doorway is 200 years younger. Facing the cathedral, the 18th-century City Hall seems to unite the whole ensemble.

➕ A2 ✉ Praza do Obradoiro

Santiago de Compostela

The baroque facade of La Catedral

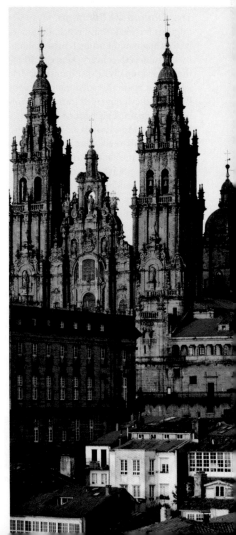

Spain

St. James and Santiago

To medieval Europeans, a pilgrimage *(peregrinación)* was a means of earning extra grace and thus attaining entry to heaven more quickly. Pilgrimages were made to many holy places, but the great goals were Jerusalem, Rome and Santiago de Compostela. The apostle St. James is known as "Sant Iago" in Spanish. The city which bears his name also is the site of his shrine and burial place. According to legend, he had preached in Spain before returning to martyrdom in Judea in AD 44. His disciples brought his body back to Spain, where it lay hidden until AD 844.

Legend tells that he appeared in a vision to Christian leaders and led them to victory against the Muslim invaders, earning him the title of *Matamoros*, the Moorslayer. His body and relics were rediscovered at Compostela, which became the center of devotion for Spain's new patron saint. By the 11th century, pilgrims arrived from all over Europe.

The *Camino de Santiago*

Pilgrims traveled from France, Britain, Germany, Italy and Scandinavia, as well as Spain and Portugal, many taking years to complete their journey. By the mid-12th century, between 500,000 and 2 million people were on the move annually, a vast number in relation to the total population.

Roads to Spain threaded their way across Europe, but once over the Pyrenees they converged into a well-organized network of routes across northern Spain. This became known as the *Camino de Santiago*, the Way of St. James. Administered by a religious military order, the *camino* was policed and marked along its length with hostels, inns and churches offering practical and spiritual sustenance to travelers. Towns grew up at the stopping points, with their own churches, hospitals and hospices.

Dressed in sandals and heavy capes and armed with stout staffs, pilgrims also wore the scallop shell emblem of the saint on their broad-brimmed hats. On arrival in Santiago, the custom was to enter the cathedral and embrace the golden effigy of the saint placed above his tomb, while giving alms and thanks in gratitude for the safe completion of the pilgrimage.

The *Camino* Today

Interest in walking the *camino* has varied over the centuries, but today thousands of people, locals and visitors alike, make the journey to Santiago on foot, as well as by car, train and plane. Those who complete the journey on foot, or by bicycle or horseback, and have fulfilled certain requirements, can receive a certificate called "La Compostela."

The Cathedral of St. James with its soaring towers dominates the city skyline

A Day in Santiago

A Spiritual Morning

Your first stop should be a visit to the excellent Pilgrimage Museum (Museo de las Peregrinacións, see page 420), where you can learn about the fascinating history of pilgrimage. It provides a sense of perspective and will pave the way for a visit to the cathedral, which should be next on the list. The worn stones of the entrance pillar show where pilgrims once touched them as a gesture on their arrival, but the stones are now protected and touching is no longer allowed.

Spend time admiring the architecture and artistic treasures, then join the line and mount the steps behind the altar to embrace the effigy of St. James, as pilgrims have done for more than 1,000 years. You could time your visit to coincide with the daily Pilgrims' Mass at noon.

A Secular Afternoon

Head up Rúa do Franco or Rúa do Vilar, Santiago's main streets, and choose one of the many restaurants for lunch – shellfish or octopus are both traditional Galician specialties. After lunch, you could head back toward the cathedral and visit the Museo y Tesoro de la Catedral (Cathedral Museum and Treasury, see page 421) before walking back across town to the Museo do Pobo Galego (Museum of the Galician People, see pages 420–421). At about 6 p.m. the streets begin to fill with shoppers and university students, and the bars become busy.

A Peaceful Evening

There's no problem finding an excellent restaurant for dinner; try some fish, such as bass, hake or turbot, or one of the flavorful Galician meat dishes, often pork-based, with potatoes and turnip tops. Be sure to order some of the local dome-shaped cheese, and finish with a slice of *tarta de Santiago*, a special almond pastry originally made only here. As you wander through the ancient streets after dinner, you'll probably hear the strains of bagpipes (*gaita* in Galician) echoing through some hidden courtyard. For the walking route, see the city map on page 418.

Restaurant terraces in Rúa San Clemente in Santiago de Compostela

Seville

Some of Spain's quintessential images are of whitewashed streets, Moorish architecture, flamenco dresses, orange trees and proud horsemen.

This mental picture actually reflects Andalucia and its capital, Seville (Sevilla). It is the fourth-largest city in Spain, the seat of a university founded in the early 16th century, an important industrial city and the center of a rich agricultural region.

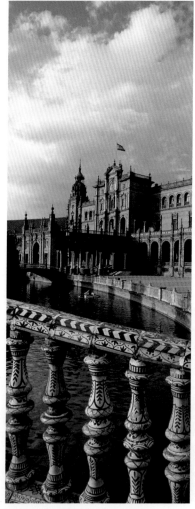

The Exposition building in Plaza de España

Renowned for architectural treasures, great festivals and a relaxed lifestyle, Seville has attracted visitors for many years, and cares for them far better than many other Spanish cities.

Seville on Foot

In Seville, every building, garden and street is designed as an escape from the sun. If you're visiting in summer, take lengthy siestas during the hottest hours. The central old core is relatively small, and you'll be able to walk to many of the main sights. The narrow, twisting streets can be confusing, so always take a city map with you; maps are free and available at the tourist office and many hotels. Blue-and-white signs direct visitors to the main sights. There's plenty of information in English, and helpful multilingual guides – often university students – offer assistance at all of the main attractions.

There's plenty to see in Seville besides the main attractions. The range of museums, fine churches and civic buildings attracts many visitors: the Casa de Pilatos, an elegant private palace, is a favorite. Also look for the Tobacco Factory (Fábrica de Tabacos), now part of the university but also where Carmen (of opera fame) worked.

Walking is only one option. Visitors can take an open-carriage drive from outside the cathedral that takes in many of the sights. Alternatively, 30-minute cruises run from the Torre del Oro on the Guadalquivir river, one of Spain's greatest waterways, and this is a relaxing way to admire Seville.

Festivals in Seville

Seville has two major festivals: the *Semana Santa* (Holy Week), the last week of Lent, and the *Feria de Abril* (April Festival), held the last week in April. If you plan to visit the city during either of these events, reserve a room months in advance as the city will be packed. Holy Week is a deeply religious time, celebrated by processions of *pasos* held by rival brotherhoods in Seville's different districts. *Pasos* are huge carriers supporting religious statues, richly decorated and carried by up to 60 men.

The April Festival is secular, a week-long celebration of Andalucia's love affair with horses, music and beautiful women. Carriages filled with girls in ruffled dresses, accompanied by horseback riders in traditional dress, parade the streets, and the graceful *sevillanas* is danced all night.

Eating Southern Style

Eating is a pleasure in Seville, with a wide range of restaurants and tapas bars. More than almost anywhere else in Spain, tapas has a special place here. There's a fabulous choice of dishes, traditionally eaten with a glass of *fino*, or white sherry, a fortified wine from nearby Jerez de la Fontera.

Mealtimes are late, particularly in summer, with lunch often finishing around 4 or 5 and dinner starting at

11 p.m. or midnight. The more touristy restaurants are geared to foreigners' dining habits. Andalucian coffee is very strong, so it's best to ask for a *café Americano* if you like it weaker.

Mantillas and Castanets

Shoppers throng Calle Sierpes – "the Serpent" – the winding pedestrian-only street running north from near the cathedral. It's a good place to shop for Sevillian fans, mantillas, shawls, flamenco dresses, castanets and gourmet candies. You'll find attractive pottery at tiny stores in Santa Cruz or across the river in the Triana district, where they also make fine wrought-iron goods, saddles and guitars.

Flamenco

Flamenco is a synthesis of dance and music, ideally performed spontaneously to express joy and sorrow about everyday life, religion and work. Its heartland lies in Andalucia, but its origins stretch as far afield as Egypt and India. It reaches its zenith in the soulful songs known as *cante jondo* (deep song), expressions of deep feelings. The profound meaning of flamenco is hard for foreigners to grasp, but the music, played on guitars *(toque)*, and dance, the distinctive costume, the rhythmic hand-clapping *(palmas)* and the click of castanets can be enjoyed by all. In 2010 UNESCO added flamenco to its list of Masterpieces of the Oral and Intangible Heritage of the World.

Essential Information

Tourist Information

Oficinas Municipales de Turismo (Municipal Tourist Offices)
Costurero de la Reine, Avenida de las Delicias 9 ☎ 95 423 4465
Castillo de San Jorge, Plaza de Altozano s/n, ☎ 95 433 2240
Paseo de las Delicias 9 ☎ 95 423 4465
Plaza del Triunfo 1 ☎ 95 421 0005
www.visitsevilla.es

Urban Transportation

Seville has a single metro (subway) line, and three more are planned. The MetroCentro is a tram which runs from Plaza Nueva to Prado. An efficient bus system services the residential suburbs. Some city-center routes run past the cathedral to the Plaza Nueva, and other lines terminate at Plaza de la Encarnación. María Luisa Park and the surrounding area is well served from the center. Buy single tickets when you board, or show your 1- or 3-day tourist pass, available at newsstands or the Tussam bus office. A rechargeable multitrip card also is available. A tourist bus *(bus turístico)* (☎ 95 456 8365) is a hop-on-and-off service covering the main sights; tickets valid all day. For summer sightseeing cruises on the Guadalquivir river, as well as trips to Sanlúca de Barrameda, go to www.crucerostorredeloro. com. White-and-yellow taxis can be hailed on the street or at a stand, or call Radio Taxi (☎ 95 458 0000), Radio Taxi Giralda (☎ 95 467 5555) or Tele-Taxi (☎ 95 462 2222).

Airport Information

Seville International Airport (☎ 902 404 704), with connections to major European cities, is 6 miles northeast of the city. An airport bus (like EA) runs every 20–30 minutes from the terminal to Prado de San Sebastián, Mon.–Fri. 4:30 a.m.–12:30 a.m.; less often on weekends.

Climate – average highs and lows for the month

Jan.	Feb.	Mar.	Apr.	May	Jun.	Jul.	Aug.	Sep.	Oct.	Nov.	Dec.
15°C	16°C	18°C	22°C	27°C	32°C	35°C	35°C	32°C	25°C	20°C	16°C
59°F	61°F	64°F	72°F	81°F	90°F	95°F	95°F	90°F	77°F	68°F	61°F
5°C	7°C	8°C	10°C	13°C	17°C	18°C	19°C	18°C	14°C	10°C	4°C
41°F	45°F	46°F	50°F	55°F	63°F	64°F	66°F	64°F	57°F	50°F	39°F

Seville Sights

Key to symbols

⊞ map coordinates refer to the Seville map on page 425 🖐 admission charge: $$$ more than €6, $$ €3–€6, $ less than €3

See page 5 for complete key to symbols

Barrio de Santa Cruz

The whitewashed Barrio de Santa Cruz (Santa Cruz Quarter), with its narrow streets, ironwork grilles and sunny squares shaded by orange trees, typifies Seville and draws many visitors. Originally the Jewish quarter, until the Jews were expelled from Spain in 1492, it was popular with 17th-century nobility, who added the huge mansions.

⊞ B3 ✉ Santa Cruz 🚌 1, 5, 21, C5; tram T1

Catedral

Seville's Catedral (Cathedral), built on the site of the Moorish mosque, is the third largest in Europe. It was built between 1401 and 1507, a magnificent blend of Gothic austerity and Spanish flamboyance. The interior is dominated by the chancel, the Capilla Mayor, its splendidly carved Flemish altarpiece glistening with gold leaf behind immense grilles. Opposite lie the choir stalls. Stand between the two and look up at the transept roof, 184 feet above your head; this riot of stone filigree is supported by massive arches and columns, but even these are dwarfed by the scale of the cathedral.

Other highlights include Christopher Columbus' tomb in the south transept; the treasury and sacristy, packed with paintings and precious altar vessels; and the domed Royal Chapel, the burial place of Alfonso X of Castille.

⊞ B3 ✉ Avenida de la Constitución s/n ☎ 90 209 9692; www.catedraldesevilla.es 🕐 Mon. 11–3:30, Tue.–Sat. 11–5, Sun. 2:30–6, Jul.–Aug.; Mon. 9:30–2:30, Tue.–Sat. 9:30–4, Sun. 2:30–6, rest of year 🚌 C5; tram T1 🖐 $$$ (combined ticket for Cathedral and La Giralda) ℹ Admission with audio guide by prior reservation on Mon. afternoon year round

Giralda

When Christians destroyed the mosque to build the cathedral, they kept the minaret and transformed it into the new cathedral's bell tower. Nicknamed the Giralda, the "weather-vane," the 322-foot-tall tower was built in the 12th century. Instead of stairs, you climb a series of interior ramps; 17 levels lead to the top, from which there are views over Seville.

Below the tower lies the lovely Patio de los Naranjos (Courtyard of the Orange Trees), once part of the mosque.

⊞ B3 ✉ Plaza Virgen de los Reyes ☎ 90 209 9692 🕐 Open same days and hours as the Catedral, via the same entrance and with the same ticket 🚌 C5; tram T1 🖐 $$$ (combined ticket for Cathedral and Giralda)

Isla Mágica

Seville hosted Expo '92 on the Isla de la Cartuja, an island between two branches of the Guadalquivir river. This is now the site of Isla Mágica, a theme park devoted to the Spanish discovery of the New World in the 15th and 16th centuries. Roller coasters, a 4D cinema and the world's largest virtual-reality theater are among the attractions.

⊞ A4 ✉ Avenida Camino de los Descubrimientos ☎ 902 16 17 16; www.islamagica.es 🕐 Daily 11–11 (midnight on Sat.), Jul. 1 to mid-Sep.; days and times vary, Apr.–Jun. and mid-Sep. to early Jan. 🚌 C1, C2 🖐 $$$ (reduction for half-day)

Museo de Bellas Artes

Seville's Fine Arts Museum, housed in an 18th-century convent, concentrates on the Golden Age of Spanish painting. The former church is devoted to the Spanish religious painter Bartolomé Murillo, and the highlight of the collection here is his painting, *Immaculate Conception*. Francisco de Zurbarán also is represented with works such as *La Virgen de las Cuevas* and *San Hugo en el Refectorio*.

⊞ A3 ✉ Plaza del Museo 9 ☎ 95 554 2942; www.museodebellasartesdesevilla.es 🕐 Tue.–Sun. 10–3:30, mid-Jun. to mid-Sep.; Tue.–Sat. 10–7:30, Sun. 10–5, rest of year 🚌 6, 43, C3, C4, C5 🖐 $

Plaza de España and Parque de María Luisa

Built as the centerpiece for the 1929 International Exhibition, the Plaza de España overlooks María Luisa Park. Traditionally styled and lavishly decorated with thousands of colored tiles, the 650-foot-wide plaza is framed by a semicircular range of buildings and encircled by a canal. The park is a tranquil area but it plays a central part in Seville's Spring Festival, when hundreds of horsemen accompany carriages of silk-robed girls around the park.

➕ B1–B2 ✉ Plaza de España 🚌 31, C2

Plaza de Toros de la Maestranza

Seville's Plaza de Toros (Bullring) is one of the oldest and most prestigious in Spain. Once built of wood, the present 14,000-seat ring was designed around the Prince's Balcony and is actually oval rather than round. Tours include the Museo Taurino, the stables, the chapel and paintings.

➕ A3 ✉ Paseo Colón 12 ☎ 95 421 0315; www.realmaestranza.com 🕐 Museum and Plaza: daily 9:30–9, Apr.–Oct.; 9:30–7, rest of year 🚌 5, 41, C3, C4 💶 $$$

Real Alcázar

The unforgettable Real Alcázar (Royal Palace) epitomizes the elegance of Mudéjar secular architecture. Little remains of the original Moorish Alcaza. Most of the palace you see today was built by Pedro the Cruel in the 1360s, long after the Moors left Spain, but the builders were Christianized Moors, the inventors of Mudéjar style, and this "Arabian Nights" complex is one of the purest examples of their art remaining today. It's a labyrinth of courtyards, delicate stucco and tile rooms, terraces and coffered chambers, fountains and arched patios. From here you pass into the 16th-century Palace of Charles V, with its tapestries and lavish rooms. Outside are gardens with terraces, pools and shady magnolia and orange trees.

➕ B2 ✉ Patio de Banderas ☎ 95 450 2324;

The spectacular Setas de Sevilla

www.alcazarsevilla.org 🕐 Tue.–Sun. 9:30–7, Apr.–Sep.; 9:30–5, rest of year 🚌 21, 23, 25, 26, 30, 31, 32, 34, 40, 41, 42, C3, C4 💶 $$$ (free to students and senior citizens) ℹ Night visits also are available

Setas de Sevilla (Metropol Parasol)

This striking building is formed by six huge, wooden parasols, which look rather like mushrooms (*setas*). Designed by German architect Jürgen Mayer, it is the largest wooden structure in the world. The interconnected parasols form a gigantic canopy for a cultural and entertainment complex, which contains everything from the Antiquarium, a high-tech museum arranged around subterranean Roman and Andalucian ruins, to a market, a restaurant and a viewing platform (*mirador*), which snakes along the top of the parasols.

➕ B3 ✉ Plaza de la Encarnación ☎ 606 635 214 🕐 Mirador: daily 10 a.m.–11 p.m. Antiquarium: Tue.–Sat. 10–8, Sun. 10–2 🚊 Plaza Nueva (T1) 🚌 27, 32 💶 Mirador $$; Antiquarium $

Active Spain

Spain is a superb destination for active visitors – whether you want to ski in the Pyrenees, hike through the hills of Mallorca or sail around pristine Galician islands, Spain has it all. Useful websites include www.spain.info and www.magrama.gob.es/es/red-parques-nacionales/nuestros-parques/.

Skiing and Winter Sports

Spain boasts Europe's most southerly ski resort in the glorious Sierra Nevada, near Granada in Andalucía. There are more ski stations in the Sierra de Guadarrama near Madrid, and in the Picos de Europa. However, the finest skiing can be had in the lofty peaks of the Catalan Pyrenees, particularly the smart resort of Baqueira-Beret, which is where the Spanish royal family spend their winter vacations. The ski season is relatively short, and is best between mid-December and late February.

Hiking

The European network of long-distance paths, called GR (*Gran Recorrido* in Spanish), provide some of the most spectacular treks in Spain. Particularly striking are the GR11, which traverses the Pyrenees from coast to coast, and the GR7, which runs the entire length of the Mediterranean coastline. Spain's 14 national parks are superb destinations for hiking. Spring and autumn are usually the best times, as summer can be overpoweringly hot, unless hiking in the cooler mountainous areas – but access may be restricted during the winter.

Sailing and Watersports

Spain's extensive coastline is dotted with marinas, while sailing, water-skiing, jet-skiing, snorkeling and diving are just some of the sports commonly offered at the main resorts along the Costa Brava, Costa Blanca, Costa del Sol, and the islands Mallorca, Menorca and Ibiza. There are more marinas along the Atlantic coast to the north, which also is a mecca for surfers. The marine reserves at Illes Medes (Costa Brava), the Islas Cies (Galicia) and the Cap de Creus (Catalunya) are ideal for sailing, snorkeling and diving.

Other Activities

Golf is popular throughout Spain, with numerous world-class courses. Facilities for horseback-riding, fishing and tennis are found throughout the country.

The clear waters off Las Salinas beach in Ibiza are popular with watersports enthusiasts

Sweden

Opposite: Kornhamnstorg Square, in the Gamla Stan area of Stockholm, with the spire of Tyska Kyrkan behind

Sweden

Sweden is the largest of the Scandinavian countries, famed for the perceived efficiency of its people and the pragmatism of its government. This is a land of wide-open spaces, where even a large city like Stockholm seems to merge urban and rural elements in a way that benefits the people.

Swedish Landscapes

Southern Sweden is an area of forests and farmland punctuated by a vast number of lakes, of which two – Vänern and Vättern – dominate the landscape. The south also is the center of Sweden's industrial powerhouse. The main cities are Gothenburg (Göteborg) and Malmö on the southwest coast.

The southernmost province, Skåne, is a rich farming area where you will find a hint of Danish features, in the people, architecture and landscape; the area was long occupied by the Danes. This is Sweden's vacation land. Off the east coast, the islands of Gotland and Öland in the Baltic Sea have superb beaches that benefit from calm waters and warm summer sunshine.

Stockholm lies on the east coast of Sweden, within a beautiful mosaic of inland lakes and offshore islands. In the surrounding provinces there is a richly varied countryside centered on mighty Lake Mälaren. North of Stockholm is Sweden's ancient capital, the university town of Uppsala. This area is accessible by ferries and cruise boats that ply a network of waterways and lakes.

Northern Sweden is known as Norrland, with similarities to northern Finland, and it enjoys the same "Land of the Midnight Sun" tag. It is a country of vast forests and tumbling rivers that are fed by icy, crystal waters from the mountains. Lapland, or Sápme (see page 434), is a vast and magnificent wilderness of mountains, moorland, birch forest and tundra.

Travel and Climate

Sweden has an extensive road network, but public transportation throughout the country also is a very efficient and convenient way to get around. Trains are modern and comfortable, and buses serve even the most remote northern parts of the country.

Sweden's climate is similar to that of its neighbors, but the country is generally much drier than Norway's western regions. Summers can be as warm and sunny as anywhere else in northern Europe, and along the southern coast you may even find yourself enjoying a Scandinavian heat wave. Conversely, visitors need to be prepared for wet weather in Sweden's maritime climate.

A remarkable number of Swedes are fluent in English, and most people in the cities have at least some command of English. The people are generally very helpful, and have a great awareness of the world in general; they are politely curious about visitors and are lively conversationalists, once their initial reserve is overcome.

Swedes are conservative by nature, and may seem overly serious about life. They are very aware that their society operates on the basis of willingness and cooperation and accepting the norm.

You may mistake Swedish directness for impatience, especially in Stockholm, but this simply reflects a national confidence about how things work.

Old merchants' houses in Gamla Stan

SWEDEN

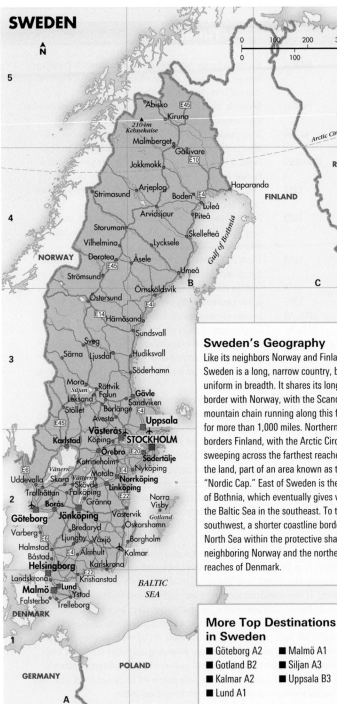

0 100 200 300km
0 100 200 miles

5

Abisko E45
Kiruna
2104m
Kebnekaise
Malmberget
Gällivare E10
Jokkmokk
RUSSIA
Arjeplog
Boden E4
Strimasund
Arvidsjaur
Piteå
Storuman
Vilhelmina
Lyckele
NORWAY
Dorotea
Åsele
E45
Strömsund
Umeå
Östersund
Örnsköldsvik B
C
E14 Härnösand
Sundsvall
Sveg
Hudiksvall
Särna Ljusdal
Söderhamn
Mora
Siljan
Rättvik
Leksand
Falun
Gävle
Stöllet
Borlänge
Sandviken
E45
Avesta E4
Uppsala
Västerås
Karlstad Köping STOCKHOLM
Örebro E20
Katrineholm Södertälje
E6 Väner Motala E4 Nyköping
Uddevalla Skara Vättern Norrköping
Trollhättan Falköping Linköping
Borås Gränna E22
Norra
Visby
Göteborg Jönköping Västervik Gotland
Oskarshamn
Varberg
Bredaryd
E6
Halmstad Ljungby Växjö Borgholm
Båstad E4 Älmhult Kalmar
Helsingborg Karlskrona
Landskrona Kristianstad E22 BALTIC
Malmö Lund SEA
Falsterbo Ystad
Trelleborg
DENMARK

Haparanda
Luleå
FINLAND
Skellefteå
Gulf of Bothnia

Arctic Circle

GERMANY

POLAND

A

Sweden's Geography

Like its neighbors Norway and Finland, Sweden is a long, narrow country, but uniform in breadth. It shares its longest border with Norway, with the Scandinavian mountain chain running along this frontier for more than 1,000 miles. Northern Sweden borders Finland, with the Arctic Circle sweeping across the farthest reaches of the land, part of an area known as the "Nordic Cap." East of Sweden is the Gulf of Bothnia, which eventually gives way to the Baltic Sea in the southeast. To the southwest, a shorter coastline borders the North Sea within the protective shadow of neighboring Norway and the northern reaches of Denmark.

More Top Destinations in Sweden

- Göteborg A2
- Gotland B2
- Kalmar A2
- Lund A1
- Malmö A1
- Siljan A3
- Uppsala B3

Timeline

8000 BC	Hunter-gatherers move throughout Scandinavia in the wake of retreating ice sheets; the Sami (Lapp) people are thought to descend from these early settlers.
1500 BC	Germanic tribes in southern Sweden develop trading links with the European lands to the south, from which they came.
AD 750	The legendary Battle of Bråvalla; the Svear emerge as the dominant tribe and give their name to the country Sverige.
800–1000	Swedish "Vikings" travel east via the great rivers of eastern Europe, as far as Constantinople.
1397	Union of Kalmar unites Denmark, Sweden and Norway under Queen Margaret of Denmark.
1523	Gustav Vasa establishes Sweden's independence; becomes King Gustav I; Lutheran Protestantism becomes the country's main religion.
1658	Treaty of Roskilde secures all of southern Swedish mainland from Danish control.
1814	Sweden wins control of Norway from Denmark.
1905	Norway achieves independence from Sweden.
1914–18	Sweden remains neutral during World War I.
1939–45	Sweden again remains neutral during World War II.
1946	Sweden maintains neutrality and joins the United Nations.
1973	Carl XVI Gustaf becomes king.
1989	The Sami people are granted their own parliament, known as the Sametinget.
1995	Sweden joins the European Union.
2000	The 10-mile Øresund tunnel and bridge linking Malmö and Copenhagen opens.
2003	In a referendum, the majority of Swedes reject the euro.
2010	Crown Princess Victoria marries Daniel Westling.
2011	Swedish surgeons carry out the first synthetic organ transplant.
2012	Crown Princess Victoria gives birth to Princess Estella.
2014	In a general election, a left-leaning coalition ousts the center-right Government.

The Sami

The Sami are the indigenous people of Sápme, the area popularly called Lapland. They are known historically as Lapps, but this is not a native name and is one that the Sami themselves feel is derogatory. The ancient name Sápme, a form of Sami which is said to mean "the people of the interior," is now considered accepted usage. Sápme covers the Scandinavian Arctic region from the Russian Kola peninsula to the northwest coast of Norway, and extends down either side of the Norwegian-Swedish border to the central area of both countries. There are an estimated 70,000 Sami people today, of which some 20,000 live in Sweden. A minority of Sami are reindeer herders, but the Sami also are developing alternative livelihoods while strengthening their self-awareness and political position within Scandinavia. Tourism is increasing in Scandinavian Lapland, but some Sami people are concerned about what they believe is too much intrusion on their fragile environment and culture.

Survival Guide

- For lunch you must experience *smörgåsbord*, a Scandinavian institution, although less common these days. The name translates as *smörgås* for "bread," *bord* for "table." The reality of a true *smörgåsbord* means much more than this simple image implies. There may be more than 100 different dishes in a true *smörgåsbord*, with items ranging from *gravad lax* (salmon slices in herbs) to *köttbullar* (tasty meatballs), *sillbullar* (herring rissoles) or *kåldolmar* (stuffed cabbage rolls).

- Like Norway and Finland, Sweden exercises tight control over alcohol sales and alcohol is expensive. The government-controlled liquor monopoly, Systembolaget, has branches throughout the country, which are generally open Mon.–Fri. 9–6, Sat. 10–3. They sell spirits, wines and strong beers; the minimum age to purchase at Systembolaget is 20. Light beers can be bought at grocery stores and supermarkets by anyone 18 or over. Try some aquavit with your food. The beverage is distilled from grain or potatoes and flavored with spices or herbs. Drink small quantities, consumed in one gulp.

- July is a popular month to travel in Sweden and the countryside and coast are very busy.

- Swedish design is world famous; the Småland area in southeast Sweden is particularly noted for its fine glassware. Stores such as NK in Stockholm's Hamngatan have good selections of glassware, or, for an education in Swedish home decor (though prices are high) check out R.O.O.M. at Täby Centrum, Stora Marknadsvägen 15, a large mall in Täby, a 15-minute hop on the train from Östra Station (East Station).

- Home furnishings are a Swedish specialty. Visit the world's biggest IKEA store at Kungens Kurva, south

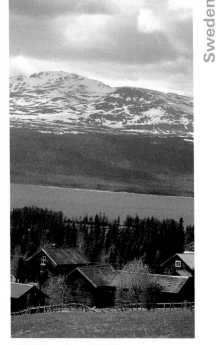

Lake Kallston in the north of the country

of Stockholm. A free bus leaves Mon.–Fri. every hour between 10 and 7 from Vasagatan 10, just outside Central Station. The return bus leaves every hour on the half hour from Kungens Kurva between 10:30 and 7:30, stopping at Hornstul, Fridhemsplan and Kungshelmstorg along the way. Or try the very stylish Nordiska Galleriet, in Nybrogatan.

- Don't miss the lively Stockholm Jazz Festival (www.stockholmjazz.com), a three- to four-day event held in early October. People flock to venues across Stockholm to listen to world-famous Swedish and international artists and groups playing jazz, blues, soul and Latin American music.

- In big cities there are public restrooms along some main streets, in main subway stations and department stores. Signs are *Damer* for ladies and *Herrar* for men. If there is an attendant, the charge can be between 5SKr and 10SKr.

Stockholm

Stockholm is one of the world's most beautiful capitals, probably the only city in the world where you can catch a salmon at a busy road intersection under the walls of a royal palace, and where the city's subway stations double as eye-catching art galleries. The salmon thrive in Stockholm's clean waters at the very heart of the city, and local anglers fish from the Strömbron bridge. The artwork that enlivens subway stations is just one expression of the vigorous cultural life that makes Stockholm one of the world's most civilized cities.

City of Islands

Modern Stockholm is a large, exhilarating city. The scale of its public buildings is monumental, the bustle of its streets all-embracing, yet the city is given a uniquely open character by the 24,000 islands in its archipelago and by the mirror images of lakes that pepper its hinterland. Stockholm stands on 14 interlocking islands; the city is a mosaic of land, lake and waterway stitched together by 50 bridges, making it a vibrant urban environment.

Gamla Stan (Old Town, see pages 442–443) lies at the heart of old Stockholm, a dramatic and fascinating expression of heritage and tradition. It stands on an island in the middle of the narrow bottleneck channel between the salty Baltic Sea and the inland freshwater lake of Mälaren, the third-largest lake in Sweden, after Vänern and Vättern. To the south is the hilly island of Södermalm, a suburban area with generous expanses of grass and trees. North of Gamla Stan and the buildings of state (the Royal Palace and the Parliament House) is Norrmalm, the business and commercial district. This is the heart of the modern city – glass, steel, concrete and good Swedish design – a cityscape of towering buildings, stylish shopping malls, busy streets and traffic-free concourses that satisfy the demands of both vehicles and pedestrians. East of Norrmalm is the residential district of Östermalm and the city's island park, Djurgården, the world's first National City Park. To the west is Kungsholmen, one of the many islands that inhabit the expanse of Lake Mälaren, Stockholm's "inland" sea.

Compass Bearings

Most visitors arrive at the city's central railroad station in Norrmalm, and the experience can be disorienting at first. The Tourist Center is opposite the station. Just east, along Klarabergsgatan is the big sunken square of Sergels Torg, with its landmark Kristall tower of glass and steel and a huge glass facade on the south side. This is Stockholm's contemporary hub. You can orient yourself here and relax in spite of the surrounding traffic and noise. Running north and south of Sergels Torg are busy shopping streets, such as the pedestrian-only Drottninggatan. The northern section of Drottninggatan runs past many additional stores.

Continuing east from Sergels Torg into the street of Hamngatan takes you past elegant NK, the best name in Swedish shopping. This huge department store

---

Subway Art

When the Stockolm *Tunnelbana* was built in the late 1940s (68 miles long) a decision was made to decorate each station with individual artworks. T-Centralen has the most, with examples ranging from sofas to wrought-iron gates. Visit the Blue Line's amazing Kungsträdgården station; it is very deep and has outstanding sculptures, some modern and some dating back several centuries. A guidebook is available from transportation and tourist offices, and online at www.sl.se. Guided tours are regularly arranged and in summer art walks (in English; free) leave from SL Center Sergels Torg at T-Centralen subway station at 3 p.m. on Tuesday, Thursday and Saturday (www.sl.se).

has floor after floor of luxury goods and such fashionable restaurants as Bobergs Matsal. Also in Hamngatan is Gallerian, a big shopping mall. Farther along is the great open swath of the Old Royal Gardens (Kungsträdgården). They sweep south to the waters of Strömmen, the magnificent Kungliga Slottet (Royal Palace, see pages 439–440) and enchanting Gamla Stan.

Seeing Stockholm

For all its size, Stockholm is a city that can be enjoyed on a human scale. You can see it by tour bus, sightseeing boat or with an organized tour accompanied by a knowledgeable guide. Try a boat trip for the wider view of Stockholm's islands, and visit some attractions, such as Djurgården (see pages 440, 441) and Drottningholms Slott (Drottningholm Palace, see page 439), by ferry boat.

Ask at the tourist center about the Stockholmskortet (Stockholm Card). Once purchased, it offers admission for one, two, three or five days (525SKr, 675SKr, 825SKr and 1,095SKr respectively), to around 80 museums and attractions; a sightseeing boat trip (Apr.–Dec.); unlimited use of public transportation in Stockholm and the surrounding area, including the SJövägen and Djurgården ferries, a bicycle tour and other benefits.

Stockholm is neatly packaged into separate entities because of its island nature, making it easy to plan your visit one day at a time. At night the city becomes even more majestic when it is lit up and vibrant with music and lively entertainment.

Stockholmers

Stockholm's confidence is infectious. Listen closely to advice and don't be afraid to ask for clarification or guidance. Then let the magic of the city take over and relax. Stockholmers have created one of the most endearing and enchanting cities in the world, and know how to enjoy it.

The setting sun casts a glow on Stockholm

Essential Information

Tourist Information

Stockholm Visitor Center
Kulturhuset, Sergels Torg 5 ☎ 08 508 285 08; www.visitstockholm.com

Urban Transportation

Stockholms Centralstation (Central Station ✉ Vasagatan ☎ 0771 75 75 75; www.sj.se) is the main railroad station. The Tunnelbana (subway) or T-Bana; has three lines: green, red and blue. T-Bana stations are indicated by signs bearing a blue "T" on a white background (the city map shows T-Bana stations as a letter "T" in a red circle). There is an efficient bus system (tickets must be bought before boarding). Public transportation in Stockholm has a unified ticket system, allowing transfer between systems. SL, responsible for the T-Bana and buses, has an information center in the T-Centralen T-Bana station (☎ 08 600 10 00; www.sl.se). For taxis contact: Taxi Kurir ☎ 08 30 00 00, Taxi Stockholm ☎ 08 15 00 00 or Taxi 020 ☎ 020 20 20 20 or 46 8 850400 (from overseas).

Airport Information

Stockholm-Arlanda Airport (☎ 0 10 109 10 00; www.swedavia.se/arlanda/) is 28 miles north of the city and is Stockholm's main air terminal. The Arlanda Express train (☎ 771 720 200; www.arlandaexpress.com) links the airport and Central Station at 10- or 15-minute intervals daily 4:35 a.m.–00:35 a.m. from Stockholm and 5:05 a.m.–1:05 a.m. from Arlanda. The trip takes 20 minutes. The Flygbussarna airport buses (☎ (0) 771 5152 52; www.flygbussarna.se) run at 10-minute intervals during peak times (less frequently at night) and take 45 minutes to reach the Cityterminalen (City Terminal) at Klarabergsviadukten. Bromma Airport (☎ 0 10 109 00 00; www.swedavia.se) is 5 miles west of Stockholm and handles domestic and some international flights. Flygbussarna buses run between the airport and the City Terminal; travel time 20 minutes. For information ☎ (0) 7715 152 52; www.flygbussarna.se.

Climate – average highs and lows for the month

Jan.	Feb.	Mar.	Apr.	May	Jun.	Jul.	Aug.	Sep.	Oct.	Nov.	Dec.
-1°C	-1°C	3°C	8°C	15°C	19°C	21°C	20°C	15°C	9°C	4°C	0°C
30°F	30°F	37°F	46°F	59°F	66°F	70°F	68°F	59°F	48°F	39°F	32°F
-5°C	-6°C	-3°C	0°C	5°C	11°C	13°C	13°C	9°C	4°C	1°C	-2°C
23°F	21°F	27°F	32°F	41°F	52°F	55°F	55°F	48°F	39°F	34°F	28°F

Stockholm Sights

ABBA The Museum

The aim of this museum is to make each visitor feel like a fifth member of the band. You will see the gold discs, scrapbooks and other memorabilia, but you also can touch the band's mixing desk in the Polar Studio, squeeze into replica costumes, and be a dancing queen on The Dance Floor alongside 3D holograms of the members of the band. A self-playing piano springs into action when the real Benny Andersson plays the piano in his studio.

➕ C2 ✉ Djurgårdsvägen 68 ☎ 08 121 328 60; www.abbathemuseum.com ⚙ Daily 10–8, May–Sep.; Sat.–Tue. 10–6, Wed.–Fri. 10–8, rest of year 🚌 44; tram 7 🚢 Slussen 🍴 Restaurant ⚙ $$$ 🛈 Guided tours $$

Drottningholms Slott

Drottningholms Slott (Drottningholm Palace) is on Lovön island. The palace, home of Sweden's royal family since 1981, is set amid its own gardens, a mix of French and English styles, and overlooks Lake Mälaren. On the grounds is the 18th-century Kina Slott (Chinese Pavilion), where Asian meets rococo.

Nearby is the 18th-century baroque Slottsteater (Palace Theater), which is a venue for opera from late May to mid-August. A museum showcases the work of Dutch sculptor Adriaen de Vries (1556–1626).

Drottningholms Slott ➕ Off map at A2 ✉ Drottningholm ☎ 08 402 62 80; www.kungahuset.se ⚙ Daily 10–4:30, May–Sep.; 11–3:30 in Apr.; Fri.–Sun. 11–3:30, in Oct.; Sat.–Sun. noon–3:30, rest of year

Kina Slott ✉ Drottningholm ☎ 08 402 62 80; www.kungahuset.se ⚙ Daily 11–4:30, May–Aug.; noon–3:30, in Sep.

Slottsteater ✉ Drottningholm ☎ 771 707 070 (box office); www.dtm.se ⚙ Guided tours daily 11–4:30, May–Aug.; noon–3:30 in Apr. and Sep.; Fri.–Sun. 12–3:30, in Oct.; Sat.–Sun. noon–3:30 p.m., Nov. to mid-Dec.

Drottningholms Slott, Kina Slott and Slottsteater: 🚇 T-Brommaplan; then bus 301 or 323 🚌 176, 177 🚢 Stadshuskajen (in summer) ⚙ $$$ for each part (includes guided tour); a combined ticket also is available in summer

Kungliga Slottet

The monumental Kungliga Slottet (Royal Palace), the official residence of the king and queen, is a stunning mix of classical styles developed throughout the 18th century on the site of the original Castle of Three Crowns. The Representationsvåningarna (Royal Apartments) within the palace are a fine expression of French baroque, rococo and imperial styles. There are several museums within the palace, including

Drottningholm Palace is a superb 17th-century baroque building in the style of Versaille

the Tre Kronor Museum, with remnants of the Tre Kronor Castle; the Skattkammaren (Treasury), where state regalia are on display; Gustav III's Antikmuseum (Gustav III's Museum of Antiquities), with a collection of classical sculptures; and the Livrustkammaren (Royal Armory), which depicts Sweden's military history.

Representationsvåningarna, Tre Kronor Museum, Skattkammaren and Gustav III's Antikmuseum
➕ B2 ✉ Slottsbacken 3 ☎ 08 402 61 30; www.kungahuset.se ⊙ Daily 10–5, mid-May to mid-Sep.; Tue.–Sun. 10–4, rest of year, depending on official royal receptions; check before you visit. Gustav III's Antikmuseum: daily 10–5, mid-May to mid-Sep. ⓠ Gamla Stan 🚌 2, 3, 43, 53, 55, 71, 76 💳 $$$ (includes guided tours). The ticket includes all three attractions and is valid for 7 days ($$$)
Livrustkammaren ✉ Slottsbacken 3 ☎ 08 402 3030; www.livrustkammaren.se ⊙ Daily 10–6, Jul. to mid-Aug.; 10–5 in Jun.; 11–5 in May; Tue.–Sun. 11–5 (also Thu. 5–8) rest of year ⓠ Gamla Stan 🚌 3, 43, 46, 53, 55, 59, 62, 65 💳 $$$ 🛈 Guided tours

Moderna museet

Stockholm's Modern Museum includes works by Andy Warhol, Willem de Kooning, René Magritte and Pablo Picasso. Look out for Salvador Dalí's startling *The Enigma of William Tell* and Marcel Duchamp's *Fountain*. There also are works by Swedish artists Vera Nilsson and Siri Derkert.
➕ B2 ✉ Slupskjulsvägen 7–9, Skeppsholmen ☎ 08

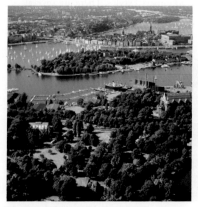

The 14 islands of Stockholm are superb for sailors

5202 3500; www.modernamuseet.se ⊙ Tue.–Sun. 10–6 (also Tue. and Fri. 6–8 p.m.) ⓠ Kungsträdgården 🚌 65 🚢 Slussen 🍴 Restaurant and café 💳 $$$ (includes guided tour and audio tour); free for under 18s

Nationalmuseum

The National Museum is a dignified Italianate building on little Blasieholmen peninsula, across the water east of Gamla Stan and facing the Royal Palace. Closed for restoration until 2017, some of the National Museum's collections will be touring Europe, while others will be on display in temporary exhibitions at Konstakademien (the Royal Swedish Academy of Fine Art).
➕ B2 ✉ Södra Blasieholmshamnen ☎ 08 5195 4300 and 08 5195 4410; www.nationalmuseum.se
Swedish Academy of Fine Arts ✉ Fredsgaten 12 ☎ 08 5195 4300 or 08 5195 4410 (recorded information) ⓠ T-Centralen 🚌 62, 65 🍴 Café 💳 $$$ 🛈 Museum shop

Nordiska museet

Standing at the entrance to Djurgården, the superb building housing the Nordiska museet (Northern Museum) has a gabled facade of brick and stone with elegant turrets and a handsome central steeple. Exhibits within illustrate Swedish and general Nordic cultural life from the medieval period onward. There is a section depicting the life of the Sami (Lapp) people (see page 434) and exhibits of traditional Swedish dress. Note as you enter the oak statue of Gustav Vasa, the 16th-century warrior who established the Swedish state and became King Gustav I.
➕ C3 ✉ Djurgårdsvägen 6–16, Djurgården ☎ 08 519 546 00; www.nordiskamuseet.se ⊙ Daily 10–5, Jun.–Aug.; Mon.–Tue. and Thu.–Sun. 10–5; Wed. 10–8, rest of year ⓠ Karlaplan 🚌 44, 69, 76; tram 7 from Sergels Torg 🚢 Slussen 🍴 Restaurant 💳 $$$ (free Wed. 5–8 p.m., Sep.–May) 🛈 Audio tours (free)

Skansen

The Skansen open-air museum is on Djurgården, Stockholm's island park, which was once the hunting domain of Swedish royalty. Other attractions include the Vasamuseet (Vasa Museum, see below) and the Nordiska Museet (Northern Museum, see page 440). At the heart of Djurgården, Skansen features more than 150 traditional buildings from the 18th to 20th centuries, and in summer it is a lively working environment for artisans. You can sample traditional Swedish delicacies, such as *smörgåsbord* and waffles with cream and cloudberries. Skansen's other attraction is its zoo, which also has an aquarium. There are several museums and art galleries scattered around Djurgården, and the Gröna Lunds Tivoli amusement park.

➕ C2 ✉ Djurgårdsslätten 49–51, Djurgården ☎ 08 442 80 00; www.skansen.se 🕐 Daily 10–10, Apr. 30 and Jun. 20; 10–4 in Apr.; 10–6, May–third week in Jun., Sep. and Dec. 13; 10–8, Jun. 6, third week Jun.–Aug.; Mon.–Fri. 10–3, Sat.–Sun. 10–4, Oct.–Mar.; 10–2 Christmas Eve; 10–4 and 8 p.m.– midnight New Year's Eve 🚌 44; tram 7 from Norrmalmstorg or Nybroplan 🚢 Slussen (year-round); Nybroplan (early Aug.–early Oct.) 🍴 Restaurants and cafés 🎟 $$$ (varies during year)

Stadshuset

Stockholm's City Hall is perhaps the city's finest example of early 20th-century Scandinavian Romantic Nationalistic style. This was the same style that produced the Jugend buildings of Helsinki. Built of red brick and with a magnificent Italianate tower, it stands on the shore of Lake Mälaren. The City Hall Tower (Stadshustornet) tapers to an upper platform that supports the gleaming Tre Kroner, the three crowns symbol of the city. Interiors are no less striking; the highlight is the Golden Hall with its marble floor. Admission to City Hall is by guided tour only (45 minutes) on a first come, first served basis. From April to September you can climb the 348-foot tower – or take the elevator halfway – for fine views over the city.

➕ A2 ✉ Hantverkargartan 1 ☎ 08 508 290 58 (for tours) or 08 508 29349 (Tower, May–Sep.); www.stockholm.se/stadshuset 🕐 Guided tours in English daily at 10, 11, 12, 1, 2 and 3, though subject to change; additional tours Jun.–Aug. Tower: daily 9:15–5:15, Jun.–Aug.; 10–4 in May and Sep. 🚇 Rådhuset 🚌 3, 62 🍴 Restaurant 🎟 City Hall $$$ ($$ Nov.–Dec.); Tower $

Stockholms Medeltidsmuseet

Stockholms Medeltidsmuseet (Museum of Medieval Stockholm) is located below the Riksdagshuset (Parliament House) on the tiny island of Helgeandsholmen, where, in the late 1970s, layers of medieval remains were uncovered during excavations for a planned underground parking lot.

Depicting the history of Stockholm from the 1250s to the 1520s, the museum is entered via steps leading down from Norrbro, the bridge between Gustav Adolfs Torg and Gamla Stan.

➕ B2 ✉ Strömparterren ☎ 08 508 316 20; www.medeltidsmuseet.stockholm.se 🕐 Tue.–Sun. noon–5 (also Wed. 5–8 p.m.) 🚇 Gamla Stan, T-Centralen or Kungsträdgården 🚌 2, 43, 62, 65, 76 🎟 Free 🛈 Guided tours in English daily at 2, Jul.–Aug.

Vasamuseet

The Vasamuseet (Vasa Museum) celebrates a unique maritime historical event. The focus of the museum is the sailing ship *Vasa*, which sank spectacularly in Stockholm harbor within minutes of starting its maiden voyage in 1628. At 230-feet long and fully restored and rigged, the *Vasa* is the only intact 17th-century ship in the world. Its finest features were well-preserved in the muddy Baltic waters for more than 330 years. The museum tells the story of the people who salvaged the *Vasa* in 1961, and exhibits 12,000 recovered artifacts.

➕ C2 ✉ Galärvarvsvägen 14, Djurgården ☎ 08 519 548 00 or 08 519 558 10; www.vasamuseet.se 🕐 Daily 8:30–6, Jun.–Aug.; 10–5 (also Wed. 5–8 p.m.), rest of year 🚇 Karlaplan 🚌 44, 69, 76 (to Djargårdsbron); tram 7 from Sergels Tor 🚢 Slussen (all year); Nybroplan (early Aug.–early Oct.) 🍴 Restaurant 🎟 $$$ (less expensive Wed. 5–8 p.m., Sep.–May); free for under 18s 🛈 Guided tours in English (included in admission fee) daily 9:30–4:30 (every 30 minutes), Jun.–Aug.; Mon.–Fri. 11:30, 1:30 and 3:30, Sat.–Sun., 10:30, 11:30, 12:30, 1:30, 2:30 and 3:30, rest of year

A Stroll Around Gamla Stan

Stockholm's Gamla Stan (Old Town) – or *staden mellan broarna*, "the city between the bridges," as it is more lyrically known to Swedes – is not a perfectly preserved medieval townscape by any means. Disastrous fires in 1407 and 1640 destroyed the original wooden buildings of medieval Gamla Stan. But the island nature of the settlement, its small area and its crowded layout have spared Gamla Stan from too much modernization. What remains today is a superb enclave of attractive old stone buildings dating from the 15th to the 18th centuries.

You can wander through the Old Town without getting lost – on this tiny island you are never far from the waterside or a bridge to reorient yourself. It is best experienced on foot, so pick up a large-scale Gamla Stan map, widely available in stores, restaurants and tourist venues, to help you find specific places.

There are many easily missed treasures hidden away from the main streets of Västerlånggatan and Österlånggatan. Pay a visit to the Cathedral of Stockholm (Storkyrkan). Dating from the 13th century, it is the city's oldest building and is just south of the courtyard of the Royal Palace. The church's finest artifact is the oak- and elkhorn-gilded sculpture of *St. George and the Dragon*, a 15th-century Gothic masterpiece of thorny carving by sculptor Bernt Notke. You may catch a lunchtime organ recital or musical performance in the church. The Riddarholmskyrkan is the memorial place and royal burial ground for past Swedish kings.

From the church, walk along the narrow street of Trångsund and then turn left past a charming old phone booth to reach Stortorget (Great Square). This was the scene in 1520 of the notorious Stockholm "Blood Bath," when Christian II of Denmark slaughtered 82 Swedish nobles and citizens in a bid to seal with blood his overlordship of Sweden. This brutal act inspired Gustav Vasa, son of a murdered nobleman, to rebel successfully against Denmark and to secure Sweden's independence. On the west side of Stortorget is a row of fine gabled houses with little cafés and restaurants on their ground floors. The 18th-century Bourse, or Stock Exchange, commands the north side of the square and contains the Nobelmuseet (Nobel Museum, open daily 10–8, Jun.–Aug.; Wed.–Sun. 11–5, Tue. 11–8, rest of year, www.nobelmuseum.se). The Swedish Academy, the body that selects Nobel prize winners, meets at the Bourse.

Leave the square via the east side and walk down Köpmangatan, "Street of the Merchants," the oldest street in the Old Town and home to several fine antiques stores with attractively painted ceilings. At the end of

Köpmangatan, in the little square of Köpmantorget, is a dramatic reprise of the Great Church's statue of *St. George and the Dragon*, this time in bronze but just as powerful. Farther east is Österlånggatan, a long, winding street that was once the Old Town's shoreline. Here you'll find many stores selling authentic Gustavian furniture.

Bear right, down the short slope of Köpmanbrinken street, and then keep right along Österlånggatan, past stylish restaurants, antiques and craft stores, and fashion salons. There are lots of gift possibilities here, especially for children, in stores such as Kalikå at Osterlånggaten 18, and Tomtar & Troll at Södra Benickebrinken 4 (www.tomtar.se), which has a wonderful array of painted wooden handicrafts. The narrow streets running east to the sea, such as Drakens Gränd, Ferkens Gränd and Packhusgränd, mark the old piers of the early medieval era. Near the end of Österlånggatan is the well-known restaurant Den Gyldene Freden (see page 491).

Soon you reach Järntorget (Iron Square), a name probably derived from the days when the Old Town's fortunes were built on its status as the main outlet for the Swedish iron and copper trade. Here, against the wall of the old Central Bank, is the remarkably lifelike statue of Swedish poet and songwriter Evert Taube, a popular performer who died in 1976. Built in the late 17th century, the Riksbank is thought to be one of the oldest bank buildings in Europe. Take a break at the nearby Sundbergs Konditori, established 1785 and making it the oldest bakery in the city.

From Järntorget, turn right onto Västerlånggatan, the busiest street in the Old Town, especially in the summer, crammed with stores and tempting restaurants and cafés. On the right, just past the Mårten Trotzig restaurant, you'll pass the narrow entrance to Mårten Trotzigs Gränd, reputed to be the narrowest alleyway in Stockholm and named after a German medieval copper trader who had a business here. In fact, German architectural influence can be easily identified in many of the winding streets and buildings of the Old Town.

All the way along Västerlånggatan you will be tempted by souvenir stores and Swedish craft stores, such as Handkraft Svea Rike at No. 24. Note the glass-paneled ceilings of many of the stores.

To end your excursion, stroll to where the bridge over the canal Stallkanalen leads through the arched passage to the gate at Riksgatan. Follow this back into Stockholm via Drottninggatan.

Above left to right: Skeppsbron waterfront glows in the early morning sun; café terraces are popular meeting places in summer

Switzerland

Opposite: The Lauterbrunnen Valley in the Bernese Oberland

Switzerland

With stunning Alpine scenery, lush meadows, a medley of beautiful lakes, attractive and neat cities and towns, Switzerland has a wonderful variety of natural and man-made attractions.

Neutral Territory

The Swiss Constitution, modeled on that of the United States, was drawn up in 1848 and revised in 1874; it is still in force today. Modern Switzerland is a federation of districts (cantons), and neutrality has traditionally been the cornerstone of state policy. Switzerland has interfered in no foreign conflicts and has made no alliances, although it became a member of the United Nations in 2002.

Remaining neutral through both world wars, Switzerland emerged in 1945 as a powerful commercial player. Banking has long thrived here due to the political stability of the country and because of Swiss financial acumen. The superb infrastructure of railroads, tunnels and roads has overcome the daunting mountainous terrain and allows the country to exploit a trading position at the center of Europe.

The Swiss Landscape

Europe's continental watershed runs through Switzerland, a landlocked country, with a central lowland sandwiched between the tree-clad slopes of the Jura mountains to the north and the mighty Alps to the south. The mountain glaciers and peaks of the Swiss Alps occupy around 60 percent of the country. Dense forests cover another quarter of the land and the rest is a delightful picture-postcard mix of lakes, winding rivers and green meadow pasture.

Switzerland's weather is typical of central Europe; Ticino canton, south of the Alps, has a pleasant, Mediterranean climate, and on some days the *Föhn* – a warm, dry wind – blows from the northern slopes of the Alps.

SWITZERLAND

More Top Destinations in Switzerland

- Ascona D1
- Baden C3
- Basel B3
- Bern B2
- Brienz C2
- Château de Chillon B1
- Engelberg C2
- Fribourg B2
- Grindelwald C2
- Gstaad B2
- Interlaken C2
- Lausanne B2
- Montreux B2

- St.-Moritz E2
- Schaffhausen C3
- Villars B1
- Wilderswil C2
- Zermatt C1

Language and Manners

Reflecting Switzerland's location in central Europe, the Swiss speak four different languages: Schwyzerdütsch, a number of Swiss-German dialects (although German is used for reading and writing); French; Italian; and Romansch (Rhaeto-Romanic), an ancient Latin tongue. This linguistic diversity results in very different types of people; you'll notice this as you travel.

On the whole, the Swiss are extremely law-abiding, and consider punctuality very important. They have a reputation for being aloof, but this is a misunderstanding. Manners are formal, with hand-shaking and serious toasts in all social circumstances. Efficient, civic-minded and polite, they make Switzerland a very well-run country.

Vacationing in Switzerland

The fabled Swiss efficiency has many positive benefits for visitors: trains run punctually, hotels are clean and comfortable, opening times for attractions are reliable, and everyone connected with tourism speaks English.

You will discover also that Switzerland is very expensive, so if you're watching your budget, don't plan on staying here too long.

There's something to enjoy throughout the year – skiing in the mountains during the winter, walking, sailing and other outdoor pursuits all summer. Late spring sees the countryside at its best, with carpets of mountain and meadow wildflowers; fall, when the leaves turn and the first snow whitens the lower peaks, also is magnificent.

Timeline

3,000 BC	Evidence of earliest neolithic settlers by Lake Neuchâtel.
circa 100 BC	Romans invade from the south, incorporating Helvetic tribes.
circa AD 400	Romans expelled southward; Burgundians occupy western areas (modern French-speaking Switzerland) and Alemans the north and east (German-speaking Switzerland).
1032	Existing country incorporated into Holy Roman Empire, followed by gradual emergence of powerful independent nobles.
1506	Formation of the Papal Swiss Guard, a force that still serves the Pope and the Vatican.
1515	Defeat at Battle of Marignano inaugurates neutrality.
1526	Zwingli's Reformation takes hold in Zurich, continued by John Calvin in Geneva beginning in 1536.
1648	Treaty of Westphalia recognizes Swiss neutrality and independence of 13 cantons.
1798	French invasion and rule under Napoleon, who establishes Helvetic Republic.
1815	Congress of Vienna guarantees Swiss independence.
1848	Adoption of Swiss Constitution, which defines political organization of the country.
1864	First Convention of Geneva is accepted and signed by 16 nations; the Red Cross is founded.
1914–18	Switzerland remains neutral during World War I.
1919	President Woodrow Wilson chooses Geneva as headquarters of the League of Nations.
1939–45	Switzerland remains neutral during World War II, but image is tarnished by pro-Nazi activities.
1946	United Nations takes over role of League of Nations; Geneva retained as European headquarters.
1990	Population votes to freeze nuclear power development.
1999	Ruth Dreifuss becomes Switzerland's first woman president.
2002	Switzerland becomes the 190th member of the United Nations.
2008–2009	The Large Hadron Collider at CERN (the European Center of Nuclear Research) near Geneva is switched on. In 2012 the LHC uncovers evidence for the existence of the Higgs boson particle.
2013	Rangers in the Graubünden region shoot dead the country's only wild bear, a brown bear *(Ursus arctos)*, on fears that it posed a growing threat to humans.
2015	Plans are announced to build Europe's tallest skyscraper (1,250 feet) at Vals in the Swiss Alps.

The Swiss Army Knife

The Swiss Army knife was first manufactured in 1891 as an accessory for soldiers in the Swiss army. More than 200 models of this versatile, world-renowned penknife now exist, each with a distinctive white cross in a shield on a red background. Its blades and attachments, ranging from tweezers and magnifying glasses to tiny hacksaws, scissors and nail files, are designed to perform a wide range of tasks. It has justifiably been called the "smallest toolbox in the world."

A restaurant and communications tower at the summit of Uetliberg mountain overlook Zurich

Survival Guide

- Keep more money available than you think you will need; cash seems to be spent alarmingly fast in Switzerland. Credit cards are widely accepted throughout the country.
- Although most Swiss are excellent linguists, it's polite to ask if they speak English before starting a conversation or asking a question.
- Be polite to everyone – *bitte, prego* or *je vous en prie* is the equivalent of "you're welcome," and it's important to use one of these expressions when you're thanked. When you use public transportation, it's customary to give up your seat for elderly people, pregnant women and people with disabilities.
- Be punctual; if you're likely to be checking in to your hotel later than planned, let them know you've been held up.
- In cities other than Zurich, Basel and Bern it is considered rude to eat or drink on the street. If you purchase food to go, find somewhere to sit down and eat it.
- Don't drop litter; it is a finable offense. When getting rid of trash, make sure you put it in the compartment designated for that particular type of waste.
- Although informality is the norm in active, health-conscious Switzerland,

very casual clothing – like beachwear – isn't usually seen in cities.
- There is no state medical health service in Switzerland; treatment must be paid for on the spot. Therefore, it is very important to carry medical travel insurance valid in Switzerland. Many drugs can be bought over the counter. If you require a prescription drug, the prescription must be written by a Swiss doctor.
- In large towns and cities, stores are often closed on Monday mornings. Museums are usually closed on Mondays.
- Always cross the street at designated crossings, and wait for the green man symbol.
- Each canton (district) and community is responsible for its own laws and law enforcement. The police uniform differs widely from place to place, as do local bylaws. Respect authority at all times, even if you see no point in what you are being requested to do.
- Use the superbly efficient public transportation system rather than the inordinately expensive taxis.
- You'll save money by eating and drinking in smaller establishments away from the more upscale areas.
- There is no need to tip in Switzerland; a service charge is automatically added to all bills.

Geneva

Sparkling Geneva (Genève), beautifully situated by the shores of the crescent-shaped Lake Geneva (Lac Léman) and backed by the Jura mountains and the Alps, is indeed an elegant city. With its key role as an important international meeting place, many visitors are in the city on business, but others come to enjoy the scenic location, excellent museums, stores and restaurants, and the lively cultural life.

The Modern City

Strategically positioned at the head of the Rhône river, Geneva joined the Swiss Confederation in 1815, after Napoleon's downfall. Since then the city has grown, prospered and become increasingly cosmopolitan.

Today Geneva hosts meetings, exhibitions, conventions and many organizations involved with humanitarian and social causes. It plays a major part in Swiss industry, finance and commerce, but has succeeded in retaining much of its French style and attitude, resulting in a pleasing blend of charm and efficiency.

An important university and scientific center, Geneva also is home to CERN, the European Center of Nuclear Research. The city is ringed with attractive countryside – the ski slopes of the French Alps are less than an hour away, and Lake Geneva offers superb watersports facilities.

Old Town and Beyond

Geneva is used to foreign visitors, and it's an easy city with which to become familiar. Getting around by public transportation is simple, and the center of the city is small enough to cover on foot, with much of the Old Town pedestrian-only. It's worth spending a couple of hours getting your bearings by walking around the town center, which lies on either side of the Rhône river.

Much of what you'll want to see is in or around the Old Town and is well marked, although with more than 30 museums to choose from, you are likely to take a bus at some point. Tourist trams run through the Old Town,

A pleasure boat on Lake Geneva (Lac Léman), with mountains rising up behind the city

leaving from place Neuve every half-hour; they're a relaxing way to enjoy the city, although guided walking tours are available.

Tour buses travel to Lausanne and Château de Chillon, and into the Alps to Mont Blanc and Gstaad. Many lake cruises are offered, most lasting from one to three hours and many with commentary in English.

Gourmet Geneva

Like all Swiss cities, Geneva has a wide range of restaurants offering cuisine from around the world. It also has its own specialties, many of which have more in common with France than the rest of Switzerland. Eating out can be expensive, although away from the city center you'll find friendly neighborhood restaurants, where prices are much lower and the food is just as good.

Many places serve Swiss specialties such as fondue, sausage and *rösti* (potato cake), but you can choose from French, Italian, Thai, Japanese, Korean, Chinese,

Festivals and Fun

Geneva's biggest traditional festival is the *Escalade*, a December commemoration of a 1602 battle. A wonderful parade in 17th-century costumes marches through the Old Town, and the whole city is out in the streets to celebrate. The *Bol d'Or* annual sailing regatta, the biggest lake sailing race in Europe, is held in June, when more than 600 boats and their crews take over the lakeshore, and early in August the city is lit up by musical fireworks displays during the renowned *Fêtes de Genève* (mid-July to mid-August) with hundreds of concerts performed all over the canton.

Russian, Spanish, Australian, Moroccan and many other types of cuisine.

You'll find all the usual fast-food outlets in the city center, and it's fun to shop for a picnic to enjoy in one of the lakeside parks.

There's a plethora of bars throughout the city; the nicest are in the Old Town and also along the lakeside.

Designer Style and Souvenirs

Geneva stores do not usually close at lunchtime and are open until 8 or 9 p.m. on Thursday evening. There are vast malls on the city outskirts, but it's likely you'll be shopping in the downtown city area, where the most attractive and elegant stores are all located. You will find many of them along rue du Rhône, rue du Mont Blanc and other elegant neighboring streets.

Don't miss Globus, on rue du Rhône, a large department store that's a Geneva institution. You'll find watches, expensive jewelry, high fashion and superb leather goods from stylish outlets such as Boucheron and Piaget, Christian Dior, Giorgio Armani, Gucci, Hermès and Chanel.

If you're looking for interesting gifts or souvenirs to take home, try the tourist boutique in Globus, Swiss Corner on rue des Alpes, or Montblanc Boutique on place du Port.

Essential Information

Tourist Information

Genève Tourisme (Geneva Tourism)
Rue du Mont-Blanc 18 🛈 Mon. 10–6, Tue.–Sat. 9–6, Sun. 10–4
☎ 022 909 7000; www.geneve-tourisme.ch

Urban Transportation

Geneva is efficiently served by trams, trolley buses and buses that cover the city's areas; Zone 10 covers the city center. Buy and validate your ticket from the machines at each bus stop, which also have route maps and instructions about using the system. A simple ticket is the Saut de Puce (Short Hop), valid for 3 stops on land, or a single boat ride. For more flexibility, the Tout Genève (All Geneva) ticket is valid for 60 minutes. The best ticket is the Geneva Transport Card, which is free when visitors check in at their hotel, hostel or campsite and allows use of all public transportation. To board or leave the vehicle, press the red button near the door; doors will open and close automatically. For information contact the Transports Publics Genevois (TPG) at offices at Geneva Cornavin Station and Rond-Point de Rive or call the Mobility Call Center (☎ 0900 022 021 toll call; www.tpg. ch). Taxis are at stands in the city center, can be hailed on the street or called: Taxi-Phone SA Genève (☎ 022 331 4133).

Airport Information

Genève Aéroport (Geneva Airport, ☎ 022 717 7111; www.gva.ch) is 3 miles north of the city center. It is linked to the central railroad station by trains departing every 12 minutes (peak times), daily 6:30 a.m.–12:30 a.m., with a 6-minute journey time. Bus No. 10 runs every 10 minutes between the airport and the city and takes 20–25 minutes. Free public transportation tickets, valid for 80 minutes, are available for arriving passengers from baggage reclaim area. Taxis wait at the airport terminal. Fares from the airport to the city are SFr30–SFr35.

Climate – average highs and lows for the month

Jan.	Feb.	Mar.	Apr.	May	Jun.	Jul.	Aug.	Sep.	Oct.	Nov.	Dec.
4°C	5°C	10°C	13°C	18°C	22°C	25°C	25°C	20°C	13°C	8°C	4°C
39°F	41°F	50°F	55°F	64°F	72°F	77°F	77°F	68°F	55°F	46°F	39°F
-2°C	0°C	2°C	3°C	7°C	12°C	14°C	14°C	11°C	6°C	2°C	0°C
28°F	32°F	36°F	37°F	45°F	54°F	57°F	57°F	52°F	43°F	36°F	32°F

Geneva Sights

Key to symbols

➕ map coordinates refer to the Geneva map on page 451 🎫 admission charge: $$$ more than SFr10, $$ SFr7–SFr10, $ less than SFr7

See page 5 for complete key to symbols

Cathédrale St.-Pierre

The vast and austere Cathédrale St.-Pierre (St. Peter's Cathedral) has been a Protestant church since 1536. It was built in the 12th and 13th centuries, and its current neoclassic facade was added in the 18th century. This is where John Calvin preached; his seat is still in the north aisle. Climb the 157 steps up the tower for views over Geneva and the lake or take a tour of the archeological site below the cathedral, telling the story of the medieval building and city.

The cathedral has a long-standing musical tradition; the Clémence, the largest bell in the tower, weighs more than 6 tons and was placed in the carillon there in 1407.

➕ B2 ✉ place du Bourg-de-Four ☎ 022 319 7190; tours 022 310 2929; www.saintpierre-geneve.ch; www.site-archeologique.ch ⏰ Cathédrale: Mon.–Sat. 9:30–6:30, Sun. 12–6:30, Jun.–Sep.; Mon.–Sat. 10–5:30, Sun. 12–5:30, rest of year. Site archéologique: Tue.–Sun. 10–5 🚊 2, 7, 9, 12, 16, 20; tram 12 🎫 Cathedral free; towers $$

Fondation Baur

An elegant 19th-century mansion houses the Fondation Baur (Baur Foundation), the extensive Asian art collection of connoisseur Alfred Baur (1865–1951). Among the many exhibits you'll find exquisite Chinese ceramics and samples of jade, snuff bottles from the 10th to the 19th centuries, prints and *netsuke* (Japanese carved toggles), and intricate Japanese and Chinese lacquerwork dating from the eighth to the 18th centuries. Spend some time marveling at the depth and translucency of the glazes on the porcelain.

➕ C1 ✉ rue Munier-Romilly 8 ☎ 022 704 3282; www.fondation-baur.ch ⏰ Tue.–Sun. 2–6 (Wed. also 6–8 p.m. for guided tours during temporary exhibitions) 🚊 1, 8, 36 🎫 $$

Jardin Anglais

Statues, trees and a riot of colorful flowers help make the lakeside Jardin Anglais (English Garden) and its mountain views the perfect place to escape the city's bustle. Admire the 1862 fountain, with numerous reclining nymphs, before spending a few minutes at the Floral Clock. This huge timepiece, made entirely of 6,500 flowers and plants, was installed in 1955 as a symbol of the Geneva watch industry. From the garden, the Jet d'Eau can be seen, a towering spray of water over the lake. A short walk along the lake will bring you to Parc de la Grange, a lovely rose garden seen at its best in mid-June.

➕ B2–C2 ✉ promenade du Lac ⏰ Daily dawn–dusk 🚊 6, 8, 29 🍴 Cafés and restaurants

Musée Ariana

The Musée Ariana is Switzerland's only public museum dedicated entirely to ceramics and glass. With some 20,000 objects, this collection is one of Europe's largest, covering seven centuries of European, Middle Eastern and Asian ceramic and glass manufacture. The main techniques represented are pottery, stoneware, faïence and porcelain.

➕ Off map at B3 ✉ avenue de la Paix 10 ☎ 022 418 5450; www.institutions.ville-geneve.ch/fr/ariana ⏰ Tue.–Sun. 10–6 🚊 5, 8, 11, 18, 22, F, V, Z; tram 15 🎫 Free; exhibitions $

Musée d'Art et d'Histoire

Behind the grandiose facade of Geneva's Musée d'Art et d'Histoire (Museum of Art and History) lies a dauntingly large collection of paintings, archeological finds and objets d'art. Ancient history fans will enjoy the Egyptian, Greek, Roman and Etruscan rooms. With 400 paintings, the galleries cover the full range of European painting, but concentrate on Swiss specialties, such as Ferdinand Hodler's powerful work

The Drinkers or Konrad Witz's 1444 altarpiece; its background is one of Europe's first accurate landscape representations. Other rooms contain applied arts collections, examples of fine furniture, silver and porcelain.

⊞ B1 ✉ rue Charles-Galland 2 ☎ 022 418 2600; www.institutions.ville-geneve.ch/mah ⏲ Tue.–Sun. 11–6 🚃 1, 3, 5, 7, 8, 36 🍴 Restaurant 🎫 Free; some exhibitions $–$$$

MAMCO (Musée d'Art Moderne et Contemporain)

The Museum of Modern and Contemporary Art showcases artistic innovation from the 1960s to today. Works by Swiss artists are featured, but the rest of the world is not forgotten, and big names like Christo can be seen.

⊞ A1 ✉ rue des Vieux-Grenadiers 10 ☎ 022 320 6122; www.mamco.ch ⏲ Tue.–Fri. noon–6, Sat.–Sun. 11–6 (to 9 p.m. first Wed. of the month) 🚃 1; tram 12, 15 🎫 $$; free first Sun. and 6–9 p.m. first Wed. of the month

Musée Barbier-Mueller

Situated in the heart of the Old Town, the Barbier-Mueller Museum was founded in 1977 to conserve, restore and exhibit an extensive collection of works of art begun by Josef Mueller in 1907. The collection consists of more than 7,000 pieces of tribal and classical art and ornaments from "primitive" civilizations, and includes pieces collected by Mueller's son-in-law, Jean Paul Barbier. The museum has earned an international reputation for its traveling exhibitions, loans to museums and the publication of catalogs and art books.

⊞ B2 ✉ rue Jean-Calvin 10 ☎ 022 312 0270; www.barbier-mueller.ch ⏲ Daily 11–5 🚃 2, 7, 12, 16, 36; tram 12 🎫 $$

Musée International de la Croix-Rouge et du Croissant-Rouge

The Musée International de la Croix-Rouge et du Croissant-Rouge (International Red Cross and Red Crescent Museum), explains the principles and history of the organization during some of the world's most serious humanitarian crises.

⊞ Off map at B3 ✉ avenue de la Paix 17 ☎ 022 748 9595; www.redcrossmuseum.ch ⏲ Tue.–Sun. 10–6, Apr.–Oct.; Tue.–Sun. 10–5, rest of year 🚃 8, 28 🎫 $$$

Muséum d'Histoire Naturelle

The splendid Natural History Museum is very popular and can be crowded, so arrive early. The exhibits cover everything from the history of the Earth through the dinosaur age to displays of animals, birds, reptiles and fish from all over the world, complete with realistic sound effects. Make time to see the relief map of Switzerland on the fifth floor.

⊞ C1 ✉ route de Malagnou 1 ☎ 022 418 6300; www.ville-ge.ch/mhng ⏲ Tue.–Sun. 10–5 🚃 1, 5, 8; tram 12 🍴 Café and snack bar 🎫 Free

Palais des Nations

Built between 1929 and 1936 to house the League of Nations, the Palais des Nations (Palace of Nations) is now the European seat of the United Nations. The vast marble and travertine-stone complex is beautifully situated on the slopes above the lake, with views of Mont Blanc. You can tour some of the interior including the 2,000-seat Salle des Assemblées, one of the world's most active conference centers.

⊞ Off map at B3 ✉ avenue de la Paix 14 ☎ 022 917 4896 or 022 917 4539; www.unog.ch ⏲ Mon.–Fri. 10–noon and 2–4, Apr.–Jun.; daily 10–noon and 2–4, Sep.–Mar.; daily 10–4, Jul.–Aug. 🚃 5, 8, 11, 28, F, V, Z; tram 15 🍴 Café 🎫 $$$ ℹ Passport or identity card required for entry

Place du Bourg-de-Four

Bourg-de-Four square is the heart of Old Geneva, historically the site of the Roman market, medieval trade fairs, and political and religious meetings. Many of the fine buildings date from the 16th century; note their extra floors, added later to accommodate the flood of Protestant religious exiles. Today it is a lovely place to enjoy a drink.

⊞ B1 ✉ place du Bourg-de-Four 🚃 3, 7, 36 🍴 Cafés and restaurants nearby

The Red Cross

In 1859, Jean Henri Dunant (1828–1910), son of a prominent Genevan family, set off to appeal to Napoleon III of France on a personal matter. Dunant caught up with Napoleon the day after the Battle of Solferino, where he saw more than 40,000 wounded men desperately in need of care and attention.

Dunant returned to Geneva and wrote a moving book, *Souvenir of Solferino*, in which he proposed the establishment of a body of volunteer male nurses to impartially care for the wounded in wartime. He further suggested that these men be recognized through an international agreement. Three friends added their support, the book was published and the International Committee of Help for the Wounded in Case of War (Comité Internationale de Secours aux Blessées en Cas de Guerre) was set up.

In 1864, the First Convention of Geneva was accepted and signed by 16 nations; a revised version of its standards of treatment for prisoners of war is still in effect today. An easily recognizable logo for the new movement was needed, and a reverse version of the colors of the Swiss flag was used; a red cross on a white background, rather than a white cross on a red background – a symbol now known the world over.

The Red Cross, present in more than 50 countries throughout the world, works hand in hand with the Red Crescent, an identical body functioning in Muslim and other non-Christian countries. Jean Henri Dunant was awarded the first Nobel Peace Prize in 1901, along with Frédéric Passy.

The Red Cross functions at both international and national levels. The international headquarters are in Geneva, and it is from here that major humanitarian relief work is coordinated. Each participating country has its own national committee that deals with day-to-day work in that particular country. The Red Cross is still manned largely by volunteers, who cover everything from terrorist attacks and natural disasters to organizing collections for war victims and refugees, as well as training the public in emergency aid procedures.

The headquarters of the International Red Cross in Geneva

Zurich

Primarily a business center, with an emphasis on international finance and banking, this prosperous and clean city has plenty for visitors to enjoy. It is dotted with fine buildings, museums, historic churches and green spaces, the perfect background for affluent stores, elegant cafés and well-dressed citizens.

Lakeside City

Zurich surrounds the northern end of Zürichsee (Lake Zurich), from which the Limmat river flows to bisect the city. The oldest part lies on either side of the river, with the 19th-century grandeur of the Bahnhofstrasse area on the west. East of the river, hills rise to the university complex, while boulevards, parks and gardens run along the lake.

ZURICH

0   100   200 meters
0   100   200 yards

A tram ride is an essential experience; these vehicles ensure that city streets are virtually traffic-free. You can borrow a free bike from several places in the city, including the main railroad station (daily 8 a.m.–9:30 p.m., ID and deposit of SFr20 required); www.zuerirollt.ch.

Evenings Out

There's a range of excellent restaurants in Zurich, most of them expensive. You can eat well and relatively cheaply on the east side of the river. You'll find fast-food outlets, cafés and tearooms, and cozy taverns and wine cellars.

Notice boards all over the city list movie theaters (often showing American films in English), concerts, theater and opera. For a relaxed evening with the locals, you'll find plenty of packed bars, open late, on and around Limmatquai; on summer nights there is an array of street performers. Zurich also has a number of cabarets and discos.

Chocolates and Watches

Bahnhofstrasse is one of Europe's great shopping streets, lined with upscale stores filled with luxury items. Schweizer Heimatwerk in Granigstraße specializes in Swiss handicraft. Don't miss Sprüngli, a mouthwatering chocolate store. The narrow old streets on each side of the river are packed with antiques stores.

Essential Information

Tourist Information

Zürich Tourismus (Tourist Service)
Hauptbahnhof (Central Station)
☎ 044 215 4000; www.zuerich.com
🕓 Mon.–Sat. 8:30–7, Sun. 9–6

Urban Transportation

Zurich's extremely efficient tram and bus system runs daily 4:30 a.m.–12:30 a.m. Tickets must be purchased and validated before boarding; all bus stops have ticket machines with transportation maps and instructions for buying and validating your ticket. Blue ticket machines accept cash or credit cards. You can buy a ZürichCARD for unlimited travel in the city for 1–3 days. These are valid for trams, buses, local trains and some boats, and offer discounts to museums, shops and restaurants. Numbers and stops (which are named) are displayed on the front of the vehicles and inside. Press the red button on the door to open it before getting off; it will close automatically. For information about public transportation ☎ 0848 988 988; www.zvv.ch. Taxis are an expensive option; call Taxi 7X7 (☎ 044 777 7777) or Taxi 444 (☎ 044 444 4444). Boats run on Lake Zurich April through October. Timetables are listed at departure points; call Wassertaxi (☎ 044 928 1811).

Airport Information

Zurich Airport (☎ 043 816 2211, or for flight information ☎ 0900 300 313 toll call; www.zurich-airport.com) is about 6 miles north of the city center. Trains run every 10 minutes from the Hauptbahnhof, daily 5:30 a.m.–12:30 a.m., with a ride time of around 10 minutes. There are two arrivals terminals, 1 and 2, which are interconnected. Taxis are available from outside the terminals; the journey from the airport to downtown costs SFr70, or telephone Airport Taxi (☎ 0848 850 852).

Climate – average highs and lows for the month

Jan.	Feb.	Mar.	Apr.	May	Jun.	Jul.	Aug.	Sep.	Oct.	Nov.	Dec.
2°C	3°C	8°C	12°C	16°C	19°C	22°C	22°C	18°C	12°C	6°C	3°C
36°F	37°F	46°F	54°F	61°F	66°F	72°F	72°F	64°F	54°F	43°F	37°F
-2°C	-2°C	2°C	4°C	8°C	11°C	14°C	14°C	11°C	7°C	2°C	0°C
28°F	28°F	36°F	39°F	46°F	52°F	57°F	57°F	52°F	45°F	36°F	32°F

Zurich Sights

Key to symbols

✚ map coordinates refer to the Zurich map on
page 456 🎟 admission charge: $$$ more
than SFr10, $$ SFr7–SFr10, $ less than SFr7
See page 5 for complete key to symbols

Altstadt

The narrow streets and peaceful squares
on either side of the Limmat river make
up the Altstadt (Old Town) with its
well-preserved old buildings. Take in
Lindenhof, a square planted with lime
trees on the site of the original Roman
settlement, then cross the river to
amble down the east side's lively
Niederdorfstrasse and Hirschengasse.

✚ A2–B2 ✉ Altstadt ☎ 044 215 4000 (tours)
🕐 Mon.–Fri. 3 p.m., Sat.–Sun. 11 a.m. and 3 p.m.,
Apr.–Oct.; Wed. and Sun. 11, Sat. 11 and 3, rest of year
🚋 Tram 3, 6, 7, 11, 13 🎟 Tours $$$

Fraumünster

The graceful spire of the Fraumünster
(Our Lady's Minster Church), founded
in the ninth century by two German
princesses, rises near the west riverbank
in the Old Town. The interior dates
from 1250 and earlier; against its gray
stone serenity, Marc Chagall's stained-
glass choir windows vibrate with green,
blue and yellow. Augusto Giacometti
designed the transept glass.

✚ A2 ✉ Münsterhof ☎ 044 221 2063; 🕐 Mon.–
Sat. 10–6, Sun. 11:15–6, Apr.–Oct.; 10–4, rest of year.
Sun. service at 10 a.m. 🚋 Trams 2, 6, 7, 8, 9, 11, 13
🎟 Free ℹ For guided tours ☎ 044 221 2063

Grossmünster

The Grossmünster (Great Cathedral)
played a major part in Zurich's
Reformation (a 16th-century movement
which aimed at reforming the Roman
Catholic Church and resulted in the
establishment of Protestant churches). It
was here that Ulrich Zwingli, the father
of Swiss Protestantism, preached and
taught. He transformed this Catholic
foundation into a theological college

that became the focal point of the
University of Zurich. The church,
galleries and three naves were built
between 1100 and 1260, a superb
Romanesque basilica with fine sculpture
on the capitals of its columns.

Be sure to visit the tranquil cloister,
where exhibits tell the story of the
Reformation, and then climb the tower
for views over Zurich and the lake.

✚ B2 ✉ Grossmünsterplatz ☎ 044 250 6650;
www.grossmuenster.ch 🕐 Mon.–Sat. 10–6, Sun.
noon–6, Mar.–Oct.; daily 10–5, rest of year. Open Sun.
when services finished 🚋 Tram 4, 15 🎟 Church free;
tower $

Kirche St. Peter

The oldest church foundation in
Zurich, Kirche St. Peter (St. Peter's
Church) stands in a quiet square at the
heart of the Old Town, its restrained
baroque interior typifying the city's
God-fearing prosperity.

Four churches predate the existing
one, which preserves the late
Romanesque choir and 13th-century
tower. All is harmony and balance, from
the richly carved choir stalls to the
superb plasterwork. The clock in the
tower is Europe's largest clockface,
measuring some 28.5 feet across.

✚ A2 ✉ St. Peterhofstatt ☎ 044 211 2588;
www.st-peter-zh.ch 🕐 Mon.–Fri. 8–6, Sat. 10–4,
Sun. noon–5 and service at 10 a.m. 🚋 Tram 4, 15
🎟 Free

Kunsthaus

Zurich's Kunsthaus (Art Gallery), a
lively museum that often mounts
important temporary exhibitions, is
mainly devoted to 19th- and 20th-
century paintings and artworks. Earlier
times are represented by a clutch of
Venetian paintings, as well as some
splendid Dutch works.

The exhibits of modern art are housed
in the newer wing. Here you'll find the
largest collection of Edvard Munch
outside Scandinavia, paintings by
Marc Chagall, and a good cross section
of modern work by Mark Rothko,

A street dominated by the clock tower of St. Peter's Church

Francis Bacon and Roy Lichtenstein, whose contribution is a piece showing a baked potato oozing with butter.

✚ B2 ✉ Heimplatz 1 ☎ 044 253 8484; www.kunsthaus.ch 🕐 Tue. and Sat.–Sun. 10–6, Wed.–Fri. 10–8 🚃 31; tram 3, 5, 8, 9 🍴 Café and restaurant 💰 $$$

Landesmuseum Zürich

Housed in a bizarre-looking castle complete with towers and turrets, the Landesmuseum Zürich (Swiss National Museum) should not be missed. This is the place to learn about Switzerland's history and development, and it is one of Europe's best organized museums.

Beginning in prehistoric times, you can follow the flowering of Swiss civilization through frescoes, religious wood carvings and exquisite jewelry, wood-paneled interiors, and furniture and costumes from every corner of the land. The 16th-century globes, showing

all that had so far been discovered, and the reconstruction of rooms from different eras, are fascinating.

✚ A4 ✉ Museumstrasse 2 ☎ 044 218 6511; www.nationalmuseum.ch 🕐 Tue.–Sun. 10–5 (also Thu. 5–7) 🚃 All buses and trams to Hauptbahnhof (main station) 🍴 Café and restaurant 💰 $$

Zoo Zürich

More than 2,000 animals are housed in the city's zoo, with special emphasis on species from South America, Africa and Asia. If you're traveling with children, arrange to be here at 10 a.m. when the elephants and monkeys are given their daily bath.

The zoo has a successful breeding program; a board near the entrance gives information about any new arrivals.

✚ Off map at B3 ✉ Zürichbergstrasse 221 ☎ 044 254 2505; www.zoo.ch 🕐 Daily 9–6, Mar.–Oct.; 9–5, rest of year 🚃 39; tram 6 🍴 Cafés and restaurant on zoo grounds 💰 $$$

Swiss Flavors

Switzerland has a range of regional dishes – German, French and Italian – rather than a national cuisine. With many foreigners working in the country, there's plenty of choice, and in the cities you'll find everything from Japanese to Tex-Mex. The Swiss call a restaurant menu the *karte* or *carte*; *menu* means the "dish of the day."

Swiss Cheese Specials

The country's best-known specialty, fondue, is made by melting a selection of Swiss hard cheeses, such as Gruyère, Emmentaler and Vacherin, in white wine spiked with garlic and then adding spices and kirsch. The bubbling pot sits in the middle of the table on a little brazier, and you help yourself by dipping forkfuls of bread into the thick mixture. Be careful not to drop the bread in the pot – traditionally the culprit has to buy the next bottle of wine. Fondues also are made by cooking cubed beef in either hot oil *(fondue bourguignonne)* or beef stock *(fondue chinoise);* these are served with a variety of tasty dipping sauces. The traditionally French *raclette* is undergoing a revival and is popular throughout Switzerland, particularly with large groups. A whole block of cheese is cut into slices and melted under a grill and then draped over boiled potatoes to be eaten with gherkins, smoked ham and sausage. It's delicious!

Main Dishes

Bündnerfleisch – raw, dried smoked beef – is well worth sampling, as are the many kinds of *Wurst*, sausages eaten cold, grilled or boiled. The traditional accompaniment is *Rösti*, a crisp potato cake studded with onions and bacon. Hungry diners might enjoy the *Berner Platte*, a groaning plate of sausage, beef and ham served with potatoes and sauerkraut. The Swiss also are fond of liver, pork and veal. Traditional fish recipes in this landlocked country involve lake trout, carp and perch.

A Little Something Sweet

Chocolate and cream feature heavily in Swiss desserts; in addition to the ubiquitous Nestlé and Cailler, Lindt, Sprüngli, Teuscher and Tobler are varieties of chocolate worth sampling. There are some splendid local cakes; try *Leckerli* (spiced bread with honey), meringues, and delicious kirsch-flavored cakes and fruit breads. Start the day with a breakfast bowl of muesli, a tasty mixture of grains, fruit and nuts.

Skiers build up a hearty appetite on the mountains for the delicious local fare

Hotels and Restaurants

Hotels and Restaurants

The hotels and restaurants in this book were selected by on-site contributing authors. Since price is often the best indication of the level of facilities and quality of service guests can expect, a three-tiered price guide appears at the beginning of the listings for each city. Prices vary widely depending on the country. Because variable rates will affect the amount of foreign currency that can be exchanged for dollars, price ranges are given in the local currency.

Although price ranges and any given days/times restaurants are closed were accurate at press time, this information is always subject to change. If you are interested in an establishment, it is always advisable to call ahead and verify amenities or hours of operation, but not all establishments will have phones.

Facilities suitable for travelers with disabilities vary greatly and you are strongly advised to contact an establishment directly. Buildings in the old areas of city centers may not be suitable for visitors with limited or impaired mobility.

Accommodations

Accommodations have been selected with two considerations in mind: a particularly attractive character or sense of local flavor, or a central location. Establishments in different price ranges are included for each city.

Map Coordinates

Map coordinates given in each listing relate to the city maps and give an idea of the approximate area in which each establishment is located. Although you may be able to find some of the street locations on these maps, it is always a good idea to pick up a more detailed city map from the local tourist office to help you find places.

City-center hotels fill up quickly, especially during summer; make reservations well in advance. In-room bathrooms (usually referred to as "en suite facilities") may not be available in smaller budget hotels.

European hotels normally provide a light breakfast of rolls or croissants and coffee (if not, the listing description is "room only"). Breakfast in British and Irish hotels, however, can be a filling meal of bacon, sausages, eggs, fried potatoes and toast.

Some hotels offer a price for their overnight accommodations that includes an evening meal (known as "half-board" in Britain and Ireland and *demi-pension* in French-speaking countries).

Eating Out

Listed restaurants range from upscale places to small cafés. Some are close to attractions; where this is the case, there is a cross-reference under the attraction listing. Other possibilities are the cafeterias and restaurants on the premises of museums and galleries.

Be sure to sample the amazing variety of indigenous European fast food: *crêpes* (filled pancakes) in France; tasty hot *Wurst* (sausages) in Germany and Austria; fish and chips (fish fillets and french fries) in Britain; savory tapas appetizers served in Spanish bars; and pizzas in Italy – served crusty and piping hot from charcoal ovens or *al taglio* (sliced to go) on street corners.

Many European hotels, especially the larger ones in big cities, are not only options for an overnight stay but also for a meal. Their lounges and bars often are comfortable, quiet places to relax.

Alcoholic beverages have a rich European heritage. France, Germany and Spain produce memorable wines; beers in the Czech Republic, Belgium and Britain are justly famed; and Guinness, of course, is an Irish institution. The nonalcoholic fruit juices (*portokalada freska*) served in Greece are wonderfully refreshing.

Cities are shown in the order that they appear in the book.

Price guide: (double room with breakfast for two people)

$	€60–€80
$$	€80–€160
$$$	over €160

Grand Hotel Wien $$$

Here you'll find the ultimate in luxury and style, with the personal service of a majestic old European hotel with modern comforts. Ask about the packages which typically include a champagne buffet breakfast, dinner for two in the hotel's restaurant, Le Ciel, and tickets to concerts, exhibitions or museums.
27 D2 ⊠ Kärntner Ring 9 ☎ 01 51 58 00; www.grandhotelwien.com 🚊 2A; tram 1, 2, D AX, DC, MC, VI

Hollmann Beletage Design & Boutique Hotel $$$

The outside of this small hotel in a 19th-century Old Town house with garden oozes wall-to-wall Vienna tradition. However, inside, you'll experience contemporary style and comforts, a touch of design humor and innovative features like its own mini movie theater.
27 D2 ⊠ Köllnerhofgasse 6 ☎ 01 96 11 960; www.hollman-beletage.at 🚊 Schwedenplatz, Stephansplatz 🚊 3A AX, DC, MC, VI

Hotel Kugel $$

In the trendy Spittelberg district, this family-run hotel in an historic building has 25 individually designed rooms. The generous buffet breakfast is included in the room rate and features hot and cold regional specialties and Viennese pastries.
27 B2 ⊠ Siebensterngasse 43 ☎ 01 523 3355; www.hotelkugel.at 🚊 Neubaugasse 🚊 13A, 49; tram 1, 1A, 1B MC, VI

Kärntnerhof $$–$$$

The Kärntnerhof, situated in the city center, is convenient for sightseeing. It occupies a 19th-century building with a roof garden and sits quietly on a cul-de-sac, where a gate leads to the beautiful courtyard of Heiligenkreuzerhof.
27 D2 ⊠ Grashofgasse 4 ☎ 01 51 21 923; www.karntnerhof.com 🚊 Stephansplatz, Schwedenplatz 🚊 3A AX, DC, MC, VI

Price guide: (dinner per person, excluding drinks)

$	€10–€15
$$	€15–€30
$$$	over €30

Augustinerkeller $$

Delicious Austrian- and Viennese-style dishes are complemented by good, locally produced wines. It's popular with foreign visitors.
27 C2 ⊠ Augustinerstrasse 1 ☎ 01 533 1026 🚊 Karlsplatz 🚊 2A AX, DC, MC, VI

Café Drechsler $–$$

This traditional coffeehouse is close to the Naschmarkt. Hot food from the classically Viennese menu is served throughout the day and international newspapers and magazines are available. On several evenings a week, DJs create a hip vibe.
27 C2 ⊠ Linke Wienzeile 22 ☎ 01 581 2044; www.cafedrechsler. at 🕐 Sun.–Thu. 8 a.m.–midnight, Fri.–Sat. 8 a.m.–2 a.m. 🚊 Karlsplatz, Kettenbrückengasse 🚊 59A No credit cards

Plachutta $$–$$$

This is one of the best restaurants for original Viennese dishes in the Old Town. Typical items include *Wiener Tafelspitz* (boiled rump of beef with apple and horseradish sauce), delicious sautéed pike or perch with garlic butter, and pork with dumplings and cabbage. Reservations are advisable.
27 D2 ⊠ Wollzeile 38 ☎ 01 512 1577; www.plachutta.at 🕐 Daily 11:30 a.m.–midnight 🚊 Stubentor 🚊 1A AX, DC, MC, VI

Steirereck $$$

This intimate (22 tables) restaurant is ideal for a special occasion or a relaxing lunch. The food here is a mix of traditional and international, and there is an outstanding wine list from the vaulted cellars. Reservations are necessary at this popular place.
27 D2 ⊠ Am Heumarkt 2A (Stadtpark) ☎ 01 71 33 168; www. steirereck.at 🕐 Closed public holidays 🚊 Stadtpark 🚊 2A AX, DC, MC, VI

Zu den 3 Hacken $$

For a traditional Austro-Hungarian menu, this place is hard to beat. You'll be able to choose from a long wine list, and to dine at a sidewalk table in good weather.
27 D2 ⊠ Singerstrasse 28 ☎ 01 512 5895; www.zuden3hacken. at 🕐 Closed Sun. 🚊 Stubentor 🚊 1A; tram 2 MC, VI

Price guide: (double room with breakfast for two people)

$	€50–€70
$$	€70–€150
$$$	over €150

Best Western Plus Hotel Goldener Adler $$–$$$

At this charming hotel in the heart of old Innsbruck, modern comfort combines with Tyrolean character. Past guests have included Mozart, Wagner and several emperors.
35 A2 ⊠ Herzog-Friedrich-Strasse 6 ☎ 0512 571111; www. goldeneradler.com 🚊 A, C, J, O, TS, W; tram 1, 3 AX, DC, MC, VI

Grand Hotel Europa $$$

Innsbruck's top hotel has a wide range of rooms at varying prices, some elegant public areas, and friendly and welcoming staff.
35 C1 ⊠ Südtiroler Platz 2 ☎ 0512 5931; www.grandhotel europa.at 🚊 J, O; tram 3 AX, DC, MC, VI

Hotel Maximiliam $$–$$$

The comfortable rooms at this welcoming hotel on the edge of the Old Town are stylish, light and modern. A breakfast buffet is included and there's a lobby bar.
35 A2 ⊠ Marktgraben 7–9 ☎ 0512 599 670; www.hotel-maximiliam.com 🚊 A, C, J, O, TS, W AX, DC, MC, VI

Weisses Kreuz $–$$

Mozart and his father once stayed at this 15th-century Old Town hotel, which combines Tyrolean charm with modern comfort. Rooms at the lower prices can be small. Restaurants are on the premises.
35 A2 ⊠ Herzog-Friedrich-Strasse 31 ☎ 0512 594790; www. weisseskreuz.at 🚊 A, C, J, O, TS, W; tram 1, 3 AX, MC, VI

Price guide: (dinner per person, excluding drinks)

$	€10–€15
$$	€15–€30
$$$	over €30

KEY TO SYMBOLS

- ✚ map page number and coordinates
- ✉ address
- ☎ telephone number
- ⊘ days/times closed
- Ⓜ nearest subway station
- 🚌 nearest bus/trolley bus/ tram/funicular route
- ⛴ ferry
- $$$ expensive
- $$ moderate
- $ inexpensive
- AX American Express
- DC Diners Club
- MC MasterCard
- VI VISA

Eating in Innsbruck

Most of Innsbruck's best – and most expensive – restaurants are located in a tiny area of Old Town, along with some excellent cafés and coffeehouses. Many of these places serve meals all day, so you can eat when you feel like it, a bonus if you've been skiing or hiking. Maria-Theresien-Strasse has a number of self-service and fast-food restaurants if you're looking for a quick lunchtime snack. For lunch with a view, take the Hungerburgbahn to Hoch-Innsbruck, where there are several restaurants with pretty terraces, or ride the cable car up to Seegrube mountain and eat on the terrace while enjoying a superb mountain panorama. The daily market, held in the Markthalle building beside the river, is an excellent place to buy provisions for a picnic.

Dengg $$

Known for its international cooking, Dengg offers contemporary fare that includes good vegetarian dishes and good service.

✚ 35 B2 ✉ Riesengasse 11–13 ☎ 0512 582347 ⊘ Closed Sun. and holidays 🚌 A, C, J, O, TS, W; tram 1, 3 AX, DC, MC, VI

Lichtblick/360° $$$

Lichtblick is a stylish wine bar, lounge and small restaurant with a wrap-around outdoor viewing terrace offering stunning, 360-degree panoramas over the city and mountains.

✚ 35 B1 ✉ Rathaus Galerien, Maria-Theresien-Strasse 18, 7th Floor ☎ 0512 566 550; www.360-grad.at ⊘ Mon.–Sat. 10 a.m.–1 a.m. 🚌 D, E, F, H, R, TS; tram 3 AX, DC, MC, VI

Ottoburg $–$$

This historic restaurant was established around 1745 in a building that some say is the oldest in Innsbruck. Dishes take in standard classics with fish, meat and noodles, but there are some innovative additions to the menu.

✚ 35 A2 ✉ Herzog-Friedrich-Strasse 1 ☎ 0512 584338; www. ottoburg.at ⊘ Daily noon–3 and 6–midnight 🚌 A, C, J, O, TS, W; tram 1, 3 AX, DC, MC, VI

Restaurant Goldener Adler $$

Its decor and friendly staff make this traditional hotel restaurant popular with locals and tourists alike. The menu of Tyrolean specialties includes steak with onions and braised saddle of lamb. The desserts are delicious.

✚ 35 A2 ✉ Herzog-Friedrich-Strasse 6 ☎ 0512 571111; www. goldeneradler.com 🚌 A, C, J, O, TS, W; tram 1, 3 AX, DC, MC, VI

Stiftskeller $$

In the heart of the Old Town, this restaurant with several dining rooms and a beer garden serves filling Tyrolean and Austrian specialties.

✚ 35 B2 ✉ Stiftgasse 1 ☎ 0512 570706; www.stiftskeller.eu 🚌 A, C, J, O, TS, W; tram 1, 3 AX, DC, MC, VI

SALZBURG HOTELS

Price guide: (double room with breakfast for two people)

$	€50–€70
$$	€70–€150
$$$	over €150

Boutiquehotel Am Dom $$–$$$

Reserve ahead to ensure one of just 15 rooms at this restored boutique hotel in the heart of Salzburg's historic center.

✚ 40 B3 ✉ Goldgasse 17 ☎ 0662 842 765; www.hotelamdom.at 🚌 3, 5, 6, 7, 8, 10, 20, 25, 28 AX, DC, MC, VI

Goldener Hirsch $$$

This luxurious, baronial-style hotel is one of Salzburg's oldest and most famous accommodations, and provides service to match. Rooms and suites are finished in vibrant colors and the restaurant is renowned throughout Austria.

✚ 40 B3 ✉ Getreidegasse 37 ☎ 0662 80 84-0; www.goldener hirsch.com 🚌 1, 4, 8, 22 AX, DC, MC, VI

Schloss Mönchstein $$$

This luxury-class hotel is beautifully situated in thickly wooded grounds high above the old center of Salzburg. Sumptuous rooms are complemented by gleaming marble bathrooms. There is a spa and a choice of dining venues, including an intimate four-seater dining room.

✚ 40 A3 ✉ Mönchsberg Park 26 ☎ 0662 848 555-0; www.monchstein. at 🚌 1, 4, 7, 8, 10, 22 AX, DC, MC, VI

Wolf-Dietrich $$–$$$

This family-run hotel near the city's historic center has a good restaurant, an indoor swimming pool, and a spa and sauna. Rooms include family suites for up to five people.

✚ 40 C4 ✉ Wolf-Dietrich-Strasse 7 ☎ 0662 871 275; www.wolf-dietrich. at 🚌 2, 4, 21, 22 AX, DC, MC, VI

SALZBURG RESTAURANTS

Price guide: (dinner per person, excluding drinks)

$	€10–€15
$$	€15–€30
$$$	over €30

Augustiner Bräu $

This huge, friendly restaurant serves beer, *Wurst* and simple Austrian fare in wood-paneled halls. The summer beer garden is extremely popular with tourists and can get very crowded.

✚ 40 A4 ✉ Lindhofstrasse 7 ☎ 0662 431 246; www. augustinerbier.at 🚌 7, 10, 20, 21, 24, 27, 28 No credit cards

Restaurant Zur Festung Hohensalzburg $$

Located in the Hohensalzburg Fortress (see page 43), this restaurant has panoramic views of the Salzburg area and serves good Austrian cooking (reservations required for dinner Jul.–Aug.).

⊞ 40 C2 ⊠ Hohensalzburg, Mönchsberg 34 ☎ 0662 841 780; www.salzburg-burgen.at ⏰ Closed mid-Jan. to late Feb. 🚋 Festungsbahn funicular AX, DC, MC, VI

St. Peter Stiftskeller $$

Said to be Europe's oldest restaurant, St. Peter Stiftskeller is a popular beer cellar serving reasonably priced beer, wine and local dishes.

⊞ 40 B2 ⊠ St. Peter Bezirk 1–4 ☎ 0662 841 2680; www.stpeter-stift skeller.at 🚋 1, 4, 5, 22 AX, MC, VI

Zirkelwirt $–$$

A small, atmospheric restaurant in a traditional building with an attractive garden terrace, the Zirkelwirt is popular for its homestyle Austrian cooking at surprisingly good prices given its location in the heart of the Old Town. The goulash with dumplings comes highly recommended.

⊞ 40 C2 ⊠ Pfeifergasse 14 ☎ 0662 842 796; www.zumzirkelwirt. at ⏰ Daily 11 a.m.–midnight 🚋 3, 5, 6, 7, 8 MC, VI

BRUSSELS HOTELS

Price guide: (double room with breakfast for two people)
$	under €100
$$	€100–€200
$$$	over €200

Amigo $$$

This charming hotel near the Grand' Place, part of the Rocco Forte group, is luxurious, offers perfect service, and is both lively and relaxed. Its excellent Italian restaurant serves Belgian specialties. Rooms have lovely central views.

⊞ 56 B2 ⊠ rue de l'Amigo 1–3, 1000 ☎ 02 547 4747; www. roccofortehotels.com 🚋 Gare Centrale 🚌 All bus and tram routes to Gare Centrale AX, DC, MC, VI

Le Dixseptième $$–$$$

This luxurious and stylish boutique hotel, in a grand 17th-century house in a great location behind the Grand' Place, was once the residence of the Spanish Ambassador. The old part of the hotel houses the breakfast room and several beautifully decorated suites, while the modern addition has 12 comfortable rooms.

⊞ 56 B2 ⊠ rue de la Madeleine 25, 1000 ☎ 02 517 1717; www. ledixseptieme.be 🚋 Gare Centrale 🚋 Tram: all routes to Gare Centrale AX, DC, MC, VI

La Grande Cloche $

Excellent value for central Brussels, La Grande Cloche is an older style hotel but rooms are pleasant and spacious. There's free WiFi in the rooms.

⊞ 56 A2 ⊠ 10 place Rouppe, 1000 ☎ 02 512 6140; www.hotel grandecloche.com 🚋 Anneessens 🚋 Tram 3, 4, 32 AX, MC, VI

Métropole $$$

Built in 1895, the Métropole's glorious and flamboyant facade and ground floor are now a protected monument. The hotel has a fine restaurant, L'Alban Chambon, a beautiful bar and a fitness center.

⊞ 56 B3 ⊠ place De Brouckère 31, 1000 ☎ 02 217 2300; www.metro polehotel.com 🚋 De Brouckère 🚌 29, 63, 126, 127, 128; tram 1, 3, 4, 5, 24 AX, DC, MC, VI

Warwick Barsey $$–$$$

One of Brussels' few boutique hotels, this is elegantly decorated with rich textiles and objets d'art. This a choice venue for visiting celebrities and a perfect location for those who have shopping in mind.

⊞ 56 off B1 ⊠ avenue Louise 381–383, 1050 ☎ 02 649 9800; www.warwickhotels.com 🚋 Louise then tram 93 and 94 (from city center) AX, DC, MC, VI

BRUSSELS RESTAURANTS

Price guide: (dinner per person, excluding drinks)
$	under €35
$$	€35–€60
$$$	over €60

Belga Queen $$–$$$

The superb Hôtel de la Poste, with its grand entrance hall and beautiful, late 19th-century stained-glass windows, is now a trendy dining complex with fine dining, oyster bar and beer bar.

⊞ 56 B3 ⊠ rue Fosse aux Loups 32, 1000 ☎ 02 217 2187; www. belgaqueen.be 🚋 De Brouckère 🚌 29, 38, 63, 66, 71 AX, DC, MC, VI

Le Chou de Bruxelles $–$$

This small bistro is *the* place for *moules* and *frites* (mussels and fries). You can choose from 30 different sauces to accompany your shellfish. There is also a lovely terrace for summer dining.

⊞ 56 off B1 ⊠ rue de Florence 26, 1050 ☎ 02 537 6995; www. lechoudebruxelles.be ⏰ Closed Sun., and Mon. lunch 🚋 Tram 93, 94 MC, VI

Comme Chez Soi $$$

Brussels' top gastronomic experience can be savored at this celebrated restaurant. New Belgian cuisine with traditional specialties is featured; reserve well in advance.

⊞ 56 A2 ⊠ place Rouppe 23, 1000 ☎ 02 512 2921; www.commechezsoi. be ⏰ Closed Sun.and Mon., and Tue.–Wed. lunch 🚋 Anneessens 🚋 Tram 3, 4, 32 MC, VI

Le Corrège $

An excellent lunch stop close to the attractions of Cinquantenaire Park. This informal restaurant serves Belgian and French dishes made with market-fresh produce.

⊞ 56 off map at C2 ⊠ rue le Corrège, 1000 ☎ 02 734 3412; www.lecorrege.be ⏰ Closed Sat. and Sun., and Mon.–Wed. dinner 🚌 21, 63, 79 MC, VI

Vincent $$–$$$

At this traditional Bruxellois restaurant, skilled waiters prepare specialties like *steak flambée* or *steak tartare* with a flourish at your table. Entrance to the atmospheric, old-fashioned tiled dining room is through the kitchen.

⊞ 56 B3 ⊠ 8–10 rue des Dominicains, off rue des Bouchers, 1000 ☎ 02 511 2607; www. restaurantvincent.com ⏰ Closed Jan. 1–12 and Aug. 1–15 🚋 De Brouckère, Gare Centrale AX, DC, MC, VI

Wine Bar Les Caves du Sablon $$

This is an excellent wine bar with a cozy dining room in the cellar. The menu is compact, concentrating on continental fare. Wines are available by the glass.

⊞ 56 B2 ⊠ rue des Pigeons, 1000 ☎ 02 513 1220; www.cavesdusablon. be ⏰ Closed Sun., daily lunch, and mid-Jul. to mid-Aug. 🚋 Grand Sablon 🚌 27, 95 DC, MC, VI

Belgium, Britain

KEY TO SYMBOLS

⊞	map page number and coordinates
✉	address
☎	telephone number
⊘	days/times closed
Ⓜ	nearest subway station
🚌	nearest bus/trolley bus/ tram/funicular route
⛴	ferry
$$$	expensive
$$	moderate
$	inexpensive
AX	American Express
DC	Diners Club
MC	MasterCard
VI	VISA

Chocolates Galore

By far the best chocolate shop in Bruges is the family-run Spegelaere at Ezelstraat 92. The house specialty is bunches of chocolate grapes filled with marzipan or *pralinée*. Here you can see the daily production of fresh chocolate in a workshop where traditional methods are used – from the preparation of the chocolate in melting cauldrons to the hand-making process, in which white, milk and dark chocolate are fashioned into a variety of forms. Choco-Story is a fascinating chocolate museum at St. Jansplein (Wijnzakstraat 2; ☎ 050 612 237; www.choco-story.be, daily 10–5). It explains the history of chocolate and the process of making chocolates. Finish your visit with a taste of freshly made chocolates by one of Belgium's master *chocolatiers*. The Museum of Cocoa and Chocolate in Brussels is at rue de la Tête d'Or 9–11 (off Grand' Place) ☎ 02 514 2048; www.choco-story-brussels.be, Tue.–Sun. 10–4:30 (also open Mon. 10–4:30 during national public holidays).

Price guide: (double room with breakfast for two people)

$	under €100
$$	€100–€200
$$$	over €200

Hotel Fevery $–$$

This small family-owned eco-label hotel is centrally located and also offers gluten-free breakfast options, WiFi and private parking.
⊞ 62 B3 ✉ Collaert Mansionstraat 3, 8000 ☎ 050 331 269; www.hotelfevery.be 🚌 4, 14 MC, VI

Hotel Patritius $–$$

The family-owned Patritius is set in a 17th-century building with large bedrooms, courtyard garden and private parking (extra charge).
⊞ 62 B3 ✉ Riddersstraat 11, 8000 ☎ 050 338 454; www.hotelpatritius.be 🚌 1 AX, MC, VI

Martin's Orangerie $$–$$$

One of Bruges' most lauded hotels is within this 15th-century canalside building, with views of the tree-lined Dijver walkway. Guests have use of the pool and sauna of the De Tuilerieën Hotel.
⊞ 62 B2 ✉ Kartuizerinnensstraat 10, 8000 ☎ 050 341 649; www.hotelorangerie.be 🚌 1, 11, 91 AX, DC, MC, VI

The Pand Hotel $$$

This hotel is hidden away on a backwater close to the Markt. Rooms are luxurious and tastefully decorated. The owners also own an antiques and objets d'art shop, Kasimir's Antique Studio.
⊞ 62 B2 ✉ Pandreitje 16, 8000 ☎ 050 340 666; www.pandhotel.com 🚌 1, 6, 11, 16, 88, 91 AX, DC, MC

Price guide: (dinner per person, excluding drinks)

$	under €30
$$	€30–€50
$$$	over €50

Bistro den Huzaar $–$$

Chef Willy Bostyn serves a mix of French and Flemish dishes including smoked eel soup and stews flavored with beer. There's a terrace for summer dining.
⊞ 62 B2 ✉ Vlamingstraat 36, 8000 ☎ 050 333 797; www.denhuzaar.be ⊘ Closed Wed. and Thu. 🚌 All buses for Markt MC, VI

Bistro Pro Deo $

This city town house has been transformed into a cozy period bistro, serving meat and fish dishes, and a good value lunch menu. Gluten-free and vegetarian options are available.
⊞ 62 C3 ✉ 161 Langestraat, 8000 ☎ 050 337 355; www.bistroprodeo.be ⊘ Closed Sun. and Mon. 🚌 6, 16, 88 MC, VI

Park $$–$$$

Classic Belgian cuisine is served in this elegant setting, including excellent seafood. There also is a very good choice of wines.
⊞ 62 B2 ✉ Minderbroedersstraat 1, 8000 ☎ 497 801 872; www.parkrestaurant.be ⊘ Closed lunch, and Mon. and Thu. dinner ⓘ No public transport AX, DC, MC, VI

Réliva $$

This modern bistro-style restaurant brings traditional dishes from around Europe to the table. It also offers vegetarian and vegan dishes.
⊞ 62 B2 ✉ Goezepuntstraat 6, 8000 ☎ 050 331 307; www.reliva.be ⊘ Closed Mon.–Thu. lunch, Tue.–Wed. dinner ⓘ No public transport MC, VI

Rock Fort $$

The owners of this restaurant put on the menu only the things they like to eat: their favorite Belgian dishes feature a touch of the Mediterranean.
⊞ 62 B2/C2 ✉ Langestraat 15, 8000 ☎ 050 334 113; www.rock-fort.be ⊘ Closed Sat. and Sun. 🚌 6, 16, 88 AX, MC, VI

Price guide: (double room with breakfast for two people)

$	under €75
$$	€75–€175
$$$	over €175

Ghent Marriott Hotel $$–$$$

Housed behind a facade of historical downtown waterside mansions, this contemporary hotel is renowned for its excellent service.
⊞ 70 A1 ✉ Korenlei 10, 9000 ☎ 09 233 9393; www.marriott.com 🚌 Tram 1, 4, 24 AX, DC, MC, VI

Hotel Erasmus $$

This charming family-run hotel is in an impressive town house, right in the center of town, but you will not be disturbed by noise. The 10 bedrooms are furnished in authentic Flemish style. Friendly service.

➕ 70 A3 ✉ Poel 25, 9000 ☎ 09 224 2195; www.erasmushotel.be
🚊 3, 17, 18, 38, 39 AX, DC, MC, VI

Hotel de Flandre $$

The cool and comfortable contemporary rooms are housed in two interconnected and renovated buildings in the city center.

➕ 70 A3 ✉ Poel 1–2, 9000
☎ 09 266 0600; www.historic-hotels-ghent.com 🚊 3, 17, 18, 38, 39
AX, DC, MC, VI

Hotel Harmony $$

A modern interior wrapped in two canalside town houses, the Harmony combines history with modern facilities, including a swimming pool. The lovely courtyard garden is an added bonus.

➕ 70 B4 ✉ Kraanlei 37, 9000
☎ 09 324 2680; www.hotel-harmony. be 🚊 Tram 1, 4, 24 AX, MC, VI

NH Gent Belfort $$

This is a large luxury hotel in the historic heart of the city, opposite the Town Hall. Its many amenities, including a restaurant and fitness room, make it a decent value.

➕ 70 B3 ✉ Hoogpoort 63
☎ 09 233 3331; www.nh-hotels.com
ℹ No public transport MC, VI

Price guide: (dinner per person, excluding drinks)
$ under €30
$$ €30–€50
$$$ over €50

Avalon $

Avalon is one of a new generation of vegetarian restaurants that sources local and organic ingredients to produce contemporary dishes.

➕ 70 B4 ✉ Geldmunt 32, 9000
☎ 09 224 3724; www.restaurant avalon.be ⓒ Closed Mon., Tue.–Sun. dinner, second week in Apr.
🚊 Tram 4 AX, MC, VI

Brasserie Pakhuis $$–$$$

Set in a large and spectacular warehouse *(pakhuis* in Flemish) is this wonderful restaurant, popular with locals for its mouthwatering French-Italian cuisine.

➕ 70 A3 ✉ Schuurkenstraat 4, 9000
☎ 09 223 5555; www.pakhuis.be
ⓒ Closed Sun. 🚊 3, 17, 18, 38, 39; tram 1, 4, 24 AX, DC, MC, VI

The House of Eliott $$$

The dining room pays homage to the heyday of the art deco and art nouveau eras, but it's the cuisine that keeps customers returning. Lobster dishes are a specialty here.

➕ 70 A3 ✉ Jan Breydelstraat 36, 9000 ☎ 09 225 2128; www.thehouse ofeliott.be ⓒ Closed Tue., Wed. and Thu. lunch 🚊 Tram 1, 24 AX, MC, VI

Volta $$–$$$

A little way out of the tourist center, this restaurant offers a modern European menu. You can kick-start your evening here with your favorite beverage at the cocktail bar upstairs.

➕ 70 off map at A3 ✉ Nieuwe Wandeling 2b 9000 ☎ 09 324 0500; www.volta-gent.be ⓒ Closed Sun. and Mon. 🚊 38, 39, 53, 65, 67; tram 4 MC, VI

Price guide: (double room with breakfast for two people)
$ £50–£100
$$ £100–£150
$$$ over £150

The Berkeley $$$

This stylish hotel, just off Knightsbridge, offers luxurious comfort in a chic setting, along with great views from the rooftop pool. Marcus Wareing's restaurant offers some of the best dining in London, and the guests can book the chef's table for an extra special experience.

➕ 86 A3 ✉ Wilton Place, Knightsbridge ☎ 020 7235 6000; www.the-berkeley.co.uk ⓒ Hyde Park Corner AX, DC, MC, VI

DoubleTree by Hilton Tower of London $$$

The Tower View suites are particularly desirable and the rooftop bar offers perhaps the best view in London.

➕ 87 F3 ✉ 7 Pepys Street ☎ 020 7709 1000; doubletree3.hilton.com
ⓒ Tower Hill AX, DC, MC, VI

Dukes London $$$

This gem of a hotel is one of Britain's most desirable boutique hotels. Don't miss either the martinis or the afternoon teas.

➕ 86 C2 ✉ St. James's Place
☎ 020 7491 4840; www.dukeshotel. com ⓒ Green Park AX, DC, MC, VI

The Goring $$$

An icon of hospitality for more than a century, this classic hotel offers

spacious comfort and friendly service all within easy reach of Buckingham Palace – so it's no wonder the now Duchess of Cambridge chose to stay here the night before her wedding to Prince William in April 2011.

➕ 86 C2 ✉ Beeston Place ☎ 020 7396 9000; www.thegoring.com
ⓒ Victoria AX, DC, MC, VI

Myhotel Chelsea $$

This small hotel in the heart of South Kensington is a great budget option. The styling is modern and quirky. It offers its own raw food café as well as a good Italian restaurant.

➕ 86 B1 ✉ 35 Ixworth Place
☎ 020 7225 7500; www.myhotels. com ⓒ South Kensington
AX, MC, VI

Price guide: (dinner per person, excluding drinks)
$ £10–£15
$$ £15–£30
$$$ over £30

Dinner by Heston Blumenthal $$$

The innovative British chef pushes fine dining to new levels, and his exciting modern twists bring the wow-factor to many classic recipes dating from 1390 to 1940. The restaurant setting is stylish, the service is charming and the experience most memorable.

➕ 86 B2 ✉ Mandarin Oriental Hyde Park, Knightsbridge ☎ 020 7201 3833; www.dinnerbyheston.com
ⓒ Knightsbridge AX, DC, MC, VI

Gillray's Steakhouse & Bar $$

Near to the London Eye, and with fabulous views across the Thames to the Houses of Parliament, this sophisticated restaurant offers an interesting British food, with top-notch steaks and superb puddings.

➕ 87 D2 ✉ Marriott Hotel County Hall, Westminster Bridge Road
☎ 020 7902 8000; www.gillrays.com
ⓒ Westminster, Waterloo AX, DC, MC, VI

Murano $$$

Expect Italian refinement at this extremely upscale restaurant, and a menu that reflects the wider European influences of owner-chef Angela Hartnett. The atmosphere here is anything but stuffy and the food is superb.

➕ 86 C2 ✉ 20–22 Queen Street

KEY TO SYMBOLS

- ⊞ map page number and coordinates
- ✉ address
- ☎ telephone number
- ⊙ days/times closed
- Ⓟ nearest subway station
- ▤ nearest bus/trolley bus/ tram/funicular route
- 🖃 ferry
- $$$ expensive
- $$ moderate
- $ inexpensive
- AX American Express
- DC Diners Club
- MC MasterCard
- VI VISA

☎ 020 7495 1127; www.murano london.com ⊙ Closed Sun. Ⓟ Green Park AX, MC, VI

Namo $

Authentic, inspiring Vietnamese food is served up in the East London setting of Victoria Park village. Go for a delicious lunch or sublime supper. ⊞ 87 off map at F4 ✉ 178 Victoria Park Road ☎ 020 8533 0639; www. namo.co.uk Ⓟ Bethnal Green, then bus 388 AX, MC, VI

Pizzaro $–$$

Top-notch authentic modern Spanish cuisine is the order here. The open kitchen sets the buzz, and look out for the daily specials. Lying south of the River Thames, the now-trendy area of Bermondsey is a foodie haven with lively street markets. ⊞ 86 F2 ✉ 194 Bermondsey Street ☎ 020 7378 9455; www.pizarro restaurant.com Ⓟ Bermondsey, Borough, London Bridge AX, MC, VI

EDINBURGH HOTELS

Price guide: (double room with breakfast for two people)
$ £50–£100
$$ £100–£150
$$$ over £150

Abbey Hotel $–$$$

Situated on the north side of Calton Hill, this small hotel in a Georgian town house offers good views to the Firth of Forth from the top floors. ⊞ 99 E3 ✉ 9 Royal Terrace ☎ 0131 557 0022; abbeyhoteledin burgh.co.uk ▤ City-center buses AX, MC, VI

The Balmoral Hotel $$$

This classic Edwardian building dominates the east end of Princes Street with superb views over the city. All rooms are elegantly furnished and air-conditioned. ⊞ 99 D3 ✉ 1 Princes Street ☎ 0131 556 2414; www.roccoforte hotels.com ▤ City-center buses AX, DC, MC, VI

Mercure Edinburgh City $$

This is a great mid-price option in the city center, offering private balconies with panoramic views, especially from the seventh floor. The Princes Street location is enviable and the views of the castle are superb. ⊞ 99 C2 ✉ Princes Street; www.mercureedinburgh.co.uk ▤ City-center buses AX, MC, VI

The Scotsman Hotel $$$

Formerly the headquarters of _The Scotsman_ newspaper, this elegant hotel has contemporary bedrooms and state-of-the-art technology. Note the stainless steel swimming pool. ⊞ 99 D2 ✉ 20 North Bridge ☎ 0131 556 5565; www.thescots manhotel.co.uk ▤ City-center buses AX, MC, VI

Waldorf Astoria Edinburgh $$$

A Waldorf Astoria Hotel, the "Caley," (formerly the Caledonian Hotel) is a haven of luxury and style. Request a bedroom with a castle view. ⊞ 98 B2 ✉ Princes Street ☎ 0131 222 8888; www.waldorfastoria edinburgh.com ▤ City-center buses AX, DC, MC, VI

EDINBURGH RESTAURANTS

Price guide: (dinner per person, excluding drinks)
$ £10–£15
$$ £15–£30
$$$ over £30

21212 $$$

Talented chef Paul Kitching serves French cuisine in this Georgian town house near Calton Hill. The set three-course lunch is a good value. ⊞ 99 E3 ✉ 3 Royal Terrace ☎ 0131 523 1030; www.21212 restaurant.co.uk ⊙ Closed Sun. and Mon.; 2 weeks in Jan. and in summer ▤ City-center buses AX, MC, VI

The Kitchin $$$

A former whisky warehouse in Leith's dockside is home to one of Scotland's most dynamic chefs, Tom Kitchin. Expect passionate attention to the flavors of the finest local and seasonal ingredients. The set lunch offers a good value. ⊞ 99 off map at E3 ✉ 78 Commercial Quay, Leith ☎ 0131 555 1755; www.thekitchin.com ⊙ Closed Sun.–Mon., first two weeks Jan. ▤ 16, 22 AX, MC, VI

Number One, The Balmoral $$$

Located in the grand baronial-style Balmoral Hotel near Waverley Station, this smart modern dining room offers dynamic Scottish cooking at its best. ⊞ 99 D3 ✉ 1 Princes Street ☎ 0131 557 6727; www.roccoforte hotels.com ⊙ Closed 2 weeks in Jan. ▤ City-center buses AX, DC, MC, VI

English Pubs

The traditional English pub, from the term "public house," is another of those treasured institutions by which an entire culture is measured. The great thing about traditional pubs is their spirit of easygoing informality. Pubs were always the focus of local life, places where people exchanged views and took their hard-earned leisure. It is no coincidence that village pub and village church often stand cheek by jowl. In medieval times, churches and monasteries often owned the local pub, or "hostelry." In and around Oxford you will find traditional pubs that have not compromised with modern fashion, while still maintaining the highest standards of comfort and service. Try the Chequers, off High Street; the King's Arms, on Holywell Street; the Turf Tavern, in Bath Place; the Isis Farmhouse on the towpath at Iffley Lock; or The Rose and Crown on North Parade Avenue.

Ondine Restaurant $$–$$$

Just off the Royal Mile, this good seafood restaurant has a lively buzz and great views over the Old Town. Pre-theater menu available.

⊞ 99 C2 ⊠ 2 George IV Bridge ☎ 0131 226 1888; www.ondinerestaurant.co.uk ⊗ Closed Sun., first week in Jan. 🚌 35 AX, DC, MC, VI

Stac Polly $$

Just off the Royal Mile, Stac Polly is a cozy, city-center bistro with the charm of a country restaurant. The traditional Scottish cuisine also features some global touches. Reservations are advised.

⊞ 99 D2 ⊠ 38 St. Mary's Street ☎ 0131 557 5754; www.stacpolly.com ⊗ Closed Sun.–Mon., and Sat. lunch 🚌 35 AX, MC, VI

OXFORD HOTELS

Price guide: (double room with breakfast for two people)
$ £50–£100
$$ £100–£150
$$$ over £150

Belmond Le Manoir aux Quat'Saisons $$$

This is one of the UK's most delightful and intimate hotels, set in a pretty Oxfordshire village. Guests here can enjoy beautifully designed rooms, lovely English gardens and a fabulous restaurant serving exquisite food.

⊞ 107 off map at C1 ⊠ Church Road, Great Milton ☎ 0184 427 8881; www.belmond.com No public transport AX, MC, VI

Macdonald Randolph Hotel $$$

This landmark hotel, with neo-Gothic architectural elegance and elegant interiors, has very comfortable rooms and luxury service. Visit the spa for treatments or its sauna and Jacuzzi. It is near to the Ashmolean Museum.

⊞ 107 A2 ⊠ Beaumont Street ☎ 01865 256400; www.macdonaldhotels.co.uk ⊟ City-center buses AX, MC, VI

Manor House Hotel $$

This small, family-run hotel in a Victorian-era building, a mile from the center, has a comfortable lounge, bar and breakfast facilities.

⊞ 107 off map at C1 ⊠ 250 Iffley Road ☎ 01865 727627; www.manorhouseoxford.com ⊟ 3 MC, VI

Mercure Oxford Eastgate $$

The scholars J.R.R. Tolkein and C.S. Lewis once favored this historic hotel, now stylishly refurbished and equipped to a high standard of comfort, with a good Italian restaurant. It's an easy stroll from the city center, and close to the Botanic Garden.

⊞ 107 C1 ⊠ 73 High Street ☎ 01865 248332; www.mercure.com ⊟ City-center buses AX, MC, VI

Old Bank Hotel $$–$$$

This skillfully restored former bank is a place of tranquility away from the bustle of High Street, yet within walking distance of all central sights and shops. The Quod Brasserie and Bar (see right) is on the premises.

⊞ 107 B2 ⊠ 92–94 High Street ☎ 01865 799599; www.oldbankhotel.co.uk ⊟ City-center buses AX, MC, VI

OXFORD RESTAURANTS

Price guide: (dinner per person, excluding drinks)
$ £10–£15
$$ £15–£30
$$$ over £30

Brasserie Blanc $$–$$$

A popular and stylish yet friendly brasserie owned by the renowned French chef Raymond Blanc. Ingredients are seasonal and of the finest quality in the restaurant.

⊞ 107 off map at C3 ⊠ 71–72 Walton Street ☎ 01865 510999; www.brasserieblanc.com ⊗ Closed Dec. 25 🚌 2, 6 AX, MC, VI

Kazbar $–$$

Kazbar is a popular and inexpensive *tapas* restaurant with a *souk*-inspired setting and great wine list. Sip a glass of Rioja while nibbling on *gambas pil pil* (prawns in chili and garlic) or oven-roasted pork ribs.

⊞ 107 off map at C1 ⊠ 25–27 Cowley Road ☎ 01865 202920; www.kazbar.com ⊗ Closed lunch Mon.–Fri. 🚌 5, 10, 12 MC, VI

The Punter $–$$

This rustic, cool pub is a gastronomic treat found on Osney Island, in the River Thames. Sample the Punter's own ale, and relax in the eclectic, informal setting, to enjoy a homestyle burger and fries, or perhaps a tasty venison steak.

⊞ 107 off map at A1 ⊠ 7 South

Street ☎ 01865 248832; www.thepunteroxford.co.uk ⊟ City-center buses MC, VI

Quod Brasserie and Bar $–$$$

This trendy and popular all-day hotel bar and grill serves breakfast and later a choice of modern British cuisine and pizzas. Enjoy live jazz here every Sunday evening.

⊞ 107 B2 ⊠ Old Bank Hotel, 92–94 High Street ☎ 01865 202505; www.quod.co.uk ⊗ Closed Dec. 25–26 ⊟ City-center buses AX, MC, VI

YORK HOTELS

Price guide: (double room with breakfast for two people)
$ £50–£100
$$ £100–£150
$$$ over £150

Cedar Court Grand Hotel and Spa $$–$$$

A central location, a superb spa with indoor pool and great facilities make this hotel one of York's best options. There are two good restaurants and afternoon tea is a special treat.

⊞ 113 B2 ⊠ Station Rise ☎ 01904 380038; www.thegrandyork.co.uk ⊟ City-center buses AX, MC, VI

Guy Fawkes Inn $–$$$

This historic inn was the birthplace in 1570 of the notorious gunpowder plotter, Guy Fawkes. Bedrooms are furnished with antiques, Italian fabrics and luxury beds. Atmospheric original features in the public areas include gas lighting and open fires.

⊞ 113 C2 ⊠ 25 High Petergate ☎ 01904 623716; www.gfyork.com ⊟ City-center buses MC, VI

Hotel du Vin York $–$$$

Enjoy being cosseted in this elegant town-house hotel, with monsoon showers in the bathrooms and quality furnishings throughout.

⊞ 113 A1 ⊠ 89 The Mount ☎ 01904 557350; www.hotelduvin.com AX, MC, VI

Mount Royale $$$

Some of the individually styled bedrooms of this friendly hotel lead out into the attractive gardens. There's a good restaurant on the spot, and it's not far from the town center.

⊞ 113 off map at A1 ⊠ 119 The Mount ☎ 01904 628856; www.mountroyale.co.uk ⊟ City-center buses AX, MC, VI

470

KEY TO SYMBOLS

- map page number and coordinates
- address
- telephone number
- days/times closed
- nearest subway station
- nearest bus/trolley bus/tram/funicular route
- ferry
- $$$ expensive
- $$ moderate
- $ inexpensive
- AX American Express
- DC Diners Club
- MC MasterCard
- VI VISA

Danish Smørrebrød

Like their fellow Scandinavians, Danes are great believers in hearty lunches, and nothing is more mouthwatering or filling than *smørrebrød*, which translates simply as "buttered bread." If it sounds like "smothering," then that's exactly what happens to the large slice of rye bread that is the basis of *smørrebrød* when it is piled high with a tasty mix of salads and garnishes, shrimp and chunks of fish, beef or pork. You can accompany this mini-banquet with a Danish lager or a small glass of chilled *akvavit* (aquavit). You also can enjoy the Danish *kolt bord*, or cold table, an array of meat and fish dishes, salads and savory dips, hot dishes, and a selection of bread and rolls.

YORK RESTAURANTS

Price guide: (dinner per person, excluding drinks)
$ £10–£15
$$ £15–£30
$$$ over £30

The Blue Bicycle $$–$$$

One of York's best-loved restaurants exudes old charm and offers a wide-ranging, modern European menu and an excellent wine list. It's situated alongside the River Foss.
113 C2 ✉ 34 Fossgate ☎ 01904 673990; www.thebluebicycle.com ⊘ Closed lunch Mon.–Wed. 🚌 City-center buses MC, VI

El Piano $–$$

There's a strong Spanish feel to this very popular *tapas* restaurant, which specializes in gluten-free vegan food, sourced locally and as ethically as possible. The flavors are as fresh and vibrant as the decor.
113 B2 ✉ 17 Grape Lane ☎ 01904 610676; www.el-piano.com 🚌 City-center buses MC, VI

The Judges Lodgings $–$$

Dine on the terrace of this historic town house close to the city's famous church, York Minster. The Cellar Bar offers a changing menu of seasonal Yorkshire fare, including a tasty beef and ale pie, and beer-battered haddock and fries, as well as lighter salad options.
113 C2 ✉ 9 Lendal ☎ 01904 638733; www. judgeslodgingyork.co.uk 🚌 2, city-center buses MC, VI

The Lamb & Lion $–$$

Built into the ancient city walls and in the shadow of the Minster, this cozy pub is a historic gem. The food is comforting and tasty, and the ales are hand-pulled. Dine al fresco in the courtyard in summer.
113 B3 ✉ 2–4 High Petergate ☎ 01904 654112; www.lamband lionyork.com 🚌 City-center buses MC, VI

Melton's Restaurant $$

Attractively presented modern British cuisine, and generous portions are on offer here. There is an appealing fixed-price lunch as well as an early evening fixed-price menu.
113 off map at B2 ✉ 7 Scarcroft Road ☎ 01904 634341; www.meltonsrestaurant.co.uk ⊘ Closed Sun. and Mon. and Dec. 23–Jan. 9 🚌 11 MC, VI

Rustique $–$$

Authentic, rustic French cooking is offered in this well-established bistro with a very decent wine list and a good-value set menu.
113 C2 ✉ 28 Castlegate ☎ 01904 612744; www.rustique restaurants.co.uk 🚌 City-center buses AX, MC, VI

PRAGUE HOTELS

Price guide: (double room with breakfast for two people)
$ 1,000Kč–2,500Kč
$$ 2,500Kč–4,500Kč
$$$ over 4,500Kč

Hotel Savoy $$$

A relaxed atmosphere prevails at this stunning, five-star top Prague hotel, located behind Prague Castle. Rooms are well designed and modernized, making it a perfect base.
124 off map at A4 ✉ Keplerova 6 ☎ 224 302 430; www.hotelsavoy.com Ⓜ Malostranská 🚊 Tram 22 AX, DC, MC, VI

Penzion U Medvídků $$

The name of this 15th-century former brewery tavern means "The Little Bear." There are 33 rooms in two categories: all have bathrooms, but the "historic rooms" cost more. There's a breakfast buffet.
125 C3 ✉ Na Perštýně 7 ☎ 224 211 916; www.umedvidku.cz Ⓜ Narodní třída 🚊 Tram 6, 9, 18, 22 AX, DC, MC, VI

Sax $$

On the steep hill leading to Prague Castle (just off Nerudova, near Charles Bridge), this hotel has a funky, retro-inspired interior and well-equipped, comfortable rooms.
124 A4 ✉ Jánský vršek 3 ☎ 257 531 268; www.hotelsax.cz Ⓜ Malostranská 🚊 Tram 12, 20, 22 AX, DC, MC, VI

U Zlaté Studně $$$

This luxury boutique hotel, perched on a hill overlooking Malá Strana, has won excellence awards around the world, meaning you will have to plan your stay well in advance. It is worth it, though, for the 17th-century period charm, the peacefulness and the chance to dine on the lovely terrace.
124 B4 ✉ U Zlaté Studně 4 ☎ 257 011 213; www.goldenwell.cz Ⓜ Malostranská 🚊 Tram 12, 20, 22 AX, DC, MC, VI

Britain, Czech Republic, Denmark

PRAGUE RESTAURANTS

Price guide: (dinner per person, excluding drinks)

$	100Kč–200Kč
$$	200Kč–600Kč
$$$	over 600Kč

Aromi $$–$$$

Aromi has been turning out arguably Prague's best high-end Italian cooking for several years and shows no sign of letting up. The setting in residential Vinohrady is elegant without being stuffy. The chef prides himself on the fish choices, but everything is delicious. Reservations are a good idea in the evening.

✚ 124 off map at E2 ✉ Mánesova 78 ☎ 222 713 222; www.aromi.cz Ⓜ Jiřího z Poděbrad 🚊 Tram 11 AX, DC, MC, VI

Francouzská Restaurace $$$

This stylish art nouveau, Czech-style pub, on the ground floor of the landmark Obecní dům (Municipal House), offers traditional specialties served amid grand, end-of-the-20th-century splendor.

✚ 125 E4 ✉ Náměstí Republiky 5 ☎ 222 002 770; www.francouzska restaurace.cz Ⓜ Náměstí Republiky 5 🚊 Tram 5, 8, 14, 26 AX, DC, MC, VI

Lokál $

Solid Czech pub fare, including good roasted pork and *Wiener Schnitzel*, plus arguably the best beer in Prague make this a tough table to get during meal times. Book in advance or try off-peak times (before 11:30 a.m. for lunch, before 6 p.m. for dinner). This great location is just five minutes on foot from Old Town Square.

✚ 125 D4 ✉ Dlouhá 33 ☎ 222 316 265; www.ambi.cz Ⓜ Staroměstská No credit cards

Lví dvůr $$

The name means "Lion's Court," after the lions that were once kept here, close to Prague Castle. Traditional Czech fare is served, including roasted suckling pig – a specialty. There is a special venison menu, too.

✚ 124 A5 ✉ U Prašného mostu 6 ☎ 224 372 361; www.lvidvur.cz 🚊 22 AX, DC, MC, VI

U modré kachničky $$$

This traditional Czech inn comes highly recommended for its excellent Czech cooking. Request a table upstairs near the piano for a perfect evening.

✚ 124 B3 ✉ Nebovidská 6 ☎ 257 320 308; www.umodrekachnicky.cz Ⓜ Malostranská 🚊 Tram 12, 20, 22 AX, DC, MC, VI

COPENHAGEN HOTELS

Price guide: (double room for two people)

$	DKr400–DKr700
$$	DKr700–DKr1,200
$$$	over DKr1,200

Axel Hotel Guldsmeden $$–$$$

The Axel is very close to the central railroad station and has individually decorated rooms with four-poster beds. Breakfasts are delicious and the on-site organic spa luxurious.

✚ 140 A1 ✉ Helgolandsgade 11 ☎ 33 31 32 66; www.guldsmeden hotels.com Ⓜ S-train 🚊 6A, 26 København H AX, MC, VI

Copenhagen Admiral Hotel $$$

This waterfront hotel, in a superbly renovated, 18th-century, red-brick granary warehouse, is located close to Amalienborg Plads. Regular rooms and family suites are available.

✚ 140 D3 ✉ Toldbodgade 24–28 ☎ 33 74 14 14; www.admiralhotel.dk Ⓜ Kongens Nytorv 🚊 1A, 11A, 15, 26, 29 AX, DC, MC, VI

Hotel Alexandra $$–$$$

If you love 20th-century Danish design, you will like this hotel. The light and airy rooms are well-equipped and furnished, and the staff are very friendly.

✚ 140 B2 ✉ H. C. Andersen Boulevard 8 ☎ 33 74 44 44; hotelalexandra.dk Ⓜ Veserport 🚊 5A, 6A, 14 AX, DC, MC, VI

Hotel Bethel Sømandshjem $$

For a very central location at a reasonable price it's hard to beat this hotel. Its rooms are full of character as well as comfortable beds, and staff are friendly.

✚ 140 D3 ✉ Nyhavn 22 ☎ 33 13 03 70; www.hotel-bethel.dk Ⓜ Kongens Nytorv 🚊 1A, 15, 20E, 26, 350S AX, DC, MC, VI

Hotel Nimb $$$

Nimb is magically placed in the Moorish Palace building in the Tivoli Gardens. It has 14 luxurious rooms, of which eight are suites and several overlook the gardens. The food here is top-notch too, with a brasserie, a steak house and an open sandwich restaurant to choose from.

✚ 140 B1 ✉ Bernstorffsgade 5 ☎ 88 70 00 00; www.nimb.dk Ⓜ S-train København H 🚊 1A, 2A, 5A, 11A, 15, 30, 40, 60, 250S AX, DC, MC, VI

COPENHAGEN RESTAURANTS

Price guide: (dinner per person, excluding drinks)

$	DKr100–DKr250
$$	DKr250–DKr500
$$$	over DKr500

Nyhavns Færgekro $$–$$$

This is one of the best restaurants on canalside Nyhavn, with a nautical theme reflecting the area's maritime history, which includes model boats hanging from the ceiling. Superb lunchtime buffets featuring a variety of herring dishes are a great deal ($); the Danish, French and Italian dinner menu is more expensive.

✚ 140/141 D2 ✉ Nyhavn 5 ☎ 33 15 15 88; www.nyhavnsfaergekro.dk Ⓜ Kongens Nytorv 🚊 1A, 11A, 15, 26, 350S MC, VI

Peder Oxe $$

Built on the foundation of an old monastery, this noted restaurant/cellar bar is on Grey Brothers Square. Traditional cuisine emphasizes hearty helpings of meat; the lunchtime *smørrebrød* is very good. The food here is locally sourced where possible.

✚ 140 C2 ✉ Gråbrødretorv 11 ☎ 33 11 00 77; www.pederoxe.dk Ⓜ Kongens Nytorv 🚊 11A, 14 DC, MC, VI

Restaurant Els $$–$$$

Original 1850s wall panels add style to this popular Nyhavn restaurant. Excellent fish choices and fine wines are served. Lunch plates and sandwiches also are available to 5 p.m. Reservations are advised.

✚ 140 D2–D3 ✉ Store Strandstræde 3 ☎ 33 14 13 41; www.restaurant-els.dk Ⓜ Kongens Nytorv 🚊 1A, 11A, 15, 26, 350S AX, DC, MC, VI

RizRaz $–$$

RizRaz takes its inspiration from world cuisine and offers delicious low-fat, healthy options. There's plenty of choice, but especially

KEY TO SYMBOLS

✚	map page number and coordinates
✉	address
☎	telephone number
⊘	days/times closed
Ⓜ	nearest subway station
🚍	nearest bus/trolley bus/ tram/funicular route
⛴	ferry
$$$	expensive
$$	moderate
$	inexpensive
AX	American Express
DC	Diners Club
MC	MasterCard
VI	VISA

Russian Restaurants

You can sample authentic Russian cuisine in Helsinki at one of the city's several Russian restaurants. Russian food is not noted for its lightness of touch, but it can be innovative. You can even start with caviar and sour cream if you want, before plunging into hearty meat dishes with cakes, fruit pies and ice cream for dessert. Two notable choices to try are Kasakka at Meritullinkatu 13 (☎ 06 135 6288; www.kasakka.fi) and Bellevue at Rahapajankatu 3 (☎ 09 179 560; www. restaurantbellevue.com).

popular is its all-you-can-eat fresh, seasonal salad buffet, to which you can add prime steak, salmon or kebabs cooked over an open-flame grill. There are two restaurants – the restaurant at Kannikstræde 19 has an attractive large courtyard which is open in summer.

✚ 140 C2 ✉ Kompagnistræde 20 ☎ 33 15 05 75; www.rizraz.dk Ⓜ Nørreport 🚍 1A, 2A, 5A, 6A, 350S DC, MC, VI

Salt $$

In a great position on the harbor promenade, Salt offers a choice of two-, three- and four-course menus in an architecturally stunning space that honors its waterfront setting. Expect updated Danish classics as well as some interesting modern European cuisine.

✚ 141 D3 ✉ Tolbodgade 24–28 ☎ 33 74 14 44; www.saltrestaurant. dk Ⓜ Kongens Nytorv 🚍 1A, 15, 20E, 350S AX, DI, MC, VI

ODENSE HOTELS

Price guide: (double room with breakfast for two people)

$	DKr400–DKr700
$$	DKr700–DKr1,200
$$$	over DKr1,200

City Hotel Odense $$

This comfortable, modern hotel is near the Hans Christian Andersen Museum, in the heart of the Old Town. Apartments also are available to rent.

✚ 146 C2 ✉ Hans Mulesgade 5 ☎ 66 12 12 58; www.city-hotel-odense.dk AX, DC, MC, VI

First Hotel Grand $$

One of Odense's most illustrious hotels, the Grand, is situated in a handsome old building just across from Brandts 13, housing the city's fine art collection, close to the city center.

✚ 146 B2 ✉ Jernbanegade 18 ☎ 66 11 71 71; www.firsthotels.com AX, DC, MC, VI

Hotel Domir $–$$

The medium-size Hotel Domir has simple but comfortable rooms. It is conveniently located in the city center, close to the railroad station and within easy walking distance of the Town Hall.

✚ 146 A3 ✉ Hans Tausens Gade 19 ☎ 66 12 14 27; www.domir.dk AX, DC, MC, VI

Pjentehus $

Located just outside the city center, this is a small, comfortable bed-and-breakfast housed in a pleasant villa near the Hans Christian Andersen Museum.

✚ 146 C3 ✉ Pjentedamsgade 14 ☎ 66 12 15 55; www.pjentehus.dk No credit cards

Radisson Blu H. C. Andersen Hotel $$–$$$

This luxurious, modern hotel is close to the Hans Christian Andersen Museum and next door to the Concert Hall and the Carl Nielsen Museum. It has spacious rooms and its own restaurant. Amenities include sauna, solarium and casino.

✚ 146 C2 ✉ Claus Bergsgade 7 ☎ 66 14 78 00; www.radissonblu. com AX, DC, MC, VI

ODENSE RESTAURANTS

Price guide: (dinner per person, excluding drinks)

$	DKr100–DKr250
$$	DKr250–DKr300
$$$	over DKr300

Den Gamle Kro $$$

This restaurant occupies a magnificent 1683 building. Meals are served in several rooms, including the brick-vaulted cellar. Expect excellent Danish cuisine.

✚ 146 B2–C2 ✉ Overgade 23 ☎ 66 12 14 33; www.dengamlekro.eu AX, DC, MC, VI

Den Grimme Ælling $

This charming little restaurant, "The Ugly Duckling," is on a cobbled lane, just across the main road from the Hans Christian Andersen Museum. The restaurant is known for its extravagant buffets.

✚ 146 B2 ✉ Hans Jensens Stræde 1 ☎ 65 91 70 30; www. grimme-aelling.dk AX, MC, VI

Jensens Bøfhus $

This lunchtime and evening favorite serves steaks, burgers and spit-roast chicken with lavish salads and french fries. They also do take-out food.

✚ 146 A2 ✉ Jernbanegade 4 ☎ 66 14 59 59; www.jensens.com AX, MC, VI

Restaurant Air Pub $–$$

This pub and restaurant has a lively atmosphere, hearty Danish cooking and a good selection of beers. Lighter dishes also are served, and there is

live music from 10 p.m. Fri. and Sat.
🚇 146 A2 ✉ Kongensgade 41
☎ 66 14 66 08; www.air-pub.dk
🕐 Closed Sun. AX, MC, VI

Restaurant Under Lindetræet $$$

Close to the Hans Christian Andersen Museum, this elegant restaurant serves inventive Scandinavian, Alsatian and Tuscan dishes. On summer weekends, the terrace here is a great choice for brunch.
🚇 146 B2 ✉ Ramsherred 2 ☎ 66 12 92 86; www.underlindetraet.dk
🕐 Closed Sun. and Mon. dinner AX, MC, VI

Price guide: (double room with breakfast for two people)
$ €50–€100
$$ €100–€150
$$$ over €150

GLO Hotel Art $–$$$

Once the elegant home of the Helsinki Students Union, this Jugend-style hotel in the Design District has thick granite walls and cool modern furnishings. Breakfast is served in the cozy cellar.
🚇 159 C4 ✉ Lönnrotinkatu 29
☎ 09 5840 9445; www.glohotels.fi
🚊 20, 20N; tram 6 AX, DC, MC, VI

Helka $$–$$$

Located in the heart of the city, this hotel is finished in a cool Finnish style. It offers good service, good value and a sauna. Special weekend rates are available.
🚇 159 B3 ✉ Pohjoinen Rautatiekatu 23 ☎ 09 613 580; www.helka.fi 🚊 All buses from Kamppi bus station and 14, 14B, 32, 39, 45, 47; tram 2 AX, DC, MC, VI

Hotel Fabian $$$

This traditional town house has been converted into a smart hotel with a contemporary feel, impeccable rooms, a cozy bar and a leafy courtyard. A stylish choice, Hotel Fabian is at the lower end of the upper price bracket.
🚇 159 C2 ✉ Fabianinkatu 7 ☎ 09 6128 2000; www.hotelfabian.fi 🚊 24, 615; tram 1, 2, 10 AX, DC, MC, VI

Scandic Grand Marina Hotel $–$$$

You can step from ferry to foyer, if you travel to Helsinki by Viking Line, and stay in this large hotel on the

western side of the harbor. Rooms are elegant and there are several bars and a restaurant. Kids stay free.
🚇 159 C2 ✉ Katajanokanlaituri 7
☎ 09 16661; www.scandichotels.fi
🚊 Tram 4 AX, DC, MC, VI

Price guide: (dinner per person, excluding drinks)
$ €10–€25
$$ €25–€50
$$$ over €50

G. W. Sundmans $$$

Located in the 19th-century house of a naval captain, this restaurant serves modern Finnish dishes such as grilled turbot with cauliflower pudding or caviar with cold cucumber soup.
🚇 159 C2 ✉ Eteläranta 16
☎ 09 6128 5400; www.sundmans.fi
🕐 Closed Sat. lunch and Sun.
🚊 Tram 1, 2, AX, DC, MC, VI

Juuri $$

This bright, unpretentious restaurant creates exciting twists on traditional Finnish dishes and ingredients. A choice of *sapas* – tasty morsels similar to *tapas* – include sugar salted trout with red currant and licorice; mains may include organic lamb from Åland.
🚇 159 B2 ✉ Korkeavuorenkatu 27
☎ 09 635 732; www.juuri.fi
🕐 Closed Sun. lunch 🚊 24; tram 10 AX, DC, MC, VI

Kappeli $$–$$$

This is a stylish restaurant and café, with outside terraces on the Esplanade, in a pavilion of cast iron and glass dating from 1867. A variety of Finnish and Scandinavian dishes are offered. In summer, music concerts take place at the bandstand.
🚇 159 B2 ✉ Eteläesplanadi 1
☎ 010 766 3880; www.kappeli.fi
🚊 13, 64S, 77S; tram 1, 1A AX, MC, VI

Kellohalli $–$$

All things foodie have found a home in Helsinki's old abattoir. Among them is Kellohalli, a permanent restaurant serving imaginative Finnish food with liberal pinches of other cuisines.
🚇 159 C4 ✉ Työpajankatu 2 rakennus 1e ☎ 050 339 5400; kellohalli.fi 🕐 Closed Mon.–Fri. dinner 🚊 Kalasatama 🚊 68 AX, MC, VI

Price guide: (double room with breakfast for two people)
$ under €150
$$ €150–€225
$$$ over €225

Bristol Paris $$$

The Louis XV-style rooms affirm the elegance of this hotel, which boasts a rooftop indoor swimming pool, pampering spa and restaurant.
🚇 174 B3 ✉ 112 rue du Faubourg-St.-Honoré, 75008
☎ 01 53 43 43 00; www.lebristolparis.com 🚇 Miromesnil AX, DC, MC, VI

Hôtel Georgette $$

This boutique hotel has compact, but well-equipped, rooms that reflect the distinct style of owners Anne Peyroux and Emmanuèle Thisy.
🚇 175 D3 ✉ 36 rue de Grenier Saint-Lazare, 75003 ☎ 01 44 61 10 10; www.hotelgeorgette.com
🚇 Rambuteau, Etienne Marcel, Châtelet AX, DC, MC, VI

Hôtel des Grandes Écoles $–$$

This typically French hotel has pretty bedrooms and is set in a garden in a narrow street in the Latin Quarter.
🚇 175 D1 ✉ 75 rue Cardinal-Lemoine, 75005 ☎ 01 43 26 79 23; www.hotel-grandes-ecoles.com
🚇 Cardinal-Lemoine MC, VI

Hôtel New Orient $–$$

Pleasantly decorated, small and personal, this is a little gem for the room prices and is located 10 minutes on foot from the Opéra.
🚇 174 B4 ✉ 16 rue de Constantinople, 75008 ☎ 01 45 22 21 64; www.hotelneworient.com
🚇 Villiers AX, MC, VI

Pavillon de la Reine $$$

This is a romantic and luxurious hotel, complete with four-poster beds in some rooms and suites. The spa offers a range of treatments and massages.
🚇 175 E2 ✉ 28 place des Vosges, 75003 ☎ 01 40 29 19 19; www.pavillon-de-la-reine.com
🚇 Saint-Paul AX, DC, MC, VI

Price guide: (dinner per person, excluding drinks)
$ under €35
$$ €35–€60
$$$ over €60

France

KEY TO SYMBOLS

✚	map page number and coordinates
✉	address
☎	telephone number
◷	days/times closed
Ⓜ	nearest subway station
🚌	nearest bus/trolley bus/tram/funicular route
⛴	ferry
$$$	expensive
$$	moderate
$	inexpensive
AX	American Express
DC	Diners Club
MC	MasterCard
VI	VISA

The *Belle Époque* in Nice

The *belle époque*, or "beautiful era," was the name the French gave to the early 20th century. During this period Nice's fame soared with the influx of up to 150,000 wealthy English and Russians who came here to while away northern winters in elegance. They expected luxury, and it was for them that sumptuous and grandiose hotels and villas were built. Some buildings survive along the promenade des Anglais. The Négresco is the most famous; enjoy a drink there in Edwardian style.

L'Ange 20 $$

This is a cozy, old-style bistro in the heart of the Marais area of the city. There is an excellent fixed-price daily French menu.

✚ 175 D3 ✉ 8 rue Geoffroy L'Angevin, 75004 ☎ 01 40 27 93 67; www.lange20.com ◷ Closed daily lunch, Mon. dinner Ⓜ Rambuteau MC, VI

Le Bistrot Lorette $–$$

This tiny, unassuming bistro with traditional decor serves a short weekly menu of French classics including a succulent *confit de canard* (slow cooked duck leg).

✚ 175 C4 ✉ 43 rue Notre Dame de Lorette, 75009 ☎ 01 42 81 13 87 Ⓜ St. Georges MC, VI

Le Cinq $$$

The three Michelin stars awarded to chef Christian Le Squer speak of the quality and attention to detail at this French restaurant. The dining room is elegant and there's a garden for summer dining.

✚ 175 B3 ✉ Hotel Four Seasons Georges V, 31 avenue Georges V, 75008 ☎ 01 49 52 71 54; www. restaurant-lecinq.com Ⓜ Georges V AX, DC, MC, VI

La Coupole $$–$$$

This sprawling art deco brasserie, renowned in the 1920s, serves seafood, fish and steaks. Sole *meunière* and *Châteaubriand* are among the specialties.

✚ 175 C1 ✉ 102 boulevard du Montparnasse, 75014 ☎ 01 43 20 14 20; www.lacoupole-paris.com Ⓜ Vavin AX, DC, MC, VI

Le Poule au Pot $$

The sumptuous 1930s decor at Le Poule au Pot hints at the age of this classic bistro that serves almost till dawn. The menu hasn't changed either and the signature *poule au pot*, a type of chicken stew, is a great choice.

✚ 175 D3 ✉ 9 rue Vauvilliers, 75001 ☎ 01 42 36 32 96; www.lapouleau pot.com ◷ Closed daily lunch, Mon. dinner Ⓜ Châtelet-Les-Halles, Rivoli MC, VI

LYON HOTELS

Price guide: (double room with breakfast for two people)
$ under €125
$$ €125–€200
$$$ over €200

Collège Hôtel $$

Styled around the theme of an old college dorm, this hotel is delightfully quirky. Rooms are brilliant white and have terraces with lovely views of the city.

✚ 186 A4 ✉ 5 place St.-Paul, 69005 ☎ 04 72 10 05 05; www.college-hotel.com Ⓜ St.-Paul, Vieux Lyon (St.-Jean) AX, MC, VI

Hotel Sofitel Lyon Bellecour $$–$$$

This deluxe hotel, centrally located on the Rhône river, is a good choice. There are two restaurants on site.

✚ 186 B1 ✉ 20 quai Gailleton, 69002 ☎ 04 72 41 20 20; www.sofitel.com Ⓜ Bellecour AX, DC, MC, VI

Mercure Lyon Centre Beaux-Arts $$

An early 20th-century building houses this comfortable hotel in the center of the Presqu'Île.

✚ 186 B3 ✉ 75 rue Président Édouard-Hérriot, 69002 ☎ 04 78 38 09 50; www.mercure.com Ⓜ Cordeliers, Bellecour AX, DC, MC, VI

St.-Paul $

Consider staying at this excellent budget choice in the Old Town. It has simple, clean and airy rooms.

✚ 186 B3 ✉ 6 rue Lainerie, 69005 ☎ 04 78 28 13 29; www.hotelsaint paul.eu AX, DC, MC, VI

La Villa Florentine $$$

A former convent, this deluxe hotel with many amenities – including a pretty garden – stands above the Old Town, on the slopes of Fourvière.

✚ 186 A3 ✉ 25–27 montée St.-Barthélémy, 69005 ☎ 04 72 56 56 56; www.villaflorentine.com Ⓜ Vieux Lyon AX, DC, MC, VI

LYON RESTAURANTS

Price guide: (dinner per person, excluding drinks)
$ under €35
$$ €35–€60
$$$ over €60

L'Auberge du Pont de Collonges $$$

Chef Paul Bocuse offers exceptional French haute-cuisine dishes at this top-notch restaurant. You will need to reserve a table.

✚ 186 off map at C4 ✉ 40 quai de la Plage, Collonges, 69660 (2.5 miles north of Lyon city) ☎ 04 72 42 90 90; www.bocuse.fr ⓘ Daily lunch and dinner AX, DC, MC, VI

Le Comptoir du Vin $

A tiny authentic *bouchon* in the heart of the Croix-Rousse district run by Daniel Perrier, where the few tables are always busy. Order from the chalkboard and enjoy a typical Lyonnais dining experience.
✛ 186 off map at B4 ✉ 9 rue Belfort, 69004 ☎ 04 78 39 89 95 ⓘ Closed Sun. ⓠ Croix-Rousse

Jérémy Galvan $$–$$$

This young chef has worked with the best chefs in Lyon and now serves his own upscale contemporary dishes in the Old Town.
✛ 186 A3 ✉ 29 rue de Boeuf, 69005 ☎ 04 72 40 91 47; www.jeremy galvanrestaurant.com ⓘ Closed Sun.–Mon., and Sat. lunch ⓠ Vieux Ville AX, MC, VI

Le Musée $

One of Lyon's most popular *bouchons* (taverns), this tiny restaurant serves a range of classic local dishes.
✛ 186 C3 ✉ 2 rue des Forces, 69002 ☎ 04 78 37 71 54 ⓘ Closed Sun. and Mon. ⓠ Cordeliers AX, MC, VI

Têtedoie $$$

Rich but light specialties are on the menu at this elegant restaurant. Large windows give wonderful views of the city.
✛ 186 A2 ✉ Montée du Chemin Neuf, 69005 ☎ 04 78 29 40 10; www. tetedoie.com ⓘ Closed Sun., Aug. ⓠ Vieux Lyon AX, DC, MC, VI

Price guide: (double room with breakfast for two people)

$	under €125
$$	€125–€200
$$$	over €200

Gounod $–$$

This moderately priced *belle époque* choice is in a quiet location, yet is just a short, 10-minute walk from the sea.
✛ 194 B1 ✉ 3 rue Gounod, 06000 ☎ 04 93 16 42 00; www.gounod-nice. fr ⓠ 3, 7, 9, 10, 22, 38 AX, MC, VI

Hotel La Perouse $$$

Overlooking the Baie des Anges and at the foot of the Vielle Ville, this well-placed, refurbished hotel offers

opulence with a personal touch.
✛ 194 D1 ✉ 11 quai Rauba Capua ☎ 04 93 62 34 63; www.leshotels duroy.com ⓠ T32 AX, DC, MC, VI

Négresco $$$

This is one of the world's great hotels in the flamboyant *belle époque* style; superb comfort, service and facilities.
✛ 194 B1 ✉ 37 Promenade des Anglais, 06000 ☎ 04 93 16 64 00; www.hotel-negresco-nice.com ⓠ 8, 11, 52, 59, 60, 62, 70, 94 AX, DC, MC, VI

Windsor $–$$

This famous hotel is centrally located and has a garden pool and beautifully frescoed rooms, each with soundproofing.
✛ 194 B1 ✉ 11 rue Dalpozzo, 06000 ☎ 04 93 88 59 35; www.hotelwindsor nice.com ⓠ 3, 7, 9, 10, 22, 27, 38, 59 AX, DC, MC, VI

Price guide: (dinner per person, excluding drinks)

$	under €35
$$	€35–€60
$$$	over €60

L'Ane Rouge $$–$$$

Typical Provençal dishes are served here. There's a lovely view over the old harbor from the terrace.
✛ 195 E1 ✉ 7 quai des 2 Emmanuel, 06300 ☎ 04 93 89 49 63; www.anerougenice.com ⓘ Closed Wed. lunch and dinner, Thu. lunch; mid-Feb. to mid-Mar. ⓠ 9, 10, T32 AX, DC, MC, VI

Boccaccio $$–$$$

Located in the city center, this restaurant offers mouthwatering seafood specialties; in summer you can dine on the terrace.
✛ 195 C1 ✉ 7 rue Masséna, 06300 ☎ 04 93 87 71 76; www.boccaccio-nice.com ⓠ 3, 7, 8, 9, 10, 14, 22, 27, 38, 52, 59, 70, 94; tram Masséna AX, DC, MC, VI

Oliviera $–$$

This compact bistro serves Provençal dishes with the freshest ingredients accompanied by excellent value local wines. They also stock and sell their own top-class olive oil on site.
✛ 195 D1 ✉ 8b rue de Collet, 06300 ☎ 04 93 13 06 45; www.oliveira.com ⓘ Closed Sun. and Mon. ⓠ Cathédrale ⓠ 3, 8, 11, 14, 38, 52, 59, 70, 98 No credit cards

Restaurant Luc Salsedo $$–$$$

Local chef Luc Salsedo did his national service cooking for the president at the Elysée Palace in Paris. Today everyone can benefit from his delicate touch with local ingredients.
✛ 195 C2 ✉ 14 rue Maccarani, 06000 ☎ 04 93 82 24 12; www. restaurant-salsedo.com ⓘ Closed lunch daily, Wed. dinner ⓠ 3, 7, 9, 10, 59, 70 AX, DC, MC, VI

Price guide: (double room with breakfast for two people)

$	under €125
$$	€125–€200
$$$	over €200

Cathédrale $$

This excellent hotel is close to Strasbourg's main sights and some of the city's best restaurants. Rooms are air-conditioned and soundproofed and there is a small bar.
✛ 200 B2 ✉ 12–13 place de la Cathédrale, 67000 ☎ 03 88 22 12 12; www.hotel-cathedrale.fr ⓠ Tram A, B, C, D, F AX, DC, MC, VI

Dragon $–$$

This cozy, renovated 17th-century town house lies just outside the canal zone but within a five-minute walk from most of the downtown sights.
✛ 200 B1 ✉ 12 rue du Dragon, 67000 ☎ 03 88 35 79 80; www. dragon.fr ⓠ 10 AX, DC, MC, VI

Hotel Cour du Corbeau $$–$$$

You'll find contemporary, cool interiors set in a 16th-century historic shell at this attractive hotel, just a stone's throw away from the main sites. A beautifully situated touch of luxury.
✛ 200 C1 ✉ 6 rue des Couples, 67000 ☎ 03 90 00 26 26; www. accorhotels.com ⓠ 10; tram A, D AX, DC, MC, VI

Hotel Rohan $–$$

This pretty hotel on a picturesque and historic street close to the cathedral is an easy stroll from the main sights and several good restaurants.
✛ 200 B1 ✉ 17–19 rue du Maroquin, 67000 ☎ 03 88 32 85 11; www.hotel-rohan.com ⓠ Tram A, B, C, D, F AX, DC, VI

KEY TO SYMBOLS

- 🔢 map page number and coordinates
- ✉️ address
- ☎️ telephone number
- 🕐 days/times closed
- Ⓜ️ nearest subway station
- 🚌 nearest bus/trolley bus/tram/funicular route
- ⛴️ ferry
- $$$ expensive
- $$ moderate
- $ inexpensive
- AX American Express
- DC Diners Club
- MC MasterCard
- VI VISA

Strasbourg Specials

Visualize French flair and imagination combined with high-quality ingredients and German influences, and you'll begin to understand the gastronomic delights that await you in Strasbourg. This is the home of *foie gras*, fatted goose liver eaten whole or made into pâté; *choucroute* (sauerkraut), assorted meats and spicy sausages served with mounds of pickled cabbage; and *kougelhupf*, yeast cake traditionally eaten for breakfast. There are other, less well-known regional dishes; look for *bæckeoffe*, a slow-cooked casserole featuring three different meats, and *tarte flambée*, a rich hot onion tart. The smooth, pungently aromatic Munster is Strasbourg's local cheese.

STRASBOURG RESTAURANTS

Price guide: (dinner per person, excluding drinks)

$	under €35
$$	€35–€50
$$$	over €50

Le Baeckeoffe d'Alsace $

An old, timbered building in the Old Town is the setting for this *winstub* (wine room). Naturally, they serve *bæckeoffe*, a slow-cooked stew of beef, lamb and pork in wine.
🔢 200 A1 ✉️ 14 rue des Moulins, 67000 ☎️ 03 88 23 05 40; www.baeckeoffe.com 🚌 Tram A, D AX, MC, VI

La Gavroche $$$

For classy French dining, this restaurant is one of the best in the city. The menu covers classics such as *foie-gras* and *tartelette aux citron*, with a range of meat and fish on the well-balanced menu.
🔢 200 C1 ✉️ 4 rue Klein, 67000 ☎️ 03 88 36 82 89; www.restaurant-gavroche.com 🕐 Closed Sat.–Sun. 🚌 Tram A, D AX, MC, VI

Au Petit Tonnelier $$

Dine in either the contemporary interior or on the summer terrace and enjoy stylishly presented regional and seasonal dishes.
🔢 200 B1 ✉️ 16 rue des Tonneliers, 67000 ☎️ 03 88 32 53 54; www.aupetittonnelier.com 🕐 Closed Sun. 🚌 Tram A, D AX, MC, VI

La Table du Gayot $–$$

In a picturesque square in the Old Town, this bistro-style eatery serves typical French dishes and salads. The lovely shaded terrace in the summer is perfect for alfresco dining.
🔢 200 C2 ✉️ 8 place du Marché Gayot, 67000 ☎️ 03 88 36 30 27 🕐 Closed Tue. 🚌 Tram B, C, F MC, VI

BERLIN HOTELS

Price guide: (double room with breakfast for two people)

$	under €75
$$	€75–€150
$$$	over €150

Hotel Aida $$

This small hotel is on a quiet side street close to Kurfürstendamm and the Savignyplatz restaurants. Guests can enjoy the graceful converted 19th-century town house away from the hustle and bustle of the crowds.
🔢 216 B2 ✉️ Knesebeckstrasse 29 ☎️ 030 881 2129; www.hotelaida.de Ⓜ️ U-Bahn to Uhlandstrasse 🚌 109, 110, 204, 209, M19, M29, X9 AX, DC, MC, VI

Kempinski Hotel Bristol $$$

This hotel features formal furnishings, sparkling chandeliers and deep-pile carpets. There are 246 opulent rooms and 55 suites, and a good restaurant.
🔢 216 B2 ✉️ Kurfürstendamm 27 ☎️ 030 884 340; www.kempinski berlin.de Ⓜ️ U-Bahn to Uhlandstrasse 🚌 109, M29, X10 AX, DC, MC, VI

Romantik Hotel Kronprinz Berlin $$$

This elegant hotel, in a 70-room, late 19th-century house surrounded by chestnut trees, is only a few steps from the Ku'damm and has an attractive terraced beer garden.
🔢 216 off map at A1 ✉️ Kronprinzendamm 1 ☎️ 030 896 030; www.kronprinz-hotel.de Ⓜ️ S-Bahn to Halensee 🚌 104, M19, M29 AX, DC, MC, VI

Scandic Berlin Kurfürstendamm $$

This is a renovated 1960s hotel, behind the KaDeWe department store. In spite of the plain exterior, it is stylish inside, with 217 rooms, a roof terrace and conservatory.
🔢 216 B2 ✉️ Augsburger Strasse 5 ☎️ 030 212 420; www.scandichotels.com Ⓜ️ U-Bahn to Augsburger Strasse 🚌 M19, M29, M46 AX, DC, MC, VI

Transit $

The Transit has pleasant rooms and is located in an attractive part of the Kreuzberg quarter. A good value choice in this city.
🔢 217 D1 ✉️ Hagelberger Strasse 53–54 ☎️ 030 789 0470; www.hotel-transit.de Ⓜ️ U-Bahn to Mehringdamm 🚌 119, 219 MC, VI

BERLIN RESTAURANTS

Price guide: (dinner per person, excluding drinks)

$	under €15
$$	€15–€30
$$$	over €30

Alt Luxemburg $$$

This is one of the city's best restaurants, with food cooked by chef Karl Wannemacher. Each month the restaurant offers a special four-course menu.

✚ 216 A2 ✉ Windscheidstrasse 31 ☎ 030 323 8730; www. alt-luxemburg.de ◷ Mon.–Sat. from 5 p.m. Ⓤ U-Bahn to Sophie-Charlotte -Platz 🚌 309 AX, DC, MC, VI

Borchardt $$$

Stylish Berliners and politicians love this attractive, 1920s-style bistro, a lunch spot where "new" and international cuisine is featured.

✚ 217 D2 ✉ Französische Strasse 47 ☎ 030 8188 6262; www.borchardt-restaurant.de Ⓤ U-Bahn to Französische Strasse 🚌 47 AX, MC, VI

Dressler $$–$$$

Fine German and French cuisine can be enjoyed inside this art deco restaurant or outside on the sun terrace. Seasonal cuisine includes game and young herring.

✚ 216 D3 ✉ Unter den Linden 39 ☎ 030 204 4422; www.restaurant-dressler.de Ⓤ U-Bahn to Friedrichstrasse, S-Bahn to Unter den Linden 🚌 100, 147, 200 TXL AX, MC, VI

Zum Nussbaum $

This little gem of a tavern-cum-restaurant in the partly restored medieval Nikolaiviertel area, "The Nut Tree," serves up hearty helpings of traditional German fare.

✚ 217 E3 ✉ Am Nussbaum 3 ☎ 030 242 3095 Ⓤ U-Bahn to Klosterstrasse 🚌 M48, 248 MC, VI

COLOGNE HOTELS

Price guide: (double room with breakfast for two people)
$ under €75
$$ €75–€150
$$$ over €150

Das Kleine Stapelhäuschen $–$$

Two adjacent town houses, in historically interesting buildings on the Rhine promenade, house a friendly hotel with a pleasant restaurant that's just a short walk from the cathedral.

✚ 225 C3 ✉ Fischmarkt 1–3 ☎ 0221 272 7777; www. kleines-stapelhaeuschen.de 🚋 Tram 1, 7, 9 MC, VI

Hotel im Kupferkessel $$

Just outside the city center, this family-run hotel in a town house

from 1900, has neatly furnished rooms in a modern style. Room rates take it just out of budget level.

✚ 225 off map at A4 ✉ Probsteigasse 6 ☎ 0221 270 7960; www.im-kupferkessel.de Ⓤ U-Bahn to Christophstrasse, Mediapark 🚌 12, 15 MC, VI

Mondial am Dom $$–$$$

Situated between the cathedral and the river, this hotel is ideally placed for exploring the Old Town. There is a good restaurant on site.

✚ 225 B3 ✉ Kurt-Hackenberg-Platz 1 ☎ 0221 20630; www.accorhotels.com Ⓤ Dom/Hbf AX, DC, MC, VI

Viktoria $$

This early 20th-century Jugendstil building by the Rhine offers some rooms with river views and a generous breakfast buffet.

✚ 225 off map at C4 ✉ Worringer Strasse 23 ☎ 0221 973 1720; hotel viktoria.com Ⓤ Reichenspergerplatz AX, DC, MC, VI

COLOGNE RESTAURANTS

Price guide: (dinner per person, excluding drinks)
$ under €15
$$ €15–€30
$$$ over €30

Bosporus $$$

Located in the multicultural quarter of Weidengasse, Bosporus has an à la carte menu offering a wide range of Turkish dishes.

✚ 225 B4 ✉ Weidengasse 36 ☎ 0221 125 265; www.bosporus.de 🚋 Tram 12, 15, 16, 18 AX, DC, MC, VI

Brauhaus Sion $$

This busy side-street brewery-tavern is popular for lunch and coffee, and for strong *Kölsch* beer. Traditionally dressed waiters roll out the barrels.

✚ 225 B3 ✉ Unter Taschenmacher 5–7 ☎ 0221 257 8540; brauhaussion.de 🚋 Tram 1, 7, 9 MC, VI

Kintaro $$–$$$

Japanese dishes are served in this popular sushi restaurant, where particularly good entrées include seaweed *(hijiki)* and octopus, and cucumber and seaweed in vinegar *(tako su)*. It is advisable to make a reservation here.

✚ 225 A3 ✉ Friesenstrasse 16 ☎ 0221 135 255; www.kintaro.de Ⓤ Friesenplatz AX, MC, VI

Pfaffen Brauerei Max Päffgen $$

This pub, belonging to Cologne's smallest brewery and centrally located, serves tasty regional dishes and *Kölsch* beer.

✚ 225 C2 ✉ Heumarkt 62 ☎ 0221 257 7765; www.max-paffgen.de ◷ Closed Mon. 🚋 Tram 1, 7, 9 No credit cards

MUNICH HOTELS

Price guide: (double room with breakfast for two people)
$ under €75
$$ €75–€150
$$$ over €150

Hotel Gästehaus Englischer Garten $$

This hotel, at the edge of the English Garden in Schwabing, is housed in a converted water mill. Breakfast is served in the garden in summer.

✚ 230 off map at D4 ✉ Liebergesellstrasse 8 ☎ 089 383 9410; hotelenglischergarten.de Ⓤ Münchner Freiheit AX, DC, MC, VI

Hotel am Viktualienmarkt $$

This family-owned hotel has a modern design and offers rooms with from one to four beds.

✚ 231 C2 ✉ Utzschneiderstrasse 14 ☎ 089 231 1090; www.hotel-am-viktualienmarkt.de 🚋 Tram 17, 18 AX, MC, VI

Mariandl $–$$

In a quiet zone between the city center and Theresienwiese, the Mariandl has elegantly furnished rooms, the graceful Café am Beethovenplatz and pretty gardens.

✚ 230 A1 ✉ Goethestrasse 51 ☎ 089 55 29 100; www.mariandl.com Ⓤ Sendlinger Tor 🚌 58 AX, DC, MC, VI

Opéra $$$

The Opéra is housed in an old mansion and has elegant arcades and a Renaissance courtyard.

✚ 231 D2 ✉ St. Anna-Strasse 10 ☎ 089 210 4940; www.hotel-opera.de Ⓤ Lehel 🚋 Tram 18 AX, MC, VI

Torbräu $$$

Torbräu is Munich's oldest hotel. On the premises are a Continental restaurant, café and 90 rooms.

✚ 231 C2 ✉ Tal 41 ☎ 089 24 23 40; www.torbrau.de Ⓤ Marienplatz, Isartor AX, MC, VI

KEY TO SYMBOLS

⊞	map page number and coordinates
✉	address
☎	telephone number
🕐	days/times closed
Ⓜ	nearest subway station
🚌	nearest bus/trolley bus/tram/funicular route
⛴	ferry
$$$	expensive
$$	moderate
$	inexpensive
AX	American Express
DC	Diners Club
MC	MasterCard
VI	VISA

Water in Greece

It's important not to waste water in Greece, especially on the islands, where it often has to be shipped in by tankers. Although Athens' tap water is drinkable, bottled water is inexpensive and tastes better. Greeks are water connoisseurs, discussing the flavor and mineral properties of favorite spring varieties. Glasses of water are served alongside every drink you order in cafés: Drink it, or pour it in your ouzo and watch the clear spirit turn milky white. Since it's often hot in Greece and most places are not air-conditioned, it's important to drink plenty of water.

MUNICH RESTAURANTS

Price guide: (dinner per person, excluding drinks)

$	under €15
$$	€15–€30
$$$	over €30

Augustiner Grossgaststätten $

Munich's oldest surviving brewery serves Bavarian dishes in the large beer hall, under the art nouveau glass dome of the Mussel Hall and in the arcaded courtyard.
✉ 231 B2 ✉ Neuhauser Strasse 27 ☎ 089 23 18 32 57; www.augustiner-restaurant.com Ⓜ Karlsplatz 🚌 Tram 16, 17, 18, 20, 27 AX, MC, VI

Halali $$$

Top quality regional cooking is offered here. Game dishes and mushrooms are seasonal specialties.
✉ 231 C3 ✉ Schönfeldstrasse 22 ☎ 089 28 59 09; www.restaurant-halali.de 🕐 Closed Sat. lunch, Sun. and holidays Ⓜ Odeonsplatz 🚌 100 AX, MC, VI

Ratskeller $$

Hearty local dishes are served in the Ratskeller tavern, situated in the New Town Hall's vaulted cellars.
✉ 231 C2 ✉ Marienplatz 8 ☎ 089 21 99 89-0; www.ratskeller.com Ⓜ Marienplatz AX, MC, VI

Spatenhaus an der Oper $$–$$$

The atmosphere is relaxed and the service good at this favored after-theater restaurant. The menu features Bavarian, regional and international dishes.
✉ 231 C2 ✉ Residenzstrasse 12 ☎ 089 290 7060; www.spatenhaus.de Ⓜ Marienplatz, Odeonsplatz; tram 19 AX, MC, VI

ATHENS HOTELS

Price guide: (double room with breakfast for two people)

$	€50–€80
$$	€80–€140
$$$	over €140

Attalos Hotel $$

The Attalos is a comfortable hotel located halfway between Omónia and Monastiráki squares. The roof garden/bar has good views of the Acropolis, just a short walk away.
✉ 244 B3 ✉ 29 Athinas ☎ 210 321 2801-3; www.attaloshotel.com

Ⓜ Omónia, Monastiráki AX, DC, MC, VI

Grande Bretagne $$$

The Grande Bretagne is Athens' most historic, grandest and very traditional hotel, offering the highest level of service and amenities.
⊞ 244 C2 ✉ Syntagmatos ☎ 210 333 0000; www.grandebretagne.gr 🚌 1, 18, 15 AX, DC, MC, VI

Pallas Athena $$

This fun boutique hotel oozes chic style and has several light and airy loft suites. Regular rooms are decorated by local artists.
⊞ 244 C3 ✉ 65 Athinas ☎ 210 325 0900; www.grecotel pallasathena.com Ⓜ Omónia AX, DC, MC, VI

Phaedra $

A location at the quieter end of Pláka makes up for one or two fairly small rooms at this pleasant hotel.
⊞ 244 C2 ✉ Cherefontos 16 & Adrianou ☎ 210 323 8461; www.hotelphaedra.com Ⓜ Akrópoli 🚌 9, 11, 15 AX, DC, VI

Saint George Lycabettus $$$

Beautifully situated on the quiet, shady slopes of Lycabettus Hill, this first-class hotel offers lovely views from its rooftop restaurant. Rooms have good, modern facilities.
⊞ 244 D3 ✉ 2 Kleomenous-Dexamini ☎ 210 729 0711; www.sglycabettus.gr 🚌 3, 8, 13 AX, DC, MC, VI

ATHENS RESTAURANTS

Price guide: (dinner per person, excluding drinks)

$	€10–€15
$$	€15–€30
$$$	over €30

Archeon Gefsis $$$

Dine at this imaginative restaurant that offers meat and fish dishes prepared from traditional recipes.
⊞ 244 A4 ✉ Kodratou 22 ☎ 210 523 9661; www.arxaion.gr Ⓜ Metaxourgio AX, DC, VI

O Platanos $

This friendly Pláka taverna serves simple and delicious food at both indoor and outdoor tables.
⊞ 244 B2 ✉ 4 Diogenous, Pláka ☎ 210 322 0666 🚌 1, 9, 11, 18 No credit cards

Psaras $$

Tucked below the Acropolis on one of Pláka's prettiest streets is this 100-year-old taverna, serving home-cooked traditional dishes.

➕ 244 B2 ✉ 16 Erekteos and Erotokritou Pláka ☎ 210 321 8733; www.psaras-taverna.gr 🚇 Thission 🚌 1, 9, 11, 18 AX, DC, MC, VI

Saita $

This popular basement restaurant in the Pláka has good food and friendly service. (The sidewalk tables close to the door belong to another restaurant.)

➕ 244 B2 ✉ 21 Kidathineon ☎ 210 322 6671 🚌 1, 5, 9, 18 No credit cards

Spondi $$$

To enjoy state-of-the-art Greek cooking, eat at the Michelin-starred Spondi and sample their "Discovery" tasting menu. Dining out gets no better than this.

➕ 244 B3 ✉ 5 Pyrronos ☎ 210 756 4021; www.spondi.gr 🚇 Agios Ioannis AX, DC, MC, VI

Carlton $$

This is a spacious and simple hotel at the foot of Castle Hill. Of the 95 rooms, only those on the upper floor have good views.

➕ 258 B2 ✉ Apor Péter utca 3 ☎ 1 224 0999; www.carltonhotel.hu 🚇 Batthyány tér AX, DC, MC, VI

Danubius Hotel Astoria $$–$$$

Set on a busy intersection in the center of Pest, this is a splendid hotel with a relaxing atmosphere in an old building. It was the headquarters of the Soviet army during the 1956 revolution.

➕ 258 C2 ✉ Kossuth Lajos utca 19–21 ☎ 1 889 6000; www.danubius hotels.com 🚇 Astoria AX, DC, MC, VI

Hilton Budapest $$$

This modern building, in a prime position on Castle Hill, incorporates the ruins of a 13th-century Dominican cloister and a 17th-century Jesuit cloister. You'll

get spectacular views over the Danube. Facilities include cafés, shops and a courtyard concert area.

➕ 258 A3 ✉ Hess András tér 1–3 ☎ 1 889 6600; www.placeshilton. com 🚇 Moszkva tér, then Várbusz (Castle Bus) AX, DC, MC, VI

Kempinski Hotel Corvinus Budapest $$$

This luxury hotel with an unusual postmodern design includes a lavish royal suite. It's popular with business travelers and has a good fitness center and pool.

➕ 258 C2 ✉ Erzsébet tér 7–8 ☎ 1 429 3777; www.kempinski.com 🚇 Deák tér AX, DC, MC, VI

Alabárdos $$$

This stylish, formal restaurant serves Hungarian dishes in ancient vaulted dining rooms. Presentations are beautiful and the staff attentive. There are only a few tables, so it's always best to reserve in advance.

➕ 258 A3 ✉ Országház utca 2 ☎ 1 356 0851; www.alabardos.hu 🕐 Mon.–Sat. 7–11 p.m., Sat. noon–3 p.m. 🚇 Moszkva tér, then Várbusz (Castle Bus) AX, DC, MC, VI

Café Astoria Restaurant $$

The restaurant in the grand, early 20th-century Danubius Hotel Astoria (see left) serves first-class Hungarian and international dishes accompanied by good wines. A pianist entertains evening diners, and there's also a charming café.

➕ 258 C2 ✉ Kossuth Lajos utca 19–21 ☎ 1 889 6022; www.cafe astoriabudapest.hu 🚇 Astoria AX, DC, MC, VI

Gundel $$$

Traditional Hungarian meals are served in this 100-year-old restaurant in City Park. It is owned by Danubius Hotels, retaining its sumptuous atmosphere.

➕ 259 D4 ✉ Gundel Károly út 4 ☎ 1 889 8111; www.gundel.hu 🚇 Hősök tere AX, DC, MC, VI

Művész Kávéház $

This coffeehouse, opposite the Opera House, has retained the

ambience of Budapest's golden era of café society. The dark wood interior and gilt candelabras evoke a sense of grandeur and charm.

➕ 258 C3 ✉ Andrássy út 29 ☎ 1 343 3544 🚇 Opera MC, VI

Panorama $$

In the art nouveau Danubius Hotel Gellért, this well-known restaurant, over a thermal spring at the foot of Gellért Hill, has fine river views. Pike, perch and veal are specialties. A band plays traditional Hungarian music in the evenings.

➕ 258 C1 ✉ Gellért tér 1 ☎ 1 889 5500; www.danubiushotels.com 🕐 Closed Mon. and Sun. dinner 🚌 Tram 18, 19, 47, 49 AX, DC, MC, VI

Ashling Hotel $$

Located on the banks of the River Liffey, this stylish contemporary hotel is to the west of the center, close to the expanse of Phoenix Park. There's a good restaurant, and great transportation links mean you can explore the city with ease.

➕ 274 off map at A3 ✉ Parkgate Street ☎ 01 677 2324; www. ashlinghotel.ie 🚇 LUAS Museum, Heuston AX, MC, VI

Barrys Hotel $

Just off O'Connell Street and near a hop-on-hop-off bus tour stop, the great location and prices make this long-established hotel a good budget choice, popular with young people. Family rooms are available.

➕ 274 B4 ✉ 2 Great Denmark Street ☎ 01 874 9407; www. barryshotel.com 🚌 16, 16A, 747 AX, VI

The Clarence $$–$$$

This is an individual and tasteful hotel owned by Bono and The Edge, of Irish rock group U2. The comfortable hotel is in the heart of the city overlooking the River Liffey. The two-bedroom penthouse is especially chic. There is a very good restaurant.

➕ 274 B3 ✉ 6–8 Wellington Quay ☎ 01 407 0800; www.theclarence.ie AX, DC, MC, VI

KEY TO SYMBOLS

🔳 map page number and coordinates
✉ address
☎ telephone number
🅾 days/times closed
Ⓜ nearest subway station
🚌 nearest bus/trolley bus/tram/funicular route
⛴ ferry
$$$ expensive
$$ moderate
$ inexpensive
AX American Express
DC Diners Club
MC MasterCard
VI VISA

Bread, Cakes and Cookies

In Italy, bread comes from a *panificio* or *forno*, cakes and cookies from a *pasticceria*. In Tuscany there is no salt in bread, a legacy of an age when baking was done once a week and saltless bread didn't get moldy. Once you're accustomed to it, it goes well with the strong, salty flavors of prosciutto or salami. Italian cakes are outstanding: luscious creations piled with fruit, filled with cream, oozing chocolate and soaked with liqueur. Italians often buy a large cake or selection of smaller ones to eat for Sunday dessert, or a piece of *panforte*, a traditional spiced fruit confection from Siena. It's acceptable to buy a single pastry or cake and eat it on the spot in the shop.

The Schoolhouse Hotel $$–$$$

A former schoolhouse has been converted into this comfortable hotel with spacious rooms in a leafy part of town, and with free parking. There's also a restaurant and a pub on-site.
🔳 274 off map at C2 ✉ 2–8 Northumberland Road ☎ 01 667 5014; www.schoolhousehotel.com Ⓜ DART Pearse Station AX, DC, MC, VI

The Shelbourne $$$

A Dublin institution, this elegant hotel offers the highest standard of accommodation and comfort. Bedrooms are first-class, some with views over St. Stephen's Green, and facilities include a spa, leisure suite and fine dining. The afternoon tea here is legendary.
🔳 274 C2 ✉ 27 St. Stephen's Green ☎ 01 663 4500; www.marriot.com Ⓜ DART Pearse Station; LUAS St. Stephen's Green AX, MC, VI

DUBLIN RESTAURANTS

Price guide: (dinner per person, excluding drinks)
$ €15–€30
$$ €30–€45
$$$ over €45

Chapter One $$$

This elegant literary-themed restaurant located in the Dublin Writers Museum serves French cuisine with an Irish influence. Just the place to discuss Shaw over salmon or Joyce over venison.
🔳 274 B4 ✉ 18–19 Parnell Square ☎ 01 873 2266; www.chapterone restaurant.com 🅾 Closed Sun.–Mon. and Sat. lunch Ⓜ DART Connolly Station; LUAS Abbey Street AX, MC, VI

Gallagher's Boxty House $–$$

This is just the place to sample authentic Irish cuisine. Choose from a selection of mains that include traditional Irish potato boxty pancake and beef stew, and finish with a dessert such as Baileys cheesecake.
🔳 274 B3 ✉ 20–21 Temple Bar ☎ 01 677 2762; www.boxtyhouse.ie 🚌 All city-centre buses MC, VI

The Lobster Pot $$–$$$

As you'd expect from the name, the accent on this 35-year-old restaurant is on fish and seafood – with crab, mussels, prawns, salmon and white fish on the menu daily. Irish chicken, beef and lamb feature for carnivores; desserts are tempting and homemade. The Early Bird dinner, served 6–7:30 p.m., is a good value.
🔳 274 off map at C1 (2 miles southeast of the city near to U.S. Embassy) ✉ 9 Ballsbridge Terrace ☎ 01 668 0025; www.thelobsterpot.ie 🅾 Mon.–Sat. dinner 🚌 4, 7 AX, DC, MC, VI

Restaurant Patrick Guilbaud $$$

French cuisine of the highest standard makes this Ireland's premier fine-dining venue. The styling and the menu are modern. Advance booking is recommended.
🔳 274 C2 ✉ 21 Upper Merrion Street ☎ 01 676 4192; www.restaurantpatrickguilbaud.ie 🅾 Closed Sun.–Mon. Ⓜ DART Pearse Station; LUAS St. Stephen's Green AX, DC, MC, VI

ROME HOTELS

Price guide: (double room with breakfast for two people)
$ under €125
$$ €125–€250
$$$ over €250

66 Imperial Inn $–$$

This centrally located bed-and-breakfast has five bedrooms. All are decorated in a quirky, colorful style and facilities include Jacuzzi showers and plasma TVs.
🔳 293 D3 ✉ Via del Viminale 66 ☎ 06 482 5648; www.66imperialinn.com Ⓜ Termini station MC, VI

Campo de Fiori $$–$$$

You'll find comfortable rooms and a pleasant roof garden at this pretty and moderately priced hotel. It is near one of Rome's liveliest squares.
🔳 292 C2 ✉ Via del Biscione 6 ☎ 06 6880 6865; www.hotelcampo defiori.com 🚌 40, 46, 62, 64, 116, 190, 571, 916 AX, DC, VI

Hotel NH Vittorio Veneto $$$

Sleek modern comfort is the hallmark of this big hotel, situated near the Borghese gardens. Some rooms are bigger than others; specify when you book. Breakfast is buffet style and there is a good restaurant.
🔳 293 D4 ✉ Corso d'Italia 1 ☎ 06 84591 (within Italy); www.nhcollection.com Ⓜ Barberini 🚌 52, 53, 116 AX, DC, MC, VI

Regina Hotel Baglioni $$$

The Baglioni combines traditional architecture with modern comfort. The ambience and service are luxurious, and there's an excellent restaurant.

➕ 292 D3 ✉ Via Vittorio Veneto 72 ☎ 06 421 111; www.baglionihotels.com 🚇 Barberini 🚌 52, 53, 116, 910 AX, DC, MC, VI

Teatropace $$

A glorious spiral stairway leads to the upper floors of this comfortable hotel, close to Piazza Navona. The rooms are varying sizes, so be sure to specify the size you wish when you make a reservation. Breakfast is served in your room.

➕ 292 C2 ✉ Via de Teatro Pace 33 ☎ 06 668 79075; www.hotelteatropace.com 🚌 30, 70, 81, 186, 492 AX, DC, MC, VI

Price guide: (dinner per person, excluding drinks)
$ under €30
$$ €30–€55
$$$ over €55

De Armando al Pantheon $$

If you want to sample traditional Roman cooking, this is the place to come. The menu features classics such as *zuppa di farro* (spelt soup) and *saltimbocca* (veal with bacon and sage). Vegetarian dishes also are available.

➕ 292 C2/C3 ✉ Salita de' Crescenzi 31 ☎ 06 6880 3034; www.armandoalpantheon.it ⏱ Closed Sat. p.m. and Sun. 🚇 Vittorio Emanuele 🚌 64, 70, 81, 119 and all services to city center AX, MC, V

Da Baffetto $$

For a quintessential Roman experience and the best pizza in town, stand in line to get a table at this tiny pizzeria. Great for partygoers, it stays open until 1 a.m.

➕ 292 B3–C3 ✉ Via del Governo Vecchio 114 ☎ 06 686 1617; www.pizzeriabaffetto.it 🚌 30, 70, 81, 87, 116, 130, 186, 492, 628 No credit cards

Checchino dal 1887 $$$

This long-established restaurant specializes in the traditional Roman dishes of tripe, brains and offal. Reservations are essential.

➕ 292 C1 ✉ Via Monte Testaccio 30 ☎ 06 574 3816 or 06 5474 6318; www.checchino-dal-1887.com ⏱ Closed Sun.–Mon., Aug. and Dec. 25 🚌 719 AX, DC, MC, VII

Ginger $–$

This light and airy all-day space is both a bistro and a juice bar, serving imaginative blends of fruit and vegetables, great baguettes, soups and the best of Italian cheese and *salumeria*; there's a fine wine list too.

➕ 292 C3 ✉ Via Borgognona 43 ☎ 06 9603 6390; www.ginger.roma.it 🚇 Spagna 🚌 All routes down Via del Corso AX, MC, VI

Price guide: (double room with breakfast for two people)
$ under €125
$$ €125–€250
$$$ over €250

Brunelleschi $$–$$$

Reserve in advance to stay in this hotel, with tastefully decorated rooms, situated around a medieval tower in the heart of Florence.

➕ 302 C3 ✉ Piazza Santa Elisabetta 3 ☎ 055 27370; www.hotelbrunelleschi.it 🚌 In the pedestrian zone. C2, C3 AX, DC, MC, VI

Casci $

This excellent mid-range hotel is just two minutes from the Duomo. The charming owners keep clean, well-appointed rooms.

➕ 302 B4 ✉ Via Cavour 13 ☎ 055 211686; www.hotelcasci.com ⏱ Closed 2 weeks Jan. 🚌 10, 11, 25, 31, 82, C1 AX, DC, MC, VI

Cestelli $

Centrally situated near the Ponte Vecchio, this friendly little place is one of the best deals in Florence, with immaculate, and surprisingly large rooms (five of the eight have bathrooms), and nice touches such as pretty chandeliers and pleasing fabrics. The owners go out of their way to make your stay pleasant. Reserve well ahead.

➕ 302 C2 ✉ Borgo SS Apostoli 25 ☎ 055 214213; www.hotelcestelli.com 🚌 C1, C2 AX, MC

Loggiato dei Serviti $$–$$$

This beautiful hotel, housed in a 16th-century building, is set on one of Florence's loveliest squares a short stroll from the Duomo. Inside, corridors and public areas have kept the original architectural features and are furnished with Tuscan antiques; bedrooms are varied and traditionally styled, with every modern comfort. There's a lovely vaulted breakfast room and a cozy bar.

➕ 303 D4 ✉ Piazza della Santissima Annunziata 3 ☎ 055 289592; www.loggiatodeiservitihotel.it 🚌 C1, 1, 7, 20 AX, DC, MC, VI

Relais Uffizi $$

This 16th-century building has lovely rooms, good bathrooms and a pleasant lounge with clear views over the piazza.

➕ 302 C2 ✉ Via Chiasso del Buco 16 ☎ 055 267 6239; www.relaisuffizi.it 🚌 C3, D AX, MC, VI

Price guide: (dinner per person, excluding drinks)
$ under €30
$$ €30–€55
$$$ over €55

Buca Mario $$

Founded in 1886, this is a truly traditional *buca*, the word used in Florence to describe characteristic restaurants tucked away in low-ceilinged ground-floor rooms. Desserts are all homemade and the wine list includes a good house red, some great Chiantis and a clutch of interesting "new wave" reds.

➕ 302 B3 ✉ Piazza degli Ottaviani 16r ☎ 055 214179; www.bucamario.com 🚌 C2, 4, 22, 36, 37 MC, VI

Dei Frescobaldi $$

Classic Tuscan dishes are complemented by superb wines produced by one of Italy's most prestigious wine-producing dynasties at this atmospheric but elegant restaurant-cum-wine bar.

➕ 302 C2 ✉ Via dei Magazzini 2–4R ☎ 055 265 6535; www.deifrescobaldi.it 🚌 C1, C2 AX, DC, MC, VI

La Martinicca $–$$

Locals and tourists alike love this restaurant near Santa Maria Novella. Classic Tuscan dishes head up the menu including *bruschetta* (toasted country bread with different toppings) or ravioli stuffed with ricotta and spinach and served with a creamy sauce.

➕ 302 B3 ✉ Via del Sole 27/r ☎ 055 218928; www.ristorante-lamartinicca.com ⏱ Closed Sun. 🚌 C2, 6, 11, 22 No credit cards

KEY TO SYMBOLS

✚	map page number and coordinates
✉	address
☎	telephone number
🚫	days/times closed
Ⓜ	nearest subway station
🚌	nearest bus/trolley bus/ tram/funicular route
🛳	ferry
$$$	expensive
$$	moderate
$	inexpensive
AX	American Express
DC	Diners Club
MC	MasterCard
VI	VISA

Plan Ahead for Venice

To enjoy a stress-free visit in Venice it is absolutely necessary to make hotel reservations ahead of time. Reservations for June to September should be made during the previous fall, as should those for the two weeks in February in which Carnival falls (although you may be able to get something closer to the time of your visit if you hunt around). Three months ahead should be enough time for other months. If you would like to eat at a specific restaurant it's also advisable to make reservations; your hotel concierge will be happy to call and set them up.

Osteria de' Benci $

This is a genuine Florentine *osteria*. Start with *crostini* (Tuscan *bruschetta* – toasted bread served with spreads, cheeses and cold meats), then choose from a daily menu.

✚ 303 D2 ✉ Via dei Benci 13r ☎ 055 234 4923; www.osteriadebenci.it 🚌 23, 71, C3 AX, DC, VI

Rosticceria La Spada $

This is an old-style Florentine *rosticceria* where you can eat in or take out. Everything is freshly prepared, with the accent on grilled meat, fresh pasta dishes, grilled vegetables and tasty *crostini*.

✚ 302 B3 ✉ Via della Spada 62r ☎ 055 218757; www.laspadaitalia.com 🚌 C1, C2 No credit cards

Trattoria al Trebbio $–$$

This neighborhood *trattoria* has been catering to locals and tourists alike for years. The staff speaks English well but the food is Tuscan pure and simple. Seasonal specials are a good value; the wine list is short and strong on Chianti.

✚ 302 B3 ✉ Via delle Belle Donne 47–49r ☎ 055 287 089; www.casatrattoria.com/trattoria-al-trebbio 🚫 Closed Tue. lunch 🚌 4, 22, 36, 37, C2 AX, DC, MC, VI

Price guide: (double room with breakfast for two people)

$	under €125
$$	€125–€250
$$$	over €250

Excelsior $$–$$$

This grand hotel in the elegant Chiaia district has rooms with period furnishings and views of Capri.

✚ 309 A1 ✉ Via Partenope 48 ☎ 081 764 0111; www.hotelexcelsiornapoli.com 🚌 R3 AX, DC, VI

Hotel Piazza Bellini $$

A 16th-century building with a lovely courtyard has had a 21st-century update, resulting in a hotel that's modern, comfortable and a little bit funky. Factor in helpful and friendly young staff, quiet rooms and a very central location and this could be the ideal choice. Free WiFi and excellent buffet breakfast.

✚ 309 B3 ✉ Via Santa Maria di Constantinopoli 101 ☎ 081 451732; www.hotelpiazzabellini.com Ⓜ Dante 🚌 C57, R4 AX, MC, VI

Miramare $$$

The Miramare is housed in an art nouveau building near the Castel dell'Ovo and offers beautifully furnished rooms and elegant public areas. However, the chief draw here is the terrace, where you can eat breakfast while gazing over the Bay of Naples towards Mount Vesuvius.

✚ 309 B1–B2 ✉ Via Nazario Sauro 24 ☎ 081 764 7589; www.hotelmiramare.com 🚌 R3 AX, DC, MC, VI

Palazzo Decumani $$

Right in the heart of Spaccanapoli, this contemporary-style boutique hotel marries cutting-edge design and comfort with the baroque backdrop of this old *palazzo*. Expect loads of comfort and cool, calm rooms together with state-of-the-art technological devices.

✚ 309 B3 ✉ Via del Grande Archivio 8 ☎ 08142 01379; www.palazzodecumani.com 🚌 R2 AX, DC, MC, VI

Price guide: (dinner per person, excluding drinks)

$	under €30
$$	€30–€55
$$$	over €55

Al 53 $$

Naples' oldest restaurant, complete with 17th-century furnishings and original mosaic floor, serves great appetizers, seafood pasta and delicious Neapolitan desserts.

✚ 309 B3 ✉ Piazza Dante Alighieri 53 ☎ 081 549 9372 🚌 R1, 24 DC, MC, VI

Le Ancore $–$$

This traditional family-run restaurant in the port area may be functional decor-wise, but there's a terrace and the food is fresh, seasonal and well-cooked, and served with unfailing cheer and efficiency. Seafood and fish are favorites here and they offer a great-value fish menu and good carafe wines.

✚ 309 B1 ✉ Calata Villa del Popolo (inside port area) ☎ 081 553 5235; www.napoliristorante.it Ⓜ Garibaldi AX, MC, VI

La Cantina di Sica $$

This is a classic family-run Neapolitan neighborhood restaurant with a loyal clientele. Menus change seasonally, but there's always homestyle pasta, fish and meat dishes, with indulgent and imaginative desserts to follow.

➕ 309 off map at A3 ✉ Via Bernini 17 ☎ 081 556 7520; www. cantinadisica.it 🚇 Closed Sun. dinner and Mon. 🚇 Vanvitelli AX, MC, VI

Osteria la Chitarra $–$$

You'll enjoy a truly Neapolitan dining experience at this restaurant, where many local specialties are on offer. Be sure to try the *limoncello* cake.

➕ 309 B3 ✉ Rampe Santo Giovanni Maggiore 1/bis ☎ 081 552 9103; www.osterialachitarra.it 🚇 Dante 🚌 R3; tram 1 🚇 Closed Sun. (except Nov. to mid-May), Mon. p.m., Sat. lunch and Aug. AX, DC, MC, VI

VENICE HOTELS

Price guide: (double room with breakfast for two people)
$	under €150
$$	€150–€250
$$$	over €250

American-Dinesen $–$$$

This hotel is in the residential area of Dorsoduro. Many of the rooms have flower-hung balconies or terraces and breakfast is served buffet-style.

➕ 314 B2 ✉ Dorsoduro 628 ☎ 041 520 4733; www.hotelamerican.it 🚤 1, 2 AX, DC, MC, VI

Hotel Monaco and Grand Canal $$$

This world-class, classically elegant hotel is set where the Grand Canal enters the Basin of St. Mark. There are breathtaking views from some rooms and suites.

➕ 314 C2 ✉ Calle Vallaresso, San Marco 1332 ☎ 041 520 0211; www.hotelmonaco.it 🚤 1, 2 AX, DC, MC, VI

Locanda ai Santi Apostoli $–$$

Two of the twelve rooms in this good value palazzo-hotel overlook the Grand Canal. There's a spacious bar area and a private landing stage.

➕ 315 C3 ✉ campo Santi Apostoli, Cannaregio 4391/A ☎ 041 099 6916; www.locandasantiapostoli.com 🚤 Vaporetto Ca d'Oro DC, MC, VI

Palazzo Stern $$–$$$

Palazzo Stern is one of the prettiest Grand Canal *palazzi* in Venice. Outside, the breakfast terrace is set right on the water. Rooms are traditionally furnished in Venetian style, and there's a fun rooftop

Jacuzzi and charming public areas.

➕ 314 B2 ✉ Calle del Traghetto, Dorsoduro 2792/A ☎ 041 277 0869; www.palazzostern.it 🚤 1 AX, DC, MC, VI

VENICE RESTAURANTS

Price guide: (dinner per person, excluding drinks)
$	under €30
$$	€30–€55
$$$	over €55

Acquapazza $$

The accent is firmly on fish at this good, reliable restaurant, set on one of San Marco's nicer *campi*.

➕ 314 C2 ✉ Campo Sant' Angelo, San Marco 3808 ☎ 041 277 0688; www.veniceacquapazza.com 🚇 Closed Mon. and Jan. 🚤 1 AX, MC, VI

Antica Locanda Montin $$–$$$

This lovely, long-established restaurant serves classic dishes in its wood-paneled dining room or under the pretty pergola in the garden.

➕ 314 B2 ✉ Fondamenta di Borgo, Dorsoduro 1147 ☎ 041 522 7151; www.locandamontin.com 🚇 Closed Mon. 🚤 Vaporetto Zattere, Accademia AX, DC, MC, VI

Antiche Carampane $$$

This off-the-beaten-track restaurant specializes in elegantly cooked and served seafood and fish. The style is a modern take on tradition, with dishes such as *spaghetti alla granseola* (pasta with spider crab) or *branzino in salsa di peperoni* (sea bass in a sweet pepper sauce).

➕ 314 C3 ✉ Ponte delle Tette, San Polo 1911 ☎ 041 524 0165; www. antichecarampane.com 🚇 Closed Sun. and Mon. lunch 🚤 1, 2 AX, DC, MC, VI

Bancogiro $–$$

Housed in a 16th-century building by the Rialto market, the Bancogiro is a well-run restaurant that doubles as a bar serving *cicchetti*, typical Venetian snacks. The brick-vaulted interior is understated and elegant, while the outside tables make it one of Venice's best alfresco dining spots.

➕ 314 C3 ✉ Campo San Giacometto, San Polo 122 ☎ 041 523 2061; www.osteriabancogiro.it 🚇 Closed Mon. 🚤 1, 2 AX, DC, MC, VI

LUXEMBOURG HOTELS

Price guide: (double room with breakfast for two people)
$	under €120
$$	€120–€180
$$$	over €180

Français $$

Ideal for strolling to the Old Town, this hotel is at the heart of the city and has its own restaurant, with a terrace on the central square.

➕ 329 B3 ✉ 14 place d'Armes ☎ 47 45 34; www.hotelfrancais.lu 🚌 All city-center buses AX, DC, MC, VI

Hotel le Châtelet $$

This family-run hotel has been in business for over 40 years and is in a good location, a short walk from both the city center and the train station.

➕ 329 A1 ✉ 2 boulevard de la Pétrusse ☎ 40 21 01; www. chatelet.lu 🚌 9 AX, DC, MC, VI

Hotel Vauban $

Location is a big selling point for this hotel, right in the heart of town. Rooms are simple and modern; some overlook the central square. Staff are helpful and friendly. Excellent value for money though some rooms are small and there can be late-evening noise from outside. Free WiFi.

➕ 329 B3 ✉ 10 place Guillame II ☎ 22 04 93; www.hotelvauban.lu 🚌 All city-center buses AX, DC, MC, VI

Simoncini $$$

Elegant modern lines are the hallmark of this hotel, just a short stroll from the place d'Armes. There are 36 spacious rooms, and the bathrooms are excellent.

➕ 329 B3 ✉ 6 rue de Notre Dame ☎ 22 28 24; www.hotelsimoncini.lu 🚌 All city-center buses AX, DC, MC, VI

LUXEMBOURG RESTAURANTS

Price guide: (dinner per person, excluding drinks)
$	under €30
$$	€30–€45
$$$	over €45

Am Tirmschen $$$

There's a choice of classic dishes on the menu here, as well as Luxembourg specialties such as boiled meats served with mustard sauce. The charming restaurant has open stonework and flagged flooring.

KEY TO SYMBOLS

🔲 map page number and coordinates
✉ address
☎ telephone number
🕐 days/times closed
🚇 nearest subway station
🚌 nearest bus/trolley bus/tram/funicular route
⛴ ferry
$$$ expensive
$$ moderate
$ inexpensive
AX American Express
DC Diners Club
MC MasterCard
VI VISA

Weekend Treats

As in other Scandinavian cities, Oslo hotels cater to businesspeople on weekdays. This makes weekday room rates some of the most expensive in Europe. On weekends and during the holiday summer months fewer reservations are made, and hotels often offer discounts. You can stay in a luxury hotel from Friday night through Monday morning for a substantially reduced rate. Outside the height of summer this can also mean that there are few fellow guests, making your weekend stay seem even more exclusive. The high standard of service does not diminish with the price. Reduced rates on weekends and during holiday periods are common in many major European cities – it's always worth asking at the hotel you are interested in.

🔲 329 B3 ✉ 32 rue de l'Eau
☎ 26 27 07 33; www.amtirmschen.lu
🕐 Closed Sun. and public holidays, Mon. and Sat. lunch 🚌 All city-center buses AX, DC, MC, VI

G L'Beguin $–$$

This tiny place in the Grund area is both brasserie and restaurant, serving an excellent value set menu, which changes weekly, as well as a more sophisticated *menu de chef*. Friendly service and a nice location add to the pleasure – you can book online in advance.
🔲 329 C3 ✉ 21 rue de la Tour Jacob
☎ 279 16112; www.g-lebe guin.lu 🕐 Closed Sun. dinner
🚌 6, 23 AX, DC, VI

Les Caves Gourmandes $$–$$$

This popular and atmospheric place in the Îlot Gastronomique complex is within part of the Old Town wall. The menu features French cuisine.
🔲 329 C3 ✉ Îlot Gastronomique, 32 rue de l'Eau ☎ 46 11 24; www. caves-gourmandes.lu 🕐 Closed Sat. lunch and Sun. 🚌 All city-center buses AX, MC, VI

La Lorraine $$$

Located on place d'Armes, this bright, attractive restaurant offers French cuisine with excellent fish dishes. You can choose your lobster from a tank by the door.
🔲 329 B3 ✉ 7 place d'Armes
☎ 47 14 36; www.lalorraine-restaurant.lu 🚌 All city-center buses AX, DC, MC, VI

Price guide: (double room with breakfast for two people)
$ €75–€150
$$ €150–€300
$$$ over €300

Ambassade Hotel $$

On the splendid Herengracht, the most elegant canal, this beautifully furnished hotel offers comfortable rooms and a good breakfast.
🔲 342 B2 ✉ Herengracht 341
☎ 020 555 0222; www.ambassade-hotel.nl 🚌 Tram 1, 2, 5 AX, DC, MC, VI

Amstel Botel $$

Moored in Amsterdam's redeveloped waterfront, this floating hotel has interesting rooms with harbor views.
🔲 342 off map at B4 ✉ NDSM Pier

3 ☎ 020 626 4247; www.amstel botel.nl ⛴ NDSM ferry from Centraal Station AX, DC, MC, VI

Hotel de L'Europe $$$

The private boat landing at this expensive luxury hotel on the Amstel river says it all. It has a fine Victorian exterior, and inside it has been renovated to offer every modern amenity. The finest *haute cuisine* and wine list can be found at the hotel's Bord'Eau restaurant.
🔲 342 C2 ✉ Nieuwe Doelenstraat 2–8 ☎ 020 531 1777; www.leurope. nl 🚌 Tram 4, 9, 14, 16, 24, 25 AX, MC, VI

Nova Hotel $$

This family-run hotel has a central location but is sheltered from street noise. The en suite rooms are spotless and the service is friendly.
🔲 342 C3 ✉ Nieuwezijds Voorburgwal 276 ☎ 020 623 0066; www.novahotel.nl 🚌 Tram 1, 2, 5 AX, DC, MC, VI

Singel Hotel $$

A short walk from Centraal Station along the Singel canal, this 32-room hotel occupies three converted canalside houses. It has an historic feel but modern amenities.
🔲 342 C2 ✉ Singel 13–17
☎ 020 626 3108; www.singelhotel.nl
🚇 Amsterdam Centraal 🚌 Tram 1, 2, 5, 13, 17 AX, DC, MC, VI

Price guide: (dinner per person, excluding drinks)
$ €10–€20
$$ €20–€30
$$$ over €30

t'Blauwe Theehuise $

If you're in the Vondelpark then a visit to this 1937 café is a must. Drinks and meals are served as well as simple sandwiches and other snacks.
🔲 342 A1 ✉ Vondelpark ☎ 020 662 0254; www.blauwetheehuis.nl
🚌 Tram 1, 2, 3, 5, 12 No credit cards

In de Waag $–$$

Come to this friendly restaurant for late-night Continental cuisine, when it is lit by hundreds of candles. The generous three-course lunch and early evening menu offer good value.
🔲 342 C3 ✉ Nieuwmarkt 4
☎ 020 422 7772; www.indewaag.nl
🚇 Nieuwmarkt AX, DC, MC, VI

De Silveren Spiegel $$–$$$

Located in a restored, redbrick building dating from 1614, this restaurant has a varied menu, from Dutch cuisine to fish.

✚ 342 C4 ✉ Kattengat 4–6 ☎ 020 624 6589; www.desilverenspiegel.com ⓘ Closed lunch and Sun. ⊞ Centraal Station ⊟ Tram 1, 2, 5, 13, 17 AX, DC, MC, VI

Toscanini $$

This stylish Jordaan district restaurant features excellent Italian food. Homemade *biscotti* is a particular specialty.

✚ 342 B4 ✉ Lindengracht 75 ☎ 020 623 2813; www.restaurant toscanini.com ⓘ Closed lunch and Sun. ⊟ Tram 3, 10 AX, DC, MC, VI

d'Vijff Vlieghen $$$

The name translates as The Five Flies, for the five canalside houses that contain nine dining rooms serving traditional Dutch fare but with contemporary flair.

✚ 342 B2 ✉ Spuistraat 294–302 ☎ 020 624 8369; www.vijffvlie ghen.nl ⓘ Closed lunch ⊟ Tram 1, 2, 5 AX, MC, VI

THE HAGUE HOTELS

Price guide: (double room with breakfast for two people)
$ €75–€150
$$ €150–€300
$$$ over €300

Best Western Delft Museumhotel and Residence $$

While in Delft, spend at least one night in this tastefully furnished hotel overlooking a tranquil canal.

✚ 350 off map at B2 ✉ Oude Delft 189 ☎ 015 215 3070; www.bestwest ern.nl ⊞ Delft Centraal Station ⊟ Tram 1 AX, DC, MC, VI

Carlton Ambassador Hotel $$–$$$

This luxury hotel in an elegant neighborhood is within easy walking distance of the city center.

✚ 350 B2 ✉ Sophialaan 2 ☎ 070 363 0363; www.carlton.nl ⊟ 4, 5, 22, 24; tram 1, 17 AX, DC, MC, VI

Hotel Mozaic $$–$$$

This renovated hotel is a short distance from the city center but it is a pleasant mid-range choice with good tram connections.

✚ 350 B2 ✉ Laan Copes van Cattenburch 38 ☎ 070 352 2335; www.mozaic.nl ⊟ Tram 9 AX, DC, MC, VI

Mercure Hotel Den Haag Central $–$$

This modern hotel is located near the railroad station and is convenient for the city center. It also has a restaurant.

✚ 350 C1 ✉ Spui 180 ☎ 070 203 9002; www.mercure.com ⊟ 18, 22, 24; tram 1, 15, 16 AX, DC, MC, VI

Steigenberger Kurhaus Hotel $$$

If you are in Scheveningen and want a hotel with a sun lounge and terrace overlooking the beach, consider this Old European-style hotel, built in the 1880s. Some of the comfortable rooms have a balcony.

✚ 350 off map at B4 ✉ Gevers Deynootplein 30, Scheveningen ☎ 070 416 2636; www.steigen berger.com ⊟ 21, 22, 23; tram 1, 9 AX, DC, MC, VI

THE HAGUE RESTAURANTS

Price guide: (dinner per person, excluding drinks)
$ €10–€20
$$ €20–€30
$$$ over €30

Bodega De Posthoorn $$

This restaurant is housed in an attractive building on the stylish Lange Voorhout. Advance reservations are advised.

✚ 350 C2 ✉ Lange Voorhout 39a ☎ 070 360 4906; www.bodega deposthoorn.nl ⊟ Tram 9 AX, MC

It Rains Fishes $$$

High-quality, expensive seafood is served in this classy and intimate restaurant. Advance reservations are advised.

✚ 350 B2 ✉ Noordeinde 123 ☎ 070 365 2598; www.itrains fishes.nl ⓘ Closed Sat. lunch and Sun. ⊟ 22, 24; tram 1, 17 AX, DC, MC, VI

Les Ombrelles $$

On attractive, historic Denneweg, this restaurant serves good seafood dishes and has a lovely terrace for summer dining.

✚ 350 C2 ✉ Hooistraat 4a ☎ 070 365 8789; www.lesombrelles.nl ⓘ Closed Sat. and Sun. lunch ⊟ 18, 22, 29; tram 9 AX, DC, MC, VI

Stadsherberg 't Goude Hooft $$$

Rebuilt in the 17th century, this popular inn serves good food.

✚ 350 B1 ✉ Dagelijkse Groenmarkt 13 ☎ 070 346 9713; www.tgoudehooft.nl ⊟ 25, tram 2, 3, 4, 6 AX, MC, VI

OSLO HOTELS

Price guide: (double room with breakfast for two people)
$ Kr800–Kr1,000
$$ Kr1,000–Kr1,400
$$$ over Kr1,400

Anker Hotel $$–$$$

Comfortable 3-star hotel, a few minutes' walk from Oslo Central Station and Karl Johans Gate.

✚ 365 C2 ✉ Storgata 55 ☎ 22 99 75 00; www.anker-hotel.no ⓦ Jernbanetorget ⊟ 30, 31, 32; tram 12, 13 AX, DC, MC, VI

First Hotel Grims Grenka $$–$$$

Norway's most fashionable hotel, boasting deluxe rooms and suites, is in the center of Oslo.

✚ 365 B1 ✉ Kongens Gate 5 ☎ 23 10 72 00; www.firsthotels.no ⓦ Stortinget ⊟ Tram 12 AX, DC, MC, VI

Grand Hotel $$$

The Grand is one of Oslo's most prestigious places to stay with well-appointed rooms, restaurants, bars and a rooftop sauna and pool.

✚ 365 B1 ✉ Karl Johans Gate 31 ☎ 23 21 20 00; www.grand.no ⓦ Stortinget ⊟ Tram 11, 17, 18 AX, DC, MC, VI

Hotel Continental $$$

Located between the Royal Palace and City Hall, this is a member of "The Leading Hotels of the World." It has four good restaurants and cafés.

✚ 365 B1 ✉ Stortingsgaten 24–26 ☎ 22 82 40 00; www.hotelcontin ental.no ⓦ Nationaltheatret ⊟ Tram 13, 19 AX, DC, MC, VI

The Thief $$$

A distinctive and elegant hotel at Tjuvholmen with direct access to the Oslo Fjord. The hotel has a bar, restaurant, rooftop terrace and spa.

✚ 365 B1 ✉ Tjuvholmen ☎ 24 00 40 00 ; thethief.com ⓦ Nationaltheatret ⊟ 21, 54, N54; tram 12 AX, DC, MC, VI

KEY TO SYMBOLS

⊞ map page number and coordinates
⊠ address
☎ telephone number
🕐 days/times closed
🚇 nearest subway station
🚌 nearest bus/trolley bus/ tram/funicular route
⛴ ferry
$$$ expensive
$$ moderate
$ inexpensive
AX American Express
DC Diners Club
MC MasterCard
VI VISA

OSLO RESTAURANTS

Price guide: (dinner per person, excluding drinks)
$ Kr50–Kr80
$$ Kr80–Kr200
$$$ over Kr200

Café Christiania $$

Traditional Norwegian food is served in museumlike surroundings here. In summer you can dine on the terrace overlooking the Parliament building.
⊞ 365 B1 ⊠ Nedre Vollgate 19
☎ 22 01 05 10; www.cafechrist iania.no 🕐 Closed Sun. year-round, Mon. in Jul. 🚇 Stortinget 🚌 Tram 11, 18, 19 AX, DC, MC, VI

Engebret Café $$

Founded in 1857 by Engebret Christoffersen, this restaurant offers Norwegian and international cuisine, including traditional fish dishes.
⊞ 365 B1 ⊠ Bankplassen 1
☎ 22 82 25 25; engebret-cafe.no 🕐 Closed Sat. lunch and Sun. 🚇 Stortinget 🚌 Tram 12 AX, DC, MC, VI

Grand Café $$$

A great heritage, including visits by Ibsen in his day, makes this restaurant in the Grand Hotel (see page 485) a firm favorite. Norwegian cuisine, from elk stew to *lutefisk* (marinated dried fish), is available.
⊞ 365 B1 ⊠ Karl Johans Gate 31
☎ 23 21 20 00; www.grand.no 🚇 Stortinget 🚌 Tram 11, 17, 18 AX, DC, MC, VI

Restaurant Det Gamle Rådhus $$$

In the 17th-century building next to Akershus Castle, this restaurant is billed as Oslo's oldest eating establishment. International cuisine and fish specialties are served. Reservations are strongly advised.
⊞ 365 B1 ⊠ Nedre Slottsgate 1
☎ 22 42 01 07; www.gamleraadhus. no 🕐 Closed Sun. and 3 weeks in Jul. 🚇 Stortinget 🚌 Tram 12 AX, DC, MC, VI

LISBON HOTELS

Price guide: (double room with breakfast for two people)
$ under €125
$$ €125–€200
$$$ over €200

Britânia $$$

This friendly, art deco-style hotel, just east of Avenida da Liberdade, was refurbished in the 1990s.
⊞ 378 off map at A5 ⊠ Rua Rodrigues Sampaio 17 ☎ 213 155 016; www.hotel-britania.com
🚇 Avenida 🚌 All buses for Avenida da Liberdade AX, DC, MC, VI

Four Seasons Ritz $$$

One of Lisbon's most luxurious hotels, with sumptuously decorated large rooms and suites, and exceptional service. Visit the spa for some pampering.
⊞ 378 off map at A5 ⊠ Rua Rodrigo da Fonseca 88 ☎ 213 811 400; www. fourseasons.com 🚇 Marquês de Pombal 🚌 All buses for Marquês de Pombal AX, DC, MC, VI

International Design Hotel $$–$$$

Situated on the Rossio and easily recognized by its striking violet color, this hotel offers design-oriented rooms, some of which are decorated in vibrant hues.
⊞ 379 B4 ⊠ Rua Betesga 30
☎ 213 240 990; www.idesignhotel. com 🚇 Rossio 🚌 All buses for Rossio AX, MC, VI

Residencial Florescente $

This is a well-managed budget hotel in the heart of the city with compact but well decorated rooms. There's a wealth of dining and entertainment options within walking distance.
⊞ 378 B5 ⊠ Rua Portas de Santo Antão 99 ☎ 213 426 609; www. residencialflorescente.com 🚇 Rossio 🚌 and tram: all services to Restauradores AX, MC, VI

Zuza $–$$$

Choose from budget rooms in the Zuza guesthouse or splurge on one of Zuza's suites or apartments dotted across the Chiado.
⊞ 378 B4 ⊠ Rua do Duque 41
☎ 934 445 500; www.zuzabed.com 🚇 Rossio, Baixa-Chiado AX, MC, VI

LISBON RESTAURANTS

Price guide: (dinner per person, excluding drinks)
$ under €25
$$ €25–€35
$$$ over €35

100 Maneiras $$$

Book in advance to savor 100 Maneiras' innovative 10-course tasting menu with ingredients sourced from the Ribeira market.
⊞ 378 A4 ⊠ Rua do Teixeira 35

☎ 910 307 575; www.restaurant100maneiras.com ⏱ Closed daily lunch Ⓜ Restauradores and Gloria elevator 🚌 758 AX, DC, MC, VI

As Salgadeiras $$–$$$

Excellent Portuguese cuisine with a contemporary twist is served in the cozy surroundings of this converted old bakery in the Barrio Alto District. ✚ 378 A3 ✉ Rua das Salgadeiras 18 ☎ 213 421 157; www.as-salgadeiras.com ⏱ Closed Mon. Ⓜ Tram 28E MC, VI

Cantinho Lusitano $

This tiny, family-run eatery serves *petiscos*, small taster-sized portions of traditional Portuguese favorites. The menu reflects seasonal produce all accompanied by a good choice of local wines. ✚ 378 off map at A4 ✉ Rua dos Prezares 52 ☎ 218 065 185; www.cantinholusitano.com ⏱ Closed lunch and Sun. Ⓜ Marquês de Pombal 🚌 727, 707 MC, VI

Gambrinus $$$

There's an old-fashioned ambience at this deluxe, formal restaurant, where fish and seafood are the specialties. Reservations advised. ✚ 378 B5 ✉ Rua das Portas de Santo Antão 23 ☎ 213 421 466; www.gambrinuslisboa.com Ⓜ Rossio AX, MC, VI

Winebar do Castelo $–$$

Come to this small and bustling traditional café/bar in the shadow of the castle for casual tapas-style eating and a delicious selection of wines and ports. ✚ 379 D3 ✉ Rua Bartolomeu de Gusmão 11–13 ☎ 218 879 093 🚌 737 MC, VI

Price guide: (double room with breakfast for two people)
$	under €100
$$	€100–€175
$$$	over €175

Hotel da Musica $–$$

Set in a refurbished market hall, this hotel has contemporary, chic spaces with light, bright rooms; some decor features "musical" accents. ✚ 387 off map at A4 ✉ Mercadi do Bom Successo, Largo Ferreira Lapa ☎ 226 076 000; www.hoteldamusica.com 🚌 402, 508, 704, 803, 907 Ⓜ Casa da Musica AX, DC, MC, VI

Infante de Sagres $$–$$$

Porto's landmark hotel has a pretty terrace and some lovely bedrooms. Stylish design is used throughout to great effect. ✚ 387 B3 ✉ Praça Filipa de Lencastre 62 ☎ 223 398 500; www.hotelinfantesagres.pt Ⓜ Aliados 🚌 All buses for Praça da Liberdade AX, DC, MC, VI

Intercontinental Porto, Palácio das Cardosas $$$

Housed in a beautifully renovated late 18th-century palace, this good, centrally located hotel has excellent service to match. ✚ 387 C3 ✉ Praça da Liberdade 25 ☎ 220 035 600; www.ihg.com Ⓜ São Bento 🚌 All buses to Liberdade AX, DC, MC, VI

Pestana Porto $$–$$$

In the heart of the historic Ribeira district, within a UNESCO heritage site, this boutique hotel offers comfortable rooms with river views and friendly staff. ✚ 387 B1 ✉ Praça da Ribeira 1 ☎ 223 402 300; www.pestana.com 🚌 500, 900, 901, 906 AX, MC, VI

Seculo Hotel $

This simple, serviceable city hotel makes a good base for budget-conscious travelers. ✚ 387 off map at C4 ✉ Rua Santa Catarina 1256 ☎ 222 099 120; www.seculohotel.com 🚌 701,702 AX, MC, VI

Price guide: (dinner per person, excluding drinks)
$	under €25
$$	€25–€35
$$$	over €35

Abadia $$

With huge portions of hearty Portuguese food, Abadia has been a favorite for many years. The food is the real draw here, not the setting. ✚ 387 C3 ✉ Rua do Ateneu Comercial do Porto 22 ⏱ Closed Sun., Mon. lunch ☎ 222 008 757; www.abadiadoporto.com Ⓜ Aliados 🚌 All buses for Praça da Liberdade AX, MC, VI

Casinha São João $–$$

The city's most authentic *tapas* bar, with local wines and sangria, in a simple vaulted dining room on the waterfront.

✚ 387 C1 ✉ Cais da Ribeira 9 ☎ 914 237 742; casinhasaojoao.com ⏱ Closed Mon. (also Sun. evening in winter) 🚌 900, 901, 906 MC, VI

Essência $$

A vegetarian restaurant is a rare thing in Portugal. This contemporary eatery near the Casa da Musica has an excellent reputation (it also serves nonvegetarian options). ✚ 387 off map at A4 ✉ Rua de Pedro Hispano 1190 ☎ 228 301 813; www.essenciarestaurantevegeteranio.com ⏱ Closed Sun. MC, VI

ODE Porto Wine House $$$

You'll find an excellent modern twist on traditional Portuguese dishes at this atmospheric eatery in a historic building close to the river. ✚ 387 C1 ✉ Largo do Terreiro 7 ☎ 913 200 010 🚌 900, 901, 906 No credit cards

Pedro Lemos $$–$$$

Head to the seafront district of Foz do Douro and this 1-Michelin star restaurant set in a traditional town house. A *tapas* menu and afternoon tea also are available. ✚ 387 off map at A2 ✉ Rua Padre Luis Cabral 974, Fox do Douro ☎ 220 115 986; www.pedrolemos.net ⏱ Closed Sun. dinner, Mon.–Tue. lunch 🚌 500; tram 1 AX, DC, MC, VI

Price guide: (double room with breakfast for two people)
$	€50–€100
$$	€100–€150
$$$	over €150

Hospedaje Romero $

This is an affordable, family-run guesthouse with well-kept rooms. ✚ 402 B2 ✉ Gran Vía 64 ☎ 92 559 76 61; www.hospedajeromero.com Ⓜ Gran Vía MC, VI•

Hotel Atlàntico $$

Occupying a splendid turn-of-the-20th-century building, this hotel has elegant and sound-proofed rooms. Guests can enjoy panoramic views from the hotel's roof terrace. ✚ 402 C2 ✉ Gran Vía 38 ☎ 91 522 64 80; www.hotelatlantico.es Ⓜ Callao No credit cards

The Principal $$$

One of Madrid's newest luxury hotels, with a spa, rooftop terrace

KEY TO SYMBOLS

✚	map page number and coordinates
✉	address
☎	telephone number
◎	days/times closed
Ⓜ	nearest subway station
🚌	nearest bus/trolley bus/tram/funicular route
⛴	ferry
$$$	expensive
$$	moderate
$	inexpensive
AX	American Express
DC	Diners Club
MC	MasterCard
VI	VISA

Andalucian Cuisine

Simplicity is all in Andalucian cooking, in which the superb quality of the ingredients, combined with a Moorish legacy of spices, almonds and oranges, has created one of Spain's most enjoyable cuisines. *Tapas* originated here, as did *gazpacho*, the cold summer soup, and sherry, a fortified wine drunk as an aperitif and used in cooking. There are tasty stews and soups, thickened with lentils, potatoes or almonds, and every dish is redolent with olive oil, garlic and tomatoes. Excellent bread and rich Arab-inspired pastries and desserts complete the picture.

---

and restaurant. It enjoys a superb location overlooking the Gran Vía.
✚ 402 C2 ✉ Calle Marqués de Valdeiglesias 1 ☎ 91 521 87 43; www.theprincipalmadridhotel.com Ⓜ Banco de España AX, MC, VI

Room Mate Alicia $$

The Room Mate Alicia is part of a rapidly expanding chain of cheap-and-chic hotels, and has a fabulous central location right on the Plaza Santa Ana.
✚ 402 C1 ✉ Calle Prado 2 ☎ 91 389 60 95; alicia.room-matehotels.com Ⓜ Puerta del Sol AX, MC, VI

Price guide: (dinner per person, excluding drinks)

$	€10–€25
$$	€25–€50
$$$	over €50

La Bola $$

This long-established tavern specializes in Madrid *cocido* – delicious stews cooked slowly in traditional clay pots.
✚ 402 B2 ✉ Calle Bola 5 ☎ 91 547 69 30; www.labola.es ◎ Closed Sun. dinner Ⓜ Santo Domingo MC, VI

Casa Patas $$

Casa Patas is one of the best flamenco venues in town offering traditional dishes or *tapas* at the bar. There are daily flamenco shows (extra charge).
✚ 402 C1 ✉ Cañizares, 10 ☎ 91 369 04 96; www.casapatas.com ◎ Closed Sun. Ⓜ Antón Martín AX, MC, VI

Mercado de San Miguel $–$$

The century-old, wrought-iron Mercado (Market) de San Miguel has been transformed into the gastronomic hub of the old city. As well as the stalls selling the finest gourmet produce (including oils, hams, cheeses, seafood and conserves), it has several wonderful bars serving fine wines accompanied by all manner of delicious treats.
✚ 402 B2 ✉ Plaza de San Miguel ☎ 91 542 49 36; www.mercadode sanmiguel.es ◎ Open Mon.–Thu. 10 a.m. to midnight, Fri.–Sun. 10 a.m.– 2 a.m. Ⓜ Sol

TriCiclo $$

Close to the Prado Museum, this bistro-style spot with scrubbed

wooden tables serves market-fresh cuisine, including local and international dishes.
✚ 403 D2 ✉ Calle Santa María 28 ☎ 91 024 47 98; www.eltriciclo.es Ⓜ Antón Martín No credit cards

Price guide: (double room with breakfast for two people)

$	€60–€120
$$	€120–€180
$$$	over €180

Hotel Arts $$$

This 44-story, luxury waterfront hotel, with superb views across the city, is still the city's premier address.
✚ 411 A1 ✉ Carrer de la Marina 19–21 ☎ 93 221 10 00 ; www. hotelartsbarcelona.com Ⓜ Ciutadella/Vila Olímpica AX, DC, MC, VI

Hotel Banys Orientals $$

This well-priced boutique hotel enjoys a superb location in the fashionable Born neighborhood. Suites are available in an annex.
✚ 411 C1 ✉ Carrer Argenteria 37 ☎ 93 269 84 60; www.hotelbanys orientals.com Ⓜ Jaume I AX, MC, VI

Hotel Neri $$$

Hotel Neri is one of the ciy's finest boutique hotels, hidden away in the Gothic heart of old Barcelona.
✚ 411 B1 ✉ Carrer Sant Sever 5 ☎ 93 304 06 55; www.hotelneri.com Ⓜ Liceu AX, MC, VI

The Praktik Bakery $$

This hotel has an in-house bakery and is located close to the Pedrera. Pay extra to stay in one of the light-filled, exterior rooms.
✚ 411 B3 ✉ Carrer Provença 279 ☎ 93 488 00 61; www.hotelpraktik bakery.com Ⓜ Diagonal No credit cards

Price guide: (dinner per person, excluding drinks)

$	€10–€25
$$	€25–€50
$$$	over €50

Café de l'Acadèmia $$

Perfect for a romantic dinner, particularly on the pretty terrace, this restaurant serves excellent Catalan fare. The cod dishes are tasty.
✚ 411 C2 ✉ Carrer Lledó 1, Plaça Sant Just ☎ 93 319 82 53 ◎ Closed Sat.–Sun. and 3 weeks in Aug. MC, VI

Kaiku $$

This is one of the best seafood restaurants in the city, although you'd never guess it from the plain exterior. It's most famous for the *arròs del xef*, a paella-style dish made with smoked rice, but this is complemented each day by a range of fabulously fresh seafood. Book a table on the terrace, and enjoy a long languid lunch with sea views.

🔲 411 C1 ✉ Plaça del Mar 1
☎ 93 221 90 82; restaurantkaiku.cat
🅲 Closed dinner and Mon.
🚇 Barceloneta MC, VI

Llamber $$

This ultra-stylish, spacious tavern serves elegant interpretations of Spanish classics, including dishes such as parmesan fondue with king prawns and asparagus.

🔲 411 C3 ✉ Carrer Fusina 5
☎ 93 319 62 50; llamberbarcelona.com 🚇 Jaume I, Barceloneta
No credit cards

Rasoterra $

High ceilings and big scrubbed tables make an inviting setting for delicious veggie and vegan cuisine, prepared, where possible, with local and organic ingredients. They offer a good set lunch, and a selection of organic wines and beers.

🔲 411 B1 ✉ Carrer de Palau 5
☎ 93 318 6926; www.rasoterra.cat
🚇 Jaume I MC, VI

Set Portes $$–$$$

One of Barcelona's best and most historic restaurants serves a wide range of excellent Catalan food and fine wines. It is famous for the quality of its paella.

🔲 411 C1 ✉ Passeig de Isabel II 14
☎ 93 319 30 33; www.7portes.com
🚇 Barceloneta AX, DC, MC, VI

Hostal Alfonso $

For location, comfort and price, it's hard to beat this friendly little *hostal*. The rooms are simple, but immaculately kept, and some have views across the square to the cathedral. Book well in advance – with just six rooms, this hotel fills up very quickly.

🔲 418 off map at A1 ✉ Rúa do Pombal 40 ☎ 981 585 685;
www.hostalalfonso.com MC, VI

Hostal Reis Católicos $$$

This *parador* is considered by many to be the finest deluxe hotel in Spain. It is magnificently situated in the cathedral square, in a beautiful 15th-century cloistered building. You will need to make reservations months in advance.

🔲 418 A3 ✉ Praza do Obradoiro 1
☎ 981 582 200; www.parador.es/en/
AX, DC, MC, VI

Hotel Costa Vella $

This enchanting hotel overlooks a beautiful garden on the edge of Santiago de Compostela's old quarter. Bedrooms are comfortable.

🔲 418 B3 ✉ Rúa da Porta da Pena 17 ☎ 981 56 95 30;
www.costavella.com MC, VI

San Miguel $$

A beautiful hotel in an historic building near the cathedral, this has light-filled, modern rooms set around a pretty garden courtyard. The excellent restaurant, with tables out on the terrace, is perfect for relaxing after a long day's sightseeing.

🔲 418 B2 ✉ Praza de San Miguel dos Agros 9 ☎ 981 555 779;
sanmiguelsantiago.com MC, VI

Casa Marcelo $$$

This chic gastro-tavern has three bar areas and serves an interesting menu of *platillos* (small plates), including many contemporary Gallego dishes.

🔲 418 A2 ✉ Rúa das Hortas 1
☎ 981 558 580; www.casamarcelo.net 🅲 Closed Mon., and dinner Sun.
MC, VI

La Cavita $

A stylish *tapas* bar which also serves original, creative main courses, this is one of the hottest addresses in town.

🔲 418 1A ✉ Rúa de San Pedro de Mezonzo 9 🅲 Closed Sun. ☎ 981 935 098; www.lacavita.com MC, VI

Pedro Roca $$–$$$

This is one of Santiago's best kept secrets. Come here to sample great Spanish cooking in a tranquil, relaxing environment.

🔲 418 off map at A3 ✉ Domingo García Sabell 1 ☎ 981 585 776;
www.pedroroca.es 🅲 Closed Sun. dinner MC, VI

Alfonso XIII $$$

Seville's top hotel, set in an attractive palm-shaded garden, offers every comfort in its elegant, luxurious rooms with exceptional service.

🔲 425 B2 ✉ Calle San Fernando 2
☎ 95 491 70 00; www.hotel-alfonso xiii-seville.com 🅲 C1, C3, C4; tram T1 AX, DC, MC, VI

Casas de la Judería $$$

This atmospheric hotel, located in the heart of Santa Cruz, features peaceful courtyards with fountains.

🔲 425 B3 ✉ Calle Santa María la Blanca 5 ☎ 95 441 51 50;
www.lascasasdelajuderiasevilla.com
🚌 5, C3, C4 AX, DC, MC, VI

Hostal Callejón del Agua $

Definitely one of the best budget choices in town, this charming *hostal* is located in a 19th-century town house in the old quarter. The elegantly furnished bedrooms are set around a tranquil, plant-filled patio. There are good views from the roof terrace.

🔲 425 B3 ✉ Calle Corral del Rey 23
☎ 95 421 20 98; www.callejondel agua.com 🚌 1, 5 MC, VI

Hotel Alminar $–$$

This modest hotel has just a dozen rooms in an ideal location near the cathedral. The decor is a little dated, but the staff are welcoming, and there are thoughtful touches such as the library of travel guides. Street noise can be a problem, so be sure to pack ear plugs.

🔲 425 A3 ✉ Calle Álvarez Quintero 52 ☎ 95 429 39 13;
www.hotelalminar.com 🚌 21–26, 30, 31, 34, 41, 42, C3, C4 MC, VI

Hotel Casa 1800 $$–$$$

This 19th-century *palacete* (small palace) has been converted into a smart boutique hotel. Rooms are sumptuously decorated, and touches

KEY TO SYMBOLS

- ⊞ map page number and coordinates
- ✉ address
- ☎ telephone number
- ◷ days/times closed
- Ⓜ nearest subway station
- 🚌 nearest bus/trolley bus/tram/funicular route
- ⛴ ferry
- $$$ expensive
- $$ moderate
- $ inexpensive
- AX American Express
- DC Diners Club
- MC MasterCard
- VI VISA

include free afternoon tea on the patio. From the roof terrace, you can enjoy views of the cathedral. To reach the hotel you will need to take a taxi and then walk the final 55 yards.
⊞ 425 B3 ✉ Calle Rodrigo Caro 6 ☎ 95 456 18 00; www.hotelcasa1800.com 🚌 1 AX, DC, MC, VI

Itaca Sevilla $$

A comfortable, great value hotel set in a traditional town house close to the cathedral. Rooms (including family rooms) are arranged around a charming central patio, and there's a sun deck and plunge pool on the roof terrace.
⊞ 425 B3 ✉ Calle Santillana 5–7 ☎ 954 22 81 56; www.itacasevilla.com 🚌 27, 32; tram T1 MC, VI

SEVILLE RESTAURANTS

Price guide: (dinner per person, excluding drinks)
$ €10–€25
$$ €25–€50
$$$ over €50

El 3 de Oro $$

This lively and friendly restaurant in Santa Cruz serves a range of Andalucian dishes and is always packed with locals.
⊞ 425 B3 ✉ Calle Santa María la Blanca 34 ☎ 954 42 27 59; www.el3deoro.com 🚌 1, C3, C4 MC, VI

Becerrita $$

This long-established restaurant serves traditional Andalucian food and prides itself on its desserts.
⊞ 425 B3 ✉ Calle Recaredo 9 ☎ 95 441 20 57; www.becerrita.com ◷ Closed Sun. dinner and 2 weeks in Aug. 🚌 1, 24, 27, A1, A2, C3 MC, VI

ConTenedor $–$$

As yet undiscovered by tourists, this stylish and relaxed local restaurant is part of the "slow food" movement. The delicious seasonal menu of mostly organic and local produce is chalked up daily on blackboards.
⊞ 425 B4 ✉ Calle San Luis 50 ☎ 95 491 63 33; www.contenedor.com 🚌 C5 MC, VI

La Flor de Toranza $

Known to locals as "Trifón," this much-loved, friendly haunt is a great spot for breakfast, a quick lunch or some *tapas*.
⊞ 425 A3 ✉ Calle Jimios 1 ☎ 95 422 93 15 🚌 C5; tram T1
No credit cards

STOCKHOLM HOTELS

Price guide: (double room with breakfast for two people)
$ 800SKr–1,500SKr
$$ 1,500SKr–2,200SKr
$$$ over 2,200SKr

Diplomat $$–$$$

This comfortable hotel in a handsome early 20th-century building overlooks the waterfront on the road to Djurgården. The on-site T/BAR is a delightful place to stop for tea.
⊞ 437 C3 ✉ Strandvägen 7C ☎ 08 459 68 00; www.diplomathotel.com Ⓜ Östermalmstorg 🚌 47, 69; tram 7 AX, DC, MC, VI

Grand Hôtel Stockholm $$$

At this hotel across from the Royal Palace, facilities are luxurious. The Mathias Dahlgren restaurant is one of the finest in the city, and the Veranda restaurant is famous for its *smörgåsbord*.
⊞ 437 B2 ✉ Södra Blasieholmshamnen 8 ☎ 08 679 35 00; www.grandhotel.se Ⓜ Kungsträdgården 🚌 2, 43, 55, 62, 76 AX, DC, MC, VI

Hotel Skepps Holmen $$

With a country-in-the-city feel, this hotel on Skeppsholmen, near the Modern Art Museum, offers waterfront views, spacious rooms filled with sleek Scandinavian furniture, and the free use of bicycles.
⊞ 437 B2 ✉ Gröna gången ☎ 08 407 23 00; www.hotelskeppsholmen.se 🚌 65 ⛴ From Slussen AX, DC, MC, VI

Mälardrottningen $–$$

Once owned by Woolworth heiress Barbara Hutton, this 1920s converted yacht, on the west side of the Old Town, is a hotel with a difference. The restaurant serves excellent international and Swedish cuisine.
⊞ 437 A2–B2 ✉ Riddarholmen ☎ 08 120 90200; www.malardrottningen.se Ⓜ Gamla Stan 🚌 3, 53 AX, DC, MC, VI

Radisson Blu Strand Hotel $$–$$$

This comfortable hotel with modern facilities is in a fine old building on the southwest side of Nybroviken inlet. Enjoy views across the water from the top-floor restaurant.
⊞ 437 B3 ✉ Nybrokajen 9

☎ 08 5066 4000; 020 238 238 in Sweden (toll free); 00 800 3333 3333 in Europe (toll free); 1 800 333 333 in US (toll free); www.radissonblu.com 🚇 Kungsträdgården or Östermalmstorg 🚌 47, 69; tram 7 AX, DC, MC, VI

Den Gyldene Freden $$$

Established in 1722, this famous Old Town restaurant attracts the rich and famous, including Nobel Prize selection committee members. Even the restroom has 18th-century poetry on the wall. The cuisine is excellent. Reservations are definitely required.
✚ 437 B2 ✉ Österlånggatan 51 ☎ 08 24 97 60; www.gyldenefre den.se 🕐 Closed Sun. 🚇 Gamla Stan, Slussen 🚌 2, 3, 53, 55 AX, DC, MC, VI

Hermans $

This vegetarian restaurant has a glassed-in terrace and open garden overlooking Stockholm Harbor and Djurgården island. Its buffet includes dishes from Asia, Mexico, India, the Mediterranean and the Middle East.
✚ 437 C1 ✉ Fjällgatan 23B ☎ 08 643 94 80 🚇 Gamla Stan MC, VI

Hjerta $$

On the waterfront, Hjerta serves flavorful Scandinavian dishes such as black pudding with potato pancakes or cod with beetroot and capers.
✚ 437 B3 ✉ Slupskjulsvägen 28, Skeppsholmen ☎ 08 520 236 70; restauranghjerta.se
🚇 Kungsträdgården 🚌 65 🚢 Slussen AX, DC, MC, VI

Oaxen Slip $$$

Combine a trip to Abba The Museum with lunch or dinner at this bustling Nordic bistro right on the waterfront. It shares premises with its more sophisticated (and pricier) sister, Oaxen Krog.
✚ 437 C2 ✉ Beckholmsvägen 26 ☎ 08 55 15 31 05; www.oaxen.com 🚌 44; tram 7 AX, DC, MC, VI

Pontus $$–$$$

Trendy Pontus has superb fish and meat dishes and great service makes it worth the money. The more

informal "Pocket Pontus" section offers great tastes at lower prices.
✚ 437 B3 ✉ Norrlandsgatan 31 ☎ 08 510 254 00; www. pontusfrithiof.com 🕐 Closed Sun., Dec. 25 and public holidays 🚇 Östermalmstorg, Hötorget 🚌 All city-center buses AX, DC, MC, VI

Beau Rivage $$$

Founded in 1865 on the shore of Lac Léman (Lake Geneva), the Beau Rivage is one of the most famous and luxurious hotels in the world. Its refined elegance and perfect service embody the dream and the qualities of "Old Europe."
✚ 451 B3 ✉ quai du Mont-Blanc 13 ☎ 022 716 6825; www.beau-rivage.ch 🚌 6, 8, 9 AX, DC, MC, VI

Central $

This is a family-run hotel in the heart of the city. Some of the bedrooms can accommodate up to five people.
✚ 451 B2 ✉ rue de la Rôtisserie 2 ☎ 022 818 8100; www.hotelcentral. ch 🚌 10; tram 16 AX, DC, MC, VI

Edelweiss $$

A popular choice with tourists, this chalet-style hotel near the lakeside has 42 attractive rooms and stages folklore evenings in its restaurant.
✚ 451 B3 ✉ place de la Navigation 2 ☎ 022 544 5151; www.hoteledelweissgeneva.com 🚌 1 AX, DC, MC, VI

Eden $$$

In a quiet area across from Mon Repos park and the lake, this hotel has a good restaurant and a friendly, relaxed atmosphere.
✚ 451 off map at C3 ✉ rue de Lausanne 135 ☎ 022 716 3700; www.eden.ch 🚌 1, 11, 28 AX, DC, MC, VI

Hotel Kipling $–$$

The Hotel Kipling is an excellent value hotel with friendly staff and plenty of frills for the price. Rooms are a good size, with well-equipped bathrooms. There's free WiFi, two restaurants and a plentiful morning breakfast buffet.

✚ 451 B3 ✉ rue de la Navigation 27 ☎ 022 544 4040; www.hotelkipling geneva.com 🚌 1 AX, DC, MC, VI

Warwick Geneva $–$$

This sleek hotel is ideally situated opposite the station, and guests receive a complimentary travel card to use during their stay.
✚ 451 A3 ✉ rue de Lausanne 14 ☎ 022 716 8000; www.warwick hotels.com/geneva 🚌 5, 8, 11, 28 AX, DC, MC, VI

Auberge de Savièse $

Enjoy a selection of Swiss specialties at this friendly restaurant, which features different types of fondue.
✚ 451 B3 ✉ rue des Pâquis 20 ☎ 022 732 8330; www.aubergede saviese.ch 🚌 1 AX, DC, MC, VI

Brasserie Lipp $$$

This popular French restaurant in the Confédération Centre shopping mall is named after a Parisian brasserie.
✚ 451 B2 ✉ rue de la Confédération 8 ☎ 022 318 8030; www.brasserie-lipp.com 🚌 2, 5, 7, 10, 36; tram 12 AX, DC, MC, VI

Café du Bourg-du-Four $$

Part café, part wine bar, part bistro, this is a charming and cozy place for a pause if you're sightseeing in the old city center.
✚ 451 B1 ✉ place du Bourg du Four 13 ☎ 022 311 9076; www. cafedubourgdufour.ch 🚌 2, 7, 9, 12; tram 12 AX, MC

Le Patara $$$

This is the best Thai restaurant in Geneva. Expect impeccable service in tasteful surroundings.
✚ 451 B3 ✉ Hôtel Beau Rivage, quai du Mont-Blanc 13 ☎ 022 731 5566; www.patara-geneve.ch 🚌 6, 8, 9 AX, DC, MC, VI

Saveurs du Liban $–$$

Head here to sample the fresh flavors of genuine Lebanese food. The menu offers traditional favorites including *fattoush*, lamb and beef *kofteh* (meatballs), and sweet *baklava*, dripping with golden honey and oozing pistachios.

KEY TO SYMBOLS

➕ map page number and coordinates
✉ address
☎ telephone number
🕐 days/times closed
Ⓜ nearest subway station
🚌 nearest bus/trolley bus/tram/funicular route
⛴ ferry
$$$ expensive
$$ moderate
$ inexpensive
AX American Express
DC Diners Club
MC MasterCard
VI VISA

➕ 451 B3 ✉ place de la Navigation 8 ☎ 022 731 0928; www.lessaveurs duliban.ch 🕐 1 No credit cards

Le VG – Restaurant des Vieux-Grenadiers $$

A typical Genevan restaurant, this specializes in regional dishes and fondues. It has a pretty summer terrace and occasional live jazz.
➕ 451 off map at B1 ✉ rue de Carouge 92 ☎ 022 320 1327; www.vgrestaurant.ch 🕐 Closed Sun. 🚌 35; tram 12 AX, MC, VI

ZURICH HOTELS

Price guide: (double room with breakfast for two people)
$ SF150–SF250
$$ SF250–SF400
$$$ over SF400

Altstadt $$

In the heart of old Zurich, this comfortable hotel has 25 sleek rooms. The bar serves breakfast, lunch or a late nightcap.
➕ 456 B2 ✉ Kirchgasse 4 ☎ 044 250 5353; www.hotel-altstadt. ch 🚌 Tram 4, 15 AX, DC, MC, VI

Bristol $$

This is a comfortable hotel near the railroad station, with modern and functional rooms.
➕ 456 B4 ✉ Stampfenbachstrasse 34 ☎ 044 258 4444; www.hotel bristol.ch 🚌 Tram 6, 7, 10, 15 AX, DC, MC, VI

Eden au Lac $$$

Stay at this elegant lakeside hotel, built in 1909, for the ultimate in comfort, luxury and service.
➕ 456 B1 ✉ Utoquai 45 ☎ 044 266 2525; www.edenaulac.ch 🚌 912, 916; tram 2, 4 AX, DC, MC, VI

Rössli $$

The Rössli is a comfortable and imaginatively designed hotel with well-equipped rooms.
➕ 456 B2 ✉ Rössligasse 7 ☎ 044 256 7050; www.hotelroessli. ch 🚌 Tram 4, 15 AX, DC, MC, VI

Storchen $–$$

The "Stork" has been welcoming travelers for over 600 years. Today, you can enjoy high comfort levels in this beautiful waterside setting. The big rooms have every modern convenience, some overlook the river, and breakfast and WiFi are included in the room rate.

➕ 456 A2 ✉ Storchengasse 16 ☎ 044 227 2727; www.storchen.ch 🚌 Tram 12, 15 AX, DC, MC, VI

ZURICH RESTAURANTS

Price guide: (dinner per person, excluding drinks)
$ SF25–SF45
$$ SF45–SF60
$$$ over SF60

Haus Hiltl $$

Reputed to be the world's oldest vegetarian restaurant, and still the the top choice in Zurich, Haus Hiltl has two main branches in the city and a take-out section.
➕ 456 A2 ✉ Haus Hiltl, Sihlstrasse 28 ☎ 044 227 7000; www.hiltl.ch 🚌 Tram 4, 15 AX, DC, MC, VI

Haus zum Rüden $$$

Overlooking the Limmat river, this historic restaurant serves the best of Swiss specialties.
➕ 456 B2 ✉ Limmatquai 42 ☎ 044 261 9566; www.hauszum rueden.ch 🕐 Closed Sat.–Sun. 🚌 Tram 4, 15 AX, DC, MC, VI

Kindli $$–$$$

Hospitality has been offered here since 1474 and today's restaurant, with its starched white table linen and paneled walls, won't disappoint.
➕ 456 A2 ✉ Pfalzgasse 1 ☎ 043 888 7378; www.kindli.ch 🕐 Closed Sun. 🚌 Tram 4, 15 AX, DC, MC, VI

Kronenhalle $$$

This long-established restaurant offers traditional dishes beneath artworks by Picasso and Matisse.
➕ 456 B2 ✉ Rämistrasse 4 ☎ 044 262 9900; www.kronenhalle.ch 🚌 912, 916; tram 2, 4, 5, 8, 9, 11, 15 AX, DC, MC, VI

Mère Catherine $$

This central garden restaurant serves good fish and seafood dishes, with an accent on Mediterranean and Provençal dishes.
➕ 456 B2 ✉ Nägelihof 3 ☎ 044 250 5940; www.commercio.ch 🚌 Tram 4, 15 AX, DC, MC, VI

Zum Kropf $$

This cheerful restaurant has been serving generous portions of local dishes since 1888.
➕ 456 A2 ✉ In Gassen 16 ☎ 044 221 1805; www.zumkropf.ch 🕐 Closed Sun. 🚌 Tram 2, 6, 7, 8, 11, 13 AX, MC, VI

Essential Information

U.S. CITIZENS

The information in this guide has been compiled for U.S. citizens traveling as tourists.

AAA recommends travelers consult online U.S. State Department travel advisories when planning travel abroad. Find this information at http://travel.state.gov/content/passports/english/alertswarnings.html.

Travelers who are not U.S. citizens, or who are traveling on business, should check with their embassies and tourist offices for information on the countries they wish to visit.

Entry requirements are subject to change at short notice, and travelers are advised to check the current situation before they travel.

National Flag

Essential for Travelers*

● Required ● Recommended ● Not required

Passport	●
Visa (check regulations before you travel)	●
Travel, medical insurance	●
Round-trip or onward airline ticket	●
Local currency	●
Traveler's checks	●
Credit cards	●
First-aid kit and medicines	●
Inoculations*	●

*see also *Health* section

Essential for Drivers*

Driver's license	●
International Driving Permit	●
Car insurance (for nonrental cars)	●
Car registration (for nonrental cars)	●

*see also *Driving* section

Important Addresses

Austrian National Tourist Office
P.O. Box 1142
New York, NY 10108-1142
☎ (212) 944-6880
Fax (212) 730-4568
www.austria.info

**Österreich Werbung
(Austrian National Tourist Office)**
Vordere Zollamtstrasse 13
A-1030 Vienna, Austria
☎ 0800 400 20000
Fax 0810 101819
www.austria.info/at

American Citizen Services
Parkring 12A
A-1010 Vienna, Austria
☎ 01 31 339-7535
Fax 01 512 5835
http://austria.usembassy.gov
Mon.–Fri. 8–5
(outside these hours ☎ 01 313 390)

Customs

✔ **Duty-free limits on goods brought in from non-European Union countries:**
200 cigarettes or 100 cigarillos or 50 cigars or 250 g. tobacco; 1 L. alcohol over 22% volume; or 2 L. alcohol under 22% volume and 4 L. non-sparkling wine, and 16 L. beer; plus any other duty-free goods (including gifts) to the value of €430 for travelers arriving by air, and €300 for all other travelers. This information applies to visitors age 17 and over. Currency worth €10,000 or more must be declared. There is no limit on the importation of tax-paid goods purchased within the European Union, provided they are for your own personal use.

✘ No unlicensed drugs, weapons, ammunition, obscene material, pets or other animals, counterfeit money or copied goods, meat or poultry.
For customs limits for returning U.S. citizens see page 16.

Money

Austria's currency is the euro (€), a currency shared by 18 other European Union countries. The euro is divided into 100 cents (¢). The denominations of euro bills are 5, 10, 20, 50, 100, 200 and 500. There are coins of 1, 2, 5, 10, 20 and 50¢ and €1 and €2. ATMs are located in most towns and cities and can be used to withdraw local currency. Credit, debit and prepaid cards are widely accepted. It is a good idea to carry a mix of large and small euro denominations.

Tips and Gratuities

Tips *(Trinkgeld)* are welcomed and expected in restaurants and cafés.

Restaurants (even when service is included)	10%
Cafés/bars	10%
Taxis	10%
Porters	at your discretion
Chambermaids	at your discretion
Hairdressers (and change to shampooer)	5%

Communications

Post Offices

Buy stamps *(Briefmarken)* at a post office *(Postamt)*, or newsstand/tobacconist *(Tabak Trafik)* or from a hotel. Post offices can be recognized by a golden trumpet symbol and can often be found close to the main square or railroad station. Hours for out-of-town post offices may vary. Mailboxes are yellow or orange.

Telephones

Use cash or prepaid phone cards *(Callingcards)* to make a call. Telephones have direct dialing for national and international calls. Buy phone cards from gas stations, newsstands, post offices and hotels. Some booths take credit cards. Check overseas cell-phone usage with your provider.

Phoning inside Austria

All Austrian telephone numbers in this book include an area code: dial the number that is listed. To call the operator dial 11 88 77.

Phoning Austria from abroad

The country code for Austria is 43. Note that Austrian numbers in this book do not include the country code; you will need to prefix this number if you are phoning from another country. To phone Austria from the United States or Canada, omit the first zero from the Austrian number, and add the prefix 011 43. (Note that the number of digits in Austrian area codes varies.) Example: 01 12 23 34-4 becomes 011 43 1 12 23 34-4.

Phoning from Austria

To phone the United States or Canada from Austria, prefix the area code and number with 00 1. Example: (111) 222-3333 becomes 00 1 111 222-3333. To call national and international information dial 11 88 77.

Emergency telephone numbers

Police *(Polizei)* **133**   Fire service *(Feuerwehr)* **122**
Ambulance *(Krankenwagen)* **144**
Mountain rescue service *(Bergrettung)* **140**
Emergency calls are free from phone booths.
General emergency number within the E.U. **112**

Hours of Operation

- Stores Mon.–Sat.
- Offices Mon.–Fri.
- Banks Mon.–Fri.
- Post Offices Mon.–Fri.
- Museums/Monuments
- Pharmacies

7 8 9 10 11 12 1 2 3 4 5 6 7

Saturday is early closing day; shops close between noon and 5 p.m. Thursday or Friday is late-night shopping (until 7 or 8).

Banks stay open until 5:30 p.m. on Thursday.

Post offices may also open 8–10 a.m. on Saturday. Main and station post offices in larger cities are open 24 hours, including weekends and public holidays.

Pharmacies usually follow store opening hours with a 2-hour lunch break. There is always one pharmacy open late in each city: details are displayed in pharmacy windows.

Facilities at tourist resorts may have special hours of operation.

National Holidays

Banks, businesses and most stores close on these days. Also, some museums may be closed or have restricted hours.

Jan. 1	New Year's Day
Jan. 6	Epiphany
Mar./Apr.	Easter Monday
May 1	Labor Day
May	Ascension Day
May/Jun.	Pentecost Monday
May/Jun.	Corpus Christi
Aug. 15	Assumption of the Virgin
Oct. 26	National Day
Nov. 1	All Saints' Day
Dec. 8	Immaculate Conception
Dec. 25	Christmas Day
Dec. 26	St. Stephen's Day

Photography

Magnificent and varied subject matter awaits the photographer in Austria. Away from the city, the Alpine peaks give enormous scope for landscape photography, and the light is generally very good. Camera batteries are readily available and there are many places offering download and CD services for digital cameras. Most museums will not allow you to take pictures; check first.

Austria

Health

Medical Insurance

The cost of medical treatment in Austria is high, and private medical insurance is recommended. Ärztekammer für Wien (Vienna Doctors' Chamber) can suggest a doctor *(Arzt)* or hospital *(Krankenhaus)*: Weihburggasse 10–12, Vienna, ☎ 01 51 501-0. Other Austrian towns and regions have their own such chambers. The south and east of the country are home to *Zecken* – a kind of tick that can transmit encephalitis. This disease is potentially lethal, therefore it is essential to seek medical advice if you are bitten. An inoculation is available.

Dental Services

A dentist *(Zahnarzt)* will charge for any treatment given. Dental work is expensive, so check that it is covered by your medical insurance. Dentists are listed in the telephone directory, or ask for English-speaking dentists at your embassy, a tourist office or hotel.

Sun Advice

Austria has strong sun during the summer months so sun protection is needed. Wear a hat, cover shoulders, drink plenty of fluids and use sunscreen.

Drugs

Pharmacies *(Apotheken)* can dispense prescriptions. Many assistants speak English, and a schedule displayed on the door enables you to find a late-opening or 24-hour pharmacy in every town.

Safe Water

Tap water is safe to drink throughout Austria. Mineral water *(Mineralwasser)* is widely available.

Restrooms

Public restrooms *(Toiletten/WC)* are generally easy to find and immaculately clean. A small charge is levied.

Electricity

Austria has a 230-volt power supply. Electrical sockets take plugs with two round pins. American appliances will need a plug adapter and will require a transformer if they do not have a dual-voltage facility.

National Transportation

Train *(Zug)*

The Austrian Federal Railways (Österreichische Bundesbahnen or ÖBB; www.oebb.at) runs a comfortable and efficient service, with connections to all European countries. If you like a slower pace try a steam-train journey through valleys along lakesides or a cable-car trip; local tourist offices can give details. For rail information ☎ 05 1717.

Bus *(Bus)*

Austria has a good network of local, federal and private bus companies. Bus travel is slower but less expensive than the train; for information contact ÖBB ☎ 05 1717.

Ferry *(Fähre)*

From Easter to the end of October you can enjoy steamer services on the Danube; some continue into neighboring countries. Steamers ply the larger Austrian lakes from May to September. Wien-Tourismus can supply details on steamer companies: ☎ 01 24-555.

Driving

Drive on the right

Speed Limits

Police impose on-the-spot fines (for which receipts are issued), although a foreign motorist may refuse and instead be asked to make a surety payment.

Limited-access highways *(Autobahnen)*
130 k.p.h. (80 m.p.h.)

Main roads
100 k.p.h. (62 m.p.h.)

Urban areas
50 k.p.h. (31 m.p.h.)

Seat Belts

Must be worn in front and back seats at all times. Children under 14 are not allowed to use a front seat, unless in a child safety seat.

Blood Alcohol

The legal blood alcohol limit is 0.049%. Random breath tests on drivers are carried out frequently, especially late at night, and the penalties for offenders are severe.

Driving (continued)

Tolls

To use toll highways, purchase a windshield sticker *(Vignette)* at automobile clubs in Austria or abroad, or at a border crossing, gas station, post office or tobacconist. There are charges for some other major roads. Nonpayment of tolls results in a fine.

Car Rental

The leading car-rental firms have offices at airports and train stations. Hertz offers discounted rates for AAA members (see page 15). For reservations:

	United States	Austria
Alamo	(877) 222-9075	01 866 1611 (Europcar)
Avis	(800) 331-1084	0800 0800 8757
Budget	(800) 472-3325	01 7007-32700
Hertz	(800) 654-3001	01 512 8677

Fuel

Many gas stations *(Tankstelle)* are self-service, and 24-hour facilities are common. Unleaded gas *(Bleifrei)* is available at 95 and 98 octane. Diesel is available.

AAA Affiliated Motoring Club

Österreichischer Automobil-, Motorrad-und Touring Club (ÖAMTC)
Schubertring 1-3, A-1010 Vienna
☎ 01 711 99 10200. If you break down while driving, call ☎ 120 (ÖAMTC breakdown service). Not all automobile clubs offer full services to AAA members.

Breakdowns and Accidents

There are 24-hour emergency phones at regular intervals on highways. All accidents involving personal injury must be reported to the police (☎ 133). Most car-rental firms provide their own free rescue service; if your car is rented, follow the instructions given in the documentation. Use of a car-repair service other than those authorized by your rental company may violate your rental agreement. You must carry a first-aid kit, warning triangle and a fluorescent vest in case of a breakdown or accident.

Other Information

The minimum age for driving a car is 18 (may be higher for some car-rental firms). An International Driving Permit (IDP) is recommended; some car-rental firms require it, and it can speed up formalities if you are in an accident. A Green Card (international motor insurance certificate) is recommended if driving a private car (see page 15). Only hands-free phone use is permitted while driving. In winter, snow tires or chains are essential, and are legal Nov. 1–Apr. 15. Rent chains at automobile clubs and border crossings.

Useful Words and Phrases

The official language in Austria is German, although Austrians are very proud of their brand of the language *(Österreichisch)*, and are offended if it is treated as a mere dialect of "standard" German *(Hochdeutsch)*. On paper, the differences between the two varieties are not obvious, but the Austrian accent is distinctive, and especially strong in rural regions.

There are numerous words that are peculiar to Austria and the south of Germany. The Austrian diminutive is *-el* or *-lein* compared with the German *-chen*, so *Mädchen* (girl) in German becomes *Mädel* in Austrian. A small number of Austrian words, such as *Fauteil* (armchair) and *Plafond* (ceiling), are in fact of French origin. See page 525 for a pronunciation and basic vocabulary guide to the German language; the following list is an eclectic sample of words peculiar to Austrian German.

Everyday life

friend, guy	*Haberer*
funny	*hetzig*
goodbye	*pfiat di*
guitar	*Klampfe*
hello	*Grüss Gott*
legs	*Laxen*
policeman	*Gendarm*
slippers	*Schlapfen*
work	*Hockn*

Food and drink

blood sausage	*Blunzn*
carrot	*Karotte*
corn	*Kukuruz*
croissant	*Kipferl*
doughnut	*Krapfen*
green beans	*Fisole*
green salad	*Häuplsalat*
lemonade	*Kracherl*
milky coffee	*Melange*
mushroom	*Schwammerl*
potato	*Erdäpfel*

Common words and phrases

breakfast	*Frühstück*
closed	*geschlossen*
excuse me	*Entschuldigen*
how much?	*Wieviel kostet es?*
I don't understand	*Ich verstehe nicht*
I'd like	*Ich möchte*
key	*Schlüssel*
no smoking	*nicht rauchen*
open	*geöffnet*
please	*bitte*
room	*Zimmer*
shower	*Dusche*
thank you	*danke*
where is...?	*Wo ist...?*

Belgium

National Flag

Essential for Travelers

● **Required** ● **Recommended** ● **Not required**

Passport	●
Visa (check regulations before you travel)	●
Travel, medical insurance	●
Round-trip or onward airline ticket	●
Local currency	●
Traveler's checks	●
Credit cards	●
First-aid kit and medicines	●
Inoculations	●

Essential for Drivers*

Driver's license	●
International Driving Permit	●
Car insurance (for nonrental cars)	●
Car registration (for nonrental cars)	●

*see also *Driving* section

Important Addresses

Belgian Tourist Office
300 East 42nd Street, 14th floor (entrance on 2nd Avenue), New York, NY 10017
☎ (212) 758-8130 Fax (212) 355-7675
www.visitbelgium.com

Belgian Tourist Office/Information Office
Flanders Belgium (Flemish-speaking areas)
620 Eighth Avenue, 44th Floor, New York, NY 10018
☎ 212 584 2336; www.visitflanders.us
Wallonie Bruxelles (French-speaking areas)
300 East 42nd Street, 14th floor, NY 10017
☎ (212) 758 8130; www.opt.be

American Embassy
Boulevard du Régent 27/Regentlaan 27, 1000 Brussels, Belgium
☎ 02 811 4000 Fax 02 811 4500
http://belgium.usembassy.gov. Open Mon.–Fri. 9–6

American Embassy Consular Service
☎ 02 811 4300. Open Mon., Tue, Thu. 2–4 p.m., Wed. 8–noon, Fri. 11 a.m.–1 pm. After hours, call the main embassy number.

Customs

✔ **Duty-free limits on goods brought in from non-European Union countries:**
200 cigarettes or 100 cigarillos or 50 cigars or 250 g. tobacco; 1 L. alcohol over 22% volume or 2 L. alcohol under 22% volume; 4 L. wine, 16 L. beer; plus any other duty-free goods (including gifts) to the value of €430 for visitors entering the E.U. (and Belgium) by air or by sea or €300 if arriving by other means. There is no limit on the importation of tax-paid goods, for personal use, purchased within the E.U. Visitors must declare cash over the value of €10,000 (or equivalent).

✘ No unlicensed drugs, weapons, ammunition, obscene material, pets or other animals, counterfeit money or copied goods, meat or poultry.
For customs limits for returning U.S. citizens see page 16.

Money

Belgium's currency is the euro (€), a currency shared by 18 other European Union countries. The euro is divided into 100 cents (¢). The denominations of euro bills are 5, 10, 20, 50, 100, 200 and 500. There are coins of 1, 2, 5, 10, 20 and 50¢ and €1 and €2. ATMs are located in most towns and cities and can be used to withdraw local currency. Credit, debit and prepaid cards are widely accepted. It is a good idea to carry a mix of large and small euro denominations.

Tips and Gratutities

Tips are not obligatory; a service charge is usually included for restaurants, cafés and taxis.

Restaurants (where service is not included)	10%
Cafés/bars	change
Taxis	change
Porters	€1 per item
Chambermaids	€1 per day
Cloakroom attendants	€1–€2

Brussels	New York	Chicago	Denver	Los Angeles	Time zones
12:00 noon	− 6 hrs	− 7 hrs	− 8 hrs	− 9 hrs	

499

Belgium

Communications

Post Offices

Buy stamps *(timbres/postzegels)* at a post office *(bureau de poste/postkantoor)*, a tobacconist or newsstand *(tabac/tabaksverkoper)*, or from a vending machine. Allow a week for mail to reach the United States. Mailboxes are painted red. Hours for out-of-town post offices may vary.

Telephones

There are some coin-operated public phones but phone card booths are more common. Phone cards *(télécartes/telefoonkaart)* are available from Belgacom Teleboutiques, post offices, railroad stations, bookstores and some newsstands, from €5. Phones accepting credit cards are available at some tourist sites. Instructions in English may be displayed in booths. Check overseas cell-phone usage with your provider.

Phoning in Belgium
All Belgian phone numbers in this book include an area code: dial the entire number. To call the operator dial 1307 for domestic numbers and 1304 for international numbers.

Phoning Belgium from abroad
The country code for Belgium is 32. Belgian numbers in this book do not include the country code; you will need to prefix this number if you are phoning from another country. To phone Belgium from the United States or Canada, dial 011 32 then omit the first zero from the Belgian number. (Note that Belgian area codes have two or three digits.) Example: 01 122 3344 becomes 011 32 1 122 3344.

Phoning from Belgium
To phone the United States or Canada from Belgium, prefix the area code and number with 00 1. Example: (111) 222-3333 becomes 00 1 111 222-3333. To call international directory assistance, dial 13 04; for local directory assistance in English, dial 13 07.

Emergency telephone numbers
Police *(Police)* 101
Fire service *(Pompiers)* 100
Ambulance *(Ambulance)* 100
Red Cross ambulance 105
General emergency number within the E.U. 112

Hours of Operation

- ■ Stores Mon.–Sat.
- ■ Offices Mon.–Fri.
- ■ Banks Mon.–Fri.
- ■ Post Offices Mon.–Fri.
- ■ Museums/Monuments
- ■ Pharmacies Mon.–Sat.

While Sunday is the official closing day, souvenir shops in many towns stay open, usually 10–4.

Many **bakeries and patisseries** open at 7:30 or 8 a.m. and also open on Sunday morning.

Department and other major stores often stay open until 7 p.m. on weekdays and 8 or 9 p.m. on Friday.

Smaller stores may close for lunch.

Some **city post offices** and **banks** open on Saturday morning. Post offices and banks outside cities and large towns may close for 2 hours at lunch.

It is common for **museums** to close on Monday (except for some small museums) and open later one evening a week. Some close for 2 hours at lunchtime.

National Holidays

Banks, businesses and most stores close on these days. Each region has its own feast day. Most cities, towns and villages celebrate their patron saint's day, but most places stay open.

Jan. 1	New Year's Day
Mar./Apr.	Easter Monday
May 1	Labor Day
May	Ascension Day
May/Jun.	Pentecost Monday
Jul. 21	National Day
Aug. 15	Assumption of the Virgin
Nov. 1	All Saints' Day
Nov. 11	Armistice Day
Dec. 25	Christmas Day

Photography

Camera batteries are readily available and there are many places offering digital equipment, download services for digital cameras and rapid developing services. Most museums will not allow you to take pictures; check first.

Health

Medical Insurance

Private medical insurance is recommended. Visitors from non-European Union countries can receive treatment in a hospital emergency room but are charged if admitted to a hospital *(hôpital/ziekenhuis)*. Doctors *(médecin/dokter)* may also charge for a consultation.

Dental Services

Dental treatment is not available free of charge; all dentists practice privately. A list of dentists *(dentiste/tandarts)* can be found in the *Yellow Pages (Pages Jaunes/Gouden Gids)*. Check that dental treatment is covered by your private medical insurance.

Sun Advice

The warmest months are July and August, with average daytime temperatures of 60°F. Belgian weather can be unpredictable and although the sun is not often very fierce, protection is still required.

Drugs

Prescription and nonprescription medicines are available from a pharmacy *(pharmacie/apotheek)*. If you need a medicine outside regular hours, the addresses of 24-hour facilities are posted on the door of all pharmacies.

Safe Water

Tap water is safe to drink and mineral water *(eau minérale/mineraalwater)* is widely available. The origin of the English word "spa" is in fact the Belgian town of Spa, especially popular during the 19th century for its mineral springs.

Restrooms

Public restrooms *(toilettes/toiletten)* are not always easy to find but are usually clean. If you need to use the facilities at a restaurant or café purchase a drink first. Restrooms in the larger restaurants and cafés sometimes have attendants; you should tip them €1–€2, which goes toward their wages.

Electricity

Belgium has a 220-volt power supply. Electrical sockets take plugs with two round pins. American appliances will need a plug adapter and will require a transformer if they do not have a dual-voltage facility.

National Transportation

Train *(Train/Trein)*

The national rail network is the SNCB/NMBS (Société Nationale des Chemins de Fer Belges in French, and Nationale Maatschappij der Belgische Spoorwegen in Flemish). Check online at www.belgianrail.be or by phone ☎ 02 528 28 28 for information or for reservations. The Eurostar trains from London arrive in the Gare du Midi (☎ 079 79 79 79; www.eurostar.com). Brussels has good connections with the Thalys network that operates high-speed trains to Paris, Amsterdam, Cologne and Geneva (☎ 079 79 79 79; www.raileurope.com or www.thalys.com).

Bus *(Bus/Bus)*

Local bus service timetables are available from local tourist offices. Open the door yourself on buses and trams or press the black strip or button. Low-cost international buses to most European capitals are operated by Eurolines (☎ 02 274 13 50; www.eurolines.com).

Driving

Drive on the right

Speed Limits

Police impose on-the-spot fines (receipts are issued), although a foreign motorist may refuse and instead be asked to make a surety payment.

Limited-access highways *(autoroutes/autoweg)* 120 k.p.h. (74 m.p.h.) Minimum speed on straight, level stretches 70 k.p.h. (43 m.p.h.)

Main roads 90 k.p.h. (56 m.p.h.)

Urban areas 50 k.p.h. (31 m.p.h.); 30 k.p.h. (18 m.p.h.) on roads in central area of Brussels (the Pentagon), cycle streets and school zones; 20 k.p.h. (12 m.p.h.) on residential streets.

Seat Belts

Must be worn in front and back seats at all times; children under 18 years and shorter than 135cm (4ft 5in) must have a seat belt/restraint/child seat suitable for their height and weight. If a child seat is unavailable for children that height, they must travel in the rear, restrained by the factory-fitted seat belt.

Blood Alcohol

The legal blood alcohol limit is 0.05%. Random breath tests on drivers are carried out often. Penalties for offenders are severe.

Belgium

Driving (continued)

Tolls

There are no tolls on Belgian highways, but there is a toll on the Liefkenshoek Tunnel to the north of Antwerp.

Car Rental

The leading car-rental firms have offices at airports, train stations and ferry terminals. Hertz offers discounted rates for AAA members (see page 15). For reservations:

	United States	Belgium
Alamo	(888) 233-8749	30 692 1399
Avis	(800) 331-1084	070 223 001
Budget	(800) 472-3325	02 720 0944
Hertz	(800) 654-3001	02 717 3201

Fuel

Gasoline *(essence/benzine)* and diesel are priced in liters and are expensive. There are two grades of unleaded gas *(sans plomb/loodvrij)*: normal (95 octane) and super (98 octane). Most gas stations are self-service, and 24-hour facilities are common.

AAA Affiliated Motoring Club

Touring Club Belgium (TCB) 44 rue de la Loi, 1040 Brussels ☎ 02 233 2202; www.touring.be. If you break down while driving, phone TCB breakdown service ☎ 070 344 777 or, on a limited-access highway, use one of the emergency telephones located every 1.2 miles. Ask for *"Touring-Secours."* Not all automobile clubs offer full services to AAA members.

Breakdowns and Accidents

Most car-rental firms have their own free rescue service; if your car is rented, follow the instructions given in the documentation. Use of a car-repair service other than those authorized by your rental company may violate your rental agreement. If you are involved in an accident phone for police assistance ☎ 101. You must carry a warning triangle and a fluorescent vest in your car.

Other Information

The minimum age for driving a car is 18 (may be 21 for some car-rental firms). An International Driving Permit (IDP) is recommended; some car-rental firms require it, and it can speed up formalities if you are involved in an accident. A Green Card (international motor insurance certificate) is recommended if you are driving a private car; see page 15 for more information. Drivers must yield the right of way to vehicles approaching from the right (except on major roads) and to vehicles on rails, public transport buses, and cycles on designated cycle streets. Beware of cobbled roads, which can be slippery in wet weather.

Useful Words and Phrases

A linguistic battle has existed in Belgium for many centuries; settlers have long entered from neighboring countries, and as a result there are three distinct language communities: French, Dutch and German.

The two dominant languages are Walloon (a form of French, spoken in the south) and Flemish (related to Dutch, spoken in the north). Passions run deep between the two groups; prosperity has moved back and forth between them over the centuries, and their relationship is still difficult to this day. The Flemish fear their language is being diminished, aware of the strength that French has as a world language. In addition, German is spoken in the east.

Both Walloon and Flemish hold equal status as official languages, and although the bilingual signs can be confusing to the visitor, English is widely spoken.

In Brussels, where Flemish and French are both spoken, the street signs also are in both languages. Place-names are not usually a problem, since the Flemish and French proper names have similarities, but there can be differences.

Following is a selection of locations:

English	Flemish	French
Aalst	Aalst	Alost
Antwerp	Antwerpen	Anvers
Bruges	Brugge	Bruges
Brussels	Brussel	Bruxelles
Ghent	Gent	Gand
Jodoigne	Geldenaken	Jodoigne
Kortrijk	Kortrijk	Courtrai
Liège	Luik	Liège
Louvain	Leuven	Louvain
Mechelen	Mechelen	Malines
Mons	Bergen	Mons
Mouscron	Moeskroen	Mouscron
Nivelles	Nijvel	Nivelles
Ostend	Oostende	Ostende
Roeselare	Roeselare	Roulers
Ronse	Ronse	Renaix
Scheldt	Schelde	Escaut
Tongeren	Tongeren	Tongres
Tournai	Doornik	Tournai
Veurne	Veurne	Furnes
Ypres	Ieper	Ypres

For useful phrases in French, see page 521; for phrases in German, see page 525; for phrases in Dutch, see page 549.

Britain

National Flag

Essential for Travelers

● Required ● Recommended ● Not required

Passport	●
Visa (check regulations before you travel)	●
Travel, medical insurance	●
Round-trip or onward airline ticket	●
Local currency	●
Traveler's checks	●
Credit or debit cards	●
First-aid kit and medicines	●
Inoculations	●

Essential for Drivers*

Driver's license	●
International Driving Permit	●
Car insurance (for nonrental cars)	●
Car registration (for nonrental cars)	●

*see also *Driving* section

Important Addresses

VisitBritain
www.visitbritain.com

City of London Information Centre
St. Paul's Churchyard
London EC4M 8BX, U.K.
☎ 020 7332 1456
Mon.–Sat. 9:30–5:30, Sun.10–4

American Embassy
24 Grosvenor Square
London W1A 2LQ, U.K.
☎ 020 7499 9000 (24hrs)
http://london.usembassy.gov
Mon.–Fri. 9:30–5:30

U.S. Consulate General
3 Regent Terrace
Edinburgh EH7 5BW, U.K.
☎ 0131 556 8315
http://edinburgh.usconsulate.gov
Mon.–Fri. 8:30–5

Customs

✔ **Duty-free limits on goods brought in from non-European Union countries:**
200 cigarettes or 100 cigarillos or 50 cigars or 250 g. tobacco; 4 L. wine; 16 L. beer; 1 L. alcohol over 22% volume or 2 L. alcohol under 22% volume; 60 ml. perfume; 250 ml. toilet water; plus any other duty-free goods (including gifts) to the value of £390. There is no limit on the importation of any currency or of tax-paid goods purchased within the European Union, provided the goods are for your own personal use.

✘ No unlicensed drugs, weapons, self-defense sprays, obscene material, counterfeit and copied goods, meat, poultry or dairy products.
For customs limits for returning U.S. citizens see page 16.

Money

Britain's currency is the pound sterling (£), which is divided into 100 pence (p). The denominations of pound bills are 1 (Scotland only), 5, 10, 20, 50 and 100 (Scotland only). There are coins of 1, 2, 5, 10, 20 and 50p and £1 and £2. You can exchange dollars or traveler's checks at banks, main post offices, exchange offices and some travel agencies. Credit, debit and prepaid cards are widely accepted throughout Britain, and ATMs are plentiful in towns and cities. When sightseeing, it is a good idea to carry a mix of large and small value coin denominations.

Tips and Gratuities

Restaurants (where service is not included)	10–15%
Cafés/bars	change
Taxis	10%
Porters	£2–£5
Hairdressers	10%
Tour guides	£2–£5
Chambermaids	£2–£5
Cloakroom attendants (where no charges)	30p–50p

London	New York	Chicago	Denver	Los Angeles	Time zones
12:00 noon	− 5 hrs	− 6 hrs	− 7 hrs	− 8 hrs	**503**

Britain

Communications

Post Offices

Buy stamps at post offices, gas stations, tobacconists and supermarkets. Out-of-town post offices often close from 1–2. Mailboxes

("pillar-boxes") are red, and are usually free-standing, though some may be set into walls. Pillar-boxes show who was monarch at the time of their installation (ER II, for instance, stands for Elizabeth Regina II).

Telephones

Public telephones can be hard to find, and the traditional red booths are rare in towns and cities. Use cash, or a credit or debit card. Most public telephones accept 10p, 20p, 50p, £1 and £2

coins, but only unused coins are returned. There is a minimum charge of 60p (includes 40p connection charge). If using a credit card there is a £1.20 minimum fee (includes £1 connection charge). Check overseas cell-phone usage with your provider.

Phoning in Britain
All British numbers in this book have an area code: dial the number listed. For the operator dial 100.

Phoning Britain from abroad
The country code for Britain is 44. British numbers in this book do not include the country code; you need to prefix it if you are phoning from another country. To phone Britain from the United States or Canada, omit the first zero from the British number, and add the prefix 011 44. Example: 011 2233 4455 becomes 011 44 11 2233 4455.

Phoning from Britain
To phone the United States or Canada from Britain, prefix the area code and number with 00 1. Example: (111) 222-3333 becomes 00 1 111 222-3333. To call the international operator dial 155.

Emergency telephone numbers
Police **999** or **112**
Fire service **999** or **112**
Ambulance **999** or **112**
Emergency calls are free from phone booths.

Hours of Operation

- Stores Mon.–Sat.
- Post Offices Mon.–Fri.
- Offices Mon.–Fri.
- Museums/Monuments
- Banks Mon.–Fri.
- Pharmacies

7 8 9 10 11 12 1 2 3 4 5 6 7

The times above are traditional hours of operation. Many malls and city-center **stores** open for longer hours (late-night hours one day a week, usually Wednesday or Thursday) and also open on Sunday (11–5). Convenience grocery stores stay open until late in the evening.

Main town **banks** and **post offices** open on Saturday mornings.

Museum opening times vary. Some major sights close on Monday and open later one evening a week; more modest sights of interest may close off season, so it is advisable to check with the local tourist office.

Note that many restaurants do not open for dinner until around 6 or 7 p.m. Before then, chain restaurants and fast-food outlets are usually the only places serving meals.

National Holidays

Banks, businesses and smaller stores close on these days, although larger stores may remain open.

Jan. 1	New Year's Day
Jan. 2	Bank Holiday (Scotland only)
Mar./Apr.	Good Friday
Mar./Apr.	Easter Monday (not in Scotland)
First Mon. of May	May Day
Last Mon. of May	Spring Bank Holiday
First Mon. of Aug.	Summer Bank Holiday (Scotland only)
Last Mon. of Aug.	Summer Bank Holiday
Dec. 25	Christmas Day
Dec. 26	Boxing Day

When December 25 and 26 fall on a weekend, the following Monday and Tuesday are public holidays. If January 1 falls on a weekend, usually the first Monday in January is a public holiday.

Photography

Memory cards and camera batteries are readily available and there are many places offering download and CD services for digital cameras.

Health

Medical Insurance

Private insurance is recommended. Visitors can receive treatment in emergency rooms but are charged if admitted to a hospital. You can seek advice from a doctor at a surgery or health center; you must make an appointment, and will be charged. Doctors are listed in the *Yellow Pages*, or ask at your hotel or a tourist office.

Dental Services

Dentists charge for consultations or treatment. Emergency treatment is available after hours in towns and cities (see the *Yellow Pages*). Check if it is covered by your medical insurance.

Sun Advice

Although not renowned for very warm weather, Britain does have its moments, and it is not unheard of for July and August to be as hot as the Mediterranean. Visiting historic sights can involve being outside for prolonged periods, so cover up, apply sunscreen and drink plenty of fluids.

Drugs

Prescription and nonprescription medicines are available from pharmacies (chemists). Pharmacists can advise on medication for common ailments. Notices in all pharmacy windows give details of emergency facilities open outside regular hours.

Safe Water

Tap water is safe to drink, even in remote areas. Mineral water is widely available in stores but can be quite expensive in restaurants.

Restrooms

Public restrooms (toilets, lavatories, WCs or, in everyday parlance, "loos") are generally easy to find and maintained to a high standard. Most are free, but there may be a charge for those at major rail stations (about 30p).

Electricity

Britain has a 240-volt power supply. Electrical sockets take plugs with three square pins, so an adapter is needed for American appliances. A transformer is also required for appliances operating on 110 or 120 volts.

National Transportation

Train

Rail services are good in Britain. First class is comfortable but considerably more expensive than standard. Intercity (high-speed) trains connect cities. A variety of discount railcards are available – check the National Rail Enquiries website in advance for eligibility and restrictions. Once you are in Britain, Rail Rover passes are good value for regional rail travel. There is online information at www.nationalrail.co.uk.

Bus

 It is cheaper to travel by bus than by rail. The main operator for long-distance bus/coach travel in Britain is National Express. There is online information at www.nationalexpress.com. Euroline's buses operate from Britain to the rest of Europe. There is online information at www.eurolines.com.

Ferry

 The busiest ferries run between southeast England and France (a high-speed train also shuttles passengers and cars through the Channel Tunnel). Service is frequent, especially in summer. Ferries also serve the smaller British islands, plus Ireland, Spain, Belgium, The Netherlands and Denmark.

Driving

Drive on the left

Speed Limits

British speed limits are stringently enforced by police patrols and also by strategically positioned cameras that detect speeding motorists.

Limited-access highways (motorways); divided highways (dual carriageways)
70 m.p.h.

Main roads
50 or 60 m.p.h.

Urban areas
20, 30 or 40 m.p.h.

Seat Belts

Must be worn in front and rear seats at all times.

Blood Alcohol

 The legal blood alcohol limit in England and Wales is 0.08%; in Scotland it is 0.05%. Random breath tests on drivers are carried out frequently. Penalties are severe.

Driving (continued)

Tolls

Limited-access highways are free except for the M6 Toll Road (junction 4 to 11a). Some bridges or tunnels levy a toll. In central London there is a weekday congestion charge (see page 16) ☎ 0343 222 1234 or visit www.tfl.gov.uk for payment information.

Car Rental

The leading car-rental firms have offices at airports, train stations and ferry terminals. Hertz offers discounted rates for AAA members (see page 15). For reservations:

	United States	Britain
Avis	(800) 331-1084	0808 284 0014
Budget	(800) 472-3325	0808 284 4444
Hertz	(800) 654-3001	877 826 8782

Fuel

Gasoline (petrol) and diesel are priced in liters and are expensive. There are two grades of unleaded gas: super (98 octane) and premium (95 octane). Most gas stations are self-service, and 24-hour facilities are common.

AAA Affiliated Motoring Club

The Automobile Association (AA) Ltd., Fanum House, Basing View Basingstoke, Hampshire RG21 4EA; www.theaa.com.

AAA members staying in the U.K. for up to 3 months get free AA Breakdown Service. If you break down while driving a privately owned car in the U.K. call ☎ 0800 887766 or 0121 275 3746 (AA Breakdown Service). If you're driving a rental car, contact the rental company's assistance partner. If you're staying for longer than 3 months, call the AA on 0800 085 2721 when you arrive in the U.K. to obtain AA Breakdown Service. You also can purchase the service online: www.theaa.com.

Breakdowns and Accidents

There are emergency telephones at intervals on limited-access and divided highways. If you have an accident ☎ 999 or 112 for police, fire and ambulance. Most car-rental firms provide their own rescue service; if your car is rented, follow the company's instructions. Use of an unauthorized car-repair service may violate your rental agreement.

Other Information

The minimum age for driving a car is 17. An International Driving Permit (IDP) is recommended. A Green Card (international motor insurance certificate) is recommended if you are driving a private car; see page 15 for more information.

Useful Words and Phrases

Spotting the differences between American and British English is fun, especially as some regional accents are almost incomprehensible to the untrained ear! Britons have become familiar with Americanisms through American television shows, but it is still possible to make a blunder. Below are some illustrations of the "Atlantic divide."

American	British
ATM	*cashpoint*
to call collect	*to reverse the charges*
check	*cheque*
check (in a restaurant)	*bill*
elevator	*lift*
first/second floor (etc.)	*ground/first floor (etc.)*
movie theater	*cinema*
phone booth	*phone box*
reserve (reservation)	*book (reservation)*
restroom	*toilet/loo (colloquial)*
Scotch™ tape	*sticky tape/Sellotape™*
trash or garbage can	*dustbin or rubbish bin*
Food and drink	
arugula	*rocket salad leaf*
(soft hamburger) bun	*bap*
beer	*bitter (dark), lager (light)*
candy	*sweets*
(potato) chips	*crisps*
cookies	*biscuits*
corn	*sweetcorn*
cotton candy	*candyfloss*
eggplant	*aubergine*
french fries	*chips*
grocery store	*supermarket*
Jell-O™	*jelly*
jelly	*jam*
liquor store	*off-licence*
oatmeal	*porridge*
Saranwrap™	*cling film*
zucchini	*courgette*
Fashion	
bangs	*fringe*
pants	*trousers*
pantyhose	*tights*
suspenders	*braces*
undershirt	*vest*
vest	*waistcoat*
Getting around	
hood (of a car)	*bonnet*
one-way trip	*single*
parking lot	*car park*
paved shoulder	*lay-by*
rotary/traffic circle	*roundabout*
round trip	*return ticket*
sidewalk	*pavement*
stick shift	*manual*
subway	*tube/underground*
truck	*lorry*
trunk (of a car)	*boot*

National Flag

Essential for Travelers

● Required ● Recommended ● Not required

Passport	●
Visa* (check regulations before you travel)	●
Travel, medical insurance	●
Round-trip or onward airline ticket	●
Local currency	●
Traveler's checks	●
Credit cards	●
First-aid kit and medicines	●
Inoculations	●

*U.S. citizens can stay in the Czech Republic for up to 90 days without a visa. For stays of longer than 90 days, visas must be obtained from an embassy outside the Czech Republic.

Essential for Drivers*

Driver's license	●
International Driving Permit	●
Car insurance (for nonrental cars)	●
Car registration (for nonrental cars)	●

*see also *Driving* section

Important Addresses

Czech Tourist Authority CzechTourism
109 Madison Avenue
New York, NY 10028
☎ (212) 288-0830
www.czechtourism.com

CzechTourism
Information Center
Staroměstské náměstí 5, Prague 1
☎ 224 861 476
www.czechtourism.com

American Embassy
Tržiště 15
118 01 Praha 1, Czech Republic
☎ 257 022 000
Fax 257 022 809
http://czech.prague.usembassy.gov

Customs

✔ **Duty-free limits on goods brought in from non-European Union countries:**
200 cigarettes or 100 cigarillos or 50 cigars or 250 g. tobacco; 1 L. alcohol more than 22% volume or 2 L. less than 22% volume; 2 L. nonsparkling wine; 50 ml. perfume or 250 ml. toilet water; plus any other duty-free goods (including gifts) to the value of 4730Kč Persons importing alcohol must be 18 and over, for cigarettes and tobacco products 16 and over. There is no restriction on the import or export of Czech or foreign currencies, but amounts in excess of 405,300Kč must be declared.

✗ No unlicensed drugs, firearms, ammunition, offensive weapons, obscene material, unlicensed animals, counterfeit or copied goods, meat and poultry.
For customs limits for returning U.S. citizens see page 16.

Money

The Czech Republic's currency is the Koruna česká (Kč) – or Czech crown – which is divided into 100 haléřů (h) – or hellers – although these tiny coins no longer circulate. The denominations of Kč bills are 100, 200, 500, 1,000, 2,000 and 5,000. There are coins of 1, 2, 5, 10, 20 and 50Kč. Credit, debit and prepaid cards are widely accepted, and ATMs are plentiful in the Czech Republic for withdrawing local currency.

Tips and Gratuities

Tips are welcomed in restaurants and cafés, although service is normally included.

Restaurants (even when service is included)	5–10%
Cafés/bars	5–10%
Taxis	5–10%
Porters	40Kč
Hairdressers	10%
Tour guides	20Kč

Communications

Post Offices

Buy stamps *(známky)* at a post office *(pošta)*, a newsstand/kiosk *(trafika/tabák)* or from a hotel. The postal service is generally reliable and not expensive.

Mailboxes are orange. Hours for out-of-town post offices may vary.

Telephones

Pay phones either accept coins (less common, usually in more remote locations) or telephone cards *(telefonní karta* or *TRICK)* which cost 200 or 300Kč. Phone cards can be bought from newsstands, tobacconists, post offices, shops, hotels and travel agencies. Most card phone booths have English instructions. Check overseas cell-phone usage with your provider.

Phoning inside the Czech Republic
There are no area codes in the Czech Republic; all numbers are nine digits: dial the number that is listed. For national directory inquiries dial 1180.

Phoning the Czech Republic from abroad
The country code for the Czech Republic is 420. You will need to prefix this number to the numbers in this book if you are phoning from another country. To phone the Czech Republic from the United States or Canada dial the prefix 011 420. Example: 112 233 445 becomes 011 420 112 233 445.

Phoning from the Czech Republic
To phone the United States or Canada from the Czech Republic, prefix the number with 00 1. Example: (111) 222-3333 becomes 00 1 111 222-3333. To call international information dial 1181.

Emergency telephone numbers
All emergencies **112**
Police – national *(Policie Česká republiky)* **158**
City police *(Městská policie)* **156**
Fire service *(požár)* **150**
Ambulance *(ambulance)* **155**
Emergency calls are free from phone booths.

Hours of Operation

- Stores Mon.–Sat.
- Offices Mon.–Fri.
- Banks Mon.–Fri.
- Post Offices Mon.–Fri.
- Museums/Monuments
- Pharmacies Mon.–Sat.

7 8 9 10 11 12 1 2 3 4 5 6 7

Stores close early on Saturday; many close at noon or 1. Some stores close for an hour for lunch, normally between noon and 1.

Food stores in the large cities open at 7 a.m., and large stores and shopping centers stay open until 8 or 10 p.m. (4 p.m. on Saturday). In Prague, most stores open all day Saturday and Sunday.

Banks may close earlier on Friday, though some stay open until 6 p.m. some days, and some are open Saturday morning. Some **post offices** open on Saturday morning. Some tourist resorts may have special opening times.

Museums often close on Monday and days following public holidays, and opening times may be reduced during the winter.

National Holidays

Banks, businesses and most stores close on these days. Monuments, museums and galleries usually open on public holidays (except Jan. 1, Easter, and Dec. 25 and 26) but are closed the following day.

Jan. 1	New Year's Day and Day of Restoration of Independent Czech State
Mar./Apr.	Easter Monday
May 1	Labor Day
May 8	Liberation Day
Jul. 5	SS Cyril and Methodius' Day
Jul. 6	Jan Hus Day
Sep. 28	Czech Statehood Day
Oct. 28	Independence Day
Nov. 17	Day of Fight for Freedom and Democracy
Dec. 24	Christmas Eve
Dec. 25	Christmas Day
Dec. 26	St. Stephen's Day

Photography

Czechs are enthusiastic photographers and you will have no difficulty in finding spare equipment for your digital camera. Several shops in Prague will do on-the-spot digital printing. An excellent shop is Foto Škoda at Vodičkova 47.

Czech Republic

Czech Republic

Health

Medical Insurance

Private medical insurance is recommended. U.S. and Canadian visitors should go to a hospital *(nemocnice)* to seek treatment for an accident or emergency. You will be asked to show a passport. Bring cash or credit card, as payment will be levied on the spot. The following clinics in Prague have English-speaking doctors: Na Homolce Hospital, Roentgenova 2 ☎ 257 271 111; www.homolka.cz. Also Canadian Medical Care, Veleslavínská 1 ☎ 235 360 133; www.cmcpraha.cz.

Dental Services

A dentist *(zubař)* will charge for any treatment given. Check if it is covered by your medical insurance. For an English-speaking dentist, ask at your hotel or embassy, at a tourist office or the Elite Dental Clinic, Vodičkova 5 ☎ 222 510 888; www.elitedental.cz.

Sun Advice

June through August is the sunniest period, when adequate sun protection should be applied.

Drugs

A pharmacy *(lékárna)* is the only place you can buy over-the-counter medicines. Pharmacies also dispense many drugs normally available only by prescription in other Western countries. However, it is advisable to bring supplies of your own medicines with you. If you need a pharmacy after regular hours, information about the nearest all-night facility is posted at some pharmacies.

Safe Water

Tap water is safe to drink but may have an unpleasant taste. Bottled water is available everywhere.

Restrooms

Public restrooms *(WC)* are scarce and usually require a payment of 5–10Kč. Metro stations in Prague will have a reasonably clean restroom. The best bet is to use the facilities of a hotel or restaurant.

Electricity

The Czech Republic has a 230-volt power supply. Electrical sockets take plugs with two round pins. American appliances will need a plug adapter, and will require a transformer if they do not have a dual-voltage facility.

National Transportation

Train *(Vlak)*

Czech Railways (České dráhy, CD) is extensive and inexpensive, but often crowded. The fast trains stop at major cities; local trains stop everywhere but usually provide only second-class service. All long-distance trains have two classes; some have dining carriages and overnight services. Reserve seats on express trains. For information: ☎ 840 112 113 (24-hours); www.cd.cz.

Bus *(Autobus)*

Buses are inexpensive and popular with Czechs. Reserve for weekends, national holidays or early morning. Purchase tickets from the bus station kiosk or the driver. For information: ☎ 900 144 444 (daily 24-hours); www.florenc.cz. Large items of luggage will be stowed for a small charge. Euroline's buses connect to other countries: ☎ 731 222 111; www.elines.cz.

Ferry *(Prévos)*

From April to September boats cruise the Vltava river as far as Troja Château to the north of Prague and Slapy Dam to the south: ☎ 224 810 030; www.evd.cz.

Driving

Drive on the right

Speed Limits

Police can give on-the-spot fines. If this should happen to you, ask for a receipt.

 Limited-access highways *(dalnice)*
130 k.p.h. (80 m.p.h.).
Minimum speed **80 k.p.h. (49 m.p.h)**

 Main roads
90 k.p.h. (56 m.p.h.)

 Urban areas
50 k.p.h. (31 m.p.h.)

Seat Belts

 Must be worn in front and back seats at all times. Children under 4 feet 11 inches or 79 pounds must not travel in the front.

Blood Alcohol

 The legal blood alcohol limit is zero. Random breath tests on drivers are carried out frequently, especially late at night, and the penalties for offenders are severe.

Czech Republic

Driving (continued)

Tolls

A tax is levied for use of highways and express roads. A sticker *(vignette)* must be purchased and displayed; failure to do so will result in a fine. Stickers can be bought for one week, one month or one year at the Czech border, ÚAMK offices, gas stations or post offices.

Car Rental

The leading car-rental firms have offices at airports and train stations. Hertz offers discounted rates for AAA members (see page 15). For reservations:

	United States	Czech Republic
Avis	(800) 331-1084	235 362 420
Budget	(800) 472-3325	220 560 443
Enterprise	(800) 261-7331	220 113 454
Hertz	(800) 654-3001	225 345 021

Fuel

Gas, sold in liters, is unleaded *(natural)* sold as 95 and 98 octane, diesel *(nafta)* or LPG *(autoplyn* or *plyn)*. Some out-of-town stations *(benzinová pumpa)* close for lunch and after 6 p.m. There are 24-hour gas stations in cities and along highways.

AAA Affiliated Motoring Club

Ústřední automotoklub České republiky **(ÚAMK; CR)** Na Strži 9, CZ-140 02 Prague 4 ☎ 261 104 111; www.uamk.cz. If you break down while driving phone ☎ 1230 (24-hours; ÚAMK breakdown service). Not all automobile clubs offer full services to AAA members.

Breakdowns and Accidents

There are 24-hour emergency phones at regular intervals on highways or ☎ 158 for police assistance. Most car-rental firms provide their own free rescue service; if you have an accident, follow the rental documentation instructions supplied with the car. Use of an unauthorized repair company may violate your rental agreement. You must carry a first-aid kit and a warning triangle in the car.

Other Information

The minimum age for driving a car is 18 (may be higher for some car-rental firms). An International Driving Permit (IDP) is formally required, though police and car-rental companies will usually accept a U.S. state driver's license. A Green Card (international motor insurance certificate) is required for a private car; see page 15 for more information. You are required by law to use dimmed headlights at all times when driving.

Useful Words and Phrases

The official language of the Czech Republic is Czech *(česky)* – a highly complex Slavic tongue. Czech sounds and looks daunting, but apart from a few special letters, each letter and sound is pronounced as it is written – the key is to stress the first syllable of a word.

Any attempt to speak Czech will be heartily appreciated, although English is spoken by many involved in the tourist trade. Below are a few words that may be helpful.

Do you speak English?	*Mluvíte anglicky?*
What is your name?	*Jak se jmenujete?*
hello, goodbye (casual)	*ahoj*
good morning	*dobré ráno*
goodbye	*na shledanou*
good night	*dobrou noc*
How much?	*Kolik?*
excuse me	*promiňte*
I am American	*Jsem Američan(ka)*
I would like	*Chtěl(a) bych*
I don't understand	*Nerozumím*
no smoking	*kouření zakazano*
okay	*dobře*
open	*otevřeno*
closed	*zavřeno*
please	*prosím*
thank you	*děkuji*
ticket	*lístek*
(one-way/round trip)	*(jednosměrnou/ zpáteční)*
Where is...?	*Kde je...?*
yes/no	*ano/ne*
you're welcome	*prosím*
the hotel	***hotel***
breakfast	*snídaně*
key	*klíč*
reservation	*reservaci*
room	*pokoj*
single/double room	*jednolužkový dvoulužkový pokoj*
Where is the toilet?	*Kde je toalet?*
bathroom	*koupelna*
shower	*sprcha*
the restaurant	***restaurace***
beef	*hovězí*
beer	*pivo*
bread	*chleb*
the check	*účet*
chicken	*kuře*
coffee	*káva*
dessert	*moučnik*
dish of the day	*nabídka dne*
fish	*ryba*
lamb	*jehněčí*
meat	*maso*
pork	*vepřové maso*
seafood	*mořské ryby*
starter	*předkrm*
wine	*víno*

Denmark

National Flag

Essential for Travelers*

● Required   ● Recommended   ● Not required

Passport	●
Visa (check regulations before you travel)	●
Travel, medical insurance	●
Round-trip or onward airline ticket	●
Local currency	●
Traveler's checks	●
Credit cards	●
First-aid kit and medicines*	●
Inoculations	●

*see also *Health* section

Essential for Drivers*

Driver's license	●
International Driving Permit	●
Car insurance (for nonrental cars)	●
Car registration (for nonrental cars)	●

*see also *Driving* section

Important Addresses

VisitDenmark
655 Third Avenue
Ste. 1810
New York, 10017
☎ (212) 885-9700
Fax (212) 885-9726
www.visitdenmark.com

VisitDenmark
Islands Brygge 43, 3rd Floor
DK-2300 København S, Denmark
☎ 32 88 99 00
Fax 32 88 99 01
www.visitdenmark.com

American Embassy
Dag Hammarskjölds Allé 24
DK-2100 København Ø, Denmark
☎ 33 41 71 00
Fax 35 38 96 16
http://denmark.usembassy.gov

Customs

✔ **Duty-free limits on goods brought in from non-European Union countries:**
200 cigarettes or 100 cigarillos or 50 cigars or 250 g. tobacco; 4 L. wine or 1 L. alcohol over 22% volume or 2 L. alcohol under 22% volume; 16 L. beer; 50 ml. perfume; 250 ml. toilet water; plus any other duty-free goods (including gifts) to the value of DKr3,250 if you arrive by plane or ship, or DKr2,250 if you arrive by other transport. There is no limit on the importation of tax-paid goods purchased within the European Union, provided they are for your own personal use. Limits for alcohol and tobacco products apply to visitors aged 17 or over. There are no currency regulations.

✘ No unlicensed drugs, weapons, ammunition, fireworks, obscene material, pets or other animals, counterfeit money or copied goods, plants, meat or poultry.
For customs limits for returning U.S. citizens see page 16.

Money

Denmark's currency is the krone (DKr), which is divided into 100 øre. The denominations of krone bills are 50, 100, 200, 500 and 1,000. There are coins of 50 øre and 1, 2, 5, 10 and 20DKr. ATMs are plentiful and credit, debit and prepaid cards are accepted in hotels, large stores and upscale restaurants; check first in small or rural establishments. Senior citizens and holders of International Student Identity Cards (ISIC) can often obtain discounts on travel and entrance fees.

Tips and Gratuities

Tips are not expected, but may be given for outstanding service.

Restaurants (service is always included)	change
Cafés/bars	change
Taxis (tips included in fare)	change
Porters	change
Chambermaids	change
Cloakroom attendants	change

Denmark

Communications

Post Offices

Stamps *(frimerker)* can be bought at a post office *(postkontoret)*, newsstand *(aviskiosk)* or stationer *(papirhandel)*.

Mailboxes *(postkasse)* are red with a horn and crown detail. Hours for out-of-town post offices may vary. For postal service inquiries telephone Post Danmark ☎ 70 70 70 30; www.postdanmark.dk.

Telephones

Danish public telephones *(telefon)* work efficiently but do not refund money if the call is not answered. Some phones require coins to be inserted after dialing – DKr5, DKr10 and DKr20

coins. Some phones also accept euro coins (10, 20 and 50 cents and €1 and €2). Phone card booths also are available; buy the cards (DKr30, DKr50 or DKr100) from a post office, train station, newsstand or gas station. Check overseas cell-phone usage with your provider. You can buy a pre-paid SIM card for use in your own cell providing your cell is compatible and isn't locked. Check with your provider before you visit.

Phoning inside Denmark

All telephone numbers are 8 digits and include the regional code. Dial all digits when making a call. To call the operator dial 110; to call collect dial 115.

Phoning Denmark from abroad

The country code for Denmark is 45. Note that Danish numbers in this book do not include the country code. To phone Denmark from the United States or Canada add the prefix 011 45.
Example: 11 22 33 44 becomes 011 45 11 22 33 44.

Phoning from Denmark

To phone the United States or Canada from Denmark, prefix the area code and number with 00 1. Example: (111) 222-3333 becomes 00 1 111 222-3333. To call directory inquiries in Denmark dial 118. To call international information dial 113.

Emergency telephone numbers

Police *(politi)* **112**   Fire service *(brandvæsen)* **112**
Ambulance *(sygevogn)* **112**
Emergency calls are free from phone booths.

Hours of Operation

- Stores Mon.–Sat.
- Offices Mon.–Fri.
- Banks Mon.–Fri.
- Post Offices Mon.–Fri.
- Museums/Monuments
- Pharmacies Mon.–Fri.

7 8 9 10 11 12 1 2 3 4 5 6 7

Shop opening times in Denmark were legally extended in October 2012 and shops may now open on Sundays and stay open later on Fridays. The exceptions to this are public holidays when they must close at 3.

Department stores and **supermarkets** often stay open later than 5:30/6. Bakeries, florists and souvenir stores are often open seven days a week.

Large **gas stations** sell convenience foods seven days a week.

Banks in Copenhagen are open until 5. On Thursday all banks are open until 6.

Post offices open at 9 or 10 and close at 5 or 6; some post offices open Saturday 9 or 10–noon or 2.

National Holidays

Banks, businesses and most stores close on these days.

Jan. 1	New Year's Day
Mar./Apr.	Maundy Thursday
Mar./Apr.	Good Friday
Mar./Apr.	Easter Monday
Apr. /May	Great Prayer Day
May/Jun.	Ascension Day
May/Jun.	Pentecost Monday
May/Jun.	Whit Sunday
May/Jun.	Whit Monday
Jun. 5	Constitution Day
Dec. 24	Christmas Eve
Dec. 25	Christmas Day
Dec. 26	St. Stephen's Day
Dec. 31	New Year's Eve

Photography

Denmark is not renowned for its sunshine and the winter months have short daylight hours. Batteries are sold throughout the city and there are plenty of places to download and print digital images. Some museums may not allow photography; check before taking photographs.

Health

Medical Insurance

Private medical insurance is recommended. In an emergency, visitors from the U.S. and Canada can receive free temporary treatment in a hospital *(hospitalet)*. You will be charged for more extensive treatment. Health offices *(kommunes social og sundhedforvaltning)* have lists of hospitals and doctors, or ask at your hotel.

Dental Services

Dentists *(tandlægen)* will charge for any treatment given. They are listed in the telephone directory, and after-hours treatment is available in some clinics. Advice can be sought at tourist and health offices. Be sure that treatment is covered by your medical insurance.

Sun Advice

The warmest months are July and August. The sun in Denmark is not fierce, but sun protection is still advised, especially on boats or near the water.

Drugs

To obtain a prescription medicine at a pharmacy *(apotek)* it must be prescribed by a Scandinavian doctor, so make sure that your supply of prescribed medicines will last your stay. If you are bringing prescription drugs for personal use into Denmark, bring a copy of your prescription to prove that the drugs relate to you. Additionally, some preparations available over the counter in the U.S. may be obtained in Denmark only with a prescription. After regular hours, the nearest all-night facility is posted at all pharmacies.

Safe Water

Tap water is safe to drink, and mineral water *(mineralvand)* is widely available.

Restrooms

Public restrooms *(toiletterne)* are easy to find, clean, well equipped and usually free. They are often indicated by a symbol, or marked WC or *Damer* (women) and *Herrer* (men).

Electricity

Denmark has a 220-volt power supply. Electrical sockets take plugs with two round pins. American appliances will need a plug adapter and will require a transformer if they do not have a dual-voltage facility.

National Transportation

Train *(Tog)*

 Copenhagen is an important meeting point for trains between Europe and the rest of Scandinavia. Danish State Railways, Danske Statsbaner (DSB), runs an efficient service with trains linking to Germany and, via the Øresund Link, to Sweden. Most domestic trains have refreshment facilities; seat reservations are recommended. Call for information (☎ 70 13 14 15; press 3 for English-language version, 1 for information and tickets, 2 for international routes; www.dsb.dk).

Bus *(Bus)*

 The domestic bus service is good; ask for details at local tourist offices. Eurolines services run between other European countries (☎ 33 88 70 00 Mon.–Fri.; www.eurolines.dk).

Ferry *(Færge)*

 There are numerous ferry services from Denmark, with year-round connections to many northern European countries. DFDS Seaways has an office in Denmark, ☎ 33 42 30 10 (Mon.–Fri. 9–5); www.dfdsseaways.com.

Driving

Drive on the right

Speed Limits

Police can impose on-the-spot fines.

Limited-access highways *(motorvej)* **130 k.p.h. (80 m.p.h.)** or **110 k.p.h. (68 m.p.h.)**

Main roads **80 k.p.h. (50 m.p.h.)** Minimum speed **40 k.p.h. (24 m.p.h.)**

Urban areas **50 k.p.h. (31 m.p.h.)** but **40 k.p.h. (24 m.p.h.)** in central Copenhagen

Seat Belts

Must be worn in front and back seats at all times. Children under 8 years must be fastened in a child's seat.

Blood Alcohol

The legal blood alcohol limit is 0.05%. Random breath tests on drivers are carried out frequently, especially late at night, and the penalties for offenders are severe.

Note: It is illegal to drive while using a hand-held cell phone.

Denmark

Driving (continued)

Tolls

There are no tolls on highways. However, the Storebælt (Great Belt) tunnel and bridge from Korsør to Nyborg, and the impressive 10-mile Øresund tunnel and bridge from Copenhagen to Malmö (Sweden) both levy a toll.

Car Rental

The leading car-rental companies have offices at airports, principal train stations and ferry terminals. Hertz offers discounted rates for AAA members (see page 15). For reservations:

	United States	Denmark
Alamo	(888) 233-8749	32 50 30 90
Avis	(800) 633-3469	33 26 80 80
Budget	(800) 527-0700	33 55 05 00
Hertz	(800) 654-3131	33 17 90 00

Fuel

Gas *(benzin)* is sold in liters; unleaded gas *(blyfri)* comes in 92 and 95 octane ratings. Self-service gas stations *(tank selv* or *selvbetjening)* are common, except on limited-access highways. Most gas stations take credit cards, and some have automatic pumps for DKr50, DKr100 and sometimes DKr200 bills.

AAA Affiliated Motoring Club

Forenede Danske Motorejere (FDM)
Firskovvej 32, 2800 Lyngby
☎ 70 13 30 40; www.fdm.dk. Not all automobile clubs offer full services to AAA members.

Breakdowns and Accidents

Report accidents to the Dansk Forening for International Motorkøretøjsforsikring (DFIM; www.dfim.dk), Philip Heymans Allé 1, DK-2900 Hellerup (☎ 41 91 91 91, 10 a.m.–3 p.m.; fax 41 91 91 92). If you are involved in an accident ☎ 112 for police, fire or ambulance services.

Most car-rental firms provide their own free rescue service; if your car is rented, follow the instructions given in the documentation. Use of a car-repair service other than those authorized by your rental company may violate your agreement. You must carry a warning triangle in your car.

Other Information

The minimum legal age for driving a car is 18 (may be 20 to 25 for some car-rental firms).

An International Driving Permit (IDP) is recommended; some car-rental firms require it, and it can speed up formalities if you are involved in an accident. A Green Card (international motor insurance certificate) is recommended if you are driving a private car; see page 15 for more information. Use dimmed headlights at all times.

Useful Words and Phrases

Danish is a Germanic language, close to Swedish and Norwegian, but it is tricky to pronounce because some letters *(d, g)* are silent in the middle or at the end of words, *h* before a *v* becomes silent, and some specifically Scandinavian vowels *(å, ø, and æ)* are awkward to say correctly. But Danes are aware of this, and most of them speak very good English. In addition, menus are often in English or German.

In the Danish alphabet, the following letters come after *z: å, ø* and *æ*. (Århus, for example, comes at the end of the alphabet.) *Å* is used in place of aa, although the city of Aalborg prefers to write the two vowels out in full.

The following words and phrases should help you:

Do you speak English?	*Taler de Engelsk?*
excuse me	*undskyld*
hello/goodbye	*hej/farvel*
how much is…?	*hvor meget koster det?*
I am American	*jeg er Amerikaner*
I'd like…	*jeg vil gerne have…*
I don't understand	*jeg forstår det ikke*
open/closed	*åben/lukket*
please/thank you	*værså venlig/tak*
ticket (one-way/ round trip)	*billet (enkeltbillet/ en tur-retur)*
where is/are…?	*hvor er…?*
yes/no	*ja/nej*
the hotel	**hotel**
breakfast	*morgenmad*
key	*nøgle*
for one/two nights	*en nat/to nætter*
for one person/ two people	*enkeltværelse/ dobbeltværelse*
room	*værelse*
shower	*brusebad*
the restaurant	**restaurant**
beef	*bøf*
bread	*brød*
butter	*smør*
cheese	*ost*
the check	*regningen*
chicken	*kylling*
cod	*torsk*
coffee/tea	*kaffe/the*
Danish pastry	*Wienerbrød*
dessert	*dessert*
fish	*fisk*
fruit salad	*frugtsalat*
herring	*sild*
pork	*suinkød*
potatoes	*kartofler*
shellfish	*skaldyr*
shrimps	*rejer*
starter	*forret*
trout	*ørred*
vegetables	*grøntsager*
wine	*vin*

National Flag

Essential for Travelers

● Required ● Recommended ● Not required

Passport	●
Visa (check regulations before you travel)	●
Travel, medical insurance	●
Round-trip or onward airline ticket	●
Local currency	●
Traveler's checks	●
Credit cards	●
First-aid kit and medicines	●
Inoculations	●

Essential for Drivers*

Driver's license	●
International Driving Permit	●
Car insurance (for nonrental cars)	●
Car registration (for nonrental cars)	●

*see also *Driving* section

Important Addresses

Visit Finland
297 York Street
Jersey City
NJ 07302
☎ (917) 863-5484
www.visitfinland.com

Visit Finland
P.O. Box 358
Porkkalankatu 1
C/O Finpro
FIN-00181, Helsinki, Finland
☎ 02 9469 5650
www.visitfinland.com

American Embassy
Itäinen Puistotie 14B
FIN-00140 Helsinki, Finland
☎ 09 616 250 (embassy);
citizen services ☎ 40 140 5957
Telephone to make appointments
Telephone inquiries Mon.–Thu. 2–4
http://finland.usembassy.gov

Customs

✔ **Duty-free limits on goods brought in from non-European Union countries:**
200 cigarettes or 100 cigarillos or 50 cigars or 250 g. tobacco; 1 L. alcohol over 22% volume or 2 L. alcohol under 22% volume; 4 L. wine; 16 L. beer; 50 ml. perfume; 250 ml. toilet water; plus any other duty-free goods (including gifts) to the value of €430 for visitors entering the E.U. by air or by sea or €300 if arriving by other means. Visitors must declare cash over the value of €10,000 (or equivalent).

✘ No unlicensed drugs, weapons, ammunition, obscene material, counterfeit money or copied goods.
For customs limits for returning U.S. citizens see page 16.

Money

Finland's currency is the euro (€), a currency shared by 18 other European Union countries. The euro is divided into 100 cents (¢). The denominations of euro bills are 5, 10, 20, 50, 100, 200 and 500. There are coins of 1, 2, 5, 10, 20 and 50¢ and €1 and €2. Credit, debit and prepaid cards are widely accepted. ATMs for withdrawing local currency are plentiful in Finland.

Tips and Gratuities

Tips are welcomed, but not expected.

Restaurants	change
Cafés/bars	change
Taxis; hairdressers	none
Porters; restroom attendants	change
Chambermaids	change
Cloakroom attendants; hotel/restaurant doormen	€1

Finland

Communications

Post Offices

Helsinki's main post office at Elielinaukio 2F is open Mon.–Fri. 8–8, Sat. 10–2. Stamps *(postimerkki)* can be bought at post offices, bookstores, newsstands (R-kiosks), train and bus stations. Mailboxes can be freestanding or set into a wall.

Telephones

Public phone boxes have been phased out in Finland. To use your own cell phone without incurring potentially high roaming charges, you can buy and insert a prepaid SIM card, providing your cell is compatible and it isn't locked. Check with your provider before leaving home. Alternatively, consider buying a very basic mobile phone with a prepaid SIM when you arrive in Finland for use during your stay.

Phoning inside Finland

All Finnish telephone numbers in this book include an area code: dial the number listed.
For directory assistance information dial 118.

Phoning Finland from abroad

The country code for Finland is 358; to phone Finland from the United States or Canada, omit the first zero from the Finnish number and prefix with 011 358. (Finnish area codes have two or three digits including the first zero.) Example: 01 122 3344 becomes 011 358 1 122 3344.

Phoning from Finland

To phone the United States or Canada from Finland, prefix with the area code and number with 00 1. (There are other numbers to dial out of the country depending on what telephone system you are using: 990, 994 or 999, followed by 1.) Example: (111) 222-3333 becomes 00 1 111 222-3333. For national information, dial 02 02 02; for international information, dial 02 02 08.

Emergency telephone numbers
Police *(poliisi)* **112**
Fire service *(palokunta)* **112**
Ambulance *(ambulanssi)* **112**

Hours of Operation

- Stores Mon.–Sat.
- Offices Mon.–Fri.
- Banks Mon.–Fri.
- Post Offices Mon.–Fri.
- Pharmacies Mon.–Fri.

7 8 9 10 11 12 1 2 3 4 5 6 7

Many **stores** close at 2 or 3 on Saturday, but department stores and shopping malls stay open until 5 or 6. During the week, large stores extend their hours to 8 or 9, and open on Sunday from June through August and during December. Grocery stores stay open until 8 or 9. Some supermarkets and convenience stores open on Sunday.

Some **gas stations** close on Sunday.

Out-of-town **post offices** and **banks** may have shorter hours, and some city post offices and banks stay open into the evening.

Museum and **monument** opening times vary according to the season. Check opening times with the local tourist office.

Some **pharmacies** *(apteekki)* close early on Saturday. In Helsinki, the Apteekki Yliopiston, Mannerheimintie 5, ☎ 0300 20200, is open daily 7 a.m.–midnight.

National Holidays

Banks, businesses and most stores close on these days.

Jan. 1	New Year's Day
Jan. 6	Epiphany
Mar./Apr.	Good Friday
Mar./Apr.	Easter Monday
May	Ascension
Jun. 21–22	Midsummer's Day Eve and Midsummer's Day
Nov. 1	All Saints' Day
Dec. 6	Independence Day
Dec. 24	Christmas Eve
Dec. 25	Christmas Day
Dec. 26	St. Stephen's Day

Photography

Camera batteries and memory cards are readily available and there are many places offering digital equipment and download services for digital cameras. Bring a tripod if you hope to photograph the northern lights *(aurora borealis)*. Check whether or not photography is permitted in museums.

Finland

Health

Medical Insurance
Private medical insurance is recommended. All treatment in a hospital *(sairaala)* has to be paid for. Foreign visitors can receive good service at a private hospital or health center *(lääkäriasema);* for 24-hour medical advice ☎ 0910023. For private medical care contact Mehiläinen, Mannerheimintie 20B, 4th Floor, 00100 Helsinki ☎ 010 414 0200 (24 hours).

Dental Services
Dentists *(hammaslääkäri)* charge for treatment and can be expensive, so find out if treatment is covered by your medical insurance. City hospitals have 24-hour clinics.

Sun Advice
Southeast Finland has the highest summer temperature in Scandinavia, so precautions are necessary. Use a suitable sunscreen and cover up sensitive skin.

Drugs
Prescription and nonprescription medicines are available from pharmacies *(apteekki)*. If you need a pharmacy outside regular hours, information about the nearest all-night facility is posted at all pharmacies.

Safe Water
Tap water is safe to drink, and mineral water *(kivennäisvesi)* is widely available.

Restrooms

Public restrooms are easy to find, immaculately clean and modern, and are designated by *Miehille/Miehet* (men) and *Naisille/Naiset* (women). There may be a small charge, but many are free. Attendants welcome loose change as a tip.

Electricity

Finland has a 230-volt power supply. Electrical sockets take plugs with two round pins. American appliances will need a plug adapter and will require a transformer if they do not have a dual-voltage facility.

National Transportation

Train *(Juna)*
The Finnish Railway (Valtion Rautatiet, or VR) extends north to southern Lapland. For timetable information *(Suomen kulkuneuvot)* ☎ 0600 41 902; www.vr.fi. If you are planning extensive rail travel, buy a Eurail Finland pass before you arrive in Finland. For information ☎ 1800 622 8600 from the U.S.;1800 361 7245 from Canada; www.raileurope.com or www.eurail.com.

Bus *(Bussi)*
Bus lines run to even the most remote corners of Finland. Bus passes (discount cards) are available for those traveling long distances (valid 2 weeks). For information contact the inner-city bus service Matkahuolto, ☎ 0200 4000.

Ferry *(Laiva)*
There are many excursions exploring Finland's eastern lake system and the country's canal network. Trips into Russia, Estonia, Latvia and Lithuania are possible; check with the tour operator whether a short-term visa is required. These can be obtained through the country's embassy or a travel agent. Contact Tallink Silja ☎ 0600 15700; www.tallinksilja.com, and Viking Line ☎ 0600 41577; www.vikingline.fi.

Driving

Drive on the right

Speed Limits
Minor fines can be imposed on the spot, but not collected. Payment can be made at banks.

 Limited-access highways *(moottoritie)* **120 k.p.h. (74 m.p.h.)** in summer **100 k.p.h. (62 m.p.h.)** in winter Divided highways **100 k.p.h. (62 m.p.h.)**

 Main roads **80 k.p.h. (49 m.p.h.)**

 Urban areas **40–60 k.p.h. (24–37 m.p.h.)**

Seat Belts
Must be worn in front and back seats at all times.

Blood Alcohol
 The legal blood alcohol limit is 0.05%. Random breath tests on drivers are carried out frequently, especially late at night, and the penalties for offenders are severe.

Finland

Driving (continued)

Tolls
There are no highway tolls in Finland.

Car Rental
The leading car-rental firms have offices at airports and train stations. Hertz offers discounted rates for AAA members (see page 15). For reservations:

	United States	Finland
Alamo	(888) 233-8749	04 0306 2803
		(Europcar)
Avis	(800) 633-3469	104 362 200
Budget	(800) 527-0700	0207 466 618
Hertz	(800) 654-3131	0205 552 100

Fuel
There is no leaded gas in Finland. There are two grades of unleaded gas, 95 and 98 octane. Diesel is available. Gas stations are open Mon.–Sat. 7 a.m.–9 p.m., shorter hours on Sunday. Credit cards are acccepted at most filling stations.

AAA Affiliated Motoring Club
Autoliitto (AL) P.O. Box 35, Hämeentie 105A, FI-00551 Helsinki ☎ 09 7258 4400; fax 09 7258 4460; www.autoliitto.fi. If you break down while driving, call ☎ 02 00 80 80 (24 hours) for the AL breakdown service. Not all automobile clubs offer full services to AAA members.

Breakdowns and Accidents
There are 24-hour emergency phones at regular intervals on highways. If you are involved in an accident, phone ☎ 112 for police, fire or ambulance. Accidents should be reported to Finnish Motor Insurers' Center (Liikenne-vakuutuskeskus), Bulevardi 28, 00120 Helsinki ☎ 040 450 4750 (administration); ☎ 040 450 4520 (claims); www.lvk.fi.

Most car-rental firms provide their own free rescue service. Use of a car-repair service other than those authorized by your rental company may violate your agreement. You must carry a warning triangle and a fluorescent vest in your car.

Other Information
The minimum age for driving a car is 18 (19–25 for car-rental firms). An International Driving Permit (IDP) is recommended; some car-rental firms require it, and it can speed up formalities if you are involved in an accident. A Green Card (international motor insurance certificate) is recommended if you are driving a private car; see page 15 for more information. Dimmed headlights must be used at all times. In winter, snow tires or chains are essential. From December through February,

Driving (continued)

winter tires (with or without studs) or tires intended for year-round use are compulsory. You can buy or rent winter driving equipment from Autoliitto. Watch out for signs warning of elk and reindeer crossing roads, indicating the approximate length of danger zones – these animals are more active at dusk.

Useful Words and Phrases

Finnish is a complex and difficult language to learn, and bears little or no resemblance to neighboring languages. However, Swedish is Finland's second, more accessible language, and most people speak some English.

Finnish uses compound words, which are pronounced exactly as they are written. The first syllable of a word is always stressed, and each letter is pronounced individually.

Do you speak English?	*Puhutteko englantia?*
excuse me	*anteeksi*
hello	*terve*
goodbye	*näkemiin*
how much?	*kuinka paljon?*
how are you?	*kuinka voitte?*
Is it near?	*Onko se lähellä?*
I'd like…	*Haluaisin…*
I don't understand	*en ymmärrä*
nonsmoking	*tupakointi kielletty*
okay	*ja lyh*
open/closed	*avoinna/suljettu*
please/thank you	*olkaa hyvä/kiitos*
ticket (one-way/	*menolippu*
round trip)	*meno-paluulippu*
where is…?	*missä on…?*
yes/no	*kyllä ei joo/ei*
the hotel	***hotelli***
breakfast	*aamiainen*
key	*avain*
room	*huone*
shower	*suihku*
it's too expensive	*se on liian kallis*
the restaurant	***ravintola***
beef	*nauta*
bread	*leipä*
chicken	*kana*
coffee	*kahvi*
dessert	*jälkiruoka*
fish	*kala*
lamb	*karitsa*
main course	*pääruoka*
milk	*maito*
pork	*sianliha*
seafood	*äyrläisiä*
soup	*keitto*
steak	*pihvl*
wine	*vini*

France

National Flag

Essential for Travelers

● Required ● Recommended ● Not required

Passport	●
Visa (check regulations before you travel)	●
Travel, medical insurance	●
Round-trip or onward airline ticket	●
Local currency	●
Traveler's checks	●
Credit cards	●
First-aid kit and medicines	●
Inoculations	●

Essential for Drivers*

Driver's license	●
International Driving Permit	●
Car insurance (for nonrental cars)	●
Car registration (for nonrental cars)	●

*see also *Driving* section

Important Addresses

French Embassy USA
4101 Reservoir Road, N.W.
Washington, D.C., 20007
☎ (202) 944-6000
www.info-france-usa.org

**Maison de la France
(French Government Tourist Office)**
79–81 rue de Clichy, 75009 Paris, France
(not open to the public)
☎ 01 42 96 70 00
www.rendezvousenfrance.com

American Embassy
2 avenue Gabriel, 75008 Paris, France
☎ 01 43 12 22 22
Fax 01 42 66 97 83
http://france.usembassy.gov

American Consulate for American Citizen Affairs
4 avenue Gabriel, 75008 Paris, France
☎ 01 43 12 22 10 for recorded information
Open by appointment only

Customs

✔ **Duty-free limits on goods brought in from non-European Union countries:**
200 cigarettes or 100 cigarillos or 50 cigars or 250 g. tobacco; 1 L. alcohol over 22% volume or 2 L. alcohol under 22% volume or sparkling wine and 4 L. still wine, 16 L. beer; plus any other goods/gifts to the value of €430 if arriving by air or sea, €300 if arriving overland (€150 for travelers under 15). See http://ec.europa.eu/taxation_customs/common/travellers/enter_eu/index_en.htm. There is no limit on the importation of tax-paid goods bought within the EU if they are for your own use. Visitors must declare cash over the value of €10,000 (or equivalent).

✘ No unlicensed drugs, weapons, ammunition, obscene material, pets or other animals, counterfeit money or copied goods, meat or poultry. **For customs limits for returning U.S. citizens see page 16.**

Money

France's currency is the euro (€), a currency shared by 18 other European Union countries. The euro is divided into 100 cents (¢). The denominations of euro bills are 5, 10, 20, 50, 100, 200 and 500. There are coins of 1, 2, 5, 10, 20 and 50¢ and €1 and €2. Credit, debit and prepaid cards are widely accepted. ATMs are plentiful throughout most of France. It is a good idea to carry a mix of large and small euro denominations.

Tips and Gratuities

Tips *(pourboires)* are welcomed, but not expected.

Restaurants (service is almost always included)	change
Cafés/bars (service is almost always included)	change
Taxis	€1–€2
Porters	€1–€2
Chambermaids	€2–€10
Hairdressers	€1–€2
Cloakroom attendants	50¢–€1

Communications

Post Offices

Buy stamps *(timbres-poste)* at a post office *(la poste)*, newsstand *(marchand de journaux)* or tobacconist *(tabac)*.

Hours of out-of-town post offices may vary. Mailboxes are yellow and wall-mounted or free-standing; there may be separate compartments for local mail *(départemental)*, for elsewhere in France, and abroad *(autres départements/destinations)*.

Telephones

The telephone system in France is efficient, and phone booths with instructions in English are easy to find. Most phones are operated solely with a phone card *(télécarte)*, which can be bought in 50 or 120 units from post offices, France

Telecom offices, news-stands, tobacconists *(tabacs)*, and SNCF (railway) counters. Most booths accept credit cards. Check overseas cell-phone usage with your provider.

Phoning inside France

All telephone numbers are 10 digits, and include the regional code. Paris and Île de France numbers begin with 01; the rest of France is divided into four zones (02, 03, 04 and 05). Dial all digits when making a call.

Phoning France from abroad

The country code for France is 33. Note that French numbers in this book do not include the country code; you need to prefix this number if you are phoning from another country. To phone France from the United States or Canada, omit the first zero from the French number, and add the prefix 011 33. Example: 01 22 33 44 55 becomes 011 33 1 22 33 44 55.

Phoning from France

To phone the United States or Canada from France, prefix the area code and number with 00 1. Example: (111) 222-3333 becomes 00 1 111 222-3333. For directory inquiries dial 118 712. For international directory inquiries dial 118 700.

Emergency telephone numbers

Police *(police)* 17; Fire service *(pompiers)* 18 Ambulance *(ambulance)* 15
112 (pan-European general emergency number) Emergency calls are free from phone booths.

Hours of Operation

- Stores Mon.–Sat.
- Offices Mon.–Fri.
- Banks Mon.–Fri.
- Post Offices Mon.–Sat.
- Museums/Monuments Tue.–Sun.
- Pharmacies Mon.–Fri.

| 7 | 8 | 9 | 10 | 11 | 12 | 1 | 2 | 3 | 4 | 5 | 6 | 7 |

Many **stores** close on Sunday and all day or a half-day Monday, although some food establishments, especially bakeries, open Sunday mornings. Hypermarkets (large all-purpose stores) are open Mon.–Sat. 9–9 or 10. Opening hours are longer in resort areas and major towns and cities.

Out-of-town **banks** may stay closed on Monday, while city banks may open on Saturday morning. **Post offices** close at noon on Saturday.

Museum times vary considerably, and it is best to check before a visit. Municipal museums close on Monday, while national museums close on Tuesday (except Versailles and Trianon Palace which close on Monday). Many museums close on national holidays.

National Holidays

Banks, businesses and most stores close on these days.

Jan. 1	New Year's Day
Mar./Apr.	Easter Monday
May 1	May Day
May 8	VE Day
May	Ascension Day
May/Jun.	Pentecost Monday
Jul. 14	Bastille Day
Aug. 15	Assumption of the Virgin
Nov. 1	All Saints' Day
Nov. 11	Armistice Day
Dec. 25	Christmas Day

Photography

The range of subjects to photograph in France is enormous. All sizeable towns will have a camera store with digital equipment and photo developing facilities, though development may not be the same day and will be expensive.

Some museums and churches will allow you to photograph inside, but permission for flash photography is usually required.

Health

Medical Insurance

Private medical insurance is recommended. Visitors from non-E.U. countries have to pay for all medical treatment; keep all receipts and medicine labels to claim on your travel insurance. If you wish to see an English-speaking doctor *(médecin)* ask at your consulate or hotel.

Dental Services

A dentist *(dentiste)* charges for treatment. Emergency help is available from dentists listed in the *Yellow Pages (pages jaunes)*. Make sure that your private medical insurance covers dental treatment.

Sun Advice

The yearly average for sunshine is high: 2,500 hours (3,000 hours along the coast). Summers, particularly July and August, can be dry and hot, especially in the south. When outside wear a hat and drink plenty of fluids. On the beach a high-SPF sunscreen is essential.

Drugs

Prescription medicines and medical advice can be obtained from a pharmacy *(pharmacie)*, designated by a green cross sign. If you need medicines after regular hours, information about the nearest 24-hour facility is posted on the door of all pharmacies.

Safe Water

It is safe to drink tap water, but never drink from a fountain marked *"eau non potable"* ("not drinking water"). Many French people prefer the taste of bottled mineral water *(l'eau minérale en bouteille)*, which is widely available. A less expensive alternative is *l'eau de source*, which is spring water.

Restrooms

It is not difficult to find a restroom *(toilettes* or *WC*, pronounced *vay-say* in French), although you may still find the old-fashioned "squat" variety. Hygiene is usually of a reasonable standard. There is a small fee to use facilities in train stations. If you need to use the restroom in a café or bar, buy a drink first.

Electricity

France has a 220-volt power supply. Electrical sockets take plugs with two round pins (occasionally with three round pins). American appliances will need a plug adapter and will require a transformer if they do not have a dual-voltage facility.

National Transportation

Train *(Train)*

The state rail company is the Société Nationale des Chemins de Fer Français (SNCF): ☎ 3635; www.sncf.com. Trains are fast, reliable and comfortable, with numerous discounts available. A round-the-clock car-carrying rail service from Calais (Le Shuttle) to Folkestone, England, and a Paris–London passenger train, Eurostar (☎ 08 92 35 35 39, toll call; www.eurostar.com) both run through the tunnel under the English Channel. International train services from Paris to cities in Belgium, The Netherlands and Germany are operated by Thalys ☎ 08 92 35 35 36; www.thalys.com.

Bus *(Autobus)*

Bus services in cities are excellent, but rural areas may be less well served. Long-distance bus stations are usually close to train stations, and major train and bus services usually coordinate (a long-distance bus is called a *car*). Bus services shown on train timetables are run by the SNCF, and rail tickets are often valid for them. The Eurolines international bus network operates in France (☎ 08 92 89 90 91, toll call; www.eurolines.com).

Ferry *(Ferry)*

There are frequent ferry sailings to Britain from ports along the English Channel. Some Mediterranean ferries operate in summer only and may need reservations in advance.

Driving

Drive on the right

Speed Limits

Traffic police can impose severe on-the-spot fines.

Limited-access toll highways
(autoroutes à péage) **130 k.p.h. (80 m.p.h.)**
Outer lane minimum **80 k.p.h. (49 m.p.h.)**
On wet roads **110 k.p.h. (68 m.p.h.)**
In fog with visibility less than 50m (55 yards)
50 k.p.h. (31 m.p.h.)
Toll-free highways *(autoroutes)* and divided
highways **110 k.p.h. (68 m.p.h.)**

Main roads **90 k.p.h. (56 m.p.h.)**
On wet roads **80 k.p.h. (49 m.p.h.)**

Urban areas. **50 k.p.h. (31 m.p.h.)**,
sometimes reduced to **30 k.p.h. (18 m.p.h.)**

France

Driving (continued)

Seat Belts

Must be worn in front and back seats at all times.

Blood Alcohol
The legal blood alcohol limit is 0.05%. Random breath tests on drivers are carried out frequently, and the penalties for drivers in excess of the legal limit are severe.

Tolls
There are tolls on many limited-access highways *(autoroutes à péage)*. Collect a ticket on entry and keep it in a safe place: you must show the ticket and pay when exiting. Cash and credit cards are accepted.

Car Rental
The leading car-rental firms have offices at airports and train stations. Hertz offers discounted rates for AAA members (see page 15). For reservations:

	United States	France
Alamo	(877) 222-9075	08 05 54 25 10
Avis	(800) 331-1084	08 21 23 07 60
Budget	(800) 472-3325	08 21 23 06 41
Hertz	(800) 654-3001	08 25 80 09 00

Fuel
Gas stations are generally easy to find, and highway service areas are open 24 hours. Gas *(essence)* is unleaded *(sans plomb)* and sold in liters. Credit cards are accepted at most filling stations; many pumps read cards directly, so the customer does not have to pay at the counter; check with your card issuer for usage in France.

AAA Affiliated Motoring Club
Automobile Club de L'Ile de France (FFAC)
9 rue d'Artois, Paris 75008
☎ 01 40 55 43 00; fax 01 40 55 43 09;
www.automobile-club.org. Not all automobile clubs offer full services to AAA members.

Breakdowns and Accidents
If you are involved in an accident, phone ☎ 17 or 112 for police assistance. There are orange emergency telephones every 2 km (1.2 miles) on highways. Most car-rental firms provide their own free rescue service; follow the instructions given in the rental documentation. Use of a car-repair service other than those authorized by your rental company may violate your agreement. Vehicles must carry an emergency pack containing a high visibility vest and luminous warning triangle in case of breakdown. In the event of a breakdown the vest must be worn when you are outside your vehicle.

Driving (continued)

Other Information
The minimum age for driving a car is 18 (between 21 and 25, for some car-rental firms). An IDP (International Driving Permit) is recommended; some car-rental firms require it. A Green Card (international motor insurance certificate) is recommended if driving a private car (see page 15). In built-up areas you must yield the right-of-way to vehicles coming from a side street on the right. All vehicles must carry a breath alcohol analyzer.

Useful Words and Phrases

You'll be well received if you try to pronounce words correctly. Final consonants are seldom pronounced. For instance, the masculine adjective *ouvert* (open) is pronounced [oo-ver]; the feminine *ouverte* [oo-vert]. The final consonant in a word like *vin*, *bon* or *grand* alters the last vowel, making it nasal.

h is silent	*hôtel* [o-tel]
th is *t* (but *ch* is *sh*)	*thé* [tay]*, chaud* [show]
ou is full	*tout* [too]
u is tight, as in cupola	*tu* [tu]*, menu* [meuh-nu]
c and *g* hard before *a, o, u,*	*car* [car]*, guide* [geed]
c and *g* soft before *i* or *e*	*cigarette, age* [arzh]
ç is soft (before an a)	*français* [frahn-say]
gn as in union	*agneau* [an-yo]
Do you speak English?	*Parlez-vous anglais?*
excuse me	*excusez-moi*
hello/goodbye	*bonjour/au revoir*
How much is this?	*C'est combien?*
I am American	*Je suis Américain/e*
I'd like…	*je voudrais…*
I don't understand	*Je ne comprends pas*
open/closed	*ouvert/fermé*
please/thank you	*s'il vous plaît/merci*
ticket	*billet*
(one-way/round trip)	*(simple/aller-retour)*
where is…?	*où est…?*
yes/no	*oui/non*
you're welcome	*de rien*
the hotel	***l'hôtel***
breakfast	*petit déjeuner*
I have a reservation	*j'ai réservé*
for one/two nights	*pour une/deux nuit(s)*
one/two people	*une/deux personne(s)*
room	*une chambre*
shower	*une douche*
with en-suite bathroom	*avec salle de bains*
the restaurant	***le restaurant***
beef	*boeuf*
bread	*pain*
the check	*l'addition*

Germany

National Flag

Essential for Travelers

● Required ● Recommended ● Not required

Passport	●
Visa (check regulations before you travel)	●
Travel, medical insurance	●
Round-trip or onward airline ticket	●
Local currency	●
Traveler's checks	●
Credit cards	●
First-aid kit and medicines	●
Inoculations	●

Essential for Drivers*

Driver's license	●
International Driving Permit	●
Car insurance (for nonrental cars)	●
Car registration (for nonrental cars)	●

*see also Driving section

Important Addresses

German National Tourist Office (Administration)
122 East 42nd Street, 52nd Floor
New York, NY 10168-0072
☎ (212) 661-7200
Fax (212) 661-7174
www.germany.travel

**Deutsche Zentrale für Tourismus e.V
(German National Tourist Office)**
Beethovenstrasse 69
60325 Frankfurt am Main, Germany
☎ 069 974 64-0
Fax 069 751 903
www.germany.travel

American Embassy
Clayallee 170
14191 Berlin, Germany
☎ 030 805 1200 (Mon., Tue. and Thu. 2–3 p.m.)
or 030 8305-0 (emergencies only)
Fax 030 8305-1215
American Citizen Services
Mon.–Fri. 8:30–noon, by appointment only
http://germany.usembassy.gov

Customs

✔ **Duty-free limits on goods brought in from
non-European Union countries:**
200 cigarettes or 100 cigarillos or 50 cigars or
250 g. tobacco; 1 L. alcohol over 22% volume and
2 L. alcohol under 22% or 2 L. sparkling or fortified
wine and 4 L. still wine, 16 L. beer; 50 ml. perfume;
250 ml. toilet water; plus any other duty-free goods
(including gifts) to the value of €430 if arriving by
air or sea, and €300 for all other travelers (€150
for travelers under 15). There is no limit on the
importation of tax-paid goods purchased within the
E.U., provided they are for personal use. Visitors
must declare €10,000 cash (or equivalent).

✘ No unlicensed drugs, weapons, ammunition,
obscene material, pets or other animals,
counterfeit money or copied goods, meat or poultry.
**For customs limits for returning U.S. citizens
see page 16.**

Money

Germany's currency is the euro (€), a currency
shared by 18 other European Union countries.
The euro is divided into 100 cents (¢). The
denominations of euro bills are 5, 10, 20, 50, 100,
200 and 500. There are coins of 1, 2, 5, 10, 20
and 50¢ and €1 and €2. Credit, debit and prepaid
cards are accepted at most larger merchants and
upscale restaurants, however, cash is still more
widely accepted throughout most of Germany.

Tips and Gratuities

Restaurants (where service is not included)	10%
Cafés/bars (where service is not included)	10%
Taxis	10%
Porters	change
Chambermaids	change
Hairdressers	change
Restroom attendants	change
Cloakroom attendants	change

Germany

Communications

Post Offices

 Buy stamps *(Briefmarken)* at a post office *(Postamt)*. Hours for out-of-town post offices may vary. Mailboxes are bright yellow.

Telephones

Black telephones have instructions in English, and most operators are bilingual. Increasingly fewer phones accept coins; most are

operated by telephone cards *(Telefonkarten)*, which can be bought at any post office. International calls can be made from any booth. Check overseas cell-phone usage with your provider.

Phoning inside Germany

German telephone numbers in this book include an area code: dial the number listed.
To call the operator dial 11833 (extra cost).

Phoning Germany from abroad

The country code for Germany is 49. Note that German numbers in this book do not include the country code; you will need to prefix this number if you are phoning from another country. To phone Germany from the United States or Canada, omit the first zero from the German number, and add the prefix 011 49. (Note that the number of digits in German area codes varies.) Example: 011 22 33 44 becomes 011 49 11 22 33 44.

Phoning from Germany

To phone the United States or Canada from Germany, prefix the area code and number with 00 1. Example: 111 222-3333 becomes 00 1 111 222-3333. For national and international information in English, ☎ 11837.

Emergency telephone numbers

Police *(Polizei)* **110**
Fire service *(Feuerwehr)* **112**
Ambulance *(Krankenwagen)* **112**
112 (pan-European general emergency number)
Emergency calls are free from phone booths.

Hours of Operation

- ■ Stores Mon.–Sat.
- ■ Offices Mon.–Fri.
- ■ Banks Mon.–Fri.
- ■ Post Offices Mon.–Sat.
- ■ Museums/Monuments. Tue.–Sun.
- ■ Pharmacies Mon.–Fri.

```
7  8  9  10  11  12  1  2  3  4  5  6  7
```

Store opening hours vary considerably, so even within cities there is no standard rule. In larger cities, some stores stay open as late as 10 p.m., but generally they close around 8.

Pharmacies tend to close earlier during the week and at 4 on Saturday.

Banks stay open until 6 on Thursday.

Post offices open 8–noon on Saturday. Post offices at airports and train stations sometimes operate longer hours.

Government offices close promptly at 4, or at 2 on Friday.

Museums often close on Monday and open late on Thursday; some outside cities close for lunch.

National Holidays

Banks, businesses and most stores close on the following days.

Jan. 1	New Year's Day
Jan. 6	Epiphany (Bavaria, Baden-Württemberg and Saxony only)
Mar./Apr.	Good Friday
Mar./Apr.	Easter Monday
May 1	Labor Day
May	Ascension Day
May/Jun.	Pentecost Monday
Aug. 15	Assumption of the Virgin (Bavaria and Saarland only)
Oct. 3	Day of German Unity
Nov. 1	All Saints' Day (Baden-Württemberg, Bavaria, North Rhine-Westphalia, Rhineland-Palatinate, Saarland and Thuringia only)
Dec. 25	Christmas Day
Dec. 26	St. Stephen's Day

Photography

Memory cards, quality brand-name batteries and other accessories are easy to find. There are stores for digital equipment and facilities for downloading and printing. Photography is generally forbidden in museums and churches or needs special permission.

Health

Medical Insurance

U.S. and Canadian visitors must pay for medical treatment from a doctor or at a hospital *(Krankenhaus)*. Keep all receipts to claim on your travel insurance. For details on emergency, weekend or English-speaking doctors, ask your hotel or consulate.

Note: Large parts of the countryside, particularly but not exclusively in the south, are home to *Zecken* – a kind of tick that can transmit a disease. It is essential to seek medical advice if you are bitten. An inoculation is available.

Dental Services

A dentist *(Zahnarzt)* always charges for treatment. Emergency help is available from dentists listed in the local telephone directory. Find out if your private medical insurance covers dental treatment.

Sun Advice

Germany's continental climate brings cold, clear winters and warm summers, when sun protection is needed. Use sunscreen; children and those with fair skin should be vigilant.

Drugs

Prescription medicines and advice can be obtained from a pharmacy *(Apotheke)*; cosmetics and toiletries at a *Drogerie*. If you need medicine outside regular hours, information about the nearest 24-hour facility is posted on the door of all pharmacies.

Safe Water

Water is safe to drink in Germany, but you may prefer to drink bottled mineral water *(Mineralwasser)*, which is widely available.

Restrooms

Finding a restroom *(Toilette)* is not difficult; they are usually identified by symbols, or are designated *Herren* (men) and *Damen* or *Frauen* (women). Most toilets in restaurants, bars and coffee shops are free. Public toilets, however, are not free and often are operated by a 50¢ coin. If there is an attendant, small change is appreciated as a tip (50¢ usual amount).

Electricity

Germany has a 230-volt power supply. Electrical sockets take plugs with two round pins or sometimes three pins in a vertical row. American appliances will need a plug adapter and will require a transformer if they do not have a dual-voltage facility.

National Transportation

Train *(Zug)*

Germany's efficient rail network is operated by Deutsche Bahn (DB), and local companies. ICE is a fast service of long-distance, high-speed trains. IC and EC trains operate between major towns and cities. Regional (IR) trains are modern and comfortable, and connect with long-distance services. Local services are called SE or S-Bahn. For fare reductions and information call ☎ 01806 996633 (24hrs; toll call).

Bus *(Bus)*

Towns and villages not served by the rail network usually have bus links, with timetables and routes coordinating with trains. German towns have their own buses, and one ticket is often good for other types of city transportation. The Eurolines (Deutsche Touring GmbH) international bus service operates in Germany: ☎ 069 7903 501.

Ferry *(Fähre)*

Ferries from the ports of Lübeck, Kiel and Rostock in the north connect to Denmark, Norway, Sweden, Finland and the Baltic countries. Boats also offer a service to German islands and on many German lakes, rivers and canals. Ask for details at your travel agency or a local tourist office, where reservations can often be made.

Driving

Drive on the right

Speed Limits

Traffic police can impose severe on-the-spot fines.

Limited-access highways *(Autobahn)*: unless signposted there is no speed limit but the suggested limit is **130 k.p.h. (80 m.p.h.)**

Main roads
100 k.p.h. (62 m.p.h.)

Urban areas
50 k.p.h. (31 m.p.h.) or **30 k.p.h. (18 m.p.h.)** or as otherwise posted

Seat Belts

Seat belts must be worn at all times. Children must use a suitable restraint or seat.

Blood Alcohol

The legal blood alcohol limit is 0.05%. Random breath tests on drivers are carried out frequently, especially late at night, and the penalties for offenders are severe.

Germany

Driving (continued)

Tolls

Autobahn (highway) tolls are expected to come into force in 2016 on some roads.

Car Rental

The leading car-rental firms have offices at airports and train stations. Hertz offers discounted rates for AAA members (see page 15). For reservations:

	United States	Germany
Alamo	(877) 222-9075	01805 462526
Avis	(800) 331-1084	01806 557755
Budget	(800) 472-3325	01805 217711
Hertz	(800) 654-3001	01805 333535

Fuel

Gas *(Benzin)* and diesel fuel are sold in liters. Gas stations are easy to find, and most highway services are open 24 hours. Self-service stations are called *Selbstbedienung* or *SB-Tanken,* and credit cards are widely accepted.

AAA Affiliated Motoring Club

Allgemeiner Deutscher Automobil-Club E.V. (ADAC) Amsinckstrasse 39–41, 20097 Hamburg ☎ 01805 101112; fax 040 239 19289; www.adac.de. If you break down while driving, phone ☎ 01802 22 22 22 (ADAC breakdown service). Not all automobile clubs offer full services to AAA members.

Breakdowns and Accidents

Most car-rental firms provide their own free rescue service; if your car is rented, follow the instructions given in the documentation. Use of a car-repair service other than those authorized by your rental company may violate your agreement. If you are involved in an accident, phone ☎ 110 or 112 for police.

Other Information

The minimum age for driving a car if you are a foreign license holder is 18 (it may be higher for some car-rental firms). You must keep an official translation with your driver's license; your embassy or a tourist office can help. An International Driving Permit (IDP) is recommended; some car-rental firms require it, and it can speed up formalities if you are involved in an accident. A Green Card (international motor insurance certificate) is recommended if you are driving a private car; see page 15 for more information. On-the-spot fines can be imposed if you run out of gas on a highway. Using a cell phone while driving is not permitted.

Useful Words and Phrases

German has many dialects. Language in the north is descended from Old Saxon, and in the south from Old High German. Their differences were resolved by Standard German *(Schriftdeutsch)*, created by Martin Luther when he translated the Bible in the 16th century.

Germans are helpful to visitors who attempt to communicate in German, although English is widely spoken.

ü is like the u in cupola	*über* (over)
ie sounds like heat	*Sie* (you)
ei sounds like height	*Eingang* (entrance)
ch is a harsh rasp…	*J. S. Bach*
j is like the English y	*ja* (yes)
r is a guttural sound	*Fräulein* (Miss)
w sounds like English v	*wo* (where)
z is like English ts	*Zeit* (time)
Do you speak English?	*Sprechen Sie Englisch?*
excuse me	*Verzeihung*
hello	*Guten Tag*
goodbye	*Auf Wiedersehen*
How much is…?	*Wieviel kostet…?*
I am American	*Ich bin Amerikaner (in)*
I'd like…	*Ich hätte gerne*
I don't understand	*Ich verstehe nicht*
nonsmoking	*Nichtraucher*
open/closed	*offen/geschlossen*
please/thank you	*bitte/danke*
one-way ticket	*einfache Fahrkarte*
round-trip ticket	*Rückfahrkarte*
where is…?	*wo ist…?*
yes/no	*ja/nein*
you're welcome	*bitte*
the hotel	***das Hotel***
breakfast	*Frühstück*
reservation	*Reservieren/ Reservierung*
key	*Schlüssel*
for one/two nights	*für eine Nacht/ zwei Nächte*
for one person/ two people	*für eine Person/ zwei Personen*
room	*Zimmer*
shower	*Dusche*
the restaurant	***das Restaurant***
beefsteak	*Steak*
bread	*Brot*
the check	*Rechnung*
chicken	*Hähnchen*
coffee	*Kaffee*
dish of the day	*Tagesgericht*
dessert	*Dessert*
entree	*Hauptgericht*
first courses	*Vorspeisen*
fish	*Fisch*
lamb	*Lamm*
pork	*Schweinefleisch*
seafood	*Meeresfrüchte*
wine	*Wein*

National Flag

Essential for Travelers*

● Required   ● Recommended   ● Not required

Passport	●
Visa (check regulations before you travel)	●
Travel, medical insurance	●
Round-trip or onward airline ticket	●
Local currency	●
Traveler's checks	●
Credit cards	●
First-aid kit and medicines*	●
Inoculations	●

*see also *Health* section

Essential for Drivers*

Driver's license	●
International Driving Permit	●
Car insurance (for nonrental cars)	●
Car registration (for nonrental cars)	●

*see also *Driving* section

Important Addresses

Greek National Tourism Organization
305 East 47th Street
New York, NY 10017
☎ (212) 421-5777
Fax (212) 826-6940
www.visitgreece.gr

**Hellenic Tourism Organization
(Greek National Tourism Organization)**
Tsoha 24
11521 Athens, Greece
☎ 210 870 7000
www.visitgreece.gr

American Embassy
91 Vassilissis Sophias Avenue
10160 Athens, Greece
☎ 210 721 2951
Mon.–Fri. 8:30–5
http://athens.usembassy.gov

Customs

✔ **Duty-free limits on goods brought in from non-European Union countries:**
200 cigarettes or 100 cigarillos or 50 cigars or 250 g. tobacco; 4 L. wine, 16 L. beer; 1 L. alcohol over 22% volume; 2 L. alcohol under 22% volume; 50 ml. perfume; 250 ml. toilet water; plus any other duty-free goods (including gifts) to the value of €175. There is no importation limit for tax-paid goods purchased within the European Union for personal use. Visitors must declare cash of €10,000 (or equivalent). Up to $1,000 in foreign currency may be exported by visitors.

✘ No unlicensed drugs, weapons, ammunition, obscene material, pets or other animals, counterfeit money or copied goods, meat or poultry.
For customs limits for returning U.S. citizens see page 16.

Money

The Greek currency is the euro (€), a currency shared by 18 other European Union countries. The euro is divided into 100 cents (¢). The denominations of euro bills are 5, 10, 20, 50, 100, 200 and 500. There are coins of 1, 2, 5, 10, 20 and 50¢ and €1 and €2. Credit, debit and prepaid cards are widely accepted. ATMs for withdrawing euros are plentiful throughout most of Greece.

Tips and Gratuities

Tips are welcomed, but not expected or obligatory.

Restaurants (where service is not included)	10–15%
Cafés/bars	change
Taxis	change
Porters	€2
Chambermaids	€2 per day
Cloakroom attendants	change

Athens	New York	Chicago	Denver	Los Angeles	Time zones
12:00 noon	− 6 hrs	− 7 hrs	− 8 hrs	− 9 hrs	

527

Greece

Communications

Post Offices

Buy stamps *(ghramatósima)* at a post office *(takhithromio)*, distinguished by a yellow "OTE" sign. Lines can be long at post office

counters; if you simply need stamps, check whether there's a window that sells stamps. A corner kiosk *(periptero)* will sell stamps if you are buying postcards. Hours for out-of-town post offices may vary.

Telephones

Most public telephones take phone cards available from kiosks, local stores and OTE *(Organismos Tilepikoinonion Ellados,* pronounced O-tay)* offices. If your calls are short and local, use a street kiosk *(periptero)* where you pay after the call. Coin-operated phones are hard to find in the more urban and resort areas of Greece. Check overseas cell-phone usage with your provider.

Phoning inside Greece
All Greek telephone numbers in this book include an area code: dial the number that is listed. To call the operator dial 132 (or 131 in Athens).

Phoning Greece from abroad
The country code for Greece is 30. Note that Greek numbers in this book do not include the country code; you will need to prefix this number if you are phoning from another country. To call a Greek number from the United States or Canada, add the prefix 011 30. Example: 210 122 3344 becomes 011 30 210 122 3344.

Phoning from Greece
To phone the United States or Canada from Greece, prefix the area code and number with 00 1. Example: (111) 222-3333 becomes 00 1 111 222-3333. To call international information dial 00 162.

Emergency telephone numbers
General emergencies **112**
Police *(astínomia)* **100**
Tourist police (Athens only) **171**
Fire service *(fotyá)* **199**
Ambulance *(asthenoforo)* **166**
Emergency calls are free from phone booths.

Hours of Operation

- Stores Mon.–Sat.
- Offices Mon.–Fri.
- Banks Mon.–Fri.
- Post Offices Mon.–Fri.
- Museums/Monuments
- Archeological sites
- Pharmacies Mon.–Fri.

7 8 9 10 11 12 1 2 3 4 5 6 7

In tourist areas **stores** open at 8 a.m. and close late; they have shorter hours off-season, and some close completely in winter.

Banks close at 1:30 Fridays. They may stay open longer hours at peak season in resort areas. *At time of press the opening hours of banks in Greece are uncertain – please check before leaving U.S.*

Post offices close at noon on Saturday.

Archeological sites usually close in the afternoon; some reopen in the evening in the summer, but all sites vary their hours depending on the time of year. It is best to check locally. Many archeologcal sites, museums and monuments close completely or partly on Monday.

Restaurants open all day in resort areas but may close off-season.

National Holidays

Banks, businesses and most stores and museums close on these days, but restaurants and some stores in tourist areas may stay open.

Jan. 1	New Year's Day
Jan. 6	Epiphany
Feb./Mar.	Shrove Monday
Mar. 25	Independence Day
***Apr./May**	Good Friday
***Apr./May**	Easter Monday
May 1	Labor Day
May/Jun.	Pentecost Monday
Aug. 15	Assumption of the Virgin
Oct. 28	Óchi Day
Dec. 25	Christmas Day
Dec. 26	St. Stephen's Day

* Greece observes the Orthodox calendar, and the date on which Easter falls may differ from that observed by other Western nations.

Photography

Camera batteries are widely available. Digital equipment and printing facilities are available in cities and large towns.
Never take photos near military bases or airports, and ask first in museums and churches.

Greece

Health

Medical Insurance

Private medical insurance is recommended. Visitors from non-E.U. countries can receive basic treatment at hospital emergency rooms. Admittance to a hospital *(nosokomío)* or consultation with a doctor *(iatrós)* will entail a fee. Ask your hotel, consulate or the tourist police for information on English-speaking doctors.

Dental Services

Dentists *(odhondoyatrós)* always charge for treatment, so find out if your medical insurance covers it; keep all receipts for insurance purposes. Treatment is available from English-speaking dentists listed in the telephone directory, or ask at your hotel.

Sun Advice

Summer, particularly July and August, can be oppressively hot and humid. Seek shelter inside a museum, or cover up, apply sunscreen and drink plenty of fluids. Be especially careful on boats or near the water.

Drugs

A pharmacy *(farmakío)*, distinguished by a green cross, has staff qualified to offer medical advice and provides a wide range of prescription medicines. Information about the nearest all-night facility is usually posted at pharmacies. Note that codeine is banned and you can be fined for carrying it.

Safe Water

Tap water is safe to drink but because of the high level of minerals it can cause upsets. Bottled water *(metaliko nero)* is available everywhere at a reasonable cost.

Restrooms

Finding a clean restroom *(toualéta)* away from tourist areas can be difficult. It is advisable to use facilities in cafés and restaurants after buying a drink. Restrooms are free. The Greek sewage system does not take toilet tissue, even in café and restaurant facilities; always use the wastebin provided.

Electricity

Greece has a 220-volt power supply. Electrical sockets take plugs with two round pins. American appliances will need a plug adapter and will require a transformer if they do not have a dual-voltage facility.

National Transportation

Train *(Tréno)*

Greek mainland trains are run by Organismos Sidirodromon Ellados (OSE; www.ose.gr) The network is limited. Reservations are essential on most express trains. For rail information in Athens: ☎ 145 (domestic services) or 147 (international services).

Bus *(Leoforío)*

Buses are popular and frequent; few villages or ferry ports are without a bus link. Buy city-to-city tickets from the bus station; in rural areas tickets *(isitirio)* are issued by a conductor on the bus. For bus information in Athens: ☎ 185.

Ferry *(Féribot)*

Ferries serve all of the Greek islands, and boat excursions run from May to October. You can take a boat from the port of Piréas to most islands. You can usually buy a ticket on the day of travel unless you are reserving a cabin or taking a car. You may need to reserve in advance in mid-August and over the Easter period; ask at a travel agency or tourist office.

Note: frequent transit strikes take place in Greece; check travel details with transportation company.

Driving

Drive on the right

Speed Limits

Police can impose on-the-spot fines but they cannot collect them.

Limited-access highways
130 k.p.h. (80 m.p.h.)

Main roads
90 k.p.h. (56 m.p.h.) or
110 k.p.h. (68 m.p.h.)

Urban areas
50 k.p.h. (31 m.p.h.)

Seat Belts

Must be worn in the front seat at all times and in the rear seat where fitted. Children over three years and under 1.5m (just under 5 feet) tall are not allowed to travel in the front seat.

Blood Alcohol

The legal blood alcohol limit is 0.05%. Random breath tests on drivers are carried out frequently, especially late at night, and the penalties for offenders are severe.

Driving (continued)

Tolls

There are some, but not many, highway tolls in Greece.

Car Rental

The leading car-rental firms have offices at airports, train stations and principal ferry terminals. Hertz offers discounted rates for AAA members (see page 15).

For reservations:

	United States	Greece
Alamo	(877) 222-9075	210 353 3323
Avis	(800) 331-1212	210 322 4951
Budget	(800) 218-7992	210 921 4771
Hertz	(800) 654-3001	210 922 0102

Fuel

Gas *(venzini)* is sold in liters and usually comes in five grades: super *(sooper)*, regular *(apli)*, unleaded *(amolyvdhi)*, super unleaded *(sooper amolyvdhi)* and diesel *(petrelaio)*. There are few stations in remote areas; they are less likely to be open on weekends and may not take credit cards.

AAA Affiliated Motoring Club

Automobile and Touring Club of Greece (ELPA) 395 Messogion Street, 153 43 Agia Paraskevi, Athens ☎ 201 606 8800; fax 201 606 8800; www.elpa.gr. If you break down while driving, phone ☎ 10400 (ELPA breakdown service). Not all automobile clubs offer full services to AAA members.

Breakdowns and Accidents

There are emergency telephones at regular intervals on highways. If you are involved in an accident, phone ☎ 100 for police. Most car-rental firms provide their own free rescue service; if your car is rented, follow the instructions given in the documentation. Use of a car-repair service other than those authorized by your rental company may violate your agreement.

Other Information

The minimum age for driving a car is 18 (may be higher for some car-rental firms). An International Driving Permit (IDP) is recommended; some car-rental firms require it, and it can speed up formalities if you are involved in an accident. A Green Card (international motor insurance certificate) is recommended if you are driving a private car; see page 15 for more information. You can be fined for unnecessary use of the horn. You must carry a fire extinguisher, a first-aid kit and a warning triangle in your car.

Useful Words and Phrases

The Greek language can be daunting to the visitor; it uses a different alphabet and is spoken with staccato rapidity. The way words and place-names are converted into English varies considerably according to which transliteration system a translator happens to prefer.

With patience and a keen ear, you should be able to recognize what sounds these unfamiliar letters stand for. Learning the Greek alphabet may enable you to deduce the meaning of signs and notices. The easiest thing to do, however, is to learn a few basic courtesy phrases.

The Greeks realize how difficult their language appears to foreigners, and they appreciate visitors' attempts to speak it.

Do you speak English?	*milate angliká?*
excuse me	*signomi*
hello/goodbye	*yásou/chérete*
how much?	*póso?*
I'd like	*tha íthela*
I do not understand	*dhen katalavéno*
nonsmoking	*khoros ya mi kapnízondes*
okay	*endáγsi*
open/closed	*aniktos/klistos*
please/you're welcome	*parakaló*
thank you	*efharistó*
ticket	*isitíro*
one-way/round trip	*apló/isitiro met epistrofis*
where is...?	*poo íne...?*
yes/no	*né/óhi*
the hotel	***xenodochio***
breakfast	*proino*
key	*klidhí*
for one/two nights	*ya mía/dýo vradhiés*
for one/two people	*yiá éna/dýo átoma*
room	*éna dhomátio*
shower	*doos*
the restaurant	***estiatorio***
beans	*fasólia*
beer	*bira*
bread	*psomi*
the check	*logariasmós*
chicken	*kotópoulo*
coffee	*kafé*
dessert	*glikisma*
food	*fagitó*
lamb	*arnáki*
lobster	*astakós*
meat balls	*kefthédes*
olives	*eliés*
pork	*hirino*
red mullet	*barboúnia*
squid	*kalamarákia*
starter	*proto piato*
stuffed vine leaves	*dolmadakia*
water	*neró*
wine	*krasí*

Greece

National Flag

Essential for Travelers

● Required   ● Recommended   ● Not required

Passport	●
Visa (check regulations before you travel)	●
Travel, medical insurance	●
Round-trip or onward airline ticket	●
Local currency	●
Traveler's checks	●
Credit cards	●
First-aid kit and medicines	●
Inoculations	●

Essential for Drivers*

Driver's license	●
International Driving Permit	●
Car insurance (for nonrental cars)	●
Car registration (for nonrental cars)	●

*see also *Driving* section

Important Addresses

Hungarian National Tourist Office
223 East 52nd Street
New York, NY 10022
☎ (212) 695-1221
www.gotohungary.com

Budapest Info
v. Sütő utca 2
H-1052 Budapest
Hungary
☎ 1 438 8080 (24 hours)
www.budapestinfo.hu

American Embassy
H-1054 Budapest
Szabadság tér 12
Hungary
☎ 1 475 4164 (8 a.m.–5 p.m.); 1 475 4400
(5 p.m.–8 a.m.; U.S. citizens only)
http://hungary.usembassy.gov

Customs

✔ **Duty-free limits on goods brought in from non-European Union countries:**
200 cigarettes or 100 cigarillos or 50 cigars or 250 g. tobacco; 2 L. still wine; 1 L. spirits or strong liqueurs over 22% volume or 2 L. fortified wine, sparkling wine or other liqueurs; 50 ml. perfume; 250 ml. toilet water; plus any other duty-free goods (including gifts) up to a value of Ft48,000. There is no limit on the importation of tax-paid goods purchased within the European Union, provided the goods are for your own personal use. If you are bringing in cash or traveler's checks to the value of $14,800, customs must be notified and proof of ownership will be required.

✘ No unlicensed drugs, weapons, ammunition, obscene material, pets or other animals, counterfeit money or copied goods, meat or poultry.
For customs limits for returning U.S. citizens see page 16.

Money

Hungary's currency is the forint (Ft or HUF), which is divided into 100 fillérs, although fillérs are no longer legal tender. The denominations of forint bills are 500, 1,000, 2,000, 5,000, 10,000 and 20,000. There are coins of 5, 10, 20, 50, 100 and 200 forints. ATMs can be found throughout Hungary. You can exchange dollars or traveler's checks *(utazasi csekket)* at a bank *(bank)*, exchange office *(penzvalto)*, post office *(posta)* and some hotels. Credit card acceptance is limited. It is a good idea to carry a mix of large and small forint denominations.

Tips and Gratuities

Tips *(borravaló)* are welcomed, but not expected, where service is not included.

Restaurants	10%
Cafés/bars	10%
Taxis	10%
Porters	to reflect quality of service
Chambermaids	to reflect quality of service
Hairdressers	10%
Gas station attendants	change
Cloakroom attendants	change

Budapest	New York	Chicago	Denver	Los Angeles	Time zones
12:00 noon	− 6 hrs	− 7 hrs	− 8 hrs	− 9 hrs	

531

Hungary

Communications

Post Offices

Buy stamps *(bélyeg)* at a post office *(posta)*, newsstand/tobacconist *(dohanyaruda)* or from a hotel. Hours for out-of-town post offices may vary. Mailboxes are wall-mounted and red with a calling-horn emblem.

Telephones

You can use cash and prepaid phone cards to make a call in Hungary. For direct dialing for national and international calls, use Ft20, Ft50 and Ft100 coins (minimum Ft20). International calls can be made from red phone booths. Phone cards of 50 and 100 units can be bought from newsstands/tobacconists, gas stations, post offices and hotels.

Check overseas cell-phone usage with your provider.

Phoning inside Hungary

Hungarian telephone numbers include an area code of one or two digits (there is no initial zero). For long-distance calls within Hungary precede the number with 06. Numbers in Budapest are seven digits, not including the area code; the area code is 1. To call the operator dial 191.

Phoning Hungary from abroad

The country code for Hungary is 36. Note that Hungarian numbers in this book do not include the Hungarian country code; prefix the country code if you are phoning from another country. To phone Hungary from the United States or Canada, add the prefix 011 36 before the area code and number. Example: 1 122 3344 becomes 011 36 1 122 3344.

Phoning from Hungary

To phone the United States or Canada from Hungary, prefix the area code and number with 00 1. Example: (111) 222-3333 becomes 00 1 111 222-3333. To call the international operator dial 190; for international directory inquiries dial 199.

Emergency telephone numbers

General emergencies **112**
Police *(rendörség)* **107** or **112**;
Fire service *(tüzoltéóság)* **105** or **112**;
Ambulance *(mentök)* **104** or **112**

Hours of Operation

- ■ Stores Mon.–Sat.
- ■ Offices Mon.–Fri.
- ■ Banks Mon.–Fri.
- ■ Post Offices Mon.–Fri.
- ■ Museums/Monuments
- ■ Pharmacies

7 8 9 10 11 12 1 2 3 4 5 6 7

Department **stores** are open Mon.–Fri. 10–6, Sat. 9–1. Saturday afternoon they close early, and few stores remain open after 1 or 2. Thursday is late-night shopping until 7 or 8.

Grocery stores and other food stores have longer hours and also open on Sunday morning. In large cities, some stores stay open 24 hours.

In smaller towns, stores close over lunchtime. Large shopping centers in cities are open Mon.–Sat. 10–9, Sun. 10–6.

The **National Bank of Hungary** is open Mon.–Fri. 10:30–2. Most other banks close at 1. on Friday. Banks are closed Dec. 24 and 31.

Post offices close at 1. on Saturday.
Many **museums** close on Monday.

National Holidays

Banks, businesses and most stores are closed on these days. If a public holiday falls on a Tuesday or a Thursday, the day between it and the weekend also becomes a holiday (e.g. the Monday or Friday).

Jan. 1	New Year's Day
Mar. 15	Day of the Nation (anniversary of 1848 revolution)
Mar./Apr.	Easter Monday
May 1	Labor Day
May/Jun.	Pentecost Monday
Aug. 20	Constitution Day
Oct. 23	Day of the Proclamation of the Republic
Nov. 1	All Saints' Day
Dec. 25	Christmas Day
Dec. 26	St. Stephen's Day

Photography

Hungary has spectacular landscapes, including the Danube bend north of Budapest, one of the most beautiful stretches of this great river, and romantic Lake Balaton, framed by vineyards. Digital camera equipment and printing services are widely available in towns and cities.

Health

Medical Insurance

Private medical insurance is recommended. U.S. and Canadian visitors can receive free essential first-aid and emergency treatment. All further treatment and care has to be paid for. Fees for medical care are set by the individual hospital or practice. There is a 24-hour private medical care service with English-speaking doctors in Budapest: SOS Hungary. It also has its own ambulance service ☎ 1 240 0475; www.soshungary.hu.

Dental Services

Dentists *(forgovos)* charge for any treatment, but quality dental work is relatively inexpensive. Check to be sure it is covered by your medical insurance. Dentists are listed in the *Yellow Pages*; ask for English-speaking dentists at your embassy or hotel, or at a tourist office. A good dental clinic in Budapest is SOS Dental Service ☎ 1 269 6010.

Sun Advice

Hungary has up to 2,500 hours of sun annually, one of the highest levels in Europe. In summer, 9 or 10 hours a day can be expected, so protection is essential.

Drugs

A pharmacy *(gyógyszetár* or *patica)* sells both prescription and nonprescription medicines (bring your own medication if you need a specific product). Most are cheaper than similar U.S. products. Information about the nearest 24-hour facility is posted at all pharmacies.

Safe Water

Although tap water is safe, you may find it causes mild upsets. Bottled mineral water *(ásvány víz)* and soda water *(szoda víz)* are widely available and advised.

Restrooms

Public restrooms *(mosdó)* are fairly easy to find, and are usually indicated by a symbol or marked WC, and designated by *férfi* for men and *nöi* for women. There may be a charge of between Ft100 and Ft200.

Electricity

Hungary has a 220/230-volt power supply. Electrical sockets take plugs with two round pins. American appliances will need a plug adapter and will require a transformer if they do not have a dual-voltage facility.

National Transportation

Train *(Vonat)*

The state railroad, MÁV-Start, serves most towns. Express trains link Budapest with provincial centers; it may be quicker to go via the capital for cross-country journeys. Fares are low, and MÁV-Start offers many discounted fares and passes, including rail cards for unlimited travel; ☎ 06 40 49 49 49 (domestic), 1 444 4499 (international); www.mav-start.hu.

Bus *(Busz)*

Long-distance buses are expensive, but can be quicker than trains. The main Budapest terminal is at Erzsébet tér. The main operator is state-owned Volánbusz, whose yellow buses serve even very small communities. Volánbusz is a member of Eurolines, who operate an international bus service; ☎ 1 382 0888 (domestic and international); www.volanbusz.hu.

Ferry *(Komp)*

Ferries run from spring to late fall on Lake Balaton, the Danube between Budapest and Esztergom, and the Tisza river (for Sárospatak, Tokaj, Szolnok, Csongrád and Szeged). Information is available from Mahart at the Vigadó tér landing stage; ☎ 1 484 4013; www.mahartpassnave.hu.

Driving

Drive on the right

Speed Limits

On-the-spot fines of up to Ft30,000 can be imposed by the police. Receipts must be issued.

 Limited-access highways *(autópályára)*
130 k.p.h. (80 m.p.h.)
Divided highways **110 k.p.h. (68 m.p.h.)**

 Main roads
90 k.p.h. (56 m.p.h.)

 Urban areas
50 k.p.h. (31 m.p.h.)
Some resorts and residential zones
30 k.p.h. (18 m.p.h.)

Seat Belts

Must be worn in front and rear seats at all times.

Blood Alcohol

The legal blood alcohol limit is zero. Random breath tests on drivers are carried out frequently, especially at night.

Hungary

Driving (continued)

Tolls

Driving on highways requires the pre-purchase of a sticker called a *matrica*, available at border crossings and gas stations.

Car Rental

The leading car-rental firms have offices at airports and train stations. Hertz offers discounted rates for AAA members (see page 15). For reservations:

	United States	Hungary
Avis	(800) 331-1084	1 318 4240
Budget	(800) 472-3325	1 214 0420
Enterprise	(800) 261-7331	1 296 6610
Hertz	(800) 654-3001	1 296 7171

Fuel

Unleaded fuel *(ólommentes benzine)* is graded 95 octane. Diesel can be bought along major routes and in cities. Many gas stations *(benzinkút)* are self-service, although you may not be able to use a credit card in smaller stations. A map of rural gas stations is available from MAK (see below).

AAA Affiliated Motoring Club

Magyar Autóklub (MAK) H-1043 Budapest, Berda Józef u. 15 ☎ 1 345 1800. If you break down while driving, phone ☎ 188 or www.autoklub.hu (MAK breakdown service). Not all automobile clubs offer full services to AAA members.

Breakdowns and Accidents

If you have an accident, phone the police ☎ 107 and ask for an interpreter at the scene. You are legally required to report personal injury. Most car-rental firms provide their own free rescue service; if you break down follow the instructions given in the documentation. Use of an unauthorized car-repair service may violate your agreement. Vehicles with damaged bodywork may only leave the country with an official certificate.

Other Information

The minimum age for driving a car is 18 (21 for some car-rental firms). An International Driving Permit (IDP) is recommended; some car-rental firms require it, and it can speed up formalities if you are involved in an accident. A Green Card (international motor insurance certificate) is needed if you are driving a private car; see page 15 for more information. Dimmed headlights must be used by cars at all times outside built-up areas. You must have a first-aid kit, a warning triangle and a fluorescent vest in your car.

Useful Words and Phrases

Hungarian, called Magyar by its speakers, is a difficult language, related to Finnish and Estonian. German is traditionally the second language, but English is gradually replacing it, especially among the younger generation.

Apart from a few international words *(posta, telefon)*, Hungarian offers few clues as to its meaning. However, pronunciation is regular – letters consistently stand for the same sounds. By learning basic words, street signs, notices and labels will begin to make sense.

Do you speak English?	*Beszél angolul?*
What is your name?	*Hogy hívnak?*
excuse me	*elnézést*
hello	*jó napot kivanok*
goodbye	*viszontlátásra*
yes/no	*igen/nem*
how much?	*mennyibe kerul?*
I am American	*Amerikai vagyok*
I don't understand	*nem értem*
nonsmoking	*nem domanyzo*
open	*nyitva*
closed	*zárva*
please	*kérem*
thank you	*köszönöm*
ticket	*jegy*
(one-way/round trip)	*(egyiranyu/retur)*
where is...?	*hol van...?*
the hotel	***szálloda***
you're welcome	*szívesen*
Where is the restroom?	*Hol a mosdó?*
breakfast	*reggeli*
reservation	*foglalás*
key	*kulcs*
room	*szoba*
shower	*zuhany*
the restaurant	***étterem/vendeglo/etkezde***
beef	*marha*
beer	*sör*
bread	*kenyer*
the check	*szamla*
coffee/tea	*kávé/tea*
dessert	*édesség*
fish	*hal*
fruit	*gyümölcs*
ice cream	*fagylalt*
meat	*hús*
pork	*sertés*
potato	*burgonya*
poultry	*csirke*
starter	*elöételek*
vegetable	*zöldség*
wine	*bor*

National Flag

Essential for Travelers

● Required ● Recommended ● Not required

Passport	●
Visa (check regulations before you travel)	●
Travel, medical insurance	●
Round-trip or onward airline ticket	●
Local currency	●
Traveler's checks	●
Credit cards	●
First-aid kit and medicines	●
Inoculations	●

Essential for Drivers*

Driver's license	●
International Driving Permit	●
Car insurance (for nonrental cars)	●
Car registration (for nonrental cars)	●

*see also *Driving* section

Important Addresses

Tourism Ireland (Republic of Ireland and Northern Ireland)
345 Park Avenue, New York, NY 10154
☎ 1 212 418 0800
www.ireland.com
Discover Ireland Information Office
14 Upper O'Connell Street, Republic of Ireland
☎ 01 850 230 330
www.ireland.com or www.discoverireland.ie
American Embassy (Republic of Ireland)
42 Elgin Road, Ballsbridge
Dublin 4, Republic of Ireland
☎ 01 668 8777
http://dublin.usembassy.gov
American Citizens Services: by appointment;
see details and make reservation via website
Visit Belfast Welcome Centre
9 Donegall Square North,
Belfast BT1 5GJ, Northern Ireland
☎ 028 9024 6609
www.visit-belfast.com
US Consulate General (Northern Ireland)
Danesfort House, 223 Stranmills Road
Belfast BT9 5GR
☎ 028 9038 6100, Mon.–Fri. 8:30–5
belfast.usconsulate.gov

Customs

✓ **Duty-free limits on goods brought in from non-European Union countries**:
200 cigarettes or 100 cigarillos or 50 cigars or 250 g. tobacco; 4 L. still wine or 16 L. beer; 1 L. spirits or strong liqueurs over 22% volume or 2 L. fortified wine, sparkling wine or other liqueur; 50 ml. perfume; 250 ml. toilet water; plus any other duty-free goods (or gifts) to the value of €430. There is no limit on the importation of tax-paid goods bought within the E.U. if they are for your own personal use. There are no currency regulations.

✗ No unlicensed drugs, weapons, ammunition, obscene material, pets or other animals, counterfeit money or copied goods, meat or poultry.
For customs limits for returning U.S. citizens see page 16.

Money

The Republic of Ireland's currency is the euro (€), a currency shared by 18 other European Union countries. The euro is divided into 100 cents (¢). The denominations of euro bills are 5, 10, 20, 50, 100, 200 and 500. There are coins of 1, 2, 5, 10, 20 and 50¢ and €1 and €2. ATMs are available in the major cities. Credit, debit and prepaid cards are accepted in hotels, large stores and upscale restaurants; check first in small or rural establishments. Exchange dollars at a bank, exchange office, post office or a hotel.
For information about currency in Northern Ireland, see page 502.

Tips and Gratuities

Restaurants (if service is not included)	10–15%
Cafés/bars (if service is not included)	10%
Taxis	€1 (IR) or round up to nearest £1 (NI)
Porters	€1 (IR) or £1 (NI) per bag
Hairdressers	€2 (IR) or £1 (NI)
Tour guides	€2 (IR) or £1 (NI)
Cloakroom attendants	€1 (IR) or £1 (NI)

Ireland

Communications

Post Offices

Buy stamps at post offices, newsstands/tobacconists, large grocery stores and hotels. Out-of-town post office times vary. Mailboxes are green in the Republic of Ireland and red in Northern Ireland.

Telephones

Public phone booths are either blue and cream or the glass-booth style, although many are now glass and metal. They take cash or prepaid phone cards bought from newsstands, post offices and local stores. Some city phones take credit cards. For phone calls made to or from Northern Ireland, except calling Northern Ireland from the Republic (see below), follow the instructions for Britain on page 503.

Check overseas cell-phone usage with your provider.

Phoning inside Ireland
All Irish phone numbers in this book include the area code; dial the number listed. To call the operator dial 10 (Republic), 100 (NI).

Phoning the Republic of Ireland from abroad
The country code for the Republic of Ireland is 353. To phone the Republic from another country, prefix 353 to the number given. To phone the Republic from the United States or Canada, omit the first zero from the Irish number, and add the prefix 011 353. (The number of digits in Irish area codes varies.) Example: 01 122 3344 becomes 011 353 1 122 3344.

Phoning from Ireland
To phone the United States or Canada from Ireland, prefix the area code and number with 00 1. Example: (111) 222-3333 becomes 00 1 111 222-3333. To phone Northern Ireland from the Republic of Ireland, replace the code 028 with 048. Example: 028 1122 3344 becomes 048 1122 3344. To call international directory inquiries dial 11818 (Republic), 153 (NI).

Emergency telephone numbers
General emergencies **112 or 999**
Police *(gardaí)* **112 or 999**
Fire service **112 or 999**
Ambulance **112 or 999**
Emergency calls are free from phone booths.

Hours of Operation

- Stores Mon.–Sat.
- Offices Mon.–Fri.
- Banks Mon.–Fri.
- Post Offices Mon.–Fri.
- Museums/Monuments
- Pharmacies Mon.–Sat.

7 8 9 10 11 12 1 2 3 4 5 6 7

Hours in chart refer to the Republic of Ireland; hours for Northern Ireland may differ slightly.
Some **stores** stay open until 8 or 9 p.m. on Thursday or Friday. On Sunday some bigger stores and many supermarkets open from noon until 5 or 6. In smaller towns and rural areas stores close in the afternoon on one day of the week.

Pharmacies may close earlier on Saturday.
Some **banks** in small towns close 12:30–1:30. Banks open until 5 p.m. one day a week (Thursdays in Dublin and Belfast). Nearly all banks are closed on Saturday and Sunday.

In larger cities and towns, **post offices** stay open during lunchtime and until 5. on Saturdays. In suburban and rural areas, they typically close for lunch (1–2:15) and are closed on Saturdays.

Hours for **museums** and tourist sights vary; always check with the local tourist office. Some places close from October to March, although most major sights are open all year.

National Holidays

Banks, businesses and most stores close on these days. Museums also may have restricted hours.

Jan. 1	New Year's Day
Mar. 17	St. Patrick's Day
Mar./Apr.	Good Friday
Mar./Apr.	Easter Monday (also day after in NI)
1st Mon. in May	May Bank Holiday
Last Mon. in May	Spring Bank Holiday (NI)
1st Mon. in Jun.	June Bank Holiday (ROI)
Jul. 12	Battle of the Boyne (NI)
1st Mon. in Aug.	August Bank Holiday (ROI)
Last Mon. in Aug.	Summer Bank Holiday (NI)
Last Mon. in Oct.	October Bank Holiday (ROI)
Dec. 25	Christmas Day
Dec. 26	St. Stephen's Day

Photography

The light is frequently poor. Bring a tripod for landscape work. Digital equipment and printing facilities are widely available. Camera batteries also are available countrywide.

Ireland

Health

Medical Insurance

Private medical insurance is recommended. U.S. and Canadian visitors can receive treatment in emergency rooms, but are charged if admitted to a hospital bed. A general practitioner also will charge for services.

Dental Services

Dental work is expensive, so check to see if it is covered by your medical insurance. Dentists are listed in the *Golden Pages* (IR) or *Yellow Pages* (NI). Alternatively, ask at your hotel or embassy. For the Irish Dental Association call ☎ 01 295 0072; www.dentist.ie.

Sun Advice

The sunniest months are May and June, with 5–6.5 hours of sun a day (the extreme southwest is the sunniest). July and August are the warmest. During these months you should take sensible precautions against the sun.

Drugs

Pharmacies (also called chemists) sell a range of prescription and nonprescription medicines. If you need medicine outside regular hours, information about the nearest 24-hour facility should be posted on the door of all pharmacies.

Safe Water

Tap water is safe to drink throughout Ireland. If, however, you prefer mineral water you will find it widely available.

Restrooms

Identify restrooms by *Fir* (men) and *Mná* (women). A small charge is levied in restrooms at some train stations, but most other facilities are free. The standards of hygiene are moderate. You will be welcomed into any local pub if you need to use their facilities, but stop for a drink and a talk while you are there.

Electricity

The Republic of Ireland has a 230-volt and Northern Ireland a 240-volt power supply.

Electrical sockets either take plugs with two round pins or three square pins. American appliances will need a plug adapter and will require a transformer if they do not have a dual-voltage facility.

National Transportation

Train

The Republic of Ireland's rail company is Iarnród Éireann (IÉ or Irish Rail). Trains are the fastest way of covering long distances and are generally reliable and comfortable, but the network is limited and one-way tickets can cost almost as much as round-trip tickets. There are many special offers on fares, and for extensive rail travel consider a Trekker or Explorer ticket. For information: ☎ 01 850 366 222; www.irishrail.ie. For Northern Ireland call Translink ☎ 028 9066 6630; www.translink.co.uk.

Bus

Bus Éireann (Irish Bus) operates a network of express bus routes serving most of the country (some run summer only). For information check online at www.buseireann.ie. Translink is the integrated service operator for Northern Ireland ☎ 028 9066 6630; www.translink.co.uk for information.

Ferry

A car ferry runs between Ballyhack (County Wexford) and Passage East (County Waterford); ☎ 051 382 480, saving 60 miles on the road trip. Another serves Killimer (County Clare) and Tarbert (County Kerry); ☎ 065 905 3124. There also are ferries to several islands; ask for details at a local tourist office. There are regular ferries from Belfast, Larne, Dublin, Dun Laoghaire and Rosslare to ports on the mainland of Britain, and from Cork, Dublin and Rosslare to France.

Driving

Drive on the left

Speed Limits

Traffic police can impose on-the-spot fines.

 Limited-access highways (motorways/blue) 120 k.p.h. (74 m.p.h.)

 Main roads (national/green) 100 k.p.h. (62 m.p.h.); in some areas 80 k.p.h. (49 m.p.h.). Regional/local/white 80 k.p.h. (49 m.p.h.)

 Urban areas (RI) 50 k.p.h. (31 m.p.h.) Northern Ireland: 50–60 k.p.h (31–37 m.p.h.)

Seat Belts

 Must be worn in front and back seats at all times.

Ireland

Driving (continued)

Blood Alcohol

The legal blood alcohol limit is 0.08%. Random breath tests on drivers are carried out frequently, especially late at night, and the penalties for offenders are severe.

Tolls

Tolls are charged at some locations: Dublin Port Tunnel; Limerick Tunnel; M50 (radial route around Dublin); East Link Bridge and West Link Bridge (both Dublin); M1 (Drogheda By-Pass); M3 (Navan–Kells); M4 (Kinnegad-Enfield-Kilcock); N6 (Galway–Ballinasloe); M7/M8 (Portlaoise); N8 (Rathcormac/Fermoy By-Pass); N25 (Waterford Bypass). For details see www.nra.ie.

Car Rental

The leading car-rental firms have offices at airports, train stations and large ferry terminals. Hertz offers discounted rates for AAA members (see page 15). Advise the car-rental company if you plan on traveling between the Republic and Northern Ireland. For reservations:

	United States	Republic of Ireland
Alamo/ Europcar	(888) 233-8749	01 648 5900
Avis	(800) 331-1084	01 605 7500
Budget	(800) 472-3325	01 844 5150
Hertz	(800) 654-3001	01 844 5466

Fuel

Gas is unleaded and sold in liters; diesel also is easily purchased. Gas stations in villages stay open until 8 or 9 p.m. and usually open after Mass on Sunday.

AAA Affiliated Motoring Club

AA Ireland 57 Drury Street, Dublin 2
01 617 9104; www.theaa.ie. If you break down while driving, 1800 66 77 88 (AAI breakdown service). Not all automobile clubs offer full services to AAA members. Northern Ireland: see Britain section (page 505).

Breakdowns and Accidents

There are 24-hour emergency phones at regular intervals on major highways. 112 or 999 if involved in an accident. Most car-rental firms provide their own free rescue service; if your car is rented, follow the instructions given in the documentation. Use of a car-repair service other than those authorized by your rental company may violate your agreement.

Other Information

The minimum age for driving a car is 17 (may be higher for some car-rental firms). An International Driving Permit (IDP) is recommended; some car-rental firms require it, and it can speed up

Driving (continued)

formalities if you are involved in an accident. A Green Card (international motor insurance certificate) is recommended if you are driving a private car; see page 15 for more information.

In the Republic of Ireland road signs are marked in kilometers, but you may find old signs in miles. In Northern Ireland all road signs are in miles.

Useful Words and Phrases

Although the Republic of Ireland is officially bilingual, and the Irish language (Gaelic or Gaeilge) is learned by all schoolchildren, English is more commonly spoken. There are around 80,000 native speakers of Irish (data from 2011 census), making it Europe's least widespread official language.

Because it often reflects expressions in Gaelic, Irish English is famed for its picturesque turns of phrase, much more poetic than American or British English.

The Gaelic language is enjoying a revival: radio, television and the Internet all stir up interest in the old language. There are Gaelic-speaking clubs as far away as the U.S. West Coast.

Following are pronunciations of words you may come across:

Bord Fáilte (Irish Tourist Board)	bord falt-cha
Ceilidh (traditional dance night)	kaylee
Gaeilge (the Irish language)	gale-geh
Gaeltacht (Irish-speaking country)	gale-tackt
Garda (policeman)	gawrdah
Fleadh (traditional music evening)	flah
Taoiseach (prime minister)	teeshock

Numbers:

1	*a haon*	a hay-on
2	*a dó*	a doe
3	*a trí*	a tree
4	*a ceathair*	a ca-hir
5	*a cuíg*	a koo-ig
6	*a sé*	a shay
7	*a seacht*	a shocked
8	*a hocht*	a huct
9	*a naoi*	a neigh
10	*a deich*	a de

Other words:

good day	*lá maith*	law mah
goodbye	*slán*	slawn
goodnight	*oíche mhaith*	ee-ha vah
How are you?	*Conas taio?*	co-nus tee?
please	*más é do thoil é*	maws eh duh hull eh
thanks	*gusmaith agat*	gurrah mah a-gut
pub	*tábhairne*	taw-er nay
water	*uisce*	ishkek
whiskey	*fuisci*	fwishgee
yes	*sea*	shah

National Flag

Essential for Travelers

● **Required** ● **Recommended** ● **Not required**

Passport	●
Visa (check regulations before you travel)	●
Travel, medical insurance	●
Round-trip or onward airline ticket	●
Local currency	●
Traveler's checks	●
Credit cards	●
First-aid kit and medicines	●
Inoculations	●

Essential for Drivers*

Driver's license	●
International Driving Permit	●
Car insurance (for private cars)	●
Car registration (for private cars)	●

*see also *Driving* section

Important Addresses

Italian National Tourist Board
686 Park Avenue, 3rd Floor
New York, NY 10065
☎ (212) 586-9249
🕐 Mon.–Fri. 9–5
www.italiantourism.com

Ente Nazionale Italiano per il Turismo (Italian State Tourist Board)
Via Marghera 2/6
00185 Rome, Italy
☎ 06 49711
www.enit.it or www.italia.it

American Embassy
Via Vittorio Veneto 121
00187 Rome, Italy
☎ 06 46741
http://italy.usembassy.gov
Non-emergency services are available through an online appointment system.

Customs

✔ **Goods brought into Italy from non-European Union countries limited to:**
200 cigarettes or 100 cigarillos or 50 cigars or 250 g. tobacco; 2 L. wine; 1 L. alcohol over 22% volume or 2 L. alcohol under 22% volume; 50 ml. perfume; 250 ml. toilet water; plus any other duty-free goods (including gifts) to the value of €300 if arriving by land, €430 if arriving by sea or air. There is no limit on the importation of tax-paid goods purchased within the European Union, provided they are for your own personal use. Foreign or local currency in excess of $10,000 must be declared on arrival.

✘ No unlicensed drugs, weapons, ammunition, obscene material, pets or other animals, counterfeit money or copied goods, meat or poultry.
For customs limits for returning U.S. citizens see page 16.

Money

Italy's currency is the euro (€), a currency shared by 18 other European Union countries. The euro is divided into 100 cents (¢). The denominations of euro bills are 5, 10, 20, 50, 100, 200 and 500. There are coins of 1, 2, 5, 10, 20 and 50¢ and €1 and €2. Exchange dollars or traveler's checks *(assegni turistici)* at a bank *(banca)* or exchange office *(ufficio di cambio)*. Hotels may exchange traveler's checks but stores do not. ATMs *(sportello automatico)* are plentiful and credit, debit and prepaid cards are accepted in hotels, large stores and upscale restaurants; check first in small or rural establishments. It is a good idea to carry a mix of large and small euro denominations.

Tips and Gratuities

Restaurants (service usually included but add 50¢ per person)	
Cafés/bars	small change
Taxis	15%
Porters	€1
Chambermaids	€1 per day
Restrooms	minimum
Cloakroom attendants	50¢

Italy

Communications

Post Offices

Buy stamps *(francobolli)* at a post office *(ufficio postale)* or at a tobacconist *(tabaccaio)*. Mailboxes (red or blue) often have two slots, one for local mail *(per la città)*, the other for out-of-town mail *(tutte le altre destinazioni)*. Mail can take up to three weeks; to speed delivery send it priority *(posta prioritaria)* or recorded *(raccomandata)* post.

Telephones

Pay phones can be found in bars and other public places. Prepaid cards *(carta or scheda telefonica)* for card-operated phones are available from tobacconists, bars, post offices, newsstands, train stations and dispensers showing a Telecom Italia (TI) logo. Use a prepaid card for international calls; tear the corner off before using it. Check overseas cell-phone usage with your provider.

Phoning inside Italy
All telephone numbers in Italy include an area code that must be dialed. To call the operator dial 10.

Phoning Italy from abroad
The country code for Italy is 39. Note that Italian numbers in this book do not include the country code; you will need to prefix this number if you are phoning from another country. To call Italy from the United States or Canada dial the prefix 011 39. Include the first zero of the regional code. There is no standard number of digits in Italian numbers. Example: 01 122 3344 becomes 011 39 01 122 3344.

Phoning from Italy
To phone the United States or Canada from Italy, prefix the area code and number with 00 1. Example: (111) 222-3333 becomes 00 1 111 222-3333. To call international information dial 4176.

Emergency telephone numbers
Police *(policia)* **113** (local) or **112** (national)
Fire service *(pompieri)* **115** or **112**
Ambulance *(ambulanza)* **118** or **112**
Emergency calls are free from phone booths.

Hours of Operation

- Stores Mon.–Sat.
- Offices Mon.–Fri.
- Banks Mon.–Fri.
- Post Offices Mon.–Fri.
- Museums/Monuments
- Architectural sites
- Churches/Pharmacies

Department **stores**, some grocery stores and stores in major cities and tourist areas may not close at lunchtime, and sometimes stay open until later in the evening. Some stores close on Monday morning and may close on Saturday afternoon in summer; most stores close on Sunday. Many stores, especially in Rome, Florence and Venice (less so in Naples) now stay open from 1 to 4.

Some **banks** close at 2 and do not reopen later in the afternoon.

Post office times may vary slightly; some may be open Saturday 8:30–noon.

Many **museums** are open in the late afternoon (typically 4–7), others are open all day, and a few stay open late into the evening. Many museums close early on Sunday (around 1), and many are closed on Monday.

National Holidays

Banks, businesses and most stores and museums close on these days. Most cities, towns and villages celebrate their patron saint's day, but generally most establishments remain open.

Jan. 1	New Year's Day
Jan. 6	Epiphany
Mar./Apr.	Easter Monday
Apr. 25	Liberation Day 1945
May 1	Labor Day
Jun. 2	Anniversary of the Republic
Aug. 15	Assumption of the Virgin
Nov. 1	All Saints' Day
Dec. 8	Immaculate Conception
Dec. 25	Christmas Day
Dec. 26	St. Stephen's Day

Photography

Digital equipment is available in towns and cities. Photography may be banned in museums and churches.

Health

Medical Insurance

Private medical insurance is strongly recommended. Visitors from non-European Union countries can receive treatment in a hospital accident and emergency room, but will be charged if admitted to a bed. A general practitioner *(medico)* can deal with less urgent cases, but also will charge for treatment.

Dental Services

Emergency dental treatment is available from English-speaking dentists listed in the *Yellow Pages (pagine gialle*; www.paginegialle.it). A fee will be charged, so check that you are covered for treatment on your private medical insurance.

Sun Advice

In summer, especially July and August, it can be oppressively hot and humid in cities. On sunny days cover your head and shoulders and use a sunscreen. Cathedrals and other stone buildings can be refreshingly cool. Take frequent breaks in the shade and drink plenty of fluids.

Drugs

A pharmacy *(farmacia)* displays a green cross symbol and has staff who can provide prescription medicines and offer advice on minor ailments. Information about the address of the nearest 24-hour facility is normally posted at every pharmacy.

Safe Water

In isolated rural areas it is not advisable to drink tap water. However, across most of the country tap water is perfectly safe, although most Italians prefer to drink bottled mineral water *(acqua minerale)*, which is inexpensive and widely available.

Restrooms

Finding a restroom *(gabinetto/bagno)* can be difficult away from airports, train and bus stations, highway service areas and museums. Leave a tip (about 50¢) for the attendant. If using the facilities in a bar you will be expected to buy a drink. Some bars have separate restrooms for men *(signori)* and women *(signore)*.

Electricity

Italy has a 220-volt power supply (in some areas, 125 volts). Electrical sockets take plugs with two round pins or three pins in a vertical row. American appliances will need a plug adapter and will require a transformer if they do not have a dual-voltage facility.

National Transportation

Train *(Treno)*

Italian State Railways provides an efficient range of services (information available online only at www.trenitalia.com). *Regionale* and *Interregionali* trains are slow for long journeys; Intercity are faster, though tickets carry a supplement. The Frecce network, traveling at speeds of up to 300 k.p.h. (186 m.p.h.), are the fastest and most expensive.

Bus *(Autobus)*

There is no national bus company, but each major city has its own company for short-, medium- and some long-distance bus travel. International Eurolines buses run from the main Italian cities: ☎ 0861 199 1900; www.eurolines.it.

Ferry *(Traghetto)*

Genoa and Naples are the main Mediterranean ports, with regular services to Sicily and Sardinia. Naples also has services to Capri and other islands. Many services are reduced off-season, and some are cut altogether. Reserve well in advance for car ferries.
Note: frequent transit strikes take place in Italy; check travel details with transportation company.

Driving

Drive on the right

Speed Limits

Police can demand up to a quarter of an imposed fine to be paid on the spot.

 Limited-access highways *(autostrada)* **130 k.p.h. (80 m.p.h.)**
Some designated stretches of *autostrada* have a **150 k.p.h. (93 m.p.h.)** limit.

Main roads
90–110 k.p.h. (56–68 m.p.h.)

Urban areas
50 k.p.h. (31 m.p.h.)

Note: keep your headlights on low beam at all times in built-up areas.

Seat Belts

Must be worn in front and back seats at all times.

Blood Alcohol

 The legal blood alcohol limit is 0.05%. Random breath tests are carried out frequently, especially late at night.

Driving (continued)

Tolls

You will be issued a toll-card on entering nearly every limited-access highway *(autostrada)*: pay on leaving. You can buy a prepaid card *(viacard)* at tollbooths, service areas, tourist offices and tobacconists.

Car Rental

The leading car-rental firms have offices at airports, train stations and ferry terminals. Hertz offers discounted rates for AAA members (see page 15). For reservations:

	United States	**Italy**
Avis	(800) 331-1084	199 100 133
Budget	(800) 472-3325 (US number only)	
Europcar	Online only; go to www.europcar.com or www.europcar.it	
Hertz	Online only; go to www.hertz.com	

Fuel

Gas *(benzina)* is unleaded *(senza piombo)* 95 and 98 octane. Outside urban areas, stations are open daily 7–12:30 and 3–7:30. Highway services are open 24 hours. Credit cards are accepted at most filling stations.

AAA Affiliated Motoring Club

Automobile Club D'Italia (ACI) Via Marsala 8, 00185 Rome ☎ 803116 in Italy (24 hours a day); or 06 491 115 or 800 000 116 (toll-free in Italy); www.aci.it. If you break down while driving, phone ☎ 803116. Not all automobile clubs offer full services to AAA members.

Breakdowns and Accidents

There are emergency phones at regular intervals on all highways. If you are involved in an accident, phone ☎ 112. Most car-rental firms provide their own free rescue service; if you have an accident, follow the rental documentation instructions. Use of an unauthorized repair company may violate your agreement. In the event of a breakdown, you must wear a fluorescent vest when outside your car. You must carry a warning triangle in your car.

Other Information

The minimum age for driving a car is 18 (may be higher for some car-rental firms). An International Driving Permit (IDP) is recommended; some car-rental firms require it, and it can speed up formalities if you are involved in an accident. A Green Card (international motor insurance certificate) is recommended if you are driving a private car (see page 15). Dimmed headlights are required by law at all times outside built-up areas and when visiblity is poor. Many historic down-town areas have a Zone a Traffico Limitato (ZTL) with automatic fines for non-approved vehicles.

Useful Words and Phrases

Italian pronunciation is consistent with spelling, and vowels are always pronounced. The letter h is always silent, but can modify the sound of letters c and g. As a general rule, accentuate the next-to-last syllable.

c is hard before a, o, u, h	*medico; Chianti*
c is soft before i or e	*ciao* [chow]
g is hard before a, o, u, h	*Gucci*, Lamborghini
g is soft before i or e	*gelati*
	[jel-ah-tee]
gl as in Amelia	*figlia* [fee-lyah]
gn as in union	*gnocchi*
	[nyee-ok-kee]
sc before i or e is soft	*prosciutto*
	[pro-shoot-toh]

Where two consonants appear together, each belongs to a different syllable.

Do you speak English?	*Parla inglese?*
excuse me	*mi scusi*
goodbye	*arrivederci*
hello	*buongiorno*
How much is…?	*Quanto costa…?*
I am American	*sono Americano/-a*
I'd like…	*vorrei…*
I don't understand	*non capisco*
nonsmoking	*per non fumatori*
okay	*va bene*
open/closed	*aperto/chiuso*
please/thank you	*per favore/grazie*
ticket (one-way/ round trip)	*biglietto (andata sola/andata ritorno)*
where is…?	*dov'è…?*
yes/no	*si/no*
you're welcome	*prego*
the hotel	***l'albergo***
breakfast	*prima colazione*
I have a reservation	*ho una prenotazione*
key	*una chiave*
for one/two nights	*per una/due notte/-i*
one/two people	*una/due persona/-e*
room	*una camera*
shower	*una doccia*
with en-suite bathroom	*con bagno privato*
the restaurant	***il ristorante***
beef	*il manzo*
bread	*il pane*
the check	*il conto*
chicken	*il pollo*
coffee	*il caffè*
dessert	*il dolce*
dish of the day	*il piatto del giorno*
entrée	*il secondo*
fish	*il pesce*
lamb	*l'agnello*
pork	*il maiale*
seafood	*i frutti di mare*
starter	*l'antipasto*
wine	*il vino*

Luxembourg

National Flag

Essential for Drivers

● Required ● Recommended ● Not required

Passport	●
Visa (check regulations before you travel)	●
Travel, medical insurance	●
Round-trip or onward airline ticket	●
Local currency	●
Traveler's checks	●
Credit cards	●
First-aid kit and medicines	●
Inoculations	●

Essential for Drivers*

Driver's license	●
International Driving Permit	●
Car insurance (for nonrental cars)	●
Car registration (for nonrental cars)	●

*see also *Driving* section

Important Addresses

Luxembourg National Tourist Office
17 Beekman Place
New York, NY 10022
☎ (212) 935-8888
www.visitluxembourg.com

**Office National du Tourisme
(Luxembourg National Tourist Office)**
P.O. Box 1001
L-1010 Luxembourg
☎ 42 82 82 10
www.visitluxembourg.com

Embassy of the United States
22 boulevard Emmanuel Servais
L-2535 Luxembourg
☎ 46 01 23
http://luxembourg.usembassy.gov
Mon.–Fri. 8:30–5:30

Customs

✓ **Duty-free limits on goods brought in from non-European Union countries:**
200 cigarettes or 100 cigarillos or 50 cigars or 250 g. tobacco; 2 L. wine; 1 L. alcohol over 22% volume or 2 L. alcohol under 22% volume; 50 ml. perfume; 250 ml. toilet water; plus any other duty-free goods (including gifts) to the value of €175 (€90 for children under 15). There is no limit on the importation of tax-paid goods purchased within the European Union, provided they are for your own personal use. There are no restrictions on the import or export of cash or traveler's checks in euros or foreign currency.

✗ No unlicensed drugs, weapons, ammunition, obscene material, pets or other animals, counterfeit money or copied goods, meat or poultry. **For customs limits for returning U.S. citizens see page 16.**

Money

Luxembourg's currency is the euro (€), a currency shared by 18 other European Union countries. The euro is divided into 100 cents (¢). The denominations of euro bills are 5, 10, 20, 50, 100, 200 and 500. There are coins of 1, 2, 5, 10, 20 and 50¢ and €1 and €2. ATMs are plentiful and credit, debit and prepaid cards are accepted in hotels, large stores and upscale restaurants; check first in small or rural establishments. It is a good idea to carry a mix of large and small euro denominations.

Tips and Gratuities

Restaurants (service is usually included)	€1 or €2
Cafés/bars (service is usually included)	€1 or €2
Taxis	15%
Porters, chambermaids	€1–€2
Hairdressers	€2
Restroom attendants	50¢–€1
Cloakroom attendants	50¢ per coat

City of Luxembourg 12:00 noon | New York – 6 hrs | Chicago – 7 hrs | Denver – 8 hrs | Los Angeles – 9 hrs | Time zones **543**

Communications

Post Offices

Buy stamps *(timbres-poste)* at a post office *(poste)*, newsstand/tobacconist *(tabac-journaux)* or at a bookstore. Mailboxes are yellow.

Luxembourg City's main post office is ✉ 25 rue Aldringen ☎ 8002-8004 🕓 Mon.–Fri. 7–7, Sat. 7–5. Another is ✉ 38 place de la Gare ☎ 4088-7610 🕓 Mon.–Fri. 6 a.m.–7 p.m., Sat. 6–noon. Hours for out-of-town post offices may vary.

Telephones

Public telephones *(cabine téléphoniques)* are easy to find. Phone booths usually have pictorial instructions, with French and German text. You can use most denominations of coins, or buy a prepaid phone card *(télécarte)* from a post office or train station. International phone booths display a

yellow sign showing a telephone dial with a receiver in the center. Check overseas cellphone usage with your provider.

Phoning inside Luxembourg
There are no area codes in Luxembourg; dial the number that is listed.

For the operator dial 118 171.

Phoning Luxembourg from abroad
The country code for Luxembourg is 352. Note that Luxembourg numbers in this book do not include the country code; you will need to prefix this number if you are phoning from another country. To phone Luxembourg from the United States or Canada, add the prefix 011 352. Example: 11 22 33 becomes 011 352 11 22 33.

Phoning from Luxembourg
To phone the United States or Canada from Luxembourg, prefix the area code and number with 00 1. Example: (111) 222-3333 becomes 00 1 111 222-3333. To call the international operator dial 11816.

Emergency telephone numbers
Police *(police)* **112** or **113**
Fire service *(pompiers)* **112**
Ambulance *(ambulance)* **112**
Emergency calls are free from phone booths.

Hours of Operation

- Stores Mon.–Sat.
- Offices Mon.–Fri.
- Banks Mon.–Fri.
- Post Offices Mon.–Fri.
- Museums/Monuments
- Pharmacies Tue.–Sat.

7 8 9 10 11 12 1 2 3 4 5 6 7

Most **stores** open at 9 a.m. Many stores and **pharmacies** do not open until noon on Monday, and most are closed on Sunday. Many establishments have long lunch breaks (typically noon–2).

Provincial **post offices** and **banks** may have shorter hours, but some stay open at lunchtime and open on Saturday morning. Some post offices open earlier and stay open in the evening.

Opening times for **museums** and **monuments** vary; they are frequently closed on Monday – check with the local tourist office.

National Holidays

Banks, businesses and most stores close on these days.

Jan. 1	New Year's Day
Mar./Apr.	Easter Monday
May 1	May Day
May/Jun.	Ascension Day
May/Jun.	Whit Monday
Jun. 23	National Day
Aug. 15	Assumption of the Virgin
First Mon. in Sep.	Luxembourg City Fete (City of Luxembourg only)
Nov. 1	All Saints' Day
Dec. 25	Christmas Day
Dec. 26	St. Stephen's Day

National holidays falling on a Sunday are normally observed on the following Monday.

Photography

Luxembourg enjoys a temperate climate, and the light is good. Make sure that photography is permitted before taking pictures in museums. Camera batteries can be bought from tourist stores. Digital equipment and printing facilities are available in major towns.

Health

Medical Insurance
Private medical insurance is recommended; U.S. and Canadian visitors can be treated in emergency rooms, but are charged if admitted to a hospital *(hôpital)*. Phone ☎ 112 for 24-hour information on hospitals and English-speaking doctors.

Dental Services
A dentist *(dentiste)* will charge a fee for treatment, so check whether this is covered by your medical insurance. Emergency clinics are available in city hospitals. To find a dentist look in the *Yellow Pages (pages jaunes)* or ask at your hotel.

Sun Advice
You will not experience extremes of temperature in Luxembourg, but the sunshine during summer months can burn, so good sun protection is essential.

Drugs
Prescription medicines and advice can be obtained from a pharmacy *(pharmacie)*, identified by a green cross. Information about the nearest 24-hour facility is posted at all pharmacies.

Safe Water
Tap water in Luxembourg is safe to drink, and bottled mineral water *(eau minérale)* is widely available.

Restrooms
Restrooms *(toilettes)* are usually clean, modern and easy to find. They may also be called "WC" (pronounced *vay-say)*. Coin-operated facilities exist; those with an attendant usually charge 50¢ or €1.

Electricity
Luxembourg has a 220-volt power supply. Electrical sockets take plugs with two round pins. American appliances will need a plug adapter and will require a transformer if they do not have a dual-voltage facility.

National Transportation

Train *(Train)*
The national rail company is the Societé Nationale des Chemins de Fer Luxembourgeois (CFL; www.cfl.lu). Most services run through the City of Luxembourg. Combined train and bus one-day travel cards (the "Billet Longue Durée") are good value at €4 and are valid until 8 a.m. the following day. "Short distance" train and bus tickets are available for €2 and are valid for 2 hours or 6 miles. At Luxembourg City train station there is an information office (🕐 daily 5 a.m.–9.30 p.m.). National information and tickets ☎ 2489-2489.

Bus *(Bus)*
Long-distance, CFL-operated buses complement the rail network (☎ 24 89 24 89; www.cfl.lu). The Eurolines European bus network serves Luxembourg, arriving at place de la Gare, in front of Gare Centrale.

River Boat *(Bateau-mouche)*
There are many excursions (mostly Easter to October) exploring Luxembourg's fine Moselle river. For details, contact Entente Touristique de la Moselle Luxembourgeoise, 115 route du Vin, L-5416 Ehnen ☎ 26 74 78 74; www.visitmoselle.lu.

Driving

Drive on the right

Speed Limits
Police impose minor on-the-spot fines.

 Limited access highways *(autoroutes)*
130 k.p.h. (80 m.p.h.), 110 k.p.h. (68 m.p.h.) when wet or in snow conditions

 Main roads
90 k.p.h. (56 m.p.h.)

Urban areas
50 k.p.h. (31 m.p.h.)

Seat Belts
Must be worn in front and back seats at all times. Children aged 3 to 18 years and/or under 4 feet 11 inches in height must use an appropriate child restraint system.

Blood Alcohol
 The legal blood alcohol limit is 0.05%. Random breath tests on drivers are carried out frequently, especially late at night, and the penalties for offenders are severe.

Luxembourg

Driving (continued)

Tolls

There are no highway tolls in Luxembourg.

Car Rental

The leading car-rental firms have offices at airports and train stations. Hertz offers discounted rates for AAA members (see page 15). For reservations:

	United States	Luxembourg
Alamo	(888) 233 8749 (US number only)	
Avis	(800) 331-1084	43 51 71
Budget	(800) 472-3325 (US number only)	
Hertz	(800) 654-3001	43 46 45

Fuel

Most gas stations *(stations de service)* are self-service, and 24-hour facilities are common. Stations on highways often have café services. The price of gas is fixed by the government, but self-service stations often offer discounts. Major credit cards are accepted.

AAA Affiliated Motoring Club

Automobile Club du Grand-Duché de Luxembourg (ACL) 54 route de Longwy, L-8007 Bertrange, ☎ 45 00 45-1 (Mon.–Fri. 8:30–6); www.acl.lu. If you break down while driving, phone ☎ 26000 (ACL 24-hour breakdown service). Not all automobile clubs offer full services to AAA members.

Breakdowns and Accidents

There are emergency phones at regular intervals on highways. If you are involved in an accident, phone for emergency assistance (☎ 112 or 113 for police or ☎ 112 for fire or ambulance). Most car-rental firms provide their own free rescue service; if your car is rented, follow the instructions given in the documentation. Use of a car-repair service other than those authorized by your rental company may violate your agreement. In the event of a breakdown, you must put on a fluorescent vest when you are outside your vehicle. You must carry a warning triangle in your vehicle.

Other Information

The minimum age for driving a car is 18 (may be higher for some car-rental firms). An International Driving Permit (IDP) is recommended; some car-rental firms require it, and it can speed up formalities if you are involved in an accident. A Green Card (international motor insurance certificate) is recommended if you are driving a private car; see page 15 for more information.

Useful Words and Phrases

Because the Grand Duchy of Luxembourg is tucked between Belgium, France and Germany, Luxembourgers often slip unconsciously between different languages.

The official language (and, unofficially, the language of the elite) is French, but German is used for many situations. In addition to this, there is a third, everyday language: Lëtzebuergesch, a symbol of both national identity and Luxembourg's ability to assimilate other cultures.

The roots of Luxembourg's own language are Germanic, but it has evolved into a dialect that Germans no longer understand. The use of Lëtzebuergesch is primarily an oral tradition. It was only in 1984 that its spelling was decreed by law; up until then Luxembourgers spelled words more or less as they pleased.

French, German and Lëtzebuergesch are taught in schools, and English also is widely spoken, especially among the young and those working in the tourist trade. Don't expect Luxembourgers in rural areas to have mastered a fourth language, however!

Lëtzebuergesch is resilient enough to exist side-by-side with such widely spoken languages as French and German, but as the patois of a tiny, landlocked duchy it's evidently not very exportable. So if you have the opportunity to speak a word or two of this country's uniting language you'll raise a smile and a welcome.

good morning/hello	*moien*
goodbye	*eddi*
thank you (very much)	*merci (villmols)*
sorry	*pardon*
excuse me	*entschellegt*
please	*wanneschglift*
I don't understand	*ech verstin nët*
Food and drink	
apple cake	*Äppelkuch*
blood sausage	*Trèipen*
cheesecake	*Kéiskuch*
chicken in Riesling sauce	*Hong am Rèisleck*
coffee	*Kaffi*
crayfish	*Kriibsen*
green bean soup	*Bou'neschlupp*
nettle soup	*Brennesselszopp*
pike in green liquor	*Hiecht mat Kraïderzooss*
pork in aspic	*Jhelli*
potato dumplings	*Gromperekniddeln*
potato soup	*Gromperenzopp*
tripe	*Kuddelfleck*
trout in Riesling sauce	*F'rell am Rèisleck*

For useful phrases in French, see page 521; for phrases in German see page 525.

National Flag

Essential for Travelers

● Required   ● Recommended   ● Not required

Passport	●
Visa (check regulations before you travel)	●
Travel, medical insurance	●
Round-trip or onward airline ticket	●
Local currency	●
Traveler's checks	●
Credit cards	●
First-aid kit and medicines	●
Inoculations	●

Essential for Drivers*

Driver's license	●
International Driving Permit	●
Car insurance (for nonrental cars)	●
Car registration (for nonrental cars)	●

*see also *Driving* section

Important Addresses

The Netherlands Board of Tourism & Conventions
215 Park Avenue South
Suite 2005
New York, NY 10003
☎ (917) 370-7360
www.holland.com

Nederlands Bureau voor Toerisme & Congressen – NBTC (Netherlands Board of Tourism & Conventions – NBTC)
Prinses Catharina-Amaliastraat 5,
2496 XD Den Haag
The Netherlands
☎ 070 370 5705
www.holland.com

American Embassy
Lange Voorhout 102
2514 EJ The Hague, The Netherlands
☎ 070 310 2209
http://thehague.usembassy.gov

Customs

✔ **Duty-free limits on goods brought in from non-European Union countries:**
200 cigarettes or 100 cigarillos or 50 cigars or 250 g. tobacco; 2 L. wine; 1 L. alcohol over 22% volume or 2 L. alcohol under 22% volume or sparkling wine and 4 L. still wine, 16 L. beer; plus any other goods/gifts to the value of €430 if arriving by air or sea, €300 if arriving overland (€150 for travelers under 15). There is no limit on the importation of tax-paid goods bought within the E.U. if they are for your own use. Currency worth more than €10,000 (or equivalent) must be declared.

✗ No unlicensed drugs, weapons, ammunition, obscene material, pets or other animals, counterfeit money or copied goods, meat or poultry. **For customs limits for returning U.S. citizens see page 16.**

Money

The Dutch currency is the euro (€), a currency shared by 18 other European Union countries. The euro is divided into 100 cents (¢). The denominations of euro bills are 5, 10, 20, 50, 100, 200 and 500. There are coins of 1, 2, 5, 10, 20 and 50¢ and €1 and €2. ATMs are plentiful and credit, debit and prepaid cards are accepted in hotels, large stores and upscale restaurants; check first in small or rural establishments. It is a good idea to carry a mix of large and small euro denominations.

Tips and Gratuities

Restaurants (service is always included)	change
Cafés/bars (service is always included)	change
Taxis (service is always included)	change
Porters	change
Hairdressers	change
Chambermaids	change
Restroom attendants	€1
Cloakroom attendants	none

The Netherlands

Communications

Post Offices

Buy stamps *(postzegels)* at a post office *(postkantoor* or *Post NL)*, tobacco shop, newsstand, souvenir shop or vending machines in

post offices. If you are buying from a counter make sure you are in a line for stamps. Mailboxes have two slots; foreign mail should be dropped into the slot marked *Overige*. Hours

for out-of-town post offices may vary.

Telephones

You can use cash (uncommon), credit cards and prepaid phone cards *(telefoonkaart)* to make calls. Phone cards can be bought from post offices, VVV tourist offices and shops displaying the phone-card symbol. Orange-and-gray-colored booths require a different phone card, available from Wizzl shops and railroad ticket offices. Calls

also can be made from post offices and *KPN Telehouse* booths. Check overseas cell-phone usage with your provider.

Phoning inside The Netherlands

All Dutch telephone numbers in this book include an area code; dial the number listed. To call the operator dial 0800 0410.

Phoning The Netherlands from abroad

The country code for The Netherlands is 31. Dutch numbers in this book do not include the country code; include the country code if you are phoning from another country. To phone The Netherlands from the United States or Canada, omit the first zero from the Dutch number and dial the prefix 011 31. Example: 011 223 3445 becomes 011 31 11 223 3445.

Phoning from The Netherlands

To phone the United States or Canada, prefix the area code and number with 00 1. Example: (111) 222-3333 becomes 00 1 111 222-3333. To call international information dial 0900 8418 (toll call). For national information dial 0900 8008 (toll call).

Emergency telephone numbers

General emergencies **112**
Police *(politie)* **112**
Fire service *(brandweer)* **112**
Ambulance *(ziekenwagen)* **112**
Emergency calls are free from phone booths.

Hours of Operation

- Stores Mon.–Sat.
- Offices Mon.–Fri.
- Banks Mon.–Fri.
- Post Offices Mon.–Fri.
- Museums/Monuments. Mon.–Sat..
- Pharmacies Mon.–Fri.

7 8 9 10 11 12 1 2 3 4 5 6 7

Stores open at 11 a.m. on Monday and close at 5 p.m. on Saturday. In Amsterdam many stores open Sunday noon–7 and in The Hague and Rotterdam noon–5. In other Dutch cities stores open one Sunday a month. Larger city stores stay open until 9 p.m. on Thursday or Friday. In rural areas many stores close for lunch.

Banks generally open at 1 p.m. on Mondays.

Post offices also are open 9–noon or 12:30 on Saturday. Some city post offices stay open into the evening (Thursday or Friday).

Museums and **monuments** usually are open 1–5 on Sunday; some may close on Monday. In rural areas they may be closed October through March.

National Holidays

Banks, businesses and most stores close on these days, except for Good Friday, when most shops remain open.

Jan. 1	New Year's Day
Mar./Apr.	Good Friday
Mar./Apr.	Easter Monday
Apr. 27	King's Day. Celebration of the birthday of King Willem-Alexander
May 5	Liberation Day (occurs every 5 years; next in 2019)
May/Jun.	Ascension Day
May/Jun.	Pentecost Monday
Dec. 25	Christmas Day
Dec. 26	St. Stephen's Day

Photography

The Dutch climate is essentially maritime; conditions for outdoor photography are gentle but changeable. Some museums do not allow photography; check before taking pictures. Camera batteries are widely available. Digital equipment and printing services are available in towns and cities.

Health

Medical Insurance
➕ Private medical insurance is recommended. U.S. and Canadian visitors can receive emergency treatment, but are charged if admitted to a hospital *(ziekenhuis)*. Doctors *(dokter)* are listed at the beginning of the telephone directory; English is widely spoken throughout the medical profession in The Netherlands.
Tourist Medical Service: doctor 📞 020 592 3355.

Dental Services
⭕ Dentists charge for treatment and can be expensive; check if this is covered by your medical insurance. Look in the telephone directory, or ask about local English-speaking dentists at your hotel or embassy.

Sun Advice
☀️ The Netherlands' maritime climate is not one of extremes, but precautions against sunburn should be taken from June through August.

Drugs
💊 For nonprescription medicines go to a pharmacy *(drogisterij)*. If you need prescription medicines you will have to go to an *apotheek*, where staff also are trained to treat minor ailments. If you need medicine after regular hours, information about all-night facilities is posted at all pharmacies.

Safe Water
💧 Tap water is safe to drink throughout The Netherlands. However, mineral water also is widely available.

Restrooms

🚻 There are not many public restrooms, although you will usually find adequate and clean facilities in museums, department stores and roadside service areas. Cafés provide restrooms for the use of customers; buy a drink if you need to use them.

Electricity

🔌 The Netherlands has a 230-volt power supply. Electrical sockets take plugs with two round pins. American appliances will need a plug adapter and will require a transformer if they do not have a dual-voltage facility.

National Transportation

Train *(Trein)*
 The Netherlands Railways, or *Nederlandse Spoorwegen (NS)*, network is fast, clean, modern, punctual and inexpensive. Information in English is widely available from stations; 📞 0900 9296 (toll call) for international train service, 📞 0900 9292 (toll call) for all domestic transportation services; www.ns.nl.

Bus *(Bus)*
 Bus travel is well-organized, with many connections to trains (bus and railroad stations are usually next to each other). If you're planning several trips ask for the *Nationale Buswijzer*, which provides maps and full route details; 📞 0900 9292 (toll call) for information. The Eurolines European bus network operates in The Netherlands 📞 088 076 1700.

Ferry *(Veerboot)*
 There are ferry services from the mainland across the Waddenzee to the Wadden islands (from Den Helder for Texel; Harlingen for Vlieland and Terschelling; Holwerd for Ameland; and Lauwersoog for Schiermonnikoog), and in summer services between the islands. For details about canal trips, contact VVV tourist information centers.

Driving

Drive on the right

Speed Limits
Police can impose on-the-spot fines.

🚸 Limited-access highways *(autoweg)*
100 k.p.h. (62 m.p.h.) or **120 k.p.h. (74 m.p.h.)**

 Main roads
80 k.p.h. (49 m.p.h.)

🔲 Urban areas
50 k.p.h. (31 m.p.h.)

Seat Belts
 Must be worn in front and back seats at all times. Children must use a suitable restraint system for their height/weight.

Blood Alcohol
🔋 The legal blood alcohol limit is 0.05%. Random breath tests on drivers are carried out frequently, especially late at night, and the penalties for offenders are severe.

The Netherlands

Driving (continued)

Tolls

There are no highway tolls in The Netherlands, but there are tolls for the Dordtse Kil tunnel near Dordrecht and the Westerschelde tunnel.

Car Rental

The leading car-rental firms have offices at airports and train stations. Hertz offers discounted rates for AAA members (see page 15). For reservations:

	United States	Netherlands
Alamo	(877) 222-9075	020 683 2123
Avis	(800) 331-1084	088 284 7020
Budget	(800) 472-3325	088 284 7620
Hertz	(800) 654-3001	020 502 0240

Fuel

Many gas stations are self-service and 24-hour facilities are common. Unleaded gas *(Super-Plus* and *Euro-Super)*, lead-replacement fuel and diesel are available, and credit cards are accepted at most garages.

AAA Affiliated Motoring Club

Koninklijke Nederlandse Toeristenbond (ANWB) Wassenaarseweg 220, 2596 The Hague ☎ 088 269 2222; www.anwb.nl. If you break down while driving, telephone ☎ 088 269 2888 (ANWB breakdown service, toll free). Not all automobile clubs offer full services to AAA members.

Breakdowns and Accidents

There are yellow 24-hour emergency phones at regular intervals on highways. All accidents involving personal injury must be reported to the police; ☎ 112. Most car-rental firms provide their own free rescue service; if your car is rented, follow the instructions given in the documentation. Use of a car-repair service other than those authorized by your rental company may violate your agreement.

Other Information

The minimum age for driving a car is 18 (usually between 21 and 25 for car-rental firms). An International Driving Permit (IDP) is recommended; some car-rental firms require it, and it can speed up formalities if you are involved in an accident. A Green Card (international motor insurance certificate) is recommended if you are driving a private car; see page 15 for more information. Drivers should yield to vehicles approaching from the right. In built-up areas, trams and buses have the right of way when leaving bus stops. Beware of cyclists and skaters.

Useful Words and Phrases

It is not easy to reproduce the guttural sounds that make up the Dutch language. There are many similarities between German and Dutch, although the Dutch go to lengths to point out the differences. English is spoken fluently by a large proportion of the population, who learn foreign languages from an early age.

Dutch pronunciation is similar to English, with some variations:

j as in *y*ellow
v like an f as in *f*ar
w like a v as in *v*at
ng as in bri*ng*
nj as in o*ni*on

Double consonants keep their separate sounds: for instance, k and n together are never pronounced as in the English "know."

Some letters and diphthongs are tricky. If the letter is doubled, the vowel sound is lengthened. For example:

a as in s*a*p,	*aa* as in *a*rt
e as in l*e*t,	*ee* as in f*a*te
o as in m*o*p,	*oo* as in m*o*pe
oe as in f*oo*d	
au, ou and *ui* as in h*ow*	
ei and *ij* as in l*i*ne	
ch as in Ba*ch*	
tje as in *ch*urch	
tie as in *tee*	

Do you speak English?	*Spreekt u Engels?*
excuse me	*pardon*
hello	*hallo or dag*
goodbye	*tot ziens*
yes/no	*ja/nee*
how much is?	*wat kost?*
I want…	*ik wil…*
I don't understand	*Ik begrijp het niet*
open/closed	*open/gesloten*
please	*alstublieft*
thank you	*bedankt*
ticket (one-way/ round trip)	*enkele reis retour*
where's the…?	*waar is…?*
the airport	*de luchthoven*
the room	*de kamer*
the breakfast	*het ontbijt*
the dinner	*het diner*
May I order?	*Mag ik even bestellen?*
steak	*biefstuk*
bread	*brood*
chicken	*kip*
coffee/tea	*koffie/thee*
dish of the day	*dagschotel*
lamb	*lamsvlees*
pork	*varkensvlees*
sandwich	*broodje*
wine	*wijn*

Norway

National Flag

Essential for Travelers

● Required　● Recommended　● Not required

Passport	●
Visa (check regulations before you travel)	●
Travel, medical insurance	●
Round-trip or onward airline ticket	●
Local currency	●
Traveler's checks	●
Credit cards	●
First-aid kit and medicines	●
Inoculations	●

Essential for Drivers*

Driver's license	●
International Driving Permit	●
Car insurance (for nonrental cars)	●
Car registration (for nonrental cars)	●

*see also *Driving* section

Important Addresses

Innovation Norway
655 Third Avenue, Suite 1810
New York, NY 10017-9111
☎ (212) 885-9700
www.visitnorway.com

Innovation Norway
P.O. Box 448, Sentrum
N-0158 Oslo, Norway
☎ 22 00 25 00
www.visitnorway.com

American Embassy
Henrik Ibsens Gate 48
N-0255 Oslo, Norway
☎ 22 44 85 50 or 21 30 85 40
http://norway.usembassy.gov
🕐 Mon.–Fri. 8:30–5

Customs

✔ **Duty-free limits on goods brought in from non-European countries:**
200 cigarettes or 250g. tobacco and 200 cigarette papers; 1 L. alcohol 23–60%; 1.5 L. alcohol up to 22%; 2 L. beer. If you have no alcohol 23–60% you are allowed 1.5 L. extra alcohol up to 22%, or 5L. beer if no other alcohol. Also goods to the value of Kr6,000, which must include your tobacco and alcohol allowances. You must be 20 and over to bring in spirits and 18 and over to bring in wine, beer and tobacco products. You may import or export local or foreign currency to the value of Kr25,000. Larger amounts must be declared to the customs authorities. This does not apply to traveler's checks.

✗ No unlicensed drugs, weapons, ammunition, fireworks, obscene material, pets or other animals, counterfeit money or copied goods, alcohol over 60%, meat or poultry.
For customs limits for returning U.S. citizens see page 16.

Money

Norway's currency is the krone (NOK or Kr), which is divided into 100 øre. The denominations of krone bills are 50, 100, 200, 500 and 1,000. There are coins of Kr1, Kr5, Kr10 and Kr20. You can exchange dollars or traveler's checks *(reisesjekk)* at an exchange office *(vekslekontor)*, post office *(posten)* or hotel; you will need ID. Credit, debit and prepaid cards are widely accepted in hotels, main stores and more expensive restaurants. ATMs are readily available for withdrawal of local currency and it is a good idea to carry a mix of large and small krone denominations for everyday expenses.

Tips and Gratuities

Restaurants (service is included)	5–10%
Cafés/bars (service is included)	5–10%
Taxis (service is included)	10% (optional)
Porters	Kr5 per bag
Hairdressers	change
Chambermaids	Kr5
Restroom attendants	Kr3

| Oslo | New York | Chicago | Denver | Los Angeles | Time zones | 551 |
| 12:00 noon | − 6 hrs | − 7 hrs | − 8 hrs | − 9 hrs | | |

Norway

Communications

Post Offices

Buy stamps *(frimerker)* at a post office *(posten)*, a newsstand/tobacconist such as Narvesen or MIX or from a hotel. Hours for out-of-town post offices may vary. Mailboxes are red.

Telephones

You can use cash or a credit card to make a call in Norway. Most phone booths have direct dialing for international calls. Use Kr1, Kr5, Kr10 and Kr20 coins (minimum charge Kr5).

Some card phones accept credit cards. International phone calls are provided by BBG, call (toll-free) ☎ 800 33 200 and follow instructions. Check overseas cell-phone usage with your provider.

Phoning inside Norway
There are no area codes in Norway; all numbers are eight digits: dial the number that is listed. To call the operator dial 117; for directory inquiry information (Norway, Sweden and Denmark) dial 1881.

Phoning Norway from abroad
The country code for Norway is 47. Note that Norwegian numbers in this book do not include the country code; you will need to prefix this number if you are phoning from another country. To phone Norway from the United States or Canada, simply add the prefix 011 47. Example: 11 22 33 44 becomes 011 47 11 22 33 44.

Phoning from Norway
To phone the United States or Canada from Norway, prefix the area code and number with 00 1. Example: (111) 222-3333 becomes 00 1 111 222-3333. To call international information dial 1882. For the international operator dial 115.

Emergency telephone numbers
Police *(politi)* **112**
Fire service *(brannvesen)* **110**
Ambulance *(ambulanse)* **113**
Sea emergency **120**
Emergency calls are free from phone booths.

Hours of Operation

- Stores Mon.–Sat.
- Offices Mon.–Fri.
- Banks Mon.–Fri.
- Post Offices Mon.–Fri.
- Museums/Monuments
- Pharmacies Mon.–Fri.

7 8 9 10 11 12 1 2 3 4 5 6 7

On Thursday most **stores** open at 9 a.m. and remain open until between 6 and 8 p.m. On Saturday most stores are closed between 1 and 3.

Supermarkets are generally open Mon.–Fri. 9–8 or 9, Sat. 9–4 or 6. Many shopping complexes are open until 8 p.m. (4 or 6 on Sat.). Kiosks are open daily and stay open until 10 or 11. Most stores are closed on Sunday. Stores around tourist attractions may have special hours.

Offices usually close at 3 p.m. in summer.

Banks generally close half an hour earlier from mid-May to mid-September, but stay open until 5 p.m. on Thursday all year and are closed weekends.

Some **post offices** may not open until 9 and close at 4. They are open 9–1 on Saturday.

Museums often close on Monday, and hours of operation may be reduced during the winter.

Pharmacies are open the same hours as stores.

National Holidays

Banks, businesses and most stores close on these days.

Jan. 1	New Year's Day
Mar./Apr.	Maundy Thursday
Mar./Apr.	Good Friday
Mar./Apr.	Easter Monday
May 1	Labor Day
May 17	Constitution Day
May	Ascension Day
May/Jun.	Pentecost Sunday and Monday
Dec. 25	Christmas Day
Dec. 26	St. Stephen's Day

Photography

Spectacular shots are possible in fjord country if the weather is right (bear in mind that Norway is susceptible to poor light, especially during the winter). Photography is not permitted in some museums and places of historic interest – check before taking pictures. Camera batteries are readily available in towns. Digital photography equipment and facilities for downloading and printing also are widely available.

Health

Medical Insurance

U.S. and Canadian visitors will be charged for medical assistance, including treatment in a hospital *(sykehus)* emergency room. For medical emergency service in Oslo contact Oslo kommune Legevakt, ☎ 22 93 22 93 (24 hours). For general practitioners, see *Lege* in the phone directory.

Dental Services

A dentist *(tannlege)* will charge you for treatment, so check your medical insurance coverage. Many dentists speak English; ask a tourist office or your hotel to find one for you. For after-hours emergency treatment *(tannlegevakten)* in Oslo contact Oslo kommunale Tannlegevakt (☎ 22 67 30 00).

Sun Advice

Despite its northerly location, Norway has warm weather during the summer months. Use an appropriate sunscreen.

Drugs

A pharmacy *(apotek)* sells prescription medicines; many pharmacists speak English. Information about the nearest late-night or 24-hour facility is posted at all pharmacies. For a 24-hour pharmacy in Oslo go to Vitus Apotek, Jernbanetorget 4B, near Oslo Central Station (☎ 23 35 81 00).

Safe Water

Tap water is safe to drink throughout Norway. Mineral water *(mineralvann)* is widely available.

Restrooms

Public restrooms *(toaletter)* are easy to find. Facilities are separate for men *(herrer)* and women *(damer)*, and are identified by symbols or a "WC" sign. They are invariably clean and modern, and a small charge (usually Kr5) may be made.

Electricity

Norway has a 220-volt power supply. Electrical sockets take plugs with two round pins. American appliances will need a plug adapter and will require a transformer if they do not have a dual-voltage facility.

National Transportation

Train *(Tog)*

The Norges Statsbaner (NSB) network operates as far north as the Arctic Circle. Travel is comfortable but not cheap. Reservations are recommended on train trips and compulsory on long-distance and overnight trains; (☎ 81 50 08 88, press 9 for information in English; for international journeys ☎ 81 50 08 88, press 4), or go online at www.nsb.no).

Bus *(Buss)*

Buses are an inexpensive way to travel in Norway. NOR-WAY Bussekspress (☎ 81 54 44 44; www.nor-way.no) is the national operator. Buy your ticket on board; it is not necessary to book in advance.

Ferry *(Ferje)*

Norway relies heavily on ferries and express boats/catamarans, which connect with trains and buses. Car ferries operate on a first-come, first-served system; payment is made on board. Some waterways have ferry services. *Hurtigruten*, a grand coastal steamer, links Bergen with Kirkenes, in northern Norway, calling at 34 ports en route over an 11-day round trip (☎ 81 00 30 30; www.hurtigruten.com).

Driving

Drive on the right

Speed Limits

Speed controls are stringent. Police can impose on-the-spot fines.

Limited-access highways *(motorvei)* **90 k.p.h. (56 m.p.h.)** or **100 k.p.h. (62 m.p.h.)**

Main roads **80 k.p.h. (49 m.p.h.)**

Urban areas **50 k.p.h. (31 m.p.h.)**; usually **30 k.p.h. (18 m.p.h.)** in residential areas

Seat Belts

Must be worn in front and back seats at all times. Children under 4 feet 5 inches or 79 pounds must use child safety equipment.

Blood Alcohol

The legal blood alcohol limit is 0.02%. Random breath tests on drivers are carried out frequently, especially late at night, and the penalties for offenders are extremely severe.

Norway

Driving (continued)

Tolls

There are tolls to enter Bergen, Oslo, Stavanger and Trondheim, as well as some highways, bridges and tunnels.

Car Rental

The leading car-rental firms *(bilutleie)* have offices at airports and train stations. Hertz offers discounted rates for AAA members (see page 15). For reservations:

	United States	Norway
Alamo	(877) 222-9075	22 83 12 42 (Europcar)
Avis	(800) 331-1212	81 53 30 44
Budget	(800) 527-0700	81 56 06 00
Hertz	(800) 654-3001	67 16 80 00

Fuel *(Olje)*

Unleaded gas is 95 and 98 octane; diesel also is available. Gas stations *(bensinstasjon)* have varying opening hours and there are few in remote areas, so keep your eye on the gauge.

AAA Affiliated Motoring Club

Norges Automobil-forbund (NAF)
Østensjøveen 14, Postboks 6682, Etterstad, NO-0609 Oslo ☎ 08505 (from abroad: 926 08505); www.naf.no. If you break down while driving, call ☎ 08 505 (24-hour NAF breakdown service). A fee is charged for the service. Not all automobile clubs offer full services to AAA members.

Breakdowns and Accidents

NAF patrols main roads and mountain passes mid-June to mid-August. There are 24-hour emergency phones on all highways. All accidents involving personal injury must be reported to the police (☎ 112). Most car-rental firms provide their own free rescue service; if you break down follow the instructions given in the documentation. Use of an unauthorized car-repair service may violate your rental agreement. You must carry a warning triangle in your car.

Other Information

The minimum age for driving a car is 18 (may be higher for car-rental firms). An International Driving Permit (IDP) is recommended; some car-rental firms require it, and it can speed up formalities if you are involved in an accident. A Green Card (international motor insurance certificate) is highly recommended if you are driving a private car (see page 15 for more information). You are required by law to use dimmed headlights at all times when driving. Snow tires and chains are advised from November 1 until the first Sunday after Easter (mid-Oct. through Apr. 30 in northern Norway); rent tires and chains from NAF or at border crossings.

Useful Words and Phrases

There are two official, and similar forms of Norwegian. Riksmal, or Bokmal ("book language"), is an old form of Norwegian. Athough many bureaucrats speak in Bokmal, it is mostly used in its written form. Landsmål, or Nynorsk, has its roots in Old Norse dialects but developed out of the wave of Norwegian nationalism in the 19th century. You will encounter both during your stay; it is not uncommon for speakers to use a combination of both, but writing rarely mixes styles. The phrases below are translated into Bokmal:

Do you speak English?	*Snakker du engelsk?*
excuse me	*unnskyld meg*
hello	*god dag*
goodbye	*ha det bra*
how much?	*hvor mye?*
I would like	*Jeg vil gjerne*
I don't understand	*Jeg forstår ikke*
nonsmoking	*røyking forbudt*
open/closed	*åpen/stengt*
please	*vær så snill*
thank you	*takk*
ticket (one-way/ round trip)	*enkeltbillett/ tur-returbillett*
Where is…?	*Hvor er…?*
yes/no	*ja/nei*
early/late	*tidlig/sent*
hot/cold	*varm/kald*
big/small	*stor/liten*
good/bad	*god/dårlig*
airport	*flyplass*
you're welcome	*vær så god*
the restaurant	**restaurant**
beef	*oksekjøtt*
bread	*brød*
breakfast	*frokost*
the check	*regningen*
chicken	*kylling*
coffee/tea	*kaffe/te*
cookies	*kjeks*
cranberries	*tranebær*
dessert	*dessert*
entree	*hovedrett*
fish	*fisk*
herring	*sild*
hot-dog	*pølse*
ice cream	*is*
lamb	*lammekjøtt*
lobster	*hummer*
pork	*svinekjøtt*
salad	*salat*
sandwich	*smørbrød*
seafood	*sjømat*
starter	*forrett*
waffles	*vafler*
wine	*vin*

National Flag

Essential for Travelers

● Required ● Recommended ● Not required

Passport	●
Visa (check regulations before you travel)	●
Travel, medical insurance	●
Round-trip or onward airline ticket	●
Local currency	●
Traveler's checks	●
Credit cards	●
First-aid kit and medicines	●
Inoculations	●

Essential for Drivers*

Driver's license	●
International Driving Permit	●
Car insurance (for nonrental cars)	●
Car registration (for nonrental cars)	●

*see also *Driving* section

Important Addresses

Portuguese National Tourist Office
886 Second Avenue, 8th Floor
New York, NY 10017
☎ (646) 723-0200
www.visitportugal.com

Turismo de Portugal (Portugal Tourist Office)
Rua Ivone Silve, Lote 6, 1050-124 Lisboa
☎ 211 140 200
www.visitportugal.com

American Embassy
Avenida Forças Armadas
1600-081 Lisbon, Portugal
☎ 217 273 300
http://portugal.usembassy.gov
🕐 Mon.–Fri. 8–5

Customs

✔ **Duty-free limits on goods brought in from non-European Union countries:**
200 cigarettes or 100 cigarillos or 50 cigars or 250 g. tobacco; 4 L. wine; 1 L. alcohol over 22% volume or 2 L. alcohol under 22% volume, 16 L. beer; 60 ml. perfume; 250 ml. toilet water; plus any other duty-free goods (including gifts) to the value of €430 (€300 if you enter by road, rail, private boat or plane). Local or foreign currency (including coins, notes, traveler's checks or other monetary securities) exceeding €10,000 must be declared on entry and when leaving the country. There is no limit on the importation of tax-paid goods purchased within the European Union if they are for personal use.

✘ No unlicensed drugs, weapons, ammunition, obscene material, pets or other animals, counterfeit money or copied goods, meat or poultry.
For customs limits for returning U.S. citizens see page 16.

Money

Portugal's currency is the euro (€), a currency shared by 18 other European Union countries. The euro is divided into 100 cents (¢). The denominations of euro bills are 5, 10, 20, 50, 100, 200 and 500. There are coins of 1, 2, 5, 10, 20 and 50¢ and €1 and €2. Credit, debit and prepaid cards are widely accepted. ATMs are plentiful throughout Portugal. It is a good idea to carry a mix of large and small euro denominations.

Tips and Gratuities

Restaurants (where service is not included)	5–10%
Cafés/bars (where service is not included)	change
Taxis	10%
Porters	50¢–€1
Hairdressers	€3–€5
Chambermaids	€3–€5
Restroom attendants	50¢
Cloakroom attendants	50¢

Portugal

Communications

Post Offices

Buy stamps *(selos)* at a post office *(correios)*, identified by a sign showing a white horse on a red background. You may also see the words "Correios." Hours for out-of-town post offices may vary.

Telephones

You can use coins or a phone card, available from post offices, in a phone booth *(cabine telefónico)*. Public phones are easily found on the street and in cafés, main post offices

and at some newsstands and tourist offices. Most public phones also take international credit cards. Check overseas cell-phone usage with your provider.

Phoning inside Portugal
All Portuguese telephone numbers in this book include an area code; dial the number listed from anywhere in the country. To call an international operator dial 120. To call information dial 118.

Phoning Portugal from abroad
The country code for Portugal is 351. Note that Portuguese numbers in this book do not include the country code; you will need to prefix this number if you are phoning from another country. To phone Portugal from the United States or Canada dial the prefix 011 351. Example: 111 223 344 becomes 011 351 111 223 344.

Phoning from Portugal
To phone the United States or Canada from Portugal, prefix the area code and number with 00 1. Example: (111) 222-3333 becomes 00 1 111 222-3333. For an international operator dial 117. To call international information dial 1820.

Emergency telephone numbers
Police *(polícia)* **112**
Fire service *(bombeiros)* **112**
Ambulance *(ambulância)* **112**
Emergency calls are free from phone booths.

Hours of Operation

- ■ Stores Mon.–Sat.
- ■ Offices Mon.–Fri.
- ■ Banks Mon.–Fri.
- ■ Post Offices Mon.–Fri.
- ■ Museums/Monuments
- ■ Pharmacies Mon.–Fri.

7 8 9 10 11 12 1 2 3 4 5 6 7

Most **stores** and **pharmacies** close at 1 p.m. on Saturday and are not open on Sunday. Stores in large malls are open Mon.–Sun. 10 a.m.–midnight. Grocery stores are usually open until 9 p.m.

Post offices and **banks** in rural areas of Portugal often close for lunch. A few banks in Lisbon stay open until 6 p.m.

Museums generally close on Monday (others close on Wednesday), and the smaller sights may have shorter hours of operation off-season.

National Holidays

Banks, businesses and most stores close on these days. There also are many local festivals when everything comes to a halt.

Jan. 1	New Year's Day
Feb./Mar.	Shrove Tuesday (unofficial holiday but widely observed)
Mar./Apr.	Good Friday
Apr. 25	Liberty Day
May 1	Labor Day
Jun. 10	Portugal Day
Aug. 15	Assumption of the Virgin
Dec. 8	Immaculate Conception
Dec. 25	Christmas Day

As part of the austerity drive, the Portuguese government has suspended the following national holidays for a period of five years, starting in 2013:

May/Jun.	Corpus Christi
Oct. 5	Republic Day
Nov. 1	All Saints' Day
Dec. 1	Independence Day

Photography

Finding adequate light is rarely a problem in Portugal; rise early for atmospheric shots of fishing ports, villages, castles and the mountains. You will not be permitted to photograph at airports or military areas, and ask permission before taking pictures in museums and churches. Digital peripherals and commercial digital printers are widely available, along with batteries.

Health

Medical Insurance
U.S. and Canadian visitors will be charged for emergency medical treatment, consultation with a doctor and/or admittance to a hospital *(hospital)*. Ask at a tourist office or your hotel to find an English-speaking doctor.

Dental Services
Dental treatment is charged for in Portugal. Ask at a tourist office or your hotel for a list of English-speaking dentists. Check whether dental treatment is covered by your medical insurance.

Sun Advice
The sun is strong during summer (and some days in winter), particularly in the south. Do not be deceived by the cooling breeze off the Atlantic. Avoid prolonged exposure and protect yourself with a sunscreen or cover up.

Drugs
Prescription medicines are available from a pharmacy *(farmácia)*, distinguished by a large green cross. Pharmacists can prescribe remedies for minor ailments, and many speak English. Information about the nearest late-night or 24-hour facility is posted at all pharmacies.

Safe Water
Tap water is generally safe, but does not always taste too pleasant. It is advisable to drink bottled water *(agua mineral)*, especially in rural areas; *sem gas* means noncarbonated, *com gas* means carbonated.

Restrooms

Public restrooms *(casa de banho* or *lavabos)* are easy to find. Ladies' *(senhoras)* restrooms may occasionally charge a small fee and are generally clean. Men's *(homens)* restrooms are usually free.

Electricity

Portugal has a 220-volt power supply. Electrical sockets take plugs with two round pins. American appliances will need a plug adapter and a transformer if they do not have a dual-voltage facility.

National Transportation

Train *(Comboios)*
The Caminhos de Ferro Portugueses (CP) operates three types of service: *regional* and *Intercidade* (which both stop at most stations) and *Alfa Pendular* (express between Braga in the north and Faro in the south). For information ☎ 707 210 220 (outside Portugal); www.cp.pt.

Bus *(Autocarros)*
Rede Expressos operates a network to all major destinations with connections to smaller towns (☎ 707 223 344; www.rede-expressos.pt). Buses are modern and comfortable. Several companies also maintain an extensive network in the regions of the country.

Ferry *(Barcos)*
Ferries cross the Rio Tejo from Cais do Sodré to Cacilhas, Seixal and Montijo; Terreiro do Paço to Barreiro; Belém to Trafaria; and Porto to Brandão (☎ 210 422 411; www.transporteslisboa.pt). From Setúbal ferries cross the Rio Sado to the Tróia peninsula. Tickets can be bought at the boat stations' ticket offices.

Driving

Drive on the right

Speed Limits
Police can impose on-the-spot fines.

 Limited-access highways *(autoestrada)* **120 k.p.h. (74 m.p.h.)**.
Minimum speed **50 k.p.h. (31 m.p.h.)**
Divided highways **100 k.p.h. (62 m.p.h.)**

 Main roads
90 k.p.h. (56 m.p.h.)

 Urban areas
50 k.p.h. (31 m.p.h.)

Seat Belts
Must be worn in front and back seats at all times.

Blood Alcohol
 The legal blood alcohol limit is 0.05%. Random breath tests on drivers are carried out frequently, especially late at night, and the penalties for offenders are severe.

Driving (continued)

Tolls

There are tolls on highways *(autoestrada)* in Portugal. Highway numbers are prefixed by the letter A. There are an increasing number of highways where tolls are calculated electronically and paid through pre-paid devices or by a credit card registered with the payment authorities. For information in English see www.portugaltolls.pt.

Car Rental

The leading car-rental firms have offices at airports and train stations. Hertz offers discounted rates for AAA members (see page 15). For reservations:

	United States	Portugal
Alamo	(877) 222 9075	218 401 163
		(Enterprise)
Avis	(800) 331-1084	800 201 002
Budget	(800) 472-3325	808 25 26 27
Hertz	(800) 654-3001	808 202 038

Fuel *(Gasolina)*

Gas and diesel are sold in liters, and most stations *(posto de gasolina)* are self-service. Gas stations, generally open daily 7 a.m.–10 p.m. (some 24 hours), are not as common in the more remote northern areas of Portugal. Credit cards are mostly accepted.

AAA Affiliated Motoring Club

Automóvel Club de Portugal (ACP)
Rua Rosa Araújo 24–26, 1250–195 Lisbon
☎ 213 180 100 or 707 509 510 for 24-hour global assistance; www.acp.pt. Not all automobile clubs offer full services to AAA members.

Breakdowns and Accidents

There are 24-hour emergency phones at regular intervals on highways. If you are involved in an accident ☎ 112 for police assistance. Most car-rental firms provide their own free rescue service; if your car is rented, follow the instructions given in the documentation. Use of a car-repair service other than those authorized by your rental company may violate your agreement.

Other Information

The minimum age for car rental is 21 (some rental firms stipulate 23). An International Driving Permit (IDP) is a good idea; some car-rental firms require it, and it can speed up formalities if you are involved in an accident. A Green Card (international motor insurance certificate) is essential if you are driving a private car; see page 15 for more information. You are required by law to carry photographic ID at all times. Carrying a fluorescent jacket is advised for all drivers of non-Portuguese registered vehicles. It is compulsory for Portuguese registered vehicles.

Useful Words and Phrases

Portuguese is a Latin language, so an acquaintance with French, Spanish or Italian makes written Portuguese quite easy to understand. Understanding spoken Portuguese, however, is more difficult. Although on paper Portuguese words look similar to Spanish, they actually sound very different. English is widely spoken in tourist areas, but using a few Portuguese words will make your trip more rewarding.

Do you speak English?	*Fala Inglês?*
I'm sorry	*desculpe*
hello/goodbye	*olá/adeus*
yes/no	*sim/não*
how much?	*quanto?*
I am American	*sou Americano*
I would like a	*queria um/uma*
I don't understand	*não entendo*
nonsmoking	*não fumadores*
okay	*está bem*
today/tomorrow	*hoje/amanhã*
open/closed	*aberto/fechado*
right/left	*direita/esquerda*
near/far	*perto/longe*
big/little	*grande/pequeno*
cheap/expensive	*barato/caro*
please	*se faz favor*
thank you	*obrigado (m.)/ obrigada (f.)*
ticket	*bilhete*
one way/return	*ida/ida e volta*
where is…?	*onde é…?*
the hotel	***hotel***
breakfast	*pequeno almoço*
lunch	*almoço*
dinner	*jantar*
I have a reservation	*tenho uma marcação*
key	*chave*
for one night	*para uma noite*
room	*quarto*
shower	*duche*
with bathroom	*com casa de banho*
the restaurant	***restaurante***
beef	*bife*
bread	*pão*
cheese	*queijo*
the check	*a conta*
chicken	*frango*
coffee/tea	*café/chà*
dessert	*sobremesa*
dish of the day	*prato do dia*
fish	*peixe*
ham	*fiambre*
lamb	*carneiro*
pork	*porco*
starter	*entrada*
veal	*vitela*
wine	*vinho*
Is the service included?	*O serviço está incluido?*

Spain

National Flag

Essential for Travelers

● Required ● Recommended ● Not required

Passport	●
Visa (check regulations before you travel)	●
Travel, medical insurance	●
Round-trip or onward airline ticket	●
Local currency	●
Traveler's checks	●
Credit cards	●
First-aid kit and medicines	●
Inoculations	●

Essential for Drivers*

Driver's license	●
International Driving Permit	●
Car insurance (for nonrental cars)	●
Car registration (for nonrental cars)	●
*see also *Driving* section	

Important Addresses

Tourist Office of Spain
60 East 42nd Street, Suite 5300
New York, NY 10165
☎ (212) 265-8822
www.spain.info
Visitors by appointment only

US Consulate Barcelona
Passeig Reina Elisenda de Montcada 23
08034 Barcelona, Spain
☎ 93 280 2227

American Embassy
Serrano 75
28006 Madrid, Spain
☎ 91 123 8866 (from within Spain);
703 439 2364 (from the U.S.)
http://madrid.usembassy.gov
Personal inquiries: Mon.–Fri. 8:30–1
Emergencies: ☎ 91 587 2200

Customs

✓ **Duty-free limits on goods brought in from non-European Union countries:**
200 cigarettes or 100 cigarillos or 50 cigars or 250 g. tobacco; 2 L. wine; 1 L. alcohol over 22% volume; 2 L. alcohol under 22% volume; 50 ml. perfume; plus any goods (including perfume and electronic goods) up to a value of €430 for air or sea travelers; up to €300 for other travelers. The import of currency of any denomination of €10,000 must be declared on arrival in Spain. There is no limit on the importation of tax-paid goods purchased within the European Union if they are for personal use.

✗ No unlicensed drugs, weapons, ammunition, obscene material, pets or other animals, counterfeit money or copied goods, meat or poultry.
For customs limits for returning U.S. citizens see page 16.

Money

Spain's currency is the euro (€), a currency shared by 18 other European Union countries. The euro is divided into 100 cents (¢). The denominations of euro bills are 5, 10, 20, 50, 100, 200 and 500. There are coins of 1, 2, 5, 10, 20 and 50¢ and €1 and €2. ATMs are plentiful and credit, debit and prepaid cards are accepted in hotels, large stores and upscale restaurants; check first in small or rural establishments. It is a good idea to carry a mix of large and small euro denominations.

Tips and Gratuities

Locals rarely tip, though they may add a few euros to a large bill. There are different expectations of visitors, however. If you receive good service, consider tipping as follows. Most hotel, restaurant and café checks will include a service charge.

Restaurants (service is normally included)	5–10%
Cafés/bars (service is normally included)	change
Taxis	5%
Porters, chambermaids	€1
Cloakroom attendants	change

Spain

Communications

Post Offices

Buy stamps *(sellos)* at a post office *(correos)*, a tobacconist *(estancos)* denoted by a "T" or at some hotels. Out-of-town post office hours may vary. Opening times for post offices are shorter in August.

Telephones

Few public telephones (except those in bars) accept coins. Most now operate with credit cards. Many public phone booths have instructions in English and lists of national and

international dialing codes posted inside them also.

In major cities, telecommunications stores offer email facilities. Check overseas cell-phone usage with your provider.

Phoning inside Spain

All Spanish phone numbers in this book include an area code; dial the number that is listed. To call the operator dial 11818.

Phoning Spain from abroad

The country code for Spain is 34. Note that Spanish numbers in this book do not include the Spanish country code; you will need to prefix this number if you are phoning from another country. To phone Spain from the United States or Canada dial the prefix 011 34. (Note that the number of digits in Spanish area codes varies.) Example: 11 122 3344 becomes 011 34 11 122 3344.

Phoning from Spain

To phone the United States or Canada from Spain, prefix the area code and number with 00 1. Example: (111) 222-3333 becomes 00 1 111 222-3333. To call international information dial 11825.

Emergency telephone numbers

General emergencies **112**
Police *(policía)* **112**
Fire service *(bomberos)* **112**
Ambulance *(ambulancia)* **112**
Emergency calls are free from phone booths.

Hours of Operation

- Stores Mon.–Sat.
- Offices Mon.–Fri.
- Banks Mon.–Fri.
- Post Offices Mon.–Fri.
- Museums/Monuments Tue.–Sat.
- Pharmacies Mon.–Fri.

```
  7  8  9  10 11 12  1  2  3  4  5  6  7
```

Department **stores** and grocery stores may operate the hours shown, especially in summer. Department stores are open Mon.–Sat. 10–10, and in Madrid also open the first Sun. of each month. In December stores in big towns also are open on Sundays. Business hours vary depending on season; many companies work *horas intensivas* (shorter, more intensive hours) from 8 to 2 or 3 in summer (particularly in August).

Some **banks** are open Saturdays 9–1 in winter. Most **museums** and **monuments** are closed on Monday, but many are open 9–2 on Sunday.

National Holidays

Banks, businesses and most stores close on these days. Days marked (*) are not national holidays but are celebrated in Catalonia, when shops and offices may close.

Jan. 1	New Year's Day
Jan. 6	Epiphany
Mar. 19	St. Joseph's Day (not Catalonia)
Mar./Apr.	Good Friday
***Mar./Apr.**	Easter Monday
May 1	Labor Day
***May/Jun.**	Pentecost Monday
***Jun. 24**	St. John's Day
Aug. 15	Assumption of the Virgin
***Sep. 11**	National Day (Catalonia)
***Sep. 24**	Our Lady of Mercy Day
Oct. 12	National Day
Nov. 1	All Saints' Day
Dec. 6	Constitution Day
Dec. 8	Immaculate Conception
Dec. 25	Christmas Day
***Dec. 26**	St. Stephen's Day
Dec. 31	New Year's Eve (some businesses close in the afternoon)

Photography

Take your pictures early in the morning or late in the evening. Ask permission before taking pictures in museums and churches. Digital camera equipment and printing facilities are widely available.

Health

Medical Insurance

U.S. and Canadian visitors can receive treatment in a hospital emergency room, but are charged if admitted to a bed. There also are private clinics, such as Unidad Médica (Conde de Aranda, Madrid ☎ 91 435 1823; www.unidadmedica.com), where English is spoken.

Dental Services

You will be charged for dental treatment, so check whether it is covered by your medical insurance. Dentists *(dentistas)* are listed in the *(páginas amarillas)* Yellow Pages.

Sun Advice

The sun is strong during summer, particularly in the south. Dress sensibly, avoid prolonged exposure and protect yourself with a sunscreen.

Drugs

Prescription medicines are available from pharmacies *(farmacias)*, designated by a red or green cross. Information about the nearest late-night or 24-hour facility is posted at all pharmacies.

Safe Water

Tap water is generally safe, although it can be heavily chlorinated. Mineral water *(agua mineral)* is inexpensive and is sold *con gas* (carbonated) and *sin gas* (noncarbonated). Drink plenty of fluids during hot weather.

Restrooms

Public restrooms *(servicios)* can usually be found in large department stores, museums and other places of interest to visitors. Elsewhere, restrooms may not be easy to find, but there is no charge. If you use the facilities in a bar you will be expected to buy a drink. Spanish words are *señores* for men and *señoras* for women.

Electricity

Most of Spain has a 220-volt power supply. Electrical sockets take plugs with two round pins. American appliances will need a plug adapter, and either a dual voltage facility or a transformer.

National Transportation

Train *(Tren)*

The Red Nacional de los Ferrocarriles Españoles (RENFE) rail network is inexpensive to use. There are express services for long-distance travel: Alaris, Euromed, Talgo 200 and AVE (reservations required/advisable for all). For information and reservations ☎ 902 320 320 (24 hours); www.renfe.com.

Bus *(Autobus)*

Spain has a good bus system. Ask at a tourist office for details. The Eurolines international bus service operates in Spain: ☎ 902 405 040 (Barcelona); www.eurolines.es.

Ferry *(Transbordador)*

Barcelona is the Mediterranean's biggest port and offers a regular ferry service to the Balearic islands. One of the largest ferry operators is Acciona Trasmediterranea: ☎ 902 45 46 45. "Mini-cruises" of two or three days operate from northern Spain to and from Britain; obtain details from a travel agent.

Driving

Drive on the right

Speed Limits

Police can impose on-the-spot fines.

 Limited-access highways *(autopistas)*
120 k.p.h. (74 m.p.h.)
Divided highways **100 k.p.h. (62 m.p.h.)**

 Main roads
100 k.p.h. (62 m.p.h.)

 Urban areas
50 k.p.h. (31 m.p.h.)

Seat belts

Must be worn in front and back seats at all times.

Blood Alcohol

The legal blood alcohol limit is 0.05% (the limit is 0.03% for drivers with less than 2 years' driving experience). Random breath tests on drivers are carried out frequently, especially late at night, and the penalties for offenders are severe.

Spain

Driving (continued)

Tolls

A toll *(peage)* is levied on limited-access highways; a toll highway is signed *autopista de peage* (AP). Take a ticket when you enter and pay when exiting.

Car Rental

The leading car-rental firms have offices at airports and train stations. Hertz offers discounted rates for AAA members (see page 15). For reservations:

	United States	Spain
Alamo	(800) 233-8749	0800 533 1196
Avis	(800) 633-3469	902 248 824
Budget	(800) 472 3325	902 112 585
Hertz	(800) 654-3001	902 402 405

Fuel

Gas *(gasolina)* and diesel are sold in liters. Many gas stations *(gasolineras)* in towns and cities and on highways are open 24 hours.

AAA Affiliated Motoring Club

Real Automóvil Club de España (RACE)
Paseo de las Delicias 97 ☎ 900 100 992; www.race.es. If you break down while driving, phone ☎ 900 112 222 (RACE members' break-down service). Not all automobile clubs offer full services to AAA members.

Breakdowns and Accidents

There are 24-hour emergency phones on highways. If you are involved in an accident, phone ☎ 112. Most car-rental firms provide their own free rescue service; if your car is rented, follow the instructions given in the documentation. Use of a car-repair service other than those authorized by your rental company may violate your agreement. In the event of a breakdown, you must put on a fluorescent vest when you are outside your vehicle. You must carry two warning triangles in your vehicle.

Other Information

The minimum age for driving a car is 18 (may be higher for most car-rental firms). An International Driving Permit (IDP) is recommended; some car-rental firms require it, and it can speed up formalities if you are involved in an accident. A Green Card (international motor insurance certificate) is recommended if you are driving a private car; see page 15 for more information. All drivers are required to carry a driver's license, car permit and insurance papers (minimum third-party coverage).

Useful Words and Phrases

Castilian is the main language in Spain, with three important regional languages: Catalan, spoken in Catalonia, the Balearics and Valencia; Basque, the official language of the Basque north; and Galician, spoken in the northwest.

Catalan is closely related to Occitan (or Provençal), and Galician has noticeable links with Portuguese. The Basque tongue is unique, having no connection with any language in Europe.

The following words and phrases are in Castilian:

Do you speak English?	*¿Habla usted inglés?*
excuse me	*perdone*
hello	*hola*
goodbye	*adiós*
yes/no	*sí/no*
how much?	*¿cuánto?*
I would like	*me gustaría*
I don't understand	*no entiendo*
no smoking	*prohibido fumar*
okay	*vale*
open/closed	*abierto/cerrado*
today/tomorrow	*hoy/mañana*
here/there	*aquí/allí*
more/less	*más/menos*
please	*por favor*
thank you	*gracias*
you're welcome	*de nada*
how/what	*cómo/qué*
left/right	*izquierda/derecha*
What time is it?	*¿Qué hora es?*
travel ticket	*el billete*
one way/return	*ida/ida y vuelta*
where is…?	*¿donde está…*
the hotel	**el hotel**
breakfast	*el desayuno*
lunch	*la comida*
dinner	*la cena*
I have a reservation	*Tengo una reserva*
key	*la llave*
room	*la habitación*
shower	*la ducha*
the restaurant	**el restaurante**
beef	*la ternera*
bread	*el pan*
the check	*la cuenta*
cheese	*el queso*
chicken	*el pollo*
coffee	*el café*
dessert	*el postre*
dish of the day	*el plato del día*
fish	*el pescado*
fixed-price lunch menu	*el menú del día*
pork	*la carne de cerdo*
starter	*el primer plato*
wine, red/white	*el vino tinto/blanco*

National Flag

Essential for Travelers

● Required ● Recommended ● Not required

Passport	●
Visa (check regulations before you travel)	●
Travel, medical insurance	●
Round-trip or onward airline ticket	●
Local currency	●
Traveler's checks	●
Credit cards	●
First-aid kit and medicines	●
Inoculations	●

Essential for Drivers*

Driver's license	●
International Driving Permit	●
Car insurance (for nonrental cars)	●
Car registration (for nonrental cars)	●

*see also *Driving* section

Important Addresses

VisitSweden
P.O. Box 4649, Grand Central Station
New York, NY 10163-4649
☎ (212) 885-9700
www.visitsweden.com

Stockholm Visitor Center
Kulturhuset, Sergels Tor 3
10327 Stockholm
☎ 08 5082 8508
www.visitstockholm.com

American Embassy
Dag Hammarskjölds Väg 31
SE-115 89 Stockholm, Sweden
☎ 08 783 53 00
http://sweden.usembassy.gov

Customs

✔ **Duty-free limits on goods brought in from non-European Union countries:**
200 cigarettes or 100 cigarillos or 50 cigars or 250 g. tobacco; 1 L. alcohol over 22% volume or 2 L. alcohol under 22% volume; 2 L. fortified or sparkling wine; 16 L. beer; a reasonable quantity of perfume or toilet water; plus any other duty-free goods (including gifts) to the value of 4,300SKr. Thre are no longer restrictions on the importation of tax-paid goods purchased within the European Union. You must be 18 years or over to import tobacco products and 20 or over to import alcohol. There is no restriction on the import of Swedish or foreign currencies, but amounts in excess of $14,800 must be declared.

✘ No unlicensed drugs, weapons, ammunition, obscene material, pets or other animals, counterfeit money or copied goods, meat, poultry, fish or shellfish.
For customs limits for returning U.S. citizens see page 16.

Money

Sweden's currency is the krona (SEK, SKr or Kr; plural kronor), which is divided into 100 öre. The denominations of krona bills are 20, 50, 100, 500 and 1,000. There are coins of 1, 5 and 10SKr. Note: 50 krona and 1,000 krona banknotes without a foil strip bacame invalid on January 1, 2014. Credit, debit and prepaid cards are widely accepted. ATMs for withdrawing local currency are plentiful throughout most of Sweden.

Tips and Gratuities

Tips are welcomed but not expected or obligatory. In restaurants it is usual to round off the check to the nearest 10SKr.

Restaurants, cafés/bars (service is included)	change
Taxis	10%
Hairdressers, chambermaids	none
Porters, restroom attendants	change
Cloakroom attendants	5SKr

Sweden

Communications

Post Offices

Buy stamps *(frimärken)* at a post office *(postkontoret)*, supermarket, newsstand *(nyhetsbyra)*, stationer *(handel)* or kiosk displaying a blue-and-yellow post sign. Blue post boxes are for local mail; yellow boxes are for national and international mail.

Telephones

Public phone booths were removed in Sweden in 2015. To avoid high roaming fees on your own cell phone, you can buy a prepaid SIM card for use in your own phone, providing your cell is compatible (some U.S. cell phones are not) and isn't SIM locked. Check with your provider before leaving home. Alternatively, consider buying a very basic mobile phone with a prepaid SIM when you arrive in Sweden for use during your stay. However, phone service operators in Sweden speak English.

Phoning inside Sweden
All Swedish numbers in this book include an area code; dial the number that is listed. To call the operator dial 90130; for directory assistance dial 118118.

Phoning Sweden from abroad
The country code for Sweden is 46. Note that Swedish numbers in this book do not include the Swedish country code; you will need to prefix this number if you are phoning from another country. To phone Sweden from the United States or Canada, omit the first zero from the Swedish number and add the prefix 011 46. For example: 01 122 33 44 becomes 011 46 1 122 33 44.

Phoning from Sweden
To phone the United States or Canada from Sweden, prefix the area code and number with 00 1. Example: (111) 222-3333 becomes 00 1 111 222-3333. For national operator assistance dial 0018. For international operator assistance dial 07977.

Emergency telephone numbers
Police *(polis)* **112**
Fire service *(brandkår)* **112**
Ambulance *(ambulans)* **112**

Hours of Operation

- Stores Mon.–Sat.
- Offices Mon.–Fri.
- Banks Mon.–Fri.
- Post Offices Mon.–Fri.
- Museums/Monuments
- Pharmacies Mon.–Fri.

7 8 9 10 11 12 1 2 3 4 5 6 7

In large towns, department **stores** stay open until 7 or 10 p.m., and some also are open Sunday from around noon to 4. Stores often close on Saturday afternoon between 2 and 4, and usually close early the day before a public holiday. Some smaller stores may close for lunch.

Banks also are open on Thursday until 4 or 5 and in some cities Monday to Friday until 6. All banks are closed on weekends.

Post offices may stay open later in main cities. They also are open Sat. 9–1. The post office at Centralstationen (Central Station) in Stockholm is open Mon.–Fri. 7 a.m.–10 p.m., Sat.–Sun. 9–6.

Some **museums** close on Monday and stay open late one or two nights a week.

Some **pharmacies** *(apotek)* in major cities are open 24 hours.

National Holidays

Banks, businesses and most stores close on these days; they also may be closed or close earlier the day before a holiday.

Jan. 1	New Year's Day
Jan. 5–6	Epiphany
Mar./Apr.	Good Friday
Mar./Apr.	Easter Monday
May 1	Labor Day
May	Ascension Day
May/Jun.	Pentecost Monday
Jun. 6	Sweden's National Day
Jun.	Midsummer's Eve (Fri. before Jun. 21)
Jun.	Midsummer's Day (Sat. nearest Jun. 21)
Nov. 1	All Saints' Day
Dec. 24	Christmas Eve
Dec. 25	Christmas Day
Dec. 26	St. Stephen's Day
Dec. 31	New Year's Eve

Photography

Poor light conditions occur in winter. Taking photographs in museums may be forbidden; check first. Digital photography equipment and printing services are available.

Sweden

Health

Medical Insurance

Private medical insurance is recommended. There are no general practitioners; go straight to a hospital clinic *(Akutmottagning* or *Vårdcentral)*, taking your passport with you. You will be charged for treatment (free for under 16s). For information contact Stockholm Care AB, ☎ 08 672 24 00; www.stockholmcare.se.

Dental Services

Dentists *(tandläkeren)* always charge for treatment; check whether it is covered by your medical insurance. Emergency treatment is available after hours in major cities. Clinics are indicated by *"Tandläkare"* or *"Folktandvård"* signs.

Sun Advice

The Gulf Stream dictates Sweden's temperate climate of warm sunshine during July and August. Although the sun is not fierce, good sun protection is necessary. Take precautions near the water.

Drugs

Prescription and nonprescription drugs and medicines are available from a pharmacy *(apotek)*. Information about the nearest all-night facility is posted at all pharmacies. A 24-hour service is available in most cities.

Safe Water

Tap water is safe to drink, and mineral water *(mineralvatten)* is widely available.

Restrooms

Public restrooms *(toalett)* are easy to find. There is a charge of 5SKr–10SKr to use some restrooms. Separate facilities for men *(Herrar)* and women *(Damer)* are always clean and modern.

Electricity

Sweden has a 220-volt power supply. Electrical sockets take plugs with two round pins. American appliances will need a plug adapter and will require a transformer if they do not have a dual-voltage facility.

National Transportation

Train *(Tåg)*

The Swedish rail network is operated by several companies: Statens Järnvägar (SJ), Tågkompaniet, ArrivaTåg and Inlandsbanan. It is an efficient and extensive system extending above the Arctic Circle. General information (timetables, prices, etc) is available from any station *(järnvägsstation)*. On some trains reservations are necessary. To obtain tickets for travel with SJ, the largest train operator, call ☎ 0771 75 75 75; www.sj.se.

Bus *(Buss)*

There is an excellent, inexpensive bus network of express services between larger towns and cities in south and central Sweden and between Stockholm and the north. The largest bus operator is Swebus Express ☎ 0771 218 218; www.swebus.se. Euroline Scandinavia buses operate to 27 destinations in Sweden ☎ 08 30 12 45; www.eurolines.se.

Ferry *(Farja)*

There are ferry services in Sweden, and you can get various island-hopping boat passes or coupons. Most depart from Stockholm. Passes are available from Waxholmsbolaget, on Strömkajen in Stockholm; ☎ 08 679 5830; www.waxholmsbolaget.se.

Driving

Drive on the right

Speed Limits

Police can impose on-the-spot fines, but cannot collect them. Pay particular attention to road signs as speed limits also are based on the quality and safety of the actual road.

 Limited-access highways **110 k.p.h. (68 m.p.h.)** Some parts of the E4 and E6 **120 k.p.h. (74 m.p.h.)** Divided highways **90 k.p.h. (56 m.p.h.)**

 Main roads **70 k.p.h. (43 m.p.h.)**

Urban areas **50 k.p.h. (31 m.p.h.)**, reduced to **30 k.p.h. (18 m.p.h.)** around schools

Seat Belts

 Must be worn in front and rear seats at all times.

Driving (continued)

Blood Alcohol

The legal blood alcohol limit is 0.02%. Random breath tests on drivers are carried out frequently, especially late at night, and the penalties for offenders are severe.

Tolls

There are no highway tolls in Sweden except when crossing the Øresund Bridge between Sweden and Denmark. Stockholm's and Gothenburg's inner city areas do have tolls that drivers of rental cars must pay. Check with your car-rental company that this is included in the price.

Car rental

The leading car-rental firms have offices at airports and train stations. Hertz offers discounted rates for AAA members (see page 15). For reservations:

	United States	Sweden
Alamo	(888) 233-8749	020 1 00531
Avis	(800) 633-3469	08 797 9970
Budget	(800) 527-0700	010 494 8400
Hertz	(800) 654-3131	08 454 6250

Fuel

Gas *(bensin)* is sold unleaded *(blyfri)* in 95 and 98 octane. Diesel also is available. Most gas stations are self-service, and on highways and in main towns they are open 24 hours. Major credit cards are accepted.

AAA Affiliated Motoring Club

Motormännens Riksförbund (M)
Fridhemsgatan 32, Stockholm, ☎ 08 690 38 00; www.motormannen.se. Not all automobile clubs offer full services to AAA members.

Breakdowns and Accidents

There are 24-hour emergency phones at regular intervals on highways. If you are involved in an accident, phone ☎ 112 for police. If you break down while driving, contact Assistancekåren: ☎ 020 912 912 (toll-free) or 08 627 57 57. Most car-rental firms provide their own free rescue service; if your car is rented, follow the instructions given in the documentation. Use of a car-repair service other than those authorized by your rental company may violate your agreement.

Other Information

The minimum age for driving a car is 18 (may be higher for some car-rental firms). An International Driving Permit (IDP) is recommended; some car-rental firms require it, and it can speed up formalities if you are involved in an accident. A Green Card (international motor insurance certificate) is recommended if you are driving a private car; see page 15 for more information.

Driving (continued)

Dimmed headlights must be turned on year-round, even during daylight hours. Be aware of moose, roe deer and reindeer appearing on roads, especially at dawn or dusk.

Useful Words and Phrases

Any effort made to speak Swedish is appreciated although most Swedes also speak English. German, Danish and Norwegian are understood.

In Swedish, a vowel sound is usually long when it is the final syllable, and verbs are the same regardless of person. Definite articles are determined by the ending of the noun: -en and -et for singular nouns and -na or -n for plural. There are an additional three letters in the Swedish alphabet – å, ä and ö – which always appear at the end in alphabetical lists.

There are two words for "you": *du* and *ni. Ni* is the polite form, *du* is the familiar form. Unlike some other European countries, it is not necessarily impolite to address a complete stranger with the familiar form. In fact, many Swedes consider the polite form to be old-fashioned.

Do you speak English?	*Talar ni Engelska?*
excuse me	*ursäkta mig*
hello	*hej*
goodbye	*adjö/hej då*
yes/no	*ja/nej*
how much is it?	*hur mycket kostar den?*
I am American	*Jag är från U.S.A.*
I'd like	*Jag skulle vilja ha*
I don't understand	*Jag förstår inte*
nonsmoking	*rökning förbjuden*
open	*öppen/öppet*
closed	*stängt*
please	*snälla, vänligen*
thank you	*tack*
(one-way) ticket	*en enkelbiljett*
the hotel	***hotell***
breakfast	*frukost*
lunch	*lunch*
dinner	*middag*
key	*nyckel*
room	*rum*
shower	*dusch*
the restaurant	***restaurang***
beef	*nötkött, oxkött*
beer	*öl*
bread	*bröd*
chicken	*kyckling*
coffee/tea	*kaffe/te*
dessert	*efterrätt*
fish	*fisk*
lamb	*lammkött*
pork	*fläsk*
wine	*vin*
please bring the check	*notan tack*

Switzerland

National Flag

Essential for Travelers

● Required ● Recommended ● Not required

Passport	●
Visa (check regulations before you travel)	●
Travel, medical insurance	●
Round-trip or onward airline ticket	●
Local currency	●
Traveler's checks	●
Credit cards	●
First-aid kit and medicines	●
Inoculations	●

Essential for Drivers*

Driver's license	●
International Driving Permit	●
Car insurance (for nonrental cars)	●
Car registration (for nonrental cars)	●

*see also *Driving* section

Important Addresses

Switzerland Tourism
Swiss Center, 608 Fifth Avenue
New York, NY 10020
☎ 1 800 794 7795 (toll free); 1 757 594 4240
www.myswitzerland.com
Note: this office is not open to the public.

Schweiz Tourismus (Switzerland Tourism)
Toedistrasse 7
8027 Zürich, Switzerland
☎ 00800 100 200 29 (toll free)
www.myswitzerland.com

American Embassy
Sulgeneckstrasse 19
CH-3007 Bern, Switzerland
☎ 031 357 7011 (Mon.–Fri. 9–12:30 and 1:30–5)
or 031 357 7777 (after hours)
http://bern.usembassy.gov

Customs

✔ **Duty-free limits on goods brought in from non-European countries:**
200 cigarettes or 50 cigarillos or cigars or 250 g. tobacco; 2 L. alcohol under 15% volume and 1 L. alcohol over 15% volume; plus any other duty-free goods (including gifts) to the value of SF100. These limits apply to visitors aged 17 and over. There are no currency regulations but amounts worth SF10,000 (or equivalent) should be declared.

✗ No unlicensed drugs, weapons, ammunition, obscene material, pets/other animals, counterfeit money or copied goods, meat or poultry.
For customs limits for returning U.S. citizens see page 16.

Money

Switzerland's currency is the Swiss franc (SF), which is divided into 100 centimes or "Rappen." The denominations of franc bills are 10, 20, 50, 100, 200 and 1,000. There are coins of 5, 10, 20 and 50 centimes and 1, 2 and 5SF. ATMs are plentiful and credit, debit and prepaid cards are accepted in hotels, large stores and upscale restaurants; check first in small or rural establishments. It is a good idea to carry a mix of large and small Swiss franc denominations.

Tips and Gratuities

Tips are welcomed but not expected, as a service charge is always included. A small tip is accepted for exceptional service.

Restaurants, cafés/bars (service included)	change
Taxis (usually includes service)	change
Porters, chambermaids	change
Hairdressers	change
Restroom/cloakroom attendants	change

Switzerland

Communications

Post Offices

Buy stamps *(timbres postaux/ Briefmarken)* at a post office *(bureau de poste/ Postamt)*, newsstand *(kiosque/Zeitungsstand)* or from a hotel. Hours for out-of-town post offices may vary.

Telephones

You can use cash or a prepaid phone card *(télecarte/Kartentelefon)* to make a call in Switzerland. Most telephones have direct dialing

for international calls. A Taxcard (phone card) can be bought from newsstands, gas stations, train stations and post offices for 10SF. Check that the phone booth is equipped with a Taxcard reader. You can also make a call with SF 1 and 5 coins at some telephones.

Check overseas cell-phone usage with your provider.

Phoning inside Switzerland

All Swiss telephone numbers in this book include an area code; dial the number that is listed. To call national information dial 1811.

Phoning Switzerland from abroad

The country code for Switzerland is 41. Note that Swiss numbers in this book do not include the country code; you will need to prefix this number if you are phoning from another country. To phone Switzerland from the United States or Canada, omit the first zero from the Swiss number and add the prefix 011 41. (Note that Swiss area codes are either one or two digits.) Example: 01 122 33 44 becomes 011 41 1 122 33 44.

Phoning from Switzerland

To phone the United States or Canada from Switzerland, prefix the area code and number with 00 1. Example: (111) 222-3333 becomes 00 1 111 222-3333. To call international information dial 1811.

Emergency phone numbers

Police *(police/Polizei)* 117
Fire service *(pompiers/Feuerwehr)* 118
Ambulance *(ambulance/Krankenwagen)* 117 or 144
Emergency calls are free from phone booths.

Hours of Operation

■ Stores Mon.–Sat.
■ Offices Mon.–Fri.
■ Banks Mon.–Fri.
■ Post Offices Mon.–Fri.
■ Museums/Monuments
■ Pharmacies Mon.–Sat.

7 8 9 10 11 12 1 2 3 4 5 6 7

Stores close on Saturday afternoon at 4 or 5. In large towns stores may close on Monday morning, while out-of-town stores often close on a Wednesday or Thursday afternoon; some also may close for lunch (noon–1:30).

The hours of operation for **banks** are varied and complicated depending on the town; ask at your hotel or a tourist office.

Post offices close at 11 on Saturday morning except for some major offices in cities, which close later; small offices have briefer hours of operation.

Museums often close on Monday and hours vary, so check locally.

National Holidays

Banks, businesses and most stores close on these days. Various cantons observe other national holidays such as Jan. 2, May 1, Corpus Christi and All Saints' Day.

Jan. 1	New Years' Day
Mar./Apr.	Good Friday
Mar./Apr.	Easter Monday
May	Ascension Day
May/Jun.	Pentecost Monday
Aug. 1	National Day
Dec. 25	Christmas Day
Dec. 26	St. Stephen's Day

Photography

Digital camera equipment and developing services are available in towns and cities. Photography is prohibited in some military areas, which includes some public footpaths, parks and forest areas. It is quite common to come across the Swiss army when you are walking, hiking or mountain biking. Some footpaths are closed during maneuvers, and temporary barriers set up by the army should be observed at all times. Photography may be forbidden in some churches and museums; ask before taking photographs if you need to obtain permission to do so.

Switzerland

Health

Medical Insurance

Private medical insurance is recommended. U.S. and Canadian visitors will have to pay for all medical treatment, including emergency assistance, consultation or admittance to a hospital *(hôpital/Krankenhaus)*. If you are planning to take part in winter sports, special sports policies are widely available. For information on medical issues dial Anglo-Phone, ☎ 0900 576 444 (toll call), from anywhere in Switzerland.

Dental Services

A dentist *(dentiste/Zahnarzt)* will charge for any treatment; dental work is expensive; check whether it is covered by your medical insurance. Dentists are listed in the telephone directory. You also can ask for English-speaking dentists at your embassy, hotel or a tourist office.

Sun Advice

Conditions vary considerably; no country in Europe combines within so small an area such marked climatic contrasts. The sun can be deceptively strong in the mountains; protection is essential. The warmest part of Switzerland is south of the Alps, which is under the influence of the Mediterranean. Sun protection is needed; it is advisable to wear a hat and apply sunscreen.

Drugs

Pharmacies sell a range of medicines and drugs and dispense prescriptions. Many pharmacists speak English. At least one pharmacy in every town stays open late; information is displayed on store doors.

Safe Water

Tap water is safe to drink throughout Switzerland. Mineral water *(eau minérale/Mineralwasser)* is widely available.

Restrooms

Most toilets *(toilettes/Toiletten)* are clean and well maintained. They are indicated by a variety of signs, such as "WC" or *Toiletten*. Women's restrooms are designated *Damen, Frauen, Femmes, Dames, Signore* or *Donne;* men's as *Herren, Männer, Hommes, Messieurs, Signori* or *Uomini*.

Electricity

Switzerland has a 230-volt power supply. Electrical sockets take plugs with two round pins. American appliances will need a plug adapter and will require a transformer if they do not have a dual-voltage facility.

National Transportation

Train *(Train/Zug)*

Swiss Federal Railways is Chemins de Fer Fédéreaux (CFF) in French, Schweizerische Bundesbahnen (SBB) in German and Ferrovie Federali Svizzere (FFS) in Italian. It runs a fast, clean and efficient service. Express trains only stop at major cities. *Trains régionales/Regionalzuge* are slow trains usually running the same routes. To reach an English-speaking operator dial ☎ 0900 300300 (toll call). There are various good-value rail passes available. Inquire at tourist offices or any large railroad station.

Bus *(Autobus/Bus)*

The bus service takes passengers to mountainous regions where railroads are unable to go. Mail bus routes encounter magnificent scenery joining villages and towns, occasionally even delivering the mail. There are many special offers; passes and cards that combine train, bus and boat are available at reduced rates. Eurolines operates in Switzerland. Go online at www.eurolines.com for information.

Ferry *(Ferry/Fähre)*

There are many excursions and some scheduled services on Switzerland's lakes. Regional tourist offices in different cantons can offer information, and some take reservations.

Driving

Drive on the right

Speed Limits

Police can impose on-the-spot fines, for which a receipt is issued. Fines are severe.

Limited-access highways *(Autobahn)*
120 k.p.h. (74 m.p.h.)
Divided highways **100 k.p.h. (62 m.p.h.)**

Main roads
80 k.p.h. (49 m.p.h.)

Urban areas
50 k.p.h. (31 m.p.h.) or
30 k.p.h. (18 m.p.h.)

Seat Belts

Must be worn in front and back seats at all times. Children under 7 are not allowed in a front seat.

Driving (continued)

Blood Alcohol

The legal blood alcohol limit is 0.05%. Random breath tests on drivers are carried out frequently, especially late at night, and the penalties for offenders are severe.

Tolls

An annual road tax of SF40 is levied on all cars and motorcycles using Swiss highways. Permits *(vignettes/Vignetten)*, available at border crossings, post offices and service areas, are valid for multiple reentry into Switzerland within the duration of the license period. To avoid border delays, it is advisable to buy the permit in advance from a Swiss tourist office.

Car Rental

The leading car-rental firms have offices at airports and train stations. Hertz offers discounted rates for AAA members (see page 15). For reservations:

	United States	Switzerland
Alamo	(877) 222-9075	022 717 8110
Avis	(800) 331-1084	0848 81 18 18
Budget	(800) 472-3325	22 929 0330
Hertz	(800) 654-3001	www.hertz.co.uk/ rentacar/car-hire/ switzerland

Fuel

Gas and diesel are sold in liters. There are 24-hour gas stations on highways and in cities; many have refreshment facilities and stores. Credit cards are accepted for payment.

AAA Affiliated Motoring Club

Touring Club Suisse (TCS) Chemin de Blandonnet 4, CH-1214 Vernier/Geneva, Switzerland ☎ 0844 888 111; www.tcs.ch. If you break down while driving ☎ 0800 140 140 (TCS breakdown service). Not all automobile clubs offer full services to AAA members.

Breakdowns and Accidents

There are 24-hour emergency phones at regular intervals on highways. If you are involved in an accident ☎ 117 for police. Most car-rental firms provide a free rescue service; if your car is rented, follow the instructions given in the documentation. Use of a car-repair service other than those authorized by your car-rental company may violate your agreement. You must use a warning triangle in the event of an accident/ breakdown; this must be kept within easy reach (not in the trunk).

Driving (continued)

Other Information

The minimum age for driving a car is 18 (may be higher for some car-rental firms). An International Driving Permit (IDP) is recommended; some car-rental firms require it, and it can speed up formalities if you are involved in an accident. A Green Card (international motor insurance certificate) is recommended if you are driving a private car; see page 15 for more information.

Dimmed headlights must be used when passing through tunnels. Yellow mail buses have priority at all times, as do vehicles ascending mountain roads. Many mountain pass roads are closed from October through June. For road conditions ☎ 163.

Useful Words and Phrases

There are four official languages spoken in Switzerland: German, French, Italian and Romansch. About 18 percent of the population in southwest Switzerland speak French. South of the Alps, Italian (12 percent) is predominant through-out Ticino and parts of the Grisons (also known as the Graubünden). Most Swiss (65 percent) speak German. A Swiss-German dialect with a variety of local variations is used in everyday conversation; traditional German is used for business purposes.

The fourth language is Romansch, an ancient hybrid of Celtic and Latin tongues spoken by about 40,000 people in the Surselva region of southeastern Switzerland.

This coexistence of distinct languages results in a true "European" nation. The Romansch area is probably the most "Swiss" part of the country. French influence is evident in Lausanne, while Lugano exhibits both Italian and Swiss influences.

Every Swiss child learns two or three languages. English is spoken throughout the country, but an attempt to say a few words in any of Switzerland's languages will always be appreciated.

See page 521 for French words, page 525 for German and page 541 for Italian.

European Distance Chart

European Distance Chart

Road distances, in kilometers (km), are calculated by the shortest or quickest routes (highways, main roads) from center to center and do not take into account seasonal weather conditions.

Miles	Km
1	1.6
10	16
20	32
30	48
40	64
50	80
100	160
200	320
300	480
400	640
500	800
1000	1600

Cities (diagonal labels, in order):
Amsterdam (NL), Athína (Athens) (GR), Barcelona (ES), Berlin (DE), Brugge/Bruges (BE), Brussel/Bruxelles (BE), Budapest (HU), Den Haag (The Hague) (NL), Dublin (IE), Edinburgh (GB), Firenze (Florence) (IT), Genève (CH), Gent (BE), Helsinki (FI), Innsbruck (AT), København (Copenhagen) (DK), Köln (Cologne) (DE), Lisboa (Lisbon) (PT), London (GB), Luxembourg (LU), Lyon (FR), Madrid (ES), München (Munich) (DE), Nápoli (Naples) (IT), Nice (FR), Odense (DK), Oslo (...)

Distance matrix (km):

Athína: 1736
Barcelona: 1600 1591
Berlin: 653 1577 1889
Brugge: 269 1680 1372 832
Brussel: 210 1568 1403 773 101
Budapest: 1413 1521 2085 874 1473 1368
Den Haag: 64 1755 1574 697 211 180 1432
Dublin: 959 2350 1958 1522 704 791 2163 930
Edinburgh: 1092 2483 2091 1655 837 924 2296 1063 538
Firenze: 1387 544 1103 1228 1331 1219 1085 1406 2001 2134
Genève: 1004 973 809 1119 769 724 1276 896 1355 1488 606
Gent: 221 1635 1367 783 52 56 1423 191 742 875 1286 764
Helsinki: 1542 2864 2929 1013 1748 1689 2449 1586 2438 2571 2515 2159 1700
Innsbruck: 1001 832 1381 750 1061 956 731 1021 1751 1884 483 574 1011 2037
København: 926 2248 2313 397 1132 1073 1833 970 1822 1955 1899 1543 1084 620 1421
Köln: 262 1481 1419 569 315 210 1158 282 1005 1138 1132 749 265 1502 747 886
Lisboa: 2370 2847 1258 2908 2161 2168 3340 2341 2747 2880 2359 2065 2156 3841 2637 3225 2345
London: 482 1873 1481 1045 227 314 1686 453 463 665 1524 878 265 1961 1274 1345 528 2270
Luxembourg: 410 1356 1190 759 324 212 1193 384 1014 1147 1007 512 279 1697 677 1081 230 2222 537
Lyon: 932 1069 652 1233 779 734 1429 906 1365 1498 693 153 774 2272 727 1656 751 1908 888 522
Madrid: 1809 2188 630 2347 1600 1607 2681 1779 2186 2319 1700 1406 1595 3279 1978 2663 1784 625 1709 1660 1249
München: 834 990 1396 583 894 789 690 854 1584 1717 641 587 844 1870 163 1254 580 2677 1107 566 740 1993
Nápoli: 1859 594 1577 1700 1803 1691 1557 1878 2473 2606 474 1080 1758 2987 955 2371 1604 2833 1996 1479 1167 2174 1113
Nice: 1396 910 681 1347 1268 1223 1403 1394 1853 1986 421 541 1263 2551 700 1935 1142 1937 1376 1011 472 1278 858 895
Odense: 765 2086 2151 599 971 911 1671 809 1660 1793 1737 1381 922 781 1260 165 724 3063 1183 919 1495 2502 1093 2209 1774
Oslo: 1510 2832 2897 981 1716 1657 2417 1554 2406 2539 2483 2127 1668 530 2005 588 1470 3809 1929 1665 2241 3247 1838 2954 2519 749

589 1980 1588 1152 334 421 1793 560 396 598 1631 985 372 2068 1381 1452 635 2377 90 644 995 1816 1214 2103 1483 1290 2036
509 1508 1067 1047 300 307 1494 480 888 1021 1141 542 295 1980 953 1364 484 1856 411 376 466 1295 831 1614 954 1202 1948
2170 2647 1213 2708 1961 1968 3140 2141 2547 2680 2159 1865 1956 3641 2437 3025 2145 318 2070 2022 1708 564 2477 2632 1737 2863 3609
967 1375 1754 343 1027 922 531 987 1717 1850 1026 984 977 1377 549 761 713 2895 1240 747 1098 2333 382 1498 1243 957 1345
1663 521 1381 1504 1607 1495 1362 1683 2277 2410 278 885 1562 2791 759 2175 1409 2637 1800 1283 971 1978 917 219 700 2014 2759
977 1007 1535 726 1037 932 553 997 1727 1860 658 725 987 2013 180 1397 723 2791 1250 722 879 2132 139 1129 1236 1981
2078 2555 1166 2616 1869 1876 3048 2049 2454 2587 2067 1773 1864 3549 2345 2933 2053 549 1977 1930 1616 646 2385 2540 1645 2771 3517
2354 2599 1041 2892 2145 2152 3092 2325 2733 2866 2111 1817 2140 3825 2389 3209 2329 408 2256 2206 1660 543 2404 2584 1689 3047 3793
1542 2864 2929 1013 1748 1689 2449 1586 2438 2571 2515 2159 1700 1800 2037 620 1502 3841 1961 1697 2273 3279 1870 2986 2551 781 530
628 1133 1147 753 543 431 1063 602 1213 1346 784 401 498 1793 471 1177 354 2335 736 219 491 1744 360 1256 794 1015 1761
1345 537 1256 1126 1289 1177 847 1364 1959 2092 256 584 1244 2413 381 1797 1090 2512 1482 965 701 1853 539 728 574 1636 2381
1157 1124 1843 637 1217 1112 244 1176 1907 2040 843 1020 1167 2193 475 1577 902 3084 1430 937 1174 2440 434 1315 1161 1415 2161
805 2196 1804 1368 550 637 2009 776 322 311 1847 1201 588 2284 1597 1668 851 2593 339 860 1211 2032 1430 2319 1699 1506 2252
831 940 1095 844 775 663 996 851 1446 1579 591 285 730 1986 284 1370 577 2351 969 451 439 1692 306 1062 600 1209 1954

European Distance Chart

Oxford (GB)	Paris (FR)	Porto (PT)	Praha (Prague) (CZ)	Roma (Rome) (IT)	Salzburg (AT)	Santiago de Compostela (ES)	Sevilla (Seville) (ES)	Stockholm (SE)	Strasbourg (FR)	Venézia (Venice) (IT)	Wien (Vienna) (AT)	York (GB)	Zurich (CH)
518													
2177	1656												
1347	1049	2695											
1907	1419	2437	1303										
1347	987	2591	377	934									
2084	1564	231	2603	2345	2499								
2363	1840	679	2762	2389	2543	910							
2068	1982	3641	1377	2791	2013	3548	3827						
843	489	2135	618	1060	516	2042	2157	1793					
1589	1119	2312	816	532	436	2219	2266	2413	742				
1537	1238	2884	294	1119	297	2791	2853	2193	807	605			
295	734	2393	1563	2123	1573	2300	2579	2284	1059	1805	1753		
1076	664	2151	712	867	445	2058	2105	1986	229	548	740	1292	

Acknowledgments

The Automobile Association wishes to thank the following photographers and organizations for their assistance in the preparation of this book.

Abbreviations for the picture credits are as follows – (t) top; (b) bottom; (l) left; (r) right; (c) center; (AA) AA World Travel Library

3 BANANA PANCAKE/Alamy, 18 AA/J Smith, 22 Jon Arnold Images Ltd/Alamy, 23 AA/J Smith, 25 imageBROKER/Alamy, 29 AA/J Smith, 30 AA/D Noble, 31 AA/M Siebert, 32 AA/D Noble, 33 AA/J Smith, 34 Aivar Mikko/Alamy, 37 Kuttig - Travel/Alamy, 38 Martin Siepmann/Photolibrary, 39 AA/M Jourdan, 43 AA/A Baker, 45 AA/J Smith, 47 AA/J Smith, 48 Chris Dorney/Alamy, 52 AA/A Kouprianoff, 53 Marc Hill/Alamy, 55 PCL/Alamy, 57 imagebroker/Alamy, 61 eye35.com/Alamy, 63 AA/A Kouprianoff, 65 Hideo Kurihara/Alamy, 66 Groeningemuseum, Bruges, Belgium/Peter Willi/The Bridgeman Art Library , 68 AA/A Kouprianoff, 69 AA/A Kouprianoff, 71 Ian Dagnall/Alamy, 73 Arterra Picture Library/Alamy, 74 Riccardo Sala/Photolibrary, 75 St. Bavo Cathedral, Ghent, Belgium/Giraudon/The Bridgeman Art Library, 76 Peter Scholey/Alamy, 81 AA/M Moody, 82 AA/J Smith, 85 AA/J Tims, 90 AA/J Tims, 93 AA/J Tims, 94 AA/N Setchfield, 95 AA/W Voysey, 97 Stefano Paterna/Alamy, 101 AA/K Blackwell, 102 AA/K Paterson, 104 AA/K Blackwell, 105 AA/K Blackwell, 106 AA/J Tims, 110 AA, 111 AA/J Wyand, 112 AA/D Clapp, 115 AA/D Clapp, 116 AA/P Bennett, 117 AA/D Clapp, 118 AA/T Woodcock, 121 AA/S McBride, 123 AA/L Noble, 126 AA/J Smith, 127 Nataliya Hora/Alamy, 128 AA/S McBride, 129 AA/J Wyand, 130 AA/S McBride, 131 AA/J Wyand, 132 AA/D Forss, 135 AA/J Wyand, 136 F1online digitale Bildagentur GmbH/Alamy, 137 Tibor Bognar/Alamy, 139 AA/D Forss, 144 Morten Svenningsen/Alamy, 148 AA/D Forss, 150 AA/D Forss, 151 The Art Archive/Alamy, 152 Layne Kennedy/Corbis, 154 Photoshot Holdings Ltd/Alamy, 155 AA, 157 Peter Lilja/Photolibrary, 158 PCL/Alamy, 163 Manfred Gottschalk/Alamy, 164 AA/I Dawson, 168 AA/J Edmanson, 169 AA/J Tims, 170 AA/C Sawyer, 171 AA/R Strange, 173 AA/K Blackwell, 176 AA/K Blackwell, 178 AA/K Blackwell, 179 AA/K Paterson, 180 AA/K Blackwell, 181 AA/M Jourdan, 182 AA/J Tims, 185 Prisma Bildagentur AG/Alamy, 187 AA/J Wyand, 189 AA/J Wyand, 191 AA/J Wyand, 192 AA/Y Levy, 193 AA/I Morejohn, 197 AA/J Tims, 198 AA/J Tims, 199 AA/J Tims, 201 Jon Arnold Images Ltd/Alamy, 203 AA, 205 AA/B Smith, 206 AA/A Kouprianoff, 211 AA/A Baker, 212 AA/C Sawyer, 213 AA/M Jourdan, 215 AA/A Kouprianoff, 219 Anne-Marie Palmer/Alamy, 222 AA/T Souter, 223 AA/A Kouprianoff, 224 AA/A Baker, 227 AA/A Hemmisen, 229 Bildarchiv Monheim GmbH/Alamy, 233 AA/M Jourdan, 235 AA/C Sawyer, 236 AA/T Souter, 237 Oliver Hoffmann/Alamy, 238 AA/Mockford & Bonetti, 243 AA/Mockford & Bonetti, 246 AA/Mockford & Bonetti, 247 Jan Wlodarczyk/Alamy, 248 AA/Mockford & Bonetti, 251 AA/R Surman, 252 AA/J Smith, 257 AA/J Smith, 260 AA/J Smith, 261 AA/J Smith, 262 AA/J Smith, 263 AA/J Smith, 265 AA/K Paterson, 266 AA/C Hill, 270 AA/C Jones, 271 AA/C Hill, 273 AA/K Blackwell, 276 AA/K Blackwell, 277 AA/K Blackwell, 278 AA/K Blackwell, 279 AA/K Blackwell, 281 AA/K Blackwell, 282 AA/Mockford & Bonetti, 287 AA/J Tims, 288 AA/Mockford & Bonetti, 289 AA/Mockford & Bonetti, 291 AA/C Sawyer, 296 AA/Mockford & Bonetti, 298 AA/Mockford & Bonetti, 299 AA/Mockford & Bonetti, 300 AA/Mockford & Bonetti, 301 AA/Mockford & Bonetti, 305 AA/J Tims, 307 AA, 308 AA/M Jourdan, 312 AA/M Jourdan, 313 Jon Arnold Images Ltd/Alamy, 317 AA/Mockford & Bonetti, 319 AA/Mockford & Bonetti, 320 AA/S McBride, 321 AA/C Sawyer, 322 Jon Arnold Images Ltd/Alamy, 324 David Robertson/Alamy, 327 Travelshots.com/Alamy, 331 blickwinkel/Alamy, 332 Lana Sundman/Alamy, 333 David Robertson/Alamy, 334 AA/A Robinson, 336 AA/A Robinson, 338/39 AA/A Robinson, 339b AA/A Robinson, 341 AA/A Robinson, 345 AA/A Robinson, 346 AA/K Paterson, 347 AA/A Robinson, 348 AA/A Robinson, 349 AA/A Robinson, 351 CW Images/Alamy, 353 David R. Frazier Photolibrary, Inc./Alamy, 354 moodboard/Alamy, 355 AA/K Paterson, 356 David Robertson/Alamy, 360 AA, 361 imagebroker/Alamy, 363 Body Philippe/Photolibrary, 364 blickwinkel/Alamy, 369 AA/K Naylor, 370 AA/P Wilson, 372 AA/M Wells, 374 AA/M Wells, 375 AA/M Wells, 377 AA/M Wells, 381 AA/T Harris, 383 AA/M Wells, 384 AA/M Wells, 385 AA/T Harris, 388 AA/Mockford & Bonetti, 390 AA/Mockford & Bonetti, 391 AA/A Kouprianoff, 392 AA/M Bonnet, 396 AA/M Jourdan, 397 AA/P Wilson, 399 AA/M Chaplow, 401 AA/M Bonnet, 405 Glyn Thomas Photography/Alamy, 406 AA/M Jourdan, 407 AA/M Jourdan, 408 AA/R Strange, 409 AA/M Chaplow, 412 AA/M Bonnet, 413 AA/M Bonnet, 414 AA/M Jourdan, 415 AA/M Bonnet, 417 AA/M Bonnet, 418 imagebroker/Alamy, 421 BANANA PANCAKE/Alamy, 422 BANANA PANCAKE/Alamy, 423 Hemis/Alamy, 424 Jon Arnold Images Ltd/Alamy, 428 Karol Kozlowski/Alamy, 429 AA/C Sawyer, 430 BANANA PANCAKE/Alamy, 432 BANANA PANCAKE/Alamy, 435 AA/K Naylor, 438 AA/K Naylor, 439 Chalermchai Chamnanyon/Alamy, 440 Chad Ehlers/Photolibrary, 441 BANANA PANCAKE/Alamy, 442 Sweden And Swedish/Alamy, 444 Tibor Bognar/Alamy, 449 imagebroker/Alamy, 450 Hemis/Alamy, 455 Andre Jenny/Alamy, 459 Cosmo Condina Western Europe/Alamy, 460 Prisma Bildagentur AG/Alamy, 494t Central Intelligence Agency, 494b www.ecb.int, 495t AA/S Montgomery, 495b AA/S Montgomery, 498t Central Intelligence Agency, 498b www.ecb.int, 499t AA/A Kouprianoff, 499b AA/A Kouprianoff, 502t Central Intelligence Agency, 502b MRI Bankers' Guide to Foreign Currency, Houston, USA, 503t AA/J Tims, 503b AA/S Montgomery, 506t Central Intelligence Agency, 506b MRI Bankers' Guide to Foreign Currency, Houston, USA, 507t AA/J Wyand, 507b AA/J Wyand, 510t Central Intelligence Agency, 510b MRI Bankers' Guide to Foreign Currency, Houston, USA, 511t AA/J W Jorgensen, 511b AA/Y Levy, 514t Central Intelligence Agency, 514b MRI Bankers' Guide to Foreign Currency, Houston, USA, 515t Wikimedia Commons/ Bart van Klaveren, 518t Central Intelligence Agency, 518b MRI Bankers' Guide to Foreign Currency, Houston, USA, 519t AA/P Bennett, 519b AA/K Blackwell, 522t Central Intelligence Agency, 522b MRI Bankers' Guide to Foreign Currency, Houston, USA, 523t AA/M Jourdan, 523b AA/M Jourdan, 526t Central Intelligence Agency, 526b MRI Bankers' Guide to Foreign Currency, Houston, USA, 527t AA/S Day, 527b AA/Mockford & Bonetti, 530t Central Intelligence Agency, 530b MRI Bankers' Guide to Foreign Currency, Houston, USA, 531t AA/K Paterson, 531b Vlad Breazu/Alamy, 534t Central Intelligence Agency, 534b MRI Bankers' Guide to Foreign Currency, Houston, USA, 535t AA/S Whitehorne, 535b AA/K Blackwell, 538t Central Intelligence Agency, 538b MRI Bankers' Guide to Foreign Currency, Houston, USA, 539t AA/Mockford & Bonetti, 539b AA/N Setchfield, 542t Central Intelligence Agency, 542b MRI Bankers' Guide to Foreign Currency, Houston, USA, 543t Nick Scott/Alamy, 543b AA/A Kouprianoff, 546t Central Intelligence Agency, 546b MRI Bankers' Guide to Foreign Currency, Houston, USA, 547t AA/A Robinson, 547b AA/A Robinson, 550t Central Intelligence Agency, 550b MRI Bankers' Guide to Foreign Currency, Houston, USA, 551t JoeFox/Alamy, 551b dk/Alamy, 554t Central Intelligence Agency, 554b MRI Bankers' Guide to Foreign Currency, Houston, USA, 555t AA/M Wells, 555b AA/Mockford & Bonetti, 558t Central Intelligence Agency, 558b MRI Bankers' Guide to Foreign Currency, Houston, USA, 559t AA/M Bonnet, 559b AA/M Bonnet, 562t Central Intelligence Agency, 562b MRI Bankers' Guide to Foreign Currency, Houston, USA, 563t Stuwdamdorp/Alamy, 566t Central Intelligence Agency, 566b MRI Bankers' Guide to Foreign Currency, Houston, USA, 567t Rob Lacey/vividstock.net/Alamy, 567b Rob Lacey/vividstock.net/Alamy.

Every effort has been made to trace the copyright holders, and we apologize in advance for any unintentional omissions or errors. We would be pleased to apply any corrections in any following edition of this publication.